Financial Econometrics

Princeton Series in Finance

Finance as a discipline has been growing rapidly. The numbers of researchers in academy and industry, of students, of methods and models have all proliferated in the past decade or so. This growth and diversity manifests itself in the emerging cross-disciplinary as well as cross-national mix of scholarship now driving the field of finance forward. The intellectual roots of modern finance, as well as the branches, will be represented in the *Princeton Series in Finance*.

Titles in the series will be scholarly and professional books, intended to be read by a mixed audience of economists, mathematicians, operations research scientists, financial engineers, and other investment professionals. The goal is to provide the finest cross-disciplinary work in all areas of finance by widely recognized researchers in the prime of their creative careers.

Financial Econometrics

PROBLEMS, MODELS, AND METHODS

Christian Gourieroux

Joann Jasiak

Princeton University Press
Princeton and Oxford

The Library of Congress has cataloged the cloth edition as follows:

Gourieroux, Christian, 1949–
    Financial econometrics / Christian Gourieroux and Joann Jasiak.
        p. cm. — (Princeton series in finance)
    Includes index
    ISBN 0-691-08872-1
        1. Econometrics.   2. Finance–Statistical methods.   3. Finance–
    Mathematical models.   I. Jasiak, Joann, 1963–   II. Title.   III. Series.

    HB139 .G685 2001
    330′.01′5195–dc21   2001036264

First paperback printing, 2022
Paperback ISBN 9780691242361
Cloth ISBN 9780691088723

British Library Cataloging-in-Publication Data is available

This book has been composed in New Baskerville

press.princeton.edu

Contents

Preface

The aim of econometrics is to make use of data, statistical inference methods and structural or descriptive modeling to address practical economic problems. The development of econometric methods in finance is quite recent and has been paralleled by fast expansion of financial markets and increasing variety and complexity of financial products. While some material covered in the book is now well established, we gave much consideration to foregoing research. The objective of this book is to report on the current state of scientific advancement and point out the accomplishments and failures of econometric methods applied to finance. Given the progress of financial econometrics and its wide scope, the content of the book necessarily reflects our subjective choice of the matters of interest. Therefore, we devote the next paragraphs to the motivations for the adopted approach and array of problems presented in the text.

Past versus Future

It is conceivable to review the theory and practice of financial econometrics in a chronological order. Such an approach seems a priori quite natural and insightful. However, its potential pitfall is to put too much emphasis on the techniques developed in the past and adapted to an environment that no longer exists. Therefore, we focus on the methods related to foregoing research, as well as on those that seem to us to be relevant for future advances. As a consequence, the reader may feel that some topics have been given much attention at the expense of other ones. For example, the arbitrage pricing theory (APT), which seeks the possibilities of making sure gains, has not been given extensive coverage as it requires a set of restrictive conditions, practically never fulfilled in the real world. Instead, APT is discussed as a particular case of a factor model with additional dynamic features and we give a brief overview of its limitations.

A similar argument motivated the limited coverage of autoregressive conditionally heteroscedastic (ARCH) models designed to accommodate time-varying risks. The advent of the ARCH model has marked the last two decades of financial econometrics and was a breakthrough in the way econometricians used to model and evaluate the returns and risks on assets. Nevertheless, due to their restrictive form, the ARCH models fail to account for several empirical features, such as asymmetric responses of volatility to rising and falling asset prices, and postulate a deterministic relationship between the risk and past returns. We believe that future research interests likely will shift toward the family of stochastic volatility models and general nonlinear models, which accordingly were given more attention in the text.

Statistics versus Finance

Most textbooks concerning finance illustrate the subjects of primary interest, both of theoretical or practical nature, by data-based empirical results. A converse approach would imply describing the statistical models and methods of analysis along with their financial applications. Neither of these two outlines has been followed in the present text. We believe that an adequate treatment of financial econometrics consists of a well-balanced synthesis of financial theory and statistical methodology. Therefore, we put much effort in the embodiment of our vision of an optimal blend of these two aspects of financial econometrics. As a consequence, some theoretical results and estimation methods are dispersed among several chapters. For example, the Capital Asset Pricing Model (CAPM) is discussed under various headings, such as portfolio management in application to risk control and the equilibrium model to highlight the CAPM-based derivative pricing. For the same reason, the generalized method of moments appears in the analysis of actuarial models, intertemporal optimization, and derivative pricing.

Case Study versus Empirical Illustration

There currently is a tendency to provide textbooks with computer disks that contain a set of financial series used for empirical illustrations. In our work, we employ a variety of data sampled at frequencies that range from intraday to monthly and comprise time series that represent both European and North American markets for stocks, bonds, and foreign currencies. Our purpose is to convince the reader that econometric methods need to be adapted to the problem and data set under study on a case-by-case basis. In this way, we try to convey the message that there does not exist a true model for each market that yields the best approximation of its price dynamics, captures most of the evidenced stylized facts, is valid at different frequencies, and provides a unifying framework to portfolio management, derivative pricing, forecasting, and risk control.

One has to remember that a statistical model is a simplified image of reality, which is much too complex to be described exactly. Therefore, an econometrician is aware of the fact that a model is necessarily misspecified. Since specification errors differ depending on the subject under study, models designed for examining various problems may not be compatible. For the same reason, one has to interpret with caution the stylized facts reported in empirical literature. These stylized facts are based on inference from imperfect models and are to a great extent influenced by the adopted research methodology. Indeed, we have seen in the past that even a very slight improvement of a model may produce evidence that contradicts the commonly recognized empirical regularities. For example, volatility persistence is significantly reduced when trading volumes are included in the conditional variance equation. As well, in contrast to a common belief, asset prices do not follow random walks when nonlinear patterns are accounted for in the dynamic specification. Especially, so-called financial puzzles often result from a narrow interpretation of inference based on misspecified models.

Descriptive Diagnostics versus Testing Theory

The above remarks lead to the conclusion that a crucial task of financial econometrics is to eradicate specification errors or at least keep them under control. There exist two instruments to this end: graphical diagnostics, including residual plots, autocorrelograms, tracking errors, and the like, and statistical tests for comparing various hypotheses. We have clearly given a priority to the first type of instruments for the two following reasons. First, graphical diagnostic methods are easier to understand for practitioners than the test statistics and thus avoid human errors in interpreting the outcomes. The focus on graphical diagnostics also eliminates heavy mathematics involved in the theory of tests. Second, the theory of tests relies on a comparison of the test statistic to a critical value that presumes correct specification of the hypothetical model. The critical values, and hence the outcomes, of a test are extremely sensitive to omitted nonlinearities, heteroscedasticity, or poor data.

Topics Covered

Chapters 1-13 outline the econometric methods and models readily applicable to forecasting financial data, to portfolio management, and to derivative pricing. Although this material lends itself to a majority of financial applications, the reader needs to be aware that econometric models are plagued by specification errors. The last three chapters of the book deal directly with misspecification problems and offer an array of solutions. Some of the specification errors concern

- microeconomic aspects such as investor heterogeneity, noncompetitive behavior of investors, market organization, and market mechanism effects;
- the computation of market indexes and the responsibility delegated to scientific committees, which decide on their composition;
- the treatment of extreme risks for risk control and determining minimal capital requirements.

Given its scope, the book is intended as a text for graduate students in statistics, mathematics, economics, and business who are interested in financial applications. It was developed from our lectures at York University; Montreal University; Schulich School of Business in Canada; INSEAD; ENSAE; Paris I, VI, VII, and IX Universities in France; and Geneva and Lausanne Universities in Switzerland. It has usefulness both at the master's level, because of its emphasis on the practical aspects of financial modeling and statistical inference, and at the doctoral level, for which detailed mathematical derivations of the deeper results are included together with the more advanced financial problems concerning high-frequency data or risk control. By establishing a link between practical questions and the answers provided by financial and statistical theory, the book also addresses applied researchers employed by banks and financial institutions.

Instructors who use the book might find it difficult to cover all included material. It is always better to have some topics in the book that instructors can choose depending on their interests or needs. A one-semester graduate course with an explicit focus on discrete time analysis might cover Chapters 1-4, 6, and possibly elements of Chapter 14 when the emphasis of the course lies on statistical analysis or Chapters 8, 13, and 15 when the main field of interest is derivative pricing. Instructors who teach continuous time modeling might consider Chapters 1 and 10-13. The material for a course in financial macroeconometrics might include chapters 1-5, 7, and possibly 9. At an advanced (doctoral) level, the following topics can be used for lectures:

1. High-frequency data analysis (Chapter 14)
2. Market and risk management (Chapters 14 and 16)
3. Factor models (Chapter 9)
4. Stochastic discount factor models (Chapters 8, 11, and 13)

We expect the ongoing progress in financial econometrics to be driven further by future advances in the domains of martingales and nonlinear time series; parametric and nonparametric estimation methods, including the simulation-based methods and methods of moments; numerical analysis for solving diffusion equations; and integral approximations for pricing the derivatives and in economics, by better explaining the market mechanisms.

Acknowledgment

This book would not have been written without the help of some of our colleagues, students, and collaborators. We are grateful to Alain Monfort, Darrell Duffie, Frank Diebold, and an anonymous referee for helpful comments. We are also indebted to Jon Cockerline, the director of Research Services of the Toronto Stock Exchange, and George Tauchen for data and valuable collaboration; and to our former students Serge Darolles, Gaelle LeFol, Christian Robert, and Xingnong Zhu, for their assistance in empirical research. As well, we thank Bonny Stevenson and Fanda Traore for technical support in preparing the text. Finally, we thank each other for the commitment, dedication, and mutual support during the time of writing this book.

Financial Econometrics

1

Introduction

1.1 Assets and Markets

1.1.1 Markets

Financial markets comprise markets for stocks, bonds, currencies, and commodities. During the last decade, these markets have grown remarkably fast in number and volume of daily concluded transactions. Their expansion was paralleled by substantial qualitative improvements. The supply of financial products has increased in size, and several new and sophisticated products have been developed. As well, trading on major stock exchanges has become much faster due to computerized order matching systems that enhance market transparency and accelerate operations.

Financial markets satisfy various commercial and productive needs of firms and investors. For instance, the forward markets of futures on commodities ensure the purchases and future deliveries of goods at prices fixed in advance. Their activity reduces uncertainty in transactions and creates a safe environment for developing businesses. Stock markets satisfy essentially the demand of national and international companies for external funds. The possibility of issuing equity tradable on domestic markets and abroad offers easy access to many investors and allows diversification of shareholders. As for investors, the market value of stocks provides information on the performance of various companies and helps efficient investment decisions to be made.

Financial markets also serve some purely financial purposes: lending, risk coverage, and refinancing. Especially, bonds issued by the Treasury, various states, or companies represent the demand of these institutions for loans. The use of organized markets to collect external funds has several advantages: It allows for a direct match between borrowers and lend-

1

ers; it extends the number of potential lenders by splitting the requested amount into the so-called bonds or notes; it facilitates the diversification of investments; and it allows financing of very risky plans with low probabilities of repayment (junk bonds and emerging markets). Moreover, the experience of past decades shows that the development of organized markets has contributed to significant growth of pension funds by providing sustained returns in the middle and long run.

Financial assets are also used by investors for coverage against various risks; in financial terminology, this is *risk hedging*. For example, a European firm that exports its production to the United States and receives its payments in US dollars within six months following a shipment, may wish to cover against the risk of a decrease in the exchange rates between the US dollar and the Euro. Similarly, an institution that provides consumption loans indexed on the short-term interest rate may need to seek insurance against a future decline of this rate. The demand for coverage of diverse types of risk has generated very specific products called *derivatives*, such as options written on exchange rates or interest rates.

Finally, we need to emphasize the role of secondary markets. A standard credit contract involves a borrower and a lender; the lender is entitled in the future to receive regular payments of interest and capital until the expiry date. Secondary financial markets provide the initial lender an opportunity to sell the rights to future repayments to a secondary lender. The trade of repayment rights is widely used by credit institutions as an instrument of refinancing. A related type of transaction involving mortgages is called *securitization*, which allows a bank or an institution that specializes in mortgages to create financial assets backed by a pool of individual mortgages and to trade them on the market. The assets created in the process of securitization are called *mortgage-backed securities* (MBS).

1.1.2 Financial Assets

Financial assets are defined as contracts that give the right to receive (or obligation to provide) monetary cash flows. Typically such a contract specifies the dates, conditions, and amounts of future monetary transfers. It has a market price and can be exchanged whenever there are sufficient potential buyers and sellers. The acquisition of a financial asset can be summarized in terms of a sequence of monetary cash flows, including the purchasing price. It is graphically represented by a bar chart with a horizontal axis that measures the times between consecutive payments and a vertical axis that measures the amounts of cash flows. The cash flows take positive values when they are received and are negative otherwise.

Figure 1.1 shows that, unlike standard real assets, the financial assets

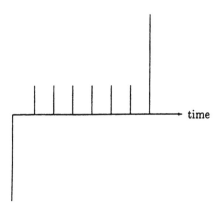

Figure 1.1 *Bar Chart*

need not exist physically. Instead, most financial assets are recorded and traded by computer systems.

Below are some examples of financial assets and the associated bar charts.

Zero-Coupon Bond (or Discount Bond)
A *zero-coupon bond* or *discount bond* is an elementary financial asset. A zero-coupon bond (Figure 1.2) with maturity date T provides a monetary unit (i.e., \$1) at date T. At date t with $t \leq T$, this zero-coupon bond has a residual maturity of $H = T - t$ and a price of

$$B(t,H) = B(t,T - t).$$

The zero-coupon bond allows for monetary transfers between the dates t and T.

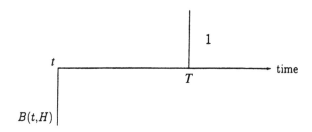

Figure 1.2 *Zero-Coupon Bond*

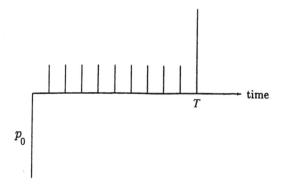

Figure 1.3 *Coupon Bond*

Coupon Bond
Coupon bonds are similar to loans with fixed interest rates and constant, regular repayment of interest. The contract specifies the lifetime of the loan (or *maturity*) and interest payments (or *coupons*) and states the method of capital repayment. The capital is usually repaid at the terminal date (or *in fine*). The coupon bond has a market price at any date after the issuing date 0. Figure 1.3 displays the bar chart at issuing date 0.

If the coupon bond is traded at any date t between 0 and the maturity date T, the bar chart needs to be redrawn. The reason is that the sequence of residual cash flows is altered since some payments prior to t have already been made. Therefore, intuitively, the price p_t differs from the issuing price p_0.

Stocks
Stocks are assets that represent equity shares issued by individual companies. They give to shareholders the power to inflict their opinion on the

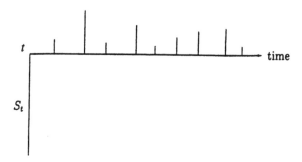

Figure 1.4 *Stock Indefinitely Held*

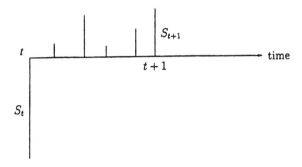

Figure 1.5 *Stock Sold at* $t + 1$

policy of the firm via their voting rights and to receive a part of the firm's profits (*dividends*). If we disregard the value of the right to vote, the current price S_t of a stock is equivalent to the sequence of future dividends, the amounts and payment dates of which are not known at t. Figure 1.4 provides the bar chart representing an indefinitely held stock, whereas Figure 1.5 provides the bar chart of a stock sold at $t + 1$.

Buying and Selling Foreign Currency
To demonstrate transactions that involve buying and selling foreign currency, let us denote by x_t the exchange rate between the US dollar and the Euro at date t. We can buy 1 Euro at t for x_t dollars and sell it at $t + 1$ for x_{t+1} dollars.

The bar chart of Figure 1.6 differs from the one that illustrates a zero-coupon bond because the future exchange rate (i.e., the amount of cash flow at $t + 1$) is not known at date t.

Forward Asset
Let us consider a simple asset, such as an IBM stock. A *forward buy contract* of this stock at date t and maturity H represents a commitment of a trader

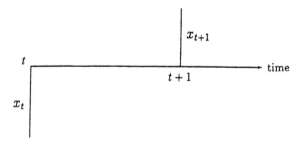

Figure 1.6 *Buying and Selling of Foreign Currency*

to buy the stock at $t + H$ at a predetermined price. Therefore, the buyer starts receiving the dividends after $t + H$. The existence of forward assets allows stripping the sequence of stock-generated cash flows before and after $t + H$ (Figure 1.7).

Options
Options are contingent assets that give the right to make a future financial transaction as described in the following example. A *European call* on IBM stock with maturity T and strike K gives the opportunity to buy an IBM stock at T at a predetermined price K. The cash flow received by the buyer at T is

$$F_T = \max(S_T - K, 0) = (S_T - K)^+,$$

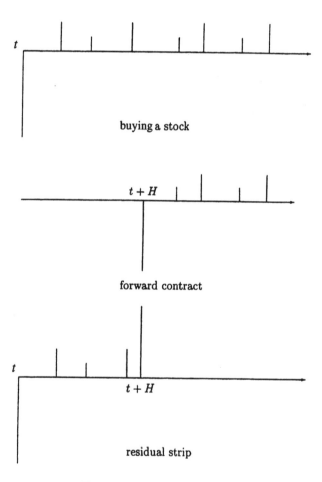

Figure 1.7   *Stripping of a Stock*

where S_T is the price at T of the IBM stock. Therefore, this cash flow is uncertain and depends on the future value S_T. It is equal to $S_T - K$ if $S_T > K$ and is zero otherwise. These two outcomes are illustrated in Figure 1.8. Here, $C_t(T,K)$ denotes the price at t of the European call.

1.2 Financial Theory

Financial theory describes the optimal strategies of portfolio management, risk hedging, and diffusion of newly tailored financial assets. Recently, significant progress has been made in the domain of market microstructures, which explore the mechanisms of price formation and market regulation. In this section, we focus attention on the theoretical aspects of dynamic modeling of asset prices. We review some basic theoretical concepts, not all of which are structural.

1.2.1 Actuarial Approach

The actuarial approach assumes a deterministic environment and emphasizes the concept of fair price of a financial asset. As an illustration, let

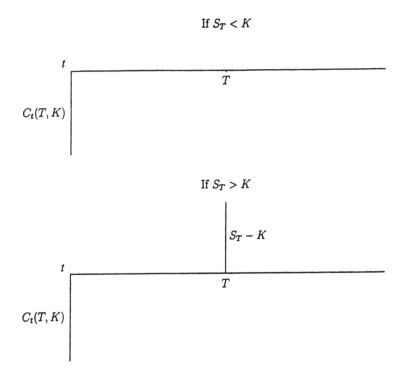

Figure 1.8 *European Call*

us consider at date 0 a stock that provides future dividends $d_1, d_2, \ldots, d_t$ at predetermined dates $1, 2, \ldots, t$. In a deterministic environment, the stock price has to coincide with the discounted sum of future cash flows:

$$S_0 = \sum_{t=1}^{\infty} d_t B(0,t), \qquad (1.1)$$

where $B(0,t)$ is the price of the zero-coupon bond with maturity t. Moreover, if the short-term interest rate r_0 is assumed to be constant at all maturities, the above formula becomes

$$S_0 = \sum_{t=1}^{\infty} \frac{d_t}{(1+r_0)^t}. \qquad (1.2)$$

Formulas (1.1) and (1.2) are the essential elements of the *actuarial calculus*. However, they are in general not confirmed by empirical evidence. The reason is that formulas (1.1) and (1.2) do not take into account the uncertainty about future dividends and the time variation of the short-term interest rate. Some ad hoc extensions of the actuarial formulas have been proposed in the literature to circumvent this difficulty in part. For instance, the literature on expectation models has come up with the formula

$$S_0 = \sum_{t=1}^{\infty} \frac{E_0(d_t)}{(1+r_0)^t}, \qquad (1.3)$$

in which future dividends are replaced by their expectations evaluated at date 0. However, the pricing formula (1.3) disregards again the uncertainty about future dividends. Intuitively, the larger this uncertainty, the greater the risk on future cash flows is. Hence, the observed price will likely include a *risk premium* to compensate investors for bearing risk.

An alternative extension assumes the existence of a deterministic relationship between the derivative prices (e.g., an option written on a stock) and the price of an underlying asset (e.g., the stock). This approach is known as the *complete market hypothesis*, which underlies, for instance, the well-known Black-Scholes formula. The existence of deterministic relations between asset prices also is not confirmed by empirical research.

Essentially, the merit of concepts such as fair price or the deterministic relationship between prices lies rather in their theoretical appeal than in their empirical relevance.

1.2.2 Absence of Arbitrage Opportunity

Let us consider two financial assets; the first one provides systematically, at predetermined dates, the cash flows of amounts smaller than the second one. Naturally, we would expect the first asset to have a lower price.

For instance the price $C_t(T,K)$ of a European call with maturity T and strike K and written on an underlying asset with price S_t should be less than S_t. Its cash flow at the maturity date $(S_T - K)^+$ indeed is less than S_T.

The inequality between prices is a consequence of the *absence of arbitrage opportunity* (AAO), which assumes the impossibility of achieving a sure, strictly positive, gain with a zero initial endowment. Thus, the AAO principle suggests imposing deterministic inequality restrictions on asset prices.

1.2.3 Equilibrium Models

In the approach of equilibrium models, market prices arise as outcomes of aggregate asset demand and supply equilibrium. The equilibrium models are rather complicated due to the presence of assumptions on investor behavior and traded volumes involved in the analysis.

Various equilibrium models can be distinguished with respect to the assumptions on individual behavior. Basic differences among them can be briefly outlined as follows. The standard *Capital Asset Pricing Model* (CAPM) assumes the existence of a representative investor. The equilibrium condition concerns only a limited number of financial assets. The *Consumption-Based Capital Asset Pricing Model* (CCAPM) instead supposes joint equilibrium of the entire market of financial assets and of a market for a single consumption good. The *market microstructure theory* focuses on the heterogeneity of economic agents by distinguishing different categories of investors. This classification is based on access to information about the market and therefore makes a distinction between the informed and uninformed investors (the so-called liquidity traders), and the market makers. Microstructure theory also explains the transmission of information between these groups during the process of convergence toward equilibrium.

1.2.4 Predictions

The efficiency of portfolio management and risk control depends on the accuracy of several forecasted variables, such as asset prices, and their time-varying variance (called the *volatility*). A significant part of financial theory relies on the *random walk hypothesis*, which assumes that the history of prices contains no information useful for predicting future returns. In practice, however, future returns can often be inferred from past prices and volumes, especially when nonlinear effects are accounted for. There exist various methods to examine nonlinear temporal dependence, such as the technical analysis or the time series analysis of autoregressive conditionally heteroscedastic processes (ARCH).

1.3   Statistical Features

Statistical methods for estimation and forecasting of prices, returns, and traded volumes exploit the informational content of past observations. We give below a few insights on various types of variables used in statistical analysis and on the selection of sampling schemes and methodology.

1.3.1   Prices

Many financial time series represent prices of financial assets. It is important to understand the nature of available data before proceeding to the statistical analysis. The mechanisms of financial markets do not differ substantially from those of standard good markets (see Chapter 14 for more details). The trades are generated by buyers and sellers, whose demand and supply are matched directly by computer systems or by an intermediary. On some stock markets, called *order driven*, the prices offered by traders who wish to buy or sell (i.e., the *quotes*), are displayed on computer screens accessible to the public. The quotes are ranked starting with the best *bid* (proposed buy price) and the best *ask* (proposed sell price). This type of market includes the Toronto Stock Exchange (TSE) and the Paris Bourse (PB), for example. On other stock markets, such as the New York Stock Exchange (NYSE) and the National Association of Securities Dealers Automated Quotation (NASDAQ), asks and bids are determined by market makers and include their commissions.

The price at which assets are effectively exchanged can therefore be equal to the bid, the ask, or even a different amount, especially in the presence of market makers. Accordingly, the price records may contain the bids, asks, and/or traded prices. Also, prices per share depend not only on the exchanged assets and times of trade, but also on the traded quantities (*volume*) and individual characteristics of investors and may eventually include the commission of an intermediary. Moreover, in particular cases, the publicly displayed prices may differ from the true trading prices. Therefore, even on well-organized financial markets for which information is accurate and available on line in real time, it is important to know the genuine content of price records. In particular, we have to consider the following questions:

1. Do the available data contain the true trading prices, quotes, or proxies for trading prices computed as geometric averages of bids and asks?
2. Empirical analysis may occasionally concern separately the buyer-initiated (ask) or seller-initiated (bid) trades. In such cases, only sequences of ask and bid prices (*signed transactions*) need to be extracted from records.

3. Do the prices include transaction costs or commissions of intermediaries? Are they corrected for the tax transfers effectuated by either the buyer or seller?
4. Is the market sufficiently liquid to eliminate noncompetitive effects in price formation? This issue arises in the empirical analysis of infrequently traded assets.
5. Have the prices been adjusted for inflation to facilitate their comparison at different dates? This question is especially important for bonds with coupon payments that commonly are discounted.

1.3.2 Frequency of Observations

Recent expansion of financial markets has entailed increasing numbers and frequencies of trades due to the implementation of electronic order-matching systems. Until the early 1980s, data on prices were registered daily at either market openings or market closures. Accordingly, daily traded volumes were also recorded. Therefore, a sample spanning, for example, four years of asset trading would amount to about 1,000 daily observed prices (there are about 250 working days per year).

The electronic systems now allow instantaneously updated records to be kept of all transactions. They register on computer screens all movements that reflect all changes in the list of queued orders (called the *order book*) and have an accuracy of a fraction of one second. Therefore, the size of data files comprising the so-called tick-by-tick data or high-frequency data may be extremely large. A four-year sample may contain more than 1 million records on trades of a liquid stock or more than 3 million records on exchange rates.

Since transaction records are made at various times and are not necessarily integer multiples of a time unit such as one day, the timing of trades requires particular consideration. It is important to distinguish the price data indexed by transaction counts from the data indexed by time of associated transactions. Empirical evidence suggests that the price dynamics in calendar time and in transaction time differ significantly. The comparison of both sampling scales provides insights into the trading activity of an asset and its liquidity.

1.3.3 Definition of Returns

Time series of asset prices display a growing tendency in the long run. Occasionally, however, price series may switch from upward to downward movements and vice-versa in the short or middle run. For this reason, prices of the same asset sampled at different periods of time may exhibit unequal means. Since this feature greatly complicates statistical inference, it needs to be eliminated. A simple approach consists in transforming the prices into returns, which empirically display more stationary behavior.

Let us consider a financial asset with price p_t at date t that produces no dividends. Its return over the period $(t, t + H)$ is defined as

$$r(t, t + H) = \frac{p_{t+H} - p_t}{p_t}. \tag{1.4}$$

The return depends on time t and the horizon H. Very often, statistical analysts investigate returns at a fixed unitary horizon:

$$r(t, t + 1) = \frac{p_{t+1} - p_t}{p_t}, \tag{1.5}$$

which in general display more regular patterns than the initial series of prices.

In theoretical or econometric analysis, the above formula is often replaced by the following approximation: Let us suppose the unitary horizon and a series of low-value returns: we obtain

$$\tilde{r}(t, t + 1) = \log p_{t+1} - \log p_t$$

$$= \log\left(\frac{p_{t+1}}{p_t}\right)$$

$$= \log\left(1 + \frac{p_{t+1} - p_t}{p_t}\right)$$

$$\simeq \frac{p_{t+1} - p_t}{p_t} = r(t, t + 1).$$

The returns defined in (1.5) are used by banks, various financial institutions, and investors in financial markets. The differences of price logarithms conventionally represent the returns examined by researchers. However, it is important to note that

$$\tilde{r}(t, t + 1) = \log\left(1 + \frac{p_{t+1} - p_t}{p_t}\right)$$

$$\simeq r(t, t + 1) - \frac{r(t, t+1)^2}{2},$$

when we consider the expansion at order two. Therefore, the approximation $\tilde{r}(t, t + 1)$ undervalues the true return and may induce a significant bias due to replacing the theoretical definition of returns in (1.5) by the approximation.

1.3.4 Historical and Dynamic Analysis

The distributional properties of returns provide valuable insights on their future values. The analysis can be carried over in two frameworks. The *static* (*historical*) approach consists of computing marginal moments such as the marginal mean and variance from a sample of past returns and using these statistics as indicators of future patterns. The *dynamic* approach concerns the conditional distribution and conditional moments, such as the conditional mean and variance. These are assumed to vary in time, so that at each date t, new estimates need to be computed conditional on past observations. The conditioning is necessary whenever there are reasons to believe that the present returns, to some extent, are determined by the past ones. By the same argument, future returns depend on present and past returns as well, and their values can be used for forecasting.

Historical Approach
The historical approach explores the marginal distribution of returns. For instance, let us consider the series of returns on a single asset $y_t = r \ (t, t + 1)$. The expected return is evaluated from the data on past returns by

$$Ey_t \simeq \frac{1}{T} \sum_{t=1}^{T} y_t = \bar{y}_T,$$

whereas the variance of the return is approximated by

$$Vy_t \simeq \frac{1}{T} \sum_{t=1}^{T} (y_t - \bar{y}_T)^2.$$

The historical approach can be refined by applying rolling estimators. Implicitly, this procedure assumes that marginal distributions of returns vary in time. It is implemented by introducing a window of a fixed length K and approximating the expected return at t by the *rolling average*:

$$Ey_t \simeq \frac{1}{K} \sum_{k=0}^{K-1} y_{t-k} = \frac{1}{K}(y_t + y_{t-1} + \ldots + y_{t-K+1}).$$

On the transition from t to $t+1$, the approximation of the expected return is updated by adding a new observation y_{t+1} and deleting the oldest one y_{t-K+1}.

Conditional Distribution
The analysis of the marginal distributions of returns is adequate for processes with a history that provides no information on their current values. In general, the expected values and variances of returns are partly predictable from the past. This property is called *temporal dependence* and requires a dynamic approach, which consists of updating the conditional moments in time by conditioning them on past observations. Very often, the analysis is limited to the first- and second-order conditional moments:

$$E(y_t \,|\, \underline{y_{t-1}}) \qquad \text{and} \qquad V(y_t \,|\, \underline{y_{t-1}}),$$

where $\underline{y_{t-1}} = (y_{t-1}, y_{t-2}, \dots)$ denotes the information available at date $t-1$. Although the conditional moments are more difficult to approximate, in practice they yield more accurate forecasts.

Horizon and Observation Frequency
The conditional distribution may be used for predicting future returns at various horizons and sampling frequencies. While the predictions of future returns may not always be improved by conditioning on the past, the conditional expectations often yield better outcomes than the historical expectations. For illustration, we discuss below the prediction accuracy in computing the conditional variance of prices, called the *price volatility*.

   Let us first assume that prices are observed at integer valued dates. The price volatilities at date t can be computed at one, two, or more units of time ahead:

$$V(p_{t+1} \,|\, p_t, p_{t-1}, p_{t-2}, \dots) \qquad \text{at horizon 1,}$$
$$V(p_{t+2} \,|\, p_t, p_{t-1}, p_{t-2}, \dots) \qquad \text{at horizon 2,}$$
$$V(p_{t+H} \,|\, p_t, p_{t-1}, p_{t-2}, \dots) \qquad \text{at horizon } H.$$

This approach allows examination of the dependence of volatility on the forecast horizon (the so-called term structure of volatilities).

   If prices are observed every two units of time and t is even, the volatility at horizon 2 is

$$V(p_{t+2} \,|\, p_t, p_{t-2}, p_{t-4}, \dots).$$

It differs from the previously given volatility at horizon 2 in terms of the content of the conditioning set, for which observations at odd dates are omitted.

   The above discussion suggests that price volatility is a complex notion comprised of the effects of time, horizon, and sampling frequency.

1.3.5 Nonlinearity

The complexity of financial time series has motivated research on statistical methods that allow accommodation of nonlinear dynamics. The nonlinear patterns result from the specificity of financial products and the complexity of strategies followed by investors. We give below some insights on the nature of nonlinearities encountered in theory and/or documented by empirical research.

Nonlinearity of the Variable to Be Predicted
Let us provide two examples of the nonlinearity of the variable to be predicted. First, market risk is related to the volatility of returns, com-

monly approximated by squared returns. Therefore, the variable to predict is a power function of the asset price. Second, there exist derivative assets with definitions that involve nonlinear transformations of the prices of underlying assets. For instance, the pricing formula of a European call is based on an expectation of $(S_T - K)^+$, which is a nonlinear transform of the stock price.

Nonlinearity of the Relationships between Prices

Even though prices of a derivative and of an underlying asset do not generally satisfy a deterministic relationship, they likely are randomly and nonlinearly related. For instance, the price of a European call $C_t(T,K)$ and the price S_t satisfy nonlinear inequality constraints due to the requirement of the AAO.

Nonlinearity with Respect to Parameters

Empirical evidence suggests that both the marginal and the conditional return distributions feature departures from normality. Essentially, research has documented the asymmetry of distributions and fat tails, implying a high probability of observing extreme returns. For this reason, standard analysis based on linear regression models, which involves the first two moments only, may be insufficient or even misleading in many financial applications.

Nonlinearity of the Dynamics

The observed dynamics of returns feature several nonlinear patterns. By looking at a trajectory of returns sampled daily or at a higher frequency, one can easily observe time-varying dispersion of returns around the mean or, equivalently, their time-varying variance (*volatility*). The first observation of this type was made by Mandelbrot in the early 1950s, who empirically found that large returns (positive or negative) have a tendency to be followed by large returns and that small returns have a tendency to be followed by small ones of either sign. This phenomenon is known as *volatility clustering* and points out not only the variation, but also the persistence of volatility. During the last twenty years, estimation and prediction of volatility dynamics have been given considerable attention and have resulted in a large body of literature on models with conditional heteroscedasticity. Technically, future squared returns are represented as functions of past squared returns, and nonlinearity arises from the presence of power functions.

In more recent developments, temporal dependence in volatility has been associated with *regime switching*, which means that episodes of high or low returns are explained by movements of a latent variable that admit a finite number of discrete states.

Nonlinearity of the Financial Strategies

The myopic or intertemporal optimizations of investors for dynamic portfolio management, hedging, and risk control are nonlinear with respect to the expected future evolution of prices. Then, at equilibrium, the behavior of investors induces nonlinear effects on future prices.

2

Univariate Linear Models:
The AR(1) Process
and Its Extensions

IN THIS CHAPTER, we introduce elementary time series models for estimation and forecasting of financial data. We begin the discussion with a simple autoregressive model that provides a good fit to various series of returns defined as logarithmic price changes sampled monthly or at a lower frequency. The so-called AR(1) (first-order autoregressive) model is extended to a general class of autoregressive moving average (ARMA) models later in the text.

Technically, two sets of basic constraints are imposed on time series for feasibility of inference and forecasting. The first one requires the time invariance of the first two moments of the marginal distribution. The second one concerns the dynamics and assumes the same type of temporal dependence across the sample. A time series that satisfies these conditions is called *second-order stationary* or simply stationary. Statistical analysis of time series consists of exploiting temporal dependence in stationary processes to build forecasts of their future values based on information available for past and present observations. This predictability property characterizes dynamic processes in the class of ARMA processes. There also exist processes that do not exhibit any relationship among their past, present, and future realizations. They are called *white noise processes*. A *weak white noise* is defined as a sequence of uncorrelated variables of mean zero and variance σ^2. It is an elementary time series, usually denoted $WN(0,\sigma^2)$; it appears in this chapter as a building block of more complex structures.

In the first section, we introduce the autoregressive process of order 1 and study its temporal dependence by means of dynamic multipliers and autocorrelations. Statistical inference is discussed in the second section; we introduce various tests of the white noise hypothesis as well. Section 2.3 presents the effects of modifications in the sampling frequency on the autoregressive representation and introduces the continuous time analogue of the AR(1) model. The limiting case of a unit root process is covered in Section 2.4 in relationship to the so-called martingale hypothesis. In the last section, we discuss the class of ARMA processes.

It has to be emphasized that linear ARMA models represent processes with time-varying conditional means and implicitly assume constant conditional variances. This assumption is not satisfied by financial series, which typically feature time-varying variances (volatility). Models that take into account the time-varying volatility are discussed in Chapter 6. In practice, however, such models are often applied to residuals of ARMA models estimated in a first step. Therefore, the reader needs to be aware of the simplifying assumption made in this chapter. This approach entails some consequences with respect to the variances of estimators, performances of test statistics, and validity of critical values and prediction intervals.

2.1   Definition and Dynamic Properties

2.1.1   *The Autoregressive Process and Its Moving Average Representation*

DEFINITION 2.1: *The series* $(y_t, t \in Z)$ *follows an autoregressive process of order 1, denoted AR(1), if and only if it can be written as*

$$y_t = \rho y_{t-1} + \varepsilon_t,$$

where $(\varepsilon_t, t \in Z)$ *is a weak white noise with variance* $V\varepsilon_t = \sigma^2$, *and* ρ *is a real number of absolute value strictly less than 1. The coefficient* ρ *is called the* autoregressive coefficient.

The dynamics of the autoregressive model are very straightforward. The current value of the series (y_t) is determined by two components. The first one represents the past effect and is determined by the history of the process. The relevant history is limited, however, to the last realization y_{t-1} only, and the impact of this variable is attenuated to some extent by the autoregressive coefficient $|\rho| < 1$. The second component can be viewed as a random shock that occurs at time t. It is called the *innovation* and is not observable. By solving the autoregressive equation recursively, the current value y_t can be expressed in terms of the current and lagged shocks.

PROPOSITION 2.1: *The autoregressive process of order 1 can be written as*

$$y_t = \varepsilon_t + \rho\varepsilon_{t-1} + \rho^2\varepsilon_{t-2} + \ldots$$

$$= \sum_{h=0}^{\infty} \rho^h \varepsilon_{t-h}.$$

This is the (infinite) moving average (MA(∞)) representation of the AR(1) process, and ρ^h is the moving average coefficient *of order h.*

The moving average coefficients can be interpreted as follows. Let us consider a "transitory shock" $\delta(\varepsilon_0)$ at time 0 (say) that adds up to the initial innovation, transforming ε_0 into $\varepsilon_0 + \delta(\varepsilon_0)$. In consequence, the future values of the process y_h accordingly become $y_h + \delta(y_h)$, where

$$\delta(y_0) = \delta(\varepsilon_0), \ \delta(y_1) = \rho\delta(\varepsilon_0), \ \ldots, \ \delta(y_h) = \rho^h\delta(\varepsilon_0), \ \ldots$$

The moving average coefficient ρ^h alters the impact of the additional shock on future values of y. Since $|\rho| < 1$, the shock effect (called the *multiplier effect*) decreases asymptotically to 0:

$$\lim_{h\to\infty} \rho^h = \lim_{h\to\infty} \frac{\delta(y_h)}{\delta(\varepsilon_0)} = 0,$$

and ultimately dies out (Figure 2.1).

REMARK 2.1: The previous results can be extended by including a constant term in the autoregressive model: $y_t = c + \rho y_{t-1} + \varepsilon_t$. Equiva-

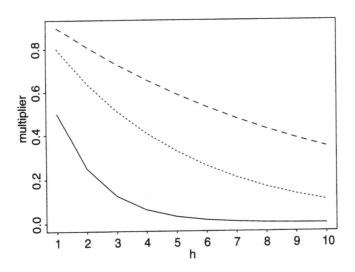

Figure 2.1 Multipliers: $\rho = 0.5, 0.8, 0.9$

lently, the autoregressive equation can be written as: $y_t - m = \rho(y_{t-1} - m) + \varepsilon_t$, where $m = c/(1-\rho)$, to show that the above results hold for the demeaned process $(y_t - m)$.

2.1.2   The First- and Second-Order Moments

The condition $|\rho| < 1$ ensures the existence of the first- and second-order marginal moments of (y_t). It also guarantees their time invariance, which is necessary for the second-order stationarity of the process defined in the following proposition.

PROPOSITION 2.2: *The autoregressive process of order 1 is such that*

(i) $Ey_t = 0, \ \forall t;$

(ii) $Cov(y_t, y_{t-h}) = \dfrac{\sigma^2 \rho^{|h|}}{1-\rho^2}, \ \forall t,h;$ *in particular,* $Vy_t = \dfrac{\sigma^2}{1-\rho^2};$

(iii) $\rho(t,h) = \rho^{|h|}, \ \forall t,h;$

(iv) (y_t) *is second-order stationary.*

PROOF:

(i) We have

$$Ey_t = E\left(\sum_{h=0}^{\infty} \rho^h \varepsilon_{t-h}\right) = \sum_{h=0}^{\infty} \rho^h E(\varepsilon_{t-h}) = 0.$$

(ii) Let us assume that $h \geq 0$. The autocovariances are defined by

$$Cov(y_t, y_{t-h}) = Cov\left(\sum_{l=0}^{\infty} \rho^l \varepsilon_{t-l}, \sum_{k=0}^{\infty} \rho^k \varepsilon_{t-h-k}\right)$$

$$= \sum_{l=0}^{\infty} \sum_{k=0}^{\infty} \rho^{l+k} Cov(\varepsilon_{t-l}, \varepsilon_{t-h-k})$$

$$= \sum_{k=0}^{\infty} \rho^{h+2k} V(\varepsilon_{t-h-k}) \qquad \text{(since the white noise is uncorrelated)}$$

$$= \sigma^2 \sum_{k=0}^{\infty} \rho^{h+2k}$$

$$= \frac{\rho^h \sigma^2}{1-\rho^2}.$$

(iii) Therefore, the autocorrelations are power functions of the auto-regressive coefficient:

$$\rho(t,h) = \frac{Cov(y_t, y_{t-h})}{Vy_t} = \frac{\sigma^2}{1-\rho^2} \rho^{|h|} \left[\frac{\sigma^2}{1-\rho^2}\right]^{-1} = \rho^{|h|}.$$

(iv) Finally, since Ey_t and $Cov(y_t,y_{t-h})$ do not depend on the time index t, the process satisfies the condition of second-order stationarity.
QED

Proposition 2.2 implies that the mean and variance of an AR(1) process remain constant in time. This follows from Proposition 2.2 (i) and (ii) since, for $h = 0$, the covariance of y_t with itself is equal to the variance of y_t. This stationarity condition concerns the marginal distribution of the process. The dynamic aspect of stationarity concerns the behavior of autocovariances at $h \neq 0$. The covariances between the realizations of a stationary time series separated by h units of time are functions of the distance in time h only. They do not depend on the timing of observasions or on their indexes in the sample. For example, in a sample of daily observations on market returns, the covariances of two consecutive returns have to be constant over the whole sample no matter how long it is and how many days it spans. As well, the covariances of each pair of observations separated by h units of time (say one, two, or three days) have to be time invariant.

The formula of autocovariances indicates that the marginal variance of (y_t) is a function of both σ^2 and ρ. As a function of ρ, it increases with $|\rho|$ and tends to infinity when ρ approaches the limiting values $+1$, -1 (Figure 2.2).

The autocorrelations are obtained by dividing the autocovariances by the variance of y_t. The sequence of autocorrelations, considered a func-

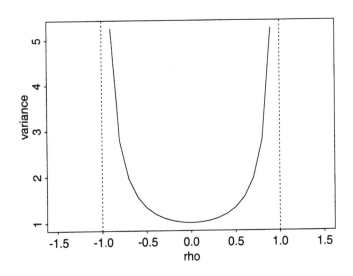

Figure 2.2 *Marginal Variance*

tion of integer valued lags h, is called the autocorrelation function (ACF) (Figure 2.3). For stationary processes, it decreases exponentially to 0. The rate of decay is slow when the absolute value of ρ is large and is fast in the opposite case. Like autocovariances, the autocorrelations describe the memory of a time series in terms of temporal dependence between realizations separated by a varying number h of time units.

As mentioned, the autoregressive parameter can be viewed as the *persistence measure* of an "additional transitory shock." This effect is observable from Figures 2.2 and 2.3. An increase of the autoregressive parameter ρ results in higher autocorrelations and stronger persistence of past shocks. It also has an immediate effect on the marginal variance $Vy_t = \sigma^2/(1 - \rho^2)$ since this expression is an increasing function of $|\rho|$.

The persistence effect of ρ can be observed in simulated trajectories of autoregressive processes. Figures 2.4 and 2.5 display various AR(1) paths generated from a Gaussian white noise with unitary variance. More precisely, we consider independent drawings u_t^i, $t = -1000, \ldots, T$ from the standard normal distribution. The simulated path for given values of the parameters ρ and σ^2 is defined recursively by $y_t^i(\rho,\sigma^2) = \rho y_{t-1}^i(\rho,\sigma^2) + \sigma u_t^i$, $t = -999, \ldots, T$, with the initial condition $y_{-1000}^i(\rho,\sigma^2) = 0$, and formed by observations with nonnegative time indexes $t \geq 0$. The stretch of simulations was initiated at the origin -1000, far away from 0, to eliminate at $t = 0$ a too strong effect of an arbitrary initial condition. For nonnegative

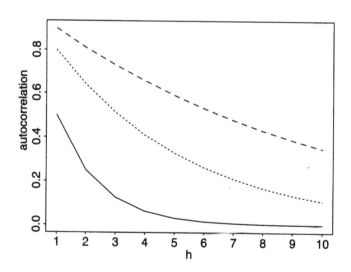

Figure 2.3 *Autocorrelation Function:* $\rho = 0.5, 0.8, 0.9$

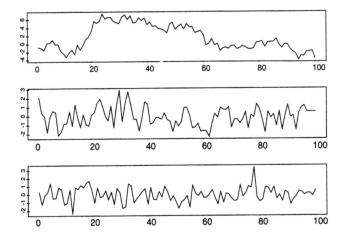

Figure 2.4   *Three Simulated Paths:* ρ = 0.95, 0.3, 0.0

ρ, the impact of past values on the current realization is stronger when ρ increases. Simultaneously, the series becomes less erratic and smoother.

The behavior of the series is different for a negative ρ. Although the autocorrelations at even lags are positive, their signs alternate, yielding negative values at odd lags. This creates pseudoperiodic patterns with period equal to two; these are easy to detect when the absolute value |ρ| is large.

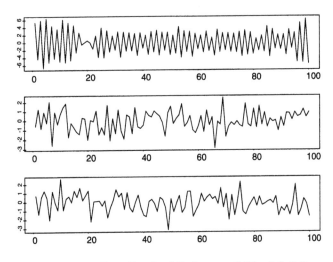

Figure 2.5   *Three Simulated Paths:* ρ = −0.95, −0.3, 0.0

REMARK 2.2: When the autoregression includes a constant term $y_t = c + \rho y_{t-1} + \varepsilon_t$, the above results hold for the process $y_t^* = y_t - m$, with $m = c/(1-\rho)$. In particular, $Ey_t = m$, $Vy_t = \sigma^2/(1-\rho^2)$, $Corr(y_t, y_{t-h}) = \rho^{|h|}$.

2.2 Estimation and Tests

The AR(1) process has two unknown parameters ρ and σ^2 that need to be estimated and tested. The inference can be performed in two ways. In a semiparametric approach, we are interested in estimating the parameters without imposing any restrictions on the distribution of the noise process (ε_t). Basic statistical results on the accuracy of estimators are valid in this framework under the assumption of a strong, or even a weak, white noise (see definition below). In a fully parametric approach, it is necessary to assume that all innovations to (y_t) follow the same parametric distribution, that is, to impose restrictions on the process (ε_t) in the class of white noise processes. Let the observations in the sample be denoted by $y_1, \ldots, y_T$.

2.2.1 Parameter Estimation

In the semiparametric framework, the parameter ρ can be approximated by either of the next two methods. First, the autoregressive parameter can be estimated by ordinary least squares (OLS) applied to the regression model:

$$y_t = \rho\, y_{t-1} + \varepsilon_t, \qquad t = 2, \ldots, T.$$

The estimator of ρ is

$$\hat{\rho}_T = \underset{\rho}{Arg\ min} \sum_{t=2}^{T} (y_t - \rho y_{t-1})^2$$

$$= \frac{\sum_{t=2}^{T} y_t y_{t-1}}{\sum_{t=2}^{T} y_{t-1}^2}.$$

Alternatively, the empirical first-order autocorrelation can be used to approximate ρ:

$$\tilde{\rho}_T = \frac{\sum_{t=2}^{T} y_t y_{t-1}}{\left(\sum_{t=2}^{T} y_t^2\right)^{1/2}\left(\sum_{t=2}^{T} y_{t-1}^2\right)^{1/2}}.$$

Proposition 2.3 summarizes the main properties of these two estimators. We call *strong white noise* a sequence of independent, identically distributed variables with mean zero and variance σ^2.

PROPOSITION 2.3: *If (y_t) is an autoregressive process of order 1 with a strong white noise, then*

(i) *The estimators $\hat{\rho}_T$ and $\tilde{\rho}_T$ are asymptotically equivalent.*
(ii) *They converge to the true value ρ when T tends to infinity.*
(iii) *They are asymptotically normal:*

$$\sqrt{T}(\hat{\rho}_T - \rho) \approx N[0, 1 - \rho^2].$$

The expression of the asymptotic variance of $\hat{\rho}_T$ is easy to derive by considering the least squares approach. Indeed, the accuracy of the least squares estimator is determined by its variance:

$$V(\hat{\rho}_T) \approx \frac{\sigma^2}{\sum_{t=2}^{T} y_{t-1}^2} \approx \frac{1}{T} \frac{\sigma^2}{V y_t} \approx \frac{1}{T} \frac{\sigma^2}{\sigma^2/(1 - \rho^2)} = \frac{1 - \rho^2}{T}.$$

This expression does not depend on the variance σ^2 of the white noise for a simple reason. The autocorrelation function is invariant with respect to the measurement unit of y_t since any change of such a measurement unit would automatically rescale the variance and the autocovariance. The final formula is obtained from the ratio of the white noise variance and marginal variance of the y_t process. The accuracy of the estimator is improved when $|\rho|$ decreases, that is, when data feature more variation and less temporal dependence.

The second parameter σ^2 can be computed from the least squares residuals which approximate the true white noise process. Let us consider an estimator $\hat{\rho}_T$ of the autoregressive parameter ρ. The OLS residuals are

$$\hat{\varepsilon}_t = y_t - \hat{\rho}_T y_{t-1}, \qquad t = 2, \ldots, T. \tag{2.1}$$

The empirical variance of the residuals approximates the true variance of the noise process:

$$\sigma^2 = V\varepsilon_t = E\varepsilon_t^2 \approx \frac{1}{T-1} \sum_{t=2}^{T} \varepsilon_t^2 \approx \frac{1}{T-1} \sum_{t=2}^{T} \hat{\varepsilon}_t^2 = \hat{\sigma}_T^2. \tag{2.2}$$

In practice, the two estimators $\hat{\rho}_T$, $\hat{\sigma}_T^2$ and their empirical variances (or standard errors) are jointly provided by standard regression software.

Finally, we can introduce a parametric model of the white noise distribution and apply a maximum likelihood (ML) method. A common approach consists of estimating the model under the normality assumption. Accordingly, the white noise is assumed to be a sequence of normally distributed variables, which are uncorrelated, with mean 0 and variance σ^2. The ML estimators are obtained by maximizing with respect to ρ, σ^2 the likelihood function

$$(\hat{\rho}_T, \hat{\sigma}_T^2 = \underset{\rho,\sigma}{Arg\ min} \sum_{t=2}^{T} \left[-\frac{1}{2} \log \sigma^2 - \frac{1}{2} \frac{(y_t - \rho y_{t-1})^2}{\sigma^2} \right].$$

The resulting formulas of estimators are

$$\hat{\rho}_T = \hat{\rho}_T,$$

$$\hat{\sigma}_T^2 = \frac{1}{T-1} \sum_{t=2}^{T} (y_t - \hat{\rho}_T y_{t-1})^2.$$

The equivalence of the ML and OLS estimators directly implies that they are consistent and asymptotically normal, even if the true distribution of innovations is not normal itself. In some sense, the normality assumption is introduced to provide an estimation criterion that yields consistent estimators. This approach is called the *quasi-maximum likelihood* (QML) method. It is especially important in financial applications since the return distributions in general exhibit departures from normality.

For Gaussian returns, the QML estimators coincide with plain ML estimators and acquire the property of asymptotic efficiency. This means that they have the highest precision (the lowest variance) among all consistent estimators when the sample size T goes to infinity. In any other case, the QML estimators have less precision and higher asymptotic variances than the ML estimators.

REMARK 2.3: When the autoregressive process includes a constant term

$$y_t = c + \rho y_{t-1} + \varepsilon_t \Longleftrightarrow y_t - m = \rho(y_{t-1} - m) + \varepsilon_t$$

the parameters c, ρ, and σ^2 need to be estimated. It is easy to verify that the OLS or QML estimators of m are asymptotically equivalent to the empirical mean:

$$\hat{m}_T = \frac{1}{T} \Sigma_{t=1}^{T} y_t$$

and that the estimators of ρ and σ^2 have the same expressions as those given above after replacing the initial series y_t by the demeaned process $y_t - \frac{1}{T} \Sigma_{t=1}^{T} y_t$. In particular, the estimator of ρ is equivalent to the empirical first-order autocorrelation.

REMARK 2.4: The asymptotic normality of the above estimators and the expressions that define the variances of their limiting distributions are in general not valid in finite samples. As an illustration, we present in Figure 2.6 a finite sample distribution of the estimator $\hat{\rho}_T$ for $T = 10$, Gaussian white noise, and various values of ρ ($\rho = 0.5$, $\rho =$

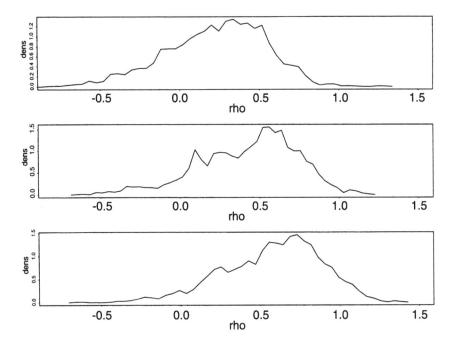

Figure 2.6 *Finite Sample Distributions of* $\hat{\rho}$

0.8, $\rho = 0.99$). We observe that the estimated autoregressive coefficients take values larger than 1 with a nonzero probability. Their probability of occurrence increases with ρ.

2.2.2 The White Noise Hypothesis

In a study of financial returns, one may be interested in testing for the absence of temporal dependence. Recall that the absence of interactions among the past, present, and future values is a characteristic of white noise processes. The corresponding null hypothesis is

$$H_0 = \{\rho = 0\}. \tag{2.3}$$

The following testing procedure is very easy to implement. Under the null hypothesis, the standard estimator of ρ is such that (Proposition 2.3)

$$\sqrt{T}\hat{\rho}_T \approx N[0, 1].$$

Therefore, with 95% probability $|\sqrt{T}\hat{\rho}_T| \leq 2$, or $T\hat{\rho}_T^2 \leq 4$.

The test consists of accepting $H_0 = \{\rho = 0\}$ if $T\hat{\rho}_T^2 \leq 4$ or of rejecting it otherwise. According to Remark 2.4, this testing procedure is valid when T is sufficiently large ($T \geq 30$ in practice).

2.2.3 Variance Ratio Analysis

The white noise hypothesis can also be verified by aggregating data sampled at various frequencies and comparing the properties of the obtained time series. Let us consider the series obtained by adding n consecutive observations:

$$y_t^n = y_t + y_{t+1} + \ldots + y_{t+n-1}.$$

The variance of this sum is equal to

$$V(y_t^n) = Vy_t[n + (n-1)\rho + (n-2)\rho^2 + \ldots + \rho^{n-1}].$$

Under the white noise hypothesis, we get

$$\frac{V(y_t^n)}{nV(y_t^1)} = \frac{V(y_t^n)}{nVy_t} = 1, \qquad \forall n.$$

Therefore, a pragmatic test of this hypothesis consists of computing the empirical ratios

$$\frac{\hat{V}(y_t^n)}{n\hat{V}(y_t^1)},$$

for different values of n ($n = 1, \ldots, N$) and in examining whether they are approximately constant and equal to 1. More details on the variance ratio tests can be found in the literature (see, e.g., Lo and McKinlay 1988, 1988b for a single ratio test and Chow and Denning 1993 for multiple ratios). The variance ratio tests are easy to perform and interpret. As such, they are often applied by practitioners to asset returns, although they are less efficient than the testing procedures based on empirical autocorrelations (see the portmanteau statistic in Section 2.5.4).

2.2.4 Application

To illustrate the previous methodology, the autoregressive parameter was estimated from various financial time series, including the stock returns, market index returns, first differences of interest rates, and exchange rates. For each series, we report in Table 2.1 the sampling frequency, number of observations, sampling period, value of $\hat{\rho}_T$, confidence interval for ρ, and outcome of the test of the white noise hypothesis.

We observe different outcomes of the test of the white noise hypothesis, depending on the sampling frequency and the type of financial asset. Such results are often difficult to interpret, especially because the test statistics and critical values are computed under the assumption of a strong white noise. Thus, the rejection may be due to the presence of a

Table 2.1 *Estimation of $\hat{\rho}_T$*

Series	Frequency	Number of Observations	Period	$\hat{\rho}_T$	Interval	Test
A	Quarterly	148	1952Q1–1988Q4	−0.1466	±0.1643	Accept
B	Quarterly	148	1952Q1–1988Q4	0.0091	±0.1643	Accept
C	Monthly	312	01.1965–12.1990	0.0538	±0.1132	Accept
D	Monthly	312	01.1965–12.1990	1.0114	±0.1132	Reject
E	Monthly	311	02.1965–12.1990	0.1437	±0.1134	Reject
F	Weekly	470	01.1980–12.1988	−0.0641	±0.0942	Accept
G	Daily	960	04.1986–12.1989	0.0956	±0.0645	Reject
H	Daily	960	04.1986–12.1989	0.1191	±0.0645	Reject

The capital letters in the first column refer to various series for T.C. Mills (1993), *The Econometric Modelling of Financial Time Series*.
Data description: A—Yield on 20 Year UK Gilts (first differences), B—91 day UK Treasury Bill Rate (first differences), C—FTA All Share price index (first differences), D—FTA All Share dividend index, E—FTA All Share nominal returns, F—Dollar/Sterling exchange rate (first differences), G—UK bond yield (first differences), H—Japanese bond yield (first differences).

significant autocorrelation, as well as to the existence of an omitted non-linear feature. To explain the results of the test, we need to take into account the following arguments:

- the probability to reject a given null hypothesis increases with the number of observations since it is easier to detect model misspecifications in large samples;
- there exist nonlinear dynamic effects that are easier to observe in data sampled at a high frequency than at a low one;
- nonlinear dynamics are more visible on markets with imperfect competition;
- finally, spurious correlation or nonlinearities may be due to some preliminary data transformations, such as aggregation, according to the rules of computing market indexes.

2.3   The Sampling Frequency

Financial data may be recorded at time intervals ranging from one second in high-frequency data (HFD) sets of stock prices registered automatically on stock markets to one month or even one year for bond prices or interest rates. These last low-frequency data have been available for research for a long time and have been well explored. In contrast, the dynamics of daily or intradaily data is a relatively new topic in the literature. The sampling frequency matters a lot at the stage of model selection and requires the use of adequate inference methods.

The autoregressive process introduced in Section 2.1 has a property of invariance with respect to the selected sampling frequency. This means that an AR(1) series of weekly returns remains an AR(1) series when we reduce the sampling frequency to monthly data or increase it to a higher frequency of, say, daily observations. Note that, while the data at the original, reduced, and increased frequencies span the same period of time, the numbers of observations retained in these samples differ.

We discuss below the consequences of reducing and increasing the sampling frequency. We also show that this issue is related to the dependence of the forecasts and forecast errors on the forecast horizon.

2.3.1 *Low Sampling Frequency*

Let us consider the time series $(y_t, \ t = 0, 1, \ldots, T)$ and assume that we construct a new one by selecting observations indexed by the multiples of an integer value δ. The new series of resampled data is defined as

$$\tilde{y}_k(\delta) = y_{k\delta}, \qquad k = 0, 1, \ldots, [T/\delta],$$

where [.] denotes the integer part.

PROPOSITION 2.4: *If (y_t) is an autoregressive process of order 1 with an autoregressive coefficient ρ and an innovation variance σ^2, then $(\tilde{y}_k(\delta))$ is an autoregressive process of order 1, with an autoregressive coefficient ρ^δ and an innovation variance $\sigma^2 \dfrac{1 - \rho^{2\delta}}{1 - \rho^2}$.*

PROOF: From the definition of the autoregressive process (y_t), we deduce

$$\begin{aligned}
\tilde{y}_k(\delta) &= \rho y_{k\delta-1} + \varepsilon_{k\delta} \\
&= \rho^2 y_{k\delta-2} + \varepsilon_{k\delta} + \rho \varepsilon_{k\delta-1} \\
&= \rho^\delta y_{(k-1)\delta} + \varepsilon_{k\delta} + \rho \varepsilon_{k\delta-1} + \ldots + \rho^{\delta-1} \varepsilon_{k\delta-\delta+1} \\
&= \rho^\delta \tilde{y}_{k-1}(\delta) + \tilde{\varepsilon}_k(\delta), \qquad \text{(say)}.
\end{aligned}$$

Since the variables $\tilde{\varepsilon}_t$ are uncorrelated, their first- and second-order moments are given by

$$E(\tilde{\varepsilon}_k(\delta)) = E(\varepsilon_{k\delta}) + \rho E(\varepsilon_{k\delta-1}) + \ldots + \rho^{\delta-1} E(\varepsilon_{k\delta-\delta+1}) = 0,$$

$$\begin{aligned}
V(\tilde{\varepsilon}_k(\delta)) &= V(\varepsilon_{k\delta}) + \rho^2 V(\varepsilon_{k\delta-1}) + \ldots + \rho^{2(\delta-1)} V(\varepsilon_{k\delta-\delta+1}) \\
&= \sigma^2 [1 + \rho^2 + \ldots + \rho^{2(\delta-1)}] \\
&= \sigma^2 \frac{1 - \rho^{2\delta}}{1 - \rho^2},
\end{aligned}$$

$$Cov[\tilde{\varepsilon}_k(\delta), \tilde{\varepsilon}_{k'}(\delta)] = 0, \qquad \text{for } k \neq k'.$$

QED

This proposition may be used to construct a specification test for evaluating the goodness of fit of an AR(1) model. Empirically, we extract from the initial data set $y_0, y_1, \ldots, y_T$ subsamples at various frequencies $\tilde{y}_0(\delta), \ldots, \tilde{y}_{[T/\delta]}(\delta), \delta = \delta_0, \delta_1, \ldots, \delta_K$. Next, we estimate the associated autoregressive coefficients corresponding to $[\tilde{y}(\delta)]$ processes with varying δ's $(\delta = \delta_0, \ldots, \delta_K)$, plot the values of $\log \hat{\rho}(\delta)$ against varying δ's, and check if the obtained function is approximately linear and passes through the origin. When linearity is accepted, the slope of the line yields an estimator of $\log \rho$. To illustrate this idea, we consider in Figure 2.7 a series of stock returns registered at each trade of the Alcatel stock on the Paris Bourse. Next, we resample these high-frequency returns at fixed intervals of 1, 5, 10, and 20 minutes to create some low-frequency series.

The estimated autoregressive coefficients are −0.237 for 1-minute, −0.025 for 5-minute, −0.078 for 10-minute, and −0.085 for 20-minute sampling schemes. This implies that the AR(1) specification is rejected. Moreover, we observe a strong negative autocorrelation at lag one in the high-frequency data, which is associated with the bid-ask bounce phenomenon (see Chapter 14).

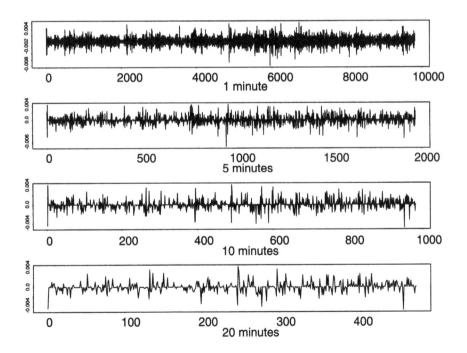

Figure 2.7 *Resampled Return Series, Alcatel*

2.3.2   Linear Forecasting

Let us consider again the autoregressive process of order 1. Assume that the records contain observations up to time T and we wish to predict an unknown future value y_{T+H} that is (say) H steps ahead. H is called the *forecast horizon*. The following discussion is restricted to *linear forecasts*, which are approximations of y_{T+H} by linear functions of $y_T, y_{T-1}, y_{T-2}, \ldots$. By definition, the best linear forecast is

$$LE[y_{T+H}|\underline{y}_T] = \hat{a}_0(H)y_T + \hat{a}_1(H)y_{T-1} + \ldots + \hat{a}_k(H)y_{T-k} + \ldots, \qquad (2.4)$$

where $\hat{a}_0(H), \hat{a}_1(H), \ldots, \hat{a}_k(H) \ldots$ minimize the square average forecast error

$$[\hat{a}_0(H), \hat{a}_1(H), \ldots] = \underset{a_0(H), a_1(H), \ldots}{Arg\ min}\ E[y_{T+H} - a_0(H)y_T - \ldots - a_k(H)y_{T-k} + \ldots]^2.$$

$$(2.5)$$

The notation LE is used to indicate the *linear* (conditional) *expectation*. Very often, the prediction $LE[y_{T+H}|\underline{y}_T]$ is denoted by $_T\hat{y}_{T+H}$ or $\hat{y}_T(H)$.

The solution to (2.5) is obtained by applying ordinary least squares and follows directly from Proposition 2.4.

PROPOSITION 2.5: *If (y_t) is an autoregressive process of order 1, the linear forecast at horizon H is*

$$LE[y_{T+H}|\underline{y}_T] = \rho^H y_T,$$

while the corresponding forecast error is

$$\hat{\varepsilon}_T(H) = y_{T+H} - \rho^H y_T.$$

PROOF: From Proposition 2.4, we get

$$y_{T+H} = \rho^H y_T + \hat{\varepsilon}_T(H),$$

where the noise is serially uncorrelated with $y_T, y_{T-1}, y_{T-2}, \ldots$. Therefore,

$$E\left[y_{T+H} - \sum_{k=0}^{\infty} a_k(H)y_{T-k}\right]^2$$

$$= E\left[\rho^H y_T - \sum_{k=0}^{\infty} a_k(H)y_{T-k} + \hat{\varepsilon}_T(H)\right]^2$$

$$= E\left[\rho^H y_T - \sum_{k=0}^{\infty} a_k(H)y_{T-k}\right]^2 + E(\hat{\varepsilon}_T(H)^2),$$

attains its minimum when $\rho^H y_T = \sum_{k=0}^{\infty} a_k(H)y_{T-k}$.
QED

When the forecast horizon increases, the forecast origin y_T becomes less and less informative. For large H, the forecast approaches zero, which

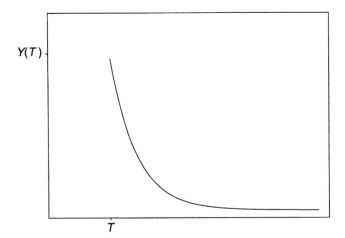

Figure 2.8 *Forecast and Prediction Horizon, Positive* ρ

is the numerical value of the marginal expectation $E(y_{T+H})$. Indeed, the marginal expected value of the series provides the best forecast in the absence of any information (Figures 2.8 and 2.9).

The accuracy of the forecast obviously depends on the horizon. Indeed, we have

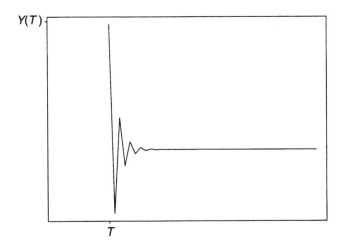

Figure 2.9 *Forecast and Prediction Horizon, Negative* ρ

$$V[y_{T+H}] = V[LE(y_{T+H}|\underline{y}_T)] + V(\hat{\varepsilon}_T(H)),$$

$$\frac{\sigma^2}{1-\rho^2} = \frac{\sigma^2}{1-\rho^2}\rho^{2H} + \sigma^2\frac{(1-\rho^{2H})}{1-\rho^2}.$$

The relative forecast accuracy can be measured by the ratio

$$1 - V(\hat{\varepsilon}_T(H))/V(y_{T+H}) = \rho^{2H}. \tag{2.6}$$

This ratio is equal to 1 for $H = 0$, that is, when the forecasted variable y_T is observed. It tends to 0 when H tends to infinity and the history up to date T is no longer informative. This means that forecasts a few steps ahead are more accurate than the long-term forecasts.

In practice, the forecast function $\rho^H y_T$ requires estimation of the unknown parameter ρ. The empirical forecast for H steps ahead is

$$_T\hat{y}_{T+H} = \hat{\rho}_T^H y_T, \tag{2.7}$$

and the associated prediction interval is

$$\left\{ _T\hat{y}_{T+H} \pm 2\hat{\sigma}_T \left[\frac{1-\hat{\rho}_T^{2H}}{1-\hat{\rho}_T^2}\right]^{1/2} \right\}. \tag{2.8}$$

REMARK 2.5: When the autoregressive model includes a constant term

$$y_t - m = \rho(y_{t-1} - m) + \varepsilon_t,$$

the prediction formulas have to be applied to the transformed process $y_t - m$. We get

$$LE(y_{T+H}|\underline{y}_T) = m + \rho^H(y_T - m),$$

which directly extends the formula in Proposition 2.5. In this framework, $LE(y_{T+H}|\underline{y}_T)$ is the best linear affine forecast (i.e., including a constant term). When H tends to infinity, the prediction tends to the unconditional mean m.

2.3.3 High Sampling Frequency and the Ornstein-Uhlenbeck Process

In Section 2.3.1, we discussed the consequences of an increase of the sampling interval (reduced frequency). The topic of this section is time disaggregation, which is a converse transformation. Assume that we have at hand a process sampled at a very high frequency, for example, of one observation per second, and another one that consists of daily observations. The question is whether the daily data were obtained from aggregating the high-frequency data. In particular, we investigate if there exists an autoregressive process of order 1 ($\tilde{y}_k(\delta)$) that generates the data at a very high frequency $\delta(\delta < 1)$ and is compatible with the process (y_t) observed at a lower frequency. In such a case, the low-frequency data arise from resampling the high-frequency process at some integer multiples of the original interval. If such a disaggregated process exists, the autoregressive representation of ($\tilde{y}_k(\delta)$) has parameters given by

$$\rho = [\tilde{\rho}(\delta)^{1/\delta}], \qquad \sigma^2 = \tilde{\sigma}^2(\delta)\frac{1 - \tilde{\rho}(\delta)^{2/\delta}}{1 - \tilde{\rho}(\delta)^2},$$

or

$$\tilde{\rho}(\delta) = \rho^\delta, \qquad \tilde{\sigma}^2(\delta) = \sigma^2\frac{1 - \rho^{2\delta}}{1 - \rho^2},$$

for a nonnegative autoregressive parameter ρ.

Let us denote by $\rho = exp(-k)$ the autoregressive parameter of the time-aggregated process. When δ is small, the regression equation becomes

$$y_{t+\delta} = \tilde{\rho}(\delta)y_t + \tilde{\sigma}(\delta)u_t(\delta),$$

where $u_t(\delta)$ is a white noise with zero mean and unitary variance, or

$$y_{t+\delta} \approx (1 - k\delta)y_t + \frac{\sigma}{(1 - \rho^2)^{1/2}}(2k)^{1/2}\delta^{1/2}u_t(\delta),$$

or

$$y_{t+\delta} - y_t \approx -ky_t\delta + \sigma^*\delta^{1/2}u_t(\delta),$$

where $\sigma^* = \dfrac{\sigma}{(1 - \rho^2)^{1/2}}(2k)^{1/2}$.

Assuming a Gaussian white noise $u_t(\delta) \sim N(0,1)$, the above regression can easily be interpreted when δ tends to 0. Let us introduce a *Brownian motion*, that is, a continuous time Gaussian process (W_t) such that $W_0 = 0$, $W_t - W_s \sim N(0, t - s)$ for any $t \geq s$. Let us also denote $\delta = dt, y_{t+\delta} - y_t = dy_t, W_{t+\delta} - W_t = dW_t$. The limiting regression equation is a (so-called) stochastic differential equation:

$$dy_t = -ky_t dt + \sigma^* dW_t. \tag{2.9}$$

This particular continuous time process is an *Ornstein-Uhlenbeck process* with mean 0. It is the continuous time equivalent of the discrete time (Gaussian) autoregressive process of order 1 (with a nonnegative autoregressive parameter) (see Chapter 11 for a more detailed analysis).

2.4   Unit Root

The aim of this section is to consider the limiting unitary value of the autoregressive coefficient ρ and discuss its relevance in financial applications. (Unit root processes are analyzed further in Chapter 5.)

2.4.1   Processes Integrated of Order 1

DEFINITION 2.2: *The process* $(y_t;\ t \in Z)$ *is* integrated of order 1, *denoted I(1), if and only if it satisfies the recursive equation*

$$y_t = y_{t-1} + \varepsilon_t,$$

where (ε_t) *is a weak white noise.*

When the regression equation includes a constant term μ, the process is called integrated of order 1 with *drift*:

$$y_t = \mu + y_{t-1} + \varepsilon_t.$$

In the limiting case when $\rho = 1$, the sum of the geometric series in ρ^h is infinite, and y_t cannot be written in terms of lagged values of the noise. Nevertheless, a kind of a moving average representation can be derived for a fixed initial date 0 and an initial condition y_0, which is assumed uncorrelated with future values of the white noise. By recursive substitutions, we get

$$y_t = y_0 + \sum_{\tau=1}^{t} \varepsilon_\tau, \tag{2.10}$$

for the $I(1)$ process and

$$y_t = y_0 + \mu t + \sum_{\tau=1}^{t} \varepsilon_\tau, \tag{2.11}$$

for the $I(1)$ process with drift. In (2.11), the current value of the process depends on three components: the initial condition, linear deterministic trend μt, and cumulated sum $\sum_{\tau=1}^{t} \varepsilon_\tau$. The mean and variance of y_t are

$$\begin{cases} Ey_t = Ey_0 + \mu t, \\ Vy_t = Vy_0 + \sigma^2 t. \end{cases}$$

The variance depends on t whenever $\sigma^2 \neq 0$, and the mean varies with t as well whenever $\mu \neq 0$. Therefore, $I(1)$ processes are nonstationary.

The autocovariance function of the $I(1)$ process is

$$\gamma(t,h) = Cov(y_t, y_{t-h})$$

$$= Cov\left(\sum_{\tau=1}^{t} \varepsilon_\tau, \sum_{\tau=1}^{t-h} \varepsilon_\tau\right) + V(y_0)$$

$$= V\left(\sum_{\tau=1}^{t-h} \varepsilon_\tau\right) + V(y_0), \qquad \text{for } t - 1 \geq h \geq 0,$$

$$= \sigma^2(t - h) + V(y_0),$$

and depends also on t, violating the stationarity condition.

The autocorrelation function is

$$\rho(t,h) = \frac{\gamma(t,h)}{(Vy_t)^{1/2}(Vy_{t-h})^{1/2}}$$

$$= \frac{\sigma^2(t - h) + V(y_0)}{(\sigma^2 t + Vy_0)^{1/2}(\sigma^2(t - h) + Vy_0)^{1/2}}$$

$$= \left[\frac{\sigma^2(t - h) + Vy_0}{\sigma^2 t + Vy_0}\right]^{1/2}. \tag{2.8}$$

It tends to 1 for large values of t.

The nonstationarity of the $I(1)$ process determines its evolution in time and features explosive patterns. Indeed, under the normality of the noise and of y_0, we can expect y_t to fall within the confidence band of length of order $t^{1/2}$, $Ey_0 + \mu t \pm 2(Vy_0 + \sigma^2 t)^{1/2}$, centered around a linear trend.

The trajectories of integrated processes can sometimes be easily recognized from their explosive patterns, as shown in the simulations displayed in Figures 2.10 and 2.11. However, this is not a rule, and many nonstationary data seem well behaved. Some integrated processes, even without drift, often display smooth patterns in some short or medium terms.

2.4.2 Estimation in the Presence of a Unit Root

The $I(1)$ specification can be represented by a regression model

$$y_t = \rho y_{t-1} + \varepsilon_t, \qquad \text{without drift,} \tag{2.12}$$

$$y_t = \mu + \rho y_{t-1} + \varepsilon_t, \qquad \text{with drift,} \tag{2.13}$$

and corresponds to the case when $\rho = 1$.

For these processes, inference is still feasible, although some properties of estimators differ from the standard ones. Especially, we can estimate the parameters of unit root processes by OLS and assess their asymptotic properties.

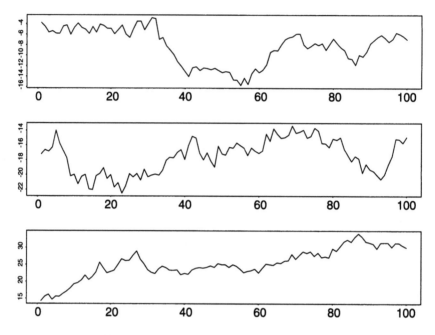

Figure 2.10   *Three Simulated Paths:* $\mu = 0$, $\sigma = 1$

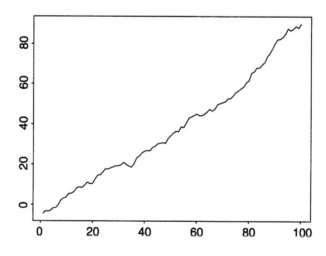

Figure 2.11   *One Simulated Path:* $\mu = 1$, $\sigma = 1$

The OLS estimators are

$$\hat{\rho}_T = \frac{\sum_{t=2}^{T} y_t y_{t-1}}{\sum_{t=2}^{T} y_{t-1}^2},$$

for the model without drift and

$$\tilde{\rho}_T = \frac{\sum_{t=2}^{T} \left(y_t - \frac{1}{T-1} \sum_{t=2}^{T} y_t \right) \left(y_{t-1} - \frac{1}{T-1} \sum_{\tau=2}^{T} y_{\tau-1} \right)}{\sum_{t=2}^{T} \left(y_{t-1} - \frac{1}{T-1} \sum_{\tau=2}^{T} y_{\tau-1} \right)^2},$$

$$\tilde{\mu}_T = \frac{1}{T-1} \sum_{\tau=2}^{T} y_\tau - \tilde{\rho}_T \frac{1}{T-1} \sum_{\tau=2}^{T} y_{\tau-1},$$

for the model with drift.

2.4.3 Test of the Integrated Process of Order 1

Similarly, we can compute the standard t statistics (also called student statistics) of $\hat{\rho}_T$ denoted by $\hat{t}_T$ and $\tilde{t}_T$ for models without and with drift, respectively, for testing the unit root hypothesis. Contrary to the stationary case, the estimator of ρ does not have a limiting normal distribution, and the t statistic is not Student T distributed either.

Exact asymptotic properties of these estimators are too complex to be covered in detail and are instead summarized in the following propositions.

PROPOSITION 2.6: *If (y_t) is an $I(1)$ process without drift*

(i) *$\tilde{\rho}_T$ tends asymptotically to 1;*
(ii) *its rate of convergence is $1/T$;*
(iii) *a test of the unit root hypothesis can be based on either $\hat{\rho}_T$ or $\hat{t}_{T_b}$ and at the 5% level, the null hypothesis is rejected if $T(1 - \hat{\rho}_T) > 14.1$ for the test based on $\hat{\rho}_T$ and is rejected if $\hat{t}_T > 2.86$ for the test based on $\hat{t}_T$.*

PROPOSITION 2.7: *If (y_t) is an $I(1)$ process with drift μ*

(i) *$\hat{\rho}_T$ tends asymptotically to 1 and $\hat{\mu}_T$ to μ;*
(ii) *the rates of convergence are $1/T$;*
(iii) *the tests of the unit root hypothesis based on $\tilde{\rho}_T$ and $\tilde{t}_T$ at the 5% level consist of rejecting the unit root hypothesis if $T(1 - \tilde{\rho}_T) > 21.8$ and rejecting the unit root hypothesis if $\tilde{t}_T > 3.41$, respectively.*

The testing procedures introduced in Propositions 2.6 and 2.7 are known as *Dickey-Fuller tests* (Dickey and Fuller 1979, 1981).

The nonstationarity of the process (y_t) explains a faster rate of convergence of the OLS estimator of $\hat{\rho}$ compared to the typical square root T convergence shown in Section 2.2. Indeed, we have asymptotically

$$V\hat{\rho}_T = \frac{\sigma^2}{\sum_{t=2}^T y_{t-1}^2} \approx \frac{\sigma^2}{\sum_{t=2}^T E y_{t-1}^2} \approx \frac{\sigma^2}{\sum_{t=2}^T [\sigma^2(t-1)]} = 0\left(\frac{1}{T^2}\right),$$

that is, the variance tends to 0 with the increasing sample size at a faster rate than in a stationary process. This is called the *superconsistency*.

2.4.4.   The Martingale Hypothesis

The $I(1)$ hypothesis is related to the so-called martingale hypothesis, which plays a crucial role in asset pricing.

DEFINITION 2.3: *A process $(y_t, t \in N)$ is a martingale if and only if $E_t y_{t+1} = y_t$, $\forall t \geq 0$, where E_t denotes the conditional expectation given the information $\underline{y_t}$. Equivalently, this condition can be written as*

$$y_t = y_{t-1} + \varepsilon_t, \tag{2.14}$$

where the process $(\varepsilon_t, t \geq 0)$ satisfies

$$E_{t-1}\varepsilon_t = 0, \qquad \forall t. \tag{2.15}$$

Here, ε is called a *martingale difference sequence*. It is easy to check that a martingale difference sequence automatically has mean zero and is uncorrelated. Therefore, whenever the variance of ε_t is time independent, the process $(\varepsilon_t, t \geq 0)$ is a weak white noise, and the martingale process $(y_t, t \geq 0)$ is integrated of order 1. Due to imposing (2.15) instead of $E\varepsilon_t = 0$, $Cov(\varepsilon_t, \varepsilon_{t-h}) = 0$, $\forall h \neq 0$, the martingale condition is stronger than the $I(1)$ condition.

The martingale condition of prices implies that the best (nonlinear) prediction of the future price is the current price. The current price conveys all information that can help to predict y_{t+1} and can be directly used as a predictor. This property is also valid for predictions at larger horizons h. Indeed, by the law of iterated expectations, we get

$$E_t y_{t+h} = y_t, \forall t \geq 0, h \geq 0. \tag{2.16}$$

The role of martingales in finance becomes clear when we consider some complex financial strategies. Let us consider a risk-free asset with a price that is constant and equal to 1 and a risky asset with a price p_t that follows a martingale process. Let w_0 denote an initial endowment. It can be invested in both assets, and the portfolio allocations can be regularly updated. Let us denote by $\alpha_{0,t}$, α_t the quantities invested at date t in the risk-free and risky asset, respectively, and by w_t the portfolio value at date t. The portfolio value is

$$w_t = \alpha_{0,t} + \alpha_t p_t. \tag{2.17}$$

The portfolio is *self-financed* if, at each date, the exact portfolio value is being reinvested. The self-financing condition can be written as

$$w_{t+1} = \alpha_{0,t} + \alpha_t p_{t+1}. \tag{2.18}$$

From (2.17) and (2.18), we deduce the updating of the portfolio value:

$$w_{t+1} - w_t = \alpha_t(p_{t+1} - p_t). \tag{2.19}$$

Whenever the decisions on allocations are based on the information $\underline{p_t}$, the updating is such that

$$E_t(w_{t+1} - w_t) = E_t[\alpha_t(p_{t+1} - p_t)]$$
$$= \alpha_t(E_t p_{t+1} - p_t)$$
$$= 0,$$

since the asset price process is a martingale. Therefore, $E_t w_{t+1} = w_t$.

PROPOSITION 2.8: *If the risk-free return is 0 and the asset price is a martingale, the portfolio value of any self-financed portfolio is also a martingale.*

Therefore, the martingale property is satisfied for any strategy of portfolio allocations no matter how complex it is. In particular, $E_0 w_t = w_0$, $\forall t \geq 0$. This equality implies that it is not possible to find a strategy ensuring a strictly positive net return with probability 1 at some fixed horizon. Indeed if $w_t > w_0$ for a time t, we get $E_0 w_t > w_0$, which is contradictory. This explains the equivalence of the terms *efficient market hypothesis* and *martingale hypothesis*. The market is efficient if even a skilled investor has no sure advantage.

2.5 The Autoregressive Moving Average Processes

The AR(1) model belongs to a wide class of models that represent conditional mean dynamics. This class of ARMA models combines the autoregressive and moving average patterns.

2.5.1 *The Wold Theorem*

The Wold theorem plays a central role in time series analysis. It implies that the dynamics of any second-order stationary process can be arbitrarily well approximated by a moving average model.

DEFINITION 2.4: *The process* (y_t) *is* second-order stationary *(or weakly stationary) if*

(i) *its mean is time independent,* $Ey_t = m$,
(ii) *the autocovariance* $Cov(y_t, y_{t-h}) = \gamma(h)$ *depends only on the absolute value of the difference of time indexes.*

Under some mild regularity conditions, a second-order stationary process can always be expressed as a linear function of current and past values of a weak white noise.

PROPOSITION 2.9, WOLD THEOREM: *Any second-order stationary process* $(y_t, t \in Z)$ *[such that* $\lim_{h \to \infty} LE(y_t | \underline{y_{t-h}}) = Ey_t]$ *can be written as*

$$y_t = m + \varepsilon_t + a_1 \varepsilon_{t-1} + \ldots + a_h \varepsilon_{t-h} + \ldots = m + \sum_{h=0}^{\infty} a_h \varepsilon_{t-h},$$

where $(\varepsilon_t, t \in Z)$ *is a weak white noise, and the coefficients are square summable, that is, they satisfy* $\Sigma_{h=0}^{\infty} a_h^2 < +\infty$.

Thus, any process can be written as a moving average of order infinity, possibly with a constant, under a regularity condition that requires that the very distant past has no impact on the current value.

2.5.2   Various Representations

Autoregressive Moving Average Model
The rationale for an ARMA representation of second-order stationary processes is approximation of the above infinite-order moving average by a model with a finite number of parameters. In the rest of this section, we assume for simplicity that all processes have zero mean. In the case when the mean m is different from zero, y_t can always be transformed into $y_t - m$, so that all results hold for the demeaned process.

DEFINITION 2.5: *A second-order stationary process* $(y_t, t \in Z)$ *is an* ARMA(p,q) *process of autoregressive order p and moving average order q if it can be written as*

$$y_t = \phi_1 y_{t-1} + \ldots + \phi_p y_{t-p} + \varepsilon_t - \theta_1 \varepsilon_{t-1} - \ldots - \theta_q \varepsilon_{t-q},$$

where $\phi_p \neq 0$, $\theta_q \neq 0$, *and* $(\varepsilon_t, t \in Z)$ *is a weak white noise.*

The coefficients ϕ_i $(i = 1, \ldots, p)$ and θ_j $(j = 1, \ldots, q)$ are the autoregressive and moving average coefficients, respectively. The description of the dynamics of the process can be simplified by introducing the lag operator L, such that

$$Ly_t = y_{t-1}, \qquad L\varepsilon_t = \varepsilon_{t-1}, \qquad \forall t. \tag{2.20}$$

The ARMA process can be written as

$$\Phi(L)y_t = \Theta(L)\varepsilon_t, \tag{2.21}$$

where the autoregressive and moving average lag polynomials are

$$\Phi(L) = 1 - \phi_1 L - \ldots - \phi_p L^p, \qquad \Theta(L) = 1 - \theta_1 L - \ldots - \theta_q L^q. \tag{2.22}$$

The pure moving average and autoregressive models arise as special cases of (2.13). A process is called a *moving average process* of order q, denoted MA(q), if it can be written

$$y_t = \varepsilon_t - \theta_1 \varepsilon_{t-1} - \ldots - \theta_q \varepsilon_{t-q},$$

that is, has the autoregressive order $p = 0$. A process is an *autoregressive process* of order p, denoted AR(p), if it can be written

$$y_t = \phi_1 y_{t-1} + \ldots + \phi_p y_{t-p} + \varepsilon_t,$$

that is, has the moving average order $q = 0$.

Infinite Moving Average Representation
As in the AR(1) case considered in Section 2.1.1, y_t can be rewritten as a function of current and lagged values of the noise by sequentially replacing $y_{t-1}, \ldots, y_{t-p}$ by their ARMA expressions. This yields an infinite moving average process whenever the a_h coefficients satisfy the condition $\sum_{h=0}^{\infty} a_h^2 < \infty$. It may be proven that this condition is satisfied if and only if the process is second-order stationary or, equivalently, the roots of the autoregressive polynomial $\Phi(z)$ lie outside the unit circle, that is, are of absolute value strictly larger than 1.

Under this condition we can write

$$y_t = \frac{\Theta(L)}{\Phi(L)} \varepsilon_t. \tag{2.23}$$

The ratio of two polynomials of finite order in L yields an infinite-order polynomial in L with the moving average a_h coefficients:

$$y_t = \frac{\Theta(L)}{\Phi(L)} \varepsilon_t = A(L)\varepsilon_t = \sum_{h=0}^{\infty} a_h \varepsilon_{t-h}.$$

PROPOSITION 2.10: *The coefficients $a_h(h = 0, \ldots)$ form dynamic multipliers that measure the effect of a transitory shock to ε on the process y at future horizons.*

PROOF: It is a direct consequence of the equality $\frac{\Delta y_{t+h}}{\Delta \varepsilon_t} = a_h$.

QED

EXAMPLE 2.1: Let us consider an ARMA(2,1) process

$$(1 - \lambda_1 L)(1 - \lambda_2 L)y_t = (1 - \theta L)\varepsilon_t,$$

where λ_1 and λ_2 are distinct real numbers with absolute values strictly less than 1. The moving average representation of the process is

$$y_t = \frac{(1 - \theta L)}{(1 - \lambda_1 L)(1 - \lambda_2 L)} \varepsilon_t$$

$$= (\lambda_1 - \lambda_2)^{-1}(1 - \theta L)\left[\frac{\lambda_1}{1 - \lambda_1 L} - \frac{\lambda_2}{1 - \lambda_2 L}\right]\varepsilon_t$$

$$= (\lambda_1 - \lambda_2)^{-1}(1 - \theta L)\left\{\lambda_1 \sum_{h=0}^{\infty} \lambda_1^h L^h - \lambda_2 \sum_{h=0}^{\infty} \lambda_2^h L^h\right\}\varepsilon_t,$$

and the dynamic multipliers arise as combinations of powers λ_1^h and λ_2^h.

The multiplier effects displayed in Figure 2.12 were computed for two sets of parameter values: $\theta = 0.3$, $\lambda_1 = -0.2$, $\lambda_2 = 0.8$; and $\theta = 0.3$, $\lambda_1 = 0.4$, $\lambda_2 = 0.6$.

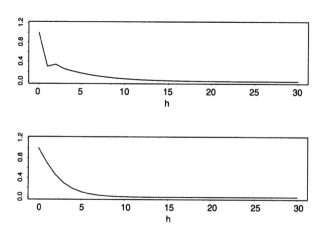

Figure 2.12   Multipliers

Infinite Autoregressive Representation
Whenever the roots of the moving average polynomial lie outside the
unit circle, the current value of the noise can also be expressed as a linear
function of the current and lagged values of the process (y_t). We get

$$\varepsilon_t = \frac{\Phi(L)}{\Theta(L)} y_t = B(L) y_t = y_t - b_1 y_{t-1} - \ldots - b_h y_{t-h} \ldots, \qquad (2.24)$$

using straightforward notation. This infinite autoregressive representation is useful for determining the prediction at horizon 1. Indeed, we
have

$$y_t = b_1 y_{t-1} + b_2 y_{t-2} + \ldots + b_h y_{t-h} + \ldots + \varepsilon_t.$$

The linear prediction yields

$$LE[y_t | \underline{y}_{t-1}] = b_1 y_{t-1} + \ldots + b_h y_{t-h} + \ldots$$

$$= -(y_t - b_1 y_{t-1} - \ldots - b_h y_{t-h} + \ldots) + y_t$$

$$= -B(L) y_t + y_t$$

$$= [1 - B(L)] y_t.$$

PROPOSITION 2.11: *The linear prediction of y_{t+1} evaluated at time t is*

$$LE(y_{t+1} | \underline{y}_t) = \left[1 - \frac{\Phi(L)}{\Theta(L)} \right] Y_{t+1}.$$

2.5.2   The Autocorrelation and Partial Autocorrelation Functions

The Autocorrelation Function
We have already seen the exponential decay pattern of the ACF for an
autoregressive process of order 1. Let us now examine the MA(q) process

$$y_t = \varepsilon_t - \theta_1 \varepsilon_{t-1} - \ldots - \theta_q \varepsilon_{t-q}, \qquad \theta_q \neq 0.$$

Since the components of the noise process are uncorrelated, the autocorrelations are

$$Cov(y_t, y_{t-h}) = 0, \qquad \text{for } h \geq q + 1,$$

$$Cov(y_t, y_{t-q}) = \theta_q \sigma^2 \neq 0.$$

PROPOSITION 2.12: *For a pure MA(q) process, the autocorrelation function vanishes at lag $q + 1$.*

This result is an outcome of the so-called Yule-Walker equations,
given in Proposition 2.13 (see, e.g., Box and Jenkins 1970; Gourieroux
and Monfort 1997). It is very useful in applied research, for which it helps
to identify the moving average order.

PROPOSITION 2.13: *A stationary process can be written as an ARMA(p,q) if and only if the autocorrelation function satisfies*

$$\rho_h - \phi_1\rho_{h-1} - \ldots - \phi_p\rho_{h-p} = 0, \qquad for\ h \geq q+1.$$

In particular, the autocorrelations satisfy a linear difference equation for h sufficiently large and therefore asymptotically become combinations of exponential functions $\lambda_j^h (j = 1, \ldots, p)$, where $1/\lambda_j$ are the roots of the autoregressive polynomial.

The Partial Autocorrelation Function

There also exists another type of autocorrelation function, called the *partial autocorrrelation function* (PACF) r_h, $h \geq 0$. It is defined by a rather complicated formula. It is not discussed in detail in this chapter, and interested readers are referred to Box and Jenkins (1970). The PACF has a property analogous to Proposition 2.12:

PROPOSITION 2.14: *For a pure AR(p), the PACF vanishes at lag p + 1.*

2.5.4   Statistical Inference

The topic of this section is estimation of ARMA models using standard software. The procedure concerns two types of parameters: the integer-valued autoregressive and moving average orders p and q and the real-valued parameters ϕ_i, θ_j, and σ^2. The estimation of p and q is called the *identification*. The next step consists of estimating the ARMA parameters and is followed by *diagnostic checking*, which involves some goodness-of-fit tests.

Identification

The starting values for the autoregressive orders p and q are inferred from the estimated autocorrelation and partial autocorrelation functions, that is, the so-called autocorrelogram and partial autocorrelogram. Generally, the autoregressive order p (or the moving average order q) is indicated by the cutoff point of the PACF (ACF), that is, the highest lag at which the partial autocorrelations (autocorrelations) remain significant, followed by statistically insignificant (close to 0) values of the autocorrelogram (or the partial autocorrelogram). Although the lags at which the PACF (or ACF) die out may overestimate the true moving average and autoregressive orders, they do not cause biased predictions and may ultimately be corrected in the final step of diagnostic checking.

Estimation

Following the identification step, p and q are considered fixed and known. The effort is now focused on finding the remaining parameters θ_i, ϕ_j, and σ^2 of the recursive representation:

$$y_t = \varphi_1 y_{t-1} + \ldots + \varphi_p y_{t-p} + \varepsilon_t - \theta_1 \varepsilon_{t-1} \ldots \theta_q \varepsilon_{t-q}, V\varepsilon_t = \sigma^2.$$

These parameters are usually estimated by the QML under the assumption of independent identically distributed (iid) normal error terms. The values of the likelihood function are computed sequentially and numerically optimized to obtain $\hat{\varphi}_i$, $\hat{\theta}_j$, and $\hat{\sigma}^2$. Recall that the QML estimators are consistent even if the true distribution of errors is not Gaussian. The QML standard errors adjusted for the loss of efficiency are provided only by some advanced software, such as Gauss, TSP, or SAS.

Diagnostics

At the diagnostic step, we identify a posteriori the autoregressive and moving average orders, which may have been previously overestimated or underestimated. To check for overestimated autoregressive order p (or moving average order q), we need to verify the significance of the parameter φ_p (or θ_q). If $\hat{\varphi}_p$ is not significant, we should assume that $\varphi_p = 0$, and that the autoregressive order is at most $p - 1$ instead of p. Next, we repeat the estimation step for an ARMA($p - 1,q$) and continue until the significance is reached. The same approach applies to the moving average order q.

If the order p or q has been underestimated, the dynamics is misspecified, and the model does not capture all temporal dependence in the data. This misspecification can be detected from the residual analysis in such a case since the residuals violate the white noise condition. Theoretically, the errors are defined by the infinite autoregressive representation $\frac{\Phi(L)}{\Theta(L)} y_t = \varepsilon_t$. In practice, the residuals are obtained by substituting the estimated coefficients into the model and computing $\hat{\varepsilon}_t = \frac{\hat{\Phi}(L)}{\hat{\Theta}(L)} y_t$. For missing dates that correspond to observations prior to the sample, the y_t values are simply set equal to 0. Next, the autocorrelogram of the residuals is computed as

$$\hat{\rho}_h(\varepsilon) = \frac{1}{T} \frac{\sum_{t=h+1}^{T} \hat{\varepsilon}_t \hat{\varepsilon}_{t-h}}{\sum_{t=1}^{T} \hat{\varepsilon}_t^2}, \qquad \text{with } h \text{ varying.} \tag{2.25}$$

When the series of residuals behaves like a white noise, its autocorrelations are close to 0. Therefore, it is natural to consider the *portmanteau statistic* (see Box and Pierce 1970; Ljung and Box 1978):

$$Q_H = T \sum_{h=1}^{H} \hat{\rho}_h^2 (\varepsilon). \tag{2.26}$$

When p and q are well specified and when the number of observations T is large, this statistic follows a chi-square distribution with $H - p -$

q degrees of freedom. When $\chi^2_{95\%}(H - p - q)$ denotes the 95% quantile, the selected orders p and q are correct if $Q < \chi^2_{95\%}(H - p - q)$, and at least one of them should be increased otherwise. In the last case, additional information can be obtained from the analysis of the autocorrelogram and the partial autocorrelogram of the residuals.

2.5.5 Application

In this section, we illustrate the approach using a series of prices and returns on the Standard and Poor's (S&P) 500 Index sampled daily between 1950 and 1992. Figure 2.13 displays the paths of the price and return series consisting of 10,876 observations. As expected, the series of returns seems more stationary than the prices. The S&P prices exhibit an upward trend over the entire sampling period, with some short episodes of declining prices. The returns display random movements around a constant mean, very close to 0. The large negative return at the end of the sample indicates the market crash on October 26, 1987.

Figure 2.14 displays the autocorrelogram and partial autocorrelogram of the S&P 500 Index. The autocorrelations of returns vanish asymptotically, while the price series features strong persistence, possibly due to the presence of a unit root (see Section 2.4.1). This conjecture can be verified by applying the Dickey-Fuller tests based on $\hat{\rho}_T$ and $\tilde{\rho}_T$. The test statistics are such that $T(1 - \hat{\rho}_T) = -2.175$, $T(1 - \tilde{\rho}_T) = 7.612$, and the unit root hypothesis cannot be rejected.

We now focus on the stationary daily S&P 500 returns. The analysis of the autocorrelogram and partial autocorrelogram (see Figure 2.15)

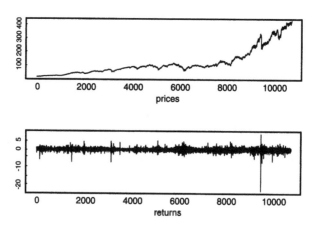

Figure 2.13 *Prices and Returns on S&P 500*

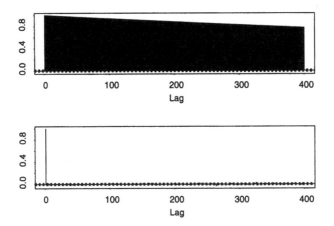

Figure 2.14 *Autocorrelogram and Partial Autocorrelation Function, Price, Daily S&P 500*

leads to the estimated autoregressive and moving average orders $p = 1$ and $q = 1$, respectively. The corresponding ARMA(1,1) model estimated by the QML is

$$(r_t - 0.0299) = -0.2194(r_{t-1} - 0.0299) + \varepsilon_t + 0.3790\varepsilon_{t-1}, \qquad (2.27)$$

with an innovation variance $\hat{\sigma}^2 = 0.6795$. The autoregressive and moving average coefficients of the largest admissible orders have standard errors

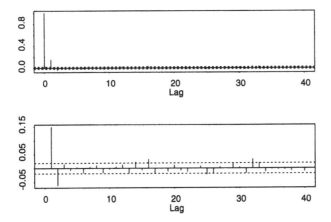

Figure 2.15 *Autocorrelogram and Partial Autocorrelation Function, Returns, Daily S&P 500*

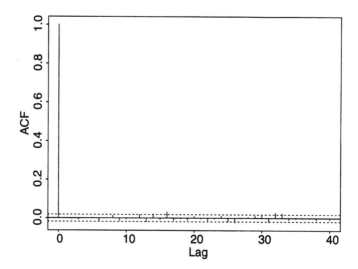

Figure 2.16 *Residual Autocorrelation Function (ACF)*

0.0529 and 0.0509, respectively, and are significant. Moreover, to evaluate the fit, we verify whether all temporal dependence has been successfully removed from the residuals by plotting the residual ACF (Figure 2.16) and computing the portmanteau statistic.

The portmanteau statistic computed with $H = 16$ lags is equal to $Q = 19.41$, whereas the critical value from the chi-square distribution with thirteen degrees of freedom is 22.36. We conclude that the ARMA(1,1) model cannot be rejected.

2.6   Summary

In this chapter, we reviewed basic concepts of time series analysis and introduced linear models for univariate processes with time-varying conditional means. In Section 2.1, we examined the autoregressive process of order 1 and defined the stationarity condition. Stationary processes are often called mean reverting because their trajectories oscillate around a constant marginal (sample) mean without exhibiting any explosive patterns. This is due to their short (finite) range of memory, reflected by fast-decaying autocorrelations (also defined in Section 2.1).

In Section 2.2, we considered how to estimate the unknown parameters of the AR(1) model and how to test the white noise hypothesis. In Section 2.3, the forecasting and sampling frequency effects were discussed. We introduced the continuous time analogue of the AR(1) model called the Ornstein-Uhlenbeck process, which is examined further in Chapters 11 and 12. We indicated that, unlike other processes, the AR(1) process preserves its dynamic structure when the sampling frequency of the process increases or decreases.

In Section 2.4, we were concerned with the presence of a unit root in the AR(1) model. Various aspects of nonstationarity and properties of integrated process are further reviewed in Chapter 5, which provides an advanced analysis of random walks. In this section, we restricted our attention to the unit root tests and to the difference between the random walk and the martingale hypothesis.

The definition of the class of ARMA models and the fundamental Wold theorem for stationary processes are given in Section 2.5. We outlined the Box-Jenkins approach to fitting ARMA models. It consists of three steps: (1) identification, in which the series is differenced to achieve stationarity, if necessary, and AR and MA orders are determined on the basis of sample autocorrelation and partial autocorrelation functions, (2) estimation, and (3) diagnostic checking. Given the estimated time series model, forecasts can be generated for future values of the financial variable. Finally, an example of an ARMA model was applied to financial data.

The approach adopted in this chapter focused on univariate time series, such as returns on individual assets. In practice, however, some processes should not be investigated regardless of their environment. For example, series of returns on assets in a portfolio should be examined jointly rather than independently. This is the rationale for extending the analysis to a multivariate framework, introduced in the next chapter.

3

Multivariate Linear Models:
VARMA Representation

THE MODELS and estimation methods introduced in Chapter 2 can be extended to multivariate time series representing jointly evolving processes. Multivariate analysis investigates temporal dependence and interactions among a set of variables in vector-valued processes. It has a wide range of applications in finance, because portfolios, that generate returns on a set of assets, typically form vector-valued processes. Therefore, multivariate models can be used as instruments for efficient portfolio updating and for revealing arbitrage opportunities. More precisely, financial portfolios contain various quantities of risky assets, which have to be regularly adjusted according to the expected future changes of asset prices. Such strategic allocation updating can be tuned to forecasts from a vector autoregressive (VAR) model of returns introduced in this chapter. Another field of application of multivariate analysis is international finance, in which domestic and foreign interest rates often need to be analyzed jointly with foreign exchange rates (see Chapter 7). By analogy, the analysis of the term structure of interest rates concerns a number of series of interest rates at different maturities and thus requires a common setup as well.

This chapter begins with basic definitions and properties of multivariate time series. In Section 3.1, we introduce a simple VAR model and show its extension to a multivariate vector autoregressive moving average (VARMA) process. The second section covers inference in the VAR model, with an emphasis on estimation of models that satisfy the conditions of seemingly unrelated regressions (SUR). The last section presents empirical examples. The first example introduces a multivariate model of high-frequency returns and volumes. The second example describes the principles of optimal portfolio management under the assumption of a VAR process of asset returns.

3.1 Definition and Dynamic Properties

We consider a multivariate time series $(Y_t, t \in Z)$ of dimension n with components denoted by $Y_{1t}, \ldots, Y_{nt}, t \in Z$. Each component $(Y_{i,t}, t \in Z)$ is a univariate process. The current value of the vector Y_t depends on the past of all component series. Therefore, statistical inference is based on information available at time t on the current and past values of all component series, denoted $\underline{Y_t}$.

3.1.1   The First- and Second-Order Moments

The mean of the multivariate process is defined by

$$m(t) = E(Y_t) = [E(Y_{1t}), \ldots, E(Y_{nt})]', \tag{3.1}$$

where the prime symbol denotes the transpose. It is an n-dimensional vector that contains the means of individual component series. The variance-covariance of Y_t is a symmetric $n \times n$ matrix of variances for the components lying on the main diagonal and of instantaneous cross-covariances for the components lying off the diagonal:

$$\Gamma(t,0) = V(Y_t) = \begin{pmatrix} V(Y_{1t}) & Cov(Y_{1t}, Y_{2t}) \ldots Cov(Y_{1t}, Y_{nt}) \\ Cov(Y_{2t}, Y_{1t}) & V(Y_{2t}) & \ddots & \vdots \\ \vdots & \ddots & \ddots & \vdots \\ Cov(Y_{nt}, Y_{1t}) & \ddots & \ddots & V(Y_{nt}) \end{pmatrix}. \tag{3.2}$$

This matrix is symmetric nonnegative, that is, for any deterministic vector of dimension n, we have

$$a'\Gamma(t,0)a = a'V(Y_t)a = V(a'Y_t) \geq 0. \tag{3.3}$$

The *multivariate autocovariance function* is defined by the expression

$$\Gamma(t,h) = Cov(Y_t, Y_{t-h}) = E(Y_t Y_{t-h}') - E(Y_t)E(Y_{t-h}'), \qquad h \text{ varying.} \tag{3.4}$$

This is a square matrix of autocovariances and cross-covariances at lag h of the components of Y_t. It summarizes both serial correlation in individual series and lagged interactions of the components:

$$\Gamma(t,h) = \begin{bmatrix} Cov(Y_{1t}, Y_{1,t-h}) Cov(Y_{1t}, Y_{2,t-h}) \ldots Cov(Y_{1t}, Y_{n,t-h}) \\ \vdots & \ddots & \ddots & \vdots \\ Cov(Y_{nt}, Y_{1,t-h}) & \cdots & \cdots Cov(Y_{nt}, Y_{n,t-h}) \end{bmatrix}. \tag{3.5}$$

On the main diagonal are the autocovariances of the component series at lag h. In particular, the first diagonal element of a $\Gamma(t, h)$ matrix is the autocovariance of the first component $(Y_{1t}, t \in Z)$ at lag h. The remaining terms determine lagged dependencies between the variables in Y_t. Note that, for a given $h \neq 0$, the $\Gamma(t, h)$ matrix does not need to be symmetric. However, for varying $h \neq 0$, the matrices that form the autocovariance function satisfy the symmetry with respect to positive and negative lags. Therefore, as in the univariate case, the autocovariance function is a symmetric function, and by definition, $\Gamma(t, -h) = \Gamma(t, h)'$.

REMARK 3.1: Let us consider two processes $(Y_{1t}, t \in Z)$ and $(Y_{2t}, t \in Z)$. The structure of joint temporal dependence of the series is quite complex. There is an instantaneous relationship, defined by $Corr(Y_{1t}, Y_{2t}) = \dfrac{Cov(Y_{1t}, Y_{2t})}{(VY_{1t})^{1/2} (VY_{2t})^{1/2}}$, representing the contemporaneous interaction of the processes. It is also possible to distinguish a lagged effect of Y_1 on Y_2 and vice-versa at any lag h. The lagged impact of Y_1 on Y_2 is measured by

$$Corr(Y_{1,t-h}, Y_{2t}) = \frac{Cov(Y_{1,t-h}, Y_{2t})}{(VY_{1,t-h})^{1/2} (VY_{2t})^{1/2}},$$

while the measure of the impact of Y_2 on Y_1 is

$$Corr(Y_{2,t-h}, Y_{1t}) = \frac{Cov(Y_{2,t-h}, Y_{1t})}{(VY_{2,t-h})^{1/2} (VY_{1t})^{1/2}}.$$

The cross effects at varying lags are discussed further in Section 4.3 in the context of causality analysis.

By analogy to univariate stationarity, there also exists a concept of multivariate stationarity. It arises as a straightforward extension of the notion of second-order stationarity for unidimensional processes $(Y_{it}, t \in Z)$, $i = 1, \ldots, n$. It requires the time invariance of the first two moments and cross moments of all component series.

DEFINITION 3.1: *The multivariate process $(Y_t, t \in Z)$ is* second-order stationary *if and only if*

(i) *the mean $m(t) = m$ is independent of t;*
(ii) *the autocovariance $\Gamma(t,h) = \Gamma(h)$ is independent of t for any h; $\Gamma(h)$ is the autocovariance function of the process.*

An elementary multivariate stationary process is called a *weak white noise.*

DEFINITION 3.2: *The multidimensional second-order stationary process $(\varepsilon_t, t \in Z)$ of dimension n is a* weak white noise *if and only if*

(i) *it is centered: $m = 0$;*
(ii) *it is serially uncorrelated: $\Gamma(h) = 0, \qquad \forall h \neq 0$.*

A multivariate white noise does not necessarily admit an identity variance-covariance matrix, and its components can be instantaneously correlated. An identity covariance matrix characterizes the standard white noise. Whenever $\Gamma(0) = \Omega$ is invertible, any white noise process can be transformed into a standard white noise $\tilde{\varepsilon}_t = \Omega^{-1/2}\varepsilon_t$, where $\Omega^{-1/2}$ is the inverse of a square root of Ω (e.g., obtained by the Choleski decomposition).

To illustrate the properties of a multivariate white noise, we show below a trajectory of a bidimensional Gaussian white noise with a variance-covariance matrix:

$$\Omega = \begin{pmatrix} 1 & \rho \\ \rho & 1 \end{pmatrix}.$$

Figure 3.1 displays the simulated paths of two component processes for $\rho = 0.5$.

The mean and the autocovariance function of a stationary process $(Y_t, t \in Z)$ are consistently estimated from their empirical counterparts:

$$\hat{m}_T = \frac{1}{T}\sum_{t=1}^{T} Y_t, \tag{3.6}$$

$$\hat{\Gamma}_T(h) = \frac{1}{T}\sum_{t=h+1}^{T} (Y_t - \hat{m}_T)(Y_{t-h} - \hat{m}_T)'. \tag{3.7}$$

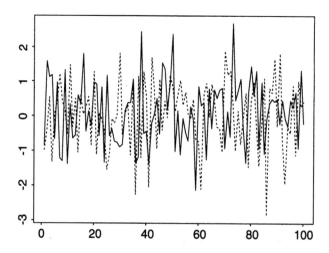

Figure 3.1 *Simulated Paths of a Bidimensional White Noise*

The basic empirical analysis consists of computing the means of individual series $\hat{m}_T$, $\hat{\Gamma}_T(0) = \hat{V}(Y_t)$, and the autocorrelation functions (ACFs) consisting of the marginal ACFs:

$$\hat{\rho}_{i,T}(h) = \hat{\gamma}_{ii}(h)/\hat{\gamma}_{ii}(0), \tag{3.8}$$

and the cross-correlation functions:

$$\hat{\rho}_{i,j,T}(h) = \hat{\gamma}_{ij}(h)/[\hat{\gamma}_{ii}^{1/2}(0)\hat{\gamma}_{jj}^{1/2}(0)], \tag{3.9}$$

where $\hat{\gamma}_{ij}(h)$ denotes the (i,j)th element of $\hat{\Gamma}_T(h)$.

3.1.2 The Vector Autoregressive Process of Order 1

As in the univariate case, the pure vector autoregressive process of order 1 [VAR(1)] provides a simple framework for exploring the multiplier effects and forecasting. Moreover, this multivariate autoregressive process can accommodate quite complex dynamics of individual component series. In empirical research, the VAR(1) model often provides a satisfactory fit to multivariate return series.

DEFINITION 3.3: *A stationary process $(Y_t, t \in Z)$ admits a VAR representation of order 1 if it can be written*

$$Y_t = \Phi Y_{t-1} + \varepsilon_t,$$

where Φ is an $n \times n$ matrix with eigenvalues of modulus strictly less than 1, and $(\varepsilon_t, t \in Z)$ is an n-dimensional weak white noise. Φ is the autoregressive coefficient matrix.

The restriction on the eigenvalues of the matrix Φ ensures that the series expansion in powers Φ^h converges to 0 when h tends to infinity. By recursive substitutions, the current value Y_t can be expressed as a function of current and past values of the noise:

$$\begin{aligned} Y_t &= \Phi Y_{t-1} + \varepsilon_t \\ &= \Phi^2 Y_{t-2} + \varepsilon_t + \Phi\varepsilon_{t-1} \\ &\vdots \\ &= \Phi^h Y_{t-h} + \varepsilon_t + \Phi\varepsilon_{t-1} + \ldots + \Phi^{h-1}\varepsilon_{t-h+1}, \end{aligned} \tag{3.10}$$

yielding

$$Y_t = \varepsilon_t + \Phi\varepsilon_{t-1} + \ldots + \Phi^h\varepsilon_{t-h} + \ldots = \sum_{h=0}^{\infty} \Phi^h\varepsilon_{t-h}, \tag{3.11}$$

which is the multivariate infinite moving average representation of the process. The moving average coefficients Φ^h, h varying, represent the multiplier effect of a transitory shock to the white noise. Let us consider a multivariate shock at date t_0, say $\varepsilon_{t_0} \to \varepsilon_{t_0} + \delta(\varepsilon_{t_0})$. Its effect on the process h steps ahead is

$$\delta(Y_{t_{0+h}}) = \Phi^h \delta(\varepsilon_{t_0}).$$

The infinite moving average representation allows derivation of the first- and second-order moments of the VAR(1). The expectation

$$EY_t = E\left(\sum_{h=0}^{\infty} \Phi^h \varepsilon_{t-h}\right) = \sum_{h=0}^{\infty} \Phi^h E\varepsilon_{t-h} = 0,$$

indicates that the Y_t process is centered at 0. Its variance is given by

$$\Gamma(0) = V(Y_t) = V\left[\sum_{h=0}^{\infty} \Phi^h \varepsilon_{t-h}\right]$$

$$= \sum_{h=0}^{\infty} \Phi^h V(\varepsilon_{t-h})\Phi'^h \qquad \text{since } \varepsilon_t\text{'s are uncorrelated}$$

$$= \sum_{h=0}^{\infty} \Phi^h \Omega \Phi'^h,$$

where $\Omega = V(\varepsilon_t)$.

The covariance function follows from (3.10). Indeed, we get

$$Cov(Y_t, Y_{t-h}) = Cov[\Phi^h Y_{t-h} + \varepsilon_t + \Phi\varepsilon_{t-1} + \ldots + \Phi^{h-1}\varepsilon_{t-h+1}, Y_{t-h}]$$

$$= Cov(\Phi^h Y_{t-h}, Y_{t-h}) \quad \text{since } \varepsilon_t, \ldots, \varepsilon_{t-h+1} \text{ are uncorrelated with } Y_{t-h}$$

$$= \Phi^h VY_{t-h},$$

or

$$\Gamma(h) = \Phi^h\Gamma(0). \tag{3.12}$$

The patterns of marginal autocorrelations and cross correlations plotted against h depend on the rate of decay of Φ^h and implicitly on the eigenvalues of Φ. Let us consider a bidimensional process and denote λ_1 and λ_2 as the eigenvalues of the autoregressive matrix Φ. Several cases may be distinguished.

CASE 1: λ_1 and λ_2 are distinct real eigenvalues (see Figure 3.2). The elements of Φ^h [and of $\Gamma(h)$] arise as linear combinations of λ_1^h and λ_2^h. Since they have absolute values strictly less than 1, we observe an exponential decay of autocovariances at a rate $\max(|\lambda_1|, |\lambda_2|)$. Eventually, the autocorrelations may feature oscillations with period equal to 2 if the largest eigenvalue in terms of its absolute value is negative.

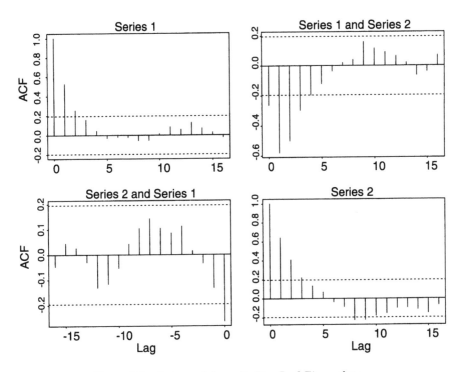

Figure 3.2 *Autocorrelations, Positive Real Eigenvalues*

CASE 2: λ_1 and λ_2 are distinct complex eigenvalues (Figure 3.3). In this case λ_1 and λ_2 are a pair of complex conjugates, and the elements of $\Gamma(h)$ are combinations of $|\lambda|^h \cos\omega h$ and $|\lambda|^h \sin\omega h$, where $|\lambda|$ and ω are the amplitude and frequency of oscillations, respectively. This creates an autocovariance function that behaves like a decreasing sine function.

CASE 3: The matrix Φ has a double real eigenvalue λ (Figure 3.4). This is the *resonance case*. The autocorrelations arise as linear combinations of λ^h and $h\lambda^h$, which leads to a pattern that features a maximum at moderate lags.

Forecasting in the context of multivariate series consists of predicting the future values conditional on the past of all individual series. The forecasts of a multivariate series at horizon h are derived from equation (3.10).

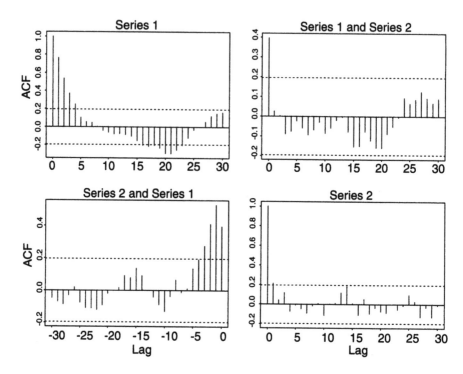

Figure 3.3 *Autocorrelations, Complex Eigenvalues*

PROPOSITION 3.1: *The forecast at horizon h evaluated at time t is*

$$LE(Y_{t+h}|\underline{Y}_t) = \Phi^h Y_t.$$

PROOF: From (3.10), we get

$$Y_{t+h} = \Phi^h Y_t + \varepsilon_{t+h} + \Phi\varepsilon_{t+h-1} + \ldots + \Phi^{h-1}\varepsilon_{t+1}.$$

By substituting for each term its best linear predictor and observing that $LE(\varepsilon_{t+k}|\underline{Y}_t) = 0$, $\forall k > 0$, we obtain

$$LE(Y_{t+h}|\underline{Y}_t) = \Phi^h Y_t.$$

QED

Thus, the dependence of the linear forecast on the past is limited to the most recent observation only.

REMARK 3.2: When (Y_t) represents a vector of price series of various financial assets, the current prices contain all information that can help forecast future prices from the VAR(1) model. (It is a form of

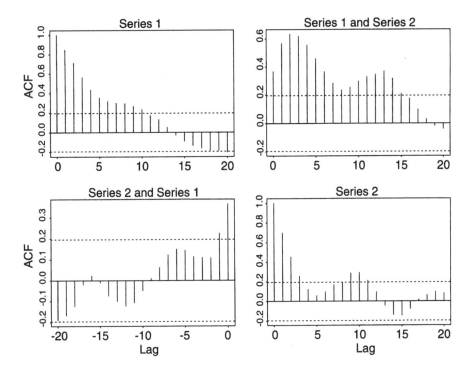

Figure 3.4 *Autocorrelations, Double-Positive Eigenvalue*

the so-called market efficiency hypothesis; see Section 2.4.4 and Chapter 7.) Generally, in the multivariate framework, the prices of financial assets $p_{2,t}, \ldots, p_{n,t}$ (say) may provide additional information to improve the prediction of the future price $p_{1,t+h}$ of asset 1. The efficiency hypothesis is contingent on the size of the market (i.e., the number of assets that are considered).

In practice, any process ($Y_{1,t}$, t varying) can be analyzed as a univariate series or as a component of a multidimensional series [($Y_{1,t}, Y_{2,t}$), t varying] say. The methodologies, discussed in Chapter 2 and here, differ mainly with respect to the information set used for conditioning at time t. In the unidimensional case, the conditioning set contains the current and past values of the series ($Y_{1,t}$) only, whereas it contains the current and past values of all component series in the second case. It is clear that the larger the information set, the more accurate are the predictions. However, it is often necessary to restrict the information set, for instance, for the sake of parsimony (i.e., to estimate a model with a small number of parameters) or to account for the lack of data on some auxiliary series. A constrained information set generally results in a more complex representation of the univariate series, as shown in Proposition 3.2.

PROPOSITION 3.2: *Let us consider an n-dimensional process with a VAR(1) representation. The component series ($Y_{1,t}$, t varying) admits generally a unidimensional ARMA(n, n − 1) representation.*

PROOF: We give the arguments of the proof for the bivariate case, $n = 2$. The VAR(1) representation is

$$Y_{1,t} = \varphi_{11}Y_{1,t-1} + \varphi_{12}Y_{2,t-1} + \varepsilon_{1,t},$$

$$Y_{2,t} = \varphi_{21}Y_{1,t-1} + \varphi_{22}Y_{2,t-1} + \varepsilon_{2,t}.$$

By introducing the lag operator, defined by $LY_t = Y_{t-1}$, we get

$$\begin{pmatrix} 1 - \varphi_{11}L & -\varphi_{12}L \\ -\varphi_{21}L & 1 - \varphi_{22}L \end{pmatrix} \begin{bmatrix} Y_{1,t} \\ Y_{2,t} \end{bmatrix} = \begin{bmatrix} \varepsilon_{1,t} \\ \varepsilon_{2,t} \end{bmatrix},$$

or

$$\begin{bmatrix} Y_{1,t} \\ Y_{2,t} \end{bmatrix} = \begin{pmatrix} 1 - \varphi_{11}L & -\varphi_{12}L \\ -\varphi_{21}L & 1 - \varphi_{22}L \end{pmatrix}^{-1} \begin{bmatrix} \varepsilon_{1,t} \\ \varepsilon_{2,t} \end{bmatrix},$$

$$= \frac{1}{(1 - \varphi_{11}L)(1 - \varphi_{22}L) - \varphi_{12}\varphi_{21}L^2} \begin{bmatrix} 1 - \varphi_{22}L & \varphi_{12}L \\ \varphi_{21}L & 1 - \varphi_{11}L \end{bmatrix} \begin{bmatrix} \varepsilon_{1,t} \\ \varepsilon_{2,t} \end{bmatrix}.$$

We find that

$$Y_{1,t} = \frac{(1 - \varphi_{22}L)\varepsilon_{1,t} + \varphi_{1,2}L\varepsilon_{2,t}}{(1 - \varphi_{11}L)(1 - \varphi_{22}L) - \varphi_{12}\varphi_{21}L^2}.$$

The process $Z_t = (1 - \varphi_{22}L)\varepsilon_{1,t} + \varphi_{12}L\varepsilon_{2,t}$ in the numerator is weakly stationary, it has mean 0, and its ACF vanishes at lags larger or equal to 2. Therefore, it admits a univariate MA(1) (moving average process of order 1) representation:

$$Z_t = \varepsilon_t + \theta\varepsilon_{t-1},$$

say. Therefore, we get

$$Y_{1,t} = \frac{1 + \theta L}{(1 - \varphi_{11}L)(1 - \varphi_{22}L) - \varphi_{12}\varphi_{21}L^2} \varepsilon_t,$$

which in general is an ARMA(2,1) representation.
QED

3.1.3 Vector Autoregressive Moving Average Representation

We present below the extension of the Wold theorem to multivariate processes (see, e.g., Doob 1953).

PROPOSITION 3.3, WOLD THEOREM: *Any second-order stationary process* $(Y_t,\ t \in Z)$ *such that* $LE(Y_t|\underline{Y}_{t-h})$ *tends to 0 when h tends to infinity admits an infinite moving average representation:*

$$Y_t = \varepsilon_t + \Theta_1 \varepsilon_{t-1} + \Theta_2 \varepsilon_{t-2} + \ldots + \Theta_p \varepsilon_{t-p} + \ldots ,$$

where $(\varepsilon_t,\ t \in Z)$ *is an n-dimensional white noise, interpreted as the linear innovation of* Y_t*:* $\varepsilon_t = Y_t - LE(Y_t|\underline{Y}_{t-1})$.

In practice, the infinite moving average can be approximated by a model of a finite order, which is easier to estimate. Indeed, there exists a linear parsimonious representation with a limited number of lags for almost any stationary process. We introduce below the centered (vector) autoregressive and moving average processes, as well as a mixed (vector) autoregressive moving average (ARMA) model.

A (vector) autoregressive process of order p, VAR(p) is

$$Y_t = \Phi_1 Y_{t-1} + \ldots + \Phi_p Y_{t-p} + \varepsilon_t. \tag{3.13}$$

A (vector) moving average process of order q, VMA(q) is defined by

$$Y_t = \varepsilon_t + \Theta_1 \varepsilon_{t-1} + \ldots + \Theta_q \varepsilon_{t-q}. \tag{3.14}$$

Finally, a (vector) autoregressive moving average process of order p and q, VARMA(p,q) is

$$Y_t = \Phi_1 Y_{t-1} + \ldots + \Phi_p Y_{t-p} + \varepsilon_t + \Theta_1 \varepsilon_{t-1} + \ldots + \Theta_q \varepsilon_{t-q}. \tag{3.15}$$

The infinite autoregressive and moving average representations of these processes are useful for evaluation of autocovariance functions or forecasting at different horizons. The notation can be simplified by introducing the lag operator L: $LY_t = Y_{t-1}$, $L\varepsilon_t = \varepsilon_{t-1}$. The VARMA model now becomes

$$\Phi(L)Y_t = \Theta(L)\varepsilon_t,$$

where

$$\Phi(L) = Id - \Phi_1 L - \ldots - \Phi_p L^p,$$
$$\Theta(L) = Id + \Theta_1 L + \ldots + \Theta_q L^q,$$

are matrices of polynomials in the lag operator L. The pure infinite representations are derived consequently by inverting the matrices. For the infinite autoregressive representation,

$$\Theta(L)^{-1}\Phi(L)Y_t = \varepsilon_t, \tag{3.16}$$

and for the infinite moving average representation,

$$Y_t = \Phi(L)^{-1}\Theta(L)\varepsilon_t. \tag{3.17}$$

The invertibility of the matrices $\Theta(L)^{-1}$ and $\Phi(L)^{-1}$ to yield converging series in nonnegative powers of the lag operator depends on the constraints imposed on the moving average and autoregressive coefficients. This concept is illustrated by the VAR(1) process. The autoregressive polynomial in L is

$$\Phi(L) = Id - \Phi L,$$

and its inverse can be written

$$\Phi(L)^{-1} = (Id - \Phi L)^{-1} = Id + \Phi L + \ldots + \Phi^h L^h + \ldots,$$

if and only if Φ^h tends to 0 when h tends to infinity. The convergence pattern is determined by the eigenvalues of Φ. Recall that the eigenvalues are solutions of the characteristic equation

$$\det(\lambda Id - \Phi) = 0,$$

or equivalently are inverses of the solution of

$$\det(Id - \Phi x) = \det\Phi(x) = 0.$$

The following conditions ensure well-behaved autoregressive and moving average processes:

For $\Theta(L)$: The roots of the characteristic equation $\det\Theta(x) = 0$ have to be strictly larger than 1 in absolute value. This condition ensures that the best linear predictor can be written as a linear combination of current and past values of Y.

For $\Phi(L)$: The roots of the characteristic equation $\det\Phi(x) = 0$ are strictly larger than 1 in absolute value. This condition ensures that the process is second-order stationary.

EXAMPLE 3.1: Let us consider a VMA(1) process:

$$Y_t = \varepsilon_t + \Theta\varepsilon_{t-1},$$

where the absolute values of the eigenvalues of Θ are strictly less than 1, and $(\varepsilon_t, t \in Z)$ is a white noise with the variance-covariance matrix Ω. The autocovariance function is easy to derive since

$$\Gamma(0) = V(Y_t) = V(\varepsilon_t + \Theta\varepsilon_{t-1})$$

$$= \Omega + \Theta\Omega\Theta',$$

$$\Gamma(1) = Cov(Y_t, Y_{t-1}) = Cov(\varepsilon_t + \Theta\varepsilon_{t-1}, \varepsilon_{t-1} + \Theta\varepsilon_{t-2})$$

$$= \Theta V\varepsilon_{t-1} = \Theta\Omega,$$

$$\Gamma(h) = Cov(Y_t, Y_{t-h}) = Cov(\varepsilon_t + \Theta\varepsilon_{t-1}, \varepsilon_{t-h} + \Theta\varepsilon_{t-h-1})$$

$$= 0, \quad \text{for } h > 2$$

The infinite VAR representation of this process is

$$Y_t = \varepsilon_t + \Theta\varepsilon_{t-1} = (Id + \Theta L)\varepsilon_t$$

$$<=> (Id + \Theta L)^{-1}Y_t = \varepsilon_t$$

$$<=> Y_t - \Theta Y_{t-1} + \Theta^2 Y_{t-2} + \ldots + (-1)^h\Theta^h Y_{t-h} + \ldots = \varepsilon_t$$

$$<=> Y_t = \varepsilon_t + \Theta Y_{t-1} - \Theta^2 Y_{t-2} + \ldots + (-1)^{h+1}\Theta^h Y_{t-h} + \ldots$$

We find the best linear forecast of Y_{t+1} computed at time t:

$$LE(Y_{t+1}|\underline{Y}_t) = \Theta Y_t - \Theta^2 Y_{t-1} + \ldots + (-1)^{h+1}\Theta^h Y_{t+1-h} + \ldots,$$

and note that this expression involves the whole past of the process.

3.2 Estimation of Parameters

Among VARMA models, the pure autoregressive process is exceptionally easy to estimate. Under standard conditions, the VAR parameters can be approximated by ordinary least squares applied to the system equation by equation. This follows from a general result on the so-called SUR model. The model is presented below, along with some remarks on the SUR representation of VAR(p) processes.

3.2.1 *Seemingly Unrelated Regressions*

Let us consider two multivariate series $Y_t = (Y_{1t}, \ldots, Y_{nt})'$ and $X_t = (X_{1t}, \ldots, X_{Kt})'$ of respective dimensions n and K. We assume that these two subsets of series satisfy a linear system

$$\begin{cases} Y_{1t} = b_{11}X_{1t} + \ldots + b_{1K}X_{Kt} + \varepsilon_{1t}, \\ \vdots \qquad\qquad\qquad\qquad \vdots \\ Y_{nt} = b_{n1}X_{1t} + \ldots + b_{nK}X_{Kt} + \varepsilon_{nt}, \end{cases}$$

where $\varepsilon_t = (\varepsilon_{1t}, \ldots, \varepsilon_{nt})'$ is a weak white noise with components uncorrelated with the X variables. Therefore, the model corresponds to n regressions with different dependent variables and identical explanatory variables. This model also admits a vector representation

$$Y_t = BX_t + \varepsilon_t, \tag{3.18}$$

using conventional notation.

Let us now denote by (X_t, Y_t), $t = 1, \ldots, T$, observations available on the two sets of variables. In this setup, the matrix of regression parameters B and the variance-covariance matrix of the noise term Ω can be estimated by the quasi-maximum likelihood method (QML). As mentioned, in this approach, we build the likelihood function as if the error terms were normally distributed. The quasi-likelihood function is

$$L = -\frac{T}{2} \log \det\Omega - \frac{1}{2} \sum_{t=1}^{T} (Y_t - BX_t)' \Omega^{-1} (Y_t - BX_t). \qquad (3.19)$$

There exists an explicit solution that maximizes this expression with respect to the regression coefficient B and the variance of the noise Ω (Zellner 1962):

PROPOSITION 3.4:

(i) *The QML estimator of B is equivalent to the ordinary least squares (OLS) estimator computed separately from each equation. Consider the equation numbered i and denote by Y^i the vector of observations of the ith endogenous variables $(Y_{i1} \ldots, Y_{iT})'$, by X the matrix of observations of the explanatory variables, and by $b^i = (b_{i1} \ldots, b_{iK})'$ the ith row of B. We get*

$$\hat{b}^i = (X'X)^{-1}X'Y^i.$$

(ii) *These estimators are consistent and asymptotically normal. Their asymptotic variance is*

$$Cov_{asy}\left[\sqrt{T}(\hat{b}^i - b^i), \sqrt{T}(\hat{b}^j - b^j)\right] = \omega_{ij}(X'X)^{-1},$$

where ω_{ij} is the (ij)th element of Ω.

(iii) *A QML estimator of ω_{ij} is*

$$\hat{\omega}_{ij} = \frac{1}{T} \sum_{t=1}^{T} \hat{\varepsilon}_{it}\hat{\varepsilon}_{jt},$$

where $\hat{\varepsilon}_{it} = Y_{it} - X_t\hat{b}^i$ is the OLS residual of equation number i.

3.2.2 Application to Vector Autoregressive Models

It is easy to see that the VAR models fit into the SUR framework. Let us, consider, for instance, a bivariate VAR(2) process:

$$Y_t = \Phi_1 Y_{t-1} + \Phi_2 Y_{t-2} + \varepsilon_t$$

$$= (\Phi_1, \Phi_2)\binom{Y_{t-1}}{Y_{t-2}} + \varepsilon_t.$$

This model satisfies the definition of the SUR model with explanatory variables $X_t = \begin{pmatrix} Y_{t-1} \\ Y_{t-2} \end{pmatrix}$ on the right-hand side (rhs). Hence, the autoregressive coefficients can be estimated by ordinary least squares. In the first equation, we have to run the regression

$$Y_{1t} \quad \text{on} \quad Y_{1,t-1}, Y_{2,t-1}, Y_{1,t-2}, Y_{2,t-2},$$

and in the second equation, we regress

$$Y_{2t} \quad \text{on} \quad Y_{1,t-1}, Y_{2,t-1}, Y_{1,t-2}, Y_{2,t-2}.$$

3.3 Joint Analysis of Intraday Prices and Volumes

3.3.1 Estimation of a Vector Autoregressive Representation

The raw data consist of daily closing values of the Standard and Poor's (S&P) composite stock index and daily volumes of shares traded on the New York Stock Exchange (NYSE). Since the market index is not directly traded, these data have to be interpreted as aggregate summaries of stock prices and market activity. The S&P 500 is a value-weighted average of

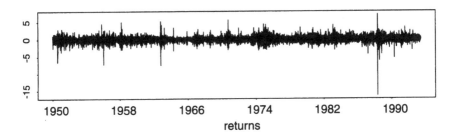

returns

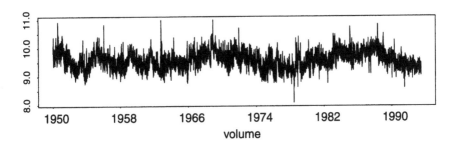

volume

Figure 3.5 The Return and Volume Series, Daily S&P 500

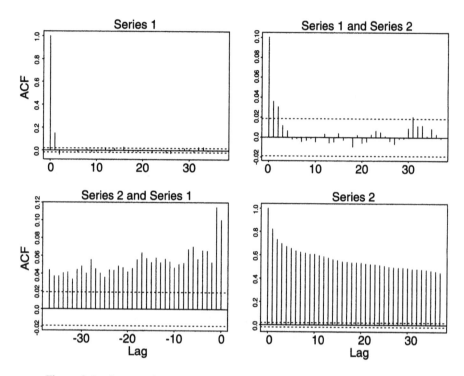

Figure 3.6 *Autocorrelations and Cross Correlations, Returns and Volumes*

prices of common stocks, most of which are traded on the NYSE. Before 1957, it included 90 stocks; it was broadened to 500 stocks on March 1, 1957. The set of stocks included in the composite index is regularly updated and so are the associated weights (see Chapter 15 for more details on market indexes). The volume data originate from the S&P Security Price Index Record. They are obtained by aggregating traded volumes of various stocks, with weights depending on stock prices. The returns are computed by differencing the log-price index, and the volumes are transformed into logarithms. As well, the raw data have been preliminarily filtered to eliminate some trend and seasonal effects (see Gallant, Rossi, and Tauchen 1992).

Figure 3.5 shows the evolution of the return and volume series over the period 1950–1995. We first compute the joint autocorrelogram of the volume and the return series (Figure 3.6). The marginal autocorrelogram of the return series is typical for autoregressive processes of a low order (likely 1), whereas the marginal autocorrelogram of volumes features a high degree of persistence. The cross correlograms show a strong impact of lagged volumes on current returns. Thus, when we consider the univar-

Table 3.1 Estimation of VAR(1)

	Volume				Return		
Valid cases	10,874	Total SS	940.889	Valid cases	10,874	Total SS	75858454.453
Degrees of freedom	10,871	R^2	0.672	Degrees of freedom	10,871	R^2	0.023
Rbar²	0.672	Residual SS	308.510	Rbar²	0.022	Residual SS	74144677.935
$F_{(2,10871)}$	11,141.586	Probability of F	0.000	$F_{(2,10871)}$	125.636	Probability of F	0.000

	Volume					Return		
Variable	Estimate	SE	t	Prob > $|t|$	Variable	Estimate	SE	t	Prob > $|t|$
Constant	1.760186	0.052783	33.347463	.000	Constant	-54.794754	25.876226	-2.117571	.034
vol_{t-1}	0.815828	0.005520	147.804709	.000	vol_{t-1}	5.998239	2.705923	2.216707	.027
r_{t-1}	0.000116	0.000019	5.988261	.000	r_{t-1}	0.146702	0.009529	15.394699	.000

SS = sum of squares
SE = standard error
t = t-value

iate series of returns, we get the impression that past market history is not relevant, whereas a joint analysis of volume and returns shows that lagged volumes can improve linear predictions of future returns. We show below that volumes also help to predict nonlinear features of return dynamics, such as the volatility. Some residual seasonal effects can also be observed.

We estimate in Table 3.1 a VAR(1) representation with a constant term. The estimated autoregressive coefficient matrix of the volume-return series is

$$\hat{\Phi} = \begin{pmatrix} 0.8158 & 0.0001 \\ 5.9982 & 0.1467 \end{pmatrix}.$$

The eigenvalues of this matrix are 0.8167 and 0.1458. The first eigenvalue is large, indicating strong persistence of the volume series.

3.3.2   Intraday Seasonality

In this section, we provide some insights on intraday regularities (called *intraday seasonalities*) observed in hourly volume and return data. The existence of such regularities implies that standard assumptions of a constant autoregressive coefficient and constant innovation variance underlying the VARMA models (see the preceding section) are not satisfied empiri-

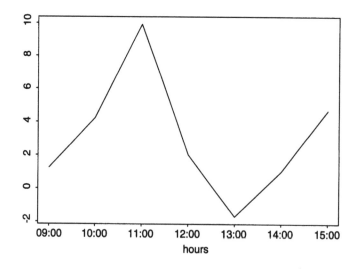

Figure 3.7   *Hourly Average Returns, Bank of Montreal*

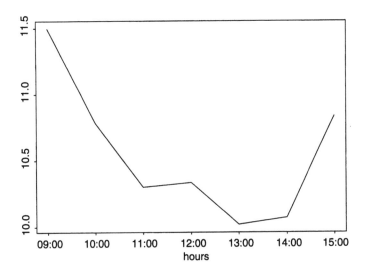

Figure 3.8 *Hourly Average Volumes, Bank of Montreal*

cally. We consider the stock of the Bank of Montreal traded on the Toronto Stock Exchange (TSE). The trading day is divided into hourly subperiods, beginning from the opening at 09:00 until the market closure at
16:00. The hourly returns and volumes averaged over several days are
plotted in Figures 3.7 and 3.8.

We observe a typical U shape for the activity curve. It shows that
traded volumes are high after the opening and before the closure. They
decrease during the lunch period.

Intraday seasonal effects also affect dynamics. Table 3.2 gives, from
the tick-by-tick data, the estimated VAR(1) coefficients as a function of
the hour of the day for October 1, 1998. The joint dynamics features
strong intraday seasonality. It is revealed by the eigenvalues of the matrices of autoregressive coefficients (Table 3.3). Depending on the hour, the
eigenvalues are real, positive or negative, or even complex, implying the
presence of cyclical movements.

3.4 Mean-Variance Efficiency

The VAR model is a useful tool for portfolio management. This section
describes the fundamentals of this approach for practical implementa-

Table 3.2   *Estimation of VAR(1) in Hourly Subsamples*

			Volume		
Hour	Variable	Estimate	SE	t	Probability > $|t|$
09:00	Constant	15.664305	1.773152	8.834157	.000
	vol_{t-1}	−0.302834	0.132568	−2.284358	.026
	r_{t-1}	−0.179635	0.337359	−0.532474	.597
10:00	Constant	13.574141	1.286492	10.551281	.000
	vol_{t-1}	−0.177135	0.102461	−1.728811	.088
	r_{t-1}	−1.074599	0.409970	−2.621169	.010
11:00	Constant	8.727931	1.403468	6.218834	.000
	vol_{t-1}	0.119328	0.120632	0.989194	.326
	r_{t-1}	0.486321	0.762924	0.637443	.526
12:00	Constant	7.513878	1.332435	5.639210	.000
	vol_{t-1}	0.066224	0.148097	0.447170	.657
	r_{t-1}	−0.002416	0.394244	−0.006128	.995
13:00	Constant	8.422337	1.656767	5.083597	.000
	vol_{t-1}	0.158842	0.143872	1.104051	.276
	r_{t-1}	−1.348326	0.711568	−1.894866	.065
14:00	Constant	10.998610	1.480554	7.428713	.000
	vol_{t-1}	−0.084764	0.130608	−0.648992	.519
	r_{t-1}	−0.380188	0.394810	−0.962965	.340
15:00	Constant	12.527214	1.584273	7.907231	.000
	vol_{t-1}	−0.002404	0.102579	−0.023438	.981
	r_{t-1}	−0.115100	0.449949	−0.255806	.799

			Returns		
Hour	Variable	Estimate	SE	t	Probability > $|t|$
09:00	Constant	−0.166868	0.702866	−0.237410	.813
	vol_{t-1}	0.004239	0.052549	0.080676	.936
	r_{t-1}	−0.183590	0.133727	−1.372870	.176
10:00	Constant	−0.381711	0.329440	−1.158667	.250
	vol_{t-1}	0.063129	0.026238	2.406025	.018
	r_{t-1}	−0.124897	0.104983	−1.189681	.238
11:00	Constant	0.175233	0.216023	0.811178	.420
	vol_{t-1}	−0.017378	0.018568	−0.935906	.353
	r_{t-1}	−0.287463	0.117430	−2.447953	.017
12:00	Constant	−0.462773	0.481662	−0.960784	.342
	vol_{t-1}	0.053552	0.053535	1.000315	.322
	r_{t-1}	−0.272268	0.142515	−1.910451	.062
13:00	Constant	−0.616406	0.338113	−1.823076	.075
	vol_{t-1}	0.048714	0.029361	1.659111	.104
	r_{t-1}	−0.124255	0.145217	−0.855654	.397
14:00	Constant	0.233328	0.465058	0.501718	.618
	vol_{t-1}	−0.021466	0.041025	−0.523224	.603
	r_{t-1}	−0.340070	0.124014	−2.742187	.008
15:00	Constant	−0.497027	0.337962	−1.470660	.145
	vol_{t-1}	0.026622	0.021882	1.216594	.227
	r_{t-1}	−0.324222	0.095984	−3.377854	.001

Table 3.3 *Eigenvalues in Hourly Subsamples*

Hour		
09:00	−0.296	−0.190
10:00	−0.151	± 0.259 i
11:00	0.097	−0.265
12:00	0.066	−0.271
13:00	0.017	± 0.214 i
14:00	−0.056	−0.368
15:00	−0.012	−0.314

tions. We begin with theoretical remarks on efficient portfolio selection and next study an empirical example involving a VAR(1) model.

3.4.1 Efficient Portfolios

Suppose the existence of a finite number of securities indexed by i, $i = 0$, $\ldots$, n. The security 0 is risk-free and has a price equal to 1 at date t, while its value at $t+1$ is $1 + r_t$, where r_t is the risk-free rate. The other securities are risky and have prices $p_{i,t}$, $i = 1, \ldots, n$, $t = 1, \ldots, T$. They pay no dividends.

A portfolio is described by an allocation vector $(\alpha_0, \alpha_1, \ldots, \alpha_n)' = (\alpha_0, \alpha')'$ (say) of quantities α_i of various securities. It defines the *portfolio allocation*. The portfolio is characterized by an acquisition cost at date t of $\alpha_0 + \alpha' p_t = w_t$ and a value at date $t+1$ of $\alpha_0(1 + r_t) + \alpha' p_{t+1} = w_{t+1}$.

At time t, this future value is partly unknown. Its expectation is $\mu_t(\alpha_0, \alpha) = E_t w_{t+1} = \alpha_0(1 + r_t) + \alpha' E_t p_{t+1}$; its variance is $\eta_t^2(\alpha_0, \alpha) = V_t w_{t+1} = \alpha' V_t p_{t+1} \alpha$.

In the mean-variance approach (Markowitz 1952, 1976; Roy 1952; Sharpe 1963), the investor selects the composition of the portfolio at time t by taking into account his initial budget constraint and tries to maximize the expected value while minimizing the risk (i.e., the variance). Since these objectives are contradictory, the investor compromises and selects the portfolio with a balanced trade-off between the conditional mean and the variance.

The investor's optimization objective is

$$\max_{\alpha_0, \alpha} \mu_t(\alpha_0, \alpha) - \frac{A}{2} \eta_t^2 (\alpha_0, \alpha), \qquad (3.20)$$

subject to

$$\alpha_0 + \alpha' p_t = w,$$

where w is the initial endowment at time t, and A is a positive scalar that measures the investor's risk aversion. From the budget constraint, we can derive the quantity of the risk-free asset: $\alpha_0 = w - \alpha' p_t$. Next, after substituting this expression into the criterion function, the objective is to maximize with respect to the allocation α in the risky assets:

$$\max_{\alpha} w(1 + r_t) + \alpha'[E_t p_{t+1} - p_t(1 + r_t)] - \frac{A}{2} \alpha' V_t p_{t+1} \alpha.$$

Let us denote by $Y_{t+1} = p_{t+1} - p_t(1 + r_t)$ the *excess gain* on the risky assets, that is, the gain corrected for the return on the risk-free asset. Since r_t and p_t belong to the information set available at time t, the expression to be maximized becomes

$$\max_{\alpha} \alpha' E_t Y_{t+1} - \frac{A}{2} \alpha' V_t Y_{t+1} \alpha. \qquad (3.21)$$

The objective function is concave in α, and the optimal allocation satisfies the first-order condition

$$E_t Y_{t+1} - A V_t Y_{t+1} \alpha_t^* = 0,$$

or

$$\alpha_t^* = \frac{1}{A} (V_t Y_{t+1})^{-1} E_t Y_{t+1}. \qquad (3.22)$$

PROPOSITION 3.5: *The solutions of the mean-variance optimization, that is, the* mean-variance efficient portfolio *allocations, consist of allocations in risky assets proportional to*

$$\alpha_t^* \propto (V_t Y_{t+1})^{-1} E_t Y_{t+1},$$

where Y_{t+1} is the excess gain: $Y_{t+1} = p_{t+1} - (1 + r_t) p_t$. The corresponding quantity of risk-free asset is

$$\alpha_{0,t}^* = w - \hat{\alpha}_t^* p_t.$$

The initial budget has an effect only on the allocation in the risk-free asset. The quantities of risky assets diminish when the risk aversion coefficient A increases.

3.4.2   Efficiency Frontier

The stochastic properties of efficient portfolios are summarized by their first- and second-order conditional moments. These are

$$\mu_t^*(A, w) = \mu_t(\alpha_{0,t}^*, \alpha_t^*)$$

$$= \alpha_{0,t}^*(1 + r_t) + \alpha_t^{*'} E_t p_{t+1}$$

$$= w(1 + r_t) + \alpha_t^{*\prime}[E_t p_{t+1} - (1 + r_t)p_t]$$

$$= w(1 + r_t) + \frac{1}{A}(E_t Y_{t+1})'(V_t Y_{t+1})^{-1}(E_t Y_{t+1}),$$

$$\eta_t^2*(A, w) = \eta_t^*(\alpha_{0,t}^*, \alpha_t^*)$$

$$= \alpha_t^{*\prime} V_t(p_{t+1})\alpha_t^*$$

$$= \frac{1}{A^2}(E_t Y_{t+1})'(V_t Y_{t+1})^{-1}(E_t Y_{t+1}).$$

When w is fixed and A, $A > 0$ varies, the moments are related by

$$\eta_t^2*(A, w) = \frac{1}{P_t}[\mu_t^*(A, w) - w(1 + r_t)]^2, \qquad (3.23)$$

where $P_t = (E_t Y_{t+1})'(V_t Y_{t+1})^{-1}(E_t Y_{t+1})$ measures the relative magnitude of the expected excess gain with respect to risk. P_t is called the *Sharpe performance* of the set of assets (Sharpe 1963; Lintner 1965).

Let us now introduce the mean-variance representation of portfolios. Each portfolio is represented by a bidimensional vector with components that are the conditional mean and variance of its future value. From (3.23), the set of efficient portfolios forms a semiparabola, which is tangent to the vertical axis at the risk-free portfolio, in which the whole budget is invested in the risk-free asset. All other portfolios are situated below this semiparabola, which justifies the term *efficiency frontier* (Figure 3.9). The efficiency frontier shifts upward when the Sharpe performance increases.

The mean-variance representation, that is, the efficiency frontier and the location of portfolios with respect to the frontier, depend on time t through the price history.

3.4.3 Expected Utility

In a special case, the mean-variance approach can be interpreted in terms of expected utility. Let us consider an exponential utility function $U(w) = -\exp(-Aw)$, where the parameter A is positive. The absolute risk aversion $-\dfrac{d^2 U(w)}{dw^2} \Big/ \dfrac{dU(w)}{dw} = A$ is independent of the wealth w. For this reason, this utility function features constant absolute risk aversion (CARA).

An investor may maximize his expected utility under the budget constraint. The optimization objective is

$$\max_{\alpha_{0,t}} E_t U(w_{t+1})$$

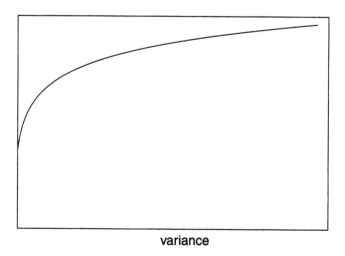

variance

Figure 3.9   *The Efficiency Frontier*

subject to

$$\alpha_0 + \alpha' p_t = w.$$

After eliminating the allocation in the risk-free asset through the budget constraint, the objective becomes

$$\max_{\alpha} - E_t[\exp - A(w(1 + r_t) + \alpha' Y_{t+1})].$$

When the vector of excess gains is conditionally Gaussian, the objective function is equivalent to the moment-generating function of a Gaussian variable and can be expressed in terms of the first- and second-order conditional moments. We get

$$\max_{\alpha} - \exp\left[-AE_t w_{t+1} + \frac{A^2}{2} V_t w_{t+1}\right].$$

This optimization is equivalent to the mean-variance optimization:

$$\max_{\alpha} \left(E_t w_{t+1} - \frac{A}{2} V_t w_{t+1}\right),$$

solved in Section 3.4.1.

3.4.4   *Vector Autoregressive Processes of Returns*

The general theory of efficient portfolios can be applied to the case of an
excess gain process with a VAR(1) representation that includes a constant:

$$Y_{t+1} = \mu + \Phi Y_t + \varepsilon_{t+1}, \tag{3.24}$$

where ε_t is conditionally centered, $E_t \varepsilon_{t+1} = 0$, and conditionally homoscedastic, $V_t \varepsilon_{t+1} = \Omega$. The first- and second-order moments of the excess
gain are

$$E_t Y_{t+1} = \mu + \Phi Y_t, \qquad V_t Y_{t+1} = \Omega.$$

Therefore, the efficient allocations are

$$\alpha_t^* = \frac{1}{A}(V_t Y_{t+1})^{-1} E_t Y_{t+1}$$

$$= \frac{1}{A}\Omega^{-1}(\mu + \Phi Y_t) \tag{3.25}$$

$$= \frac{1}{A}\Omega^{-1}\mu + \frac{1}{A}\Omega^{-1}\Phi Y_t.$$

They depend on the price history through the current values Y_t. These
allocations are generated by a limited number of basic portfolios $\Omega^{-1}\mu$ and
the columns of $\Omega^{-1}\Phi$. The number of independent generating portfolios,
often called the *benchmark portfolios*, is equal to the rank of $[\mu, \Phi]$.

The investor has to update his or her portfolio regularly by taking
into account the available information. It is interesting to compare this
behavior with the behavior of an investor who fails to perform the updating. Such an investor will select an allocation based on the marginal moments:

$$\alpha^* = \frac{1}{A}(V Y_{t+1})^{-1} E Y_{t+1},$$

$$= \frac{1}{A}\Omega^{-1}(Id - \Phi)^{-1}\mu.$$

As a result, the investor obtains a static portfolio allocation equivalent to
the expected value of the dynamic allocation $\alpha^* = E\alpha_{t+1}^*$. In the (conditional) mean-variance representation, this set of "marginally" efficient
portfolios (i.e., determined by the marginal moments) is represented by a
semiparabola located below the efficiency frontier and tangent to it at the
risk-free portfolio (Figure 3.10).

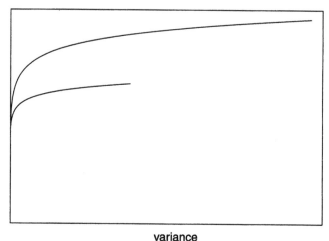

variance

Figure 3.10 *Marginally Efficient Portfolios and the Frontier*

Indeed, the equation of the subefficient semiparabola is

$$\eta_t^2 = \frac{1}{\tilde{P}_t}[\mu_t - w(1 + r_t)]^2,$$

where

$$1/\tilde{P}_t = \frac{(EY_{t+1})'(VY_{t+1})^{-1}V_tY_{t+1}(VY_{t+1})^{-1}(EY_{t+1})}{[(EY_{t+1})'(VY_{t+1})^{-1}(E_tY_{t+1})]^2}.$$

From the Cauchy-Schwartz inequality, we get

$$[(EY_{t+1})'(VY_{t+1})^{-1}(E_tY_{t+1})]^2 = [E(Y_{t+1})'(VY_{t+1})^{-1}V_tY_{t+1}(V_tY_{t+1})^{-1}(E_tY_{t+1})]^2$$

$$\leq [E(Y_{t+1})'(VY_{t+1})^{-1}V_tY_{t+1}(VY_{t+1})^{-1}(EY_{t+1})]$$

$$[(E_tY_{t+1})'(V_tY_{t+1})^{-1}(E_tY_{t+1})],$$

or, equivalently,

$$\tilde{P}_t \leq P_t.$$

The two semiparabolas overlap if and only if the Cauchy-Schwartz condition is satisfied with an equality. This arises when the two portfolios $(V_tY_{t+1})^{-1}E_tY_{t+1}$ and $(VY_{t+1})^{-1}EY_{t+1}$ are proportional.

3.5 Summary

In this chapter, we examined linear dynamic models for two or more time series. A multivariate setup can be used, for example, for short-term forecasting of portfolio returns or for joint analysis of asset returns and volumes. Most results in the multivariate framework arise as extensions of their univariate analogues. Thus, a scalar mean of a univariate series is replaced by a vector of means of the individual series. The counterpart of a scalar variance of a univariate series is a symmetric, positive, semi-definite matrix of variances of the component series and their covariances. Finally, the autocovariance function, which remains an essential tool of analysis in a multivariate setup, becomes a sequence of square matrices that captures serial correlation of the components, as well as lagged interactions between them. By analogy, VARMA and VAR models arise as multivariate analogues of ARMA and AR models for which, instead of scalar coefficients, we find matrices of autoregressive and/or moving average coefficients. These issues are covered in Section 3.1.

Section 3.2 is devoted to estimation of the parameters of the VAR model. Our interest in the VAR is motivated by its relatively simple structure and empirically evidenced good fit to financial data. In the special case of identical right-hand-side variables in all equations of the reduced form, the estimation procedure simplifies to least squares applied separately to each equation in the model. An empirical application of a VAR model to high-frequency return and volume data is given in Section 3.3. It reveals strong intraday variation of the parameters estimated from hourly samples due to intraday seasonal effects.

Section 3.4 highlights the use of the VAR in determining the mean-variance efficient portfolios. We have shown the advantage of using the VAR-based forecasts of the conditional means of returns in dynamic updating of portfolio allocations. The VAR-based strategy outperforms a static approach that relies on the marginal means of returns, which disregards the dynamic aspect.

The structure of serial correlations and lagged interactions in a multivariate model is quite complex. We documented this complexity in our empirical example illustrating the return-volume relationship. Sometimes, however, it remains unclear whether the current values of both variables are determined simultaneously or instead are subject to a leader-follower type of behavior. To investigate this issue, we need to uncover the existence of causal relationships, which are examined in the next chapter.

4

Simultaneity, Recursivity, and Causality Analysis

IN THE PREVIOUS CHAPTERS, we focused our attention on dynamic models for vectors or univariate time series with current values that depend on their past. In this chapter, we introduce systems of equations that emphasize both feedback and simultaneity effects, which arise when a current value of a time series simultaneously determines and is determined by a current value of another time series. This class of models, called *simultaneous equations*, is widely used in economics, especially for modeling supply-and-demand equilibria. In finance, simultaneous equation models provide a convenient framework to study, for example, jointly or interdependently determined asset prices and volumes. This leads to the dynamic Capital Asset Pricing Model (CAPM), which provides an explicit formula for the trade-off between risk and expected returns on assets.

The nature of dynamic interactions between variables in simultaneous equation models can be explored further using the causality analysis. It is aimed at distinguishing variables that at date t determine other variables in the system from those that respond to the system with a lag.

In the first section, we introduce the structural model, discuss its dynamics, and study the properties of ordinary least squares (OLS) estimators. For clarity of exposition, we consider models involving only two endogenous series and one exogenous series. In the second section, we present the CAPM equilibrium model of asset prices and derive the equilibrium condition of asset demand and supply. Various procedures for testing the equilibrium hypothesis are also provided. In the third section, we explain the concept of causality and show how causal relations between variables can be modeled in a vector autoregressive (VAR) framework. We apply the causality analysis for empirical study of the relation between high-frequency returns and volumes.

81

4.1 Dynamic Structural Model

We denote by $(Y_t, t \in Z)$ and $(X_t, t \in Z)$ the two endogenous time series of interest and by $(Z_t, t \in Z)$ the exogenous one. The series are assumed jointly weakly stationary. For inference, we use three information sets $\underline{Y}_t$, $\underline{X}_t$, and $\underline{Z}_t$, which represent all available information contained in the current and past values of Y, X, and Z, respectively.

4.1.1 Structural, Reduced, and Final Forms

Structural Form
Structural models represent interactions between variables implied by economic or financial theory. In general, we distinguish two sets of variables with respect to their role in the model. Variables with current values that are simultaneously determined by the system are called *endogenous*. They do not necessarily appear on the left-hand side of equations as their current or past values may determine some other endogenous processes. Among explanatory variables on the right-hand side of an equation in the system, we distinguish the *exogenous* variables, which are given or determined outside the system and the lagged endogenous variables. The form of a structural model is often based on some equilibrium conditions. These conditions can entail a quite complex structure involving interactions of the current values of endogenous processes with the lagged values of endogenous and exogenous processes, as well as instantaneous feedback effects between the current values of various endogenous variables.

A typical structural form is

$$Y_t = -a_{12}X_t + b_{11}Y_{t-1} + b_{12}X_{t-1} + c_{10}Z_t + c_{11}Z_{t-1} + u_{1t},$$
$$X_t = -a_{21}Y_t + b_{21}Y_{t-1} + b_{22}X_{t-1} + c_{20}Z_t + c_{21}Z_{t-1} + u_{2t}, \tag{4.1}$$

where the error terms u_{1t}, u_{2t} form a bivariate weak white noise and are uncorrelated with Z_t, Z_{t-1}, X_{t-1}, and Y_{t-1}. These equations jointly determine two variables, X_t and Y_t. For this reason, the system in (4.1) is called a *simultaneous equation model*.

The model may be rewritten using vector notation:

$$A\begin{pmatrix} Y_t \\ X_t \end{pmatrix} = B\begin{pmatrix} Y_{t-1} \\ X_{t-1} \end{pmatrix} + C_0 Z_t + C_1 Z_{t-1} + u_t. \tag{4.2}$$

EXAMPLE 4.1, THE EQUILIBRIUM SYSTEM: A classical example of a simultaneous equation model is the demand-supply equilibrium model. Let us consider an asset and introduce the corresponding aggregate demand and supply functions at date t. They depend on the current price, exogenous variable Z_t, and eventually lagged price and exchanged quantity. They are given by

$$d_t = a_1 p_t + b_{11} p_{t-1} + b_{12} q_{t-1} + c_1 z_t + u_{1,t},$$
$$s_t = a_2 p_t + b_{21} p_{t-1} + b_{22} q_{t-1} + c_2 z_t + u_{2,t},$$

assuming linearity with respect to prices. At equilibrium, the demand and supply are equal, and their common value determines the traded quantity:

$$q_t = d_t = s_t.$$

By introducing explicitly the equilibrium condition into the system, we obtain a bivariate simultaneous equation model with current price and traded quantity as the endogenous variables:

$$q_t = a_1 p_t + b_{11} p_{t-1} + b_{12} q_{t-1} + c_1 z_t + u_{1,t},$$
$$q_t = a_2 p_t + b_{21} p_{t-1} + b_{22} q_{t-1} + c_2 z_t + u_{2,t}.$$

EXAMPLE 4.2, EQUILIBRIUM AND ABSENCE OF ARBITRAGE OPPORTUNITY: There is a link between the notion of equilibrium and the condition of the absence of arbitrage opportunity. Let us consider two risk-free assets with respective risk-free returns $r_{1,t}$ and $r_{2,t}$, say. We denote by $s_{1,t}$, and $s_{2,t}$, respectively, the finite exogenous supplies of these assets. The total demand of investors is intuitively infinite for the asset with higher returns and thus is degenerate of the following form:

$$\begin{bmatrix} d_{1,t} \\ d_{2,t} \end{bmatrix} = \begin{bmatrix} +\infty \\ -\infty \end{bmatrix} 1_{r_{1,t} > r_{2,t}} + \begin{bmatrix} -\infty \\ +\infty \end{bmatrix} 1_{r_{1,t} < r_{2,t}} + \begin{bmatrix} d_1(r_t) \\ d_2(r_t) \end{bmatrix} 1_{r_{1,t} = r_{2,t}},$$

where $r_t = r_{1,t} = r_{2,t}$ in the regime where both risk-free returns are equal. The investors try to benefit from the arbitrage opportunity by leveraging the demanded quantities. The equilibrium condition

$$s_{1,t} = d_{1,t}, \quad s_{2,t} = d_{2,t},$$

implies the equality $r_{1,t} = r_{2,t}$ of risk-free returns. Therefore, at equilibrium, the system is degenerate with a deterministic restriction on asset returns.

Reduced Form
We have seen from previous examples that current values of the endogenous variables Y_t and X_t may be obtained as simultaneous outcomes of an equilibrium condition. The equilibrium is unique whenever the system (4.2) admits a unique solution. The condition ensuring its uniqueness is the invertibility of the A matrix. Under this restriction, there exists a reduced form of the simultaneous equation model in which current values

of endogenous variables are represented as functions of lagged endogenous and predetermined variables and of current values of exogenous variables and error terms:

$$\begin{pmatrix} Y_t \\ X_t \end{pmatrix} = A^{-1}B\begin{pmatrix} Y_{t-1} \\ X_{t-1} \end{pmatrix} + A^{-1}C_0Z_t + A^{-1}C_1Z_{t-1} + A^{-1}u_t. \tag{4.3}$$

It can be rewritten as

$$\begin{pmatrix} Y_t \\ X_t \end{pmatrix} = \tilde{B}\begin{pmatrix} Y_{t-1} \\ X_{t-1} \end{pmatrix} + \tilde{C}_0Z_t + \tilde{C}_1Z_{t-1} + \tilde{u}_t, \tag{4.4}$$

where $\tilde{B} = A^{-1}B$, $\tilde{C}_0 = A^{-1}C_0$, and $\tilde{C}_1 = A^{-1}C_1$ are the reduced form parameters, and $\tilde{u}_t = A^{-1}u_t$ is the reduced form error term. Note that the error term is uncorrelated with all explanatory variables appearing on the right-hand side of the system in (4.4).

REMARK 4.1: If $\tilde{C}_0 = \tilde{C}_1 = 0$, expression (4.4) is simply a VAR(1) representation of the bivariate process $\begin{pmatrix} Y_t \\ X_t \end{pmatrix}$. By including current and lagged values of an exogenous process, we obtain a so-called ARMAX model (X for exogenous) (Hannan 1970). Therefore, the reduced form is a VARX representation of the bivariate process.

EXAMPLE 4.3, THE EQUILIBRIUM SYSTEM: Let us consider the equilibrium model introduced in Example 4.1. The bivariate system can be solved with respect to p_t, q_t. We get

$$q_t = \frac{1}{a_2 - a_1}\{(a_2b_{11} - a_1b_{21})p_{t-1} + (a_2b_{12} - a_1b_{22})q_{t-1}$$
$$+ (a_2c_1 - a_1c_2)z_t + a_2u_{1,t} - a_1u_{2,t}\},$$

$$p_t = \frac{1}{a_2 - a_1}\{(b_{11} - b_{21})p_{t-1} + (b_{12} - b_{22})q_{t-1} + (c_1 - c_2)z_t + u_{1,t} - u_{2,t}\}.$$

Even though the error terms of the demand and supply functions are uncorrelated, $Cov(u_{1,t}, u_{2,t}) = 0$, the equilibrium price and quantity, in general, are conditionally correlated due to the equilibrium condition. Indeed, we get

$$Cov_{t-1}[q_t,p_t] = \frac{1}{(a_2 - a_1)^2}Cov_{t-1}[a_2u_{1,t} - a_1u_{2,t}, u_{1,t} - u_{2,t}]$$

$$= \frac{1}{(a_2 - a_1)^2}[a_2V(u_{1,t}) + a_1V(u_{2,t})].$$

Final Form
By recursive substitution, lagged values of endogenous processes may be eliminated from the reduced form. This yields the final form of the structural model, in which current values of endogenous processes appear as functions of current and lagged exogenous variables and error terms. The final form is

$$\begin{pmatrix} Y_t \\ X_t \end{pmatrix} = (Id - A^{-1}BL)^{-1}[A^{-1}C_0Z_t + A^{-1}C_1Z_{t-1} + A^{-1}u_t],$$

where L is the lag operator, or in explicit form,

$$\begin{pmatrix} Y_t \\ X_t \end{pmatrix} = A^{-1}C_0Z_t + (A^{-1}C_1 + A^{-1}BA^{-1}C_0)Z_{t-1}$$

$$+ \ldots + (A^{-1}B)^{h-1}(A^{-1}C_1 + A^{-1}BA^{-1}C_0)Z_{t-h} + A^{-1}u_t$$
$$+ \ldots + (A^{-1}B)^h A^{-1}u_{t-h} + \ldots$$

4.1.2 From a Structural Model to a Time Series Model

None of the specifications presented above belongs to the class of models discussed in Chapter 3, in which present values of vector autoregressive moving average (VARMA) processes were determined by their own past. The difference is due to the presence of current and lagged exogenous variables on the right-hand side (rhs) of equations in the system. Unless future values of these exogenous variables are known, a simultaneous equations model cannot be used to make predictions. Even the final form is not appropriate for forecasting at large horizons. To see that, consider the prediction of $\begin{pmatrix} Y_{T+2} \\ X_{T+2} \end{pmatrix}$ evaluated at time T. From (4.4), we infer that

$$\begin{pmatrix} Y_{T+2} \\ X_{T+2} \end{pmatrix} = \tilde{C}_0Z_{T+2} + (\tilde{C}_1 + \tilde{B}\tilde{C}_0)Z_{T+1} + \tilde{B}\tilde{C}_1Z_T + \tilde{B}^2\begin{pmatrix} Y_T \\ X_T \end{pmatrix} + \tilde{u}_{T+2} + \tilde{B}\tilde{u}_{T+1.}$$

Therefore, for I_T denoting all information available at time T, we get

$$E\left[\begin{pmatrix} Y_{T+2} \\ X_{T+2} \end{pmatrix} | I_T\right] = \tilde{C}_0 E(Z_{T+2}|I_T) + (\tilde{C}_1 + \tilde{B}\tilde{C}_0)E(Z_{T+1}|I_T) + \tilde{B}\tilde{C}_1 Z_T + \tilde{B}^2\begin{pmatrix} Y_T \\ X_T \end{pmatrix},$$

whenever I_T includes current and past values of the relevant variables. Since the structural model contains no information about the dynamics of the exogenous variables, it is not possible to evaluate $E(Z_{T+1}|I_T)$ and $E(Z_{T+2}|I_T)$. A straightforward remedy to this problem consists of adding

yet another equation to describe the dynamics of the exogenous processes. The initial structural model now becomes

$$A\begin{pmatrix}Y_t\\X_t\end{pmatrix}=B\begin{pmatrix}Y_{t-1}\\X_{t-1}\end{pmatrix}+C_0Z_t+C_1Z_{t-1}+u_t,$$
$$Z_t=DZ_{t-1}+v_t,$$

(4.5)

where the error term v_t is uncorrelated with u_t and the lagged values of
other processes. The system can be rewritten as

$$\begin{pmatrix}Y_t\\X_t\end{pmatrix}=A^{-1}B\begin{pmatrix}Y_{t-1}\\X_{t-1}\end{pmatrix}+(A^{-1}C_1+A^{-1}C_0D)Z_{t-1}+u_t+C_0v_t,$$
$$Z_t=DZ_{t-1}+v_t,$$

or, equivalently,

$$\begin{pmatrix}Y_t\\X_t\\Z_t\end{pmatrix}=\begin{pmatrix}A^{-1}B & A^{-1}C_1+A^{-1}C_0D\\0 & D\end{pmatrix}\begin{pmatrix}Y_{t-1}\\X_{t-1}\\Z_{t-1}\end{pmatrix}+\begin{pmatrix}u_t+C_0v_t\\v_t\end{pmatrix}.$$

(4.6)

This is a VAR(1) representation of the bivariate process. Some features of a structural model are still preserved under this specification. For
example, the constraints on the structural parameters A, B, C_0, and C may
imply restrictions on the autoregressive matrix. Moreover, the autoregressive matrix has to include a subset of zeros in the lower left corner to
accommodate the dynamics of the predetermined Z variable. Note that
model (4.6) represents causal relations between variables in the system. If
we disregard the noise effect at time t, Z_t is determined by Z_{t-1} and $\begin{pmatrix}Y_t\\X_t\end{pmatrix}$
are jointly determined by $\begin{pmatrix}Y_{t-1}\\X_{t-1}\end{pmatrix}$, Z_t, Z_{t-1}, and so on (Figure 4.1).

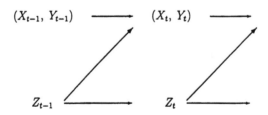

Figure 4.1   *The Causal Chain*

4.1.3   The Properties of the Ordinary Least Squares Estimators

The structural, reduced, and final forms, as well as the extended structural form (4.6), define various linear functions of explanatory (rhs) variables. Therefore, it seems natural to use OLS for estimation of these linear models without taking into account structural constraints that they may need to satisfy. However, we have to remember that the least squares method yields consistent estimators of the parameters only in equations with error terms that are uncorrelated with the explanatory variables. This condition is satisfied by the reduced and final forms only.

PROPOSITION 4.1: *The reduced form parameters $\tilde{B}$, $\tilde{C}_0$, and $\tilde{C}_1$ can be consistently estimated by OLS applied to (4.4).*

The system in (4.4) is a seemingly unrelated regressions (SUR) model, discussed in Chapter 3. In the absence of structural constraints on the coefficients $\tilde{B}$, $\tilde{C}_0$, and $\tilde{C}_1$, the same explanatory (rhs) variables are present in all equations. In this particular case, we know from Zellner (1962) that OLS estimators obtained from separate least squares estimation of each equation are equivalent to the general least squares estimator applied to the entire SUR model in (4.4).

The estimation of structural form (4.1) is more complicated due to simultaneity. Although $u_{1,t}$ and $u_{2,t}$ are assumed uncorrelated with the lagged values of endogenous processes and the current and lagged values of exogenous processes, they may still remain correlated with the current values of the endogenous processes that appear among the explanatory (rhs) variables.

PROPOSITION 4.2: *The OLS estimators of the structural coefficients in the first equation of (4.1) are consistent if and only if $Cov(X_t, u_{1,t}) = 0$.*

This condition can be written in terms of structural parameters. Let us introduce the linear prediction errors of X_t and Y_t given $\underline{X}_{t-1}$ and $\underline{Y}_{t-1}$:

$$\varepsilon_{1,t} = Y_t - LE(Y_t | \underline{X}_{t-1}, \underline{Y}_{t-1}),$$

$$\varepsilon_{2,t} = X_t - LE(X_t | \underline{X}_{t-1}, \underline{Y}_{t-1}).$$

We deduce from (4.1) that

$$\begin{cases} \varepsilon_{1t} = -a_{12}\varepsilon_{2t} + u_{1t} \\ \varepsilon_{2t} = -a_{21}\varepsilon_{1t} + u_{2t} \end{cases} \Leftrightarrow \begin{cases} \varepsilon_{1t} = \dfrac{u_{1t} - a_{12}u_{2t}}{1 - a_{12}a_{21}} \\ \varepsilon_{2t} = \dfrac{-a_{21}u_{1t} + u_{2t}}{1 - a_{12}a_{21}} \end{cases}$$

The condition for the consistency of the OLS estimators becomes

$$Cov(X_t, u_{1t}) = 0 \iff Cov(\varepsilon_{2t}, u_{1t}) = 0.$$

COROLLARY 4.1: *The OLS estimators of the first structural equation are consistent if and only if*

$$-a_{12}Vu_{1t} + Cov(u_{1t},u_{2t}) = 0,$$

or, equivalently, if

$$Cov(\varepsilon_{1t},\varepsilon_{2t}) + a_{12}V\varepsilon_{2t} = 0.$$

The consistency condition involves both the structural parameters a_{21} and the slope coefficient from a regression of u_{2t} on u_{1t}. In particular, this condition is satisfied when

$$a_{21} = Cov(u_{1t}, u_{2t}) = 0.$$

In this case X_t is a function of its own lags and of the shock u_{2t} uncorrelated with the shock u_{1t} from the equation defining Y_t. Hence, X_t is determined prior to Y_t (or predetermined). We obtain a causal chain in which the variables are recursively determined (Figure 4.2).

4.2   The Capital Asset Pricing Model

In this section, we present an equilibrium model of asset prices widely known as the CAPM and interpret its various representations. The CAPM provides an explicit formula for the trade-off between risk and expected returns and shows the important role of the market portfolio.

4.2.1   *Derivation of the Capital Asset Pricing Model*

The CAPM model was derived independently by Sharpe (1964), Lintner (1965), and Mossin (1966). It assumes an optimizing behavior of investors and an equilibrium condition of asset supply and demand. We consider the framework introduced in Section 3.4 with one risk-free asset and n risky assets. We also denote by $Y_{t+1} = p_{t+1} - (1+r_t)p_t$ the vector of excess gains on risky assets. Suppose that there are M investors, $i = 1, \ldots, M$,

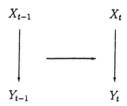

Figure 4.2   *The Causal Chain in the Recursive Scheme*

who possess the same information at time t. Their behavior obeys the mean-variance optimization described in Section 3.4. The traders are characterized by absolute individual risk aversion coefficients A_i, $i = 1, \ldots,$ M, and their total demand is (see Proposition 3.5):

$$\alpha_t^D = \sum_{i=1}^{M} \alpha_{it}^*$$

$$= \sum_{i=1}^{M} \frac{1}{A_i} [V_t(Y_{t+1})]^{-1} E_t(Y_{t+1})$$

$$= \frac{1}{A} [V_t(Y_{t+1})]^{-1} E_t Y_{t+1},$$

where A, equal to the harmonic average $\left[\sum_{i=1}^{M} \frac{1}{A_i} \right]^{-1}$ of individual risk aversion coefficients, may be interpreted as the absolute risk aversion coefficient of a representative investor. In addition, let us denote by $\alpha_t^S = Z_t b$ the asset supply and assume that it is linearly driven by a set of exogenous regressors Z_t with the sensitivity parameter b. The exogeneity assumption is justified if the supply shocks are due to the issue of new asset shares at a frequency assumed to be much lower than the trading frequency of investors. It has to be emphasized that, in the literature, exogenous supply is traditionally assumed to be time independent, $\alpha_t^s = b_0$ (say). This is a strong assumption that needs to be tested since it eliminates from the analysis all dynamics due to the quantity effects.

The equilibrium condition implies

$$\alpha_t^D = \alpha_t^S$$

$$\Leftrightarrow \frac{1}{A} (V_t Y_{t+1})^{-1} E_t Y_{t+1} = \alpha_t^S$$

$$\Leftrightarrow E_t Y_{t+1} = A (V_t Y_{t+1}) Z_t b \qquad (4.7)$$

$$\Leftrightarrow Y_{t+1} = A (V_t Y_{t+1}) Z_t b + \varepsilon_{t+1},$$

where the expectation error ε_{t+1} satisfies the martingale difference condition $E_t \varepsilon_{t+1} = 0$. At equilibrium, the expected excess gain depends on three components:

- The representative absolute risk aversion coefficient A: If this coefficient increases, the expected excess gain has to grow to compensate investors with a higher risk aversion.
- The risk effect $V_t Y_{t+1}$: A higher risk implies a higher reward for risk bearing; the relation between the expected excess gain and the volatility $V_t Y_{t+1}$ determines the *risk premium*.
- The supply $Z_t b$: When the exogenous supply increases, the expected

price also has to increase to attract investors and to ensure the matching of demand and supply.

REMARK 4.2: A similar equilibrium condition can be derived in terms of excess returns. Let us denote the excess returns by

$$y_{t+1} = [diag(p_t)]^{-1}[p_{t+1} - (1 + r_t)p_t] = [diag(p_t)]^{-1}Y_{t+1}.$$

The total demand becomes

$$\alpha_t^D = [diag(p_t)]^{-1}\frac{1}{A}[V_t(y_{t+1})]^{-1}E_t(y_{t+1}),$$

and the equilibrium condition

$$\frac{1}{A}[V_t(y_{t+1})]^{-1}E_t(y_{t+1}) = \bar{\alpha}_t^S,$$

where $\bar{\alpha}_t^S = diag(p_t)\alpha_t^S$ gives the value of the allocation vector.

4.2.2 Case of Vector Autoregressive Net Gain of Order 1

The previous structural CAPM model can be nested in a dynamic VAR representation. Let us assume that the excess gains are conditionally homoscedastic:

$$V_t Y_{t+1} = V_t \varepsilon_{t+1} = \Omega, \qquad \text{say,} \tag{4.8}$$

and that the predetermined supply is a function of excess gains, that is, the issuing of new shares depends on the observed excess gains:

$$Z_t b = b_0 + \gamma' Y_t. \tag{4.9}$$

The equilibrium condition becomes

$$Y_{t+1} = A\Omega b_0 + A\Omega \gamma' Y_t + \varepsilon_{t+1}, \tag{4.10}$$

which is an autoregressive model of order 1.

The underlying equilibrium model implies no restrictions on the parameters of the VAR representation. In fact, the number of parameters in the descriptive VAR representation is $\frac{3}{2}n(n+1)$ [n for the constant terms, n^2 for the autoregressive matrix, and $\frac{n(n+1)}{2}$ for the variance-covariance matrix of the error term] and is less than the number of structural parameters $\frac{3}{2}n(n+1) + 1$ [n for b_0, n^2 for γ, $\frac{n(n+1)}{2}$ for the variance-covariance matrix, and 1 for the risk aversion coefficient].

4.2.3 Static Supply and Market Portfolio

For illustration, let us consider a static asset supply $\alpha^S = b_0$ as is traditional in the literature. The relationship between the number of parameters in the VAR representation of the excess gains [now equal to $n + \dfrac{n(n+1)}{2}$] and the number of structural parameters is different when the total number of shares $\alpha_t^S = b_0$ is known. In such a case, there are $\dfrac{n(n+1)}{2} + 1$ independent parameters, and the equilibrium condition implies $n - 1$ constraints on the autoregressive parameters. These implicit constraints can be found easily.

Let us introduce the market portfolio, with allocation in risky assets $\alpha_t^S = b_0$. This portfolio generates an excess gain equal to $Y_{m,t+1} = (\alpha_t^S)'Y_{t+1} = b_0'Y_{t+1}$.

PROPOSITION 4.3: *In the affine regression of Y_{t+1} on $Y_{m,t+1}$*

$$Y_{t+1} = c + \beta Y_{m,t+1} + u_{t+1},$$

with $Eu_{t+1} = 0$, $Cov(u_{t+1}, Y_{m,t+1}) = 0$, the constant term c is equal to 0.

PROOF: From (4.10) with $\gamma = 0$, we have $Y_{t+1} = A\Omega b_0 + \varepsilon_{t+1}$, and we deduce $EY_{t+1} = A\Omega b_0$, $VY_{t+1} = V\varepsilon_{t+1} = \Omega$. In the regression of Proposition 4.3, the coefficient vector β is equal to

$$\begin{aligned}
\beta &= \frac{Cov(Y_{t+1}, Y_{m,t+1})}{V(Y_{m,t+1})} \\
&= \frac{Cov(Y_{t+1}, b_0'Y_{t+1})}{V(b_0'Y_{t+1})} \\
&= \frac{\Omega b_0}{b_0'\Omega b_0}.
\end{aligned}$$

The constant term is equal to

$$\begin{aligned}
c &= EY_{t+1} - \beta E(Y_{m,t+1}) \\
&= A\Omega b_0 - \frac{\Omega b_0}{b_0'\Omega\, b_0} A b_0'\,\Omega b_0 \\
&= 0.
\end{aligned}$$

QED

Therefore, the initial static model

$$Y_{t+1} = A\Omega b_0 + \varepsilon_{t+1},$$

can also be written as

$$Y_{t+1} = \beta Y_{m,t+1} + u_{t+1},$$

$$Y_{m,t+1} = Ab_0' \, \Omega b_0 + b_0' \varepsilon_{t+1}.$$

This is a kind of "recursive" form, with the excess gain of the market portfolio being determined from the second equation. On substituting into the first subsystem, it yields the excess gains of basic assets. The reader should be aware that this interpretation is misleading since Y_{t+1} and $Y_{m,t+1} = b_0' Y_{t+1}$ are simultaneously determined.

The following proposition may be viewed as the reciprocal of Proposition 4.3.

PROPOSITION 4.4: *Let us consider the static model defined by (4.10) with $\gamma = 0$ and introduce a portfolio with allocations a. The excess gain of this portfolio is $Y_{t+1}(a) = a' Y_{t+1}$. The constant term in the regression*

$$Y_{t+1} = c(a) + \beta(a) Y_{t+1}(a) + u_{t+1}(a),$$

is equal to 0 if and only if the portfolio a is proportional to b_0, that is, it is a mean-variance efficient portfolio.

PROOF: The regression coefficients are

$$\beta(a) = \frac{Cov(Y_{t+1}, Y_{t+1}(a))}{V(Y_{t+1}(a))} = \frac{\Omega a}{a' \Omega a},$$

$$c(a) = E(Y_{t+1}) - \beta(a) E[Y_{t+1}(a)]$$

$$= A \Omega b_0 - \frac{\Omega a}{a' \Omega a} A a' \Omega b_0.$$

The constant term $c(a)$ vanishes if and only if

$$\Omega b_0 = \frac{\Omega a}{a' \Omega a} a' \Omega b_0$$

$$\Leftrightarrow a = \frac{a' \Omega a}{a' \Omega b_0} b_0$$

$$\Leftrightarrow a \text{ is proportional to } b_0,$$

which completes the proof.
QED

REMARK 4.3: We obtain similar properties for excess returns instead of excess gains if the total value of supplied assets $\tilde{\alpha}^S$ is constant (see Remark 4.1). Since $\tilde{\alpha}^S = diag(p_t) \alpha^S$ and prices are not constant, only one of the static assumptions on α^S and $\tilde{\alpha}^S$ can be satisfied.

4.2.4   Test of the Capital Asset Pricing Model Hypothesis

As shown in Section 4.2.2, a complete analysis of the equilibrium condition requires the specification of exogenous supply and includes a joint study of prices and volumes. In the literature, the following three implications of the equilibrium condition are emphasized:

1. The efficiency of the market portfolio;
2. The fact that cross-sectional variation of expected excess returns is entirely captured by betas;
3. The nonnegativity of the market risk premium.

We discuss below the procedures for testing the two first equilibrium implications. They all require a precise choice of the risk-free asset and of the market portfolio. Usually, a 1-month T-bill is used as proxy for the risk-free asset and a market index is the proxy for the market portfolio (see Chapter 15). However, this choice is conventional, and other proxies can be selected. It is important to realize, however, that the test results can significantly depend on the choice of proxies and can become invalid in the presence of heteroscedasticity (see Chapter 6).

As a framework, we use regressions of excess gains and excess returns associated with the CAPM. We use the same notation Y.

Efficiency of the Market Portfolio
This testing procedure is based on Propositions 4.3 and 4.4. We consider the regressions of excess gains or excess returns of assets $Y_{j,t}$ on the market excess gains on returns $Y_{m,t}$:

$$Y_{j,t} = c_j + \beta_j Y_{m,t} + u_{j,t}, \qquad j = 1, \ldots, n, t = 1, \ldots, T. \tag{4.11}$$

The market portfolio is mean-variance efficient if and only if

$$H_0 = \{c_1 = c_2 = \ldots = c_n = 0\}. \tag{4.12}$$

Model (4.11) is a SUR model with parameters that can be estimated by OLS. Standard software can provide the estimate $\hat{c} = (\hat{c}_1, \ldots, \hat{c}_n)'$ and the estimated variance-covariance matrix of estimators $\hat{V}\hat{c}$. At this point, it is advantageous to use a heteroscedasticity-adjusted variance estimator for $\hat{V}\hat{c}$ to take into account possible conditional heteroscedasticity of the error term $u_{j,t}$ (see, e.g., Gibbons 1982; Jobson and Korkie 1982; Kandel and Staumbaugh 1987). The test of the null hypothesis H_0 is based on the Wald statistic:

$$\xi_W = \hat{c}'(\hat{V}\hat{c})^{-1}\hat{c}, \tag{4.13}$$

which measures the distance of $\hat{c}$ from 0 (Gibbons 1982; Jobson and Korkie 1982; Kandel and Staumbaugh 1987).

It may be proven that, under the null hypothesis, this statistic asymptotically follows a chi-square distribution with $n-1$ degrees of freedom: $T\xi_W \sim \chi^2(n-1)$. Therefore, the testing procedure consists of accepting the efficiency hypothesis if $T\xi_W < \chi^2_{95\%}(n-1)$ or rejecting it otherwise, where $\chi^2_{95\%}$ is the 95th percentile of the $\chi^2(n-1)$ distribution.

REMARK 4.4: Let us explain why the degrees of freedom are $n-1$ instead of n. The CAPM is a degenerate SUR model. Indeed, the explanatory variable $Y_{m,t} = \alpha'Y_t$ is a linear combination of the endogenous variables Y_t. It implies that, under the null hypothesis, H_0, $u_t = (Id - \beta\alpha')Y_t$. It may be checked easily that $Id - \beta\alpha'$ is not of full rank, and that the variance-covariance matrix of u_t is not invertible. Nevertheless, it is possible to apply a standard estimation technique and to correct only the number of degrees of freedom to $n-1$ instead of n (see Gourieroux et al. 1997, Section IV.3.4).

Cross-Sectional Regressions

Cross-sectional regressions were first developed by Blume and Friend (1973) and Fama and McBeth (1973). Under the CAPM hypothesis, we deduce from Proposition 4.3 that the marginal expectation of the excess gain satisfies an exact linear relationship with the beta:

$$\mu_j = E(Y_{j,t}) = \lambda\beta_j, \qquad j = 1, \ldots, n, \tag{4.14}$$

where $\lambda = E[Y_{m,t}] > 0$. This is called the *security market line*.

When the series $(Y_{j,t})$ is stationary, in the first step we can approximate μ_j and β_j by their historical counterparts:

$$\hat{\mu}_{j,T} = \frac{1}{T}\sum_{t=1}^{T} Y_{j,t}, \qquad \hat{\beta}_{j,T} = \frac{Cov_e(Y_{j,t}, Y_{m,t})}{V_e(Y_{m,t})}. \tag{4.15}$$

To test the null hypothesis $H_0 = \{\exists \lambda > 0: \mu_j = \lambda\beta_j, \forall j\}$, in the second step we run a cross-sectional regression of $\hat{\mu}_{j,T}$ on $\hat{\beta}_{j,T}$ for $j = 1, \ldots, n$:

$$\hat{\mu}_{j,T} = a_0 + a_1\hat{\beta}_{j,T} + v_{j,T}, \qquad j = 1, \ldots, n. \tag{4.16}$$

Then, given the OLS estimators $\hat{a}_0$ and $\hat{a}_1$ and the associated residuals $\hat{v}_{j,T}$, we check if (1) $\hat{a}_0$ is statistically nonsignificant, (2) $\hat{a}_1$ is significantly positive, and (3) the residuals are close to 0.

When we compare regression model (4.16) to the constraint in expression (4.14), we see that the error term is equal to

$$v_{j,T} = \hat{\mu}_{j,T} - \mu_j - \lambda(\hat{\beta}_{j,T} - \beta_j),$$

under the CAPM hypothesis. Therefore, regression (4.16) involves two variables μ_j and β_j with measurement errors.

A large body of financial literature on regression model (4.16) has been focused on approximating the explanatory variable β_j by $\hat{\beta}_{j,T}$ (see, e.g., the discussion on Huang and Litzenberger 1988). It is a common belief that OLS estimators are not consistent and have to be replaced by the instrumental variable estimators (see Chapter 8). A typical approach proposed by Fama and McBeth (1973) consists of dividing the assets into subsets. Let us partition the set of assets into different subsets $J_1, \ldots, J_K$ of a sample size J (say). Then, we aggregate the $\hat{\mu}_{j,T}$ and $\hat{\beta}_{j,T}$ within the subsets to get $\bar{\mu}_{k,T} = \frac{1}{J}\Sigma_{j\in J_k}\hat{\mu}_{j,T}$, $\bar{\beta}_{k,T} = \frac{1}{J}\Sigma_{j\in J_k}\hat{\beta}_{j,T}$, and run the OLS regression of $\bar{\mu}_{k,T}$ on $\bar{\beta}_{k,T}$. The aim is to reduce the error in variable $\bar{\beta}_{k,T} - \bar{\beta}_k$ by collecting assets into portfolios. Alternative bias correction methods have also been proposed by Litzenberger and Ramaswamy (1979) and Shanken (1985).

Despite common belief, the OLS estimators are consistent. Indeed, the OLS estimator of a_1 is

$$\hat{a}_{1,T} = \frac{\Sigma_{j=1}^n \hat{\beta}_{j,T}\hat{\mu}_{j,T} - \frac{1}{n}\Sigma_{j=1}^n \hat{\beta}_{j,T}\Sigma_{j=1}^n \hat{\mu}_{j,T}}{\Sigma_{j=1}^n \hat{\beta}_{j,T}^2 - \frac{1}{n}\left(\Sigma_{j=1}^n \hat{\beta}_{j,T}\right)^2}.$$

When T tends to infinity, this expression tends to

$$\lim_T \hat{a}_{1,T} = \frac{\Sigma_{j=1}^n \beta_j\mu_j - \frac{1}{n}\Sigma_{j=1}^n \beta_j\Sigma_{j=1}^n \mu_j}{\Sigma_{j=1}^n \beta_j^2 - \frac{1}{n}\left(\Sigma_{j=1}^n \beta_j\right)^2} = \lambda,$$

under the CAPM constraint (4.14). In fact, for large T, the error in variable $\hat{\beta}_{j,T} - \beta_j$ is small, and there is no need for bias correction.

The argument given above is based on asymptotic theory and requires a large number of observations, such as $T \geq 300$. In finite samples, the aggregation procedure proposed by Fama and McBeth (1973) may increase the accuracy of estimators, although this effect has not been thoroughly examined. In any case, it is sensitive with respect to the partition $J_1, \ldots, J_K$.

Finally, note that it is necessary to take into account the heteroscedasticity of the error term $v_{j,T}$ while computing the variance of the OLS estimators, aggregates, and test statistics. Under the CAPM hypothesis, we get

$$Cov(v_{j,T}, v_{k,T}) = Cov_e(\hat{\mu}_{j,T} - \lambda\hat{\beta}_{j,T}, \hat{\mu}_{k,T} - \lambda\hat{\beta}_{k,T}),$$

and a nondiagonal covariance matrix of the error terms.

4.3 Causality

The aim of *causality theory* is to describe dynamic interactions between time series and to reveal their independent movements. To simplify the exposition, we consider a bivariate VAR process:

$$\begin{cases} Y_{1,t} = \mu_1 + \varphi_{1,1}Y_{1,t-1} + \varphi_{1,2}Y_{2,t-1} + \varepsilon_{1,t}, \\ Y_{2,t} = \mu_2 + \varphi_{2,1}Y_{1,t-1} + \varphi_{2,2}Y_{2,t-1} + \varepsilon_{2,t}, \end{cases} \qquad (4.17)$$

where the weak white noise admits a variance-covariance matrix

$$\Omega = \begin{pmatrix} w_{11} & w_{21} \\ w_{21} & w_{22} \end{pmatrix}.$$

We also introduce the additional regressions of each series on its own past:

$$\begin{cases} Y_{1,t} = \bar\mu_1 + \bar\varphi_1 Y_{1,t-1} + \tilde\varepsilon_{1,t}, \\ Y_{2,t} = \bar\mu_2 + \bar\varphi_2 Y_{2,t-1} + \tilde\varepsilon_{2,t}, \end{cases} \qquad (4.18)$$

and the following regressions that account for the effects of other contemporaneous endogenous components:

$$\begin{cases} Y_{1,t} = m_1 + \psi_{1,0}Y_{2,t} + \psi_{1,1}Y_{1,t-1} + \psi_{1,2}Y_{2,t-1} + u_{1,t}, \\ Y_{2,t} = m_2 + \psi_{2,0}Y_{1,t} + \psi_{2,1}Y_{1,t-1} + \psi_{2,2}Y_{2,t-1} + u_{2,t}. \end{cases} \qquad (4.19)$$

4.3.1 The Noncausality Hypotheses

The noncausality hypotheses are defined in terms of linear predictions. We say that, first, Y_2 does not Granger cause Y_1 if and only if the best linear prediction of $Y_{1,t}$ given $Y_{1,t-1}$ and $Y_{2,t-1}$ does not depend on $Y_{2,t-1}$. In the VAR(1) framework, this hypothesis is equivalent to the nullity constraint on $\varphi_{1,2}$:

$$H_{2\to1} = \{\varphi_{1,2} = 0\}.$$

It may also be characterized by comparing regressions (4.17) and (4.18) since

$$H_{2\to1} = \{V\varepsilon_{1,t} = V\tilde\varepsilon_{1,t}\}. \qquad (4.20)$$

Both residual variances coincide if and only if the regressor $Y_{2,t-1}$ is not relevant, that is, has no explanatory power.

Second, similarly, the process Y_1 does not Granger cause Y_2 if and only if the best linear prediction of $Y_{2,t}$ given $Y_{1,t-1}$ and $Y_{2,t-1}$ does not depend on $Y_{1,t-1}$. In the above framework, this hypothesis is

$$H_{1\to2} = \{\varphi_{2,1} = 0\} = \{V\varepsilon_{2,t} = V\tilde\varepsilon_{2,t}\}. \qquad (4.21)$$

Third, we can introduce a test for the absence of an instantaneous relationship (or *simultaneity*) between the two processes. We say that Y_1 does not instantaneously cause Y_2 if and only if the best linear predictor of $Y_{2,t}$ given $Y_{1,t}$, and $Y_{1,t-1}$, $Y_{2,t-1}$ does not depend on $Y_{1,t}$. This hypothesis can be expressed by the following equivalent formulas:

$$\begin{aligned} H_{1\leftrightarrow 2} &= \{\psi_{2,0}=0\} = \{Vu_{2,t}=V\varepsilon_{2,t}\} \\ &= \{\psi_{1,0}=0\} = \{Vu_{1,t}=V\varepsilon_{1,t}\} \\ &= \{w_{1,2}=0\} = \left\{\det V\begin{bmatrix}\varepsilon_{1,t}\\\varepsilon_{2,t}\end{bmatrix} = V\varepsilon_{1,t}V\varepsilon_{2,t}\right\}. \end{aligned} \tag{4.22}$$

In particular, under this hypothesis both processes play a symmetric role: Y_1 does not instantaneously cause Y_2 if and only if Y_2 does not instantaneously cause Y_1.

Fourth, when the three noncausality hypotheses are satisfied, the VAR(1) representation (4.17) simplifies to

$$\begin{cases} Y_{1,t} = \mu_1 + \varphi_{1,1}Y_{1,t-1} + \varepsilon_{1,t}, \\ Y_{2,t} = \mu_2 + \varphi_{2,2}Y_{2,t-1} + \varepsilon_{2,t}, \end{cases}$$

where $V\varepsilon_{1,t}=w_{1,1}$, $V\varepsilon_{2,t}=w_{2,2}$, $\mathrm{cov}(\varepsilon_{1,t},\varepsilon_{2,t})=0$. We get distinct evolutions of both processes, and $\tilde\mu_1=\mu_1$, $\tilde\varphi_1=\varphi_{1,1}$, $\tilde\varepsilon_{1,t}=\varepsilon_{1,t}$, $\tilde\mu_2=\mu_2$, $\tilde\varphi_2=\varphi_{2,2}$, $\tilde\varepsilon_{2,t}=\varepsilon_{2,t}$. The hypothesis of the absence of a linear link between Y_1 and Y_2 is

$$\begin{aligned} H_{1,2} &= H_{1\to 2}\cap H_{2\to 1}\cap H_{1\leftrightarrow 2} \\ &= \left\{\det V\begin{pmatrix}\varepsilon_{1,t}\\\varepsilon_{2,t}\end{pmatrix}=V\tilde\varepsilon_{1,t}V\tilde\varepsilon_{2,t}\right\}. \end{aligned} \tag{4.23}$$

4.3.2 Causality Measures and Test Procedures

Generally, various causal links can be found in a pair of time series, and it is interesting to measure the magnitude of causalities. For this purpose, we recall the formula of the likelihood ratio statistic in a Gaussian regression model. Next, we show how it is used as a causality measure.

Test of Significance in a Gaussian Regression Model
Let us consider a regression model with two explanatory variables X_1 and X_2 and Gaussian error terms

$$Y_i = a + X_{1,i}b_1 + X_{2,i}b_2 + \varepsilon_i, \ i=1,\dots,n, \tag{4.24}$$

where ε_i are independent identically distributed (i.i.d.) with normal distribution $N(0,\sigma^2)$. The log-likelihood function corresponding to this model is

$$\log L = -\frac{n}{2}\log 2\pi - \frac{n}{2}\log\sigma^2 - \frac{1}{2\sigma^2}\sum_{i=1}^{n}(y_i - a - x_{1,i}b_1 - x_{2,i}b_2)^2.$$

The maximum likelihood estimators of the parameters a, b_1, b_2, and σ^2 are identical to the OLS estimators. They satisfy

$$\hat{\sigma}^2 = \frac{1}{n} \sum_{i=1}^{n} (y_i - \hat{a} - x_{1,i}\hat{b}_1 - x_{i,i}\hat{b}_2)^2.$$

The maximal value of the log-likelihood is obtained by replacing the parameters by their OLS estimators. It is equal to

$$\log \hat{L} = -\frac{n}{2} \log 2\pi - \frac{n}{2} \log \hat{\sigma}^2 - \frac{n}{2}. \tag{4.25}$$

Let us now consider the regression model constrained by $b_2 = 0$, with X_1 as the single regressor:

$$Y_i = \alpha + X_{1,i}\beta_1 + u_i, \qquad i = 1, \ldots, n,$$

where u_i are i.i.d. with normal distribution $N(0, \sigma_0^2)$. The constrained OLS estimators are $\hat{\alpha}$, $\hat{\beta}_1$, and $\hat{\sigma}_0^2 = \frac{1}{n} \Sigma_{i=1}^{n} (Y_i - \hat{\alpha} - X_{1,i}\hat{\beta}_1)^2$. The associated constrained log-likelihood is equal to

$$\log \hat{L}_0 = -\frac{n}{2} \log 2\pi - \frac{n}{2} \log \hat{\sigma}_0^2 - \frac{n}{2}. \tag{4.26}$$

It is possible to test the null hypothesis of irrelevance of X_2, that is, $H_0 = \{b_2 = 0\}$, by the likelihood ratio test. The idea is to accept the null hypothesis if the constrained likelihood is close to the unconstrained one. The test statistic is

$$\xi_{LR} = 2(\log \hat{L} - \log \hat{L}_0), \tag{4.27}$$

and is asymptotically chi-square distributed with 1 degree of freedom. The test consists of accepting H_0, if $\xi_{LR} \leq 4 = \chi^2_{95\%}(1)$ and of rejecting H_0 otherwise.

It follows directly from (4.25) and (4.26) that the test statistic is a simple function of the residual variances:

$$\begin{aligned} \xi_{LR} &= 2(\log \hat{L} - \log \hat{L}_0) \\ &= n \log[\hat{\sigma}_0^2/\hat{\sigma}^2]. \end{aligned} \tag{4.28}$$

This quantity is nonnegative and is equal to 0 if and only if $\hat{\sigma}_0^2 = \hat{\sigma}^2$.

Causality Measures

By considering the expression of the likelihood ratio statistic and the characterizations of various causality hypotheses in terms of residual variances, the following causality measures can be proposed.

- Measure of causality from Y_2 to Y_1:

$$C_{2\to1} = \log[V\tilde{\varepsilon}_{1,t}/V\varepsilon_{1,t}];$$

- Measure of causality from Y_1 to Y_2:

$$C_{1\to2} = \log[V\tilde{\varepsilon}_{2,t}/V\varepsilon_{2,t}];$$

- Instantaneous causality measure between Y_1 and Y_2:

$$C_{1\leftrightarrow2} = \log\left[V(\varepsilon_{1,t})V(\varepsilon_{2,t})/\det V\binom{\varepsilon_{1,t}}{\varepsilon_{2,t}}\right];$$

- Dependence measure between Y_1 and Y_2:

$$C_{1.2} = \log\left[V(\tilde{\varepsilon}_{1,t})V(\tilde{\varepsilon}_{2,t})/\det V\binom{\varepsilon_{1,t}}{\varepsilon_{2,t}}\right].$$

These measures admit nonnegative values. They are equal to 0 if and only if the corresponding noncausality hypothesis is satisfied. Moreover, we get the decomposition formula

$$C_{1.2} = C_{2\to1} + C_{1\to2} + C_{1\leftrightarrow2}. \tag{4.29}$$

Test Procedures

The causality measures are easily estimated by replacing the theoretical variances of the error terms by the residual variances from appropriate regression models. We denote by $\hat{C}$ the residual variances and obtain the following empirical decomposition formula:

$$\hat{C}_{1.2} = \hat{C}_{2\to1} + \hat{C}_{1\to2} + \hat{C}_{1\leftrightarrow2}, \tag{4.30}$$

where, for instance,

$$\hat{C}_{2\to1} = \log(\hat{V}\tilde{\varepsilon}_{1,t}/\hat{V}\varepsilon_{1t})$$
$$= \log\left(\Sigma_{t=1}^{T}\hat{\tilde{\varepsilon}}_{1,t}^2/\Sigma_{t=1}^{T}\hat{\varepsilon}_{1,t}^2\right).$$

From general results on the theory of tests and the discussion in the section on test of significance, we infer the following proposition (see Granger 1969; Geweke 1982):

PROPOSITION 4.5: *Under the null hypothesis* $H_{1.2} = H_{1 \to 2} \cap H_{2 \to 1} \cap H_{1 \leftrightarrow 2}$, *the statistics* $T\hat{C}_{1 \to 2}$, $T\hat{C}_{2 \to 1}$, *and* $T\hat{C}_{1 \leftrightarrow 2}$ *are asymptotically independent and have the same limiting chi-square distribution with 1 degree of freedom. Under* $H_{1.2}$, *the statistic* $T\hat{C}_{1.2}$ *asymptotically follows a chi-square distribution with 3 degrees of freedom.*

The components of the decomposition formula in (4.30) can be compared directly since they have the same asymptotic distribution. For instance, if we observe that $T\hat{C}_{1.2} > \chi^2_{95\%}(3)$ (i.e., find some linear dependence between the series), we can directly point out the largest component creating this dependence or detect the components that do not contribute to the linear relationship.

These testing procedures can easily be implemented using standard regression software and are included in the causality analysis, at least at a preliminary stage. Obviously, they have to be adjusted whenever a series features conditional heteroscedasticity or intraday seasonals.

4.3.3   Term Structure of Causality

The results above for causality measures can easily be extended to a bidimensional process with a VAR(p) representation:

$$\begin{cases} Y_{1,t} = \mu_1 + \Sigma_{j=1}^{p} \varphi_{1,1,j} Y_{1,t-j} + \Sigma_{j=1}^{p} \varphi_{1,2,j} Y_{2,t-j} + \varepsilon_{1,t}, \\ Y_{2,t} = \mu_2 + \Sigma_{j=1}^{p} \varphi_{2,1,j} Y_{1,t-j} + \Sigma_{j=1}^{p} \varphi_{2,2,j} Y_{2,t-j} + \varepsilon_{2,t}, \end{cases} \tag{4.31}$$

where the weak white noise admits a variance-covariance matrix
$$\Omega = \begin{pmatrix} w_{11} & w_{12} \\ w_{21} & w_{22} \end{pmatrix}.$$

By introducing the additional marginal regressions

$$Y_{1,t} = \bar{\mu}_1 + \Sigma_{j=1}^{p} \bar{\varphi}_{1,j} Y_{1,t-j} + \bar{\varepsilon}_{1,t},$$
$$Y_{2,t} = \bar{\mu}_2 + \Sigma_{j=1}^{p} \bar{\varphi}_{2,j} Y_{2,t-j} + \bar{\varepsilon}_{2,t},$$

we get as before the decomposition formula

$$C_{1.2} = C_{2 \to 1} + C_{1 \to 2} + C_{1 \leftrightarrow 2},$$

where the causality measures are defined as in Section 4.3.2. The only difference with the VAR(1) case are the degrees of freedom of the limiting chi-square distribution equal to $2p + 1$, p, p, 1, respectively. Indeed, p constraints arise, for instance, from the hypothesis of noncausality from Y_1 to Y_2:

$$H_{1 \to 2} = \{\varphi_{2,1,1} = \ldots = \varphi_{2,1,p} = 0\}.$$

In this case, it is not possible to compare directly the estimated causality measures $\hat{C}_{1\to2}$ and $\hat{C}_{1\leftrightarrow2}$, which do not admit the same limiting distribution under the null. However, it is possible to decompose the unidirectional causality measures and to find the magnitude of causality at a fixed lag h (Gourieroux, Monfort, and Renault 1987).

Let us first consider the causality from Y_1 to Y_2 and introduce the following regression models:

$$(M_h^2): Y_{2,t} = \mu_2(h) + \sum_{j=h}^{p} \varphi_{2,1,j}^{(h)} Y_{1,t-j} + \sum_{j=1}^{p} \varphi_{2,2,j}^{(h)} Y_{2,t-j} + \varepsilon_{2,t}(h), \qquad (4.32)$$

where the lagged values of Y_1 at lags larger than h appear as explanatory variables.

We can study the effect of $Y_{1,t-h}$ on $Y_{2,t}$ given the past of Y_2 and the previous values of Y_1, that is, $Y_{1,t-h-1}$, $Y_{1,t-h-2}, \ldots$

The magnitude of this effect is measured by

$$C_{1\to2}^{(h)} = \log[V\varepsilon_{2,t}(h+1)/V\varepsilon_{2,t}(h)], \qquad (4.33)$$

and it is easily checked that

$$C_{1\to2} = \sum_{h=1}^{p} C_{1\to2}^{(h)}. \qquad (4.34)$$

Similarly, we can introduce the regression models

$$(M_h^1): Y_{1,t} = \mu_1(h) + \sum_{j=1}^{p} \varphi_{1,1,j}^{(h)} Y_{1,t-j} + \sum_{j=h}^{p} \varphi_{1,2,j}^{(h)} Y_{2,t-j} + \varepsilon_{1,t}(h), \qquad (4.35)$$

and the unidirectional causality measures at lag h

$$C_{2\to1}^{(h)} = \log[V\varepsilon_{1,t}(h+1)/V\varepsilon_{1,t}(h)]. \qquad (4.36)$$

Therefore, we get a more informative decomposition formula:

$$C_{1,2} = \sum_{h=1}^{p} C_{1\to2}^{(h)} + \sum_{h=1}^{p} C_{2\to1}^{(h)} + C_{1\leftrightarrow2}. \qquad (4.37)$$

The components of this decomposition formula can be compared directly due to the following proposition.

PROPOSITION 4.6: *Under the null hypothesis $H_{1,2}$, the statistics $T\hat{C}_{1\to2}^{(h)}$ with h varying, $T\hat{C}_{2\to1}^{(h)}$ with h varying, and $T\hat{C}_{1\leftrightarrow2}$ are asymptotically independent and have the same limiting chi-square distribution with 1 degree of freedom.*

4.3.4 Causality Analysis between Returns and Volumes

The data represent returns and volumes of trades of the Alcatel stock, recorded on the Paris Stock Exchange (Paris Bourse) in July and August

1996. Prior to estimation, the opening trades (respectively the simultaneous trades concealing split orders) were deleted (respectively aggregated). The sample consists of 9,813 observations recorded at 1-minute intervals. The returns have mean $-2.87E\text{-}7$ and variance $1.079E\text{-}6$, while the average of the volume is 6.4429 and of the variance is 80.2347.

We perform the unidirectional causality tests based on the regressions of volumes (returns) on past volumes and returns using an autoregressive specification of order 1. The regressions for testing the linear causality are

$$r_t = 0.000003 - \mathbf{0.2372}r_{t-1} - 0.000001v_{t-1}$$
$$v_t = \mathbf{5.9789} - \mathbf{4.2148}r_{t-1} + \mathbf{0.0720}v_{t-1}$$
$$v_t = \mathbf{5.9805} - \mathbf{476.6650}r_t - 117.2836r_{t-1} + \mathbf{0.0716}v_{t-1},$$

Since the relevant coefficient is not significant (the significant ones are in bold), the null hypothesis of the absence of unidirectional causality from r to v can be rejected. There is, however, strong evidence in favor of instantaneous causality.

Let us briefly comment on the signs of the estimated coefficients. In the first regression, the negative sign of r_{t-1} is due to a negative autocorrelation at lag 1 often found in high-frequency returns as a consequence of the bid-ask bounce phenomenon (see Chapter 14). The positive sign of the autoregressive coefficient on lagged volume in the second regression suggests a positive correlation between subsequent volumes, which indicates, for example, that a high volume for the present transaction will often entail a high volume for the next transaction. The negative and significant coefficient on current return in the last regression can also be easily explained. Dramatically decreasing returns have a tendency to increase the volume of transactions, for psychological reasons, during market crashes. We observe here an analog of this effect for "typical" intraday returns and volumes.

Let us now proceed to the estimation of the causality measures. We have

$$
\begin{array}{cccc}
T\hat{C}_{r.v} & T\hat{C}_{r \to v} & T\hat{C}_{v \to r} & T\hat{C}_{r \leftrightarrow v} \\
14.8377 = 5.9272 & + \ 0.0000 & + \ 8.9105 \\
(7.815) & (3.841) & (3.841) & (3.841)
\end{array}
$$

The second line gives the estimated causality measures, while the third one displays the critical value of $\chi^2_{95\%}(3) = 7.815$ and $\chi^2_{95\%}(1) = 3.841$. The causality decomposition suggests the presence of linear dependence between volumes and returns due to the causality from returns to volumes and instantaneous causality between them.

It has to be stressed that the above causality analysis is performed in a linear framework, and the causality measures introduced here do not accurately account for nonlinear links between returns and volumes. Nonlinear relationships, such as the dependence between traded volumes and squared returns, used as proxies for volatility are likely much stronger than the linear ones.

4.4 Summary

In this chapter, we examined sets of dynamic relations characterized by the presence of feedback effects and simultaneity between endogenous variables. A feedback effect can easily be explained in the context of supply-demand equilibrium. In Section 4.1, it is assumed that the system is in equilibrium, so that a change in quantity changes price, which then feeds back to quantity and then to price and so on. The feedback effects have implications on the specification of the model that represents the data-generating process. Since endogenous variables appearing on the left-hand side and the right-hand side of equations in the system are correlated with the equation errors, we recognized that we could no longer apply ordinary least squares to estimate the structural parameters without bias. We then developed a model representation called the reduced form, by which the least squares method yields consistent estimates.

In Section 4.2, we used the concept of the equilibrium model to represent the trade-off between risk and expected returns, widely known as the Capital Asset Pricing Model (CAPM). In particular, we investigated instantaneous correlation of excess gains on individual assets with the excess gain on the market portfolio, determined by the beta coefficient. Under the CAPM, the expectation of excess gains satisfies a linear relationship with beta, which represents the sensitivity with respect to the gain of the market portfolio. The CAPM hypothesis implies several constraints on the model specification, while it leaves the price dynamics partly undetermined. We show in Chapter 7 that the CAPM-implied equilibrium is compatible with infinity possible price processes. The multiplicity of equilibria is directly related to the incomplete market hypothesis.

Section 4.3 developed various measures of causality, reflecting the magnitude of interdependence among variables in a dynamic system. We explained Granger causality and illustrated its application to an empirical study of a dynamic return-volume relationship. We observed that linear causality measures are insufficient to capture nonlinear dependence between squared returns and volumes or squared returns on various assets, possibly involving their lagged values. This remark suggests that a study of nonlinear patterns could provide further insights. Nonlinear analysis of squared returns is related to the topic of Chapter 6, which examines asset volatility. Comovements and common patterns characterize not only stationary processes considered so far, but also other processes, including the nonstationary ones. Parallel evolution of nonstationary time series relates to the topic of the next chapter, which covers integrated univariate and multivariate processes.

5

Persistence and Cointegration

IN SECTION 2.4, we introduced examples of processes integrated of order 1, denoted $I(1)$, and discussed their role in modeling asset prices. We observed that asset prices often admit a nonstationary component, whereas asset returns seem to be stationary. In the first section of this chapter, we extend the notion of processes integrated of order 1 to multivariate processes with integrated components. Next, we introduce processes that admit fractional orders of integration, called *fractional processes*. The fractionally integrated processes are characterized by strong persistence and possibly explosive trajectories.

Despite that univariate asset prices often feature nonstationary behavior, this property is not necessarily shared by values of asset portfolios. Let us, for instance, consider the exchange rates between European currencies. Although the logarithms of the exchange rates of the Euro and British pound with respect to US dollars seem nonstationary, we expect that there exists a linear combination of these log–exchange rates that is stationary. Indeed, the value of the British pound in terms of the Euro has to be stabilized around a fixed level a before the United Kingdom joins the Euro zone. Therefore, the linear combination $y_{1,t} - ay_{2,t}$, where $y_{1,t}$ and $y_{2,t}$ are the log–exchange rates of the pound/US dollar and of the Euro/US dollar, respectively, is not explosive. In Section 5.2, we analyze how nonstationary properties can be eliminated by linear combinations of nonstationary series. Next, we discuss the cointegration theory and introduce the Error Correction Model (ECM) of cointegrated series.

5.1 Unit Root

Financial data, such as asset prices or squared returns, often feature slow decay of empirical autocorrelation functions. This property is called *long-*

range persistence or *long memory* since it implies long-term multiplier effects of transitory shocks. It is often due to the presence of a nonstationary component in a series, although it may also be exhibited by stationary processes. In this section, we first consider processes integrated of order 1, which have a random walk component. Next, we introduce fractional processes that bridge autoregressive moving average (ARMA) and $I(1)$ processes.

5.1.1 Integrated Process

We consider a multivariate series (Y_t) with n components and defined for $t \geq 0$. We assume a zero initial condition, $Y_0 = 0$.

DEFINITION 5.1: *The process (Y_t) is integrated of order 1, denoted by I(1) if it is stationary after differencing.*

Therefore, we get

$$\Delta Y_t = (1-L)Y_t = Y_t - Y_{t-1} = u_t, \qquad t \geq 1, \tag{5.1}$$

where (u_t) is a stationary process. We infer the representation of Y_t in terms of cumulated past shocks:

$$Y_t = \sum_{\tau=1}^{t} u_\tau, \tag{5.2}$$

which is an extension of the random walk, allowing the elements of the sum to be correlated. It is easy to see that (Y_t) is nonstationary and has an explosive behavior at a rate of divergence given as follows: (1) If $Eu_t \neq 0$, we know that $\frac{1}{t}\sum_{\tau=1}^{t} u_\tau = \frac{Y_t}{t} \to E(u_t)$. Therefore, Y_t diverges at rate t. (2) If $Eu_t = 0$, we know that $\frac{Y_t}{\sqrt{t}} = \frac{1}{\sqrt{t}}\sum_{\tau=1}^{t} u_\tau$ tends to a Gaussian variable. Therefore, Y_t diverges at the rate $\sqrt{t}$.

EXAMPLE 5.1, UNIDIMENSIONAL PROCESS: If (u_t) admits an ARMA representation,

$$\varphi(L)u_t = \theta(L)\varepsilon_t,$$

where (ε_t) is a weak white noise and the roots of φ and θ lie outside the unit circle, (Y_t) satisfies the autoregressive integrated moving average representation with orders p, 1, q, denoted ARIMA $(p,1,q)$:

$$(1-L)\varphi(L)Y_t = \theta(L)\varepsilon_t, \qquad t \geq p+1.$$

It differs from the standard ARMA representation by the presence of a unit root in the autoregressive polynomial.

EXAMPLE 5.2, MULTIDIMENSIONAL PROCESS: Let us consider a multivariate autoregressive representation of order 1 of the process (Y_t):

$$\Phi(L)Y_t = (Id - \Phi L)Y_t = \varepsilon_t.$$

We assume that the eigenvalues of the autoregressive matrix Φ have a modulus strictly less than 1, except for one of them, which is equal to 1. This condition can be written using the determinant of $\Phi(L)$:

$$\det \Phi(L) = (1 - L)p(L),$$

where $p(L)$ is a lag polynomial of degree $n - 1$ with roots lying outside the unit circle.

Let us now introduce the adjoint matrix $\psi(L)$ of $\Phi(L)$ defined by

$$\psi(L)\Phi(L) = \det \Phi(L)Id = (1 - L)p(L)Id.$$

$\psi(L)$ is a matrix of lag polynomials of degree $n - 1$, which may be decomposed into

$$\psi(L) = \psi(1) + (1 - L)\tilde{\psi}(L).$$

By inverting the autoregressive representation, we get

$$Y_t = \Phi(L)^{-1}\varepsilon_t$$

$$= \frac{\psi(L)}{\det \Phi(L)}\varepsilon_t$$

$$= \frac{\psi(1) + (1 - L)\tilde{\psi}(L)}{(1 - L)p(L)}\varepsilon_t,$$

or

$$Y_t = \psi(1)\frac{1}{(1 - L)p(L)}\varepsilon_t + \frac{\tilde{\psi}(L)}{p(L)}\varepsilon_t.$$

The first term of the decomposition is integrated of order 1, whereas the second term is stationary. The presence of the nonstationary component in the decomposition of (Y_t) implies that (Y_t) is $I(1)$. Indeed, we have

$$(1 - L)Y_t = \frac{\psi(1)}{p(L)}\varepsilon_t + (1 - L)\frac{\tilde{\psi}(L)}{p(L)}\varepsilon_t,$$

which is stationary.

5.1.2   *Fractional Process*

In this section, the notion of integrated processes is extended by introducing a unit root of a fractional order. We restrict our attention to univariate time series.

DEFINITION 5.2: *The process (Y_t) is ARIMA (p,d,q) if $(1-L)^d Y_t$ is a stationary ARMA(p,q) process where*

$$(1-L)^d = 1 + \Sigma_{j=1}^{\infty} \frac{d(d-1)\ldots(d-j+1)}{j!}(-1)^j L^j$$

$$= \Sigma_{j=0}^{\infty} \frac{\Gamma(-d+j)}{\Gamma(-d)} \frac{1}{j!} L^j,$$

and the Γ function is defined by $\Gamma(v) = \int_0^{\infty} exp(-x)x^{v-1}dx$. We consider below the fractional order d taking values in [0,1].

For $d=0$, we obtain a stationary ARMA process, whereas we get a nonstationary ARIMA$(p,1,q)$ process for $d=1$. By allowing d to take any value between 0 and 1, we close a gap between stationary and nonstationary processes. Proposition 5.1 provides the limiting value of d that separates the regions of stationary and nonstationary dynamics (see, e.g., Granger 1980; Hosking 1981).

PROPOSITION 5.1: *The fractional process is (asymptotically) stationary if and only if $d < 1/2$.*

When this condition is satisfied, we can derive the limiting behavior of the autocorrelation function for large lags. We get

$$\rho(h) \sim const\ h^{2d-1}, \qquad \text{for large } h. \tag{5.3}$$

For $d < 1/2$, we have $2d - 1 < 0$, and the autocorrelations tend to 0 at a hyperbolic rate, much slower than the geometric rate associated with standard ARMA models. The persistence increases with the fractional order d.

The asymptotic expansion given in (5.3) suggests a crude estimation method for the fractional order d in the stationary case. It is a two-step procedure outlined below:

1. Estimate the autocorrelations by computing their empirical counterparts $\hat{\rho}(h)$, h varying.
2. Recognize that expression (5.3) implies that

$$\log|\rho(h)| \sim \alpha + (2d-1)\log h, \qquad \text{for large } h,$$

and estimate its empirical counterpart by regressing

$$\log|\hat{\rho}(h)| \text{ on } 1, \log h, \qquad \text{for large } h.$$

The estimator of the fractional order is defined by $\hat{d} = (1+\hat{\beta})/2$, where $\hat{\beta}$ is the ordinary least squares (OLS) estimator of the coefficient on $\log h$.

This estimator is not very accurate and its asymptotic properties are difficult to derive (see, e.g., Geweke and Porter-Hudak 1982). More advanced estimation methods can be found in the literature (see, e.g., Robinson 1992). However, the asymptotic properties of fractional order estimators are known, but only for (ε_t) being a (Gaussian) strong white noise. Obviously, this assumption is violated by financial data. Moreover, the fractional order is sensitive to nonlinear transformations of time series. For example, while returns may appear uncorrelated, their squares typically display a long range of temporal dependence.

5.1.3 Persistence and Nonlinearity

Nonlinear Transformation
Let us illustrate the dependence of the fractional order of integration on nonlinear transformations. We consider the univariate process defined by

$$y_t = \text{sng}(\varepsilon_t)\,|x_t|,$$

where $(1-L)^d x_t = \varepsilon_t$, (ε_t) is a Gaussian strong white noise, and sng $\varepsilon_t = +1$ if $\varepsilon_t \geq 0$ and is -1 otherwise. Both $|y_t|$ and (y_t) feature long-range persistence since they depend on the fractional process x_t. However, sng $(y_t) =$ sng (ε_t) is a strong white noise without memory.

Strong dependence of the fractional order on nonlinear transformations of the data is well documented in return series (see, e.g., Ding, Engle, and Granger 1993). Figure 5.1 shows the autocorrelation function

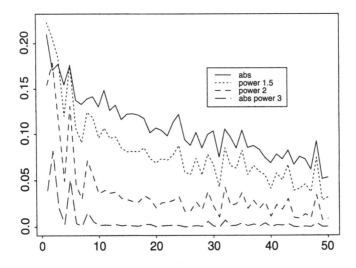

Figure 5.1 *Transformed Autocorrelogram*

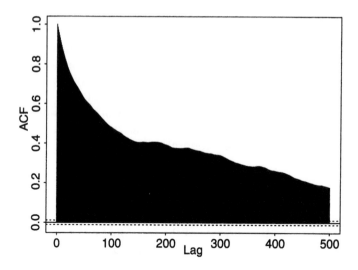

Figure 5.2   *Autocorrelation Function (ACF) of Regime Switching*

(ACF) for different power transformations of the absolute values of re-turns on the Standard and Poor's (S&P) Index sampled daily from 1950 until 1992. The empirical autocorrelations are decreasing functions of the exponent.

Infrequent Switching Regimes
Strong persistence may also be due to occasional shifts of the conditional distribution, called *switching regimes*. Let z_t be a qualitative process that admits two values, 0 and 1, depending on the regime pertaining at t. Each regime is allowed to last for a random number of time units, called a *regime duration*, until the next switch occurs. The process (y_t) featuring re-gime switches is defined by $y_t = g(x_t, z_t)$, where (x_t) and (z_t) are independent processes, (x_t) being a Gaussian ARMA process. Thus, $y_t = g(x_t, 1)$ in regime $z_t = 1$, and $y_t = g(x_t, 0)$ in regime $z_t = 0$. If the durations between regime switches are independent and come from a thick-tail distribution of a Pareto type, (y_t) behaves like a fractional process (see, e.g., Granger and Terasvirta 1999; Diebold and Inoue 1999; Gourieroux and Jasiak 2001). Figure 5.2 is the autocorrelogram of the qualitative process (z_t).

5.2   Cointegration

Empirical evidence suggests that several price series, such as prices of various stocks or bond yields at different maturities, display common nonstationary patterns in the long run. These common patterns are difficult to detect in the associated returns. Therefore, by modeling stationary returns, we lose information on the long-term comovements of prices. To account jointly for the long- and short-term aspects of price dynamics, Engle and Granger (1987) introduced the notion of cointegrated processes and explained how to model jointly log prices and their differences (i.e., returns). In the literature, this approach is known as the *Error Correction Model* (ECM).

5.2.1 Definition

We consider a multivariate process (Y_t) with components that are integrated of order 1. Hence, each component is a nonstationary process. To simplify the exposition, we assume that it follows an integrated autoregressive model of order 1 of the type described in Example 5.2:

$$\Phi(L)Y_t = (Id - \Phi L)Y_t = \varepsilon_t,$$

where $\det \Phi(L) = (1 - L)p(L)$.

DEFINITION 5.3: *The components of process Y are cointegrated if and only if there exists a nondegenerate linear combination $a'Y_t$ with $a \neq 0$, such that $a'Y_t$ is stationary. Such a linear combination is called a* cointegrating vector.

The presence of a cointegrating relationship is very easy to detect graphically in the bivariate case. Indeed, both components display parallel nonstationary movements since $a'Y_t = a_1 y_{1,t} + a_2 y_{2,t}$ is small compared to the values of $y_{1,t}$ and $y_{2,t}$. Figure 5.3 shows the plots of short-term and long-term interest rates (quarterly data). They feature similar patterns, except less variation is displayed by the long-term interest rate (solid line). This illustrates the long-term interest rate interpretation as a smooth equivalent of the future short-term interest rates and explains the observed cointegration relationship with cointegrating coefficients such that $a_2/a_1 = -1$.

5.2.2 Characterization of Cointegrating Vectors

From the moving average representation described in Example 5.2,

$$Y_t = \psi(1)\frac{1}{(1-L)p(L)}\varepsilon_t + \frac{\tilde{\psi}(L)}{p(L)}\varepsilon_t,$$

we deduce

$$a'Y_t = a'\psi(1)\frac{1}{(1-L)p(L)}\varepsilon_t + a'\frac{\tilde{\psi}(L)}{p(L)}\varepsilon_t.$$

This linear combination is stationary if the nonstationary component vanishes, that is, if $a'\psi(1) = 0$.

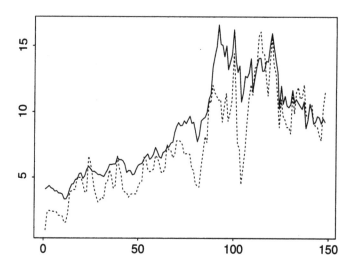

Figure 5.3 *Short- and Long-Term Interest Rates*

PROPOSITION 5.2:

(*i*) *The components of process Y are cointegrated if and only if the matrix* $\psi(1)$
is not of full rank.
(*ii*) *The cointegrating vectors are the nonzero elements of the kernel of* $\psi(1)'$,
that is, they satisfy $\psi(1)'a = 0$.

EXAMPLE 5.3: In the bivariate case, the matrix $\psi(1)$ is of dimension
(2,2). Three cases can be distinguished:

- rank $\psi(1) = 2$: The components of Y are not cointegrated, that is,
  any linear combination is nonstationary.
- rank $\psi(1) = 1$: There exists a multiplicity of cointegrating vectors
  defined up to a multiplicative scalar.
- rank $\psi(1) = 0$, that is, $\psi(1) = 0$: The process Y is stationary, which
  contradicts the assumption of $I(1)$ components.

5.2.3   Error Correction Model

In the general case, where rank $\psi(1) = n - K$, the vector space of cointegrating vectors has dimension K. Then, the matrix $\psi(1)$ can be written as

$$\psi(1) = \beta\gamma', \qquad (5.4)$$

where β and γ are matrices of the same dimension (n,r), r is the rank of
$\psi(1)$, and the columns of β form a basis of the range of $\psi(1)$ (see Appen-

dix 9.1 for a proof). Similarly, we can introduce a matrix α of dimension $n - r = K$, with columns that form a basis of the space of cointegrating vectors. From the definition of cointegrating vectors, it follows that

$$\alpha'\beta = 0. \tag{5.5}$$

Let us now consider the relation between $\Phi(L)$ and $\psi(L)$:

$$\Phi(L)\psi(L) = (1 - L)p(L)Id.$$

This implies that $\Phi(1)\psi(1) = 0 \Leftrightarrow \Phi(1)\beta = 0$. Therefore, the matrix $\Phi(1)$ can be decomposed into

$$\Phi(1) = \delta\alpha' \tag{5.6}$$

where δ has the dimension $(n, n - r)$. This decomposition provides an alternative specification of the autoregressive equation for a cointegrated system.

PROPOSITION 5.3, ERROR CORRECTION MODEL: *For a cointegrated system, the autoregressive equation*

$$\Phi(L)Y_t = (Id - \Phi L)Y_t = \varepsilon_t,$$

is equivalent to $\Delta Y_t + \delta\alpha' Y_{t-1} = \varepsilon_t.$

PROOF: We have $\Phi(1) = Id - \Phi = \delta'\alpha$. Therefore,

$$\Phi(L)Y_t = [Id(1 - L) + \delta\alpha' L]Y_t$$
$$= \Delta Y_t + \delta\alpha' Y_{t-1} = \varepsilon_t.$$

QED

In this multivariate system, the differences ΔY_t are functions of the noise and of the lagged Y_t levels. The Y_t levels appear in the linear combinations $\alpha' Y_{t-1}$. It is important to note that the dimension of $\alpha' Y_{t-1}$ is often less than the dimension of Y_{t-1}. Moreover, the system involves only stationary series ΔY_t and $\alpha' Y_{t-1}$. $\alpha' Y_{t-1}$ can be considered the deviation at $t - 1$ from the steady relation $\alpha' y = 0$. The short-term dynamics of the system represent the adjustments of Y_t in response to these deviations. In particular, the process of temporary deviations from the long-run relation has to be stationary to ensure that the steady relation prevails in the long run.

5.2.4 Factor Representation

Let us consider the moving average representation. We get

$$Y_t = \beta\gamma' \frac{1}{(1 - L)p(L)}\varepsilon_t + \frac{\bar{\psi}(L)}{p(L)}\varepsilon_t$$
$$= \beta F_t + u_t,$$

where the r dimensional factor F_t features a trend, whereas u_t is stationary. The matrix β gives the sensitivities of the components of Y with respect to various underlying factors.

5.2.5 Statistical Inference

Statistical analysis of cointegrated systems is a difficult topic (see, e.g., Johansen 1988, 1996; Phillips 1991). We provide here only a few basic insights on the estimation method based on the ECM representation. We first consider the unconstrained seemingly unrelated regression (SUR) model:

$$\Delta Y_t = \pi Y_{t-1} + \varepsilon_t,$$

comprising the regressions of differenced variables on lagged levels. Then, we examine the rank of the matrix of coefficients π, which is equal to $\pi = -\Phi(1)$. Under the cointegration hypothesis, we get a constrained SUR model, where $\pi = -\Phi(1) = -\delta\alpha'$ and has rank r. The unconstrained and constrained SUR models can be estimated by the quasi-maximum likelihood (QML), which maximizes a Gaussian likelihood function with respect to the free parameter. The optimization of the constrained Gaussian log-likelihood is necessary to estimate the cointegrating vectors for a fixed K. Then the comparison of the constrained and the unconstrained likelihoods is used for determining the number of cointegrating vectors K. The estimation of the dimension K and of the cointegrating vectors requires the solution of an eigenvalue problem:

$$S_{10}S_{00}^{-1}S_{01}e = \lambda S_{11}e,$$

where

$$S_{00} = \frac{1}{T}\Sigma_{t=1}^T \Delta y_t \Delta y_t',$$

$$S_{01} = \frac{1}{T}\Sigma_{t=1}^T \Delta y_t y_{t-1}',$$

$$S_{11} = \frac{1}{T}\Sigma_{t=1}^T y_{t-1} y_{t-1}',$$

and λ and e denote the generic eigenvalue and eigenvector, respectively. If the eigenvalues are ranked in a descending order, $\lambda_1 \geq \lambda_2 \geq \ldots$, the dimension of the space of cointegrating vectors is approximated by the number $\hat{K}$ of significant eigenvalues, whereas the cointegrating vectors are estimated by the associated eigenvectors. This standard method is valid in a linear framework. It needs to be adjusted in the presence of conditional heteroscedasticity.

5.3 Summary

Long and infinite memory patterns are frequently observed in financial data. Infinite memory characterizes integrated processes introduced in Section 5.1 and can be inferred from slowly, linearly decaying empirical autocorrelations. The class of random walks representing asset prices shown in Chapter 2 is a special case of processes that combine nonstationary and stationary components. Therefore, we introduced a general class of ARIMA processes that allow for the presence of short-term dependence expressed by autoregressive and moving average terms along with an explosive unit root. The distinction between infinite and long memory is determined by the power of the unit root. In the case when a fractional exponent is found instead of an integer value, a process displays autocorrelations that die out at a hyperbolic, rather than a linear, rate. Fractional roots are empirically documented in asset volatilities.

Synchronized movements of asset prices motivate Section 5.2 on cointegration. Under this approach, asset prices are assumed to display a common stochastic trend in the long run. Deviations from the long run are only temporary and form a stationary process. This mechanism prevents the processes from diverging from each other. This type of behavior characterizes series of forward and spot prices and long-term and short-term interest rates, for example.

There is a growing body of literature suggesting that long memory patterns detected from autocorrelations may be spurious and due to nonlinearities. A classical example of a nonlinear model is the autoregressive conditionally heteroscedastic (ARCH) model introduced in the next chapter.

6

Conditional Heteroscedasticity: Nonlinear Autoregressive Models, ARCH Models, Stochastic Volatility Models

THE PORTFOLIO mean-variance optimizing investors are assumed to evaluate the performance of their investments in terms of two summary statistics that represent the expected gain of a portfolio and its expected risk determined from asset volatility. These statistics, which correspond to the first two conditional moments of asset returns or prices, can be estimated using autoregressive moving average (ARMA) models discussed in Chapter 2. However, linear ARMA models provide a poor assessment of risk. The reason is that, while they successfully capture the movements of conditional means, they rely on the assumption of time-invariant conditional variances of the series. To accommodate the variation of risk, an approach involving conditional heteroscedasticity is required.

In this chapter, we introduce various time series models that represent the dynamics of both conditional means and conditional variances. In the first section, we extend the autoregressive process of order 1 and express its first two conditional moments as nonlinear functions of lagged returns. We describe several properties of this class of models and highlight its link with the technical analysis. Autoregressive conditionally heteroscedastic (ARCH) models are introduced in the second section. A basic ARCH specification consists of two ARMA equations, the first representing the dynamics of the series and the second its squared values. In particular, the second equation accommodates the dynamics of volatility approximated by squared returns. Major advantages and drawbacks of

ARCH models are discussed in the sequel. We point out that ARCH models fail to capture the so-called leverage effect and do not admit a straightforward continuous time representation, unlike the AR(1) (autoregressive process of order 1) process, for example. The stochastic volatility models, covered in Section 6.3, have been proposed in the literature as an alternative approach that is free of such limitations. Finally, all models mentioned are extended to a multivariate setup that allows for an analysis of multiple assets, discussed in the last section.

6.1 Nonlinear Autoregressive Models

6.1.1 Definitions

The linear AR(p) process satisfies the linear recursive equation

$$y_t = \mu + \phi_1 y_{t-1} + \ldots + \phi_p y_{t-p} + \sigma \varepsilon_t.$$

Let us now assume that the innovation process $(\varepsilon_t, t \in Z)$ is a strong white noise with mean zero and unitary variance. Then, the conditional mean of the AR(p) can be written as a linear function of lagged y's

$$E(y_t | \underline{y_{t-1}}) = \mu + \phi_1 y_{t-1} + \ldots + \phi_p y_{t-p},$$

and its conditional variance remains constant in time:

$$V(y_t | \underline{y_{t-1}}) = \sigma^2.$$

The nonlinear autoregressive models extend the previous specification in two aspects. First, they express the conditional mean as a nonlinear function of the past of the process. Second, they accommodate the volatility movements by conditioning the variance on lagged observations. A nonlinear autoregressive model can be written as

$$y_t = \mu(y_{t-1}, \ldots, y_{t-p}) + \sigma (y_{t-1}, \ldots, y_{t-p}) \varepsilon_t, \tag{6.1}$$

where $(\varepsilon_t, t \in Z)$ is a strong white noise with $E\varepsilon_t = 0$ and $V\varepsilon_t = 1$. Depending on the functional forms of the drift function μ and volatility function σ, various extensions of the general specification (6.1) can be derived. For example, the drift and volatility functions may be a priori constrained to belong to a given parametric class under a semiparametric setup. Otherwise, the drift and volatility functions may be left unconstrained under a nonparametric approach.

6.1.2 Leptokurtosis

In the early 1960s, Mandelbrot (1963) and Fama (1963) documented empirical evidence on heavy tails of the marginal distributions of asset re-

Table 6.1 *Marginal Kurtosis*

Asset	Sampling Frequency	Period	Kurtosis
Bank of Montreal	5 minutes	October 1998	7.00
	10 minutes		6.34
	20 minutes		6.89
S&P 500 (adjusted)	Daily	1950–1992	1.48
FTA Index	Monthly	1965–1990	15.96
Yield on 20-year UK gilts	Quarterly	1952–1988	5.93
Yield on 91-day UK gilts	Quarterly	1952–1988	4.22
Pound/dollar exchange rate	Daily	1974–1982	8.40

FTA: Financial Times Actuaries. All shares.

turns. This finding had crucial implications for risk management since thick-tailed distributions entail frequent occurrence of extremely valued observations (see Chapter 16). The thickness of tails is measured by the marginal kurtosis:

$$k = \frac{E(y_t - Ey_t)^4}{(Vy_t)^2},$$ (6.2)

which is the ratio of the centered fourth-order moment and squared variance. It is known that the kurtosis of a normally distributed variable is equal to 3. In Table 6.1, we report the empirical marginal kurtosis computed for various asset returns.

Table 6.1 shows that the tails of return distributions are heavier than the tails of the normal. Distributions sharing this property are called *leptokurtic*. Our evidence confirms that returns feature departures from normality. The normality assumption is violated by the marginal distributions of returns.

Let us now explain how the conditionally heteroskedastic models may reconcile this stylized fact with the normality assumption by distinguishing between the marginal and conditional kurtosis. To illustrate this approach, let us consider an autoregressive process of order 1 with a Gaussian white noise:

$$y_t = \mu(y_{t-1}) + \sigma(y_{t-1})\varepsilon_t, \qquad \varepsilon_t \sim IIN(0, 1).$$ (6.3)

The conditional distribution of y_t given y_{t-1} is normal and has conditional kurtosis equal to 3. Let us now compute the statistic

$$C(y_t) = E(y_t - Ey_t)^4 - 3(Vy_t)^2.$$

It is equal to zero if the marginal kurtosis is equal to 3. By substituting expression (6.3) for y_t, we get:

$$C(y_t) = E\{[\mu(y_{t-1}) - E\mu(y_{t-1})] + \sigma(y_{t-1})\varepsilon_t\}^4$$
$$- 3[E\{\mu(y_{t-1}) - E\mu(y_{t-1}) + \sigma(y_{t-1})\varepsilon\}^2]^2$$
$$= C[\mu(y_{t-1})] + 6E\{\sigma^2(y_{t-1})[\mu(y_{t-1}) - E\mu(y_{t-1})]^2\}$$
$$- 6E[\mu(y_{t-1}) - E\mu(y_{t-1})]^2 E\sigma^2(y_{t-1}) + 3V\sigma^2(y_{t-1}),$$

where $C(\mu(y_{t-1}))$ denotes the C-type moment of the variable $\mu(y_{t-1})$. Therefore, the marginal kurtosis of y_t depends on the marginal kurtosis of $\mu(y_{t-1})$ and on the variation of the volatility $\sigma^2(y_{t-1})$. In particular, when $\mu(y_{t-1})$ is constant (for instance, if it is equal to 0), the formula becomes

$$C(y_t) = 3V[\sigma^2(y_{t-1})] \geq 0. \tag{6.4}$$

Therefore, conditionally Gaussian errors in (6.3) are compatible with a leptokurtic marginal distribution of returns, and the thickness of tails is related to the dispersion of volatility.

6.1.3   Parametric and Nonparametric Inference

A standard estimation method for dynamic models of non-Gaussian series is the quasi (pseudo) maximum likelihood applied as if the errors were conditionally Gaussian. For clarity of exposition, we consider below a nonlinear autoregressive process of order 1.

Parametric Model
The model is defined by the equation

$$y_t = \mu(y_{t-1}; \theta) + \sigma(y_{t-1}; \theta)\varepsilon_t,$$

where the drift and volatility functions depend on the unknown parameter θ. The quasi-maximum likelihood estimator (QMLE) of θ is obtained by maximizing the log-likelihood function computed as if the errors (ε_t, $t \in Z$) were Gaussian:

$$\hat{\theta}_T = \text{Arg } \min_{\theta} L_T(\theta)$$
$$= \text{Arg } \min_{\theta} \sum_{t=1}^{T} \log l(y_t | y_{t-1}; \theta), \tag{6.5}$$

with

$$\log l(y_t|y_{t-1};\theta) = -\frac{1}{2}\log 2\pi - \frac{1}{2}\log \sigma^2(y_{t-1};\theta) - \frac{[y_t - \mu(y_{t-1};\theta)]^2}{2\sigma^2(y_{t-1};\theta)}. \quad (6.6)$$

PROPOSITION 6.1: *If $(\varepsilon_t, t \in Z)$ is a strong white noise with $E\varepsilon_t = 0$ and $V\varepsilon_t = 1$, then the QML estimator $\hat{\theta}_T$ is consistent: $\lim_{\to\infty} \hat{\theta}_T = \theta$ and asymptotically normal:*

$$\sqrt{T}(\hat{\theta}_T - \theta) \overset{d}{\to} N(0, J^{-1}IJ^{-1}),$$

where

$$J = E_\theta \left\{ -\frac{\partial^2 \log l(y_t|y_{t-1};\theta)}{\partial\theta\partial\theta'} \right\},$$

$$I = E_\theta \left\{ \frac{\partial \log l(y_t|(y_{t-1};\theta)}{\partial\theta} \frac{\partial \log l(y_t|y_{t-1};\theta)}{\partial\theta'} \right\}.$$

Although the two matrices I and J are generally different, they coincide when the error term ε_t is Gaussian, that is, when the QML is identical to the maximum likelihood (ML).

Other estimation methods may also be used, such as two-step least squares. Let us assume that the drift and volatility functions depend on distinct subsets of parameters:

$$y_t = \mu(y_{t-1}, \theta_1) + \sigma(y_{t-1}; \theta_2)\varepsilon_t. \quad (6.7)$$

The approach consists of the two steps outlined below.

In the first step, estimation of θ_1 is done by nonlinear ordinary least squares. The estimator is

$$\hat{\theta}_{1T} = \underset{\theta_1}{\text{Arg min}} \sum_{t=1}^{T} [y_t - \mu(y_{t-1}; \theta_1)]^2.$$

In the second step are computed the first-step residuals:

$$\hat{u}_{t,T} = y_t - \mu(y_{t-1}; \hat{\theta}_{1T}), \qquad t = 1, \dots, T,$$

and estimation of θ_2 is made by nonlinear least squares applied to squared residuals. The estimator of θ_2 is

$$\hat{\theta}_{2,T} = \underset{\theta_2}{\text{Arg min}} \sum_{t=1}^{T} \left[\hat{u}_{t,T}^2 - \sigma^2(y_{t-1}; \theta_2) \right]^2.$$

In practice a one-step QML method is preferred for two reasons. First, it is in general more accurate. Second, in financial applications, the existence of a risk premium implies that the parameters of the volatility equation are likely to appear in the conditional mean.

Nonparametric Model

Let us now consider the autoregressive specification

$$y_t = \mu(y_{t-1}) + \sigma(y_{t-1})\varepsilon_t,$$

where the drift and volatility functions are a priori left unconstrained except for the positivity restriction on the volatility function. They are considered as two functional parameters that can be estimated by a kernel-based quasi-maximum likelihood method (Pagan and Schwert 1990; Hardle and Vieu 1992).

A *kernel* is a weighting function used for local analysis of μ and σ. It is defined by a real function K that integrates up to 1: $\int K(u)du = 1$. A standard example is the Gaussian kernel (Figure 6.1) defined by $K(u) = \frac{1}{2\pi} \exp\left(-\frac{u^2}{2}\right)$.

The kernel-based QML estimators of μ and σ are defined by

$$\begin{bmatrix} \hat{\mu}(y) \\ \hat{\sigma}(y) \end{bmatrix} = \underset{\mu,\sigma}{\text{Arg max}} \sum_{t=1}^{T} \frac{1}{Th_T} K\left[\frac{y_{t-1}-y}{h_T}\right] l(y_t|y_{t-1}; \mu,\sigma)$$

$$= \underset{\mu,\sigma}{\text{Arg max}} \sum_{t=1}^{T} \frac{1}{Th_T} K\left[\frac{y_{t-1}-y}{h_T}\right]\left[-\frac{1}{2}\log\sigma^2 - \frac{1}{2}\frac{(y_t-\mu)^2}{\sigma^2}\right], \quad \forall y,$$

(6.8)

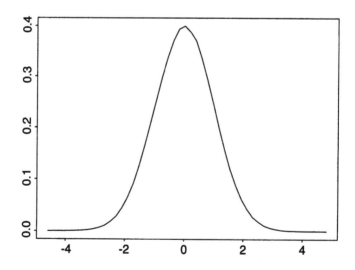

Figure 6.1   Gaussian Kernel

where h_T, called the *bandwidth*, tends to 0 when T tends to infinity. The estimators have the explicit forms

$$\hat{\mu}(y) = \sum_{t=1}^{T} y_t K\left[\frac{y_{t-1}-y}{h_T}\right] \bigg/ \left[\sum_{t=1}^{T} K\left[\frac{y_{t-1}-y}{h_T}\right]\right], \qquad (6.9)$$

$$\hat{\sigma}^2(y) = \sum_{t=1}^{T} y_t^2 K\left[\frac{y_{t-1}-y}{h_T}\right] \bigg/ \left(\sum_{t=1}^{T} K\left[\frac{y_{t-1}-y}{h_T}\right]\right) - \hat{\mu}^2(y). \qquad (6.10)$$

They can be interpreted as weighted empirical mean and variance, with weights $K\left[\frac{y_{t-1}-y}{h_T}\right] \bigg/ \left[\sum_{t=1}^{T} K\left(\frac{y_{t-1}-y}{h_T}\right)\right]$ depending on the point y and on the number of observations. The asymptotic properties of the estimators follow from general properties of kernel M-estimators (see, e.g., Gourieroux, Monfort, and Tenreiro 2000).

PROPOSITION 6.2: *If $(\varepsilon_t, t \in Z)$ is a strong white noise with $E\varepsilon_t = 0$ and $V\varepsilon_t = 1$, if $T \to \infty$ and $Th_T \to \infty$, then*

(i) $\hat{\mu}$ and $\hat{\sigma}^2$ are consistent estimators of μ and σ^2.
(ii) They are pointwise asymptotically normal:

$$\sqrt{Th_T}\,[\hat{\theta}_T - \theta] \xrightarrow{d} N\left[0, \frac{J(y)^{-1}I(y)J(y)^{-1}}{f(y)} \int K^2(v)dv\right],$$

where $\theta = \begin{pmatrix} \mu(y) \\ \sigma^2(y) \end{pmatrix}$,

$$J(y) = E\left[-\frac{\partial^2 \log l(y_t|y_{t-1}; \theta)}{\partial\theta\partial\theta'}\bigg|_{y_{t-1}=y}\right],$$

$$I(y) = E\left[\frac{\partial \log l(y_t|y_{t-1}; \theta)}{\partial\theta}\frac{\partial \log l(y_t|y_{t-1}; \theta)}{\partial\theta'}\bigg|_{y_{t-1}=y}\right],$$

$f(y)$ is the value of the marginal probability density function (pdf) of y_t evaluated at y.

The formula of the asymptotic variance is similar to the formula derived in the parametric approach. A distinctive feature is the presence of a multiplicative factor $\frac{1}{f(y)} \int K^2(v)dv$ and the expressions of information matrices I and J conditioned on $y_{t-1} = y$.

6.1.4   Asymmetric Reactions

The nonlinear autoregressive specification allows for an asymmetric response of volatility to the sign of price changes (the so-called leverage effect, see Section 6.3.2). Indeed, stock market investors seem to react differently depending on whether the asset prices rise or fall. Moreover, these reactions may generate price discontinuities due to psychological factors, such as traders' preferences for round numbers or the slowdown of market indexes before exceeding thresholds of integer multiples of 100 (say).

To examine these issues, Gourieroux and Monfort (1992) introduced a nonlinear autoregressive model with thresholds called the *Qualitative Threshold Autoregressive Conditionally Heteroscedastic* (QTARCH) Model. The specification, including two lags, is

$$y_t = \sum_i \sum_j \alpha_{ij} 1_{y_{t-1} \in A_i} 1_{y_{t-2} \in A_j} + \left(\sum_i \sum_j \beta_{ij} 1_{y_{t-1} \in A_i} 1_{y_{t-2} \in A_j} \right) \varepsilon_t, \tag{6.11}$$

where A_i, i varying, are fixed intervals defining the partition of the real line, and α_{ij} and β_{ij} are the parameters to be estimated. Under this approach, the drift and volatility functions are stepwise functions. They provide an accurate approximation of the unconstrained μ and σ whenever the partition of the real line is sufficiently fine.

The QTARCH Model was applied to daily increments of the exchange rate for French francs/US dollars (FF/US$), with intervals set by the limits -0.8, -0.6, $-.4$, -0.2, 0, 0.2, 0.4, 0.6, and 0.8. The α_{ij} coefficients were found insignificant. This result is compatible with the assumption of a lagged exchange rate being fully informative in determining a future one. The estimated volatilities β_{ij} pertaining to various regimes are plotted in Figure 6.2, which reveals the asymmetry of the volatility response. We observe that the volatility is more influenced by falling exchange rates than by rising ones.

6.1.5   Technical Analysis

Nonlinear forecasting of future returns from observations on their current and lagged values is an old topic in finance. For example, it is the essential task of the *technical analysis* (also called *chartism*), which detects regularities in the dynamics of returns and exploits them for designing financial strategies. This approach leads to a pragmatic typology of return patterns, with a prediction scheme associated with each element of the typology. It implicitly provides various specifications of the conditional mean of returns (see Appendix 6.1. for examples) (Kaufman 1980; Prechter-Frost 1985; Lofton

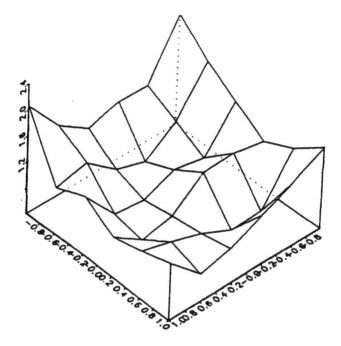

Figure 6.2 *Volatility Pattern*

1986; Murphy 1986). The nonlinear dynamic models described in Chapter 6 improve on the technical analysis in three aspects:

1. They contain a forecast error $\sigma(y_{t-1}, \ldots, y_{t-p})$ that may depend on the return history. Therefore, the point prediction is supplemented by the prediction interval, for assessing the accuracy of prediction.
2. The approach based on estimation of (functional) parameters μ and σ is more rigorous. The performance of estimators can be evaluated from the confidence intervals, with stability in time that can be examined as well.
3. Finally, nonlinear autoregressive models can be extended to a multivariate framework, while the technical analysis is limited to individual series. Indeed, typical patterns are extremely hard to detect in multivariate data.

Like the technical analysts, the nonlinear autoregressive models implicitly postulate that the future replicates (stochastically) the past. However, investors can modify their prediction formulas by incorporating complex nonlinearities and then select new strategies based on these predictions, which they believe to be more accurate. By modifying their behavior endogenously, investors alter in consequence the nonlinear dynamics of asset returns at equilibrium.

6.2 Autoregressive Conditionally Heteroscedastic Models

6.2.1 *Definitions*

The ARCH class of models was introduced by Engle (1982) to accommodate the dynamics of conditional heteroscedasticity. Its advantages are simplicity of formulation and ease of estimation. The ARCH models have been extensively used in financial empirical research and have been extended in various respects. The basic ARCH-type models are presented below in chronological order of development.

ARCH(q)
The ARCH(q) of Engle (1982) is defined by

$$E(y_t|\underline{y}_{t-1}) = 0,$$
$$V(y_t|\underline{y}_{t-1}) = c + \sum_{i=1}^{q} a_i y_{t-i}^2. \tag{6.12}$$

This is a nonlinear autoregressive specification:

$$y_t = 0 + \left(c + \sum_{i=1}^{q} a_i y_{t-i}^2\right)^{\frac{1}{2}} \varepsilon_t, \tag{6.13}$$

where the error term $(\varepsilon_t, t \in Z)$ is such that

$$E(\varepsilon_t|\underline{y}_{t-1}) = 0, \qquad V(\varepsilon_t|\underline{y}_{t-1}) = 1,$$

(a conditionally standardized martingale difference sequence).

In this simple version of the model, the past has an impact on the present volatility, which is assumed to be a quadratic function of lagged innovations. This specific functional form has the advantage of being easy to estimate. Indeed, the coefficients $c, a_1, \ldots, a_q$ can be consistently estimated by regressing y_t^2 on $1, y_{t-1}^2, \ldots, y_{t-q}^2$. To ensure nonnegative volatility, we require $c \geq 0$, $a_i \geq 0$, $\forall i = 1, \ldots, q$.

To illustrate the dynamic properties of ARCH models, we consider the model with $q = 1$ and $c = 1$ and select different values of the a_1 parameter (Figure 6.3). Intuitively, the larger the a_1 parameter, the greater the autocorrelations of volatilities (*volatility persistence*). This feature is even more apparent when squared variables are considered (Figure 6.4).

GARCH(p,q)
In the generalized autoregressive conditionally heteroscedastic (GARCH(p,q)) extension of Bollerslev (1986), the autoregressive representation of squared

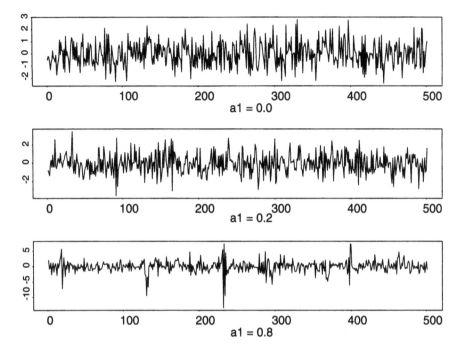

Figure 6.3 *Simulated Paths of ARCH(1) Model*

values of $(y_t, t \in Z)$ in the ARCH model is replaced by an ARMA type of specification. The GARCH process is defined by

$$E(y_t|\underline{y}_{t-1}) = 0,$$
$$V(y_t|\underline{y}_{t-1}) = \sigma_t^2 = c + \sum_{i=1}^{q} \alpha_i y_{t-i}^2 + \sum_{j=1}^{p} \beta_j \sigma_{t-j}^2, \tag{6.14}$$

where the volatility is a linear function of both lagged squares of returns and lagged volatilities. Let us introduce the innovation of the squared returns process:

$$u_t = y_t^2 - \sigma_t^2 = y_t^2 - E\left(y_t^2|\underline{y}_{t-1}\right). \tag{6.15}$$

The innovation process $(u_t, t \in Z)$ is a weak white noise [whenever (y_t) is stationary]. Replacing in equation (6.14) the conditional variance σ_t^2 by $y_t^2 - u_t$ yields

$$y_t^2 = c + \sum_{i=1}^{\max(p,q)} (\alpha_i + \beta_i) y_{t-1}^2 + u_t - \sum_{j=1}^{p} \beta_j u_{t-j}, \tag{6.16}$$

where by convention $\alpha_i = 0$ for $i > q$ and $\beta_j = 0$ for $j > p$.

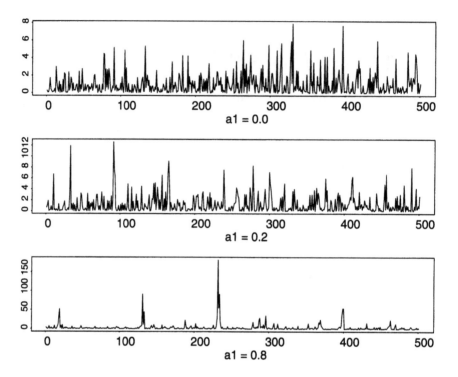

Figure 6.4   *Squares of Simulated Paths of ARCH(1) Model*

This is an ARMA representation for the transformed process (y_t^2, $t \in Z$) of an autoregressive order max(p,q) and a moving average order p. However, we need to be cautious about applying standard software designed for estimation of ARMA models to the series (y_t^2, $t \in Z$). Indeed, the innovation (u_t) of squared returns is, in general, conditionally heteroscedastic and also conditionally non-Gaussian (due to the positivity of y_t^2). Therefore, standard software packages often provide erroneous standard errors of estimators and erroneous test statistics and prediction intervals.

ARMA-GARCH

The ARCH and GARCH models introduced above represent processes with zero conditional means. Let us now examine processes with path dependent means, whose errors follow an ARCH or a GARCH process (ARMA-GARCH; Weiss 1984). For example, we can consider a linear regression model with GARCH errors:

$$\begin{cases} y_t = x_t b + u_t, \\ \text{where } (u_t) \text{ is a GARCH,} \end{cases}$$

or an ARMA model with GARCH errors:

$$\begin{cases} \Phi(L)y_t = \Theta(L)u_t, \\ \text{where } (u_t) \text{ is a GARCH.} \end{cases}$$

ARCH-M

The ARCH-M model (Engle, Lilien, and Robbins 1987) accounts for the risk premium by introducing the volatility into the conditional mean equation. For this reason the process is called ARCH-M for ARCH effect in the mean. This model can be written as

$$\begin{cases} y_t = x_t b + c\sigma_t^2 + u_t, \\ \text{where } (u_t) \text{ is a GARCH and } \sigma_t^2 = V(u_t | \underline{u_{t-1}}). \end{cases}$$

The coefficient c can be interpreted as the unitary price of risk.

6.2.2 How to Detect the Autoregressive Conditionally Heteroscedastic Effect

Before estimating the GARCH-type models, it is necessary to test for the presence of conditional heteroscedasticity. A straightforward approach follows.

1. We select a specification for the conditional mean by considering either a linear regression model

$$y_t = x_t b + u_t,$$

or an ARMA model

$$\Phi(L)y_t = \Theta(L)u_t,$$

where $(u_t, t \in Z)$ is assumed to be a weak white noise. The QML estimators of the parameters of the conditional mean are consistent (even if their standard errors produced by computer software are not correct).

2. The first-step estimators can be used to approximate the error terms by either

$$\hat{u}_t = y_t - x_t \hat{b},$$

or

$$\hat{u}_t = \frac{\hat{\Phi}(L)}{\hat{\Theta}(L)} y_t,$$

residuals, where the hat indicates that the parameters were replaced by the estimated values.

3. We analyze the ARMA properties of the series $(u_t^2, t \in Z)$ by examining the autocorrelation function (ACF) and partial autocorrelation function (PACF) of the approximating series $(\hat{u}_t^2, t = 1, \ldots, T)$ to see if the standard identification test reveals statistically significant autoregressive or moving average patterns.

The following is the rationale for this approach: If we are interested in the evolution of risk (in general, measured by the second-order conditional moment), it is insufficient to examine the standard autocorrelogram

$$\rho(y; h) = Cov(y_t, y_{t-h})/Vy_t.$$

We also have to examine temporal dependence between squared errors:

$$\rho^2(u, h) = Cov(u_t^2, u_{t-h}^2)/Vu_t^2$$

$$= \frac{Cov\{[y_t - E(y_t|y_{t-1})]^2[y_{t-h} - E(y_{t-h}|y_{t-h-1})]^2\}}{V[(y_t - E(y_t|y_{t-1}))^2]}. \qquad (6.17)$$

This expression is called the *autocorrelogram of order 2.*

6.2.3   Statistical Inference

Two-Step Estimation Method
The quadratic specification of the volatility equation can be estimated using a software package designed for estimation of ARMA models. Let us consider an ARMA model with GARCH errors:

$$\Phi(L)y_t = \Theta(L)u_t, \qquad (6.18)$$

where $\sigma_t^2 = V_{t-1}u_t$ satisfies

$$\sigma_t^2 = c + \alpha(L)u_t^2 + \beta(L)\sigma_t^2$$

$$\Leftrightarrow u_t^2 = c + [\alpha(L) + \beta(L)]u_t^2 + \eta_t - \beta(L)\eta_t. \qquad (6.19)$$

In the first step, the autoregressive and moving average parameters Φ and Θ are estimated using a computer package for estimation of ARMA models. Then, we evaluate the associated residuals $\hat{u}_t^2$. In the second step, the ARMA representation in (6.19) is estimated by again applying ARMA software to the series of squared residuals $\hat{u}_t^2$.

Although this approach is not very accurate, it is easy to implement and provides consistent estimators. They may be used later as initial values in an algorithm optimizing the quasi likelihood.

Quasi-Maximum Likelihood
The parameter estimators are derived by optimizing a log-likelihood function computed as if the innovations (u_t) were conditionally Gaussian. The

asymptotic properties of the method are similar to the properties given in Proposition 6.1. Generally, the quasi-likelihood function has a complicated analytical expression and its values have to be computed numerically.

6.2.4 Integrated Generalized Autoregressive Conditionally Heteroscedastic Models

Very often, the estimated parameters of the volatility equation are such that $\Sigma_{i=1}^{q} \hat{\alpha}_i + \Sigma_{j=1}^{p} \hat{\beta}_j \approx 1$, that is, they suggest the presence of a unit root in the volatility equation. This is evidence of the so-called volatility persistence (see, e.g., Poterba and Summers 1986). However the interpretation of a unit root in the volatility equation is very different from its interpretation in the conditional mean equation. As shown below, it implies an infinite marginal variance of y_t without violating the stationarity property, whereas a unit root in the mean equation leads to a nonstationary process (see Chapter 5).

To understand this phenomenon, we consider an example of the GARCH(1,1) model studied by Nelson (1990). The process is defined by

$$l(y_t | \underline{y_{t-1}}) = N(0, \sigma_t^2),$$

where $\sigma_t^2 = c + \beta \sigma_{t-1}^2 + \alpha y_{t-1}^2$, $\alpha \geq 0$, and $\beta \geq 0$.

Equivalently, the volatility equation can be written

$$\sigma_t^2 = c + \left(\beta + \alpha Z_{t-1}^2 \right) \sigma_{t-1}^2, \tag{6.20}$$

where (Z_t) is a reduced Gaussian white noise. Therefore, the volatility follows a nonlinear autoregressive process of order 1 with a stochastic autoregressive coefficient. Its dynamic properties can be analyzed by examining the *impulse response function*, which measures the effect of a transitory shock to σ_0^2 on future volatilities. The shock effect may quickly dissipate or persist. In our study, we distinguish the shock effect in average across many admissible trajectories and along a single path. The effect of an initial shock $\delta(\sigma_0^2)$ at horizon t is

$$\delta(\sigma_t^2) = \prod_{\tau=1}^{t} \left(\beta + \alpha Z_{\tau-1}^2 \right) \delta(\sigma_0^2). \tag{6.21}$$

Average Multiplier
For the average multiplier, we get

$$E(\delta(\sigma_t^2)) = E\left[\Pi_{\tau=1}^{t} \left(\beta + \alpha Z_{\tau-1}^2 \right) \right] \delta(\sigma_0^2)$$

$$= \Pi_{\tau=1}^{t} E\left(\beta + \alpha Z_{\tau-1}^2 \right) \delta(\sigma_0^2)$$

$$= [E(\beta + \alpha Z^2)]' \delta(\sigma_0^2)$$

$$= (\beta + \alpha)' \delta(\sigma_0^2),$$

since the variables Z_t^2, t varying, are independent with the same distribution such that $EZ^2 = 1$. Therefore, the multiplier vanishes asymptotically if and only if

$$\alpha + \beta < 1. \tag{6.22}$$

This is a standard condition of short-term persistence, which also ensures the existence of

$$Vy_t = E\sigma_t^2 = c[1 + (\alpha + \beta) + (\alpha + \beta)^2 + \ldots] = c/(1 - \alpha - \beta).$$

Along-the-Path Multiplier
From (6.21), the along-the-path multiplier is given by

$$\Pi_{\tau=1}^t(\beta + \alpha Z_{\tau-1}^2) = \exp \Sigma_{\tau=1}^t \log(\beta + \alpha\, Z_{\tau-1}^2)$$

$$\approx \exp\{tE \log(\beta + \alpha Z^2)\},$$

where the last equivalence follows by the law of large numbers. Thus, the multiplier tends to 0 over a long horizon if and only if

$$E \log(\beta + \alpha Z^2) < 0. \tag{6.23}$$

It can be proved that this condition ensures the strong stationarity of the volatility process.

Comparison of Shock Persistence Conditions
We will now discuss the persistence of shocks, and give the conditions ensuring that the multipliers do not tend to 0.
    From Jensen's inequality,

$$E \log(\beta + \alpha Z^2) < \log E(\beta + \alpha Z^2) = \log(\beta + \alpha).$$

Therefore, the stability condition in (6.22) implies the stability condition in (6.23). The discussion is summarized as follows:

PROPOSITION 6.3: *Let us consider a conditionally Gaussian GARCH(1,1) model.*

(i) *If $\alpha + \beta < 1$, there is no persistence in average or along the path (Region 1). The process is weakly stationary.*
(ii) *If $\alpha + \beta > 1$ and $E \log(\alpha + \beta Z^2) < 0$, the shock is persistent in average, but*

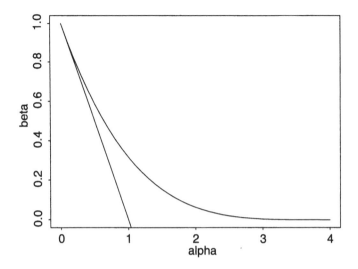

Figure 6.5 *Stationarity Regions of a GARCH(1,1)*

not along a single path (Region 2). The process is strongly stationary despite that its marginal variance does not exist.

(iii) If $E \log(\alpha + \beta Z^2) > 0$, the process is nonstationary.

In particular, the processes with a unit root in the volatility equation, called Integrated Generalized Autoregressive Conditionally Heteroscedastic Process (*IGARCH*) (where *I* stands for integrated) are strongly stationary (Figure 6.5). However, their marginal distributions feature so heavy tails that their marginal variance does not exist.

6.2.5 Application

We examine a sample of 4,044 daily observations on the returns of the Standard and Poor's (S&P) 500 Index, defined as log differences of prices recorded between January 1977 and December 1992. The data exhibit a significant, although weak, autocorrelation at lag 1, suggesting an AR(1) structure. Figure 6.6 displays the autocorrelations of squared returns, which are significant up to lag 8, except for lags 4 and 7. The dynamics suggest the presence of an ARCH effect, but require fitting an ARCH model with a fairly high number of coefficients.

Knowing that, in such a case, the GARCH model provides a parsimonious representation, we estimate instead the following AR(1)-GARCH(1,1) model: The estimation results are provided in Table 6.2:

Table 6.2   *Estimation of AR(1)-GARCH(1,1)*

Parameters	Estimates	SE	Estimate/SE	Probability
ρ	0.0926	0.0167	5.547	.0000
c	0.0188	0.0049	3.853	.0001
α	0.0590	0.0070	8.432	.0000
β	0.9217	0.0108	85.590	.0000

$$\varepsilon_t = y_t - \rho y_{t-1} \tag{6.24}$$

$$h_t = c + \alpha \varepsilon_{t-1}^2 + \beta h_{t-1} \tag{6.25}$$

The t ratios in the fourth column correspond to Wald test statistics based on the heteroscedasticity adjusted standard errors. Their p values, given in the fifth column, indicate that all estimated coefficients are significantly different from 0. Moreover, the sum of the α and β coefficients is close to 1. We mentioned above that this result is often found in empirical research.

Figure 6.7 presents the fitted trajectory of volatility over the sample period of 4,044 days. Note there is a sudden spike of volatility due to the Black Monday effect.

Finally, we compute the standardized residuals obtained as ratios $\varepsilon_t/\sqrt{(h_t)}$. Their estimated density is displayed in Figure 6.8.

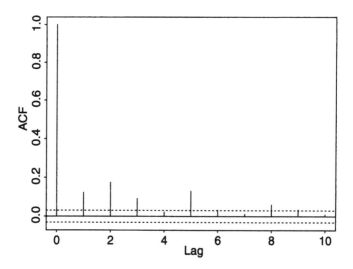

Figure 6.6   *Autocorrelations of Squared Returns*

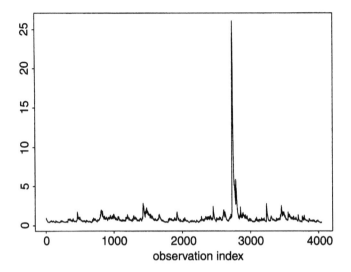

Figure 6.7 *Fitted Volatility*

The empirical density features strong departures from normality. It possesses heavy tails, indicating excess kurtosis. Especially, its left tail is very long, suggesting that extremely low returns were frequently recorded during the sampling period.

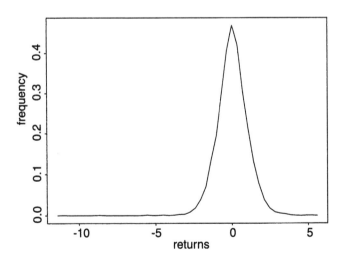

Figure 6.8 *Estimated GARCH Density*

6.3 Stochastic Volatility Models

The stochastic volatility (SV) models in discrete time were initially introduced by Melino and Turnbull (1989) and Taylor (1990) as the discrete time counterpart of the Hull and White (1987) continuous time model; they were conceived as an alternative to ARCH models (see, e.g., Harvey, Ruiz, and Shephard 1994). It is known that they are similar to selected modified ARCH models [see exponential generalized autoregressive conditionally heteroscedastic (EGARCH) models in Section 11.3.4]. We first present and discuss the basic stochastic volatility model. Then, we compare the properties of SV and ARCH models with respect to the cross moments of returns and volatility and analyze the so-called leverage effect.

6.3.1 Definition

The basic SV model is defined by

$$y_t = \sigma_t \varepsilon_t, \tag{6.26}$$

where the log-volatility satisfies the autoregressive equation

$$\log \sigma_t = \varphi \log \sigma_{t-1} + \eta u_t. \tag{6.27}$$

Here, (ε_t) and (u_t) are independent Gaussian white noises with unitary variances. Like ARCH models, this process also features conditional heteroscedasticity. However, the volatility dynamics is not solely determined by the current and lagged values of y, but is also driven by an additional noise (u_t). Therefore, the notions of volatilities in both types of models are not identical since they do not correspond to the same information set. For ARCH models, we have

$$h_t = V(y_t | \underline{y_{t-1}});$$

while for SV models, we have

$$\sigma_t^2 = V(y_t | \underline{\varepsilon_{t-1}}, \underline{u_{t-1}}) = V(y_t | \underline{y_{t-1}}, \underline{u_{t-1}}),$$

where distinct notations h_t and σ_t^2 are used to distinguish between volatilities based on different conditioning sets. In particular, σ_t^2 is a latent (i.e., unobserved) volatility process. The observable volatility is

$$h_t = V(y_t | \underline{y_{t-1}})$$

$$= E[V(y_t | \underline{y_{t-1}}, \underline{u_{t-1}}) | \underline{y_{t-1}}] + V[E(y_t | \underline{y_{t-1}}, \underline{u_{t-1}}) | \underline{y_{t-1}}]$$

$$= E(\sigma_t^2 | \underline{y_{t-1}}),$$

by the variance-decomposition equation.

Intuitively, the sign of the process (y_t) contains no useful information about the unknown parameters φ and η. By taking the absolute value on both sides of equation (6.24) and applying a logarithmic transformation, we get

$$\log|y_t| = \log \sigma_t + \log|\varepsilon_t|$$
$$= \log \sigma_t + E \log|\varepsilon_t| + (\log|\varepsilon_t| - E \log|\varepsilon_t|),$$

with $\log \sigma_t = \varphi \log \sigma_{t-1} + \eta u_t$.

This is a linear state-space model, with the state variable $\log \sigma_t$. The unknown parameters can be estimated consistently by the quasi-maximum likelihood, where (u_t) and $\log|\varepsilon_t| - E \log|\varepsilon_t|$ are treated as Gaussian white noises. The computation of the quasi-likelihood function is performed numerically by a Kalman filter (see Chapter 9.)

REMARK 6.1: The basic model is very restrictive since it assumes, for instance, a zero conditional mean. When a nonzero conditional mean is introduced and assumed constant, the first equation becomes $y_t = \mu + \sigma_t \varepsilon_t$. This model is no longer a linear state-space model since the logarithm of the absolute value $\log|y_t| = \log|\mu + \sigma_t \varepsilon_t|$ cannot be decomposed.

6.3.2 The Leverage Effect

Empirical evidence reported by Black (1976), Christie (1982), and Schwert (1989b) suggests that stock price movements are negatively correlated with the change in volatility. This stylized fact is called the *leverage effect*. In this section, we discuss the existence of this effect conditional on the information on lagged returns in the frameworks of ARCH and stochastic volatility models.

ARCH(1) Model

Let us consider an ARCH(1) model

$$y_t = (c + ay_{t-1}^2)^{1/2} \varepsilon_t, \quad c > 0, \ a > 0,$$

where (ε_t) is a standardized strong white noise. We have

$$\text{Cov}_{t-1}(y_t - y_{t-1}, h_{t+1} - h_t)$$
$$= \text{Cov}_{t-1}(y_t, h_{t+1})$$
$$= \text{Cov}_{t-1}\left(y_t, c + ay_t^2\right)$$
$$= a\text{Cov}_{t-1}\left(y_t, y_t^2\right)$$
$$= a\left(c + ay_{t-1}^2\right)^{3/2} \text{Cov}\left(\varepsilon_t, \varepsilon_t^2\right)$$
$$= a\left(c + ay_{t-1}^2\right)^{3/2} E\varepsilon_t^3.$$

The leverage effect exists if and only if the distribution of the noise is left skewed. This is due to the volatility representation in the basic ARCH model, which is a square function of y_{t-1}. Thus, a leverage effect can only be generated by an asymmetrically distributed noise.

Stochastic Volatility Model
In a stochastic volatility model (see Section 6.3.1), the analysis of the leverage effect is more complicated. Indeed, we can consider different volatilities, either the latent σ or the observable h, and different information sets, that is, either (y_{t-1}, u_{t-1}) or (y_{t-1}).

Due to the independence assumption for the noise processes (ε_t) and (u_t), we know that

$$\text{Cov}(y_t, \sigma_t^2 | y_{t-1}, u_{t-1})$$

$$= \text{Cov}(\sigma_t \varepsilon_t, \sigma_t^2 | y_{t-1}, u_{t-1})$$

$$= E(\varepsilon_t \sigma_t^3 | y_{t-1}, u_{t-1}) - E(\sigma_t \varepsilon_t | y_{t-1}, u_{t-1}) E\left(\sigma_t^2 | y_{t-1}, u_{t-1}\right)$$

$$= E(\varepsilon_t | y_{t-1}, u_{t-1}) E\left(\sigma_t^3 | y_{t-1}, u_{t-1}\right) - E(\sigma_t | y_{t-1}, u_{t-1}) E(\varepsilon_t | y_{t-1}, u_{t-1}) E\left(\sigma_t^2 | y_{t-1}, u_{t-1}\right)$$

$$= 0.$$

Thus, no leverage effect is obtained by conditioning on the latent variables. The same result holds if we consider the conditional covariance

$$\text{Cov}\left(y_t, \sigma_{t+1}^2 | y_{t-1}, u_{t-1}\right) = 0.$$

Let us now consider the observable covariance

$$\text{Cov}(y_t, h_{t+1} | y_{t-1})$$

$$= E(y_t h_{t+1} | y_{t-1}), \text{ since } E(y_t | y_{t-1}) = 0,$$

$$= \left\{ \{ y_t E\left(\sigma_{t+1}^2 | y_t\right) | y_{t-1} \right\}.$$

This variable is path dependent and generally different from 0.

These examples show that the concept of leverage effect has to be considered with caution. It heavily depends on the type of volatility under examination and on the selected information set.

6.4   Extensions to the Multivariate Framework

The mean-variance portfolio management rules require knowledge of both the conditional mean and the conditional volatility-covolatility matrix of the excess gains (or returns) of n risky assets included in a portfolio. For this reason, it is important to extend the idea of ARCH models to a multidimensional framework. In the first section, we observe that a natural extension of the ARCH model inflates the number of parameters in the multivariate model. Next, we discuss the constraints that can be imposed to reduce the number of parameters and to achieve a more parsimonious specification. In the second section, we delineate the constraints implied by the Capital Asset Pricing Model (CAPM) equilibrium condition.

6.4.1 Multivariate Autoregressive Conditionally Heteroscedastic Models

The Unconstrained Model
Let us consider an n-dimensional process (Y_t). Under the ARCH(1) specification, this process has a 0 conditional mean and a volatility-covolatility matrix H_t:

$$E(Y_t|\underline{Y_{t-1}}) = 0, \ V(Y_t|\underline{Y_{t-1}}) = H_t, \tag{6.28}$$

where the elements of H_t are affine functions of squared lagged observations. More precisely, for any symmetric matrix H, let us denote by Vech (H) the operator that represents the lower part of the matrix H in a vector form. The volatility equation is

$$\text{Vech } (H_t) = c + A \text{ Vech } (Y_{t-1}Y'_{t-1}). \tag{6.29}$$

The system of (6.29) defines any volatility and covolatility as an affine function of the squared values $Y_{i,t-1}^2$ and the cross products $Y_{i,t-1}Y_{j,t-1}$, $i \neq j$.
The drawback of the unconstrained specification is the large number of parameters to estimate equal to $\dfrac{n(n+1)}{2} + \left(\dfrac{n(n+1)}{2}\right)^2$ (associated with c and A, respectively). For instance, if the model is applied to a portfolio including $n = 10$ risky assets, we end up with 3,080 parameters to be estimated, which is not feasible. In practice, we have to impose constraints on the parameters of the volatility equation to reduce the dimension of the parameter space and simplify the dynamics. Several constraints have been considered in the literature. They are presented below in the bivariate ARCH(1) framework for ease of exposition.

Diagonal Model
It is assumed that the elements of (H_t) depend only on the elements of $Y_{t-1}Y'_{t-1}$ with the same coefficient indexes. As an illustration, the volatility equations in the bidimensional case $n = 2$ are

$$h_{1,1,t} = c_{1,1} + a_{1,1} Y_{1,t-1}^2,$$

$$h_{1,2,t} = c_{1,2} + a_{1,2} Y_{1,t-1} Y_{2,t-1},$$

$$h_{2,2,t} = c_{2,2} + a_{2,2} Y_{2,t-1}^2.$$

The number of unknown parameters is reduced to $n(n+1) = 6$. This formula is easy to estimate, despite its several drawbacks. For instance, it does not account for risk substitution effects among assets, that is, an increased volatility of asset 2 has no impact on volatility of asset 1. Moreover, the nonnegativity of the volatility-covolatility matrix H_t also implies constraints on the parameters. It may be checked that these constraints are $a_{1,2} = 0$ whenever $a_{1,1} > 0$ and $a_{2,2} > 0$. It is impossible to model the dynamics of volatilities and covolatilities simultaneously while satisfying the positivity requirement.

However, the main drawback of the diagonal model is its structure, which is not invariant with respect to linear combinations. This invariance requirement is important for a number of financial applications. Let us consider an application to the exchange rate among the Euro, US dollar, yen, and British pound expressed in logarithms. If the currency of reference is the Euro instead of the US dollar, the new variables are $y_1 - y_2$, $-y_2$, and $y_3 - y_2$. This specification is against common intuition since a constrained model should remain valid regardless of the basic currency.

Similarly, if we are interested in equity returns, then we generally have to consider asset aggregation into mutual funds. It is preferable to introduce constrained models with a structure invariant with respect to portfolio composition.

If (α_1, α_2) is a portfolio allocation, the portfolio volatility in the diagonal model is:

$$h_{\alpha,t} = \alpha_1^2 h_{1,1,t} + \alpha_2^2 h_{2,2,t} + 2\alpha_1 \alpha_2 h_{1,2,t}$$

$$= \alpha_1^2 c_{1,1} + \alpha_2^2 c_{2,2} + 2\alpha_1 \alpha_2 c_{1,2} + \alpha_1^2 a_{1,1} Y_{1,t-1}^2$$

$$+ \alpha_2^2 a_{2,2} Y_{2,t-1}^2 + 2\alpha_1 \alpha_2 a_{1,2} Y_{1,t-1} Y_{2,t-1},$$

which cannot be written in a diagonal form:

$$h_{\alpha,t} = c_\alpha + a_\alpha (\alpha_1 Y_{1,t-1} + \alpha_2 Y_{2,t-1})^2.$$

Model with Constant Conditional Correlations

These models (Bollerslev 1987) are built by assuming that the conditional correlations are time independent. In the bidimensional framework, the volatilities and covolatilities are

$$h_{1,1,t} = c_{1,1} + a_{1,1} Y_{1,t-1}^2,$$

$$h_{2,2,t} = c_{2,2} + a_{2,2} Y_{2,t-1}^2,$$

$$h_{1,2,t} = \rho_{1,2} h_{1,1,t}^{1/2} h_{2,2,t}^{1/2}.$$

This type of model is quite easy to estimate by quasi-maximum likelihood. It allows for substitution effects and provides a nonnegative volatility matrix. However, it does not satisfy the property of invariance with respect to portfolio composition. Note also that the covolatility $h_{1,2,t}$ is not a quadratic function of lagged values. Thus, this model does not belong to the class of multivariate ARCH(1) models.

Model Based on a Spectral Decomposition
The spectral decomposition of the conditional variance-covariance matrix may also be used to build a multivariate ARCH model. This approach has been adopted by Baba et al. (1987), who proposed the so-called BEKK (Baba-Engle-Kraft-Kroner) model. Let us consider the ARCH(1) case with $n = 2$. The elements of the matrix H_t can be written as

$$h_{ij,t} = c_{ij} + Y'_{t-1} A_{ij} Y_{t-1}, \qquad i, j = 1,2.$$

where A_{ij} is a nonnegative symmetric matrix. Under a matrix form, we get

$$H_t = C + \begin{bmatrix} Y'_{t-1} A_{11} Y_{t-1} & Y'_{t-1} A_{12} Y_{t-1} \\ Y'_{t-1} A'_{12} Y_{t-1} & Y'_{t-1} A_{22} Y_{t-1} \end{bmatrix}$$

$$= C + \begin{pmatrix} Y'_{t-1} & 0 \\ 0 & Y'_{t-1} \end{pmatrix} \begin{pmatrix} A_{11} & A_{12} \\ A'_{12} & A_{22} \end{pmatrix} \begin{pmatrix} Y_{t-1} & 0 \\ 0 & Y_{t-1} \end{pmatrix}.$$

Then, we can introduce a spectral decomposition of the matrix

$$A = \begin{pmatrix} A_{11} & A_{12} \\ A'_{21} & A_{22} \end{pmatrix} = \sum_{j=1}^{2n} \lambda_j \begin{pmatrix} a_{j,1} a'_{j,1} & a_{j,1} a'_{j,2} \\ a_{j,2} a'_{j,1} & a_{j,2} a'_{j,2} \end{pmatrix},$$

where $a_{j,1}$ and $a_{j,2}$, j varying, are bidimensional vectors. Thus, we get

$$H_t = C + \sum_{j=1}^{2n} \lambda_j \begin{pmatrix} Y'_{t-1} a_{j,1} a'_{j,1} Y_{t-1} & Y'_{t-1} a_{j,1} a'_{j,2} Y_{t-1} \\ Y'_{t-1} a_{j,2} a'_{j,1} Y_{t-1} & Y'_{t-1} a_{j,2} a'_{j,2} Y_{t-1} \end{pmatrix}$$

$$= C + \sum_{j=1}^{2n} \lambda_j \begin{pmatrix} a'_{j,1} Y_{t-1} Y'_{t-1} a_{j,1} & a'_{j,2} Y_{t-1} Y'_{t-1} a_{j,1} \\ a'_{j,1} Y_{t-1} Y'_{t-1} a_{j,2} & a'_{j,2} Y_{t-1} Y'_{t-1} a_{j,2} \end{pmatrix}$$

$$= C + \sum_{j=1}^{2n} \lambda_j \begin{pmatrix} a'_{j,1} \\ a'_{j,2} \end{pmatrix} Y_{t-1} Y'_{t-1} (a_{j,1}, a_{j,2})$$

$$= C + \sum_{j=1}^{2n} \lambda_j A'_j Y_{t-1} Y'_{t-1} A_j,$$

where $A_j = (a_{j,1}, a_{j,2})$ is a 2×2 matrix.

The constrained BEKK model is defined by assuming a small number of terms of the spectral decomposition:

$$H_t = C + \sum_{j=1}^{J} \lambda_j\, A'_j\, Y_{t-1} Y'_{t-1} A_j,$$

where $J \ll n^2$.

This specification is rather complex and difficult to interpret in financial terms. However, it is invariant with respect to linear combinations since

$$\alpha' H_t \alpha = \alpha' C \alpha + \sum_{j=1}^{J} \lambda_j (A_j \alpha)' Y_{t-1} Y'_{t-1} (A_j \alpha),$$

admits the same structure.

Factor ARCH Model

The factor ARCH models were introduced by Diebold and Nerlove (1989) (see also Engle, Ng, and Rothschild 1990; King et al. 1994) and arise as special cases of nonlinear dynamic factor models. They are studied in Chapter 9, in which we analyze their dynamic properties and discuss statistical inference. In these models, each component of the process is expressed as a linear function of a few latent processes (called *factors*) and of a noise. A bidimensional ARCH(1) model with one factor is defined by

$$y_{1,t} = \beta_1 f_t + \varepsilon_{1,t},$$
$$y_{2,t} = \beta_2 f_t + \varepsilon_{2,t},$$

where (f_t) and $(\varepsilon_t = (\varepsilon_{1,t}, \varepsilon_{2,t})')$ are independent, and ε_t is a conditionally homoscedastic white noise:

$$E(\varepsilon_t | \underline{f_{t-1}}, \underline{\varepsilon_{t-1}}) = 0, \quad V(\varepsilon_t | \underline{f_{t-1}}, \underline{\varepsilon_{t-1}}) = \Omega,$$

and (f_t) satisfies an ARCH(1) model

$$E(f_t | \underline{f_{t-1}}, \underline{\varepsilon_{t-1}}) = 0, \quad V(f_t | \underline{f_{t-1}}, \underline{\varepsilon_{t-1}}) = \alpha_0 + \alpha_1 f_{t-1}^2.$$

Thus, all conditional heteroscedastic properties of the process (Y_t) are captured by the single factor (f_t).

6.4.2 Capital Asset Pricing Model

Relation between Conditional Mean and Variance

The CAPM was introduced in Section 4.2, in which we pointed out the CAPM implied constraints on the AR(1) dynamics of excess gains under a static supply assumption. This approach can be extended to accommodate excess gains featuring conditional heteroscedasticity.

The equilibrium condition is

$$\frac{1}{A}(V_tY_{t+1})^{-1}E_tY_{t+1} = \alpha^s,$$

where the left-hand side is the mean-variance efficient demand for risky assets, and α^s is the static supply. We obtain a relation between the conditional mean and variance at equilibrium:

$$E_t(Y_{t+1}) = AV_tY_{t+1}\alpha^s. \tag{6.30}$$

At equilibrium, the process of excess gains admits a nonzero conditional mean that depends on the measures of risk and corisks between assets. It is a kind of multivariate ARCH-M specification, where

$$Y_t = AH_t\,\alpha^s + H_t^{1/2}\,\eta_t, \tag{6.31}$$

and (η_t) is a conditionally standardized white noise.

Expression (6.31) suggests a simple test of the CAPM hypothesis when the dimension n is not too large. We consider the multivariate ARCH-M model

$$Y_t = c + B \text{ Vech } H_t + H_t^{1/2}\eta_t, \tag{6.32}$$

where c and B are matrices of dimension $(n,1)$ and $\left(n, \dfrac{n(n+1)}{2}\right)$, respectively. Then, we test the constraints implied by the CAPM, that is, the nullity of the constant term and the constraints on the elements of B. These constraints are easily described in the bidimensional framework. The unconstrained conditional expected excess gains are

$$\begin{cases} \mu_{1,t} = c_1 + b_{1,1,1}h_{1,1,t} + b_{1,1,2}h_{1,2,t} + b_{1,2,2}h_{2,2,t}, \\ \mu_{2,t} = c_2 + b_{2,1,1}h_{1,1,t} + b_{2,1,2}h_{1,2,t} + b_{2,2,2}h_{2,2,t}. \end{cases}$$

The constrained expected excess gains are (with $A = 1$ since A is not identifiable when the static supply is not observed):

$$\begin{cases} \mu_{1,t} = h_{1,1,t}\alpha_1 + h_{1,2,t}\alpha_2, \\ \mu_{2,t} = h_{1,2,t}\alpha_1 + h_{2,2,t}\alpha_2. \end{cases}$$

Therefore, the implied constraints are

$$c_1 = c_2 = 0, b_{1,2,2} = b_{2,1,1} = 0, b_{1,1,1} = b_{2,1,2}, b_{1,1,2} = b_{2,2,2}.$$

The Market Portfolio

The above discussion was based on the joint dynamics of asset excess gains. It is also possible to introduce models that include the market portfolio. In such a framework, the tests of the CAPM hypothesis are based on Proposition 6.4, which extends Proposition 4.3 (the proof is similar).

PROPOSITION 6.4: *Let us consider a static asset supply* α^s *and denote by* $Y_{m,t} = \alpha^s Y_t$ *the excess gain of the market portfolio. At equilibrium, the "constant" term in the conditional affine regression of* Y_{t+1} *on* $Y_{m,t+1}$ *is equal to 0.*

Analytically, it is possible to decompose the vector of excess gains as

$$Y_{t+1} = c_t + \beta_t Y_{m,t+1} + u_{t+1}, \tag{6.33}$$

where $E_t u_{t+1} = 0$, $\mathrm{Cov}_t(u_{t+1}, Y_{m,t+1}) = 0$, and c_t and β_t are functions of the past. At equilibrium, $c_t = 0$. Note that, in the presence of heteroscedasticity, β's are generally path dependent. This may explain the poor accuracy of β's estimated from a misspecified homoscedastic model (see Chapter 4).

Proposition 6.4 suggests simple testing procedures of the CAPM hypothesis. We can consider a given asset i, say, and specify a model

$$Y_{i,t+1} = X_t c + Z_t d Y_{m,t+1} + u_{t+1},$$

where X_t and Z_t are observed variables, functions of lagged values of Y. Then, we estimate this equation for asset i and test the significance of the components of c.

6.5 Summary

The body of literature on asset volatility and risk management has grown considerably in the last 20 years. Especially, the ARCH model was a scientific breakthrough and has triggered intense research in the domain of financial econometrics. It allowed empirical researchers to come up with new evidence against some basic assumptions of theoretical finance, such as the unpredictability of returns. Let us recall that in Chapter 2 we discussed results contradicting this assumption and indicating that asset returns are not independent, but instead are serially correlated in conditional means. Moreover, Chapters 3 and 4 revealed the feedback and simultaneity relations among a set of asset returns. The present chapter brought more evidence against the independence, and thus unpredictability, of asset returns by documenting serial correlation in squared returns and the clustering effects. This term refers to a tendency of large returns to be followed by large returns and of small returns to be followed by additional small ones. We showed that this phenomenon, reflecting the persistence of volatility, is related to the heavy tails of marginal and conditional distributions of returns.

Since financial risk is commonly assessed in terms of asset volatility, the ability of providing accurate forecasts of future risks acquires great importance. In Section 6.1, we introduced an autoregressive nonlinear model that is conceptually simpler than ARCH. We gave empirical examples of heavy-tailed return distributions and explained the parametric and nonparametric estimation of nonlinear models. We pointed out yet another stylized fact reported in return series, the asymmetric response of volatility to rising and falling prices, called the *leverage effect*. The family of ARCH models presented in Section 4.2 comprises a fairly large number of various extensions of the initial model proposed by Engle. We restricted our attention to some basic models. We omitted, for example, the EGARCH model, which unlike other ARCH-type models, accounts for the leverage effect. We review the EGARCH model in Chapter 12 in the context of a discrete time counterpart of the continuous Hull-White model. Asymmetric volatility responses, which refer simply to correlation between squared returns and the sign of their last lag, are accommodated in the stochastic volatility model shown in Section 6.3. Despite their methodological appeal, SV models are difficult to implement. The presence of a latent variable, representing unobserved volatility, significantly complicates estimation of these models. Their merit lies in modeling volatility as a random process rather than a deterministic function of past squared returns, assumed in ARCH models. Some SV models admit a state-space representation, in financial terminology called a factor model. Mixed models combining ARCH and latent variable patterns are called factor ARCH. They are discussed in Chapter 9.

Appendix 6.1:   A Typology of Patterns

Technical analysts build catalogues of frequently observed return patterns and assign standard reference names to them. These catalogues are used for short-term predictions. When a particular pattern of returns is observed, technical analysts search in the catalogue for the closest standardized pattern and predict future returns following the approximation from the catalogue. This heuristic approach is not very efficient, but provides summary statistics of the return history that may be introduced into the nonlinear autoregressive models. We describe below some typical patterns.

Channel
The *channel* pattern corresponds to an evolution of returns inside a band of a fixed width called a channel (Figure 6.9). The channel can become wider or narrower.

Triangle
The triangle (Figure 6.10) corresponds to an evolution inside a linear band of varying length. The upper and lower bounds of the bands can be increasing or decreasing, leading to various schemes. It is interesting to note that technical analysis has always been aware of the importance of volatility (related to the width of the band) and its evaluation.

Head and Shoulders
The head and shoulders (Figure 6.11) is a pattern with three consecutive peaks, the second one being larger than the others. The discovery of this pattern by the technical analysts has led to market interventions between the second and third peaks, resulting in the disappearance of this pattern.

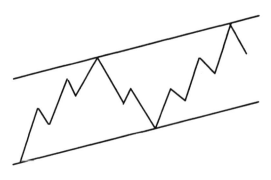

Figure 6.9   Channel

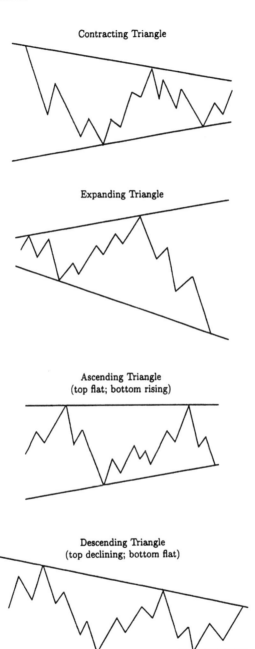

Figure 6.10   *Triangle*

Before Interventions

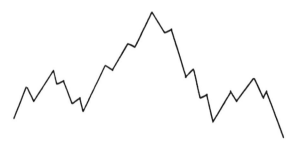

After Interventions

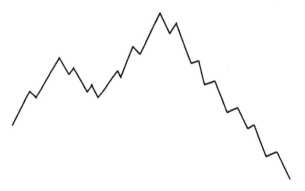

Figure 6.11   *Head and Shoulders*

Bear and Bull Markets
Bear and bull markets (Figure 6.12) are patterns that feature upward or downward (linear) trends, respectively.

Cycles
Cycles correspond to repetitive subpatterns and are classified according to their basic subpatterns. For instance, the Fibonacci cycle chart (Figure 6.13) corresponds to successive M-shape subpatterns.

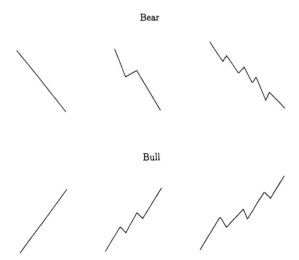

Figure 6.12   *Bull and Bear Markets*

Figure 6.13   *The Fibonacci Cycle Chart*

7

Expectation and
Present Value Models

DEMAND FOR ASSETS depends on predictions of future returns and volatilities made by investors. Therefore, the market equilibrium price determined by aggregate demand and supply is influenced by the predictions of investors as well. In previous chapters, we showed various techniques of forecasting from univariate and multivariate autoregressive moving average (ARMA) and generalized autoregressive conditionally heteroscedastic (GARCH) models. This chapter extends the concept of model-based forecasting to dynamic predictive schemes of asset returns involving exogenous variables and introduces the prediction optimality criteria. In finance, predictions appear in the Capital Asset Pricing Model (CAPM) and present value models and in the context of rational expectations. Consequently, these topics are of primary interest in this chapter.

Section 7.1 gives the definitions of various prediction schemes considered in the literature. Among them, we distinguish the so-called rational expectations satisfying an optimality criterion. A computational simpler although less powerful prediction scheme is called adaptive expectation. We compare the rational and adaptive expectations and summarize their properties. In the second section, we consider the CAPM, in which the expected future price and its volatility determine the current price of an asset. We also discuss the multiplicity of price processes that satisfy the CAPM equilibrium condition and provide some examples. Section 7.3 covers the so-called present value models. We illustrate their application to the analysis of the term structure of interest rates. Statistical inference is covered in Section 7.4, in which various tests of the rational expectation hypothesis are introduced.

7.1 Expectation Scheme

7.1.1 Basic Notions

Prediction making consists of approximating a variable y by a function of some other variables x. The *prediction* is defined as $\hat{y} = g(x)$, whereas the difference between the variable to be predicted and the prediction $\hat{\varepsilon} = y - \hat{y} = y - g(x)$ is called the *prediction error*. The accuracy of a prediction is measured by the mean square error $E(y - \hat{y})^2$. Accordingly, a prediction depends on the following three components: (1) the variable y to be predicted, (2) the variables x used to predict, (3) the function g, called the *prediction function*.

This approach can be extended to dynamic predicting in consecutive time periods. Let us introduce the processes $y = (y_t, t \in Z)$ and $x = (x_t, t \in Z)$. Suppose that, at time t, we wish to predict the future value of the process y, h steps ahead, using the available information on the present and past of x, that is, $I_t = (x_t, x_{t-1}, \ldots) = (\underline{x}_t)$. The predictions h steps ahead depend on the date t and the horizon h. The prediction of y_{t+h} made at time t is

$$_t\hat{y}_{t+h} = g_{t,h}(\underline{x}_t), \tag{7.1}$$

whereas the prediction errors are

$$_t\hat{\varepsilon}_{t+h} = y_{t+h} - {_t\hat{y}_{t+h}} = y_{t+h} - g_{t,h}(\underline{x}_t). \tag{7.2}$$

In this framework, the prediction functions $g_{t,h}$ are doubly indexed by the prediction origin t and prediction horizon h and so are the processes of predictions and prediction errors. Depending on the approach to prediction making, the following scenarios can be considered:

1. A fixed forecast origin t and a varying prediction horizon h yields the *term structure of predictions*. It shows how a prediction made at time t depends on the horizon h (or term).
2. A varying (increasing) prediction origin and a varying (shrinking) prediction horizon for predicting the same future value y_T illustrates the *prediction updating* for y_T. It displays the evolution of predictions of the terminal value y_T, where $T = t + h$ is fixed, whereas t and $h = T - t$ are jointly varying.
3. A fixed prediction horizon and a varying prediction origin result in a sequence of predictions at a fixed horizon h. This type of prediction is often made "in-sample" (as opposed to "out-of-sample" predictions) to assess their accuracy. The approach consists of comparing the true observed values of a series (y_t) to a sequence of in-sample predictions. For example, for $h = 1$, we would compare (y_t) to $(_{t-1}\hat{y}_t)$.

Table 7.1 *Approaches to Prediction Making*

Date of Prediction	Variable to Be Predicted					
	y_T	y_{T+1}	y_{T+2}	y_{T+3}	y_{t+4}	$\ldots$
T	y_T	$_T\hat{y}_{T+1}$	$_T\hat{y}_{T+2}$	$_T\hat{y}_{T+3}$	$_T\hat{y}_{T+4}$	$\ldots$
$T+1$	y_T	y_{T+1}	$_{T+1}\hat{y}_{T+2}$	$_{T+1}\hat{y}_{T+3}$	$_{T+1}\hat{y}_{T+4}$	$\ldots$
$T+2$	y_T	y_{T+1}	y_{T+2}	$_{T+2}\hat{y}_{T+3}$	$_{T+2}\hat{y}_{T+4}$	$\ldots$
$\ldots$	$\ldots$	$\ldots$	$\ldots$	$\ldots$	$\ldots$	$\ldots$

The described approaches to prediction making are summarized in Table 7.1.

In prediction updating, it is important to distinguish between the increasing sequence of information sets $I_t = (\underline{x}_t)$, which comprise the whole history of x and grow with each arriving observation, and the sequence of information sets effectively used for repeated predicting. Intuitively, it may become technically cumbersome to build predictions based on the entire history of x. Instead, we can select a prediction function based, for example, only on the last (i.e., the most recent) observation on x. In this case, we disregard the remaining available information and at each prediction updating use an information set containing the same number of elements (i.e., one element in our example). Thus, unlike the sequence of information sets comprising the growing history of x, the sequence of information sets effectively used for predicting is not necessarily increasing.

Moreover, the information sets may contain endogenous components, that is, lagged values of the process of interest y. Let us introduce an additional process z and decompose the process x into $x_t = (y_{t-1}, z_t)$. The predictions take the form

$$_t\hat{y}_{t+h} = g_{t,h}(\underline{y}_{t-1}, \underline{z}_t), \tag{7.3}$$

that is, they include an autoregressive component representing the past dependence on lagged values $\underline{y}_{t-1}$ and exogenous component $\underline{z}_t$.

Finally, there exist *stationary expectation schemes*, for which the prediction function $g_{t,h} = g_h$ depends on the prediction horizon and is independent of the prediction origin t. To this category belongs the adaptive scheme discussed below.

7.1.2 Adaptive Scheme

The adaptive scheme was the first prediction scheme introduced in economic literature. It still remains popular among practitioners. It was originally proposed by Fisher (1930a, 1930b) (see also Arrow 1959; Nerlove

1958; Friedman 1957 for historical applications). The adaptive scheme consists of simple prediction updating, with a fixed horizon:

$$\hat{y}_{t+h} = \lambda_h {}_{t-1}\hat{y}_{t+h-1} + (1 - \lambda_h)y_t. \tag{7.4}$$

The prediction made at time t is a weighted average of the previously made prediction at horizon h and the last available observation of the process. The smoothing coefficient λ_h may depend on the horizon and is assumed to lie between 0 and 1. Since the smoothing coefficient is time invariant, the expectation scheme is stationary. In the limiting case $\lambda_h = 0$, we obtain the naive expectation scheme $\hat{y}_{t+h} = y_t$, for which the prediction is equal to the current value of the process.

For the horizon $h = 1$, the adaptive scheme admits the following equivalent interpretations. An equivalent form of equation (7.4) is the error correction mechanism:

$$\hat{y}_{t+1} - {}_{t-1}\hat{y}_t = (1 - \lambda_1)(y_t - {}_{t-1}\hat{y}_t). \tag{7.5}$$

When the prediction error at time t is positive, the prediction is adjusted to a larger value using the adjustment coefficient $(1 - \lambda_1)$. The larger λ_1 is, the smaller is the necessary correction.

Predictions can also be recursively substituted into (7.4) to obtain the extrapolation formula

$$\hat{y}_{t+1} = (1 - \lambda_1)y_t + (1 - \lambda_1)\lambda_1 y_{t-1} + \ldots + (1 - \lambda_1)\lambda_1^p y_{t-p} + \ldots, \tag{7.6}$$

where the prediction is expressed as a geometrically weighted average of current and lagged observations of the process. This approach is called *exponential smoothing*.

Any expectation scheme unrelated to the dynamics of the series of interest is expected to have undesirable properties, such as bias or poor accuracy. The performance of the adaptive scheme depends on the process to be predicted. The following examples illustrate this issue.

EXAMPLE 7.1: Let us consider a constant series $y_t = c$. By applying (7.6), we get

$$\hat{y}_{t+1} = (1 - \lambda_1)\left(\sum_{p=0}^{\infty} \lambda_1^p\right)c = c = y_{t+1}.$$

This is a *perfect foresight* with a zero-expectation error.

EXAMPLE 7.2: Let us consider a deterministic exponential growth $y_t = c\rho^t$, with $\rho > 1$. We get

$$\hat{y}_{t+1} = \lambda_1 {}_{t-1}\hat{y}_t + (1 - \lambda_1)c\rho^t.$$

This is a linear recursive equation with solutions of the type:

$$\hat{y}_{t+1} = \frac{(1 - \lambda_1)c\rho^{t+1}}{\rho - \lambda_1} + A\lambda_1^{t+1},$$

where A is an arbitrary constant. For large t, we get approximately
$$\hat{y}_{t+1} \approx \frac{(1-\lambda_1)c\rho^{t+1}}{\rho-\lambda_1} = \frac{1-\lambda_1}{\rho-\lambda_1}\, y_{t+1}$$ and observe that the relative expectation
error is constant.

EXAMPLE 7.3: If $y_t = \varepsilon_t - \theta\varepsilon_{t-1}$ admits a moving average representation of order 1, the "optimal" prediction is $\hat{y}_{t+1} = -\theta y_t - \theta^2 y_{t-1} - \theta^3 y_{t-2} \dots - \theta^{p+1} y_{t-p} \dots$. Thus, the weights of the adaptive and the optimal prediction schemes are different, especially for a negative moving average coefficient.

REMARK 7.1: The efficiency of the adaptive scheme depends on the smoothing parameter. The expectation error can be reduced by adequately setting its value. In particular, for a fixed horizon h, the smoothing parameter can be estimated by

$$\hat{\lambda}_h = \underset{\lambda_h}{\text{Arg min}} \sum_{t=t_0}^{T} \left(y_{t+h} - (1-\lambda_h)\sum_{p=0}^{\infty} \lambda_h^p y_{t-p} \right)^2,$$

where the values of y_t are set to 0 for negative dates, and t_0 is chosen sufficiently large to alleviate the effect of this truncation.

7.1.3 Rational Scheme

The *rational scheme* yields the most accurate predictions among all admissible ones. It relies on the following proposition:

PROPOSITION 7.1: *Let y be a variable to be predicted and x denote variables used for predicting. The solution to the minimization*

$$\min_g E[y - g(x)]^2$$

exists and is equal to the conditional expectation of y given x: $\hat{y} = E(y\,|\,x)$.

The conditional expectation, or equivalently the *rational expectation*, can be viewed as a projection. Therefore, it satisfies the orthogonality condition, admits a variance decomposition, and obeys the law of iterated expectations, explained below.

PROPOSITION 7.2: *The (rational) expectation error is orthogonal (uncorrelated) to any function of the conditioning variables:*

$$E[(y - \hat{y})g(x)] = E\{[y - E(y\,|\,x)]g(x)\} = 0, \ \forall g.$$

In particular, by choosing a constant function, we find that

$$E(y - \hat{y}) = 0 \Leftrightarrow Ey = E\hat{y} \Leftrightarrow E\hat{\varepsilon} = 0,$$

that is, the rational expectations are unbiased. Moreover, the condition of Proposition 7.2 implies the absence of correlation between the expectation error and the conditioning variable.

PROPOSITION 7.3, VARIANCE DECOMPOSITION: *The rational expectations satisfy the following equality:*

$$Vy = V\hat{y} + V\hat{\varepsilon}.$$

PROOF: We get

$$Vy = V[\hat{y} + y - \hat{y}]$$
$$= V\hat{y} + V(y - \hat{y}) + 2 \operatorname{Cov}(\hat{y}, y - \hat{y})$$
$$= V\hat{y} + V(y - \hat{y}),$$

because the prediction error and the conditioning variable are uncorrelated.
QED

PROPOSITION 7.4, LAW OF ITERATED EXPECTATIONS: *Let us assume a partition of the set of conditioning variables into two subsets $x = (x_1, x_2)$. We have*

$$\hat{y} = E(y|x) = E(E(y|x_1)|x) = E(\hat{y}_1|x).$$

The prediction of y based on the variables x_1 and x_2 can be derived in two steps. We first compute the expectation with respect to the restricted information set x_1, which yields $\hat{y}_1$. In the second step, we compute the expectation of $\hat{y}_1$ with respect to x.

Propositions 7.2–7.4 can be extended to a dynamic framework. At this point, we need to define the martingale process.

DEFINITION 7.1: *Let $I_t = (\underline{x}_t)$, t varying, be an increasing sequence of information sets.*

  (i) *A process $M = (M_t, t \in Z)$ is a martingale with respect to (I_t) if and only if:*

$$E(M_{t+1}|I_t) = E(M_{t+1}|\underline{x}_t) = M_t, \ \forall t.$$

  (ii) *A process $\eta = (\eta_t, t \in Z)$ is a* martingale difference sequence *with respect to (I_t) if and only if*

$$E[\eta_{t+1}|I_t] = E[\eta_{t+1}|\underline{x}_t] = 0, \ \forall t.$$

A martingale is a stochastic process for which the rational and naive expectations coincide.

The martingales and martingale difference sequences are related. Indeed, it is easily checked that, if (M_t) is a martingale, then $(\eta_t = M_t - M_{t-1})$

is a martingale difference sequence. Conversely, if (η_t) is a martingale difference sequence, $(M_t = \Sigma_{\tau=0}^t \varepsilon_\tau)$ is a martingale.

Let us now consider the process of interest (y_t), the sequence of increasing information sets $(I_t) = (\underline{x}_t)$, and the associated rational expectations $_t\hat{y}_{t+h} = E(y_{t+h}|\underline{x}_t)$. We can introduce the rational expectation errors

$$\hat{\varepsilon}_{t+h} = y_{t+h} - E(y_{t+h}|\underline{x}_t), \tag{7.7}$$

and the subsequent (rational) updating errors

$$\hat{\varepsilon}_t^h = E(y_{t+h}|\underline{x}_t) - E(y_{t+h}|\underline{x}_{t-1}). \tag{7.8}$$

By applying the law of iterated expectations to y_{t+h}, the updating error can be rewritten as

$$\hat{\varepsilon}_t^h = E(y_{t+h}|\underline{x}_t) - E[E(y_{t+h}|\underline{x}_t)|\underline{x}_{t-1}],$$

that is, as one step-ahead prediction error from the prediction $E(y_{t+h}|\underline{x}_t)$. It follows that the updating errors are uncorrelated with all elements of the information set $I_{t-1} = (\underline{x}_{t-1})$

PROPOSITION 7.5: *For any fixed horizon h, the sequence of updating errors $(\varepsilon_t^h$, t varying) is a martingale difference sequence.*

In general, the prediction errors $(_t\hat{\varepsilon}_{t+h}$, t varying, h fixed) do not form a martingale difference sequence, except for $h = 1$. This becomes obvious when the expectation error at horizon h is written in terms of expectation errors at horizon 1. We get

$$\hat{\varepsilon}_{t+h} = y_{t+h} - E(y_{t+h}|\underline{x}_t)$$

$$= y_{t+h} - E(y_{t+h}|\underline{x}_{t+h-1})$$

$$+ E(y_{t+h}|\underline{x}_{t+h-1}) - E(y_{t+h}|\underline{x}_{t+h-2})$$

$$+ \ldots$$

$$+ E(y_{t+h}|\underline{x}_{t+1}) - E(y_{t+h}|\underline{x}_t),$$

or

$$\hat{\varepsilon}_{t+h} = \sum_{i=0}^{h-1} \hat{\varepsilon}_{t+h-i}^i. \tag{7.9}$$

EXAMPLE 7.4: To illustrate the differences between the expectation errors and the updating errors, we consider a Gaussian AR(1) process:

$$y_t = \rho y_{t-1} + \varepsilon_t,$$

with a Gaussian white noise, and $|\rho| < 1$. If the information set contains the lagged values of y, the rational expectation at horizon h is

$$\hat{y}_{t+h} = E(y_{t+h}|\underline{y_t}) = \rho^h y_t.$$

The prediction errors are

$$_t\hat{\varepsilon}_{t+h} = y_{t+h} - \rho^h y_t = \varepsilon_{t+h} + \rho\varepsilon_{t+h-1} + \ldots + \rho^{h-1}\varepsilon_{t+1},$$

and the updating errors are $\hat{\varepsilon}_t^h = \rho^h \varepsilon_t$; they all are functions of the white noise process.

The next proposition describes the dynamics of predictions of the value of y_T made at different origins t. It arises as a crucial element in the discussion of martingale properties of spot and forward prices on financial markets (Samuelson 1965).

PROPOSITION 7.6: *The rational expectation sequence $[\hat{y}_T = E(y_T|\underline{x_t}), t \text{ varying}]$ is a martingale.*

PROOF: It is a direct consequence of the law of iterated expectations:

$$E(y_T|\underline{x_{t-1}}) = E(E(y_T|\underline{x_t})|\underline{x_{t-1}})$$

$$\Leftrightarrow{}_{t-1}\hat{y}_T = E(\hat{y}_T|\underline{x_{t-1}}).$$

QED

Let us now comment briefly on Samuelson's argument. If y_T denotes the spot price of an asset at time T, we can expect that the forward price at date t with residual maturity $T - t$ is equal to $y_{t,T}^F = E(y_T|\underline{y_t})$. We deduce that the sequence of forward prices is a martingale. This property is a direct consequence of the law of iterated expectations. It differs from the efficient market hypothesis, which assumes that the sequence of spot prices (y_t) is a martingale.

In practice, the information set includes the lagged values of y. Therefore, the in-sample predictions become perfect foresights: $\hat{y}_T = y_T$, $\forall T \leq t$. The out-of-sample predictions (with $t < T$) become more accurate when t increases, and the prediction origin approaches T since

$$V(\hat{y}_T) = V({}_{t-1}\hat{y}_T) + V(\hat{y}_{T-t+1}\hat{y}_T)$$

$$\geq V({}_{t-1}\hat{y}_T),$$

by the variance decomposition equation; the direction of this inequality is reversed for the expectation errors:

$$V(y_T) - V(\hat{y}_T) \leq V(y_T) - V({}_{t-1}\hat{y}_T).$$

In conclusion, under the optimal expectation scheme, the prediction accuracy is improved when the predictions are made at dates closer to maturity.

REMARK 7.2: Section 7.1.3 is entirely focused on rational expectations. We do not analyze in detail suboptimal expectations, although some results established in Propositions 7.2–7.4 may hold for them as well. At this point, researchers need to be cautioned against a commonly committed error, by which suboptimal expectations are reported and mistakenly interpreted as the rational ones. This happens when the set of solutions of the optimization problem in Proposition 7.1 is restricted to linear affine functions of x, yielding as a result a theoretical linear regression of y on x: $\hat{y} = LE(y|x)$. In the literature, this suboptimal outcome is often erroneously viewed as the rational expectation. However, we must realize that, although basic Propositions 7.2, 7.3, and 7.4 can easily be extended to this framework, a linear regression does not yield martingale prediction errors, which is an important feature in financial theory (see, e.g., 2.4.4).

7.1.4 Optimality of the Adaptive Scheme

For some specific dynamic processes, the adaptive scheme may become equivalent to the rational one. This class of processes has been described by Muth (1961). Let us consider the adaptive scheme of predictions at horizon 1 for an unspecified process y:

$$_t\hat{y}_{t+1} = \lambda_{1t-1}\hat{y}_t + (1 - \lambda_1)y_t. \tag{7.10}$$

Let us also introduce the expectation errors at horizon 1:

$$\hat{\varepsilon}_t^1 = y_t - {}_{t-1}\hat{y}_t.$$

Equation (7.10) can be written as

$$y_{t+1} - \hat{\varepsilon}_{t+1}^1 = \lambda_1\big(y_t - \hat{\varepsilon}_t^1\big) + (1 - \lambda_1)y_t$$
$$\Leftrightarrow y_{t+1} = y_t + \hat{\varepsilon}_{t+1}^1 - \lambda_1\hat{\varepsilon}_t^1. \tag{7.11}$$

The adaptive scheme yields rational expectations if and only if $_{t-1}\hat{y}_t = E(y_t|\underline{x}_{t-1}) \Leftrightarrow (\hat{\varepsilon}_t^1)$ is a martingale difference sequence.

PROPOSITION 7.7: *The adaptive scheme is equivalent to the rational one for a sequence of information sets $(I_t) = (\underline{x}_t)$, t varying, if and only if the process y is an autoregressive integrated moving average ARIMA(0,1,1) with a martingale difference error term.*

In the past, for quite a long time, the adaptive scheme was a very popular tool of analysis. The reason was that the ARIMA(0,1,1) models featuring both a stochastic trend and a short-term temporal dependence fit a significant number of monthly sampled time series. At that time, this type of data was commonly used in empirical research; this was before data sampled at higher frequencies became available.

7.2   Price Dynamics Associated with the Capital Asset Pricing Model

In Section 4.2, we derived the constraints on price dynamics implied by the CAPM. In this section we further investigate the equilibrium condition to reveal that there exists a multiplicity of price dynamics compatible with the CAPM. Among the CAPM-compatible processes are, for example, the conditionally heteroscedastic processes presented in Chapter 6. To simplify the presentation, we consider a single risky financial asset. Let us recall the CAPM-implied restriction

$$\alpha_t^S = \frac{1}{A} \, (V_t y_{t+1})^{-1} \, E_t y_{t+1}, \tag{7.12}$$

where y_t is the excess gain on the risky asset, and E_t and V_t denote the conditional expectation and variance of an information set I_t, respectively. (We denote the excess gain by y_t rather than Y_t to emphasize that it is a scalar.) The supply (α_t^S) is assumed adapted with respect to (I_t), that is, α_t^S is a function of I_t.

7.2.1   *The Multiplicity of Equilibrium Dynamics*

Let us introduce β_t, a positive function of information available at date t, and a martingale difference sequence (η_t) with respect to I_t with unitary conditional variance $V_t \eta_{t+1} = 1$.

PROPOSITION 7.8: *The processes (y_t) satisfying the equilibrium condition in (7.12) are such that*

$$y_{t+1} = A\alpha_t^S \, \beta_t^2 + \beta_t \eta_{t+1}, \tag{7.13}$$

where (β_t) and (η_t) are a positive adapted sequence and a conditionally standardized martingale difference sequence, respectively.

PROOF: (1) For the sufficient condition, if $y_{t+1} = A\alpha_t^S\beta_t^2 + \beta_t\eta_{t+1}$, where β_t is positive adapted and η_t is a conditionally standardized martingale difference sequence, by taking the conditional expectation on both sides we get

$$E_t y_{t+1} = E_t\!\left(A\alpha_t^S\beta_t^2\right) + E_t(\beta_t\eta_{t+1})$$

$$= A\alpha_t^S\beta_t^2.$$

Therefore, we find that $\beta_t \eta_{t+1} = y_{t+1} - E_t y_{t+1}$ is the prediction error of y_{t+1}, and $V_t(\beta_t \eta_{t+1}) = \beta_t^2 = V_t y_{t+1}$. By substituting it into equation (7.13), we get

$$E_t y_{t+1} = A \alpha_t^S \beta_t^2 = A \alpha_t^S V_t y_{t+1},$$

that is, the CAPM condition.

(2) For the necessary condition, let us define $\beta_t = (V_t y_{t+1})^{1/2}$ and consider $\eta_{t+1} = \dfrac{y_{t+1} - E_t y_{t+1}}{(V_t y_{t+1})^{1/2}}$ the conditionally standardized expectation error. Then, (β_t) is positive adapted, and (η_t) is a conditionally standardized martingale difference sequence. Moreover, (7.12) becomes

$$\alpha_t^S = \frac{1}{A} (\beta_t)^{-2} [y_{t+1} - \beta_t \eta_{t+1}],$$

which is the previously derived equation (7.13).

QED

Proposition 7.8 implies a multiplicity of price dynamics compatible with the CAPM equilibrium condition due to arbitrary choices of the volatility and standardized innovation sequence.

7.2.2 *Selected Price Dynamics*

Let us now examine the CAPM-compatible price dynamics under the assumption of a supply process following a strong white noise, up to an additive constant

$$\alpha_t^S = \alpha + \varepsilon_t \quad \text{(say)}. \tag{7.14}$$

The admissible solutions are defined as processes satisfying

$$y_{t+1} = A(\alpha + \varepsilon_t)\beta_t^2 + \beta_t \eta_{t+1}. \tag{7.15}$$

We discuss below some selected examples from a variety of processes that obey equation (7.15).

Linear Solutions

Let us first consider linear solutions of the type

$$y_{t+1} = m + \sum_{j=0}^{\infty} a_j \varepsilon_{t-j}.$$

We deduce from the interpretations of β_t, η_{t+1} (see the proof of Proposition 7.8)

$$\beta_t^2 = V_t y_{t+1} = a_0^2 \sigma^2, \qquad \eta_{t+1} = \frac{y_{t+1} - E_t y_{t+1}}{(V_t y_{t+1})^{1/2}} = \frac{\varepsilon_{t+1}}{\sigma}, \tag{7.16}$$

where $\sigma^2 = V \varepsilon_t$. By substituting into equation (7.15), we get

$$y_{t+1} = A(\alpha + \varepsilon_t)a_0^2\sigma^2 + a_0\varepsilon_{t+1},$$

$$y_{t+1} = a_0\varepsilon_{t+1} + Aa_0^2\sigma^2\varepsilon_t + A\alpha a_0^2\sigma^2. \tag{7.17}$$

There exists an infinite set of linear solutions indexed by the volatility parameter a_0. They all admit a moving average representation of order 1 based on the same standardized innovation as the supply process. Their first- and second-order moments are

$$Ey_t = A\alpha a_0^2\sigma^2,$$

$$Vy_t = a_0^2 + A^2a_0^4\sigma^4,$$

$$\text{Cov}(y_t,y_{t-1}) = Aa_0^3\sigma^2, \qquad \text{Cov}(y_t,y_{t-h}) = 0, \qquad \text{if } h \geq 2.$$

Conditional Heteroscedasticity

Some of conditionally heteroscedastic price processes are CAPM compatible as well. Let us restrict our attention to models with GARCH(1,1) errors and set: $\eta_t = \varepsilon_t/\sigma$. We obtain

$$y_{t+1} = A(\alpha + \varepsilon_t)\beta_t^2 + \frac{\beta_t}{\sigma}\varepsilon_{t+1},$$

where

$$\beta_t^2 = c_0 + c_1\beta_{t-1}^2 + c_2\beta_{t-1}^2\varepsilon_t^2.$$

The set of solutions is parametrized by c_0, c_1, and c_2.

Speculative Bubble

Finally, there exist also solutions that feature more complex dynamics. For example, let us consider the martingale difference sequence defined by

$$\tilde{\eta}_{t+1} = \begin{cases} (2|\tilde{\eta}_t| + 1) \text{ sng } \varepsilon_{t+1}, & \text{with probability } 1/2, \\ 0, & \text{with probability } 1/2. \end{cases}$$

We immediately find that

$$E_t(\tilde{\eta}_{t+1}) = \frac{1}{2} E_t((2|\tilde{\eta}_t| + 1) \text{ sng } \varepsilon_{t+1})$$

$$= \frac{1}{2} (2\tilde{\eta}_t + 1)E_t \text{ sng } \varepsilon_{t+1} = 0,$$

if (ε_t) has a symmetric distribution. Moreover, the path of the process $(|\tilde{\eta}_t|)$ has a particular pattern. To see that, denote by τ the first point in time after $t = 0$ when the $(\tilde{\eta}_t)$ process takes value 0. We have

$$P[\tau = T] = \left(\frac{1}{2}\right)^T,$$

and, until this date, $|\tilde{\eta}_t|$ has an explosive behavior described by the recursive equation $|\tilde{\eta}_{t+1}| = 2|\tilde{\eta}_t| + 1$. Therefore, the pattern of $|\tilde{\eta}_t|$ is a succession of explosive patterns with random returns to 0. This is called the *speculative bubble effect* (Figure 7.1). A speculative bubble keeps growing until it bursts (Gourieroux, Laffont, and Monfort 1982).

7.3 Expectation Hypothesis

The analysis of returns and interest rates in macroeconomics is often based on models that assume a deterministic environment. The dynamics of these models is constrained by relations between current and future prices under the absence of arbitrage opportunities. Such an approach is called the *actuarial calculus*. In a stochastic framework, the same relations between current and future prices can still be modeled, although with future variables replaced by their current expectations. For this reason, such models belong to the category of rational expectation models. In this section, we present two models of this type, called the *present value models*. They represent the relation between the current stock price and

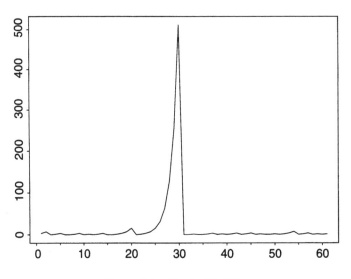

Figure 7.1 *The Bubble Effect*

the sequence of expected future dividends. Next, we introduce the *expectation hypothesis* and show various term structure models based on this hypothesis.

7.3.1   The Present Value Model

In this section, we introduce some basic present value models that are derived directly from the deterministic actuarial approach by replacing future variables by their expectations. These models are widely used, especially in financial macroeconomics. It is interesting to relate these models to other financial models, such as the CAPM. Indeed, we show that the present value models generally disregard the price of risk, which may induce errors in asset pricing. Moreover, the replacement of deterministic future values by their rational expectations implies an infinite number of admissible price paths. This is due to market incompleteness in an uncertain environment.

The Model

Let us assume a deterministic environment and consider two assets: (1) a zero-coupon bond with time-independent interest rate r_f and (2) a security with a price at date t that is p_t and that produces dividends d_t shortly before the trading date t. The perfect arbitrage opportunity is eliminated whenever the returns on both assets are identical:

$$1 + r_f = \frac{p_{t+1} + d_{t+1}}{p_t}, \tag{7.18}$$

or, equivalently,

$$p_t = \frac{1}{1 + r_f}(p_{t+1} + d_{t+1}) = a[p_{t+1} + d_{t+1}], \qquad \text{(say)}. \tag{7.19}$$

If the environment becomes uncertain, the future price and dividend could be roughly replaced by their conditional expectations. If the zero-coupon bond is a risk-free asset, we obtain the present value model:

$$p_t = a(E_t p_{t+1} + E_t d_{t+1}), \tag{7.20}$$

where $a = (1 + r_f)^{-1}$. After successive substitutions and by applying the law of iterated expectations, the present value equation may be written as

$$p_t = aE_t d_{t+1} + a^2 E_t d_{t+2} + \ldots + a^n E_t d_{t+n} + \ldots \tag{7.21}$$

The current price is equal to the expected sum of discounted future dividends. In the literature, this result is known as the *expectation hypothesis*.

There is an obvious relation between the present value model and other asset pricing theories, based on either the equilibrium condition (see the CAPM discussion in Section 7.2) or the absence of arbitrage opportunity condition (see Chapter 11). The present value model does not take into account the risk effect and determines the current price in the same way as a risk-neutral investor would do.

Variance Bounds
Let us introduce the discounted sum of future dividends

$$p_t^* = \sum_{h=1}^{\infty} a^h d_{t+h}. \tag{7.22}$$

The present value model $p_t = E_t p_t^*$ implies the following constraints on the joint dynamics of the series (p_t, p_t^*):

- Both series must have the same mean.
- Their variances must satisfy the variance bound inequalities

$$V p_t \leq V p_t^*,$$

$$V_{t-1} p_t \leq V_{t-1} p_t^*,$$

with respect to the marginal and conditional distributions, respectively.

In practice, the sequence of future dividends is not observed, and formula (7.22) cannot be used to compute the auxiliary price p_t^*. However, the same type of constraints holds with p_t^* replaced by

$$p_{t,H}^* = \sum_{h=1}^{H} a^h d_{t+h} + a^H p_{t+H}. \tag{7.23}$$

For example, we get

$$p_{t,1}^* = a d_{t+1} + a p_{t+1},$$

$$p_{t,2}^* = a d_{t+1} + a^2 d_{t+2} + a^2 p_{t+2}.$$

7.3.2   Term Structure of Interest Rates

The expectation hypothesis is used, in particular, to derive some models of the term structure of interest rates (see, e.g., Shiller 1981, 1989, 1990). We first review basic relations involving the expectations and next show their approximations used commonly in practice.

Basic Equations
The central point of this concept is the relation between the price of a bond and its sequence of future cash flows in a deterministic environ-

ment. Let us consider a coupon bond k that provides predetermined cash flows $m_{k,h,t}$ at future dates $t+h$, $h=1,\ldots,H$. Its price at date t is

$$P_{k,t} = \Sigma_{h=1}^{H} m_{k,h,t} B(t,t+h)$$

$$= \Sigma_{h=1}^{H} m_{k,h,t} \{[1+r(t;t+1)]\ldots[1+r(t+h-1,\,t+h)]\}^{-1}$$

$$= \frac{m_{k,1,t}}{1+r(t,t+1)} + \frac{1}{1+r\,(t,t+1)}\,P_{k,t+1},$$

where $B(t,t+h)$ is the price at t of the zero-coupon bond that provides one monetary unit at date $t+h$, and $r(t,t+1)$ is the short-term interest rate between dates t and $t+1$.

In a stochastic environment, the expectation hypothesis implies the following relations:

$$P_{k,t} = \Sigma_{h=1}^{H} m_{k,h,t} B(t,t+h)$$

$$= \Sigma_{h=1}^{H} m_{k,h,t} E_t\{[1+r(t;t+1)]\ldots[1+r(t+h-1,\,t+h)]\}^{-1}$$

$$= \frac{m_{k,1,t}}{1+r(t,t+1)} + \frac{1}{1+r(t,t+1)}\,E_t P_{k,t+1},$$

where the available information includes the current and lagged observations on the prices of the zero-coupon bonds for all maturities.

The expectation models can be written explicitly for the zero-coupon bonds. For example, we get

$$\begin{cases} B(t,t+1) = \dfrac{1}{1+r(t,t+1)}, \\ B(t,t+h) = \dfrac{1}{1+r(t,t+1)}\,E_t B(t+1,t+h),\ h=2,\ldots,H, \end{cases} \quad (7.24)$$

or, equivalently,

$$B(t,t+h) = E_t\{[1+r(t,t+1)]\ldots[1+r(t+h-1,t+h)]\}^{-1},$$
$$h=1,\ldots,H. \quad (7.25)$$

Approximated Models

The expectation models are specified in terms of prices. However, when the short-term interest rates are small, a first-order expansion provides an approximated linear relation between the interest rates. Obviously, disregarding the second-order term of this expansion may induce a convexity bias, that is, the omission of a variance effect and of a risk premium.

Let us define the interest rate at horizon h, $r(t,t+h)$ (say) by

$$B(t,t+h) = [1+r(t,t+h)]^{-h}. \quad (7.26)$$

We deduce from (7.25):

$$[1 + r(t,t + h)]^{-h} = E_t\{[1 + r(t,t + 1)]^{-1} \ldots [1 + r(t + h - 1,t + h)]^{-1}\}.$$

A first-order expansion provides the formula

$$1 - hr(t,t + h) \simeq E_t[1 - r(t,t + 1) \ldots - r(t + h - 1,t + h)],$$

$$r(t,t + h) \simeq \frac{1}{h} \sum_{k=1}^{h} E_t r(t + k - 1, t + k). \tag{7.27}$$

Thus, the interest rate with maturity h is approximately equal to the average of the expected short-term interest rates over the period $\{1,h\}$. This relation can also be written as

$$r(t,t + h) = \left(1 - \frac{1}{h}\right) r(t,t + h - 1) + \frac{1}{h} E_t r(t + h - 1, t + h), \tag{7.28}$$

where the interest rate at maturity h is a weighted average of the rate with maturity $h - 1$ and the expected short-term rate at $t + h - 1$.

Forward Rates
We can also introduce relations involving the forward rates. A forward zero-coupon bond with date of payment $t + l$ and maturity $t + l + h$ generates a unitary cash flow at $t + l + h$ that is paid at date $t + l$. In a deterministic environment, the price asked at date t to be paid at date $t + l$ is given by

$$B^f(t,t + l,t + l + h) = \frac{B(t,t + l + h)}{B(t,t + l)}.$$

The associated forward rate is defined by

$$B^f(t,t + l,\ t + l + h) = [1 + r^f(t,t + l,t + l + h)]^{-h}.$$

In a stochastic environment, the approximated relation between interest rates implied by the expectation hypothesis is

$$r^f(t,t + l,t + l + h) = \frac{1}{h} \sum_{k=1}^{h} E_t[r(t + l + k - 1, t + l + k)].$$

This equation extends relation (7.27) corresponding to $l = 0$. In particular, the short-term forward interest rates are such that

$$r^f(t,t + l,t + l + 1) = E_t[r(t + l, t + l + 1)], \tag{7.29}$$

and they coincide with the expected spot short-term interest rates.

7.4   Statistical Issues

The statistical analysis of expectation models depends on the observability of variables appearing in (7.19). Let us consider the basic model introduced in Section 7.3.1, that is,

$$p_t = \frac{1}{1 + r_{f,t}} (E_t p_{t+1} + E_t d_{t+1}).$$

If the asset price, the dividend, and the short-term interest rate are all observable, the relation becomes

$$p_t = E_t \left[\frac{1}{1 + r_{f,t}} (p_{t+1} + d_{t+1}) \right]. \tag{7.30}$$

It involves the bivariate series

$$y_t = p_t, \qquad z_t = \frac{1}{1 + r_{f,t-1}} (p_t + d_t),$$

and the following constraint on their joint distribution

$$E_{t-1} z_t = p_{t-1}. \tag{7.31}$$

If the asset price and the dividend are observable, but the short-term interest rate is unobservable and assumed constant, the model becomes

$$p_t = a E_t (p_{t+1} + d_{t+1}), \tag{7.32}$$

where a is an unknown parameter. The model involves the bivariate series

$$y_t = p_t, \qquad z_t = p_t + d_t,$$

and the following constraint on their joint distribution:

$$\exists a : a E_{t-1} z_t = p_{t-1}.$$

Let us examine these two types of constraints. To simplify the presentation, we first assume that the bivariate series $(y_t, z_t)'$ is stationary. Next, we consider nonstationary series and the implied cointegration relationships (see Chapter 5). The stationarity of the individual series of interest depends on the preliminary transformation of the variables and on the problem under study.

EXAMPLE 7.5, THE PRESENT VALUE MODEL: If all the variables are observed, the constraint may be written as $p_t = E_t \left[\dfrac{1}{1 + r_{f,t}} (p_{t+1} + d_{t+1}) \right]$,

which likely involves two nonstationary series, $y_t = p_t$ and $z_t = \dfrac{p_t + d_t}{1 + r_{f,t-1}}$.

Alternatively, it may also be written as

$$E_t \left(\frac{1}{1 + r_{f,t}} (p_{t+1} + d_{t+1}) - p_t \right) = 0,$$

and involves the stationary series

$$y_t = \frac{1}{1 + r_{f,t-1}} (p_t + d_t) - p_{t-1} \quad \text{and } z_t = 0.$$

EXAMPLE 7.6, THE EXPECTATION MODELS OF THE TERM STRUCTURE: In this problem, we can assume that interest rates are stationary. The approximated model

$$r^f(t,t+l,t+l+1) = E_t[r(t+l,t+l+1)],$$

corresponds to the bivariate series $y_t = r^f(t,t+l,t+l+1)$ and $z_t = r(t,t+1)$ and an expectation condition $y_t = E_t z_{t+l}$ at a larger horizon l.

7.4.1 Test of the Rational Expectation Hypothesis

Let us consider a bivariate stationary series (y_t, z_t) and the expectation hypothesis $y_t = E_t z_{t+1} \Leftrightarrow E_t(z_{t+1} - y_t) = 0$. The rational expectation hypothesis can be tested either from the implied moment restrictions on the means, variances, and so on, or in the framework of a vector autoregressive (VAR) model.

Restrictions on Cross Moments
Let the variable x_t be a function of the information set $(\underline{y_t}, \underline{z_t})$. The rational expectation hypothesis implies the following condition:

$$E[x_{t-1}(z_t - y_{t-1})] = E[x_{t-1}E_{t-1}(z_t - y_{t-1})] = 0.$$

Therefore, the test consists of investigating if the empirical cross moment between the so-called instrumental variable x_{t-1} and the difference $z_t - y_{t-1}$ is close to 0. For this purpose, we need to regress by ordinary least squares (OLS) the variable $z_t - y_{t-1}$ on the variable x_{t-1} (without a constant term) and test the significance of the slope parameter. A statistically nonsignificant slope coefficient provides evidence in favor of the rational expectation hypothesis. This method is easily extended to a joint analysis of various cross-moment restrictions: $E[x_{k,t-1}(z_t - y_{t-1})] = 0$, $k = 0, 1, \ldots, K$, where $x_{0,t} = 1$. Again, we need to run a regression of $z_t - y_{t-1}$ on the explanatory variables $x_{0,t-1} = 1$, $x_{1,t-1}, \ldots, x_{K,t-1}$, and to test the significance of all regression coefficients. Nonsignificant regression coefficients suggest that the rational expectation hypothesis cannot be rejected.

Note that these testing procedures have to take into account possible conditional heteroscedasticity of the disturbances of the regression equations.

Restriction on the Variances

The expectation condition implies an inequality between the variances of the series $Vy_t \leq Vz_t$. It is common to draw inference from the empirical counterpart of this inequality, with or without introducing a formal testing procedure. If the inequality is not satisfied, the expectation condition has to be rejected. However, if it is satisfied, the outcome is inconclusive. In fact, the inequality underlying this procedure is less informative compared to the cross-moment conditions, which underlie the expectation condition, since these conditions characterize the rational expectation hypothesis

$$E_{t-1}z_t = y_{t-1} \Leftrightarrow E[x_{t-1}(z_t - y_{t-1})] = 0, \qquad \forall x_t \in I_t = (\underline{y}_t, \underline{z}_t).$$

Vector Autoregressive Framework

Finally, we can introduce a VAR representation of the bivariate series, for example, a VAR(1) representation:

$$\begin{cases} y_t = c_1 + \varphi_{1,1}y_{t-1} + \varphi_{1,2}z_{t-1} + u_{1,t}, \\ z_t = c_2 + \varphi_{2,1}y_{t-1} + \varphi_{2,2}z_{t-1} + u_{2,t}. \end{cases} \tag{7.34}$$

The test of the expectation hypothesis can be performed by testing the following constraint:

$$H_0 = \{c_2 = \varphi_{22} = 0, \varphi_{2,1} = 1\}.$$

which involves only the parameters of the second equation.

7.4.2   *Test of an Expectation Model with Unknown Parameter*

In this setup, the expectation constraint becomes $aE_t z_{t+1} = y_t$ or $E_t z_{t+1} = \alpha y_t$, where $\alpha = 1/a$. Since a is unknown, we now need to test first the expectation constraint and, if it is accepted, to estimate the unknown parameter a. We outline below two testing and estimation procedures. The first approach is based on testing the nullity of cross moments, and the second one is developed in a VAR framework.

Cross Moments

We give a few insights on this method, which is discussed more extensively in Chapter 8. The estimation method is called the *generalized method of moments* (GMM), and the test is called the *overidentification test* (Szroeter 1983).

The approach requires the use of two instrumental variables. Let us denote by $x_{1,t}$ the first instrumental variable. The cross-moment restriction is

$$E(z_t x_{1,t-1}) = \alpha E(y_{t-1} x_{1,t-1}).$$

Equivalently, the parameter α arises as the regression coefficient in a regression of $z_t x_{1,t-1}$ on $y_{t-1} x_{1,t-1}$. It can be consistently estimated by its empirical counterpart, that is,

$$\hat{\alpha}_1 = \frac{\frac{1}{T}\sum_{t=1}^{T} z_t x_{1,t-1}}{\frac{1}{T}\sum_{t=1}^{T} y_{t-1} x_{1,t-1}},$$

which is called an instrumental variable (IV) estimator of α.

Let us now introduce a second instrumental variable $x_{2,t}$. The parameter can also be estimated by

$$\hat{\alpha}_2 = \frac{\frac{1}{T}\sum_{t=1}^{T} z_t x_{2,t-1}}{\frac{1}{T}\sum_{t=1}^{T} y_{t-1} x_{2,t-1}},$$

that is, the IV estimator based on x_2.

Accordingly, the expectation hypothesis can be tested by checking if the two IV estimators produce close outcomes. The test statistic is

$$\xi = \frac{\hat{\alpha}_1 - \hat{\alpha}_2}{\hat{\sigma}_{\hat{\alpha}_1 - \hat{\alpha}_2}},$$

where $\hat{\sigma}_{\hat{\alpha}_1 - \hat{\alpha}_2}$ denotes the estimated standard error of the difference $\hat{\alpha}_1 - \hat{\alpha}_2$. The expectation hypothesis is rejected if $\xi > 2$ and accepted otherwise.

Finally, when it is accepted, we can improve the estimators of the unknown parameter α by optimally combining $\hat{\alpha}_1$ and $\hat{\alpha}_2$. This optimal combination yields the so-called GMM estimator (see Chapter 8).

Vector Autoregressive Framework
In the VAR model (7.34), the test of the expectation hypothesis consists of testing the constraints $c_2 = \varphi_{2,2} = 0$. If this hypothesis is accepted (i.e., the constraint is binding), the parameter α is equal to $\alpha = \varphi_{2,1}$.

7.4.3 Nonstationary Observations

The rational expectation hypothesis can also be tested in the framework of nonstationary processes. Let us consider the present value model with the unknown parameter α:

$$E_t(p_{t+1} + d_{t+1}) = \alpha p_t.$$

It is likely the asset prices to follow a nonstationary process, whereas the dividends and the excess gains are stationary processes. Therefore, the series $y_t = p_t$ and $z_{t+1} = p_{t+1} + d_{t+1}$ likely feature unit roots, whereas the series $z_{t+1} - \alpha_0 y_t$, where α_0 is the true value of the parameter, is stationary. The series (y_t) and (z_{t+1}) are cointegrated, with a cointegrating vector equal to $(1, -\alpha_0)'$.

Therefore, we first perform a cointegration analysis of the bivariate series (y_t, z_{t+1}). If these processes are cointegrated, we get an estimator of the parameter α (see Campbell and Shiller 1987). Then, there is evidence in favor of the expectation hypothesis if the cross moments between the "equilibrium error" $z_t - \hat{\alpha}_T y_{t-1}$ and the instrumental variables are close to 0.

7.5 Summary

In this chapter, we reviewed various prediction schemes with the rational and adaptative expectations of particular interest in finance. The rational expectation and present value models are often used in financial macro-economics to examine exchange rates or interest rates in monthly sampled series. These models shed light on various concepts that are reconsidered in the following chapters. For example, a multiplicity of admissible price dynamics in the rational expectation model or the occurrence of speculative bubbles turn out to be related to the impossiblity of pricing the possible future states of economy without ambiguity (the so-called market incompleteness). This idea becomes clear in the deterministic actuarial models, which yield unique price dynamics. Introducing expectations into an actuarial model would automatically result in a multiplicity of admissible price dynamics. Therefore, the impossibility of anticipating future prices without error is equivalent to the failure of markets to provide perfect insurance against future uncertainty.

In the last sections, we investigated various tests and estimation procedures for expectation models. The present value models have simple structures and consequently are easy to estimate. Under a VAR dynamics, the estimation methods rely on the maximization of a quasi log-likelihood function. A semiparametric method of moments is considered when the conditional moment conditions are employed, and instrumental variables are used. These methods are discussed further in Chapters 8 and 13 in the context of stochastic discount factors.

8

Intertemporal Behavior and the Method of Moments

THE CAPITAL ASSET PRICING MODEL (CAPM) introduced in Chapter 4 assumes a myopic behavior of investors, who optimize with regard to the outcomes of their present decisions on the portfolio value at the next date only. An extension of this procedure that allows for dynamic portfolio management can be achieved by repeating the CAPM optimizations successively in time. This approach is commonly used in practice, despite its several drawbacks. In particular, it makes an investor aim at a moving target by optimizing each time at a fixed horizon and considering a changing maturity date, while a fixed maturity date and a diminishing horizon seem more natural. Also, each asset allocation is selected regardless of its effect on the future updating, yielding therefore a suboptimal outcome.

In Section 8.1, we describe the intertemporal choice problem of a consumer who optimizes the expectation of a time separable utility function and uses financial assets to transfer wealth between different periods and states of the world. The matching between the consumer's demand and exogenous supply is represented by an equilibrium model, called the Consumption-Based Capital Asset Pricing Model (CCAPM). There exist various versions of the CCAPM, depending on the parametric specification of the utility function. In general, the CCAPM relies on an intertemporal utility function that assumes an inverse relationship between intertemporal substitutability and risk aversion.

In Section 8.2, we extend this setup to an intertemporal utility function of a recursive form that allows separation of the risk and time substitution effects. Next, we derive the first-order conditions of the investor's optimization objective. In intertemporal models, individual asset demands and price dynamics do not admit, in general, tractable analytical

173

expressions. However, the parameters of these processes can be identified from the first-order conditions of the intertemporal optimization. These conditions, called the *Euler conditions*, involve a number of associated conditional moments.

The estimation methods are introduced in Section 8.3. The principal one arises as an extension of the standard instrumental variable approach introduced in Chapter 7 and is called the *generalized method of moments* (GMM). We discuss its implementation for the so-called stochastic discount factor models.

8.1   Intertemporal Equilibrium Model

The myopic approach to optimization of the expected utility of a portfolio value, discussed in Section 3.4, is aimed at augmenting future wealth. Therefore, the utility function is an indirect utility function measured in monetary units at time t. The same interpretation does not hold in the intertemporal framework since the value of money is not time invariant. Therefore, a main question that has to be adressed is how to price today the future wealth, or equivalently, how to anticipate the term structure of interest rates. The consumption is introduced into the CAPM to facilitate the analysis of intertemporal behavior. Indeed, the utility expressed as a function of the consumption at date t depends on the quantity of physical goods rather than their monetary value. The advantage of this approach is that a unit of a consumption good provides a common denominator valid at all dates.

8.1.1   Intertemporal Choices

The Optimization Problem
Let us consider a single consumption good with price q_t at date t. At this date, each individual possesses an external income R_t and a portfolio of assets, with allocation vector α_{t-1} which has been decided at a previous date. This endowment allows the individual to consume a quantity C_t and to update the portfolio to a new allocation α_t. The budget constraint at time t is

$$q_t C_t + \alpha_t' p_t = R_t + \alpha_{t-1}' p_t. \tag{8.1}$$

In general, the individual portfolio is not self-financed since the value of consumption spending does not necessarily balance the income pattern. The budget constraint linking the physical and financial assets yields a uniquely defined consumption:

$$C_t = R_t/q_t - (\alpha'_t - \alpha'_{t-1})p_t/q_t. \tag{8.2}$$

The intertemporal choice problem of the individual is to maximize at time t the expectation of a time-separable utility function under the future budget constraints. The maximization can be written as

$$\max E_t \left(\sum_{j=0}^{\infty} \delta^j U(C_{t+j}) \right), \tag{8.3}$$

subject to: $q_{t+j}C_{t+j} + \alpha'_{t+j}p_{t+j} = R_{t+j} + \alpha'_{t+j-1}p_{t+j}, \qquad j = 0, 1, \ldots,$

where δ, $0 \leq \delta < 1$, is the *subjective discount factor*. The direct utility function U is increasing, reflecting a desire for more consumption, and concave, reflecting the declining marginal value of additional consumption units. It is optimized with respect to the future consumption and portfolio plans and is used to determine the current consumption and portfolio allocation. By solving for C_{t+j} from the constraint and substituting into (8.3), the maximization can be rewritten in terms of portfolio allocations:

$$\max E_t \left[\sum_{j=0}^{\infty} \delta^j U(R_{t+j}/q_{t+j} - (\alpha'_{t+j} - \alpha'_{t+j-1})p_{t+j}/q_{t+j}) \right]. \tag{8.4}$$

This expression needs to be maximized with respect to the portfolio allocation plan only.

Euler Conditions
We can easily find the first-order conditions for the current allocation α_t from the portfolio plan. Note that α_t appears in the first and second components of the intertemporal utility:

$$U[R_t/q_t - (\alpha'_t - \alpha'_{t-1})p_t/q_t] + \delta E_t U[R_{t+1}/q_{t+1} - (\alpha'_{t+1} - \alpha'_t)p_{t+1}/q_{t+1}].$$

By computing the first-order derivative with respect to α_t, we get

$$-p_t/q_t \frac{dU}{dc}[R_t/q_t - (\alpha'_t - \alpha'_{t-1})p_t/q_t] + \delta E_t \left\{ p_{t+1}/q_{t+1} \frac{dU}{dc}[R_{t+1}/q_{t+1} \right.$$

$$\left. - (\alpha'_{t+1} - \alpha'_t)p_{t+1}/q_{t+1}] \right\} = -p_t/q_t \frac{dU}{dc}(C_t) + \delta E_t \left[p_{t+1}/q_{t+1} \frac{dU}{dc}(C_{t+1}) \right].$$

The first-order condition, called the *Euler condition*, is

$$p_t/q_t \frac{dU}{dc}(C_t) = \delta E_t \left[p_{t+1}/q_{t+1} \frac{dU}{dc}(C_{t+1}) \right]. \tag{8.5}$$

REMARK 8.1: The above demonstration is heuristic. Indeed, the allocation α_t also influences other components of utility through the conditioning information set. It may be proved that this effect can be disregarded in the first-order conditions whenever the exogenous processes R_t, p_t, and q_t are Markov.

The Euler conditions can be rearranged to express the asset prices in terms of expectations:

$$p_{j,t} = E_t\left[p_{j,t+1}\frac{q_t}{q_{t+1}}\delta\frac{\frac{dU}{dc}(C_{t+1})}{\frac{dU}{dc}(C_t)} \right],$$ (8.6)

where $j = 0, 1, \ldots, J$ is the asset index. By analogy to the formula $p_{j,t} = E_t\left(\frac{p_{j,t+1}}{1+r_f}\right)$ of the expectation model (see Section 7.3.1), the variable

$$M_{t+1} = \frac{q_t}{q_{t+1}}\delta\frac{\frac{dU}{dc}(C_{t+1})}{\frac{dU}{dc}(C_t)},$$ (8.7)

is known as the *stochastic discount factor*. In particular, if we assume for $j = 0$ a risk-free asset, we obtain

$$1 = (1 + r_f)E_t\left[\frac{q_t}{q_{t+1}}\delta\frac{\frac{dU}{dc}(C_{t+1})}{\frac{dU}{dc}(C_t)} \right]$$ (8.8)

$$= (1 + r_f)E_tM_{t+1}.$$

By combining (8.6) and (8.8), we find

$$p_{j,t} = E_t\left[\frac{p_{j,t+1}}{1+r_f}\frac{q_t}{q_{t+1}}\delta\frac{\frac{dU}{dc}(C_{t+1})}{\frac{dU}{dc}(C_t)} \right]\left[E_t\left(\frac{q_t}{q_{t+1}}\frac{\frac{dU}{dc}(C_{t+1})}{\frac{dU}{dc}(C_t)}\right) \right]^{-1}$$

$$= E_t\left[\frac{p_{j,t+1}}{1+r_f}M_{t+1} \right]/E_tM_{t+1}.$$

Since q_t, δ, and $\frac{dU}{dc}$ are positive, the function

$$M_{t+1}/E_t M_{t+1} = \frac{q_t}{q_{t+1}} \delta \frac{\frac{dU}{dc}(C_{t+1})}{\frac{dU}{dc}(C_t)} \left[E_t \left(\frac{q_t}{q_{t+1}} \frac{\frac{dU}{dc}(C_{t+1})}{\frac{dU}{dc}(C_t)} \right) \right]^{-1}, \qquad (8.9)$$

defines a probability density function that corresponds to a conditional distribution at date t. Then, we can write

$$p_{j,t} = E_t^* \left(\frac{p_{j,t+1}}{1 + r_f} \right), \qquad (8.10)$$

where E_t^* denotes the conditional expectation with respect to the modified probability distribution. Relation (8.10) shows that current price is the expected discounted future price with respect to a modified distribution. This interpretation is similar to the expectation hypothesis except for the presence of the modified distribution. This modified distribution is called the *pricing probability* or *risk-neutral probability*. It depends on the inflation rate q_{t+1}/q_t and the intertemporal rate of substitution $\delta \frac{dU}{dc}$ $(C_{t+1})/\frac{dU}{dc}(C_t)$.

REMARK 8.2: It is often assumed in the literature that the inflation rate is negligible with respect to the movements of asset prices (see, e.g., Cochrane 2001, Chap. 2). In this special case, the Euler condition becomes

$$p_{j,t} = E_t \left[p_{j,t+1} \delta \frac{\frac{dU}{dc}(C_{t+1})}{\frac{dU}{dc}(C_t)} \right], \qquad j = 1, \ldots, n. \qquad (8.11)$$

REMARK 8.3: The introduction of the consumption plans for a physical good into the optimization objective indicates that this approach is not designed for direct use by fund managers. Instead, it is more suitable for individual behavior analysis, for building macrodynamic models that link the real and financial sectors under the assumption of a representative agent, or else for asset pricing.

8.1.2 Consumption-Based Capital Asset Pricing Model

Individual Demand
The Euler conditions are used at the individual level to derive the consumption and portfolio allocation for a given price dynamics. It is interest-

ing to introduce explicitly the indexes of individual investors into the Euler conditions. If assets and good prices are identical for all individuals, we get

$$p_t = E_{i,t} \left[p_{t+1} \frac{q_t}{q_{t+1}} \delta_i \frac{\dfrac{dU_i}{dc}(C_{i,t+1})}{\dfrac{dU_i}{di}(C_{it})} \right] \tag{8.12}$$

$$= E_{i,t}[p_{t+1}M_{i,t+1}].$$

The stochastic discount factors vary across individuals. Indeed, the individuals may have different expectations, different access to information, various time preferences, and different income patterns, for example.

The individual Euler conditions are written in an implicit form, which is difficult to solve analytically for individual consumptions and portfolio allocations. Thus, we cannot explicitly aggregate individual demands for financial assets and consumption goods to derive the condition of equilibrium of aggregate demand and supply.

Representative Investor and Equilibrium Condition
This difficulty is often circumvented by assuming the existence of a single investor, called the *representative investor*, who has rational expectation. Relation (8.12) becomes

$$p_t = E_t \left[p_{t+1} \frac{q_t}{q_{t+1}} \delta \frac{\dfrac{dU}{dc}(C_{t+1})}{\dfrac{dU}{dc}(C_t)} \right] = E_t[p_{t+1}M_{t+1}], \tag{8.13}$$

and can be applied at the aggregate level. δ and U are the time discount factor and the utility function of the representative investor, respectively; q_t is a retail price index, and C_t is the quantitative equivalent of the aggregate consumption of physical goods, aggregated with respect to both individuals and goods. Finally, E_t denotes the conditional expectation of the true conditional distribution. Relation (8.13) is part of a complete equilibrium system that involves three endogenous variables: p_t, q_t, and C_t. It is known in the literature as the *Consumption-Based Capital Asset Pricing Model* (CCAPM).

8.1.3 Basic Pricing Model

Equation (8.13) is an essential asset pricing formula. It provides the market price to be accepted when the future evolution of aggregate consumption, inflation, and asset prices are known.

It is common to rearrange the basic equations in the following way. We have

$$1 = E_t\left(\frac{p_{j,t+1}}{p_{j,t}}M_{t+1}\right) = \text{cov}_t\left(\frac{p_{j,t+1}}{p_{j,t}}, M_{t+1}\right) + E_t\left(\frac{p_{j,t+1}}{p_{j,t}}\right)E_t M_{t+1}, \qquad \forall j.$$

By the law of iterated expectation, we also get

$$1 = E\left(\frac{p_{j,t+1}}{p_{j,t}}M_{t+1}\right) = \text{cov}\left(\frac{p_{j,t+1}}{p_{j,t}}, M_{t+1}\right) + E\left(\frac{p_{j,t+1}}{p_{j,t}}\right)E M_{t+1}, \qquad \forall j.$$

We derive the conditional and unconditional equations

$$E_t\left(\frac{p_{j,t+1}}{p_{j,t}}\right) = \frac{1}{E_t M_{t+1}}\left[1 - \text{Cov}_t\left(\frac{p_{j,t+1}}{p_{j,t}}, M_{t+1}\right)\right], \qquad \forall j. \qquad (8.14)$$

and

$$E\left(\frac{p_{j,t+1}}{p_{j,t}}\right) = \frac{1}{E M_{t+1}}\left[1 - \text{Cov}\left(\frac{p_{j,t+1}}{p_{j,t}}, M_{t+1}\right)\right], \qquad \forall j. \qquad (8.15)$$

Let us interpret equation (8.14). We have

$$p_{j,t} = E_t(M_{t+1})E_t p_{j,t+1} + \text{Cov}_t\left(p_{j,t+1}, M_{t+1}\right), \qquad \forall j.$$

or, if there is a risk-free asset

$$p_{j,t} = \frac{1}{1+r_f}E_t p_{j,t+1} + \text{Cov}_t\left(p_{j,t+1}, M_{t+1}\right), \qquad \forall j. \qquad (8.16)$$

This is a decomposition of the price into a standard discounted present value and a risk premium. The risk premium can have any sign. If the asset price evolution is positively correlated with the discount factor (i.e., loosely speaking with the consumption growth), at equilibrium, investors need to pay a premium. Intuitively, the more assets are demanded for intertemporal transfers, the higher their price.

The pricing formula in (8.16) shares some similarities with the pricing formula derived from the CAPM (see Chapter 4). Indeed, the optimization provides an explicit expression of the risk premium, linked with the market portfolio return in the CAPM, and consumption growth in the CCAPM. They both point out the presence of an underlying factor and the opportunity to decompose the risk into a systematic and an idiosyncratic risk. Moreover, in the CCAPM, a more risky asset does not necessarily have a higher price. For instance, let us consider an asset with a gross return that is

$$p_{0,t+1}/p_{0,t} = 1 + r_f + \xi_{t+1},$$

where ξ_{t+1} is conditionally uncorrelated with the stochastic discount factor $Cov(\xi_{t+1}, M_{t+1}) = 0$. Then, the pricing formula in (8.16) implies $E[p_{0,t+1}/p_{0,t}] = 1 + r_f$, that is, the same return as the risk-free asset. In some sense, the component ξ is an *idiosyncratic risk*, while only the *systematic risk* (i.e., a risk component conditionally correlated with the stochastic discount factor) can be corrected for.

In particular in the CCAPM framework, all discounted asset prices $(1 + r_f)^{-t} p_{j,t}$, j varying, can be martingales if the returns include only idiosyncratic components.

8.1.4 Special Utility Functions

For illustration, let us present the Euler conditions associated with exponential and power utility functions.

Exponential Utility Function
Let us consider the utility function $U(c) = -\exp(-Ac)$, where A is positive. Its derivative is $\dfrac{dU}{dc}(c) = A \exp(-Ac)$, and the Euler condition becomes

$$p_t = E_t\left[p_{t+1}\frac{q_t}{q_{t+1}}\delta \, \exp - A(C_{t+1} - C_t) \right]. \qquad (8.17)$$

It involves the prices of financial assets, the inflation rate, and the increment of the consumption level.

Power Utility Function
Let us now consider a representative agent with the power utility function

$$U(c) = \frac{c^{1-\gamma} - 1}{1 - \gamma},$$

where γ is the coefficient of relative risk aversion. When γ approaches 1, the utility function is close to the logarithmic utility function $u(c) = \log c$. The marginal utility is: $\dfrac{dU}{dc}(c) = c^{-\gamma}$, and this expression is also valid in the limiting case $\gamma = 1$. By substituting into the Euler condition, we get

$$1 = E_t\left[\frac{p_{j,t+1}}{p_{j,t}} \frac{q_t}{q_{t+1}} \delta \left(\frac{C_{t+1}}{C_t} \right)^{-\gamma} \right], \qquad \forall j, \qquad (8.18)$$

an expression that involves the rate of increase of the aggregate consumption. The practical advantage of the power utility function is combining various rates of growth in the following expression:

$$1 = E_t \left[\delta \exp\left(\log \frac{p_{j,t+1}}{p_{j,t}} - \log \frac{q_{t+1}}{q_t} - \gamma \log \frac{C_{t+1}}{C_t}\right)\right], \qquad \forall j. \qquad (8.19)$$

Log-Normal Model

A priori various asset price dynamics are compatible with Euler conditions (8.19) based on an associated power utility function (see Chapter 7 for the discussion of the multiplicity of solutions in rational expectation models). Let us restrict our attention to joint conditional log-normal distributions of various growth rates: $p_{j,t+1}/p_{j,t}, j = 0, 1, \ldots, J, q_{t+1}/q_t$, and C_{t+1}/C_t. Then, we infer from the moment-generating function of a Gaussian variable X, that is, $E(\exp X) = \exp(EX + \frac{1}{2}VX)$, that

$$1 = \delta \exp\left\{ E_t[\log(p_{j,t+1}/p_{j,t}) - \log(q_{t+1}/q_t) - \gamma \log(C_{t+1}/C_t)] + \frac{1}{2} V_t[\log(p_{j,t+1}/p_{j,t})\right.$$
$$\left. - \log(q_{t+1}/q_t) - \gamma \log(C_{t+1}/C_t)]\right\}, \qquad j = 1, \ldots, J.$$

By taking the logarithms on both sides, we obtain

$$E_t[\log(p_{j,t+1}/p_{j,t})] = -\log \delta + E_t \log(q_{t+1}/q_t) + \gamma E_t \log(C_{t+1}/C_t)$$
$$- \frac{1}{2} V_t[\log(p_{j,t+1}/p_{j,t}) - \log(q_{t+1}/q_t) - \gamma \log(C_{t+1}/C_t)], \qquad \forall j. \qquad (8.20)$$

Therefore, the (jointly) conditional log-normal model is compatible with the restriction implied by CCAPM if and only if the first- and second-order conditional moments of the various growth rates are related by (8.20).

As for the CAPM model (see Chapter 6), condition (8.20) can be tested under a joint ARCH in mean (ARCH-M) specification for $\log(p_{j,t+1}/p_{j,t})$, $j = 1, \ldots, n$, $\log(q_{t+1}/q_t)$, and $\log(C_{t+1}/C_t)$. The multivariate specification involves at least three series: the returns of a market index (if $n = 1$), the inflation rate, and consumption growth.

REMARK 8.4: For a risk-free asset, equation (8.20) becomes

$$\log(1 + r_f) = -\log \delta + E_t \log(q_{t+1}/q_t) + \gamma E_t \log(C_{t+1}/C_t) - \frac{1}{2} V_t[\log(q_{t+1}/q_t)$$
$$+ \gamma \log(C_{t+1}/C_t)].$$

The equilibrium risk-free rate is a decreasing function of δ. If the investor is impatient (δ is small), the risk-free rate increases to compensate the investor's lack of interest in the future and to ensure the existence of a market for the risk-free asset. It is an increasing function of the expected consumption growth since the risk-free asset is used for intertemporal transfers. It decreases with the volatility of consumption growth, making these transfers less efficient *ex ante*.

8.1.5   Mean-Variance Frontier

We derive from the Euler conditions

$$1 = E_t\left(\frac{p_{j,t+1}}{p_{j,t}}M_{t+1}\right), \qquad \forall j,$$

a *mean-variance frontier*, which is an analog of the efficiency frontier derived under the standard Markovitz approach (see Chapter 4). Let us consider a portfolio allocation at time t, α_t, say; we get

$$\alpha_t'p_t = E_t[\alpha_t'p_{t+1}M_{t+1}]$$

$$\Leftrightarrow W_t(\alpha_t) = E_t[W_{t+1}(\alpha_t)M_{t+1}]$$

$$\Leftrightarrow 1 = E_t\left[\frac{W_{t+1}(\alpha_t)}{W_t(\alpha_t)}M_{t+1}\right]$$

$$\Leftrightarrow 1 = Cov_t\left[\frac{W_{t+1}(\alpha_t)}{W_t(\alpha_t)}, M_{t+1}\right] + E_t\left[\frac{W_{t+1}(\alpha_t)}{W_t(\alpha_t)}\right]E_tM_{t+1}$$

$$\Leftrightarrow \left(1 - E_t\left[\frac{W_{t+1}(\alpha_t)}{W_t(\alpha_t)}\right]E_tM_{t+1}\right)^2 = Cov_t^2\left[\frac{W_{t+1}(\alpha_t)}{W_t(\alpha_t)}, M_{t+1}\right].$$

By applying the Cauchy-Schwartz inequality, we obtain

$$\left(1 - E_t\left[\frac{W_{t+1}(\alpha_t)}{W_t(\alpha_t)}\right]E_tM_{t+1}\right)^2 \le V_t\left[\frac{W_{t+1}(\alpha_t)}{W_t(\alpha_t)}\right]V_tM_{t+1}$$

$$\Leftrightarrow \frac{[E_tW_{t+1}(\alpha_t) - (1 + r_f)W_t(\alpha_t)]^2}{V_tW_{t+1}(\alpha_t)} \le \frac{V_tM_{t+1}}{(E_tM_{t+1})^2}. \tag{8.21}$$

This inequality defines a mean-variance frontier, that is, an upper bound of the ratio of the portfolio squared excess gain and its volatility.

However, it is important to note that, in general, (8.21) is satisfied with a strict inequality. In contrast, the frontier can only be reached if the Cauchy-Schwartz relation is an equality, that is, if there exists an allocation α_t^* such that M_{t+1} and $W_{t+1}(\alpha_t^*)/W_t(\alpha_t^*)$ are proportional, with a proportionality factor being a function of the information at time t. It is easy to verify that this condition is equivalent to the existence of a portfolio allocation α_t^* such that $M_{t+1} = W_{t+1}(\alpha_t^*)$. Such a portfolio is called a *numeraire portfolio*.

A necessary condition for interpreting the stochastic discount factor as a portfolio value is

$$W_t(\alpha_t^*) = E_t[W_{t+1}(\alpha_t^*)M_{t+1}] = E_t\left[M_{t+1}^2\right],$$

If α_t^* is time independent, the condition becomes

$$E_t\left[M_{t+1}^2\right] = M_t.$$

REMARK 8.5: For a power utility function and conditionally uncorrelated dynamics of q_t/q_{t+1} and $(C_{t+1}/C_t)^{-\gamma}$, the slope of the mean-variance frontier is

$$V_t M_{t+1}/(E_t M_{t+1})^2 = \frac{E_t\left[(q_t/q_{t+1})^2\right]}{[E_t(q_t/q_{t+1})]^2} \frac{E_t\left[(C_{t+1}/C_t)^{-2\gamma}\right]}{E_t\left[(C_{t+1}/C_t)^{-\gamma}\right]^2} - 1.$$

It is intuitively higher if the economy in terms of inflation rate or consumption growth is more volatile and, if the investor is more risk averse, due to the γ coefficient. In such an environment the assets are more attractive.

The efficiency frontier based on the stochastic discount factor M_t corresponding to the CCAPM is not necessarily attainable. Thus, a natural question to address is the following one: Does another stochastic discount factor M_t^* exist that is attainable and satisfies the pricing formula:

$$1 = E_t\left[\frac{p_{j,t+1}}{p_{j,t}}M_{t+1}^*\right], \qquad \forall j? \tag{8.22}$$

The answer is straightforward. It was first given by Hansen and Jagannathan (1991). We assume a risk-free asset and an information set that includes the asset prices. Let us define $M_{t+1}^* = LE_t(M_{t+1}|p_{t+1})$ as the best approximation of M_{t+1} by a linear function of $p_{j,t+1}$, $j = 0, 1, \ldots J$, with coefficients that depend on the information at time t. It follows from the definition of linear regression (see Chapter 7) that $E_t[p_{j,t+1}M_{t+1}] = E_t[p_{j,t+1}LE_t(M_{t+1}|p_{t+1})] = E_t[p_{j,t+1}M_{t+1}^*]$ Therefore, we have the pricing formula

$$p_{j,t} = E_t[p_{j,t+1}M_{t+1}^*], \qquad \forall j.$$

Moreover, M_{t+1}^* can be written as

$$M_{t+1}^* = \alpha_{0,t}^*(1 + r_f) + \sum_{j=1}^{J} \alpha_{j,t}^* p_{j,t+1}, \tag{8.23}$$

that is, it is a portfolio value.

As a by-product, the conditional variance of the attainable stochastic discount factor

$$V_t(M_{t+1}^*) = Cov_t(M_{t+1}, p_{t+1})(V_t p_{t+1})^{-1} Cov_t(p_{t+1}, M_{t+1}), \tag{8.24}$$

where p_t includes the prices of risky assets only, is smaller than the conditional variance of the initial stochastic discount factor $V_t(M^*_{t+1}) \leq V_t(M_{t+1})$. It provides a lower bound of the volatility of stochastic discount factors.

8.2 The Nonexpected Utility Hypothesis

8.2.1 Risk Aversion and Intertemporal Substitution

The individual preferences concern consumption plans across various states of the world and at various dates. There are two conceptually distinct aspects of preferences: (1) the attitude toward the variation in consumption across different states of the world (at a given date) and (2) the attitude toward the variation in consumption between different time periods (in the absence of risk). The time-separable utility function defines the following intertemporal utility:

$$V_t = E_t\left[\sum_{j=0}^{\infty} \delta^j U(C_{t+j}) \right].$$

The risk aversion is usually measured by the relative risk aversion coefficient $A(C) = -C \, U''(C)/U'(C)$.

The effect of intertemporal substitution can be evaluated by considering a stationary deterministic environment. In a deterministic environment, risky assets are not used at all, while all transfers are performed by means of a risk-free asset only. Moreover, the budget constraints at different dates can be aggregated into a single intertemporal budget constraint. Let us assume a constant pattern of income R, a constant risk-free rate r_f, and a constant inflation rate β.

The individual optimization objective at date t becomes

$$\max_{C_t} \Sigma_{j=0}^{\infty} \delta^j U(C_{t+j}),$$

$$\text{subject to: } \Sigma_{j=0}^{\infty} q_t \frac{\beta^j}{(1+r_f)^j} C_{t+j} = \Sigma_{j=0}^{\infty} \frac{R}{(1+r_f)^j} = R\frac{1+r_f}{r_f}.$$

The first-order conditions are

$$\delta^j U'(C_{t+j}) - \lambda q_t \frac{\beta^j}{(1+r_f)^j} = 0, \qquad \forall j \geq 0,$$

where λ is a Lagrange multiplier. They imply

$$\delta U'(C_{t+j})/U'(C_{t+j-1}) = \beta/(1+r_f), \qquad \forall j$$

$$\Leftrightarrow \quad \log U'(C_{t+j}) - \log U'(C_{t+j-1}) = -\log\left(\frac{1+r_f}{\beta}\right) - \log \delta.$$

If the time unit is rather small, and $C_{t+j} \simeq C_{t+j-1}$, the left-hand side can be expanded:

$$C_{t+j-1} \frac{d \log U'}{dc}(C_{t+j-1})(\log C_{t+j} - \log C_{t+j-1}) \simeq -\log\left(\frac{1+r_t}{\beta}\right) - \log \delta,$$

$$\log C_{t+j} - \log C_{t+1-1} \simeq -\frac{U'(C_{t+j-1})}{C_{t+j-1}U''(C_{t+j-1})}\left(\log\left(\frac{1+r_t}{\beta}\right) + \log \delta\right).$$

(8.25)

The *elasticity of intertemporal substitution* is defined as the derivative of the log of the planned consumption growth with respect to the log of the real interest rate. From formula (8.25), this elasticity is approximately equal to the inverse of the relative risk aversion coefficient $A(C_{t+j-1})$. Therefore, the additive specification of expected utility is considered as very restrictive. It implicitly assumes that the only admissible combinations are either (1) a high-risk aversion and a low intertemporal substitutability or (2) a low-risk aversion and a high intertemporal substitutability.

As a consequence, more flexible specifications are preferred, even at the expense of being less parsimonious. In particular, we are interested in such utility functions that would allow for a separate analysis of risk aversion and intertemporal substitution.

8.2.2   Recursive Utility

Let us consider the standard intertemporal additive expected utility. At date t, we get

$$V_t = E_t\left[\sum_{j=0}^{\infty} \delta^j U(C_{t+j})\right].$$

(8.26)

Let us also distinguish the current consumption and the future consumption plan.

$$V_t = U(C_t) + \delta E_t\left[\sum_{j=0}^{\infty} \delta^j U(C_{t+j+1})\right]$$

$$= U(C_t) + \delta E_t E_{t+1}\left[\sum_{j=0}^{\infty} \delta^j U(C_{t+j+1})\right],$$

(8.27)

$$V_t = U(C_t) + \delta E_t V_{t+1}.$$

Thus, the intertemporal utility at time t is the sum of the current utility $U(C_t)$ and the discounted expected future intertemporal utility. This recursive definition of V_t can be extended in two respects. First, we can relax the assumption on additivity of the present and future utilities.

Second, we can summarize the distribution of the future random utility by an indicator that includes a risk premium. Indeed, in (8.27), this distribution is summarized by the conditional expectation, which assumes a "risk-neutral" individual.

Kreps and Porteus (1978), Epstein and Zin (1989), and Weil (1989) introduced a recursive intertemporal utility function. It is defined by

$$V_t = W[C_t, \mu_t], \tag{8.28}$$

where μ_t is a certainty equivalent of the future intertemporal utility V_{t+1} evaluated at t, and W is an aggregator function, which aggregates the current consumption with a summary of the future to determine the current utility. The certainty equivalent is often assumed of the type

$$\mu_t = \begin{cases} (E_t[V_{t+1}^\alpha])^{1/\alpha}, & \text{if } 0 < \alpha < 1, \\ \exp E_t(\log V_{t+1}), & \text{if } \alpha = 0, \end{cases} \tag{8.29}$$

whereas the aggregator is a Constant Elasticity of Substitution (CES) function:

$$W(C, \mu) = \begin{cases} \left[(1-\beta)C^\rho + \beta\mu^\rho\right]^{1/\rho}, & \text{if } 0 < \rho < 1 \\ \exp[(1-\beta)\log C + \beta \log \mu], & \text{if } \rho = 0. \end{cases} \tag{8.30}$$

Thus, the parametric recursive utility function becomes

$$V_t = \left\{(1-\beta)C_t^\rho + \beta\left[E_t\left(V_{t+1}^\alpha\right)\right]^{\rho/\alpha}\right\}^{1/\rho}. \tag{8.31}$$

The recursive intertemporal utility depends on three parameters (β, α, ρ), in contrast to the two parameters of the additive expected power utility. As a consequence, we gain one degree of freedom.

8.2.3 The Euler Condition

Epstein and Zin (1989) considered the optimization of the recursive intertemporal utility in (8.31) under the intertemporal budget constraint (8.1). Under the Markov assumption for p_t, q_t, and R_t, they used a complicated dynamic programming argument to derive the first-order conditions

$$1 = E_t\left\{\left[\delta\left(\frac{C_{t+1}}{C_t}\right)^{-(1-\rho)}\right]^{\alpha/\rho}\left[\frac{W_t(\alpha_t)}{W_{t+1}(\alpha_{t+1})}\frac{q_{t+1}}{q_t}\right]^{1-\alpha/\rho}\frac{q_t}{q_{t+1}}\frac{p_{j,t+1}}{p_{j,t}}\right\}, \quad \forall j, \tag{8.32}$$

where $W_t(\alpha_t) = \alpha_t' p_t$ is the portfolio value at the optimum. This condition extends the CCAPM with a power utility function in the limiting case $\alpha = \rho$ [see Section 8.1.4, equation (8.17)], whereas the stochastic discount factor involves the portfolio returns as in the standard CAPM in the case when $\alpha/\rho = 0$. Generally, the stochastic discount factor

$$M_{t+1} = \left[\delta \left(\frac{C_{t+1}}{C_t} \right)^{-(1-\rho)} \right]^{\alpha/\rho} \left[\frac{W_{t+1}(\alpha_t)}{W_{t+1}(\alpha_{t+1})} \right]^{1-\alpha/\rho} \left(\frac{q_{t+1}}{q_t} \right)^{-\alpha/\rho}, \qquad (8.33)$$

involves the evolutions of consumption, portfolio value, and price of the consumption good.

REMARK 8.6: In the literature, it is common to consider the case of log-normal relative increments of consumption, portfolio values, and prices and to write the Euler conditions as a relation among the conditional expectations, volatilities, and covolatilities. It is similar to the approach described in Section 8.1.4 concerning the log-normal model. Note that the log-normality assumption is not compatible with a fixed portfolio allocation since we cannot have the joint normality of

$$\log(p_{j,t+1}/p_{j,t}), \quad j = 1, \ldots, J \quad \text{and} \quad \log \frac{W_{t+1}(\alpha)}{W_t(\alpha)} = \log \left(\frac{\sum_{j=1}^{J} \alpha_j p_{j,t+1}}{\sum_{j=1}^{J} \alpha_j p_{j,t}} \right).$$

8.3 The Generalized Method of Moments

The intertemporal equilibrium models, based on either the additive expected utility or the recursive utility do not yield analytical formulas of price dynamics. The Euler conditions, however, involve the unknown preference parameters, which may be estimated and used to derive the pricing formulas. The GMM, which is a semiparametric estimation method, exploits the information contained in the Euler conditions and produces consistent estimators of the preference parameters. In Section 8.3.1, we explain how the conditional moment restrictions can be transformed into marginal moment conditions by introducing instrumental variables. The GMM estimation method is described in Section 8.3.2.

8.3.1 *Moment Conditions and Instrumental Variables*

Let us consider a multivariate process (Y_t), with an unknown distribution that depends on a vector of parameters θ. Knowing these parameters is not sufficient to characterize the distribution of (Y_t), which implies the need for a semiparametric approach. We assume that the process (Y_t) and the parameter θ satisfy the following conditional moment restrictions:

$$E_t g(Y_{t+1};\theta) = 0, \qquad (8.34)$$

where g is a known function of dimension L. The function g depends on the problem under study, as shown in the examples below.

EXAMPLE 8.1: For the CCAPM model with an exponential utility function [see (8.16)], we have

$$Y_{t+1} = (p_{t+1}, p_t, q_{t+1}, q_t, C_{t+1}, C_t)', \qquad \theta = (\delta, A),$$

$$g(Y_{t+1};\theta) = p_{t+1}\frac{q_{t+1}}{q_t}\delta \exp - A(C_{t+1} - C_t) - p_t.$$

For a power utility function, we get [see (8.17)]

$$Y_{t+1} = (p_{t+1}/p_t, q_{t+1}/q_t, C_{t+1}/C_t)', \qquad \theta = (\delta, \gamma),$$

$$g(Y_{t+1};\theta) = (p_{t+1}/p_t)(q_{t+1}/q_t)\delta(C_{t+1}/C_t)^{-\gamma} - 1.$$

We see from Example 8.1 that the g function is not uniquely defined. For instance, for the power utility function, we can equivalently consider the function $\tilde{g}(\tilde{Y}_{t+1};\theta) = p_{t+1}(q_{t+1}/q_t)\delta(C_{t+1}/C_t)^{-\gamma} - p_t$ with the associated process $\tilde{Y}_{t+1} = (p_{t+1}, p_t, q_{t+1}/q_t, C_{t+1}/C_t)$. Intuitively, the first choice is preferable since the associated process (Y_t) represents rates of growth and is more likely stationary than the process $(\tilde{Y}_t)$, which represents price processes.

EXAMPLE 8.2: More generally, the approach outlined above can be applied to any parameterized stochastic discount factor $M_{t+1} = m(x_{t+1};\theta)$, where x contains observable variables. The Euler conditions become

$$E_t[(p_{t+1}m(x_{t+1};\theta) - p_t)] = 0,$$

or

$$E_t[p_{t+1}/p_t m(x_{t+1};\theta) - 1] = 0.$$

Note that the integrand of the second condition is more likely stationary than the integrand of the first condition.

Since it is easier to estimate a marginal expectation than a conditional expectation, the set of conditional moment restrictions is usually transformed into a set of marginal moment conditions. For this purpose, let us consider a variable z_t, defined as a function of the information at date t, denoted $\underline{Y}_t$. We deduce from (8.34) that

$$E[z_t g(Y_{t+1};\theta)] = E[z_t E_t g(Y_{t+1};\theta)]$$
$$= 0.$$

This is a marginal moment condition for the product of functions $z_t g(Y_{t+1}; \theta)$. The variable z_t is called the *instrumental variable* or *instrument*.

Then, we select K instruments, $z_{1t}, \ldots, z_{Kt}$, and replace the initial set of L conditional restrictions by a set of KL marginal moment conditions:

$$E[z_{k,t}g_l(Y_{t+1};\theta)] = 0, \qquad \forall k = 1, \ldots, K, \qquad l = 1, \ldots, L. \qquad (8.35)$$

8.3.2   The Estimation Method

For ease of exposition, we assume $L = 1$ so that the set of marginal moment restrictions becomes

$$E[z_t g(Y_{t+1};\theta)] = 0, \tag{8.36}$$

where $z_t = (z_{1,t}, \ldots, z_{K,t})'$.

The *method of moments* consists of approximating the previous moment conditions and solving the approximate set of equations for θ to obtain an estimator. Three cases can be distinguished, depending on the number K of instruments and the dimension p of the parameter vector.

1. *Underidentification.* If the number of instruments is too small, $K < p$, there are not enough relations to determine a unique value of the parameter. The parameters are unidentified.
2. *Exact identification.* When $K = p$, there exists in general a unique solution.
3. *Overidentification.* When $K > p$, there are more equations than unknown parameters, and we cannot find an exact solution of the system. We will find instead an approximate solution.

Let us assume that (z_t, Y_{t+1}) is a stationary process. The theoretical expectation in (8.36) can be estimated by its empirical counterpart:

$$E[z_t g(Y_{t+1};\theta)] \simeq \frac{1}{T}\sum_{t=1}^{T} z_t g(Y_{t+1};\theta). \tag{8.37}$$

Let us introduce a symmetric positive definite matrix Ω of dimension (K,K).

DEFINITION 8.1: *A moment estimator of θ based on the estimating equations in (8.36), the instruments z_t, and the weighting matrix Ω is the solution of*

$$\hat{\theta}_T = \operatorname*{Arg\,min}_{\theta} \left[\frac{1}{T}\sum_{t=1}^{T} z_t g(Y_{t+1};\theta)\right]' \Omega \left[\frac{1}{T}\sum_{t=1}^{T} z_t g(Y_{t+1};\theta)\right].$$

For a given set of conditional restrictions, we obtain a multiplicity of moment estimators. They depend on the selected instruments, their number, and the weighting matrix. These estimators are consistent, but their efficiency depends on Ω and z.

PROPOSITION 8.1: *The moment estimator of θ is consistent, asymptotically normal:*

$$\sqrt{T}(\hat{\theta}_T - \theta) \sim N[0, \Sigma(\Omega)],$$

where

$$\Sigma(\Omega) = \left\{ E\left[\frac{\partial g}{\partial \theta}(Y_{t+1};\theta)z_t' \right] \Omega E\left[\frac{\partial g}{\partial \theta'}(Y_{t+1};\theta)z_t \right] \right\}^{-1}$$

$$E\left[\frac{\partial g}{\partial \theta}(Y_{t+1};\theta)z_t' \right] \Omega V_{as} \left[\frac{1}{\sqrt{T}} \sum_{t=1}^{T} z_t g(Y_{t+1};\theta) \right] \Omega E\left[\frac{\partial g}{\partial \theta'}(Y_{t+1};\theta) \right]$$

$$\left\{ E\left[\frac{\partial g}{\partial \theta}(Y_{t+1};\theta)z_t \right] \Omega E\left[\frac{\partial g}{\partial \theta'}(Y_{t+1};\theta)z_t \right] \right\}^{-1},$$

where V_{as} denotes the limiting variance for large T.

For a given set of instruments, there exists an optimal choice of Ω. This choice provides the most efficient moment estimator given the instrument z. It is called the *generalized moment estimator* (see Hansen 1982). Its properties are described below.

PROPOSITION 8.2: *There exists a weighting matrix Ω^* that optimizes the efficiency of the moment estimator*

$$\Omega^* = V_{as} \left[\frac{1}{\sqrt{T}} \sum_{t=1}^{T} z_t g(Y_{t+1};\theta) \right]^{-1}.$$

The associated estimator (i.e., the GMM estimator) has the asymptotic variance-covariance matrix

$$\Sigma(\Omega^*) = \left\{ E\left[\frac{\partial g}{\partial \theta}(Y_{t+1};\theta)z_t' \right] \Omega^* E\left[\frac{\partial g}{\partial \theta'}(Y_{t+1};\theta)z_t \right] \right\}^{-1}.$$

In practice, the optimal weighting matrix is unknown and has to be estimated. We get

$$= V_{as} \left[\frac{1}{\sqrt{T}} \sum_{t=1}^{T} z_t g(Y_{t+1};\theta) \right]$$

$$= \lim_{T\to\infty} E\left[\frac{1}{T} \sum_{t=1}^{T} \sum_{\tau=1}^{T} z_t z_\tau' g(Y_{t+1};\theta)g(Y_{\tau+1};\theta) \right]$$

$$= \lim_{T\to\infty} E\left[\frac{1}{T} \sum_{t=1}^{T} \sum_{k=-\infty}^{+\infty} z_t z_{t-k}' g(Y_{t+1};\theta)g(Y_{t+1-k};\theta) \right]$$

$$= \sum_{k=-\infty}^{+\infty} E[z_t z_{t-k}' g(Y_{t+1};\theta)g(Y_{t+1-k};\theta)]$$

$$= E\left[z_t z_t' g(Y_{t+1};\theta)^2 \right], \text{ since } E_t g(Y_{t+1};\theta) = 0.$$

A consistent estimator is

$$\hat{\Omega}* = \left[\frac{1}{T}\sum_{t=1}^{T} z_t z_t' g(Y_{t+1};\hat{\theta})^2\right]^{-1}.$$

where $\hat{\theta}$ is a moment estimator computed with a simple Ω matrix, such as $\Omega = Id$.

Even with an optimal choice of the weighting matrix, the accuracy of the GMM estimator still depends on the selected instruments. The estimators may not be fully efficient if the instruments are selected in an inappropriate way.

EXAMPLE 8.3: For instance, let us assume a one-dimensional parameter θ in a stochastic discount factor model. We can use in the estimation a single "bad" instrument $z_t = 1$. The estimating restriction is simply the marginal pricing formula

$$E[p_{t+1}/p_t m(x_{t+1};\theta) - 1] = 0.$$

Intuitively, a constant instrument does not contain much information on the dynamic of the discount factor, and the estimator of θ is not very efficient. It is preferable to introduce several instruments, such as $z_{1,t} = 1$, $z_{2,t} = p_t/p_{t-1}$, $z_{3,t} = x_t$, and $z_{4,t} = (p_t/p_{t-1})^2$, including the lagged values of the processes and their squares.

8.3.3 Implementation

The Euler conditions and associated GMM estimators can be used to analyze the individual behaviors of investors and to study asset prices. These two types of applications require different data. We discuss the approaches in relation to the CCAPM model with a power utility function.

Individual Behavior
We show in Section 8.1.2 that the Euler conditions are valid at the individual level. Let us consider a set of individuals $i = 1, \ldots, n$, with portfolios invested in the same assets $j = 1, \ldots, J$. The Euler conditions for an individual i are

$$1 = E_t\left[\frac{p_{j,t+1}}{p_{j,t}}\frac{q_t}{q_{t+1}}\delta_i\left(\frac{C_{i,t+1}}{C_{i,t}}\right)^{-\gamma_i}\right], \qquad j = 1, \ldots, J, \tag{8.38}$$

where $C_{i,t}$ is the consumption at t of the individual i when all individuals have the same information, consisting for example, of asset and consumption good prices.

Thus, if the individual consumption data are available, we can apply a GMM approach based on the conditional moments corresponding to individual i. We find $\hat{\delta}_i$ and $\hat{\gamma}_i$, which approximate the individual subjective discount factor and relative risk aversion coefficient, respectively. Then, the individuals can be compared in terms of pairs $(\hat{\delta}_i, \hat{\gamma}_i)$, $i = 1, \ldots,$ n to derive a segmentation of the population of investors into homogeneous groups with similar preferences.

We can also compute for any individual the empirical differences

$$\frac{1}{T}\sum_{t=1}^{T}\left[\frac{p_{j,t+1}}{p_{j,t}}\frac{q_t}{q_{t+1}}\hat{\delta}_i\left(\frac{C_{i,t+1}}{C_{i,t}}\right)^{-\hat{\gamma}_i}-1\right]=\hat{\xi}_{i,j}, \qquad \text{(say)}.$$

If these differences $\hat{\xi}_{i,j}$, $j = 1, \ldots, J$, are close to 0, the hypothesis of the behavior of individual i being optimal cannot be rejected. It is rejected otherwise. Thus, we are able to identify the optimally behaved individuals in the sample.

Asset Price Analysis
We can also follow a macroeconomic approach, which implicitly assumes a single representative investor, to find a pricing formula of the type

$$1 = E_t\left[\frac{p_{j,t+1}}{p_{j,t}}\frac{q_t}{q_{t+1}}\delta\left(\frac{C_{t+1}}{C_t}\right)^{-\gamma}\right], \qquad j = 1, \ldots, J. \qquad (8.39)$$

In this approach, we focus on the possible model misspecification before estimating the parameters δ and γ and using the estimated values to price more complex assets. The idea is to apply the GMM method with different sets of instruments: $Z^l = (Z^l_1, \ldots, Z^l_{k_l})$, $l = 1, \ldots, L$, say. We derive the associated GMM estimators $(\hat{\delta}_l, \hat{\gamma}_l)$, $l = 1, \ldots, L$. Then, by comparing these estimators we find (1) what instruments are included in the information set and (2) among the instruments, which are the most informative ones.

This approach is described in detail in Chapter 13, in which we also explain how the estimated stochastic discount factors can be used to price derivative assets.

8.4 Summary

This chapter generalized the CAPM model to an intertemporal equilibrium model, called the Consumption-Based CAPM. An important feature of this approach is the presence of a behavioral equation defining consumer preferences. A consumer is supposed to hold assets to maximize utility, measured in units of a consumption good, and to take into account consumption in future periods. The first-order conditions of the maximization objective, called the Euler conditions, can be solved empirically using the generalized method of moments. The behavior of individuals can be described by various forms of the utility functions. Especially, investors vary with respect to their risk aversion and discount rate of future states. The GMM relies on moment conditions that involve instrumental variables. Among problems often encountered in empirical research is the choice of instruments, which need to be orthogonal to the transformation involved in the Euler equation to ensure good performance of the GMM estimator.

9

Dynamic Factor Models

IN CHAPTERS 3 AND 5, we investigated linear models of returns (prices) on various financial assets. We have pointed out several aspects of joint dynamics, such as feedback effects and cointegration. In this chapter, we present yet another specification that involves multiple time series, called a *factor model*. Under this approach, the dynamics of returns on a set of assets is explained by a common effect of a limited number of variables, called *factors*, which may or may not be observed.

In the first section, we present the models with observable factors and discuss their role in empirical finance. We show that factor models can be used to construct benchmark portfolios or to diversify investments. Linear factor models with unobservable factors are examined in Section 9.2. The approach is extended to nonlinear factor models in Sections 9.3 and to Markov models with finite dimensional dependence in Section 9.4.

It is important to mention that a significant number of factor models are considered in the financial literature in a static framework. A common practice consists of performing singular value decomposition of a sample-based variance-covariance matrix of returns. This approach implicitly assumes independent identically distributed (i.i.d.) returns and disregards temporal dependence and dynamic nonlinearities, such as conditional heteroscedasticity. Essentially, these factors are not dynamic. Genuine dynamic factor models have been introduced into the literature quite recently.

In this chapter, we focus on the factor model specifications and factor interpretations. Empirical applications of factor models to liquidity analysis (see Chapter 14) and extreme risk dynamics (see Chapter 16) are also described. In the last Section we explain how to introduce cross-sectional factors and discuss in detail the arbitrage pricing theory (APT).

9.1 Linear Factor Models with Observable Factors

9.1.1   The Model

We first examine the model, in which factors are simple linear functions of some observable variables. More precisely, a multivariate process (Y_t), of dimension n, is represented by a system of seemingly unrelated equations:

$$Y_t = BX_t + u_t, \tag{9.1}$$

where B is an (n,L) matrix, X_t is an L-dimensional vector of observable explanatory variables, and u_t is an n-dimensional error term, such that

$$E(u_t|\underline{Y_{t-1}}, \underline{X_t}) = 0, V(u_t|\underline{Y_{t-1}}, \underline{X_t}) = \Omega. \tag{9.2}$$

The number L of explanatory variables may be greater than or less than the dimension n of the vector of endogenous series. The unknown parameters B and Ω, estimated by ordinary least squares (OLS) applied separately for each equation, are denoted by $\hat{B}$ and $\hat{\Omega}$, respectively.

It follows from (9.1) that the components of X are explanatory variables in a linear seemingly unrelated regressions (SUR) model of Y. In this section, we explore the particular cases when the dimension of X can be reduced so that the common explanatory effect of variables in X can be summarized by a smaller number of variables, called *factors*. More precisely, let us assume that the matrix B is not of full rank. Proposition 9.1 can be used to rewrite relation (9.1).

PROPOSITION 9.1:

(i) *The matrix B has rank K if and only if it may be decomposed as $B = \beta\alpha'$, where the matrices α and β have dimensions (L,K) and (n,K), respectively, and the same rank K.*

(ii) *The elements of the decomposition can be derived from a joint spectral analysis of the "squared" matrices BB' and $B'B$.*

PROOF: See Appendix 9.1.

If the rank of B is rank $B = K < n$, the initial system can be written as

$$\begin{aligned} Y_t &= \beta\alpha'X_t + u_t \\ &= \beta F_t + u_t, \end{aligned} \tag{9.3}$$

where F_t has dimension K and the following components:

$$F_{k,t} = \sum_{l=1}^{L} \alpha_{lk} X_{l,t}.$$

Therefore, the links between Y_t and the past, that is, $(\underline{Y}_{t-1}, \underline{X}_t)$, are determined by a limited number of variables F_{kt}, $k = 1, \ldots, K$, which arise as linear combinations of the initial explanatory variables. Expression (9.3), in which the number of explanatory variables has been reduced, is called a *factor representation*: The variables $(F_{k,t})$, $k = 1, \ldots, K$, are the factors, whereas the coefficient β_{ik} is the *sensitivity* or beta of the endogenous variable Y_i with respect to the factor F_k.

Whenever the dimension of the factor space $K = \text{rank } B$ is uniquely defined, the factors are known up to a one-to-one linear transformation. Indeed, if $B = \beta\alpha'$ is a decomposition of B, and Q is an invertible square matrix of dimension (K,K), we get $B = BQQ^{-1}\alpha' = \beta Q[\alpha Q^{-1}]'$ and another factor representation, where $\tilde{\beta} = \beta Q$ and $\tilde{F}_t = \tilde{\alpha}'X_t = Q^{-1}\alpha'X_t$. The *factor space*, that is the space generated by the factors, comprises all linear combinations belonging to the range of B'. Therefore, this space is uniquely defined, although the basis of this space (i.e., the set of factors) can be selected in various ways.

There exist various possible choices of the set of observable explanatory variables in asset price models. For instance,

(i) The explanatory variables can consist of contemporaneous macroeconomic variables. This setup would allow study of the links between the financial and real sectors of the economy and estimation of the dimension K of this relationship.

(ii) The explanatory variables can include lagged values of endogenous processes leading to a vector autoregressive (VAR) specification:

$$Y_t = \Phi_1 Y_{t-1} + \ldots + \Phi_p Y_{t-p} + \varepsilon_t$$

$$= (\Phi_1, \ldots, \Phi_p) \begin{pmatrix} Y_{t-1} \\ \vdots \\ Y_{t-p} \end{pmatrix} + \varepsilon_t.$$

By decomposing the matrix $B = (\Phi_1, \ldots, \Phi_p)$, we search for a minimal number of sufficient statistics that summarize the asset price history.

(iii) It is also possible to select as explanatory variables the values of some specific portfolios (see Sharpe 1964). In this case, we get $X_t = \gamma'Y_t$ and attempt to combine these portfolios without any loss of information.

The linear factor model (9.1) and (9.2) of excess gains on assets with observable factors implies a particular interpretation of portfolio management, mentioned Section 3.4.3. Indeed, under a factor model representation, the mean-variance optimal portfolio has the following composition:

$$\alpha_t = (V_t Y_{t+1})^{-1} E_t Y_{t+1}$$
$$= \Omega^{-1} B X_t$$
$$= \Omega^{-1} \beta F_t.$$

Therefore, by making the individual factor components explicit, we get

$$\alpha_t \propto \sum_k F_{k,t} \alpha(k), \tag{9.4}$$

where the $\alpha(k)$, $k = 1, \dots, K$, are the columns of $\Omega^{-1}\beta$.

The vectors of allocations $\alpha(k)$, $k = 1, \dots, K$, define the *benchmark portfolios*, which arise as elementary components of efficient portfolios in various environments. Their compositions are time independent. Therefore, any modifications of the mean-variance efficient portfolio (9.4) can be accomplished by updating the relative weights $F_{k,t}$ of the benchmark portfolios. Loosely speaking, the portfolio management can be based on a limited number of well-chosen mutual funds so that the efficient portfolio is simply a fund of funds.

9.1.2 Estimation of the Factors

The initial model in (9.1) is a SUR model with parameters that can be estimated by OLS equation by equation. The estimator is

$$\hat{B} = \left[\frac{1}{T} \sum_{t=1}^{T} Y_t X_t' \right] \left[\frac{1}{T} \sum_{t=1}^{T} X_t X_t' \right]^{-1}, \tag{9.5}$$

obtained as the empirical counterpart of the theoretical regression coefficient

$$B = E(YX')E(XX')^{-1}. \tag{9.6}$$

According to Proposition 9.1, the number of factors and their expressions can be derived from a joint spectral decomposition of BB' and $B'B$. In practice, we apply the spectral decomposition to the estimates $\hat{B}\hat{B}'$ and $\hat{B}'\hat{B}$ (see Appendix 9.1). Let us denote by $\hat{\lambda}_1 \geq \hat{\lambda}_2 \geq \dots$ the first common eigenvalues of these matrices arranged in descending order. The number K of factors corresponds to the lowest rank $\hat{K}$, which appears as the index of the first statistically nonsignificant eigenvalue $\hat{\lambda}_k$ or of an eigenvalue of a considerably lower value than the preceding ones. The factor estimates are obtained as the eigenvectors of the matrix decomposition.

The statistical inference can be improved by taking into account the accuracy of the OLS estimators $\hat{B}$, which depends on $\left[\frac{1}{T} \Sigma_{t=1}^{T} X_t X_t' \right]^{-1} \approx$

$[E(XX')]^{-1}$. Then, the spectral decomposition can be performed on the matrix

$$BE(XX')B' = E(YX')E(XX')^{-1}E(XY'),$$

or, up to a linear transformation of the eigenvectors, on the matrix

$$R^2 = E(YY')^{-1/2}E(YX')E(XX')^{-1}E(XY')E(YY')^{-1/2}.$$

The matrix R^2 is a kind of multivariate correlation matrix, and the spectral decomposition will necessarily produce the most correlated pair of combinations of Y and X, respectively, followed by a pair of the next most correlated combinations, and so on. In statistics, this approach is called the *linear canonical analysis*.

9.2 Linear Factor Models with Unobservable Factors

9.2.1 The Model

Like in the previous section, the model is defined in term of first- and second-order conditional moments, although the factors are now assumed to be no longer observed. Due to the presence of latent variables, the initial setup has to be transformed into a state-space model, involving a measurement equation and a set of transition equations that describe the dynamics of the observed and unobserved variables, respectively. The initial SUR model in (9.1) is therefore replaced by the linear measurement equation

$$Y_t = BF_t + u_t, \tag{9.7}$$

where B is a (n, K) matrix, F_t is a vector of unobserved factors of dimension K, and the n-dimensional error term (u_t) satisfies

$$E(u_t | \underline{Y_{t-1}}, \underline{F_t}) = 0, \qquad V(u_t | \underline{Y_{t-1}}, \underline{F_t}) = \Omega. \tag{9.8}$$

The model is completed by expressions that specify the dynamics of the factors. It is assumed that

$$E[F_t | \underline{Y_{t-1}}, \underline{F_{t-1}}] = E(F_t | F_{t-1}) = m(F_{t-1}; \theta), \tag{9.9}$$

$$V[F_t | \underline{Y_{t-1}}, \underline{F_{t-1}}] = V(F_t | F_{t-1}) = \Sigma(F_{t-1}; \theta), \tag{9.10}$$

that is, the first- and second-order conditional moments of F_t depend on F_{t-1} only. The temporal dependence is parametrized and represented by the transition equations (9.9), (9.10). More precisely, they are the so-called first- and second-order transition equations.

The set of assumptions (9.8)–(9.10) ensures that the dynamics of the process (Y_t) is completely determined by the factors (F_t) whenever the first- and second-order conditional moments are the only ones considered.

REMARK 9.1: Assumptions (9.9) and (9.10) can easily be extended to temporal dependence at any higher lag. If the conditional mean and variance of F_t depend on F_{t-1} and F_{t-2} (say), the definition of the factor can be changed to $F_t^* = (F_t', F_{t-1}')'$.

REMARK 9.2: The factors are not uniquely defined. Indeed, if Q is an invertible matrix of dimension (K, K), an equivalent factor representation can be obtained with $F_t^* = QF_t$ and $B^* = BQ^{-1}$, which requires appropriate transformations of m and Σ.

EXAMPLE 9.1, FACTOR ARCH MODELS: The factor autoregressive conditionally heteroscedastic (ARCH) models have been introduced to reduce the number of parameters to estimate in multivariate ARCH models (see Chapter 6 and Diebold and Nerlove 1989). As an illustration, let us consider a one-factor ARCH model with ARCH(1) factor. We have

$$Y_t = bF_t + u_t,$$

where

$$E(F_t | \underline{Y_{t-1}}, \underline{F_{t-1}}) = 0,$$
$$V(F_t | \underline{Y_{t-1}}, \underline{F_{t-1}}) = a_0 + a_1 F_{t-1}^2.$$

9.2.2   Constraints on the First- and Second-Order Moments

Let us now discuss the specifications of first- and second-order conditional moments of Y_t in the framework of factor models. Depending on the informational content, two types of conditioning sets have to be distinguished. The first one encompasses the past and present of both the observed Y_t and latent factors F_t:

$$J_t = (\underline{Y_t}, \underline{F_t}).$$

Although J_t underlies the construction of the factor model, it is not available to an econometrician. Instead, the available information set contains the past of Y_t only: $I_t = (\underline{Y_t})$. As a consequence, we obtain two sets of conditional moments of Y_t conditioned on either J_t or I_t.

Moments of Y_t Conditional on the Global Information
From (9.8)–(9.10), we directly infer the conditional mean and variance of Y_t:

$$E(Y_t | J_{t-1}) = BE(F_t | J_{t-1}) = Bm(F_{t-1}; \theta), \tag{9.11}$$

$$V(Y_t | J_{t-1}) = BV(F_t | J_{t-1})B' + \Omega$$
$$= B\Sigma(F_{t-1}; \theta)B' + \Omega. \tag{9.12}$$

Moments Conditional on the Available Information
The conditional mean and variance are derived by applying the law of iterated expectations:

$$E(Y_t|I_{t-1}) = E[E(Y_t|J_{t-1})\ |I_{t-1}],$$

and the variance decomposition equation

$$V[Y_t|I_{t-1}] = V[E(Y_t|J_{t-1})\ |I_{t-1}] + E[V(Y_t|J_{t-1})\ |I_{t-1}].$$

We get

$$E(Y_t|I_{t-1}) = BE(m(F_{t-1};\theta)\ |I_{t-1}), \tag{9.13}$$

$$V(Y_t|I_{t-1}) = B\{V[m(F_{t-1};\theta)\ |I_{t-1}] + E(\Sigma(F_{t-1};\theta)\ |I_{t-1})\}B' + \Omega. \tag{9.14}$$

Except for some specific factor models, it is not possible to obtain analytical expression of these two conditional moments. However they can be calculated from a given history of (Y_t) by applying numerical procedures (see Section 9.3.2).

9.2.3 Mimicking Portfolios

The latent factors can be approximated by their expectations conditioned on observable variables, for instance, $E(F_t|\underline{Y_t})$ or $E(F_t|\underline{Y_T})$. While these approximations are rather difficult to find (see Section 9.3.2), linear approximation based only on the current value of (Y_t), that is, $LE[F_t|Y_t] = \hat{F}_t$ (say), are much easier to compute. Even though this approach is less accurate, it is computationally less involving and admits an interesting financial interpretation.

Let us assume that the observable process represents asset prices. By definition, $\hat{F}_t$ is the best affine approximation of the factor F_t based on Y_t. It can be written

$$\hat{F}_t = \hat{\alpha} + \hat{A}Y_t, \tag{9.15}$$

where α and A minimizes

$$(\hat{\alpha},\hat{A}) = \text{Arg} \min_{\alpha,A} E(F_t - \alpha - AY_t)^2. \tag{9.16}$$

Therefore, we get

$$\hat{F}_t = EF_t - \text{Cov}(F_t,Y_t)(VY_t)^{-1}(Y_t - EY_t)$$
$$= E(F_t) - BV(F_t)[B(V(F_t)B' + \Omega]^{-1}[Y_t - BE(F_t)]. \tag{9.17}$$

Any component of the approximation $\hat{F}_t$ is an affine function of Y_t and can be interpreted as a value of a portfolio that contains the risk-free asset (due to the constant term). Therefore, in a first step, we can assign to each factor its mimicking portfolio and next obtain information on the dynamics of the factor by examining the dynamics of the associated portfolio value.

9.2.4   *White Noise Directions and Codependence*

White Noise Directions

Although the conditional moments $E[Y_t|I_{t-1}]$ and $V[Y_t|I_{t-1}]$ are difficult to derive explicitly, they admit a particular structure, which may provide information on the number of factors and on the matrix B. Indeed, let us consider a vector c belonging to the kernel of B': $B'c = 0 \Leftrightarrow c'B = 0$. We apply a linear transformation to the factor model by premultiplying both its sides by c transpose. We get

$$c'Y_t = c'BF_t + c'u_t = c'u_t.$$

We deduce that the combinations $c'Y_t$ are such that

$$E(c'Y_t|J_{t-1}) = E(c'Y_t|I_{t-1}) = 0,$$

$$V(c'Y_t|J_{t-1}) = V(c'Y_t|I_{t-1}) = c'\Omega c.$$

$(c'Y_t)$ is a conditionally homoscedastic martingale difference sequence. Therefore, since these combinations are unrelated to the past, they allow identification of

- the kernel of B' or, equivalently, the range of B (since $\text{Ker}(B') = [\text{Range } B]^{\perp}$),
- the number of independent factors equal to n minus the dimension of $\text{Ker}(B')$.

Such combinations are called *white noise directions*. They do not depend on the factor.

We use the following example of a vector moving average (VMA) to explain how white noise directions can be determined in practice. A pure VMA process is a simple factor model with unobservable factors. The observable series is defined by

$$Y_t = \varepsilon_t + \Theta_1\varepsilon_{t-1} + \ldots + \Theta_q\varepsilon_{t-q}, \tag{9.18}$$

where $\Theta_q \neq 0$, and q is the moving average order. The unobservable factors consist of present and past innovations $F_t = [\varepsilon'_{t-1}, \ldots, \varepsilon'_{t-q}]'$. The white noise directions are such that

$$\begin{aligned} c'Y_t &= c'\varepsilon_t + c'\Theta_1\varepsilon_{t-1} + \ldots + c'\Theta_q\varepsilon_{t-q} \\ &= c'\varepsilon_t. \end{aligned}$$

Equivalently, they satisfy $c'\Theta_1 = \ldots = c'\Theta_q = 0$. However, since the estimation of moving average coefficients is technically involved [numerical maximum likelihood (ML) optimization is required], it is preferable to consider an equivalent condition based on the autocovariance function:

$$c'\Gamma(1) = \ldots = c'\Gamma(q) = 0$$
$$\Leftrightarrow c'[\Gamma(1)\Gamma(0)^{-2}\Gamma(1)' + \ldots + \Gamma(q)\Gamma(0)^{-2}\Gamma(q)']c = 0 \qquad (9.19)$$
$$\Leftrightarrow c \text{ belongs to Ker } [\Gamma(1)\Gamma(0)^{-2}\Gamma(1)' + \ldots + \Gamma(q)\Gamma(0)^{-2}\Gamma(q)'].$$

To obtain the first equivalence, we observe that the terms $c'\Gamma(h)\Gamma(0)^{-2}$ $\Gamma'(h)c$ are nonnegative and are equal to 0 if and only if $\Gamma(0)^{-1}\Gamma(h)'c = 0 \Leftrightarrow$ $\Gamma(h)'c = 0$. The matrix $\Gamma(0)^{-1}$ is used for normalization.

The last autocovariance-based condition suggests an estimation method for the dimension of the factor space and the space of white noise directions. The procedure consists of the following three steps:

1. Replace the theoretical autocovariances by their empirical counterparts and compute the matrix:

$$\hat{A} = \hat{\Gamma}(1)\hat{\Gamma}(0)^{-2}\hat{\Gamma}(1)' + \ldots + \hat{\Gamma}(q)\hat{\Gamma}(0)^{-2}\hat{\Gamma}(q)'.$$

2. Perform a spectral decomposition of the matrix $\hat{A}$. Let us denote by $\hat{\lambda}_1 \geq \hat{\lambda}_2 \geq \ldots \geq \hat{\lambda}_n$ the eigenvalues ranked in descending order. The estimator of K corresponds to the first-order k at which the eigenvalues become statistically nonsignificant or that corresponds to a cutoff point in the sequence of eigenvalues.
3. The space of white noise directions is generated by eigenvectors associated with the nonsignificant eigenvalues $\hat{\lambda}_{K+1}, \ldots, \hat{\lambda}_n$.

Codependence
The previous approach can be extended to reveal the differences between univariate moving average orders in a VMA process. Indeed, let us consider the process defined by

$$\begin{cases} Y_{1,t} = \varepsilon_{1,t} + 2\varepsilon_{2,t-1}, \\ Y_{2,t} = \varepsilon_{2,t}, \\ Y_{3,t} = \varepsilon_{3,t} + \varepsilon_{2,t-1} + 0.5\varepsilon_{3,t-3}. \end{cases}$$

This process admits a VMA representation of order 3, but clearly $Y_{1,t} = (1,0,0)Y_t$ has a MA(1) representation, whereas $Y_{2,t} = (0,1,0)Y_t$ is a white noise direction. Intuitively, the moving average orders are not equal in all directions; therefore, the vector moving average representation has orders $(3,1,0)$. More precisely, it is possible to define the multivariate order $q_1 \leq q_2 \ldots \leq q_n = q$ of a VMA process by the following method (see Gourieroux and Peaucelle 1992; Vahid and Engle 1997).

Let us consider the matrices

$$A_h = \Gamma(h+1)\Gamma(0)^{-2}\Gamma(h+1)' + \ldots + \Gamma(q)\Gamma(0)^{-2}\Gamma(q)',$$

$$h = 1, \ldots, q-1. \tag{9.20}$$

We obtain a decreasing sequence of nonnegative symmetric matrices. Therefore, the spaces $E_h = \mathrm{Ker} A_h$, $h = 1, \ldots, q-1$ form an increasing sequence of vector spaces. Moreover, c belongs to E_h if and only if $c'\Gamma(h+1) = \ldots = c'\Gamma(q) = 0$, that is, the linear combination $c'Y_t$ has a moving average representation of order less or equal to h.

Let us denote by q_j, $j = 1, \ldots, J$, the increasing sequence of indexes such that $E_q \neq E_{q-1}$; assume by convention that $E_{-1} = \{0\}$; and denote by n_j, $j = 1, \ldots, J$, the differences between dimensions $n_j = dim E_{q_j} - dim E_{q_{j-1}}$. Then, the process admits a moving average representation of a multivariate order: $\underbrace{q_1, \ldots, q_1}_{n_1}$ $\underbrace{q_2, \ldots, q_2}_{n_2}, \ldots, \underbrace{q_J, \ldots, q_J}_{n_J}$.

In practice, the analysis of multivariate moving average orders is performed for the following purpose. Let us assume that q_J is rather large, whereas q_1 is small and close to 0, and let us denote by c the direction associated with the order q_1. The linear combination $c'Y_t$ responds to a transitory shock only during a very short time since the multiplier effect vanishes after the lag $q_1 + 1$, whereas the shock has an effect for q_J lags on each component. Therefore, temporary shocks to $c'Y_t$ are short lived, and $c'Y_t$ defines a stable relation between the variables called the *codependence direction*.

To conclude the discussion, let us point out that codependence directions of stationary time series are the analogues of cointegration directions of nonstationary time series. This technique is used for exhibiting stable relations of stationary series such as the relative purchasing power parity, which implies that a relative increment of an exchange rate between two currencies is approximately equal to the difference between inflation rates of the two countries.

9.3 Nonlinear Factor Models

9.3.1 *The Measurement and Transition Equations*

These models are generally defined by a state-space representation involving nonlinear measurement and transition equations.

The *measurement equation* explains how the variables of interest depend on lagged values of the process, unobservable factors, and an additional strong white noise. Typically, this equation is

$$Y_t = a(F_t, Y_{t-1}, u_t; \theta), \tag{9.21}$$

where the (multivariate) error term (u_t) is assumed to be i.i.d. with a known distribution.

The *transition equation* describes the factor dynamics

$$F_t = b(F_{t-1}, \varepsilon_t; \theta), \tag{9.22}$$

where (ε_t) is a strong white noise with known distribution and is independent of (u_t). The functions a and b are known up to a parameter θ.

The system (9.21) and (9.22) implicitly assumes that, except for the effect of Y_{t-1}, the entire dynamics is completely determined by the current factor F_t. It is easy to check that the system can be alternatively represented in terms of conditional distributions.

The measurement equation specifies the conditional distribution of Y_t given $\underline{F_t}, \underline{Y_{t-1}}$, which depends on the past through F_t, Y_{t-1} only:

$$l(y_t | \underline{f_t}, \underline{y_{t-1}}) = g(y_t | f_t, y_{t-1}; \theta). \tag{9.23}$$

The transition equation specifies the conditional distribution of F_t given $\underline{F_{t-1}}, \underline{Y_{t-1}}$, which depends on the past through F_{t-1} only:

$$l(f_t | \underline{f_{t-1}}, \underline{y_{t-1}}) = \pi(f_t | f_{t-1}; \theta). \tag{9.24}$$

From these conditional distributions, we deduce

$$l(y_t, f_t | \underline{f_{t-1}}, \underline{y_{t-1}})$$
$$= l(y_t | \underline{f_t}, \underline{y_{t-1}}) \, l(f_t | \underline{f_{t-1}}, \underline{y_{t-1}})$$
$$= g(y_t | f_t, y_{t-1}; \theta) \, \pi(f_t | f_{t-1}; \theta),$$

and recursively find the distribution of the bivariate process (Y_t, F_t).

EXAMPLE 9.2, STOCHASTIC MEAN AND VOLATILITY MODEL: Let (y_t) be the return series of a financial asset. The stochastic mean and volatility "parameters" m_t and σ_t can be introduced into the return equation

$$y_t = m_t + \sigma_t u_t,$$

where (u_t) is independent identically $N(0,1)$ distributed ($IIN(0, 1)$). As well, we can impose a dynamic structure of the stochastic parameters m_t and σ_t, such as

$$\begin{pmatrix} m_t \\ \log \sigma_t \end{pmatrix} = \begin{pmatrix} a_1 \\ a_2 \end{pmatrix} + \Phi \begin{pmatrix} m_{t-1} \\ \log \sigma_{t-1} \end{pmatrix} + \Omega^{1/2} \varepsilon_t,$$

where (ε_t) is $IIN(0, Id)$. This specification extends the stochastic volatility model with $m_t = 0$ (see Section 6.3). This is a factor representation, where the factor components $F_t = (m_t, \sigma_t)'$ have straightforward financial interpretations. Moreover, the transition equation allows us to study various effects, such as the impact of log σ_{t-1} on m_t reflected by the coefficient φ_{12} or the effect of log σ_t on m_t reflected by the off-diagonal elements of $\Omega^{1/2}$. These effects are ARCH-M effects, which can be interpreted as risk premia and examined at various lags. Finally, note that the parameters a, Φ, and Ω appear in the transition equation only. The conditional distribution of Y_t given F_t, that is, measurement equation (9.23), corresponds to a normal distribution $N(m_t,\sigma_t^2)$, while the conditional distribution of F_t given F_{t-1}, that is, transition equation (9.24), is immediately deduced from a Gaussian autoregressive model by a logarithmic transformation of the volatility component.

EXAMPLE 9.3, SWITCHING REGIMES: Alternatively, the conditional mean and volatility can follow switching regime processes. As an illustration, let us consider a two-regime process. The transition equation is

$$y_t = m_0(1 - Z_t) + m_1 Z_t + [\sigma_0(1 - Z_t) + \sigma_1 Z_t]u_t,$$

where (u_t) is a standardized Gaussian white noise. The factor $F_t = Z_t$ is a qualitative process admitting the values 0 and 1. It follows a Markov chain (see Chapter 10) with transition probabilities $p_{ij} = P[Z_t = i | Z_{t-1} = j]$. This model includes two types of parameters: the transition probabilities describing the regime dynamics and the means and variances pertaining to the two regimes.

9.3.2   Filtering

The nonlinear factor model is defined by the measurement equation $l(y_t|f_t,\underline{y_{t-1}}) = g(y_t|f_t,\underline{y_{t-1}};\theta)$ and the transition equation $l(f_t|\underline{f_{t-1}},\underline{y_{t-1}}) = \pi(f_t|\underline{f_{t-1}};\theta)$. These conditional distributions suggest that the variables Y_t and F_t could potentially be predicted from the information sets $(\underline{F_t},\underline{Y_{t-1}})$ and $(\underline{F_{t-1}},\underline{Y_{t-1}})$, respectively. However, such predictions are not feasible since factors are not observed, although it is possible to build in-sample predictions based on the information limited to past Y_t's. In this section, we explain how the conditional distributions can be determined in practice given available information on lagged values of (Y_t) only. Two aspects have to be distinguished: (1) the prediction of the endogenous variable, that is, the determination of the conditional distribution $l(y_t|\underline{y_{t-1}})$; and (2) the prediction of the factor, that is, the determination of the conditional distribution $p(f_t|\underline{y_t})$. These predictions are computed iteratively following the two-step algorithm outlined below. At each iteration step t, the input is the predictive distribution of the factor $p(f_t|\underline{y_t})$.

1. Compute the conditional distribution $l(y_{t+1}, f_{t+1}|\underline{y_t})$.
    We get

$$l\left(y_{t+1}, f_{t+1} \mid \underline{y_t}\right)$$

$$= \int l\left(y_{t+1}, f_{t+1} \mid f_t, \underline{y_t}\right) p\left(df_t \mid \underline{y_t}\right)$$

$$= \int l\left(y_{t+1} \mid f_{t+1}, f_t, \underline{y_t}\right) l\left(f_{t+1} \mid f_t, \underline{y_t}\right) p\left(df_t \mid \underline{y_t}\right) \qquad (9.25)$$

$$= \int l\left(y_{t+1} \mid f_{t+1}, \underline{y_t}\right) l\left(f_{t+1} \mid f_t\right) p\left(df_t \mid \underline{y_t}\right)$$

$$= \int g\left(y_{t+1} \mid f_{t+1}, y_t; \theta\right) \pi\left(f_{t+1} \mid f_t; \theta\right) p\left(df_t \mid \underline{y_t}\right).$$

2. We deduce $p\left(f_{t+1} \mid \underline{y_{t+1}}\right)$ and $l\left(y_{t+1} \mid \underline{y_t}\right)$ by integrating out the conditioning variables in (9.25). Consequently, we obtain

$$l\left(y_{t+1} \mid \underline{y_t}\right) = \int l\left(y_{t+1}, df_{t+1} \mid \underline{y_t}\right), \qquad (9.26)$$

and

$$p\left(f_{t+1} \mid \underline{y_{t+1}}\right) = \frac{l(y_{t+1}, f_{t+1} \mid \underline{y_t})}{l(y_{t+1} \mid \underline{y_t})}. \qquad (9.27)$$

The conditional distributions $l\left(y_t \mid \underline{y_{t-1}}\right)$ and $p\left(f_t \mid \underline{y_t}\right)$, t varying, derived from this iterative procedure depend on the forms of distributions g and π and especially on the value of the parameter θ. Unfortunately, the algorithm in (9.25), (9.26), and (9.27) is, in general, not tractable. The reason for this is that, at each date t, it is necessary to integrate (9.25) with respect to all admissible values of the unobservable factor f_{t+1}. Therefore, the algorithm requires computation of an infinite number of K-dimensional integrals, which is not feasible. The good news is that, in some special cases, the algorithm simplifies.

EXAMPLE 9.4, KITAGAWA'S ALGORITHM (Kitagawa 1987; Hamilton 1989, 1990). When the factor takes values from a finite state space, the integral in (9.25) is replaced by a sum and has to be computed a finite number of times only. This case is known in the literature as the *Kitagawa's filter*. For illustration, let us assume that the factor F_t is a binary process (Z_t) with values 0 and 1. Equations (9.25) become

$$l\left(y_{t+1}, 1 \mid \underline{y_t}\right) = g\left(y_{t+1} \mid 1, y_t; \theta\right) \left[\pi(1 \mid 0; \theta) p(0 \mid \underline{y_t}) + \pi(1 \mid 1; \theta) p(1 \mid \underline{y_t})\right],$$

$$l\left(y_{t+1}, 0 \mid \underline{y_t}\right) = g\left(y_{t+1} \mid 0, y_t; \theta\right) \left[\pi(0 \mid 0; \theta) p(0 \mid \underline{y_t}) + \pi(0 \mid 1; \theta) p(0 \mid \underline{y_t})\right].$$

Thus, formula (9.27) is reduced to

$$p\left(1 \mid \underline{y_{t+1}}\right) = \frac{l\left(y_{t+1}, 1 \mid \underline{y_t}\right)}{l\left(y_{t+1}, 1 \mid \underline{y_t}\right) + l\left(y_{t+1}, 0 \mid \underline{y_t}\right)}.$$

EXAMPLE 9.5, KALMAN FILTER: The general algorithm can also be simplified whenever the processes (Y_t, F_t) are jointly Gaussian. In such a case, the updating of the predictive distributions can be replaced by the updating of the conditional mean and conditional variance only. The corresponding updating formulas were initially derived by Kalman (1960) and Kalman and Bucy (1961), and interested readers can find them, for instance, in Harvey (1989) or Gourieroux and Monfort (1997).

EXAMPLE 9.6, MARKOV FACTORS WITH FINITE-DIMENSIONAL DEPENDENCE: A tractable algorithm may also be derived when the factor follows a Markov process with nonlinear predictions that depend on a finite number of path summaries. These processes are described in Section 9.4, and the corresponding algorithm is given in Gourieroux and Jasiak (2000a).

9.3.3 Estimation

Common estimation methods require a fully parametric specification of the factor model when either the measurement equation or the transition equation feature nonlinear dynamics.

Maximum Likelihood Method
The estimator $\hat{\theta}$ is obtained by maximizing the observable log-likelihood function

$$\hat{\theta} = \text{Arg} \min_{\theta} \sum_{t=1}^{T} \log l(y_t | \underline{y_{t-1}}; \theta), \tag{9.28}$$

where the values of the lagged endogenous variables prior to the sampling period, that is, y_t, $t < 0$, are set equal to the sample average of y_t. The estimate $\hat{\theta}$ is computed numerically whenever the components of the log-likelihood $\log l(y_t | \underline{y_{t-1}}; \theta)$ can be evaluated from the observed values and for any parameter value. Therefore, the ML approach can be used to estimate discrete factor models requiring a Kitagawa's filter, for Gaussian processes requiring a Kalman filter, or for factors with finite-dimensional dependence. Nevertheless, in some other cases, it is still possible to approximate numerically the log-likelihood function, for instance, using the particle algorithm (see, e.g., Carpenter et al. 1996; Shepard and Pitt 1997).

Simulation-Based Methods
Despite the complexity of the dynamics, nonlinear factor models are easy to simulate. More precisely, a simulated path of (Y_t) can be generated from simulations of white noises whenever their distributions are specified in the model. Let us denote by u_t^i, $t = 1, \ldots, J$, and ε_t^i, $t = 1, \ldots, T$ the simulated noise paths. For an initial vector of parameter values, the simulated observations of the endogenous process and the factors are given by

$$Y_t^S(\theta) = a\left[F_t^S(\theta), Y_{t-1}^S(\theta), u_t^S; \theta\right],$$

$$F_t^S(\theta) = b\left[F_{t-1}^S(\theta), \varepsilon_t^S; \theta\right], \qquad t = 1, \dots, T.$$

Then, we search for a value of θ that ensures similar distributional properties of the simulated and the observed paths. The estimation criterion can concern some selected moments (see Duffie and Singleton 1993; Gourieroux and Monfort 1996, Chap. 2) or else can rely on an auxiliary model, as in the indirect inference method (see Gourieroux and Monfort 1996, Chap. 4; and Section 12.5 of the present book).

9.4 Markov Models with Finite-Dimensional Dependence

Another extension of the linear factor model proposed in the literature (see Gourieroux and Jasiak 2000a), is based on the analysis of finite-dimensional predictor spaces.

In a linear framework, the prediction formula in (9.13) implies that any predictor of a linear combination $c'Y_t$ can be computed from a reduced number of summary statistics of the history of the process, which consist of the components of $E[m(F_{t-1}; \theta) | I_{t-1}]$. In this section, we characterize the processes for which predictions of any nonlinear transformation of their current and future values depend on a finite number of summary statistics. This property is especially useful for derivative pricing, for which the price is the expectation of the discounted future cash flows. As a consequence, the derivative price depends on the past asset price in terms of a finite number of summary statistics independently of the cash flow patterns. For convenience, we consider a Markov process of order 1. In the first section, we introduce the nonlinear canonical decomposition of the joint distribution of (Y_t, Y_{t-1}), which is used in the second section to derive the factor model.

9.4.1 Nonlinear Canonical Decomposition

Let us consider a strong stationary process with the marginal probability density function (pdf) denoted $f(y_t)$ and joint bivariate pdf $f(y_t, y_{t-1})$. The joint distribution can be decomposed in the following way (Lancaster 1968).

PROPOSITION 9.2: *If* $\int\int \left[\dfrac{f(y_t, y_{t-1})}{f(y_t)f(y_{t-1})}\right]^2 f(y_t)f(y_{t-1})dy_t dy_{t-1} < \infty$, *the joint pdf can be written as*

$$f(y_t, y_{t-1}) = f(y_t)f(y_{t-1})\left\{1 + \sum_{j=1}^{\infty} \lambda_j \varphi_j(y_t)\psi_j(y_{t-1})\right\},$$

where the scalars λ_j, *j varying, are nonnegative, and the functions* φ_j *and* ψ_j *are such that*

$$E\varphi_j(Y) = E\psi_j(Y) = 0, \ \forall j,$$

$$V\varphi_j(Y) = V\psi_j(Y) = 1, \ \forall j,$$

$$cov[\varphi_j(Y),\varphi_k(Y)] = Cov[\psi_j(Y),\psi_k(Y)] = 0, \ \forall j \neq k.$$

The decomposition given in Proposition 9.2 is called *nonlinear canonical decomposition*. Accordingly, the scalars λ_j are called *canonical correlations*, whereas φ_j and ψ_j are the current and lagged *canonical directions*, respectively. This terminology results from the following interpretation. Let us arrange the canonical correlations in descending order $\lambda_1 \geq \lambda_2 \geq \ldots$ and consider the optimization problem

$$\max_{\varphi,\psi} \mathrm{Corr}[\varphi(Y_t),\psi(Y_{t-1})]. \tag{9.29}$$

The method consists of finding a pair of nonlinear functions of the current value Y_t and the lagged one Y_{t-1} that are the most correlated ones. It extends the linear canonical analysis (see Section 9.1.2), for which the transformations are linear functions. As solutions to this problem, we obtain nonlinear functions φ_1 and ψ_1, whereas the objective function is equal to λ_1 at the optimum. This approach can be pursued to find the following terms of the canonical decomposition: In the second step, we search for the second most correlated pair and solve

$$\max_{\varphi,\psi} \mathrm{Corr}[\varphi(Y_t),\psi(Y_{t-1})] \tag{9.30}$$

$$\text{subject to: } \mathrm{Cov}[\varphi(Y),\varphi_1(Y)] = \mathrm{Cov}[\psi(Y),\psi_1(Y)] = 0. \tag{9.31}$$

The solutions are functions φ_2 and ψ_2, whereas the objective function is equal to λ_2 at optimum. The analysis can be carried on to yield further terms of the canonical decomposition.

All temporal dependence of the series is captured by $\dfrac{f(y_t,y_{t-1})}{f(y_t)f(y_{t-1})} - 1 = \sum_{j=1}^{\infty} \lambda_j \varphi_j(y_t)\psi_j(y_{t-1})$, which is a functional measure of the difference between serial dependence and independence. It can be summarized by a scalar measure

$$E_0\left[\frac{f(Y_t, Y_{t-1})}{f(Y_t)f(Y_{t-1})}\right]^2 - 1 = \sum_{j=1}^{\infty} \lambda_j^2, \tag{9.32}$$

where E_0 indicates that the expectation is computed under the independence hypothesis.

Therefore, the amount of temporal dependence captured by the K first canonical directions can be measured by

$$\pi_K = \sum_{j=1}^{K} \lambda_j^2 \Big/ \sum_{j=1}^{\infty} \lambda_j^2.$$

There exist various nonparametric estimation methods for the terms of the nonlinear canonical decomposition. They mainly consist of replacing the unknown bivariate pdf $f(y_t, y_{t-1})$ by a nonparametric estimator $\hat{f}(y_t, y_{t-1})$ and, next, in performing the canonical decomposition of $\hat{f}(y_t, y_{t-1})$. The estimator of the bivariate pdf can be based on polynomial approximations, in the so-called sieve method (see Chen et al. 1998), or on kernel smoothing of the empirical distribution (see Darolles et al. 1998).

9.4.2   Finite-Dimensional Predictor Space

Let us consider a Markov process with a finite number K of nonzero canonical correlations. We get

$$f(y_t, y_{t-1}) = f(y_t)f(y_{t-1})\left[1 + \sum_{j=1}^{K} \lambda_j \varphi_j(y_t)\psi_j(y_{t-1})\right], \qquad (9.33)$$

$$f(y_t|y_{t-1}) = \frac{f(y_t, y_{t-1})}{f(y_{t-1})} = f(y_t)\left[1 + \sum_{j=1}^{K} \lambda_j \varphi_j(y_t)\psi_j(y_{t-1})\right]. \qquad (9.34)$$

Therefore, for any nonlinear function g, we have

$$E[g(Y_t)|Y_{t-1}] = \int g(y_t)f(y_t)\left[1 + \Sigma_{j=1}^{K} \varphi_j(y_t)\psi_j(y_{t-1})\right] dy_{t-1}$$

$$= Eg(Y_t) + \Sigma_{j=1}^{K} \lambda_j \, \mathrm{Cov}[g(Y_t), \varphi_j(Y_t)]\psi_j(Y_{t-1}).$$

These predictions are all linear combinations of the $K+1$ summary statistics $1, \psi_j(Y_{t-1}), j = 1, \ldots, K$. We extend this result to a more general proposition (Gourieroux and Jasiak 2000a).

PROPOSITION 9.3: *The predictor space, including all predictors of future paths, that is, $E(g(Y_{t+1}, \ldots, Y_{t+H})|Y_t)$, H and g varying, has a finite dimension if and only if the canonical decomposition admits a finite number of nonzero canonical correlations. Then, the predictor space is generated by $1, \psi_j(Y_t), j = 1, \ldots, K$.*

Note that model (9.33) with finite-dimensional canonical decomposition is a special case of a nonlinear factor model (see Section 9.3) for which the factors $1, \psi_j(Y_t), j = 1, \ldots, K$ are deterministic nonlinear functions of the endogenous process.

9.5   Cross-Sectional Factors

The success of factor models in finance is largely due to the idea that risk can be eliminated by choosing an appropriate portfolio allocation (see the arbitrage pricing theory, [APT] below). More precisely, the effect of the limited number of factors can be eliminated by considering only port-folios that are not sensitive with respect to shocks to the factors, whereas the residual (the idiosyncratic) risk can be eliminated by holding a large number of assets in the portfolio. However, it is very unwise to let an investor believe that there exist perfect arbitrage opportunities on the markets. The aim of this section is to discuss the restrictive (and unrealis-tic) hypotheses necessary for the existence of such opportunities.

9.5.1 *The Model*

Let us return to the linear factor model with observable or unobservable factors:

$$Y_t = BF_t + u_t, \tag{9.35}$$

where $E[u_t|\underline{Y}_{t-1},\underline{F}_t] = 0$, $V[u_t|\underline{Y}_{t-1},\underline{F}_t] = \Omega$. The factors are supposed to capture the whole dynamics of the endogenous series and represent all common dynamic patterns of the Y_t components. However, the components of Y may still be linked through the nonzero autocovariances of the error terms in (9.35). In general, an analysis of such relationships that combines both dynamic and cross-sectional aspects is quite complex. To simplify the task, we impose a structure on the residuals by decomposing the residual variance Ω so that

$$\Omega = \text{diag}(\sigma_j^2) + \Omega^*, \tag{9.36}$$

where Ω^* is a nonnegative symmetric matrix, and $\text{diag}(\sigma_j^2)$ a diagonal matrix as large as possible. Then, if rank $\Omega^* = J$, we can write a spectral decompo-sition of Ω^*:

$$\Omega^* = \sum_{j=1}^{J} \mu_j \gamma_j \gamma_j', \quad \text{(say)},$$

to get

$$\Omega = \text{diag}(\sigma_j^2) + \sum_{j=1}^{J} \mu_j \gamma_j \gamma_j', \tag{9.37}$$

where $\mu_j > 0$, $\forall j$, and γ_j, $j = 1, \ldots, J$, are n-dimensional vectors. Hence, the initial model can also be written as

$$Y_t = BF_t + \sum_{j=1}^{J} \gamma_j v_{j,t} + u_t^*, \tag{9.38}$$

where the components of the error terms, that is, $v_{j,t}$, $j = 1, \ldots, J$, u_t^* are conditionally zero mean, uncorrelated, with variance:

$$V[v_{j,t}|\underline{Y}_{t-1},\underline{F}_t] = \mu_j, \quad j \text{ varying},$$

$$V[u_t^*|\underline{Y}_{t-1},\underline{F}_t] = \text{diag}(\sigma_j^2).$$

The factor decomposition (9.38) separates the dynamic factors F_t from the cross-sectional factors $v_{1,t}, \ldots, v_{J,t}$. By collecting the dynamic and cross-sectional factors, we get

$$Y_t = B^* F_t^* + u_t^*, \tag{9.39}$$

where the number of factors is $K + J$, and u_t^* is an error term with a diagonal conditional variance-covariance matrix. The factor model in (9.38) and (9.39) extends the standard arbitrage pricing theory (APT) model, for which the dynamic factors (F_t) are omitted.

9.5.2 Diversification and the Arbitrage Pricing Theory

We now discuss financial applications of the model, including both dynamic and cross-sectional factors, with relative price changes

$$Y_{i,t} = (p_{i,t} - p_{i,t-1})/p_{i,t-1}, \qquad i = 1, \ldots, n$$

as the endogenous process. The initial concept of the APT was introduced by Ross (1976) and later refined by Huberman (1982), Chamberlain (1983), Chamberlain and Rothschild (1983), Chen and Ingersoll (1983), and Ingersoll (1984). Depending on the assumptions on the residual error term u_t^*, the APT model either involves (1) the exact or (2) the approximate condition of no arbitrage.

Residual Error Term Equal to Zero
When one factor represents a constant term, the factor model becomes

$$Y_t = a + \tilde{B}\tilde{F}_t.$$

Consider a portfolio of budget shares c, where $c'e = \Sigma_{i=1}^{n} c_i = 1$, and e denotes the vector of ones. If c belongs to $\text{Ker}\tilde{B}'$, the portfolio return is equal to $c'Y_t = c'a$ and is predetermined. Therefore, this portfolio defines a risk-free asset. By the absence of arbitrage condition, two risk-free assets produce necessarily equal returns. We deduce that

$$\forall c \text{ subject to } c'e = 1, \qquad c \in \text{Ker}\tilde{B}', \qquad \text{then } c'a = r_f,$$

where r_f is the risk-free rate.
    In particular, we find

$$\tilde{B}'c = 0 \Rightarrow c'(a - r_f e) = 0. \tag{9.40}$$

We can now apply *Farka's lemma*:

PROPOSITION 9.4: *Let us consider linear forms $a_1, \ldots, a_K, b$ such that*

$$\forall c : a_1'c = \ldots = a_K'c = 0 \Rightarrow b'c = 0,$$

then b is a linear combination of $a_1, \ldots, a_K$.

PROPOSITION 9.5: *The expected excess returns are linear combinations of betas associated with factors.*

Analytically, if $\beta_k, k = 1, \ldots, K$ denote the columns of $\tilde{B}$, there exist scalars $\gamma_1, \ldots, \gamma_K$ such that

$$a_i - r_f = E\left(\frac{p_{i,t} - p_{i,t-1}}{p_{i,t-1}}\right) - r_f = \sum_{k=1}^{K} \beta_{i,k}\gamma_k, \qquad i = 1, \ldots, n.$$

Loosely speaking, each asset can be considered as a "portfolio" of factors, which are priced by the multipliers $\gamma_k, k = 1, \ldots, K$.

Homoscedastic Residual Error Term

The assumption of zero residual term implies deterministic linear relationships between the returns on financial assets. This condition is not compatible with empirical findings. To circumvent this difficulty, a theory has been developed involving a large number n of assets (see, e.g., Chamberlain and Rothschild 1983). The idea is to eliminate the residual risk by portfolio diversification. More precisely, we assume that the linear factor model holds for an infinite number of assets:

$$Y_{i,t} = a_i + \sum_{k=1}^{K} \beta_{ik}\tilde{F}_{k,t} + u^*_{i,t}, \qquad i = 1, 2, \ldots$$

with conditionally homoscedastic residual errors $V(u^*_{i,t}|F_t, Y_{t-1}) = \sigma^2$.

Then, let us consider a portfolio of the n first assets with equal budget shares. Its return is

$$\frac{1}{n}\sum_{i=1}^{n} Y_{i,t} = \frac{1}{n}\sum_{i=1}^{n} a_i + \sum_{k=1}^{K}\left(\frac{1}{n}\sum_{i=1}^{n}\beta_{i,t}\right)\tilde{F}_{k,t} + \frac{1}{n}\sum_{i=1}^{n} u^*_{i,t}.$$

The variance of the error term is equal to σ^2/n. Therefore, if n tends to infinity, this diversified portfolio features no residual risk.

More generally, a diversified portfolio is defined by budget shares $\alpha_{i,n} \sim \alpha_i/n$ (say), where $\frac{1}{n}\Sigma_{i=1}^{n} \alpha_i \to 1$ for large n.

The return on the portfolio of n assets is

$$\frac{1}{n}\sum_{i=1}^{n} \alpha_i Y_{i,t} = \frac{1}{n}\sum_{i=1}^{n} \alpha_i a_i + \sum_{k=1}^{K}\left(\frac{1}{n}\sum_{i=1}^{n}\alpha_i\beta_{i,k}\right)\tilde{F}_{k,t} + \frac{1}{n}\sum_{i=1}^{n}\alpha_i u^*_{i,t}.$$

Let us assume the existence of the following limits of the empirical moments:

$$\frac{1}{n} \Sigma_{i=1}^{n} \alpha_i a_i \to E(\alpha a),$$

$$\frac{1}{n} \Sigma_{i=1}^{n} \alpha_i \beta_{i,k} \to E(\alpha \beta_k), \qquad k = 1, \ldots, K,$$

$$\left(\frac{1}{n^2} \Sigma_{i=1}^{n} \alpha_i^2\right) \sigma^2 \to 0.$$

Consequently, when n tends to infinity, the return on the limiting portfolio is $E(\alpha a) + \Sigma_{k=1}^{K} E(\alpha \beta_k) \tilde{F}_{k,t}$. The absence of arbitrage argument can be applied to this limiting portfolio. If the allocations are selected such that $E(\alpha \beta_k) = 0$, $\forall k = 1, \ldots, K$, the portfolio is risk free, and its return is equal to r_f: $E(\alpha a) = r_f$. We get a condition

$$E(\alpha \beta_k) = 0, \qquad \forall k = 1, \ldots, K \Rightarrow E[\alpha(a - r_f)] = 0,$$

similar to the condition used in Proposition 9.5.

However, in practice, the assumptions of this limiting APT are not satisfied. First, the assets in a portfolio are not randomly selected, but rather are selected with respect to a criterion of decreasing liquidity. This may induce a lack of convergence of the empirical moments. Second, the number of underlying factors K increases with n and does not seem to tend to a finite value.

9.6 Summary

The term *factor* is widely employed in finance and statistics. However, this terminology may refer to different concepts. Especially in methods such as singular value decomposition, principal component analysis, and state-space models, the term *factor* is unrelated to financial concepts. As well, factor models in finance commonly appear in a static setup, although dynamic factor models seem more adequate. The limited number of factors included in a model is often interpreted as a limitation that creates arbitrage opportunities. Instead, it should be viewed from the perspective of portfolio management based on a small number of well-chosen mutual funds.

In this chapter, we reviewed various concepts of factors that appear in financial applications and discussed the estimation of factor models. The estimation methods include linear and nonlinear canonical analysis, the Kalman filter, and the Kitagawa filter. In particular, we distinguished the observable and unobservable factors and the static and dynamic factors. They may appear in linear or nonlinear specifications. In particular, to the class of dynamic factor models with a single unobservable factor belongs the stochastic volatility model introduced in Chapter 6. Also, in

Chapter 6 we saw the multivariate ARCH model, which is cumbersome in empirical research due to its lack of parsimony. Instead, the volatility of a set of assets can be modeled in the more convenient framework of an ARCH factor model introduced in Section 9.2.

Appendix 9.1: Joint Spectral Decomposition of BB' and $B'B$

To simplify the presentation, we assume that B is a square matrix (n, n).

Spectral Analysis of BB'
The matrix BB' is a symmetric matrix. It is nonnegative since for any vector c: $c'BB'c = \|B'c\|^2 \geq 0$. Therefore, it may be diagonalized with nonnegative eigenvalues μ_j^2, $j = 1, \ldots, n$, and orthonormal eigenvectors b_j, $j = 1$, $\ldots, n$. We have

$$BB'b_j = \mu_j^2 b_j, \qquad j = 1, \ldots, n.$$

Spectral Analysis of $B'B$
We have $B'BB'b_j = \mu_j^2 B'b_j$. Therefore, $a_j = \dfrac{1}{\mu_j}B'b_j$ is an eigenvector of $B'B$ associated with the eigenvalues μ_j^2. Moreover, these eigenvectors are orthonormal since

$$
\begin{aligned}
a_j'a_k &= \frac{1}{\mu_j\mu_k}b_j'BB'b_k \\
&= \frac{\mu_j\mu_k}{\mu_j\mu_k}b_j'b_k \\
&= \begin{cases} 0, & \text{if } j \neq k, \\ 1, & \text{otherwise.} \end{cases}
\end{aligned}
$$

Decomposition of B
It can be proved that

$$B = \sum_{j=1}^{n} \mu_j b_j a_j'.$$

Rank Condition

(i) Let us assume that Rank $B = K$. It is known that Rank $(B) =$ Rank (BB'). Therefore, the number of nonzero eigenvalues is K, and we can write

$$
\begin{aligned}
B &= \Sigma_{j=1}^{K}\, \mu_j b_j a_j' \\
&= \Sigma_{j=1}^{K}\, \beta_j \alpha_j',
\end{aligned}
$$

where $\beta_j = \mu_j b_j$ and $\alpha_j = a_j$. We deduce $B = \beta\alpha'$, where β and α have the same rank K.

(ii) Conversely, let us assume that $B = \beta\,\alpha'$, where β and α have rank K. We can look for the kernel of B.

We have

$$C \in KerB$$

$$\Leftrightarrow Bc = 0$$

$$\Leftrightarrow \|Bc\|^2 = 0$$

$$\Leftrightarrow c'B'Bc = 0$$

$$\Leftrightarrow c'\alpha\beta'\beta\alpha'c = 0.$$

Since $\beta'\beta$ is symmetric definite positive, the condition is equivalent to $\alpha'c = 0 \Leftrightarrow c \in Ker\alpha'$. Thus, the dimension of $KerB$ is $n - K$, that is, the rank of B is K.

10

Dynamic Qualitative Processes

IN THIS CHAPTER, we study qualitative processes that admit a limited number of discrete values. In social sciences, qualitative variables often arise from various surveys, in which they are used to characterize the sampled individuals. For example, the variable "gender" has two outcomes, male or female, while the variable "age" takes a continuum of values with a domain that is often divided into intervals of 10–20 years, 20–30 years, and so on. Qualitative variables also describe the behavior of individuals, such as their choice of a preferred means of transportation (a car, a bus, etc.) or a response of an individual to a question, limited to either "yes," "no," or "has no opinion," for example.

In finance, we investigate the behavior of qualitative characteristics of price and return processes in time. This analysis requires specific modeling and inference techniques, different from those introduced in previous chapters. The reason is that autoregressive moving average (ARMA) models typically assume a linear structure of time series and require inference methods applicable only to processes with conditional distributions close to the Gaussian ones. Thus, ARMA models are suitable for continuously valued quantitative variables and are not adequate for categorical or discretely valued data.

Qualitative variables are often encountered in finance. Especially, the technical analysis is a field of research in which the signs of price movements are given more attention than their size. The sign variable is dichotomous qualitative, that is, it distinguishes only two categories of movements: $Y_t = 1$ if $\Delta p_t = p_t - p_{t-1} > 0$ and $Y_t = 0$ otherwise. The dummy values 0, 1 assigned to the variable Y have no direct interpretation and serve only to classify the price movements into these two categories. The use of dummies is convenient for empirical analysis of samples that include both quantitative and qualitative data. While character strings "up" and "down" (see the binomial tree, Chapter 11) could be used instead, mixed data are technically more difficult to handle. Qualitative processes also originate from various characteristics of the trading process. Besides the types of movement classified as "up," "stable," and "down" generated by the price dynamics, each transaction entails a number of descriptive features. Indeed, we can study buyer- or seller-initiated trades, differentiate between small or large traded volumes, or identify the traders from the list of authorized dealers. Accordingly, the outcomes may be purely qualitative (dealer names), naturally ordered (transaction volumes), or else associated with numerical dummies 0,1,2 for price movements with three alternatives: "up," "stable," "down." In this case, the dummies are related to the latent quantitative variable by nonlinear transformations:

$$Y_t = \text{``up,''} \qquad \text{if } p_t > p_{t-1},$$

$$Y_t = \text{``stable,''} \qquad \text{if } p_t = p_{t-1},$$

$$Y_t = \text{``down,''} \qquad \text{if } p_t < p_{t-1}.$$

In Section 10.1, we present the basic model of a multistate qualitative process, called the *homogeneous Markov chain*. We discuss the stationarity conditions and spectral decomposition of the transition matrix and derive a linear representation of the process.

In Section 10.2, we characterize the path of the qualitative process with respect to successively occupied states and durations of these states. This approach allows us to establish a relationship between the qualitative analysis and the duration analysis. Furthermore, we discuss the choice of the timescale of reference and derive the continuous time analog of the homogeneous Markov chain, called the *multistate Poisson process.*

The probabilities of transitions between states form a transition (probability) matrix. Statistical inference on the transition matrix may be performed either by the maximum likelihood (ML) method or by the least squares applied to a linear representation of the process. These two methods are compared in Section 10.3. Finally, we explain in Section 10.4 how Markov chains are used to represent qualitative factor models. We also show examples of this type of model such as the Qualitative Threshold Autoregressive Conditionally Heteroscedastic (QTARCH) and Markov switching regimes models and discuss the state aggregation of a Markov chain.

10.1 Homogeneous Markov Chain

10.1.1 Definition

The stochastic process is defined in discrete time over a finite number of states denoted by $j, j = 1, \ldots, J$. The states may be purely qualitative, eventually ordered, or even quantitative. The assumption of a finite state space implies that the marginal or conditional probability distributions of the process are discrete and characterized by the elementary state probabilities.

We denote

$$p(t;i;\underline{y}_{t-1}) = P_t[Y_t = i \,|\, Y_{t-1} = y_{t-1}, Y_{t-2} = y_{t-2}, \ldots]$$

$$= P_t[Y_t = i \,|\, \underline{Y}_{t-1} = \underline{y}_{t-1}],$$

the conditional probability of being in state i at date t given the history of the process.

DEFINITION 10.1: *The process (Y_t) is a homogeneous Markov chain if it satisfies:*

(i) *the* Markov property*: the conditional probability depends only on the last occupied state and does not depend on the previous history of the process;*
(ii) *the* homogeneity property*: the conditional probability is time invariant.*

These two conditions imply

$$P_t[Y_t = i \,|\, \underline{Y}_{t-1} = \underline{y}_{t-1}] = P_t[Y_t = i \,|\, Y_{t-1} = y_{t-1}] \qquad \text{(Markov property)}$$

$$= P[Y_t = i \,|\, Y_{t-1} = y_{t-1}] \qquad \text{(homogeneity property)}.$$

The conditional probabilities are represented by the transition matrix. This matrix P is a square matrix of dimension $J \times J$ with a generic element:

$$p_{ij} = P[Y_t = i \,|\, Y_{t-1} = j], \tag{10.1}$$

which is the transition probability from state j to state i in one step.

From the above interpretations of the elements of the transition matrix as conditional probabilities, we infer the following proposition:

PROPOSITION 10.2: *The transition probability matrix is a* stochastic matrix, *that is, it satisfies*

(i) $p_{ij} \geq 0, \; \forall i, j;$
(ii) $\sum_{i=1}^{J} p_{ij} = 1, \; \forall j.$

The one-step transition matrix in (10.1) can be used to determine the conditional probabilities of transitions between states in more than one step. For example, let us consider a transition in h steps; we get

$$P_t[Y_{t+h-1} = i \,|\, \underline{Y}_{t-1} = \underline{y}_{t-1}]$$

$$= \sum_{i_1} \cdots \sum_{i_{h-1}} P_t[Y_{t+h-1} = i, Y_{t+h-2} = i_{h-1}, \ldots Y_t = i_1 \,|\, \underline{Y}_{t-1} = \underline{y}_{t-1}]$$

$$= \Sigma_{i_1} \cdots \Sigma_{i_{h-1}} \{P_t[Y_{t+h-1} = i \,|\, Y_{t+h-2} = i_{h-1}, \ldots, \underline{Y_{t-1} = y_{t-1}}] P_t[Y_{t+h-2} = i_{h-1} \,|\, Y_{t+h-3} = i_{h-2}, \ldots,$$

$$\underline{Y_{t-1} = y_{t-1}}] \ldots P_t[Y_t = i_1 \,|\, \underline{Y_{t-1} = y_{t-1}}]\}$$

$$= \Sigma_{i_1} \cdots \Sigma_{i_{h-1}} \{P[Y_{t+h-1} = i \,|\, Y_{t+h-2} = i_{h-1}] P[Y_{t+h-2} = i_{h-1} \,|\, Y_{t+h-3} = i_{h-2}] \ldots$$

$$P[Y_t = i_1 \,|\, Y_{t-1} = y_{t-1}]\}$$

$$= \Sigma_{i_1} \cdots \Sigma_{i_{h-1}} [p_{i,i_{h-1}} \cdots p_{i_1, y_{t-1}}].$$

PROPOSITION 10.3:

(i) *The transition probabilities* h *steps ahead depend only on the most recently occupied state out of the entire history of the process:*

$$P[Y_{t+h-1} = i \,|\, Y_{t-1} = j, Y_{t-2} = y_{t-2}, \ldots] = p_{ij}^{(h)} \qquad (\text{say}).$$

(ii) *The transition matrix in* h *steps,* $P^{(h)}$ *with elements* $p_{ij}^{(h)}$ *is equal to* $P^{(h)} = P^h$.

Therefore, the probabilities of transitions in multiple steps arise as powers of the one-step transition matrix.

10.1.2 Stationarity Conditions

For any nonnegative date, $t \geq 0$, the distribution of the homogeneous Markov chain is entirely characterized by the transition matrix P and marginal distribution $\mu^{(0)}$ of Y_0. Indeed, let us denote $\mu_i^{(0)} = P[Y_0 = i]$. We can write

$$P[Y_0 = i_0, \ldots, Y_t = i_t] = P[Y_0 = i_0] P[Y_1 = i_1 \,|\, Y_0 = i_0] P[Y_t = i_t \,|\, Y_{t-1} = i_{t-1}]$$

$$= p_{i_t i_{t-1}} \cdots p_{i_1 i_0} \mu_{i_0}^{(0)}. \qquad (10.2)$$

In particular, the marginal distribution $\mu^{(t)}$ of Y_t is obtained by summing over $i_0, \ldots, i_{t-1}$. Let us denote by $\mu^{(t)}$ the J-dimensional vector with elements $\mu_i^{(t)}, i = 1, \ldots, J$, we get from (10.2) the *Chapman-Kolmogorov equation*:

$$\mu^{(t)} = P^t \mu^{(0)}. \qquad (10.3)$$

This equation implies that the process (Y_t) is strongly stationary if it is possible to select a marginal distribution $\mu^{(0)}$ such that

$$\mu^{(t)} = \mu^{(0)}, \qquad \forall t \geq 0.$$

PROPOSITION 10.4: *The stochastic process is strongly stationary if and only if* $\mu^{(0)} = \mu$, *where* $\mu = P\mu$.

Therefore, $\mu^{(0)}$ has to be equal to an eigenvector of the transition matrix associated with the unitary eigenvalue. Such a probability measure, if it exists, is called an *invariant measure* of the Markov chain. The eigenvector interpretation of the marginal distribution points to the spectral decomposition of the transition matrix P as a topic of further investigation.

10.1.3 *Spectral Decomposition of a Stochastic Matrix*

It is possible to show that a stochastic matrix can always be diagonalized (see Kemeny-Snell 1976). There always exists a $J \times J$ diagonal matrix Λ and a $J \times J$ invertible matrix Q with complex elements such that

$$P = Q\Lambda Q^{-1}. \tag{10.4}$$

The diagonal elements λ_i of Λ are the eigenvalues of P, while the column vectors $u_j, j = 1, \ldots, J$, of Q contain the associated eigenvectors.

The decomposition in (10.4) yields

$$P' = [Q']^{-1} \Lambda Q', \tag{10.5}$$

where the prime denotes a transpose. Therefore, the transposed transition matrix has the same eigenvalues as P, and the associated eigenvectors may be set equal to the columns $v_j, j = 1, \ldots, J$, of $[Q']^{-1}$. From these decompositions, we infer that the transition matrix may always be written as

$$P = \sum_{j=1}^{J} \lambda_j u_j v_j', \tag{10.6}$$

where the eigenvectors $u_j, j = 1, \ldots, J$, of P and the eigenvectors $v_j, j = 1, \ldots, J$, of P' may be selected such that

$$u_i' v_j = 0, \quad \text{if } i \neq j,$$
$$1, \quad \text{if } i = j,$$

which is a consequence of the relation $QQ^{-1} = Id$.

Let us now point out some constraints satisfied by the eigenvalues of the transition matrix.

PROPOSITION 10.5:

   (i) *The eigenvalues of a stochastic matrix are of absolute value less than or equal to 1.*
   (ii) *A stochastic matrix has at least one eigenvalue equal to 1.*

   PROOF:

   (i) Let us consider an eigenvalue λ and an associated eigenvector x of P' with components $x_j, j = 1, \ldots, J$. They satisfy the equation

$$\sum_{i=1}^{J} (p_{ij}x_i) = \lambda x_j.$$

We deduce that

$$|\lambda|\,|x_j| \le \sum_{i=1}^{J} (p_{ij}|x_i|) \le \left(\sum_{i=1}^{J} p_{ij}\right) \max_i |x_i| = \max_i |x_i|.$$

Since this inequality holds for any index j, we find that

$$|\lambda|\,\max_j |x_j| \le \max_i |x_i|,$$

or

$$|\lambda| \le 1.$$

(ii) Finally, the condition $\Sigma_{i=1}^{J} p_{ij} = 1, \forall j$, means that $\lambda = 1$ is an eigenvalue of P' associated with the eigenvector e, which has components that all are equal to 1.

QED

An eigenvector of P associated with the unitary eigenvalue may be selected such that $u_1'e = 1 \Leftrightarrow \Sigma_{i=1}^{J} u_{1i} = 1$. This eigenvector defines an invariant probability measure whenever its components are nonnegative.

It is interesting to consider a special case in which all eigenvalues have an absolute value strictly less than 1, except for the first one being equal to 1. We obtain

$$P = u_1e' + \sum_{j=2}^{J} \lambda_j u_j v_j', \qquad \text{with } |\lambda_j| < 1, j = 2, \dots, J,$$

and, by considering the horizon h

$$P^h = u_1e' + \sum_{j=2}^{J} \lambda_j^h u_j v_j'.$$

The matrix P^h tends to a limit when h tends to infinity

$$\lim_{h \to \infty} P^h = u_1e'. \tag{10.7}$$

Since the matrix P^h has only nonnegative elements, the same result holds for u_1, which may be considered an invariant measure. As a consequence, we obtain the following proposition.

PROPOSITION 10.6: *When all eigenvalues, except for the unitary one, have an absolute value strictly less than 1*

$$\lim_{h \to \infty} P[Y_{t+h} = i \,|\, Y_{t-1} = j] = P[Y_{t+h} = i], \forall j.$$

This means that the process is asymptotically stationary.

EXAMPLE 10.1: Let us consider the special case of a process admitting two states 0 and 1, say. The transition matrix is $P = \begin{pmatrix} p_{00} & p_{01} \\ p_{10} & p_{11} \end{pmatrix}$. It has two eigenvalues, 1 and $\alpha = p_{00} + p_{11} - 1$. α is a stability measure of the process in the states. The invariant distribution is $\mu = (\mu_0, \mu_1)'$, where $\mu_0 = \dfrac{p_{01}}{p_{01} + p_{10}}$. Therefore, it is conceptually equivalent to parameterize the Markov chain in terms of the elements of the transition matrix (with only two independent parameters due to the constraints of columns summing to 1) or in terms of the parameters α and μ_0. As well, it is important to realize that μ_0 is a long-run parameter (see Proposition 10.6), whereas α is an adjustment parameter.

10.1.4 Linear Representation of the Qualitative Process

It is possible to represent the univariate qualitative process (Y_t), admitting J possible outcomes, as a multivariate process with dichotomous qualitative components. Let us introduce $Z_{j,t}$, an indicator function defined by

$$Z_{j,t} = 1, \quad \text{if } Y_t = j,$$
$$0, \quad \text{otherwise.} \tag{10.8}$$

It is equivalent to examine either the process (Y_t) or the multivariate process (Z_t) with $Z_t = [Z_{1,t}, \ldots, Z_{J,t}]'$ since $Y_t = \Sigma_{j=1}^{J} (jZ_{j,t})$. Let us assume that (Y_t) is stationary with the transition matrix P and marginal distribution μ. We may easily derive the marginal and conditional expectations of Z_t. First, we get

$$E(Z_{i,t}) = P[Z_{i,t} = 1] = P[Y_t = i] = \mu_i,$$

or, in a vector form

$$E(Z_t) = \mu; \tag{10.9}$$

Second, we get:

$$E[Z_{i,t} | \underline{Z_{t-1}}] = E[Z_{i,t} | \underline{Y_{t-1}}]$$

$$= E[Z_{i,t} | Y_{t-1}] = P[Y_t = i | Y_{t-1}]$$

$$= \Sigma_{j=1}^{J} p_{ij} Z_{j,t-1}.$$

We find that

$$E[Z_t | \underline{Z_{t-1}}] = PZ_{t-1} = \mu + P[Z_{t-1} - \mu], \tag{10.10}$$

where the last equality results from the condition $P\mu = \mu$. Therefore, the multivariate qualitative process (Z_t) admits a linear vector autoregressive

(VAR) representation of order 1, with an autoregressive matrix equal to the transition matrix P. Moreover, the nonlinear conditional expectation $E[Z_t|Z_{t-1}]$ coincides with the linear affine regression of Z_t on Z_{t-1}. This property holds for both the Gaussian processes and pure qualitative ones.

The relation $Y_t = \Sigma_{j=1}^{J} (jZ_{j,t})$ implies that the initial qualitative process (Y_t) admits a linear ARMA representation of orders $J \times J$ (see Appendix 10.1).

Third, we can also derive the conditional variance to reveal possible ARCH effects. We get

$$E[Z_{i,t}Z_{k,t}|\underline{Z_{t-1}}] = E(Z_{i,t}|\underline{Z_{t-1}}), \qquad \text{if } k = i,$$

$$0, \qquad \text{otherwise,}$$

since the $Z_{i,t}$ variables are indicator variables corresponding to disjoint alternatives. Therefore,

$$V(Z_t|\underline{Z_{t-1}}) = \text{diag}(PZ_{t-1}) - PZ_{t-1}Z'_{t-1}P'. \tag{10.11}$$

The conditional variance-covariance matrix depends on the lagged states, and this dependence is defined by a quadratic form in Z_{t-1}.

EXAMPLE 10.2 In the two-state case, we get

$$E(Z_{0,t}|Z_{t-1}) = p_{0,1}Z_{1,t-1} + p_{0,0}Z_{0,t-1}$$

$$= p_{0,1}(1 - Z_{0,t-1}) + p_{0,0}Z_{0,t-1}$$

$$= p_{0,1} + (p_{0,0} - p_{0,1})Z_{0,t-1}$$

$$= \mu_0 + \alpha(Z_{0,t-1} - \mu_0).$$

The adjustment coefficient α is equal to the autoregressive coefficient of the $AR(1)$ representation.

10.1.5 *Application to Intraday Price Movements*

In the analysis of price dynamics, it is important to distinguish between intraday price changes with respect to the opening price on a given day and daily price changes computed as differences between the opening price on a given day and the closing price on the day before. Indeed, the type of investors and investor behaviors are different at the market opening, during a trading day, and at market closure. Typically during the preopening period, financial analysts meet to decide on a general strategy to be followed on that day, including market interventions at the opening, the repartition of budget among traders, and portfolio structure they want to achieve before the end of the trading day. Then, after the opening, traders follow their own strategies, which can be speculative, and rebalance the portfolio allocation according to the target before the closure. In the following application, we study the intraday price changes only. Therefore, its results cannot be used to predict the price changes at a horizon of 1 month, say, since we have no information on the price changes at market openings and closures. Intraday price changes have distinctive features, especially a discrete state space (i.e., a limited number of possible price changes between consecutive ticks), and short memory dynamics. The data on intraday prices allow a thorough study of the conditional tick-by-tick distribution of price, much more detailed than a simple analysis of expected returns and volatility. Especially, it can be used for intraday portfolio updating.

Our sample contains observations on differences computed between each trading price and the market opening price on the pertaining day. This variable, denoted y_t, admits a discrete set of values since the admissible price increments on stock markets are integer multiples of a basic unit called the tick (1 French franc [FF] on the French Market [presently quoted in Euros], $\$1/8$ on US market, 5 cents on the Toronto Stock Exchange [TSE]). Moreover, the state space of price increments is finite since security devices, called *circuit breakers*, automatically halt the trading process whenever the price difference y_t exceeds a predetermined upper limit. In our study, we examine the buyer-initiated trades of a liquid asset, for which the price changes $y_t - y_{t-1}$ are at most 1 tick. Consequently, if the values y_t are measured in integer multiples of ticks, the set of admissible values is of the type $\{-\bar{x}, \ldots, 0, \ldots, \bar{x}\}$, where $\bar{x}$ is the maximal admissible movement. The transition matrix admits nonzero elements on the main diagonal and on the two bordering diagonals:

$$P = \begin{matrix} p(-\bar{x},-\bar{x})\ p(-\bar{x},-\bar{x}+1)\ 0\ldots\ldots\ldots\ldots0 \\ 0\ldots0p(x,x-1)p(x,x)p(x,x+1)0\ldots0 \\ 0\ldots\ldots\ldots\ldots0p(\bar{x},\bar{x}-1)p(+\bar{x},+\bar{x}) \end{matrix} \qquad (10.12)$$

Figure 10.1 displays the approximated values of the elementary probabilities $p(x+1,x)$, $p(x,x)$, and $p(x-1,x)$ as a function of the initial state x. They are computed from the buy trades of the Elf-Aquitaine stock traded on Paris Bourse and recorded during the month of May 1998. The lower and upper limits of price changes are not symmetric around 0. More precisely, they are -5 for the lower bound and 45 for the upper bound.

We also observe that the transition probabilities are almost independent of the initial state, and that the probability of a "zero price" change is high, whereas the probabilities of up and down movements are almost equal. This characteristic is compatible with the property of a random walk.

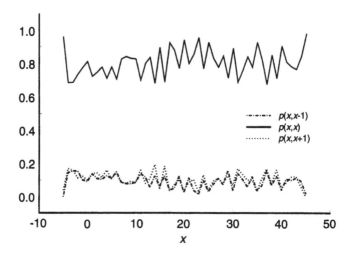

Figure 10.1   *Transition Probabilities*

The corresponding marginal (invariant) measure is plotted in Figure 10.2. It features several peaks at various tick multiples, revealing the preference of investors for round numbers.

The smoothed distribution is unimodal with a right skewness. This is due to bullish market activity, revealed by the transition probabilities.

Finally, we perform a spectral decomposition of the estimated transition matrix. Due to the specific form of the transition matrix, the eigen-

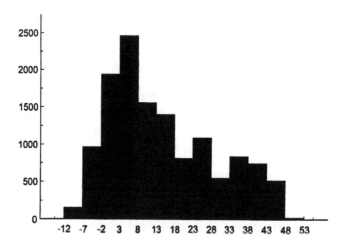

Figure 10.2   *Marginal Distribution of the Price*

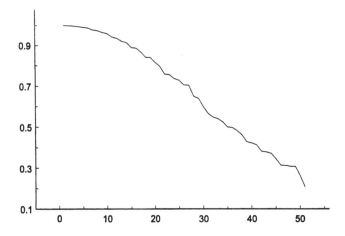

Figure 10.3 *Eigenvalues in a Descending Order*

values are all real positive. We report them in descending order in Figure 10.3 and display the first associated eigenvectors in Figure 10.4. In our case, these eigenvectors are such that $u_j = v_j, \forall j$.

The eigenvectors V_2, V_3, and V_4 provide the first nonlinear canonical functions for the intraday price process (see Chapter 9). The eigenvector V_2 is almost affine, which means that the largest possible correlation is

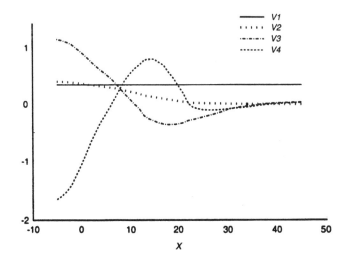

Figure 10.4 *Eigenvectors*

observed between affine price transformations; the eigenvector V_3 has an asymmetric parabolic pattern. It reveals time dependence of some risk measure, different from a quadratic function, such as the variance, which would show up as a symmetric parabola.

10.2 Duration Analysis

The behavior of a qualitative process may be examined in various ways. For example, in the above empirical study, instead of the sequence of states occupied by the process, we could have investigated the sequence of durations, that is, the times spent by the process in each state. This section provides an introduction to the duration analysis and some insights on the choice of adequate approach. We first derive the distribution of durations for a homogeneous Markov chain and present their properties. Next, we consider the limiting behavior of the Markov chain and of the durations when time interval tends to 0 to highlight the relationship between Markov chains and continuous time Poisson models. Continuous time Poisson processes are building blocks of jump processes, examined in Chapter 11. Finally, we give an alternative representation of the qualitative process. The duration models and point processes are exposed in this chapter at an introductory level. Extensions to more complicated dynamic structures are found in Chapter 14.

10.2.1   *Distribution of the Durations*

Let us consider a fixed initial date t_0. At this date, the process is in a given state y_{t_0} and will remain in this state for a random residual time τ_{t_0} (say), starting from the date t_0. The conditional distribution of τ_{t_0} given the state occupied at t_0 can easily be derived. Indeed, we get

$$P[\tau_{t_0} \geq d + 1 \,|\, Y_{t_0} = y_{t_0}]$$

$$= P[Y_{t_0+1} = y_{t_0}, Y_{t_0+2} = y_{t_0}, \ldots, Y_{t_0+d} = y_{t_0} \,|\, Y_{t_0} = y_{t_0}]$$

$$= P[Y_{t_0+1} = y_{t_0} \,|\, Y_{t_0} = y_{t_0}] P[Y_{t_0+2} = y_{t_0} \,|\, Y_{t_0+1} = y_{t_0}] \ldots P[Y_{t_0+d} = y_{t_0} \,|\, Y_{t_0+d-1} = y_{t_0}]$$

$$= p_{y_{t_0}, y_{t_0}}^d \qquad \text{for } d \in I\!N.$$

Moreover, let us denote by $\tilde{\tau}_{t_0}$ the time spent in state y_{t_0} strictly before the date t_0. By the Markov property

$$P[\tau_{t_0} \geq d + 1 \,|\, Y_{t_0} = y_{t_0}, \tilde{\tau}_{t_0}]$$

$$= P[\tau_{t_0} \geq d + 1 \,|\, Y_{t_0} = y_{t_0}]$$

$$= p_{y_{t_0}, y_{t_0}}^d.$$

PROPOSITION 10.7:

(i) *Conditional on the entry into state j, the time spent in this state follows a geometric distribution with a parameter p_{jj}.*

(ii) *The durations feature lack of memory since the distribution of the residual duration given the time already spent in the state does not depend on this time.*

Let us recall that a geometric distribution with parameter p has the elementary probabilities

$$P[\tau = d] = (1 - p)p^{d-1}, \qquad d = 1, 2, \ldots,$$

and the mean $1/(1 - p)$.

10.2.2 Continuous Time Qualitative Processes

In the previous sections, we examined discrete time processes with time intervals between successive observations measured by integer multiples of a time unit. Let us consider now very short time intervals of an order of a fraction of the time unit. This setup allows us to introduce a continuous time analog of the homogeneous Markov chain with observations separated by time δ, such that δ tends to 0. More precisely, we study a continuous time Markov process $(Y_t, t \geq 0)$, with $P^{(\delta)}$ the transition matrix, over a very short interval δ:

$$P[Y_{t+\delta} = i \,|\, Y_t = j] = p_{ij}^{(\delta)}.$$

When δ tends to 0, the transitions between different states are less and less likely. We assume that

$$p_{ij}^{(\delta)} = \lambda_{ij}\delta + o(\delta), \qquad \text{for small } \delta, i \neq j,$$

and

$$p_{jj}^{(\delta)} = 1 - \left(\sum_{i \neq j} \lambda_{ij}\right)\delta + o(\delta). \qquad (10.13)$$

$$= 1 + \lambda_{jj}\delta + o(\delta), \qquad \text{(say)}.$$

$\lambda_{ij}, i \neq j$, is the *infinitesimal transition* (or *hazard*) *rate*, also called the *transition intensity* from j to i. Note that $\lambda_{ij} \geq 0$, $\forall i \neq j$, and $\lambda_{jj} \leq 0$.

Therefore, it is implicitly assumed that, during a short time interval $(t, t + \delta)$, at most one transition takes place, and that the probability of such transition is proportional to the length of that time interval and independent of the past. These are the standard assumptions of the *multistate Poisson process*, which is the simplest example of a continuous time jump process. The dynamics of this process is summarized by the matrix

$$\Lambda = (\lambda_{ij}), \qquad (10.14)$$

where the columns of Λ sum to 0.

Moreover, the transition matrices $P^{(\delta)}$, δ varying, preserve the horizon compatibility. By Proposition 10.3, we can write

$$P^{(\delta)} = \exp(\delta Q), \qquad \text{for some matrix } Q,$$

and by considering the expansion for a small δ, we find that $Q = \Lambda$.

PROPOSITION 10.8:

   (i) *The distribution of a multistate Poisson process is characterized by the intensity matrix Λ.*
   (ii) *The transition matrix at horizon δ is $P^{(\delta)} = exp(\delta\Lambda)$.*

Let us now consider the durations spent in different states. In the present framework, the durations are continuous variables. By considering the discrete time analog, we get

$$P(D_j \geq d) \simeq P\left[\tau_j^{(\delta)} \geq [d/\delta]\right]$$

$$= \left[p_{jj}^{(\delta)}\right]^{[d/\delta]}$$

$$\simeq [1 + \lambda_{jj}\delta]^{[d/\delta]} \simeq \exp(\lambda_{jj}d),$$

where D_j is the duration spent in j for the continuous time process, $\tau_j^{(\delta)}$ is the duration for the discrete time process with time unit δ, and square brackets denote the integer part.

PROPOSITION 10.9: *In the multistate Poisson process, the duration spent in state j follows an exponential distribution with parameter $(-\lambda_{jj})$, $\lambda_{jj} < 0$.*

We may directly verify that the exponential distribution also satisfies the lack of memory property since

$$P[D_j - d \geq h \,|\, D_j \geq d] = \frac{P[D_j \geq d+h, D_j \geq d]}{P[D_j \geq d]}$$

$$= \frac{P(D_j \geq d+h)}{P[D_j \geq d]} = \frac{\exp[\lambda_{jj}(d+h)]}{\exp(\lambda_{jj}d)}$$

$$= \exp(\lambda_{jj}h) = P[D_j \geq h].$$

10.2.3   An Alternative Representation of the Qualitative Process

The knowledge of the jump process is equivalent to the knowledge of both successively occupied states i_1, i_2, i_3, ... and corresponding durations D^1, D^2, D^3, ... (Figure 10.5). Therefore, we can equivalently define the distribution of the jump process directly in terms of the transition matrix or do it rather with respect to the joint distribution of i_1, i_2, i_3, ..., D^1, D^2, D^3,

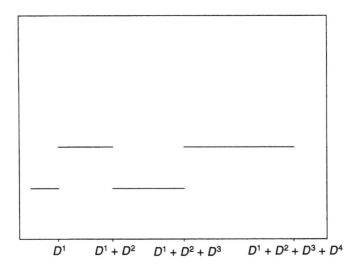

$$D^1 \qquad D^1 + D^2 \qquad D^1 + D^2 + D^3 \qquad D^1 + D^2 + D^3 + D^4$$

Figure 10.5 *The Path of the Multistate Process*

.... We describe below this last approach for a homogeneous Markov chain. Note that a similar proposition holds for the continuous multistate Poisson process.

PROPOSITION 10.10: *The distribution of the process conditional on the initial state i_1 is defined by*

(i) *the transition probabilities for the successive states* $q(i_j | \underline{i_{j-1}}) = q(i_j | i_{j-1}) = \dfrac{p_{i_j, i_{j-1}}}{1 - p_{i_j, i_{j-1}}}$, *that is, the probability that the new state is i_j conditional on the last occupied state i_{j-1},*

(ii) *the joint distribution of the durations D_j conditional on the occupied state i_j, which are independent and geometrically distributed with parameter p_{i_j, i_j}.*

PROOF: This result is a direct consequence of the form of the log-likelihood function conditioned on the initial state. It is given by

$$L = \sum_{t=1}^{T} \sum_{ij} [Z_{i,t} \, Z_{j,t-1} \log p_{ij}].$$

By introducing the occupied states k and associated durations D_k, we get

$$L = \sum_{k=1}^{K} \{ D_k \log p_{i_k, i_k} + \log p_{i_{k+1}, i_k} \}$$

$$= \sum_{k=1}^{K} [D_k \log p_{i_k, i_k} + \log(1 - p_{i_k, i_k})] + \sum_{k=1}^{K} \log \frac{p_{i_{k+1}, i_k}}{1 - p_{i_k, i_k}}.$$

The first sum corresponds to a product of exponential distributions with parameters p_{i_s,i_s}, and the second one corresponds to the probabilities of transitions between states.
QED

10.3   Statistical Inference

In Section 10.1.4, we recognized that the multivariate process Z_t with qualitative dichotomous components admits a vector autoregressive representation with conditionally heteroscedastic errors. Therefore, the parameters of the Markov chain can be estimated using semiparametric methods such as least squares or quasi-maximum likelihood. We know, however, that these methods may be inefficient. We propose instead the maximum likelihood estimators, which are derived in the sequel and are compared to ordinary least squares (OLS).

10.3.1   Maximum Likelihood Approach

Let us assume a sample of observations on the qualitative process indexed by $t = 1, \dots, T$. The elements of the transition matrix can be estimated by the maximum likelihood method. The estimators arise as solutions to the following optimization:

$$\max_{p} \sum_{t=1}^{T} \sum_{i,j} Z_{i,t} Z_{j,t-1} \log p_{ij},$$

under the constraints

$$p_{ij} \geq 0 \qquad \forall i,j,$$
$$\sum_{i=1}^{J} p_{ij} = 1, \qquad \forall j.$$

The log-likelihood may be rewritten as

$$L = \sum_{j=1}^{J} \sum_{t=1}^{T} Z_{j,t-1} \left(\sum_{i=1}^{J} Z_{i,t} \log p_{ij} \right)$$
$$= \sum_{j=1}^{J} L_j \qquad \text{(say)},$$

where L_j only depends on the parameters through p_{ij} $i = 1, \dots, J$.
Therefore, we can optimize separately

$$\max_{p} L_j = \sum_{t=1}^{T} Z_{j,t-1} \left(\sum_{j=1}^{J} Z_{i,t} \log p_{ij} \right),$$

subject to: $p_{ij} \geq 0, \qquad \forall i, \qquad \text{and} \qquad \sum_{i=1}^{J} p_{ij} = 1.$

Explicit solutions are immediately obtained. Their asymptotic independence follows from the additive decomposition of the log-likelihood function.

PROPOSITION 10.11:

(i) *The maximum likelihood estimators of the transition probabilities are given by their empirical counterparts:*

$$\hat{p}_{i,j} = \frac{\sum_{t=1}^{T} Z_{i,t} Z_{j,t-1}}{\sum_{t=1}^{T} Z_{j,t-1}}.$$

(ii) *The vectors* $[\hat{p}_{1,j}, \ldots, \hat{p}_{J,j}]'$, $j = 1, \ldots, J$, *are asymptotically independent.*

10.3.2 Least Squares Approach

Rather than using the maximum likelihood method and performing the standard derivation of the asymptotic variance-covariance matrix of estimators, we can consider the linear representation of the Markov process (see Section 10.1.4) and estimate the parameters by least squares. Indeed, we know that

$$E(Z_t \mid Z_{t-1}) = P \, Z_{t-1}.$$

Therefore, we have a system of linear regressions

$$Z_{i,t} = \sum_{j=1}^{J} p_{i,j} Z_{j,t-1} + u_{i,t}, \qquad i = 1, \ldots, J,$$

where $E(u_t \mid Z_{t-1}) = 0$, with the regression coefficients $p_{i,j}$ and the same explanatory variables in all equations. By standard results on seemingly unrelated regressions (SUR) (see Chapter 3), the generalized least squares (GLS) estimators of the regression coefficients coincide with the OLS estimators of each equation one by one. Moreover, since the explanatory variables $Z_{j,t-1}$, $j = 1, \ldots, J$, are mutually orthogonal, these estimators are

$$\tilde{p}_{i,j} = \frac{\sum_{t=1}^{T} Z_{i,t} Z_{j,t-1}}{\sum_{t=1}^{T} Z_{j,t-1}^2} = \frac{\sum_{t=1}^{T} Z_{i,t} Z_{j,t-1}}{\sum_{t=1}^{T} Z_{j,t-1}} = \hat{p}_{i,j}.$$

PROPOSITION 10.12: *The ML estimators of the transition probabilities coincide with the least squares estimators of the linear representation of the process.*

Proposition 10.12 suggests use of the standard error estimates provided by OLS software (possibly corrected them for conditional heteroscedasticity) instead of reporting the Hessian-based variances that are commonly computed under the ML approach.

10.4   Qualitative Factor Model

In this section, we introduce various models of quantitative or qualitative processes with dynamics that depend on some latent (hidden) Markov chains (see, e.g., MacDonald and Zucchini 1997). This class of models has potential applications to portfolio management. For example, the underlying qualitative factors may characterize various unobserved market regimes. The approach would consist of developing portfolio management strategies for each possible regime and of implementing the strategy corresponding to the most likely regime.

10.4.1   *Qualitative Threshold Autoregressive*
Conditionally Heteroscedastic Model

Let us consider a quantitative time series (X_t) that satisfies the Markov property. We can write the general autoregressive form (see Chapter 6)

$$X_t = m(X_{t-1}) + \sigma(X_{t-1})u_t, \tag{10.15}$$

where m and σ are two given functions, and (u_t) is a strong white noise with zero mean and unitary variance. This nonlinear model includes both the conditional mean $m(X_{t-1})$ and conditional variance $\sigma^2(X_{t-1})$ without constraining their functional forms. Therefore, they may be estimated by nonparametric techniques, although the unknown functions may also be approximated parametrically, for instance, using stepwise functions. Let us introduce a partition of the real line A_i, $i = 1, \ldots, J$. The nonlinear autoregressive form above may be approximated by

$$X_t = \sum_{i=1}^{J} \alpha_i 1_{A_i}(X_{t-1}) + \left[\sum_{i=1}^{J} \beta_i 1_{A_i}(X_{t-1}) \right] u_t, \tag{10.16}$$

where 1_{A_i} is the indicator function of A_i.

In this last specification, the effect of the past is captured by the qualitative indicators $Z_{i,t} = 1_{A_i}(X_t)$:

$$X_t = \sum_{i=1}^{J} \alpha_i Z_{i,t-1} + \left(\sum_{i=1}^{J} \beta_i Z_{i,t-1} \right) u_t \tag{10.17}$$

$$= \alpha' Z_{t-1} + (\beta' Z_{t-1})u_t.$$

It is easily checked that the qualitative process (Z_t) is a Markov chain. Indeed, we get

$$P[Z_{i,t} = 1 \,|\, \underline{X_{t-1}}] = P[X_t \in A_i \,|\, \underline{X_{t-1}}] = P\left[u_t \in \frac{A_i - \alpha'Z_{t-1}}{\beta'Z_{t-1}}\right]$$

$$= Q\left[\frac{A_i - \alpha'Z_{t-1}}{\beta'Z_{t-1}}\right], \qquad \text{where } Q \text{ denotes the distribution of } u_t.$$

Therefore, the quantitative process is defined as a function

$$X_t = g(Z_{t-1}, u_t),$$

where only the Markov chain (Z_t) features temporal dependence.

As an illustration of model (10.16), let us discuss the mean-variance portfolio management when (X_t) denotes the excess gain of a risky asset. The quantity of risky asset to include in the portfolio at time t is

$$\alpha_t^* = \frac{1}{A} \frac{m(x_{t-1})}{\sigma^2(x_{t-1})}$$

$$= \frac{1}{A} \frac{\sum_{i=1}^{J} \alpha_i \mathbf{1}_{A_i}(x_{t-1})}{\sum_{i=1}^{J} \beta_i^2 \mathbf{1}_{A_i}(x_{t-1})}$$

$$= \sum_{i=1}^{J} \mathbf{1}_{A_i}(x_{t-1}) \left(\frac{1}{A} \frac{\alpha_i}{\beta_i^2}\right),$$

where A is the risk aversion coefficient. Thus, we get different management strategies $\frac{1}{A} \frac{\alpha_i}{\beta_i^2}$, i varying, in the admissible regimes; we select the strategy $\frac{1}{A} \frac{\alpha_i}{\beta_i^2}$ if we predict that the regime prevailing on the market is the regime i, that is, $\mathbf{1}_{A_i}(x_{t-1}) = 1$.

10.4.2 Markov Switching Regimes

The popularity of these models in econometrics stems from their ability to represent business cycle fluctuations (Hamilton 1989) and their tractability due to the existence of recursive estimation algorithms (Kitagawa 1987, Chap. 9). An example of such a model is the autoregressive process of order 1 with switching regimes. Let us denote by (X_t) the quantitative process of interest. The following autoregressive equation defines its dynamics:

$$X_t = c(Y_t) + \varphi(Y_t)X_{t-1} + u_t, \tag{10.18}$$

where (u_t) and (Y_t) are independent processes, (Y_t) is a Markov chain, and (u_t) is a strong white noise.

If, at date t, the state occupied by the chain is j, then the autoregressive specification is

$$X_t = c(j) + \varphi(j)X_{t-1} + u_t.$$

Therefore, the average value of X_t, as well as the autoregressive coefficient, depend on the randomly occupied state.

This model differs from the model discussed in Section 10.4.1 in several aspects. Indeed, the underlying Markov chain is not a deterministic function of the process of interest, and the dynamics depends on two independent sources of randomness that correspond to the white noise (u_t) and to the chain (Y_t).

It is often assumed that the underlying states are not observable. A typical example is a business cycle process, where (X_t) represents a vector of observed variables, whereas the underlying Markov process describes the evolution of the two regimes of recession and expansion. Therefore, it is necessary to study the conditional distribution of X_t given only the past of the observed variables $\underline{X_{t-1}}$. In general, all lagged values are found to be significant, and thus the (X_t) process violates the Markov property.

The existence of a finite number of regimes allows derivation of the values of the conditional pdf along with predictions of the latent regimes (see Chapter 9) by iterative algorithms.

10.4.3   State Aggregation

In a qualitative Markov chain setup, we may introduce qualitative factors under the condition that the factors admit a number of admissible states less than the number of states of the chain. This problem is related to the state aggregation of the initial Markov chain.

Let us consider such a chain (Y_t) with possible states $j = 1, \ldots, J$ and a partition A_k, $k = 1, \ldots, K$, of the state space. We can introduce the qualitative process $F_t = (F_{1,t}, \ldots, F_{K,t})'$, where $F_{k,t} = \mathbf{1}_{A_k}(Y_t)$.

PROPOSITION 10.13: *It is possible to aggregate the states of the Markov chain into the partition $(A_k, k = 1, \ldots, K)$ if and only if*

  (i) *the qualitative process (F_t) is a Markov chain;*
  (ii) *F_t contains all the relevant information to predict Y_{t+1}: $l(Y_{t+1}|Y_t) = l(Y_{t+1}|F_t)$.*

Hence, it is possible to map the states into a new partition, depending on the transition matrix, which has to be of a specific form. Let us assume that the states are ordered so that A_1 corresponds to the first J_1 states, A_2 to the next J_2 states, and so on. Let us denote by Q the transition matrix of the qualitative factor process (F_t) and by $\mu_k = [\mu_{k,1}, \ldots, \mu_{k,J_k}]'$ the conditional probabilities $\mu_{k,j} = P[Y_t = j + \sum_{l=1}^{k-1} J_l | Y_t \in A_k]$, $j = 1, \ldots, J_k$. The conditions of Proposition 10.13 give the following block decomposition of the transition matrix P:

$$P = (q_{k,l}\mu_k e_l'), \tag{10.19}$$

where e_l is a J_l dimensional vector of ones. In a study of a multistate qualitative process, it is important to verify whether some states may be aggregated so that the final number of regimes can be reduced. Equivalently, we need to check if the transition matrix P admits a factorization specified in equation (10.19). The state aggregation may be performed using Proposition 10.14.

PROPOSITION 10.14: *The states may be aggregated into a partition with K subsets A_k, $k = 1, \ldots, K$, if and only if*

(i) *the transition matrix P admits $J - K$ eigenvalues equal to 0;*
(ii) *the left-hand side eigenvectors of P associated with the nonzero eigenvalues belong to the subspace generated by*

$$\begin{pmatrix} e_1 \\ 0 \\ \vdots \\ 0 \end{pmatrix}, \begin{pmatrix} 0 \\ e_2 \\ 0 \\ 0 \end{pmatrix}, \ldots, \begin{pmatrix} 0 \\ 0 \\ 0 \\ e_k \end{pmatrix} \text{ (after a possible reordering of the states).}$$

Therefore, qualitative factor analysis of the Markov chain may be performed through a spectral decomposition of the estimated transition matrix $\hat{P}$.

The qualitative factor analysis can be used for determining informative price patterns. More precisely, let us consider $Y_t = (y_t, y_{t-1}, \ldots, y_{t-5})'$, say, where $y_t = $ "up" if $\Delta p_t > 0$ and is $y_t = 0$ otherwise. The analysis can show, for example, that sufficient information is contained in the most recent state and the duration of that state. While the initial state space contains $2^5 = 32$ different patterns that correspond to various admissible sequences of ups and downs, the reduced state space will include 10 states only. The set corresponding to an up state of duration 1 consists of the following eight patterns:

up, down, up, up, up
up, down, up, up, down
up, down, up, down, up
up, down, up, down, down
up, down, down, up, up
up, down, down, up, down
up, down, down, down, up
up, down, down, down, down.

10.5 Summary

This chapter discussed the qualitative representation of financial data. The approach consists of dividing the value space of a process into distinct states and assigning a dummy variable to each of them. Accordingly, the dynamics of the new process consists of transitions between various states. This approach can be applied to asset returns, which admit states of high and low values, for example, or to squared returns that approximate the volatility process, in which the regimes of moderate, high, and low volatility can be distinguished. On one hand, this approach can be criticized for omission of information contained in the initial series. On the other hand, the transformation of a series into a qualitative process allows isolation of non-linear dynamic features that are essential to the subject of research. In this way, all valuable information is retained, and unwanted patterns are eliminated. Volatility and return transitions between various regimes are a topic of ongoing research. Recently, it has been revealed, for example, regime switches are a potential cause of spurious long memory in return volatility, mentioned in Chapter 5. As well, the interstate transition dynamics leads to jump processes that may be considered an additional source of randomness in continuous time price processes, examined in Chapter 11. The random times spent by a qualitative process in various states form a stochastic process with interesting features. They can be modeled using dynamic duration models, which are discussed in Chapter 14 in the context of modeling the times between trades on stock markets.

Appendix 10.1: Autoregressive Moving Average Representation of the Process (Y_t)

The matrix autocovariances of the multivariate process (Z_t) at order h, $\Gamma(h) = \mathrm{Cov}(Z_t, Z_{t-h})$, is a linear transformation of P^h. Therefore, since the transition matrix may be diagonalized, every covariance $\gamma_{j,k}(h) = \mathrm{Cov}(Z_{j,t}, Z_{k,t-h})$ is a linear combination of the powers of the eigenvalues:

$$\gamma_{j,k}(h) = \sum_{i=1}^{J} a_{j,k}^{(i)} \lambda_i^h.$$

Since Y_t is a linear transform of Z_t, the same property holds for the autocovariance:

$$\gamma(h) = \mathrm{Cov}(Y_t, Y_{t+h}) = \sum_{i=1}^{J} a(i) \lambda_i^h \quad \text{(say).}$$

The existence of a linear ARMA(J,J) representation for the (Y_t) process is a consequence of this form.

11

Diffusion Models

CONTINUOUS TIME MODELS that assume that asset prices follow stochastic differential equations (SDEs) were introduced into the literature by Bachelier (1900), Working (1934), and Osborne (1959) in the first half of the last century. This approach, however, was not pursued in finance until the 1970s. At that time, it was recognized that continuous time models provide a convenient framework for determining the prices of derivative assets under the so-called complete market hypothesis. In this chapter, we present the continuous time models and explain their application to derivative pricing. In particular, we derive and discuss the well-known Black Scholes formula (Black and Scholes 1973). The theoretical concepts are further extended in Chapters 12 and 13, in which we examine estimation of continuous time models and computation of derivative prices.

11.1 Stochastic Differential Equations

This section contains a comprehensive overview of stochastic differential equations, along with basic insights into their practical implementation. In some sense, we introduce the class of continuous time processes along the same lines as the class of autoregressive moving average (ARMA) processes. We first introduce an elementary continuous time process, called *Brownian motion*, with increments that behave like a Gaussian standard white noise. Next, we define other, more complex, continuous time processes using Brownian motion as an elementary building block.

11.1.1 Brownian Motion

Brownian motion was first defined by Wiener (1923, 1924) and since has also been known as the *Wiener process*. Let us denote it by $(W_t, t \in R^+)$.

Since Brownian motion is an extension of a Gaussian random walk to the continuous time framework, let us recall at this point some basic properties of the Gaussian random walk.

A standardized Gaussian random walk is a discrete time process satisfying

$$y_t = y_{t-1} + \varepsilon_t, \qquad t \geq 1, \tag{11.1}$$

where $y_0 = 0$, and ε_t, $t \geq 1$, is a sequence of independent variables with standard normal distribution $N(0,1)$. The moving average representation of the random walk is

$$y_t = \sum_{\tau=1}^{t} \varepsilon_\tau, \qquad t \geq 1. \tag{11.2}$$

Therefore, y_t can be written as a sum of all past errors. The process (y_t) is Gaussian since its components are linear combinations of the Gaussian white noise. It has mean 0,

$$Ey_t = \sum_{\tau=1}^{t} E\varepsilon_\tau = 0,$$

and its autocovariances are

$$Cov(y_t, y_{t'}) = Cov\left(\sum_{\tau=1}^{t} \varepsilon_\tau, \sum_{\tau'=1}^{t'} \varepsilon_{\tau'}\right)$$

$$= \sum_{\tau=1}^{Min(t,t')} Cov(\varepsilon_\tau, \varepsilon_{\tau'}) \tag{11.3}$$

$$= Min(t,t').$$

Thus, the random walk is a nonstationary process with basic increments $\Delta y_t = y_t - y_{t-1} = \varepsilon_t$ that are independent. We now show that Brownian motion is a continuous time process with similar properties.

DEFINITION 11.1: *Brownian motion is a Gaussian, continuous time, real-value process $(W_t, t \in R^+)$ with mean 0 and covariance given by*

$$Cov(W_t, W_{t'}) = Min(t,t'), \qquad \forall t, t' \in R^+.$$

In particular, its variance is

$$VW_t = t. \tag{11.4}$$

Therefore, the process is nonstationary, and $W_0 = 0$.

PROPOSITION 11.1: *Brownian motion has independent increments*

$$\forall t_1 < t_2 < t_3 : W_{t_3} - W_{t_2}, \text{ and } W_{t_2} - W_{t_1} \text{ are independent.}$$

PROOF: Since $(W_t, t \in R^+)$ is a Gaussian process, $(W_{t_3} - W_{t_2}, W_{t_2} - W_{t_1})$ is a bidimensional Gaussian vector. To verify the independence, it is sufficient to check whether these two variables are uncorrelated. We have

$$Cov(W_{t_3} - W_{t_2}, \; W_{t_2} - W_{t_1})$$

$$= Cov(W_{t_3}, W_{t_2}) - Cov(W_{t_2}, W_{t_2}) + Cov(W_{t_2}, W_{t_1}) - Cov(W_{t_3}, W_{t_1})$$

$$= Min(t_3, t_2) - Min(t_2, t_2) + Min(t_2, t_1) - Min(t_3, t_1)$$

$$= t_2 - t_2 + t_1 - t_1 = 0.$$

QED

Brownian motion has continuous trajectories that are almost nowhere differentiable. This result can be explained intuitively. First, for any t and dt, we have

$$E(W_{t+dt} - W_t)^2 = V(W_{t+dt} - W_t)$$

$$= V(W_{t+dt}) + V(W_t) - 2Cov(W_{t+dt}, W_t)$$

$$= t + dt - t = dt.$$

Therefore, if dt tends to 0, $\dfrac{1}{dt^2} E(W_{t+dt} - W_t)^2$ tends to infinity, which implies that $\dfrac{1}{dt}(W_{t+dt} - W_t)$ does not exist (almost surely). The nondifferentiability is due to a series of independent shocks arising between t and dt.

A typical pattern of a trajectory of a Brownian motion is given in Figure 11.1.

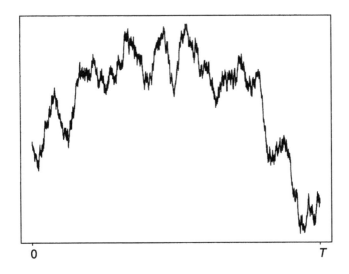

0   T

Figure 11.1 *Trajectory of a Brownian Motion*

11.1.2 Stochastic Integrals and Stochastic Differential Equations

The stochastic calculus extends the standard integration theory to stochastic integrands and measures. The stochastic integrals are defined as limits of Riemann sums. Let us consider a stochastic function g_t such that g_t depends on past and current values of the Brownian motion (W_t). We can define, under some integrability conditions,

$$\int_0^t g_u du \quad \text{and} \quad \int_0^t g_u dW_u.$$

In the first integral, g_u is stochastic, but the "weights" du are deterministic, whereas they are both stochastic in the second integral. Accordingly, these integrals are defined as

$$\int_0^t g_u du = \lim_{n \to \infty} \sum_{i=1}^n g_{t_i}(t_{i+1} - t_i),$$

$$\int_0^t g_u dW_u = \lim_{n \to \infty} \sum_{i=1}^n g_{t_i}\left(W_{t_{i+1}} - W_{t_i}\right),$$

(11.5)

where $t_1 = 0 < \ldots < t_{n+1} = t$ is a partition of $[0,t]$ such that $\sup_i |t_{i+1} - t_i|$ tends to 0 when n tends to infinity. It is interesting to note that the right-hand side (rhs) of equation (11.5) is a kind of moving average representation. Indeed, let us denote $\varepsilon_{t_i} = W_{t_{i+1}} - W_{t_i}$ and approximate g_{t_i} by $g(\varepsilon_{t_{i-1}}) = g(\varepsilon_{t_{i-1}}, \varepsilon_{t_{i-2}}, \ldots, \varepsilon_{t_1})$ so that the rhs becomes $\sum_{i=1}^n g(\varepsilon_{t_{i-1}})\varepsilon_{t_i}$. This is a moving average representation, with moving average coefficients being nonlinear functions of the lagged values of the noise.

The definition of the stochastic integral as the limit of Riemann sums allows us to determine the first- and second-order moments. We have

$$E \int_0^t g_u dW_u = \lim_{n \to \infty} \sum_{i=1}^n E\left[g_{t_i}\left(W_{t_{i+1}} - W_{t_i}\right)\right],$$

$$= \lim_{n \to \infty} \sum_{i=1}^n \left[g_{t_i} E\left(W_{t_{i+1}} - W_{t_i} | \underline{W_{t_i}}\right)\right],$$

$$= 0.$$

Similarly,

$$Cov\left[\int_0^t g_u dW_u, \int_0^t h_u dW_u\right]$$

$$= E\left(\int_0^t g_u dW_u \int_0^t h_u dW_u\right)$$

$$= \lim_{n \to \infty} \sum_{i=1}^n \sum_{j=1}^n E\left[g_{t_i} h_{t_j}\left(W_{t_{i+1}} - W_{t_i}\right)\left(W_{t_{j+1}} - W_{t_j}\right)\right]$$

$$= \lim_{n \to \infty} \sum_{i=1}^{n} E\left\{g_{t_i} h_{t_i} E\left[\left(\left(W_{t_{i+1}} - W_{t_i}\right)^2 \mid W_{t_i}\right)\right]\right\}$$

$$+ \lim_{n \to \infty} \sum \sum_{i<j} E\left[g_{t_i} h_{t_j}\left(W_{t_{i+1}} - W_{t_i}\right) E\left[\left(W_{t_{j+1}} - W_{t_j}\right) \mid W_{t_j}\right]\right]$$

$$+ \lim_{n \to \infty} \sum \sum_{j<i} E\left\{g_{t_i} h_{t_j}\left(W_{t_{j+1}} - W_{t_j}\right) E\left[\left(W_{t_{i+1}} - W_{t_i}\right) \mid W_{t_i}\right]\right\}$$

$$= \lim_{n \to \infty} \sum_{i=1}^{n} E\left(g_{t_i} h_{t_i}\right)\left(t_{i+1} - t_i\right)$$

$$= \int_0^t E\left(g_u h_u\right) du.$$

$$Cov\left(\int_0^t g_u dW_u, \int_0^t h_u dW_u\right) = \int_0^t E\left(g_u h_u\right) du. \tag{11.6}$$

Once the stochastic integrals are well defined, we can introduce the notion of a stochastic differential equation (SDE).

DEFINITION 11.2: *A stochastic process* (y_t) *satisfies the SDE*

$$dy_t = \mu(t, y_t) dt + \sigma(t, y_t) dW_t,$$

if and only if it is a solution of the integral equation

$$y_t - y_0 = \int_0^t \mu(u, y_u) du + \int_0^t \sigma(u, y_u) dW_u.$$

The notation dy_t or dW_t is conventional; it is not meant to imply that the trajectories of (y_t) and (W_t) are differentiable, as in the example of Brownian motion.

Similar notation is used in the formulas of the first- and second-order conditional moments. We get

$$E[y_{t+dt} - y_t \mid \underline{y_t}] \approx E[dy_t \mid \underline{y_t}] = \mu(t, y_t) dt.$$

Therefore,

$$\mu(t, y_t) = \lim_{dt \to 0} \frac{E(dy_t \mid \underline{y_t})}{dt}. \tag{11.7}$$

The function μ is called the *drift* function. It measures the expected instantaneous change of y_t.

Similarly, we get

$$V[dy_t \mid \underline{y_t}] = E([dy_t - E(dy_t \mid \underline{y_t})]^2 \mid \underline{y_t})$$

$$\approx E[\sigma(t, y_t) dW_t \mid \underline{y_t}]$$

$$= \sigma^2(t, y_t) dt.$$

Therefore,

$$\sigma^2(t,y_t) = \lim_{dt \to 0} \frac{V(dy_t | y_t)}{dt}. \tag{11.8}$$

The function σ is called the (*instantaneous*) *volatility* function. It can be interpreted as a measure of local uncertainty about the movements of y_t.

11.1.3   Ito's Lemma

As in standard deterministic calculus, the expressions of stochastic integrals and differential equations can be modified by a change of variable. The change of variable formula for stochastic differential equations is called *Ito's lemma* (Ito 1951).

Let us first consider a deterministic differential equation of order 1:

$$dy_t = \mu(t,y_t)dt, \tag{11.9}$$

and a differentiable one-to-one transformation of y_t into ζ_t (say):

$$\zeta_t = f(t,y_t) \Leftrightarrow y_t = f^{-1}(t,\zeta_t).$$

We have

$$d\zeta_t = \frac{\partial f}{\partial t}(t,y_t)dt + \frac{\partial f}{\partial y}(t,y_t)dy_t$$

$$\Leftrightarrow d\zeta_t = \frac{\partial f}{\partial t}(t,f^{-1}(t,\zeta_t))dt + \frac{\partial f}{\partial y}(t,f^{-1}(t,\zeta_t))\mu(t,f^{-1}(t,\zeta_t))dt$$

$$\Leftrightarrow d\zeta_t = \left[\frac{\partial f}{\partial t}(t,f^{-1}(t,\zeta_t)) + \frac{\partial f}{\partial y}(t,f^{-1}(t,\zeta_t))\mu(t,f^{-1}(t,\zeta_t))\right]dt,$$

which provides the deterministic differential equation satisfied by ξ_t. Ito's lemma implies that, in the case of a stochastic differential equation, it is necessary to introduce into the previous formula a correcting term of second order (called the *convexity effect*).

PROPOSITION 11.2, ITO'S LEMMA: *Let us consider a SDE* $dy_t = \mu(t,y_t)dt + \sigma(t,y_t)$ dW_t *and a differentiable transformation of* y_t *into* ζ_t:

$$\zeta_t = f(t,y_t) \Leftrightarrow y_t = f^{-1}(t,\zeta_t).$$

Then, the process (ζ_t) *also satisfies an SDE, and we have*

$$d\zeta_t = \frac{\partial f}{\partial t}dt + \frac{\partial f}{\partial y}dy_t + \frac{1}{2}\frac{\partial^2 f}{\partial y^2}(dy_t)^2$$

$$= \left[\frac{\partial f}{\partial t} + \frac{\partial f}{\partial y}\mu + \frac{1}{2}\frac{\partial^2 f}{\partial y^2}\sigma^2\right]dt + \frac{\partial f}{\partial y}\sigma dW_t,$$

where the subscripts have been suppressed for clarity of exposition.

This formula differs from the standard deterministic one by the presence of the correcting term $\frac{1}{2}\frac{\partial^2 f}{\partial y^2}\sigma^2 dt$. Let us provide a brief explanation of this modification. An SDE decomposes the increments dy_t into two terms: a deterministic term $\mu(t,y_t)dt$ of order dt and a random term $\sigma(t,y_t)dW_t$, which conditional on y_t, is of mean 0 and of order $dt^{1/2}$, to the standard error of dW_t. Let us now consider the second-order expansion of ζ_t. We get

$$d\zeta_t \approx \frac{\partial f}{\partial t}dt + \frac{\partial f}{\partial y}dy_t + \frac{1}{2}\frac{\partial^2 f}{\partial y^2}(dy_t)^2 + \frac{1}{2}\frac{\partial^2 f}{\partial t^2}(dt)^2 + \frac{\partial^2 f}{\partial t\partial y}dtdy_t.$$

We need now to examine the orders of the various deterministic and random terms, each being of mean 0. For instance, dt^2 is deterministic and negligible with respect to dt; hence, it can be omitted. The component $dtdy_t = \mu dt^2 + \sigma dtdW_t$ contains a deterministic term of order dt^2 and a zero-mean random term of order $dt^{3/2}$; so, it also may be disregarded. Let us now consider $(dy_t)^2$. We get

$$(dy_t)^2 = \mu^2 dt^2 + \sigma^2 (dW_t)^2 + 2\mu\sigma dtdW_t$$
$$\approx \sigma^2 (dW_t)^2,$$

since the two other terms are negligible. The term $(dW_t)^2$ is random, but has a nonzero mean. Therefore, we have to separate its mean from the zero-mean stochastic component:

$$(dy_t)^2 \approx \sigma^2 E[(dW_t)^2] + \sigma^2\left[dW_t^2 - E\left(dW_t^2\right)\right]$$
$$= \sigma^2 dt + \sigma^2\left[dW_t^2 - E\left(dW_t^2\right)\right]$$
$$\approx \sigma^2 dt.$$

This term cannot be disregarded, which justifies the presence of the correcting term.

EXAMPLE 11.1, GEOMETRIC BROWNIAN MOTION: Let us consider the process $\zeta_t = \exp W_t$. It is a transformation by an exponential function of the Brownian motion, which satisfies the diffusion equation $dy_t = 0dt + 1dW_t$. We infer the diffusion equation satisfied by ζ_t:

$$d\zeta_t = \frac{1}{2}\exp W_t + \exp W_t dW_t,$$

$$d\zeta_t = \frac{1}{2}\zeta_t dt + \zeta_t dW_t.$$

248

Diffusion Models

11.2 Diffusion Models with Explicit Solutions

It is generally impossible to find a closed-form solution of a diffusion equation written as a function of current and lagged values of Brownian motion. Analytical solutions exist only in some special cases, and the most important ones are described in this section. Obviously, the closed-form solutions also exist for all SDEs derived from those described below by a change of variables (Ito's lemma). Their analytical tractability has contributed to their success in financial literature despite the fact that they rely on very restrictive assumptions.

11.2 *Geometric Brownian Motion with Drift*

The geometric Brownian motion with drift satisfies the diffusion equation

$$dy_t = \mu y_t dt + \sigma y_t dW_t, \tag{11.10}$$

where μ and σ are the drift and volatility parameters, respectively. By applying Ito's formula, we find

$$d \log y_t = \left(\mu - \frac{\sigma^2}{2}\right) dt + \sigma dW_t, \tag{11.11}$$

which may be directly integrated since the (y_t) process no longer appears on the rhs. We get

$$\log y_t - \log y_0 = \int_0^t \left(\mu - \frac{\sigma^2}{2}\right) du + \int_0^t \sigma dW_u$$

$$\Leftrightarrow \log y_t = \log y_0 + t\left(\mu - \frac{\sigma^2}{2}\right) + \sigma W_t \tag{11.12}$$

$$\Leftrightarrow y_t = y_0 \exp t\left(\mu - \frac{\sigma^2}{2}\right) \exp \sigma W_t.$$

From this analytical expression, we deduce the distributional properties of the solution. For instance, the conditional distribution of y_t given y_0 is a log-normal distribution with parameters $\log y_0 + t\left(\mu - \frac{\sigma^2}{2}\right)$ and σ^2. Its conditional mean is

$$E(y_t|y_0) = y_0 \exp t\left(\mu - \frac{\sigma^2}{2}\right) E(\exp \sigma W_t)$$

$$= y_0 \exp t\left(\mu - \frac{\sigma^2}{2}\right) \exp \frac{\sigma^2}{2} t, \tag{11.13}$$

$$E(y_t|y_0) = y_0 \exp \mu t.$$

The trajectories of the solution feature an exponential trend. The conditional variance is given by

$$V(y_t|y_0) = E(y_t^2|y_0) - [E(y_t|y_0)]^2$$
$$= y_0^2 \exp t(2\mu - \sigma^2)E(\exp 2\sigma W_t) - y_0^2 \exp(2\mu t).$$
$$= y_0^2 \exp(2\mu t)[\exp(\sigma^2 t) - 1].$$
$$V(y_t|y_0) = E(y_t|y_0)^2[\exp(\sigma^2 t) - 1].$$

(11.14)

The last equation implies an exponentially increasing ratio of the variance and squared mean. Figure 11.2 displays a simulated path of a geometric Brownian motion where $\mu = 0.5$ and $\sigma = 1$.

11.2.2 The Ornstein-Uhlenbeck Process

The stochastic differential equation for the Ornstein-Uhlenbeck (OU) process is

$$dy_t = (\phi - \lambda y_t)dt + \sigma dW_t.$$

(11.15)

To solve this equation, it is useful to consider first a deterministic equation corresponding to (11.15) without noise, that is, under the constraint $\sigma = 0$. This equation

$$dy_t = (\phi - \lambda y_t)dt,$$

(11.16)

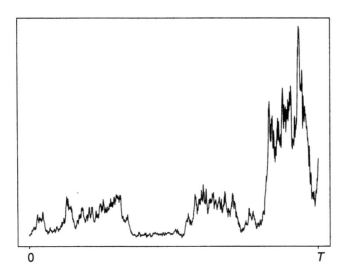

Figure 11.2   *Simulated Path of a Geometric Brownian Motion*

is an ordinary differential equation that is linear in y_t. Therefore, its general solution admits the form

$$y_t = k \, \exp(-\lambda t) + \frac{\phi}{\lambda}, \qquad (11.17)$$

where k is an arbitrary constant.

To solve the initial stochastic differential equation, we introduce the change of variable $y_t \to \zeta_t$, where:

$$y_t = \zeta_t \, \exp(-\lambda t) + \frac{\phi}{\lambda}. \qquad (11.18)$$

By Ito's lemma, the second-order correction term is not required since the relation between y_t and ζ_t is linear. We get

$$dy_t = d\zeta_t \, \exp(-\lambda t) - \lambda \zeta_t \, \exp(-\lambda t)dt$$

$$= d\zeta_t \, \exp(-\lambda t) - \lambda \left(y_t - \frac{\phi}{\lambda} \right) dt$$

$$= d\zeta_t \, \exp(-\lambda t) + (\phi - \lambda y_t)dt.$$

From (11.15), we deduce

$$\sigma dW_t = d\zeta_t \, \exp(-\lambda t)$$

$$\Leftrightarrow d\zeta_t = \sigma \, \exp(\lambda t)dW_t.$$

Therefore, for any pair of dates $t < t'$, we can express ζ_t as a function of $\zeta_{t'}$ and of the noise realizations between t' and t:

$$\zeta_t = \zeta_{t'} + \int_{t'}^{t} \sigma \, \exp(\lambda u)dW_u, \qquad t' < t.$$

A similar relation is derived from (11.18) for the initial process

$$y_t = \zeta_t \, \exp(-\lambda t) + \frac{\phi}{\lambda}$$

$$= \zeta_{t'} \, \exp(-\lambda t) + \frac{\phi}{\lambda} + \exp(-\lambda t) \int_{t'}^{t} \sigma \, \exp(\lambda u)dW_u$$

$$= \left[y_{t'} \, \exp(\lambda t') - \frac{\phi}{\lambda} \, \exp(\lambda t') \right] \exp(-\lambda t) + \frac{\phi}{\lambda} + \sigma \, \exp(-\lambda t) \int_{t'}^{t} \exp(\lambda u)dW_u$$

$$= y_{t'} \, \exp - \lambda(t - t') + \frac{\phi}{\lambda} \left[1 - \exp - \lambda(t - t') \right] + \sigma \, \exp(-\lambda t) \int_{t'}^{t} \exp(\lambda u)dW_u.$$

PROPOSITION 11.3: *The solutions of the stochastic differential equation* $dy_t = (\phi - \lambda y_t)dt + \sigma dW_t$ *satisfy, for any* $t' < t$,

$$y_t = \exp[-\lambda(t-t')]y_{t'} + \frac{\phi}{\lambda}[1 - \exp - \lambda(t-t')] + \sigma \int_{t'}^{t} \exp -\lambda(t-u)dW_u.$$

Several important results can be inferred from this expression. They are given below as corollaries.

COROLLARY 11.1: *For an OU process,* $y_t - \exp[-\lambda(t-t')]y_{t'}$ *is independent of* $y_{t'}$.

PROOF: Indeed, $y_t - \exp[-\lambda(t-t')]y_{t'}$ is a function of infinitesimal increments of the Brownian motion on (t',t), whereas the values y_τ, $\tau < t'$, depend on the value of the Brownian motion prior to t'. Then, the corollary is a consequence of the property of independent increments of the Brownian motion.
QED

We now explicitly describe the relation when $t' = t - 1$. We get

$$y_t = (\exp - \lambda)y_{t-1} + \phi \frac{1 - \exp - \lambda}{\lambda} + \sigma \int_{t-1}^{t} \exp - \lambda(t-u)dW_u.$$

The variables $\int_{t-1}^{t} \exp - \lambda(t-u)dW_u$, t varying, are Gaussian and independent, with mean 0 and variance given by

$$\sigma^2 \int_{t-1}^{t} \exp - 2\lambda(t-u)du = \frac{\sigma^2}{2\lambda}(1 - \exp - 2\lambda).$$

Therefore, we can write

$$y_t = (\exp - \lambda)y_{t-1} + \phi \frac{1 - \exp - \lambda}{\lambda} + \sigma\left(\frac{1 - \exp - 2\lambda}{2\lambda}\right)^{\frac{1}{2}}\varepsilon_t, \quad (11.19)$$

where $(\varepsilon_t, t \in Z)$ is a Gaussian white noise with unitary variance. We get the following corollary:

COROLLARY 11.2: *For* $\lambda > 0$, *the discrete time process* $(y_t, t \in Z)$ *is a Gaussian autoregressive process of order 1, with mean* ϕ/λ, *autoregressive coefficient* $\exp(-\lambda)$, *and innovation variance* $\sigma^2 \dfrac{1 - \exp - 2\lambda}{2\lambda}$.

This result can be extended to prove that, for $\lambda > 0$, the continuous time process $(y_t, t \in R)$ is also stationary and Gaussian. Thus, the OU process is the continuous time analog of the Gaussian AR(1) autoregressive process (see also Chapter 2).

11.2.3   The Cox-Ingersoll-Ross Model

The model of Cox, Ingersoll, and Ross (1985) was introduced to represent the dynamics of short-term interest rate. The stochastic differential equation is

$$dy_t = (a - by_t)dt + \sigma \sqrt{y_t}dW_t. \tag{11.20}$$

While the drift is a linear function of y_t as in the Ornstein-Uhlenbeck process, the volatility is a square root of y. For this reason, the CIR (Cox-Ingersoll-Ross) process is often called a *square root process*.

PROPOSITION 11.4: *Let us denote* $c(t) = \dfrac{\sigma^2}{4b}[1 - exp(-bt)]$. *Then, the conditional Laplace transform of the process* $x_t = y_t/c(t)$ *is given by*

$$E[\exp - \lambda x_t|y_0] = \frac{1}{[2\lambda + 1]^{2a/\sigma^2}} \exp\left[-\frac{\lambda}{2\lambda + 1}\frac{4y_0 b}{\sigma^2(\exp bt - 1)}\right].$$

The conditional distribution of $x_t = y_t/c(t)$ *given* y_0 *is a noncentered chi-square distribution with* $\delta = 4a/\sigma^2$ *degrees of freedom and the noncentrality parameter*
$$\xi = \frac{4y_0 b}{\sigma^2(\exp bt - 1)}.$$

Let us recall that the chi-square distribution $\chi^2 (\delta, \xi)$ admits a density function

$$f(x) = \frac{\exp - (\xi/2)}{2\xi^{\delta/4 - 1/2}} \exp(-x/2)x^{\delta/4 - 1/2}I_{\delta/2 - 1}(\sqrt{x\xi}), \tag{11.21}$$

where $I_v(x)$ is a Bessel function

$$I_v(x) = (x/2)^v \sum_{n=0}^{\infty} \frac{(x/2)^{2n}}{n!\Gamma(v + n + 1)}. \tag{11.22}$$

This result is valid when δ and ξ are positive or, equivalently, if $a > 0$ and $b > 0$. Then, the CIR process takes positive values. Moreover, the condition $2a/\sigma^2 < 1$ is also imposed for stationarity. The marginal distribution is derived by setting $t = \infty$. We see that

$$y_t\, 4b/\sigma^2 \sim \chi^2(4a/\sigma^2). \tag{11.23}$$

The first- and second-order conditional moments are easily derived from the second-order expansion of the log-Laplace transform. Indeed, it is easily checked that

$$\log E[\exp -\lambda x_t|y_0] = -\lambda E(x_t|y_0) + \frac{\lambda^2}{2}V(x_t|y_0) + 0(\lambda^2). \tag{11.24}$$

We find

$$\log E[\exp - \lambda x_t | y_0] = -\frac{2a}{\sigma^2} \log(2\lambda + 1) - \frac{\lambda}{2\lambda + 1}\xi$$

$$= -\lambda\left(\frac{4a}{\sigma^2} + \xi\right) + \frac{\lambda^2}{2}\left(\frac{8a}{\sigma^2} + 4\xi\right) + 0(\lambda^3).$$

Therefore, we get

$$E(y_t | y_0) = c(t)\left(\frac{4a}{\sigma^2} + \xi\right), \qquad V(y_t | y_0) = c(t)^2\left(\frac{8a}{\sigma^2} + 4\xi\right). \qquad (11.25)$$

The conditional mean and variance are both linear functions of ξ and thus of y_0. The marginal moments correspond to the limiting case $t = +\infty$:

$$E(y_t) = a/b, \qquad V(y_t) = \frac{a\sigma^2}{2b^2}. \qquad (11.26)$$

11.3 Approximation of Diffusion Models

When a diffusion equation does not admit a closed-form solution, it is generally also impossible to find the analytical formula of the conditional distribution of y_t given y_0, say. The knowledge of this distribution is, however, necessary for derivative asset pricing and estimation. In this section, we present various approximations of a diffusion model, such that the conditional distribution of the approximated model is easy to derive and close to the true one.

11.3.1 Euler Discretization

The Euler discretization approach consists of replacing the initial diffusion model

$$dy_t = \mu(y_t)dt + \sigma(y_t)dW_t, \qquad y_0 \text{ given}, \qquad (11.27)$$

by a recursive equation in discrete time. More precisely, let us introduce a small time interval δ and consider the process $(y_t^{(\delta)}, t \in R^+)$ such that

$$y_t^{(\delta)} = y_{[t/\delta]}^{(\delta)},$$

where $[x]$ denotes the greatest integer less than or equal to x, and

$$y_n^{(\delta)} - y_{n-1}^{(\delta)} = \mu\left(y_{n-1}^{(\delta)}\right)\delta + \sigma\left(y_{n-1}^{(\delta)}\right)\delta^{\frac{1}{2}}\varepsilon_n^{(\delta)}, \qquad y_0^{(\delta)} = y_0, \qquad (11.28)$$

where $\varepsilon_n^{(\delta)}$, n varying, is a Gaussian standard white noise.

This equation represents the Euler discretized version of the continuous time diffusion (11.27). A transition from date $n-1$ to date n takes time δ; dy_t has been replaced by the corresponding increment $\Delta y_n^{(\delta)}$, dt by δ, and dW_t, which is $N(0,\delta)$, has been standardized, that is, divided by $\delta^{1/2}$. This discretization is interesting to us because of the following proposition:

PROPOSITION 11.5: *The conditional distribution of $y_t^{(\delta)}$ given y_0 tends to the conditional distribution of y_t given y_0 when δ tends to 0.*

11.3.2. Binomial Tree

Approximation (11.28) has been derived by time discretization that preserved the normality of the noise. It is also possible to discretize both time and the value space of the noise. A *binomial tree* is obtained when the noise admits only two values, denoted u_δ and d_δ, for up and down movements, respectively (see Section 11.4). The approximated model is

$$y_n^{(\delta)} = y_{n-1}^{(\delta)} + \varepsilon_n^{(\delta)},$$

where

$$\varepsilon_n(\delta) = \begin{cases} u_\delta\!\left(y_{n-1}^{(\delta)}\right), & \text{with probability } p_\delta\!\left(y_{n-1}^{(\delta)}\right), \\ d_\delta\!\left(y_{n-1}^{(\delta)}\right), & \text{with probability } 1 - p_\delta\!\left(y_{n-1}^{(\delta)}\right). \end{cases}$$

The admissible values of the shock may depend on the lagged price, as does the probability of an up movement. The proposition below gives a condition for the convergence in distribution of $y_t^{(\delta)}$ to y_t that is easy to interpret (Stroock and Varadhan 1979; Nelson and Ramaswamy 1990).

PROPOSITION 11.6: *The conditional distribution of $y_t^{(\delta)}$ given y_0 tends to the conditional distribution of y_t given y_0, when δ tends to 0, if the two processes have asymptotically the same instantaneous drift function and volatility function and the instantaneous third-order moment tends to 0.*

For instance, we can set the average drift and volatility over a period of time of length δ equal to their continuous time counterparts. The conditions are

$$\begin{cases} \dfrac{1}{\delta} E\!\left[y_n^{(\delta)} - y_{n-1}^{(\delta)} \,\middle|\, y_{n-1}^{(\delta)}\right] = \mu\!\left[y_{n-1}^{(\delta)}\right], \\[2ex] \dfrac{1}{\delta} V\!\left[y_n^{(\delta)} - y_{n-1}^{(\delta)} \,\middle|\, y_{n-1}^{(\delta)}\right] = \dfrac{1}{\delta} V\!\left[y_n^{(\delta)} \,\middle|\, y_{n-1}^{(\delta)}\right] = \sigma^2\!\left[y_{n-1}^{(\delta)}\right], \end{cases}$$

or, equivalently,

$$\begin{cases} p_\delta\big(y_{n-1}^{(\delta)}\big)\big[u_\delta\big(y_{n-1}^{(\delta)}\big) - y_{n-1}^{(\delta)}\big] + \big(1 - p_\delta\big(y_{n-1}^{(\delta)}\big)\big)\big[d_\delta\big(y_{n-1}^{(\delta)}\big) - y_{n-1}^{(\delta)}\big] = \delta\mu\big(y_{n-1}^{(\delta)}\big), \\ p_\delta\big(y_{n-1}^{(\delta)}\big)\big(1 - p_\delta\big(y_{n-1}^{(\delta)}\big)\big)\big\{u_\delta\big[y_{n-1}^{(\delta)}\big] - d_\delta\big[y_{n-1}^{(\delta)}\big]\big\} = \delta\sigma^2\big(y_{n-1}^{(\delta)}\big). \end{cases}$$

We get a system of two equations with three unknowns p_δ, u_δ, and d_δ. Now, we need to select all admissible solutions with trajectories that are sufficiently smooth to ensure that the limiting path of y_t is continuous (see Section 11.6.2 for the discontinuous case). This is the reason for introducing an additional condition on the instantaneous third moment, which may be written as

$$\frac{1}{\delta} E\Big[\big(y_n^{(\delta)} - y_{n-1}^{(\delta)}\big)^3 \,\big|\, y_{n-1}^{(\delta)}\Big] \to 0, \qquad \text{when } \delta \to 0.$$

In particular, we can introduce the third equation

$$p_\delta\big[y_{n-1}^{(\delta)}\big]\big[u_\delta\big(y_{n-1}^{(\delta)}\big) - y_{n-1}^{(\delta)}\big]^3 + \big[1 - p_\delta\big(y_{n-1}^{(\delta)}\big)\big]\big[d_\delta\big(y_{n-1}^{(\delta)}\big) - y_{n-1}^{(\delta)}\big]^3 = 0.$$

11.3.3 Simulation of a Path of a Diffusion Process

Instead of simulating a path of a diffusion process, which would require determination of a continuum of values y_t, $t \geq 0$, and is practically infeasible, a simulated discrete time path can be based on one of the approximated models. This approach was used to plot Figures 11.1 and 11.2. Let us consider the Euler discretization. We first select a time unit $\delta = 1/100$ (say) and then compute recursively

$$y_n^s = y_{n-1}^s + \mu\big(y_{n-1}^s\big)\frac{1}{100} + \sigma\big(y_{n-1}^s\big)\frac{1}{10}\,\varepsilon_n^s, \qquad n = 1, \dots,$$

where ε_n^s, $n = 0, 1, \dots$, is a sequence of independent drawings from the standard normal distribution, and $y_0^s = 0$ (say). Next, we plot the values y_n^s against the associated times $t = n/100$ and link the points by segments of a straight line.

This approach can be repeated several times, producing a number of different trajectories. In particular, we may consider another sequence of drawings $\varepsilon_n^{s'}$, n varying, and generate another simulated path $y_n^{s'}$, s' varying. Such a repetition is called a *replication*.

As an illustration, we have drawn 200 simulated paths of the continuous time process with length $N = 1000$ [$\approx t = 10$],

$$dy_t = 2(1 - y_t)dt + dW_t.$$

We display in Figure 11.3 the estimated marginal distribution of y_{10} inferred from the repeated simulations. Note that it is an approximation of a normal distribution with mean 1 and standard error 0.5 [see (11.19)].

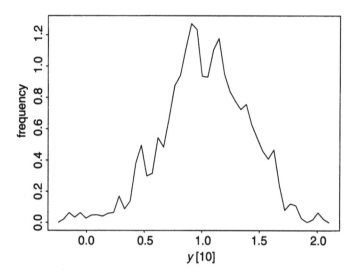

Figure 11.3 *Monte-Carlo Approximation of Marginal Distribution*

The accuracy of this approximation depends on the selected time unit δ. The smaller the time unit, the more accurate is the approximation to a continuous time trajectory. We provide in Figure 11.4 the approximations obtained with $\delta = 1/100$, $\delta = 1/10$, and $\delta = 1$. Their comparison shows clearly that the accuracy of the approximation is very sensitive to the selected δ, which needs to be fixed at a sufficiently small value.

Sometimes, the accuracy of the estimated marginal distribution may be improved by introducing either dependent replications or a different Euler discretization scheme. For instance, instead of independent drawings of the sequence $(\varepsilon_1^s, \ldots, \varepsilon_N^s)$, for varying s, we can perform a single drawing and produce the additional ones by reverting the sign of a subset of components. We still obtain drawings in the same distribution; however, they are dependent. This simulation technique is called *antithetic*.

We can also perform the simulation under a different Euler discretization. Recall that the Euler discretization depends on a preliminary transformation applied to the data. If g is a one-to-one transformation, we deduce from Ito's formula

$$dg(y_t) = \left[\frac{\partial g}{\partial y}(y_t)\mu(y_t) + \frac{1}{2}\frac{\partial^2 g}{\partial y^2}(y_t)\sigma^2(y_t) \right] dt + \frac{\partial g}{\partial y}(y_t)\sigma(y_t)dW_t,$$

with the following Euler discretization:

$$g\left[y_n^{(\delta)}\right] - g\left[y_{n-1}^{(\delta)}\right] = \left[\frac{\partial g}{\partial y}\left[y_{n-1}^{(\delta)}\right]\mu\left[y_{n-1}^{(\delta)}\right] + \frac{1}{2}\frac{\partial^2 g}{\partial y^2}\left[y_{n-1}^{(\delta)}\right]\sigma^2\left[y_{n-1}^{(\delta)}\right] \right] \delta \frac{\partial g}{\partial y}\left[y_{n-1}^{(\delta)}\right]\sigma\left[y_{n-1}^{(\delta)}\right] \sqrt{\delta}\; \varepsilon_n^{(\delta)}.$$

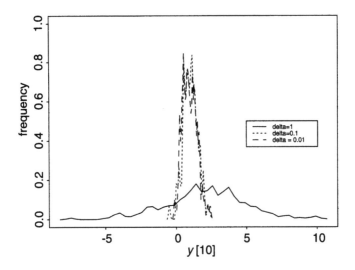

Figure 11.4 *Comparison of Marginal Distributions (δ Varying)*

This result is a nonlinear recursive equation for $y_n^{(\delta)}$, which is different from (11.28).

11.3.4 Diffusion Approximation of an Autoregressive Conditionally Heteroscedastic Model

In the previous sections, we searched for discretized versions of diffusion models, which allowed us to compute conditional or marginal distributions by simulation. We can also consider a converse problem. Which diffusion model provides an approximation to a given discrete time process?

An answer is easily obtained when we introduce a sequence of Markov processes indexed by the time unit δ. Let us denote by $y_n^{(\delta)}$, n varying, the process sampled at time unit δ. This process can be multidimensional. As in Section 11.3.2, we define the average drift and volatility at horizon δ:

$$\frac{1}{\delta} E\left[Y_n^{(\delta)} - Y_{n-1}^{(\delta)} \,|\, Y_{n-1}^{(\delta)} \right] = \mu_\delta\left(Y_{n-1}^{(\delta)} \right),$$

$$\frac{1}{\delta} V\left[Y_n^{(\delta)} - Y_{n-1}^{(\delta)} \,|\, Y_{n-1}^{(\delta)} \right] = \Sigma_\delta\left(Y_{n-1}^{(\delta)} \right).$$

The analog of Proposition 11.6 is given below.

PROPOSITION 11.7: *The process* $Y_t^{(\delta)} = Y_{[t/\delta]}^{(\delta)}$, *t varying, converges in distribution to a diffusion process* (Y_t) *when* δ *tends to 0 if the average drift and volatility functions converge:*

$$\lim_{\delta \to 0} \mu_\delta = \mu, \ \lim_{\delta \to 0} \Sigma_\delta = \Sigma,$$

(and the average third-order moment at horizon δ *tends to 0). The limiting process satisfies the stochastic differential system*

$$dY_t = \mu(Y_t)dt + \Sigma(Y_t)^{1/2}dW_t,$$

where the components of (W_t) *are independent Brownian motions.*

This technique was used by Nelson (1990) to prove that the ARCH(1) (autoregressive conditionally heteroscedastic process of order 1) model does not admit a nondegenerate continuous time analog. However, some ARCH-M (ARCH in mean) models admit continuous time limits.

PROPOSITION 11.8: *Let us consider the GARCH in mean (GARCH-M)(1,1) model defined by*

$$\begin{cases} y_t = y_{t-1} + f(\sigma_t^2) + \sigma_t \varepsilon_t, \\ \sigma_{t+1}^2 = w + \sigma_t^2(\beta + \alpha \varepsilon_t). \end{cases}$$

Then, its continuous time analog is

$$\begin{cases} dy_t = f(\sigma_t^2)dt + \sigma_t dW_{1,t}, \\ d\sigma_t^2 = (w - \theta\sigma_t^2)dt + \alpha\sigma_t dW_{2,t}. \end{cases}$$

PROOF: See Nelson (1990) or Gourieroux (1997, Sec. 5.2).

The continuous time approximation has a recursive form: The second equation describes the dynamics of the instantaneous volatility, and its outcome substituted into the first equation determines the dynamics of the entire series. Such a bivariate model is called a *stochastic volatility* (SV) *model* (see Chapter 9 for its discrete time analog). It may seem surprising that the continuous time SV model includes two independent noise processes $(dW_{1,t})$ and $(dW_{2,t})$, whereas the discrete time GARCH-M model depends on one noise only. In fact, an ARCH specification contains a linear and a quadratic function of the noise (ε_t). The two Brownian motions $W_{1,T}$ and $W_{2,T}$ arise as continuous time counterparts of the two partial sums $\tilde{W}_{1,T} = \frac{1}{\sqrt{T}} \Sigma_{t=1}^{T} \varepsilon_t$ and $\tilde{W}_{1,T} = \frac{1}{\sqrt{T}} \Sigma_{t=1}^{T}(\varepsilon_t^2 - 1)$. These partial sums are asymptotically Gaussian and independent by the central limit theorem (if ε_t has a symmetric distribution). Therefore, the dimension of the limiting continuous time system is determined by the degree of nonlinearity of the initial discrete time model.

11.4 Derivative Pricing in Complete Market

In this section, we consider price processes of financial assets that determine unique derivative prices. We first consider a setup involving up and down price movements (the so-called binomial tree) analyzed by Cox, Ross, and Rubinstein (1979). Next, we examine the limiting case when time between the consecutive price changes tends to 0. The outcome of this approach is the well-known Black-Scholes formula. Finally, we discuss derivative pricing in the general framework of complete markets.

11.4.1 The Binomial Tree

Description of the Binomial Tree
We consider an economy with two financial assets, which may be traded at discrete dates $n = 0, 1, 2, \ldots, N, \ldots$. The risk-free asset has an initial value equal to 1 and a gross return $R = 1 + r$, independent of the date. The risky asset pays no dividends. Its price at date n is denoted by S_n. This price process satisfies the binomial scheme

$$S_{n+1} = S_n[1 + u\varepsilon_n + d(1 - \varepsilon_n)], \tag{11.29}$$

where ε_n, $n = 0, 1, \ldots$, is a sequence of independent identically distributed (i.i.d.) variables with the same Bernoulli distribution $B(1,p)$, and u and d are two scalars. Therefore, at date n, S_n is known, and the future price can take two values. For the high value,

$$S_{n+1} = S_n(1 + u), \quad \text{if } \varepsilon_n = 1, \text{ with probability } p,$$

For the low value,

$$S_{n+1} = S_n(1 + d), \quad \text{if } \varepsilon_n = 0, \text{ with probability } 1 - p.$$

The terminology *high value* or *low value* (or *up* and *down*) is determined by the absence of arbitrage opportunity (AAO) condition. Indeed, these high and low values of the asset price are necessarily above and below the value associated with the risk-free asset, so that

$$1 + d < 1 + r < 1 + u. \tag{11.30}$$

Indeed, if we had $1 + d < 1 + u < 1 + r$, the risk-free asset would always have a return greater than the return on the risky asset. Thus, deterministic gains would be obtained by investing S_0 units of risk-free asset and -1 unit of the risky asset.

By recursive substitutions, we deduce from (11.29)

$$\log S_n = \log S_0 + n \log(1 + d) + \log \frac{1 + u}{1 + d} \sum_{i=1}^{n} \varepsilon_i. \tag{11.31}$$

The price logarithm has two components: a deterministic trend $n \log(1+d)$ and a random term $\Sigma_{i=1}^{n} \, \varepsilon_n$, which is binomially distributed $B(n,p)$. It is a random walk with a drift equal to $p \log(1+u) + (1-p) \log(1+d)$. The price evolution is displayed in Figure 11.5.

The successive prices are

$$S_1 = \begin{cases} (1+u)S_0, & \text{with probability } p, \\ (1+d)S_0, & \text{with probability } (1-p), \end{cases}$$

$$S_2 = \begin{cases} (1+u)^2 S_0, & \text{with probability } p^2, \\ (1+u)(1+d)S_0, & \text{with probability } 2p(1-p), \\ (1+d)^2 S_0, & \text{with probability } (1-p)^2. \end{cases}$$

In general, we denote the number of up movements in n trials by y, obtaining

$$S_n = (1+u)^y (1+d)^{n-y} S_0,$$

with probability

$$C_n^y p^y (1-p)^{n-y}, \qquad y = 0, \ldots, n,$$

where $C_n^y = n!/[y!(n-y)!]$. Except for the initial and terminal values, each admissible S_n (or *node*) can be reached in various ways. For instance, $S_2 = (1+u)(1+d)S_0$ can be reached either by the sequence $\varepsilon_1 = 1$, $\varepsilon_2 = 0$, or by the sequence $\varepsilon_1 = 0$, $\varepsilon_2 = 1$.

Contingent Assets
Prices of complex derivatives or contingent assets can be deduced from prices of some elementary products, called *state-contingent claims*, *Arrow-Debreu securities*, or *digital options* (Arrow 1964).

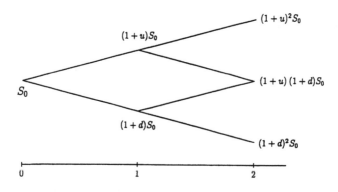

Figure 11.5 *Binomial Tree*

There exist two digital options with maturity 1. The first one pays \$1 at date 1 if $\varepsilon_1 = 1$, that is, if an up movement is observed; it pays \$0 otherwise. The second one pays \$1 at date 0 if $\varepsilon_1 = 0$, that is, if a down movement is observed; it pays \$0 otherwise.

The definition of the digital options with maturity n is similar. There exist 2^n different options associated with various possible paths. Let us consider a set of n values $0,1$: $\varepsilon_1^0, \ldots, \varepsilon_n^0$. The corresponding option pays \$1 at date n if $\varepsilon_1 = \varepsilon_1^0, \ldots, \varepsilon_n = \varepsilon_n^0$, it pays \$0 otherwise. We denote this digital option $\{n; \varepsilon_1^0, \ldots, \varepsilon_n^0\}$.

Any derivative written on the underlying asset S_n can be viewed as a portfolio of digital options. A derivative asset is defined by the cash flows received at future dates. At date n, this cash flow is $g_n(S_1, \ldots, S_n)$, a function of current and past prices or, equivalently, $\tilde{g}_n(\varepsilon_1, \ldots, \varepsilon_n)$, a function of current and past shocks. This asset has the same cash flow as a portfolio that includes the digital options $\{n; \varepsilon_1^0, \ldots, \varepsilon_n^0\}$ with allocations $\tilde{g}_n(\varepsilon_1^0, \ldots, \varepsilon_n^0)$, n, $\varepsilon_1^0, \ldots, \varepsilon_n^0$ varying.

EXAMPLE 11.2: Let us consider a European call option (see Chapter 1) with maturity 2 and a strike price K slightly less than $(1+u)(1+d)S_0$. This option gives the right to buy at date 2 a unit of the underlying asset at price K fixed in advance. It provides $S_2 - K$ dollars at date 2 if $S_2 \geq K$ and \$0 otherwise. It may be viewed as a portfolio that includes the digital options

$$\{2; 1, 1,\}, \qquad \{2; 1, 0\}, \qquad \{2; 0, 1\},$$

with respective weights $(1+u)^2 S_0 - K$, $(1+u)(1+d)S_0 - K$, and $(1+u)(1+d)S_0 - K$.

Digital Option Pricing

In the framework of the binomial tree, a digital option may be viewed as a portfolio that includes the risk-free asset and the risky asset, with an allocation that is regularly updated at each trading date without cash infusions or withdrawals until the option expires (the *self-financing condition*). By applying the condition of AAO, we infer the price of the digital option from the value of the associated portfolio. Any derivative of the underlying asset is a portfolio of digital options; therefore, its price is unique and can be determined.

We first apply this approach to the digital option. In the next section, we generalize it to all derivatives.

PROPOSITION 11.9: *The prices of the digital options with maturity 1 are*

$$C(1;\, 1) = \frac{1}{1+r}\,\pi, \qquad C(1,\, 0) = \frac{1}{1+r}(1-\pi),$$

where $\pi = \dfrac{r-d}{u-d}$ *is between 0 and 1.*

PROOF: Let us consider the digital option $\{1;\varepsilon_1 = 1\}$, which pays \$1 at date 1 if and only if an up movement is observed. The portfolio containing α units of the risk-free asset and β units of the risky asset generates the same cash flow as the digital option if

$$\begin{cases} \alpha(1+r) + \beta S_0(1+u) = 1, & \text{(up movement)} \\ \alpha(1+r) + \beta S_0(1+d) = 0. & \text{(down movement)} \end{cases}$$

This system has the unique solution

$$\alpha = -(u-d)^{-1}\frac{1+d}{1+r}, \qquad \beta = \frac{1}{S_0}(u-d)^{-1},$$

and the price of the digital option $\{1;1\}$ is

$$C(1;\,1) = \alpha 1 + \beta S_0$$
$$= \frac{1}{1+r}\frac{r-d}{u-d}.$$

A similar computation performed for the second digital option gives

$$C(1;\,0) = \frac{1}{1+r}\frac{u-r}{u-d}.$$

QED

The prices of digital options do not depend on the initial price S_0, the probability p, or the risk aversion of the investors. They are essentially deduced from the AAO conditions, which balance the payoffs.

PROPOSITION 11.10: *The prices of the digital options with maturity n are*

$$C(n;\,\varepsilon_1, \ldots, \varepsilon_n) = \prod_{j=1}^{n} C(1;\varepsilon_j)$$
$$= \frac{1}{(1+r)^n}\pi^{\sum_{j=1}^n \varepsilon_j}(1-\pi)^{n-\sum_{j=1}^n \varepsilon_j}$$
$$= \frac{1}{(1+r)^n}\pi^{H_n}(1-\pi)^{n-H_n}.$$

where $H_n = \sum_{j=1}^n \varepsilon_j$ counts the number of up movements in the associated path.

PROOF: We give only a brief insight on the proof by considering the digital option $\{2;\,1,\,0\}$ with maturity 2. A recursive procedure allows us to construct a portfolio with the same cash flow at date 2.

At date 1, in the case when $\varepsilon_1 = 1$, we have to be able to buy a digital option $\{1;\,0\}$ with a price that is

$$dS_t = \mu S_t dt + \sigma S_t dW_t, \qquad (11.33)$$

or, equivalently, by applying Ito's formula,

$$d \log S_t = \nu dt + \sigma dW_t, \qquad (11.34)$$

with $\nu = \mu - \sigma^2/2$.

We are interested in pricing assets with cash flows that are functions of the current and past values of S. To simplify the exposition, we consider a derivative asset with a unique payoff $g(S_T)$ at a fixed date T. The price $C(t;g(S_T))$ of this derivative at date t is unique under the set of assumptions given below:

ASSUMPTION A.11.1: *There are no transaction costs.*

ASSUMPTION A.11.2: *It is possible to construct a portfolio in the risk-free and risky assets, with allocations of any sign (no short-sell constraint) and any amount.*

ASSUMPTION A.11.3: *This portfolio can be updated continuously.*

ASSUMPTION A.11.4: *A price of the derivative exists and depends only on the past and current values of S.*

PROPOSITION 11.12: *Under Assumptions A.11.1–A.11.4 and if the price dynamic satisfies (11.33),*

(i) *There exists a portfolio in the risk-free and risky assets that is self-financed, continuously updated, and provides the same payoff $g(S_T)$ at date T as the derivative. It is called the* hedging *portfolio.*
(ii) *The price of the derivative is unique.*
(iii) *The derivative price is given by*

$$C(t;g(S_T)) = \exp[-r(T-t)]E^\pi[g(S_T)|S_t],$$

where the pricing probability corresponds to the distribution of a process satisfying

$$dS_t = rS_t dt + \sigma S_t dW_t^*,$$

or, equivalently,

$$d \log S_t = (r - \sigma^2/2)dt + \sigma dW_t^*.$$

PROOF: See Appendix 11.1.

The uniqueness of the derivative price is a consequence of the AAO condition and is mainly due to Assumptions A.11.3 and A.11.4. Indeed, a multiplicity of prices may occur if the derivative price depends on some external shocks unrelated to the price of the underlying asset, or if the updating frequency of the hedging portfolio is not sufficient to offset the continuous shocks to the price S_t. The set of conditions ensuring the uniqueness of the derivative price is often called the *complete market hypothesis*.

The price formula given in (iii) of Proposition 11.12 expresses the price as the expectation of the (continuously) discounted cash flow with respect to a modified probability. Under this risk-neutral probability, the price process is still a geometric Brownian motion with the same volatility σ and a modified drift r.

This drift is selected so that the discounted price is locally a martingale under π since

$$E[dS_t|S_t] \approx rS_t dt$$

$$<=> E[S_{t+dt}|S_t] \approx (1+rdt)S_t.$$

Black-Scholes Formula for European Call Options
The general pricing formula of Proposition 11.12 can be applied to specific derivatives. Let us consider a European call option with the strike price K and maturity T. It pays $g(S_T) = (S_T - K)^+$ at date T. Its price at date t will be denoted by $C(t; H, K)$, where $H = T - t$ is the *residual maturity*.

PROPOSITION 11.13: *The Black-Scholes price of the call is*

$$C(t;H,K) = \exp(-rH)E^\pi[(S_{t+H} - K)^+|S_t]$$

$$= S_t\Phi(x_t) - K\exp(-rH)\Phi(x_t - \sigma\sqrt{H})$$

where $x_t = \dfrac{\log[S_t/(K\exp-rH)]}{\sigma\sqrt{H}} + \dfrac{1}{2}\sigma\sqrt{H}$, *and* Φ *is the cdf of the standard normal distribution.*

PROOF: See Appendix 11.2

11.4.3   General Result

Pricing Formula
The previous approach can be extended to risky assets with more complex dynamics. We still consider a risk-free asset with a risk-free rate r and a risky asset with a price (S_t) that follows a Markov process. The market is complete if there exists a unique pricing formula for any derivative written on S. Let us consider a derivative asset providing the cash flow $g(S_T)$ at date T and denote by $C(t,T-t,g)$ its price at date t, $t \leq T$. It is possible to show that the pricing formula can only be of the type

$$C(t,T-t,g) = \exp-r(T-t)E^\pi[g(S_T)|S_t], \qquad (11.35)$$

where π is a unique modified distribution of the process (S_t).

The conditional risk-neutral density, that is, the probability density function (pdf) of S_T given S_t, denoted $\pi_{T-t}(s|S_t)$, is directly related to prices of digital options. Let us introduce the derivative associated with the cash flow $g(S_T) = 1_{(s,s+ds)}(S_T)$. From (11.35), the price of this digital option is approximately equal to $\exp - r(T - t)\pi_{T-t}(s|S_t)ds$. Therefore, $\pi_{T-t}(s|S_t)ds$ is a normalized price of a digital option, that is, its price divided by the price of the zero-coupon bond with residual maturity $T - t$.

Determination of the Risk-Neutral Probability
Let us assume that the asset price satisfies a stochastic differential equation

$$dS_t = \mu(S_t)dt + \sigma(S_t)dW_t. \tag{11.36}$$

There exist three methods of computing the risk-neutral probability. The first one approximates the continuous time dynamics by an appropriate binomial tree and computes the risk-neutral probability associated with this tree. This approach is frequently used by practitioners. The second approach is based on a theorem about martingales that characterizes the change of probability measure that leads to a martingale price process. This theorem, called the *Girsanov theorem*, is given below in the framework of asset prices determined by (11.36) (see, e.g., Karatzas and Shreve 1988, p. 184; Pham and Touzi 1996).

PROPOSITION 11.14, GIRSANOV THEOREM: *The change of probability measure is such that*

$$E^\pi[g(S_T)|S_t]$$

$$= E[\exp\left\{-\int_t^T \frac{\mu_\tau - rS_\tau}{\sigma_\tau} dW_\tau - \frac{1}{2}\int_t^T \left(\frac{\mu_\tau - rS_\tau}{\sigma_\tau}\right)^2 d\tau\right\}g(S_T)|S_t],$$

where $\mu_\tau = \mu(S_\tau)$, $\sigma_\tau = \sigma(S_\tau)$, and E is the expectation with respect to the historical probability.

Finally, the risk-neutral probability may also be derived by solving partial differential equations. More precisely, let us fix the maturity T and the cash flow g and denote $G(t) = C(t,T - t;g)$ the price at t. The function G will satisfy a partial differential equation. The coefficients of this equation are independent of T and g, that is, of the derivative to be priced. The effect of the derivative is taken into account only by the terminal condition $G(T) = g(S_T)$. The differential equation satisfied by the option price is derived by arbitrage conditions (Merton 1973b). The idea is to construct a risk-free self-financed portfolio based on both the asset and the derivative. By the absence of arbitrage condition, its return will be equal to the risk-free rate.

Let us denote by $a(t)$ and $a_g(t)$ the allocations in the basic asset and the derivative at date t. They are selected depending on the price history. The self-financing condition is

$$a(t)S(t+dt) + a_g(t)G(t+dt) = a(t+dt)S(t+dt) + a_g(t+dt)G(t+dt),$$

for small dt. This is equivalent to

$$da(t)S(t) + da_g(t)G(t) = 0, \qquad \forall t. \tag{11.37}$$

Let us now assume that the derivative price is a function of the current value of the asset $G(t) = G[S_t, t]$, say. Then, by Ito's lemma, we get

$$dG(t) = \mu_G(t)dt + \sigma_G(t)dW_t, \tag{11.38}$$

where

$$\mu_G = \frac{\partial G}{\partial S}\mu + \frac{\partial G}{\partial t} + \frac{1}{2}\frac{\partial^2 G}{\partial S^2}\sigma^2, \tag{11.39}$$

$$\sigma_G = \frac{\partial G}{\partial S}\sigma. \tag{11.40}$$

The value $V(t)$ of the self-financed portfolio is also a function of $S(t)$ and satisfies a stochastic differential equation. We get

$$dV(t) = da(t)S(t) + da_g(t)G(t) + a(t)dS(t) + a_g(t)dG(t)$$

$$= a(t)dS(t) + a_g(t)dG(t), \qquad \text{by the self-financing condition,}$$

$$= (a\mu + a_g\mu_g)dt + (a\sigma + a_g\sigma_g)dW_t.$$

The portfolio is riskless if $a\sigma + a_g\sigma_g = 0$, $\forall t$. Under this condition, its expected return is equal to the risk-free return: $a\mu + a_g\mu_g = r(aS + a_gG)$.
We deduce the condition

$$\frac{\mu(t) - S(t)r}{\sigma(t)} = \frac{\mu_g(t) - G(t)r}{\sigma_g(t)}, \tag{11.41}$$

that is, the equality of the instantaneous excess performance of the two risky assets. By substituting the expressions of the instantaneous drift μ_g and volatility σ_g, we deduce

$$\frac{\mu - Sr}{\sigma} = \frac{(\partial G/\partial S)\mu + \partial G/\partial t + 0.5(\partial^2 G/\partial S^2)\sigma^2 - Gr}{(\partial G/\partial S)\sigma},$$

or, equivalently,

$$\frac{\partial G}{\partial S}Sr + \frac{\partial G}{\partial t} + \frac{1}{2}\frac{\partial^2 G}{\partial S^2}\sigma^2 - Gr = 0, \tag{11.42}$$

which is a second-order linear parabolic partial differential equation of G. It is important to note that the coefficients of this equation depend on neither the transformation g nor the maturity T. The solution $G[S,t]$ is subject to the boundary conditions

$$G[S_T,T] = g(S_T),$$

and

$$G[0,t] = 0, \qquad \forall t \le T.$$

The second condition means that the market for the derivative cannot exist when the market for the underlying asset is eliminated.

11.5 Derivative Pricing in Incomplete Markets

The possibility of pricing derivatives without ambiguity in complete markets is due to the dimension of the underlying dynamic model. Indeed, for the binomial tree, the number of admissible states one period ahead equals the number of assets; similarly, the movements of the log-normal process are driven by two shocks dt and dW_t, a number equal to the number of assets. In this section, we discuss the *incomplete market*, in which the number of tradable assets is less than the number of shocks. We first extend the tree by considering a double binomial tree. By using this simple approach, we describe the problem of multiple admissible pricing formulas. Then, we provide the general pricing formula and apply it to a stochastic volatility model.

11.5.1 A Double Binomial Tree

We introduce a tree in which two binary movements can take place between consecutive trading dates. We focus on the pricing at horizon 1, where 1 denotes the first trading date after date 0. Between 0 and $t = 1/2$, we can have up or down movements with probabilities p and $1 - p$, respectively, and independently between $t = 1/2$ and 1, the same type of movements with the same weights. Using the notation of Section 11.4.1, the price evolution between 0 and 1 is defined as

$$S_1 = \begin{cases} (1+u)^2 S_0, & \text{with probability } p^2, \\ (1+u)(1+d)S_0, & \text{with probability } 2p(1-p), \\ (1+d)^2 S_0, & \text{with probability } (1-p)^2. \end{cases}$$

Moreover, we assume a risk-free asset, which may be traded at integer-valued dates. Its price at date 0 is 1, whereas its price at date 1 is $(1+r)^2$.

We have three digital options (Arrow securities) with maturity 1, associated with the movements (up, up), (up, down) or (down, up), (down, down). Let us denote by $c(1,1)$, $c(1,0)$, and $c(0,0)$ their admissible prices.

By the no arbitrage argument, we get for the risky asset,

$$S_0 = (1+u)^2 S_0 \, c(1, 1) + (1+u)(1+d)S_0 \, c(1, 0) + (1+d)^2 S_0 \, c \, (0, 0),$$

and for the risk-free asset,

$$1 = (1+r)^2 [c(1, 1) + c(1, 0) + c(0, 0)].$$

We get two linear equations for the three unknown digital prices, which have to be solved under the price nonnegativity constraint:

$$\begin{cases} 1 = (1+u)^2 c(1, 1) + (1+u)(1+d)c(1, 0) + (1+d)^2 c(0, 0), \\ \dfrac{1}{(1+r)^2} = c(1, 1) + c(1,0) + c(0, 0), \end{cases} \tag{11.43}$$

where $c(1, 1) \geq 0$, $c(1, 0) \geq 0$, and $c(0, 0) \geq 0$. This system admits infinity solutions. Moreover, with any solution $c(1, 1)$, $c(1, 0)$, $c(0, 0)$, we can associate a risk-neutral probability $\pi(1, 1)$, $\pi(1, 0)$, $\pi(0, 0)$, where $\pi(i,j) = (1+r)^2 c(i,j)$. The admissible prices of a contingent asset written on the risky asset S_1 and delivering at date 1 the cash flow $g(S_1)$ is:

$$c(g) = g((1+u)^2 S_0)c(1, 1) + g((1+u)(1+d)S_0)c(1, 0) + g((1+d)^2 S_0)c(0, 0)$$

$$= \frac{1}{(1+r^2)} [g((1+u)^2 S_0)\pi(1, 1) + g((1+u)(1+d)S_0)\pi(1, 0)$$

$$+ g((1+d)^2 S_0)\pi(0, 0)]$$

$$= \frac{1}{(1+r)^2} E^{\pi}(g(S_1)|S_0).$$

Thus, we get an infinite number of admissible contingent prices when the digital prices vary under constraints (11.43).

The price multiplicity can be handled in various ways. For instance, we can search for a subset of admissible prices, that is, prices that do not allow for an arbitrage among the risk-free asset, the risky asset, and the derivative g. The interval is given by $[\underline{c}(g), \bar{c}(g)]$, where $\underline{c}(g)$ and $\bar{c}(g)$ are the minimal and maximal admissible prices, respectively:

$$\underline{c}(g) = \min_{c \in C} c(g), \bar{c}(g) = \min_{c \in C} c(g),$$

where C denotes the set of digital prices (11.43).

We also can study all admissible prices and try to interpret their expressions.

EXAMPLE 11.3: It is easy to check the digital prices at horizon 2 of the binomial tree (see Section 11.4.1)

$$c(1,1) = \frac{\pi^2}{(1+r)^2}, \ c(1,0) = \frac{2\pi(1-\pi)}{(1+r)^2}, \ c(0,0) = \frac{(1-\pi)^2}{(1+r)^2},$$

where $\pi = \dfrac{r-d}{u-d}$ are solutions of the system in (11.35).

EXAMPLE 11.4: More generally, we can price differently the first and second bifurcations of the tree, $(\pi_1, 1 - \pi_1)$ and $(\pi_2, 1 - \pi_2)$, respectively. The associated digital prices are

$$c(1,1) = \frac{\pi_1\pi_2}{(1+r)^2}, \ c(1,0) = \frac{\pi_1(1-\pi_2) + \pi_2(1-\pi_1)}{(1+r)^2}, \ c(0,0) = \frac{(1-\pi_1)(1-\pi_2)}{(1+r)^2}.$$

Conditions (11.43) are satisfied if and only if

$$(1+r)^2 = (1+u)^2\pi_1\pi_2 + (1+u)(1+d)[\pi_1(1-\pi_2) + \pi_2(1-\pi_1)]$$
$$+ (1+d)^2(1-\pi_1)(1-\pi_2)$$
$$= [(1+u)\pi_1 + (1+d)(1-\pi_1)][(1+u)\pi_2 + (1+d)(1-\pi_2)].$$

We get an infinite number of pricing probabilities of this type. The differences arise from different pricing of the zero coupon at horizon 1/2, with rates r_1 and r_2 at the first and second subperiods, respectively, where $(1+r)^2 = (1+r_1)(1+r_2)$.

11.5.2. General Result

In an incomplete market framework, the derivative pricing formula is not unique. We still can write the relation

$$C(t, T-t, g) = \exp[-r(T-t)]E^*[g(S_T)|I_t], \tag{11.44}$$

where I_t is the information available to investors at date t, but we need to be aware that there exists an infinite number of admissible risk-neutral probabilities. This set of risk-neutral probabilities can be described case by case using any of the three methods considered in Section 11.4.3.

The multiplicity of pricing formulas is related to the number of independent shocks, which affects the price of the underlying asset. Let us consider the special case of a tradable risky asset and a tradable derivative. We cannot construct a self-financed porfolio containing this asset and derivative, which would be insensitive (immune) to two or more independent shocks.

As an illustration, let us consider a model of the type

$$dS_t = \mu(S_t,\eta_t)dt + \sigma(S_t,\eta_t)dW_{1,t}, \tag{11.45}$$

where the drift and volatility are driven by an additional factor satisfying a stochastic differential equation

$$d\eta_t = a(S_t,\eta_t)dt + b(S_t,\eta_t)dW_{2,t}, \tag{11.46}$$

with another Brownian motion. We can reapply the argument of Section 11.4.3 with a derivative price of the type $G(t) = G(S_t,\eta_t,t)$, a function of the two types of information on the price and the latent factor. We assume that the investor observes both S_t and η_t and may use this information to update the portfolio. The value of the self-financed portfolio satisfies the equation

$$dV(t) = (a\mu + a_g\mu_g)dt + (a\sigma + a_g\sigma_{1,g})dW_1(t) + a_g\sigma_{2,g}dW_2(t).$$

using obvious notation. We cannot choose nondegenerate allocations a and a_g to jointly eliminate the effects of the shocks dW_1 and dW_2. However, we obtain restrictions on the derivative prices if we include two tradable derivatives in the portfolio with cash flows $g(S_T)$ and $f(S_T)$, say. The portfolio value satisfies

$$dV(t) = (a\mu + a_g\mu_g + a_f\mu_f)dt + (a\sigma + a_g\sigma_{1,g} + a_f\sigma_{1,f})dW_1(t) + (a_g\sigma_{2,g} + a_f\sigma_{2,f})dW_2(t).$$

The absence of arbitrage condition implies

$$\begin{cases} a_g\sigma_{2,g} + a_f\sigma_{2,f} = 0 \\ a\sigma + a_g\sigma_{1,g} + a_f\sigma_{1,f} = 0 \end{cases} \Rightarrow a\mu + a_g\mu_g + a_f\mu_f = r(aS + a_gG + a_fF).$$

or, equivalently,

$$\mu - rS = \lambda_1\sigma,$$

$$\mu_g - rG = \lambda_1\sigma_{1,g} + \lambda_2\sigma_{2,g}, \tag{11.47}$$

$$\mu_f - rF = \lambda_1\sigma_{1,f} + \lambda_2\sigma_{2,f}, \tag{11.48}$$

where λ_1 and λ_2 are multipliers that depend on the information I_t. The system has a simple interpretation. Indeed, at any date, the instantaneous expected excess returns capture the risk premia associated with the two types of risk, that is, dW_1 and dW_2. The multipliers λ_1 and λ_2 provide the prices of these risks. If S is the only traded asset, $\lambda_1 = (\mu - rS)/\sigma$ is defined unambiguously, whereas λ_2 can be arbitrarily selected. The multiplicity of pricing formulas is due to this arbitrary multiplier λ_2. If there also exists a derivative (g, say) traded on the market, λ_2 is determined by the observed derivative price.

It is also possible to apply the Girsanov theorem to the bidimensional system in (11.45) and (11.46) (see Pham and Touzi 1996). Let us first make the two Brownian motions orthogonal and write

$$
\begin{cases}
dS_t = \mu(S_t,\eta_t)dt + \sigma(S_t,\eta_t)\left(\sqrt{1 - \beta^2(S_t,\eta_t)}dW_t^S + \beta(S_t,\eta_t)dW_t^\sigma\right), \\
d\eta_t = a(S_t,\eta_t)dt + b(S_t,\eta_t)dW_t^\sigma,
\end{cases}
\tag{11.49}
$$

where $W_t^\sigma = W_{2t}$ and W_t^S are independent Brownian motions.

PROPOSITION 11.15, GIRSANOV THEOREM: *The admissible changes of probability compatible with the differential system (11.49) are such that*

$$
E^\pi(g(S_T)|I_t)
$$

$$
= E\left[\exp\left\{-\int_t^T \lambda_\tau dW_\tau^s - \frac{1}{2}\int_t^T \lambda_\tau^2 d\tau\right\}\exp\left\{-\int_t^T v_\tau dW_\tau^\sigma - \frac{1}{2}\int_t^T v_\tau^2 d\tau\right\}g(S_T)|I_t\right],
$$

where the processes (λ_t) and (v_t) satisfy the constraint

$$
\left(\lambda_t\sqrt{1 - \beta_t^2} + v_t\beta_t\right)\sigma_t = \mu_t - rS_t.
$$

The multipliers λ_t and v_t can be interpreted as the path-dependent premia with respect to the two sources of uncertainty W_t^S and W_t^σ.

11.5.3   Stochastic Volatility Model

The Model
Stochastic volatility models in continuous time were introduced by Hull and White (1987) and Scott (1987) and later extended by many authors (see, e.g., Follmer and Schweizer 1991). They admit the following structure:

$$
dS_t = \mu(t,S_t,\sigma_t)S_t dt + \sigma_t S_t dW_{t}^S,
$$

$$
df(\sigma_t) = a(t,\sigma_t)dt + b(t,\sigma_t)dW_t^\sigma,
$$

where (W_t^S) and (W_t^σ) are independent Brownian motions. Thus, the model allows the stochastic volatility σ_t to influence the drift.

EXAMPLE 11.5: The initial model introduced by Hull and White (1987) is

$$
dS_t = \mu S_t dt + \sigma_t S_t dW_{t}^S,
$$

$$
d\sigma_t^2 = a\sigma_t^2 dt + b\sigma_t^2 dW_t^\sigma.
$$

The price equation resembles a geometric Brownian motion except for the varying volatility. The volatility equation does not ensure, however, the nonnegativity of σ_t^2. Therefore, the second equation is often replaced by an Ornstein-Uhlenbeck process for the log volatility. It corresponds, for instance, to the limit of the ARCH-type process derived by Nelson (1990; see Section 11.3.4). The model becomes

$$dS_t = \mu S_t dt + \sigma_t S_t dW_t^S,$$

$$d \log \sigma_t = a_0(a_1 - \log \sigma_t) dt + b dW_t^\sigma.$$

A Pricing Formula
Let us assume a Black-Scholes type of price equation

$$dS_t = \mu S_t dt + \sigma_t S_t dW_t^S. \tag{11.50}$$

We can intuitively derive a pricing formula for the stochastic volatility model from the Black-Scholes formula (see Proposition 11.11). Let us restrict our attention to European call options. In the standard Black-Scholes formula, the volatility is constant, so that $\sigma\sqrt{H}$ is the cumulated volatility between the current date t and maturity T. When volatility is time varying, this cumulated volatility becomes $[\int_t^T \sigma_\tau^2 d\tau]^{1/2}$. Therefore, it is natural to use the Black-Scholes option pricing formula after replacing σ^2 in the usual expression by $(1/H)\int_t^T \sigma_\tau^2 d\tau$.

Let us denote by $g_{BS}(S_t,H,K,r,\sigma)$ the standard Black-Scholes formula (see Proposition 11.11). The proposed derivative price becomes:

$g_{BS}\left(S_t,H,K,r,\left(\dfrac{1}{H}\int_t^T \sigma_\tau^2 d\tau\right)^{1/2}\right)$. However, the time-varying volatility is not observed and has to be predicted. Thus, we propose, for the price of the European call, the expression

$$C(t,H,K) = E_t\left(g_{BS}\left(S_t,H,K,r,\left(\frac{1}{H}\int_t^T \sigma_\tau^2 d\tau\right)^{1/2}\right)\right), \tag{11.51}$$

where the conditional expectation is evaluated with respect to the historical distribution of the stochastic volatility. It can be proved that this pricing formula is admissible and corresponds to a zero price of the volatility risk (see the next section). This explains why the last conditional expectation is taken with respect to the historical dynamics of the volatility and not to a modified one. Finally, note that this price dynamics does not admit an analytical form. In practice, it can be computed by conditional simulations of a future volatility path.

Pricing Formulas with Volatility Premium
The general pricing formula for a price dynamics given by

$$dS_t = \mu S_t dt + \sigma_t S_t dW_t^s,$$

$$df(\sigma_t) = a(\sigma_t) dt + b(\sigma_t) dW_t^\sigma,$$

is implied by the Girsanov theorem (Proposition 11.15). Since the Brownian motions (W_t^S) and (W_t^σ) are independent, we have $\beta_t = 0$, and the constraint on the risk premia becomes

$$\lambda_t = \frac{\mu S_t - r S_t}{\sigma_t S_t} = \frac{\mu - r}{\sigma_t}.$$

The admissible prices of the European call with strike K and residual maturity H are

$$C(t;H,K) = \exp(-rH)E^\pi[(S_{t+H} - K)^+ | I_t]$$

$$= \exp(-rH) \ E\bigg[\exp\bigg\{-(\mu - r)\int_t^{t+H} \frac{dW_\tau^S}{\sigma_\tau} - \frac{1}{2}(\mu - r)^2 \int_t^{t+H} \frac{d\tau}{\sigma_\tau^2}\bigg\}$$

$$\exp\bigg\{-\int_t^{t+H} v_\tau dW_\tau^\sigma - \frac{1}{2}\int_t^{t+H} v_\tau^2 d\tau\bigg\} (S_{t+H} - K)^+ | I_t\bigg],$$

where the volatility premium is any process, such that v_t depends on the information I_t.

When the volatility premium is equal to 0, $v_t = 0$, we get

$$C(t;H,K) = \exp(-rH)E\bigg[\exp\bigg\{-(\mu - r)\int_t^{t+H}\frac{dW_\tau^S}{\sigma_\tau} - \frac{1}{2}(\mu - r)^2 \int_t^{t+H} \frac{d\tau}{\sigma_\tau^2}\bigg\}(S_{t+H} - K)^+ | I_t]$$

$$= \exp(-rH)E\bigg(E\bigg[\exp\bigg\{-(\mu - r)\int_t^{t+H}\frac{dW_\tau^S}{\sigma_\tau} - \frac{1}{2}(\mu - r)^2 \int_t^{t+H} \frac{d\tau}{\sigma_\tau^2}\bigg\}$$

$$(S_{t+H} - K)^+ | S_t, \underline{\sigma}\bigg] | S_t, \sigma_t\bigg),$$

where $\underline{\sigma} = (\sigma_t)$ denotes the information included in the past, current, and future values of the volatility process. The conditional expectation in the expression can be computed analytically to get the Black-Scholes formula. Finally, we get

$$C(t;H,K) = E\bigg[g_{BS}\bigg(S_t, H, K, r, \sigma\bigg(\frac{1}{H}\int_t^{t+H} \sigma_\tau^2 d\tau\bigg)^{1/2}\bigg) | S_t, \sigma_t\bigg].$$

11.6 An Introduction to Jump Processes

The previous sections explained how to use stochastic differential equations based on a Brownian motion to define price evolution and to derive derivative pricing formulas. This approach requires continuous price paths and is inadequate when the price process features big jumps. The financial literature has proposed accommodating the possibility of jumping prices by introducing an additional discontinuous component. In this section, we present elements of this approach with reference to the standard case of a Brownian motion price process. The corresponding continuous time models are descriptive and do not explain why the jumps occur. A more structural analysis of price jumps is developed in Chapter 14, in which we discuss the effects of illiquidity and block trading.

11.6.1   The Jump Process and the Associated Stochastic Integrals

DEFINITION 11.3: *A jump process $(N(t), t \in R^+)$ is an increasing process such that*

(i) $N(0) = 0$,

(ii)
$$P[N(t + dt) - N(t) = 1 \,|\, \underline{N(t)}] = \lambda_t dt + o(dt),$$

$$P[N(t + dt) - N(t) = 0 \,|\, \underline{N(t)}] = 1 - \lambda_t dt + o(dt),$$

where $o(dt)$ tends to 0 when t tends to 0, and λ_t, called the intensity, *is a function of the information available at time t.*

Thus, the path of a jump process in an increasing stepwise function with jumps equal to 1 at random dates $D_1, D_2, \ldots, D_n, \ldots$, say. Therefore, it may be considered a cumulative function and be used to construct integrals

$$\int_0^t g_u dN(u) = \sum_{n=1}^{\infty} g_{D_n} 1_{D_n} \leq t,   \tag{11.52}$$

where $1_{D_n \leq t}$ denotes the indicator function of $D_n \leq t$. For a varying t, the integral defines a stepwise function with stochastic jumps of size g_{D_n}. The jumps can be up or down.

The first- and second-order moments of the stochastic integral are easy to compute. We have

$$E\left[\int_0^t g_u dN(u)\right] = \int_0^t E[g_u dN(u)]$$

$$= \int_0^t E\{g_u E[dN(u) \,|\, \underline{N(u)}]\}$$

$$= \int_0^t E\{g_u \lambda_u\} du.$$

$$V\left[\int_0^t g_u dN(u)\right] = \int_0^t V[g_u dN(u)]$$

$$= \int_0^t \{VE[g_u dN(u) \,|\, \underline{N(u)}] + EV[g_u dN(u) \,|\, \underline{N(u)}]\}$$

$$= \int_0^t \left[V(g_u \lambda_u du) + E(g_u^2 \lambda_u du) \right]$$

$$= \int_0^t E(g_u^2 \lambda_u) du,$$

since the terms of order 2 in du are negligible.

EXAMPLE 11.6: A special case of jump process is the Poisson process, which corresponds to a constant intensity $\lambda_t = \lambda$. Then, the expressions of the moments become

$$E\left[\int_0^t g_u dN(u) \right] = \lambda \int_0^t E[g_u] du,$$

$$V\left[\int_0^t g_u dN(u) \right] = \lambda \int_0^t E\left[g_u^2 \right] du.$$

Since the stochastic integrals are well defined, we can introduce the stochastic differential equation with jump. Its key ingredients are (1) a Brownian motion (W_t) and (2) a jump process $(N(t))$, which are assumed independent. In particular, the intensity depends on the lagged values of the jump process only.

DEFINITION 11.4: *A stochastic process (y_t) satisfies the following stochastic differential equation with jump:*

$$dy_t = \mu(t,y_t)dt + \sigma(t,y_t)dW_t + c(t,y_t)dN(t),$$

if and only if it is a solution of the integral equation

$$y_t - y_0 = \int_0^t \mu(u,y_u)du + \int_0^t \sigma(u,y_u)dW_u + \int_0^t c(u,y_u)dN(u).$$

The first- and second-order conditional moments of dy_t are

$$E[dy_t \mid \underline{y_t}] = \mu(t,y_t)dt + c(t,y_t)\lambda_t dt,$$

$$V[dy_t \mid \underline{y_t}] = \sigma^2(t,y_t)dt + c^2(t,y_t)\lambda_t dt.$$

11.6.2 Limit Behavior of the Binomial Tree

We have seen in Section 11.3.2 how a diffusion model can be approximated by a binomial tree when the time δ between the consecutive trading dates tends to 0. Moreover, this approximation can be used to derive the Black-Scholes formula (see Section 11.4.2 and Appendix 11.1). This is a consequence of the convergence of the binomial distribution toward a normal distribution under appropriate regularity conditions.

However, it is well known that the binomial distribution can also converge toward a Poisson distribution if these regularity conditions are modified. This second framework is examined in this section and is used in the next section to derive the risk-neutral probability.

We consider the standard binomial tree with a zero risk-free rate $r = 0$ for notational simplicity. These binary shocks occur at dates that are the multiples of a time unit δ. $S_{n\delta}$ denotes the price of the risky asset at date $n\delta$. The evolution of the asset price is defined by

$$S_{(n+1)\delta} = S_{n\delta}\, \varepsilon_{n\delta}, \qquad (11.53)$$

with

$$\varepsilon_{n\delta} = \begin{cases} 1 + \delta u & \text{with probability } 1 - p_\delta,\ u > 0, \\[2mm] 1 + \dfrac{\delta d}{p_\delta} & \text{with probability } p_\delta,\ d < 0. \end{cases}$$

We consider the limit of the binomial tree, when δ and p_δ jointly tend to 0, in such a way that p_δ/δ converges to $\lambda > 0$, with $d/\lambda > -1$.

We get

$$\log S_{(n+1)\delta} - \log S_{n\delta} = \log \varepsilon_{n\delta},$$

$$\log S_t - \log S_0 = \sum_{n=0}^{[t/\delta]-1} \log \varepsilon_{n\delta}$$

$$= [t/\delta]\, \log(1 + \delta u) + \left[\log\!\left(1 + \frac{\delta d}{p_\delta}\right) - \log(1 + \delta u)\right] N_{t,\delta}$$

where $N_{t,\delta}$ is the sum of $[t/\delta]$ independent Bernoulli variables with parameter p_δ. Proposition 11.16 follows directly from a (functional) convergence theorem to a Poisson process.

PROPOSITION 11.16: *Let us assume that* $\delta \to 0$, $p_\delta \to 0$, *and* $p_\delta/\delta \to \lambda > 0$, *then the process* $\log S_t - \log S_0$ *weakly converges to the process* $\left[\mu t + \log\!\left(1 + \dfrac{d}{\lambda}\right) N_t(\lambda)\right]$, *where* $N_t(\lambda)$ *is a Poisson process with constant intensity* λ.

Thus, by changing the condition on the probability p_δ, the binomial tree can converge to the solution of a pure differential equation with jump:

$$d \log S_t = u dt + \log[1 + d/\lambda] dN_t(\lambda). \qquad (11.54)$$

11.6.3 Risk-Neutral Probability

The corresponding risk-neutral probability can be derived by considering the limit of the binomial tree corrected for the risk (see Appendix 11.1

for the standard case). The risk-neutral probabilities of the two states $1 - \pi_\delta$ and π_δ are given by

$$1 = (1 + \delta u)(1 - \pi_\delta) + \left(1 + \frac{d\delta}{p_\delta}\right)\pi_\delta$$

$$\Leftrightarrow \pi_\delta = u / \left(u - \frac{\delta}{p_\delta}\right)$$

(11.55)

This probability is such that

$$\lim_{\delta \to 0} \pi_\delta / \delta = \lim_{\delta \to 0} 1/\delta \frac{u}{u - d/p_\delta} = -\frac{\lambda u}{d}.$$

(11.56)

This directly implies the following proposition.

PROPOSITION 11.17: *Let us assume* $r = 0$, $\delta \to 0$, $p_\delta \to 0$, *and* $p_\delta / \delta \to \lambda > 0$, *then under the risk-neutral probability, the process* $(\log S_t - \log S_0)$ *weakly converges to the process* $\left[\mu t + \log\left(1 + \frac{d}{\lambda}\right)N_t\left(-\frac{\lambda u}{d}\right)\right]$, *where* $N_t\left(-\frac{\lambda u}{d}\right)$ *is a Poisson process with intensity* $-(\lambda u/d)$.

Thus, for a zero risk-free rate, the risk-neutral probability is derived by modifying the intensity of the Poisson process and keeping unchanged the infinitesimal drift and the jump sizes. The risk-neutral probability is unique, which is the complete market hypothesis.

11.7 Summary

This chapter introduced basic concepts in derivative asset pricing and continuous time modeling. Continuous time asset price processes provide a convenient framework for pricing the derivatives given the information on past asset prices. In general, price processes in continuous time display either smooth trajectories and are consequently modeled using diffusion processes or else feature jumps and need to be modeled by processes with jumps. The price process underlying the Black-Scholes approach to derivative pricing follows a simple diffusion, called the geometric Brownian motion. The analysis of a geometric Brownian motion can be carried out using a tree representation under the assumption that transitions between the nodes of the tree are instantaneous. This method allowed us to derive the Black-Scholes formula of derivative pricing. It has to be emphasized that the Black-Scholes formula relies on a strong and unrealistic assumption of constant price volatility, implied by the fixed parameters of the geometric Brownian motion. In Chapter 6, we showed extensive empirical evidence contradicting this assumption. Despite this shortcoming, the Black-Scholes formula is widely used in practice. A basic continuous time model accommodating time-varying price volatility is known as the Hull-White stochastic volatility model. Its discrete time analog was introduced in Chapter 6. However, relaxing the assumption of constant volatility results in an incomplete market and infinity of derivative prices.

The determination of derivative prices requires knowledge of the distribution of the underlying continuous time price process. Therefore, in the next chapter, we present various estimation procedures for diffusion processes.

Appendix 11.1:   Black-Scholes Risk-Neutral Probability

We follow an approach by which the continuous time model is approximated by a sequence of binomial trees with nodes. The transition between the nodes takes time δ. We consider successively these approximations for the historical and risk-neutral dynamics.

Historical Dynamics
We consider a binomial tree (see Section 11.4.1) with the distance between subsequent nodes defined by time δ. The probabilities of up and down movements are p and $1 - p$, respectively. An up movement of price results in the next price value

$$S_{t+\delta} = S_t \left[1 + \delta\mu + (1 - p) \frac{\sqrt{\delta}\sigma}{\sqrt{p(1 - p)}} \right],$$

whereas a down movement yields the price

$$S_{t+\delta} = S_t \left[1 + \delta\mu - p \frac{\sqrt{\delta}\sigma}{\sqrt{p(1 - p)}} \right].$$

To apply Proposition 11.7, let us consider the drift and volatility per time unit. We get

$$\frac{1}{\delta}\{E[S_{t+\delta}|S_t] - S_t\} = S_t\mu,$$

$$\frac{1}{\delta}V(S_{t+\delta}|S_t) \quad = \frac{1}{\delta} S_t^2 \left\{ p(1 - p)^2 \frac{\delta\sigma^2}{p(1 - p)} + (1 - p)p^2 \frac{\delta\sigma^2}{p(1 - p)} \right\} = \sigma^2 S_t^2.$$

When δ tends to 0, the drift and volatility per time unit converge to $S_t\mu$ and $S_t^2\sigma^2$, respectively. Thus, the limit of the sequence of binomial trees is the diffusion equation

$$dS_t = \mu S_t dt + \sigma S_t dW_t,$$

that is, the geometric Brownian motion, which underlies the Black-Scholes approach.

Risk-Neutral Dynamics

If r is the interest rate per time unit, the interest rate over a short time period of length δ is approximately $r\delta$. Let us now consider the risk-neutral binomial tree associated with the historical binomial tree. The up and down movements are

$$S_{t+\delta} = S_t \left[1 + \delta\mu + (1-p)\frac{\sqrt{\delta}\sigma}{\sqrt{p(1-p)}} \right], \qquad \text{with probability } \pi_\delta,$$

$$S_{t+\delta} = S_t \left[1 + \delta\mu - p\frac{\sqrt{\delta}\sigma}{\sqrt{p(1-p)}} \right], \qquad \text{with probability } 1 - \pi_\delta,$$

where

$$\pi_\delta = \frac{r_\delta - d_\delta}{u_\delta - d_\delta}$$

$$= \frac{r\delta - \mu\delta + \dfrac{p\sqrt{\delta}\sigma}{\sqrt{p(1-p)}}}{\dfrac{\sqrt{\delta}\sigma}{\sqrt{p(1-p)}}}$$

$$= p + \frac{(r-\mu)}{\sigma}\sqrt{p(1-p)}\sqrt{\delta}.$$

Let us compute the drift and volatility per time unit for the risk-neutral probability. We get, for instance,

$$\frac{1}{\delta}(E_\pi(S_{t+\delta}|S_t) - S_t)$$

$$= \frac{1}{\delta}\pi_\delta S_t \left[\delta\mu + \frac{(1-p)\sqrt{\delta}\sigma}{\sqrt{p(1-p)}} \right] + \frac{1}{\delta}(1-\pi_\delta)S_t \left[\delta\mu - p\frac{\sqrt{\delta}\sigma}{\sqrt{p(1-p)}} \right]$$

$$\approx S_t\mu + S_t(r-\mu) = S_t r, \qquad \text{for small } \delta.$$

Similarly, we get

$$\frac{1}{\delta}V_\pi(S_{t+\delta}|S_t) \approx \sigma^2 S_t^2.$$

We deduce that the risk-neutral continuous time model associated with the historical geometric Brownian motion is the limit of this tree, that is,

$$dS_t = rS_t dt + \sigma S_t dW_t.$$

Appendix 11.2: Black-Scholes Price of a Call

Under the risk-neutral probability π, the price process satisfies the stochastic differential equation

$$d \log S_t = (r - \sigma^2/2)dt + \sigma dW_t.$$

By integrating, we get

$$\log S_{t+H} - \log S_t = (r - \sigma^2/2)H + \sigma\sqrt{H}u,$$

where u is a standard normal variable. Then,

$$S_{t+H} = S_t \exp(r - \sigma^2/2)H \exp(\sigma\sqrt{H}u).$$

The Black-Sholes price of the call is

$$C(t;H,K)$$
$$= \exp(-rH)E^\pi[(S_{t+H} - K)^+|S_t]$$
$$= \exp(-rH)E\left[\left(S_t \exp(r - \sigma^2/2)H \exp\left(\sigma\sqrt{H}u\right) - K\right)^+|S_t\right]$$
$$= E\left[\left(S_t \exp - \frac{\sigma^2 H}{2} \exp\left(\sigma\sqrt{H}u\right) - K \exp(-rH)\right)^+|S_t\right].$$

The integrand is positive if and only if

$$S_t \exp - \frac{\sigma^2 H}{2} \exp \sigma\sqrt{H}u - K \exp(-rH) \geq 0$$

$$\Leftrightarrow \sigma\sqrt{H}u \geq \log[K \exp(-rH)/S_t] + \frac{\sigma^2 H}{2}$$

$$\Leftrightarrow u \geq -\frac{\log[S_t/(K \exp - rH)]}{\sigma\sqrt{H}} + \frac{\sigma\sqrt{H}}{2} = -x_t + \sigma\sqrt{H}.$$

Therefore, we get

$C(t;H,K)$

$$= E\left[\left(S_t \, \exp -\frac{\sigma^2 H}{2} \, \exp\left(\sigma\sqrt{H}u\right) - K \, \exp -rH\right)\mathbf{1}_{u \geq -x_t + \sigma\sqrt{H}}\,\middle|\,S_t\right]$$

$$= S_t \, \exp\left(-\frac{\sigma^2 H}{2}\right)\int_{-x_t + \sigma\sqrt{H}}^{\infty} \exp\left(\sigma\sqrt{H}u\right)\varphi(u)du - K \, \exp(-rH)\int_{-x_t + \sigma\sqrt{H}}^{\infty}\varphi(u)du$$

$$= S_t \int_{-x_t + \sigma\sqrt{H}}^{\infty} \varphi\left(u - \sigma\sqrt{H}\right)du - K \, \exp(-rH) \int_{-x_t + \sigma\sqrt{H}}^{\infty}\varphi(u)du$$

$$= S_t[1 - \Phi(-x_t)] - K \, \exp(-rH)\left[1 - \Phi\left(-x_t + \sigma\sqrt{H}\right)\right]$$

$$= S_t\Phi(x_t) - K \, \exp(-rH)\Phi\left(x_t - \sigma\sqrt{H}\right)$$

12

Estimation of Diffusion Models

IN CHAPTER 11, we pointed out the theoretical advantages of continuous time modeling of asset prices by diffusion equations. Indeed, under the complete market hypothesis and continuous updating strategy, the allocations of a hedging portfolio are easily obtained as solutions of partial differential equations. As well, prices of derivative assets, which are unique under the complete market hypothesis, can be expressed as either solutions of partial differential equations or expectations of the discounted cash flows taken with respect to a modified probability (the risk-neutral probability), often equivalent to a distribution of a modified diffusion equation. A typical example is the Black-Scholes model, which provides an explicit pricing formula for a European call under the assumption of a geometric Brownian motion of asset prices.

Allocations of hedging portfolios, risk-neutral probability, and prices of derivatives depend, however, on the parameters of the diffusion equation that describes the dynamics of the underlying asset price. Thus, the theoretical results can be exploited in practice only, when the unknown parameters are replaced by adequate estimates. Estimation in continuous time is rather difficult, mainly because the price of the underlying asset is not observed continuously, but at discrete points in time. In this chapter, we assume that observations on asset prices are regularly spaced, $t = 1, 2, \ldots, T$, such as for observations in a sample of daily stock prices, disregarding the weekend effect. Such an observation scheme is displayed in Figure 12.1.

All information about the unknown parameters is contained in the likelihood function computed from the sample of observations $l(y_1, \ldots, y_T; \theta)$. In general, however, it is not possible to derive an explicit expression of the likelihood function from the distribution of a continuous path of y_t, $t \in [1, T]$.

285

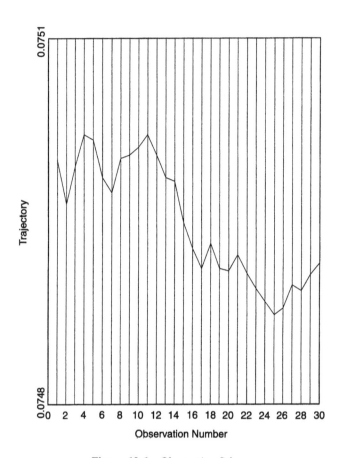

Figure 12.1 *Observation Scheme*

In the first section, we describe some restrictive diffusion models, such as the geometric Brownian motion, the Ornstein-Uhlenbeck process, and the Cox-Ingersoll-Ross (CIR) model, for which the likelihood function admits an analytical expression. These models can be estimated by the maximum likelihood (ML) method, and the explicit formulas of the associated ML estimators are often known.

When the likelihood function does not admit an analytical expression, some consistent, although inefficient, estimation methods can still be applied. In particular, we discuss the infinitesimal generator based method of moments for diffusion models (see, e.g., Hansen and Scheinkman 1995), the simulated method of moments (see, e.g., Duffie and Singleton 1993; Gourieroux and Monfort 1996), and indirect inference (see, e.g., Gourieroux, Monfort, and Renault 1993; Gallant and Tauchen 1996).

We restrict the exposition to outlining the principles and essential concepts of these methods. Interested readers will find more details, and especially the asymptotic properties of estimators (see Gourieroux and Monfort 1996 for a review), in the literature referenced at the end of this book.

12.1 Maximum Likelihood Approach

The analytical expressions of the likelihood functions exist only for a limited number of diffusion processes. Because of their tractability, these models have been extensively studied in the literature (see Section 11.2), despite that they provide a poor fit to the observed asset prices. Indeed, these diffusions do not account for features such as stochastic volatility or leverage effect. To these processes belong the geometric Brownian motion, appearing in the Black-Scholes formula; the Ornstein-Uhlenbeck model, used by Vasicek to specify the dynamics of the short-term interest rate (Vasicek 1977); and the CIR model (Cox, Ingersoll, and Ross 1984).

12.1.1 Geometric Brownian Motion

Exact Discretization
The price process satisfies the diffusion equation

$$dp_t = \mu p_t dt + \sigma p_t dW_t, \tag{12.1}$$

where (W_t) is a standard Brownian motion. Its dynamics depends on a drift parameter μ and a volatility parameter σ. The estimation of volatility is essential since it allows determination of the risk-neutral probability and consequently the prices of derivatives on (p_t) (see Chapter 11).

By applying Ito's formula, we deduce the diffusion equation satisfied by the logarithm of the price. We get

$$d \log p_t = \left(\mu - \frac{\sigma^2}{2}\right)dt + \sigma dW_t. \tag{12.2}$$

We find by direct integration

$$\log p_t - \log p_{t-1} = \mu - \frac{\sigma^2}{2} + \sigma(W_t - W_{t-1}),$$

or, equivalently,

$$\Delta \log p_t = \mu - \frac{\sigma^2}{2} + \sigma\varepsilon_t, \tag{12.3}$$

where (ε_t) is a standard Gaussian white noise. Therefore, the discretized version of the geometric Brownian motion corresponds to a Gaussian random walk with drift for the price logarithm.

Maximum Likelihood Estimator

The ML method (conditioned on the first observation p_0) provides the estimators of the mean and variance of $\Delta \log p_t$:

$$\hat{m}_T = \frac{1}{T} \sum_{t=1}^{T} \Delta \log p_t, \qquad \hat{s}_T^2 = \frac{1}{T} \sum_{t=1}^{T} (\Delta \log p_t - \hat{m}_T)^2. \qquad (12.4)$$

The ML estimators of the drift and volatility parameters are derived from their relations to the mean and variance parameters. They are given by

$$\hat{\mu}_T = \hat{m}_T + \frac{\hat{\sigma}_T^2}{2}, \qquad \hat{\sigma}_T^2 = \hat{s}_T^2. \qquad (12.5)$$

It is known that the asymptotic variances of $\hat{m}_T$ and $\hat{s}_T^2$ are such that

$$V_{asy}(\hat{m}_T) = \frac{\sigma^2}{T},$$

$$V_{asy}(\hat{s}_T^2) = \frac{2\sigma^4}{T},$$

$$Cov_{asy}(\hat{m}_T, \hat{s}_T^2) = 0.$$

We infer the asymptotic variance-covariance matrix of the pair $\hat{\mu}_T, \hat{\sigma}_T^2$:

$$V_{asy}\hat{\mu}_T = \frac{\sigma^2}{T} + \frac{\sigma^4}{2T},$$

$$V_{asy}\hat{\sigma}_T^2 = \frac{2\sigma^4}{T},$$

$$Cov_{asy}(\hat{\mu}_T, \hat{\sigma}_T^2) = \frac{\sigma^4}{T}.$$

We observe that the estimators of μ and σ^2 are correlated.

Effect of the Sampling Frequency

The previously given properties were derived by assuming an interval of one unit of time between consecutive observations. Let us examine what happens when data are sampled at a shorter interval h instead. We get

$$\log p_t - \log p_{t-h} = \Delta_h \log p_t = h\left(\mu - \frac{\sigma^2}{2}\right) + \sigma\sqrt{h}\varepsilon_t^{(h)}, \qquad (12.6)$$

where $(\varepsilon_t^{(h)})$ is a standard Gaussian white noise. As before, we compute the estimators $\hat{m}_{h,T}$ and $\hat{s}_{h,T}^2$ of the mean and variance of $\Delta_h \log p_t$ based on T observations sampled at interval h. The estimators of μ and σ are now given by

$$\hat{\sigma}^2_{h,T} = \frac{1}{h}\,\hat{s}^2_{h,T}, \qquad \hat{\mu}_{h,T} = \frac{\hat{m}_{h,T}}{h} + \frac{\hat{\sigma}^2_{h,T}}{2} = \frac{\hat{m}_{h,T}}{h} + \frac{\hat{s}^2_{h,T}}{2h}.$$

Their asymptotic variances are modified accordingly:

$$V_{asy}(\hat{\sigma}^2_{h,T}) = \frac{1}{h^2}\,\mathrm{Var}(\hat{s}^2_{h,T}) = \frac{1}{h^2}\frac{2h^2\sigma^4}{T} = \frac{2\sigma^4}{T},$$

$$V_{asy}(\hat{\mu}_{h,T}) = \frac{1}{h^2}\frac{h\sigma^2}{T} + \frac{1}{4}\frac{2\sigma^4}{T} = \frac{\sigma^2}{hT} + \frac{\sigma^4}{2T}.$$

The variance of the volatility parameter depends only on the number T of observations and does not depend on the sampling frequency h. On the contrary, the variance of the drift parameter depends on both h and T. In the limiting case, when T increases and h decreases so that $hT \to 1$, we have

$$\lim_{\substack{T\to\infty \\ h\to 0}} V_{asy}(\hat{\mu}_{h,T}) = \sigma^2.$$

Therefore, the drift parameter cannot be consistently estimated even from an infinite number of observations. This result is easy to explain. The drift parameter represents the trend effect and can be recovered only if the observations span a long period. However, the condition $hT = 1$ can be satisfied even when the observations are separated by h and recorded over the interval $[0, 1]$. In that case, we observe the trend effect only within a bounded interval, which does not convey sufficient information.

12.1.2 Ornstein-Uhlenbeck Process

Exact Discretization

The dynamics of the process is described by the stochastic differential equation

$$dy_t = (\Phi - \lambda y_t)dt + \sigma dW_t \qquad (12.7)$$

$$= \lambda(\mu - y_t)dt + \sigma dW_t, \qquad (12.8)$$

where (W_t) is a standard Brownian motion. This equation has a simple discrete time counterpart (see Section 11.2.2):

$$y_t = \mu[1 - \exp(-\lambda)] + \exp(-\lambda)y_{t-1} + \sigma\left(\frac{1 - \exp(-2\lambda)}{2\lambda}\right)^{1/2}\varepsilon_t, \qquad (12.9)$$

where (ε_t) is a standardized Gaussian white noise. This equation corresponds to a Gaussian AR(1) (autoregressive process of order 1) representation for the $(y_t, t \in Z)$ process (see also Chapter 2).

Maximum Likelihood Estimators

We can easily apply the ML method to the autoregressive model in (12.9). Let us first reparametrize the autoregressive representation as

$$y_t = \mu(1 - \rho) + \rho y_{t-1} + \eta \varepsilon_t, \tag{12.10}$$

where $\rho = \exp - \lambda$.

The ML estimators of the parameters μ, ρ, and η are asymptotically independent and equivalent to

$$\hat{\mu}_T = \frac{1}{T} \sum_{t=1}^{T} y_t = \bar{y}_T,$$

$$\hat{\rho}_T = \frac{1}{T} \sum_{t=1}^{T} (y_t - \bar{y}_T)(y_{t-1} - \bar{y}_T) / \frac{1}{T} \sum_{t=1}^{T} (y_t - \bar{y}_T)^2, \tag{12.11}$$

$$\hat{\eta}_T^2 = \frac{1}{T} \sum_{t=1}^{T} \hat{\varepsilon}_t^2,$$

where the residuals are defined by $\hat{\varepsilon}_t = y_t - \bar{y}_T - \hat{\rho}_T(y_{t-1} - \bar{y}_T)$. Their asymptotic variances are given by

$$V_{\text{asy}}\hat{\mu}_T = \frac{\eta^2}{T(1 - \rho^2)}, \qquad V_{\text{asy}}\hat{\rho}_T = \frac{1}{T}(1 - \rho^2), \qquad V_{\text{asy}}\hat{\eta}_T = \frac{2\eta^4}{T}.$$

From the ML estimators of the parameters μ, ρ, and η, we easily infer the ML estimators of the parameters of interest

$$\hat{\lambda}_T = -\log \hat{\rho}_T, \qquad \hat{\sigma}_T^2 = -\frac{2 \log \hat{\rho}_T}{1 - \hat{\rho}_T^2} \hat{\eta}_T^2. \tag{12.12}$$

Their asymptotic variances are derived by the δ-method. For instance, we get

$$V_{\text{asy}}(\hat{\lambda}_T) = \left[\frac{\partial(-\log \rho)}{\partial \rho} \right]^2 V_{\text{asy}}\hat{\rho}_T,$$

$$= \frac{1}{T} \frac{1 - \rho^2}{\rho^2},$$

$$= \frac{1}{T} \frac{1 - \exp - 2\lambda}{\exp - 2\lambda}.$$

The estimators $\hat{\lambda}_T$ and $\hat{\sigma}_T^2$ are asymptotically correlated since they both depend on $\hat{\rho}_T$. This is a consequence of time aggregation.

12.1.3   *Cox-Ingersoll-Ross Process*

The CIR process satisfies the stochastic differential equation

$$dy_t = (a - by_t)dt + \sigma \sqrt{y_t} dW_t. \tag{12.13}$$

In Section 12.2.3, we derive the conditional distribution of y_t given y_{t-1} by exploiting its Laplace transform. Recall that it is a noncentral chi-square distribution, up to a scale factor. Expression (11.21) and (11.22) of the conditional probability density function (pdf) of y_t can be used to build the log-likelihood function, which requires an adequate truncation of the Bessel function. The resulting ML estimators have no explicit expressions, and the optimization of the log-likelihood function has to be performed numerically.

12.2 Method of Moments and Infinitesimal Generator

When the likelihood function cannot be computed explicitly, we can use less efficient estimators obtained by optimizing an alternative criterion which admits an analytical form. A natural candidate for an optimization criterion arises from the moment conditions associated with a stochastic differential equation. In this section, we review various methods proposed in the literature in the context of unidimensional diffusion processes. Note that this framework implies a complete market and unique pricing formula of the derivatives, which is not compatible with stochastic volatility, for example.

12.2.1 *Moment Conditions*

The moment conditions studied by Hansen and Scheinkman (1995) are based on the following proposition:

PROPOSITION 12.1: *Let us consider a unidimensional process (y_t) that satisfies the stochastic differential equation*

$$dy_t = \mu(y_t)dt + \sigma(y_t)dW_t,$$

and let us introduce the infinitesimal generator A associated with this equation. It transforms a function Φ of y into

$$A\Phi(y) = \lim_{h \to 0} \frac{1}{h} E[(\Phi(y_{t+h}) - \Phi(y_t)) | y_t = y]$$

$$= \frac{d\Phi(y)}{dy} \mu(y) + \frac{1}{2} \frac{d^2\Phi(y)}{dy^2} \sigma^2(y).$$

Then, for a large set of functions Φ, $\check{\Phi}$, the following moment conditions are satisfied:

(i) $EA\Phi(y_t) = 0, \ \forall \Phi.$

(ii) $E[A\Phi(y_{t+1})\check{\Phi}(y_t) - \Phi(y_{t+1})A\check{\Phi}(y_t)] = 0, \ \forall \Phi, \check{\Phi}.$

By definition, the infinitesimal generator represents the infinitesimal drift of a transformed process. The differential expression of the generator follows from Ito's formula applied to $\Phi(y_t)$.

The moment conditions given in Proposition 12.1 concern the marginal moments of nonlinear functions of y_t (condition i) and cross moments of nonlinear functions of y_t and y_{t+1} (condition ii).

This set of moment conditions seems to be quite large since the functions Φ, $\tilde{\Phi}$ are not constrained (except for the second-order differentiability restriction). As an illustration, we detail the moment conditions for the exponential functions of y: $\Phi(y) = \exp(-ay)$, $\tilde{\Phi}(y) = \exp(-by)$. For condition (i), we get

$$E\left\{\exp(-ay_t)\left[\mu(y_t) - \frac{a}{2}\sigma^2(y_t)\right]\right\} = 0, \qquad \forall a.$$

for condition (ii),

$$E\left\{a\,\exp(-ay_{t+1} - by_t)\left[\mu(y_{t+1}) - \frac{a}{2}\sigma^2(y_{t+1})\right] - b\,\exp(-by_{t+1} - ay_t)\right.$$

$$\left.\left[\mu(y_t) - \frac{b}{2}\sigma^2(y_t)\right]\right\} = 0, \qquad \forall a,b.$$

12.2.2   Identification

A method of moments provides estimators that may not be fully efficient. Therefore, it is important to check whether the above set of moment conditions is sufficiently informative about the drift and volatility functions μ and σ. In fact, some identification problems may arise. For example, let us consider the drift and volatility parameterized as follows:

$$\mu(y;\theta) = \theta_0\tilde{\mu}(y;\theta_1), \qquad \sigma^2(y;\theta) = \theta_0\tilde{\sigma}^2(y;\theta_1), \qquad \text{with } \theta = \begin{pmatrix} \theta_0 \\ \theta_1 \end{pmatrix}.$$

The conditions (i) and (ii) can be simplified with respect to θ_0. Thus, this parameter cannot be identified from the previously given moment conditions.

By considering all admissible Φ functions, it may be shown that the marginal distribution of y_t is identifiable up to a scale factor. Yet, the set of conditions (ii) does not allow us to identify the joint distribution of (y_t,y_{t+1}) up to a scale factor.

To illustrate the identification problems, let us consider the following diffusion model:

$$dy_t = (\alpha + \beta y_t) + \sigma y_t^\gamma dW_t,$$

which has been proposed by Chan et al. (1992) for the short-term interest rate. This specification encompasses a number of well-known continuous time models (see Broze, Scaillet, and Zakoian 1995). Its dynamics depends on four parameters: α, β, σ, and γ. The condition (*i*) for the exponential functions is

$$E\left[\exp(-ay_t)\left(\alpha + \beta y_t - \frac{a}{2}\sigma^2 y_t^{2\gamma}\right)\right] = 0, \qquad \forall a.$$

The parameters that are identifiable from conditions (*i*) are only γ, α/σ^2, and β/σ^2.

12.2.3 Method of Moments

The method of moments is a widely used econometric procedure (see Hansen 1982; or Chapter 8). We present its implementation for restrictions of type (*i*). Let us select a priori n functions Φ_i, $i = 1, \ldots, n$. The moment conditions

$$E\left[\frac{d\Phi_i}{dy}(y_t)\mu(y_t;\theta) + \frac{1}{2}\frac{d^2\Phi_i}{dy^2}(y_t)\sigma^2(y_t;\theta)\right] = 0, \qquad i = 1, \ldots, n, \quad (12.14)$$

are satisfied for the true value of the parameter. We assume that some identifying restrictions are imposed to eliminate the effect of the scale factor (for instance, $\theta_0 = 1$; see 12.2.2). A moment estimator is a parameter value for which conditions (12.14) match their empirical counterparts. Let us denote

$$\frac{d\Phi}{dy}(y_t) = \left[\frac{d\Phi_1}{dy}(y_t), \ldots, \frac{d\Phi_n}{dy}(y_t)\right]',$$

and

$$\frac{d^2\Phi}{dy^2}(y_t) = \left[\frac{d^2\Phi_1}{dy^2}(y_t), \ldots, \frac{d^2\Phi_n}{dy^2}(y_t)\right]'.$$

The moment estimator is derived as a solution of the optimization

$$\hat{\theta}_T = \text{Arg} \min_\theta \sum_{t=1}^{T}\left\{\left[\mu(y_t;\theta)\frac{d\Phi'}{dy}(y_t) + \frac{1}{2}\sigma^2(y_t;\theta)\frac{d^2\Phi'}{dy^2}(y_t)\right]\right.$$

$$\left.\Omega\left[\mu(y_t;\theta)\frac{d\Phi}{dy}(y_t) + \frac{1}{2}\sigma^2(y_t;\theta)\frac{d^2\Phi}{dy^2}(y_t)\right]\right\},$$

(12.15)

where Ω is a positive definite matrix of weights. When this matrix is an identity matrix, the optimization yields

$$\hat{\theta}_T = \underset{\theta}{\text{Arg min}} \sum_{i=1}^{n} \left[\sum_{t=1}^{T} \mu(y_i;\theta) \frac{d\Phi_i}{dy}(y_t) + \frac{1}{2} \sigma^2(y_i;\theta) \frac{d^2\Phi_i}{dy^2}(y_t) \right]^2. \quad (12.16)$$

EXAMPLE 12.1: Let us consider the model of Chan et al. with the identifying constraint $\alpha = 1$. The optimization criterion is

$$\sum_{i=1}^{n} \left[\sum_{t=1}^{T} (\exp - a_i y_t) \left(1 + \beta y_t - \frac{a_i}{2} \sigma^2 y_t^{2\gamma} \right) \right]^2,$$

where $a_1, \ldots, a_n$ are given real numbers. This is a quadratic objective with respect to the parameters β and σ^2 and hence it may first be concentrated (i.e., optimized) with respect to these parameters. The concentrated objective function depends only on the parameter γ, which may be numerically found by a grid search method.

12.2.4 *Spectral Decomposition of the Infinitesimal Generator*

As shown in Section 12.2.2, the previous method does not allow identification of all the parameters of interest. To circumvent this drawback, it has been proposed to analyze the properties of the infinitesimal generator by considering its spectral decomposition (see Demoura 1993; Hansen, Scheinkman, and Touzi 1998; Darolles, Florens, and Gourieroux 1998; Chen, Hansen, and Scheinkman 1999). Moreover, this approach provides nonparametric estimators of the drift and volatility functions.

Under weak regularity conditions, the infinitesimal operator admits a spectral decomposition, that is, a sequence of eigenvalues and eigenfunctions λ_j, Φ_j, $j \geq 1$ (say), such that

1. $A\Phi_j(y) = \lambda_j \Phi_j(y)$, $j \geq 1$.
2. λ_j, $j \geq 1$, are positive real numbers.

Let us now rank the eigenvalues and denote by λ_1 the largest eigenvalue and by λ_2 the second largest one. The conditions defining the pairs (λ_j, Φ_j), $j = 1, 2$, are

$$\begin{cases} A\Phi_1(y) = \lambda_1 \Phi_1(y), \\ A\Phi_2(y) = \lambda_2 \Phi_2(y), \end{cases} \quad (12.17)$$

or, equivalently,

$$\begin{cases} \dfrac{d\Phi_1(y)}{dy}\mu(y) + \dfrac{1}{2}\dfrac{d^2\Phi_1(y)}{dy^2}\sigma^2(y) = \lambda_1\Phi_1(y), \\[3mm] \dfrac{d\Phi_2(y)}{dy}\mu(y) + \dfrac{1}{2}\dfrac{d^2\Phi_2(y)}{dy^2}\sigma^2(y) = \lambda_2\Phi_2(y). \end{cases} \qquad (12.18)$$

This is a bivariate system with respect to the drift and volatility. Therefore, it is equivalent to estimate the functions μ and σ or to estimate the two first pairs (λ_1, Φ_1) and (λ_2, Φ_2) and next solve the system in (12.18).

In fact, it is possible to estimate (λ_1, Φ_1) and (λ_2, Φ_2) nonparametrically from discrete time observations. The approach is based on the prediction interpretation of the infinitesimal generator

$$A\Phi(y) = \lim_{h\to 0}\frac{1}{h}E[(\Phi(y_{t+h}) - \Phi(y_t))|y_t = y], \qquad (12.19)$$

which represents the infinitesimal drift of the transformed process. Next, we note that the spectral decomposition of A is related to the spectral decomposition of the conditional expectation operator T, which is associated with the function Φ:

$$T : \Phi \to T\Phi(y_t) = E[\Phi(y_{t+1})|y_t]. \qquad (12.20)$$

The eigenfunctions of the conditional expectation operator coincide with the eigenfunctions of the infinitesimal generator, whereas its eigenvalues are given by $\tilde{\lambda}_i = \exp \lambda_i$.

REMARK 12.1: The system in (12.18) gives a possibility of identifying nonparametrically the drift and volatility functions. Alternatively, Ait-Sahalia (1996) has proposed the use of the marginal density function for identifying nonparametrically the volatility function under the assumption of a restrictive affine form of the drift function.

12.2.5 *Nonlinear Canonical Decomposition*

The spectral decomposition of the expectation operator is related to the nonlinear canonical decomposition of the joint pdf of (y_t, y_{t-1}). Let us denote by $f(y_t, y_{t-1})$ and $f(y_t)$ the joint and marginal pdf, respectively. If

$$\int\int\left[\frac{f(y_t, y_{t-1})}{f(y_t)f(y_{t-1})}\right]^2 f(y_t)f(y_{t-1})dy_t dy_{t-1} < \infty,$$

the bivariate pdf can be decomposed as (Lancaster 1968)

$$f(y_t, y_{t-1}) = f(y_t)f(y_{t-1})\left[1 + \sum_{j=1}^{\infty}\lambda_j\Phi_j(y_t)\psi_j(y_{t-1})\right], \qquad (12.21)$$

where the canonical correlations λ_j, j varying, are nonnegative, and the canonical directions Φ_j and ψ_j, j varying, satisfy the constraints

$$E\Phi_j(y_t) = E\psi_j(y_t) = 0, \forall j, V\Phi_j(y_t) = V\psi_j(y_t) = 1, \qquad \forall j,$$

$$\text{cov}[\Phi_j(y_t), \Phi_k(y_t)] = 0, \forall j \neq k, \ \text{cov} \ [\psi_j(y_t), \psi_k(y_t)] = 0, \qquad \forall j \neq k.$$

In particular, we deduce

$$f(y_t|y_{t-1}) = f(y_t)\left[1 + \sum_{j=0}^{\infty} \lambda_j \Phi_j(y_t)\psi_j(y_{t-1})\right].$$

If (y_t) is a Markov process of order 1, we get

$$E(\Phi_j(y_t)|y_{t-1}) = E\Phi_j(y_t) + \sum_{k=1}^{\infty} \lambda_k E[\Phi_j(y_t)\Phi_k(y_t)]\psi_k(y_{t-1})$$

$$= \lambda_j \psi_j(y_{t-1}). \tag{12.22}$$

The unidimensional diffusion processes are reversible, that is, their distributional properties are identical in the ordinary and reverse times (Revuz and Yor 1990). This implies that the current and lagged canonical directions are identical $\Phi_j = \psi_j, \forall j$ (up to a change of sign). Thus, the non-linear canonical decomposition becomes

$$f(y_t, y_{t-1}) = f(y_t)f(y_{t-1})\left[1 + \sum_{j=1}^{\infty} \lambda_j \Phi_j(y_t)\Phi_j(y_{t-1})\right]. \tag{12.23}$$

Moreover, the conditional expectation operator is such that

$$E[\Phi_j(y_t)|y_{t-1}] = \lambda_j \Phi_j(y_{t-1}), \qquad \forall j. \tag{12.24}$$

This suggests that the spectral elements of the conditional expectation operator can be derived from the nonlinear canonical decomposition of the bivariate distribution.

12.2.6   *Estimation of the Spectral Decomposition*

Two types of nonparametric estimation methods have been proposed in the literature. The Sieve method approximates the conditional expectation operator on a finite dimensional subspace and requires spectral decomposition of this approximated operator. The second approach relies on nonlinear canonical decomposition of a kernel-based estimator of the joint pdf $f(y_t, y_{t-1})$.

Sieve Method
The first step approximation consists of projecting the functions Φ on a finite-dimensional space (Chen, Hansen, and Scheinkman 1999).
    Let us consider the finite dimensional space of stepwise functions

$$\Phi(y) = \sum_{k=1}^{K} b_k \mathbf{1}_{[a_k,a_{k+1}]}(y), \qquad (12.25)$$

where $[a_k,a_{k+1}]$, $k = 1, \ldots, K$, is a given partition of the real line. We can approximate the conditional expectation operator by projecting these functions on the space generated by $\mathbf{1}_{(a_k,a_{k+1})}(y_{t-1})$, $k = 1, \ldots, K$. Its empirical counterpart is easily obtained by estimating by ordinary least squares (OLS) the seemingly unrelated regressions (SUR) model:

$$Z(t) = BZ(t-1) + u_t, \qquad (12.26)$$

$Z(t) = [\mathbf{1}_{[a_1,a_2]}(y_t), \ldots, \mathbf{1}_{(a_K,a_{K+1})}(y_t)]'$. Then, we perform the spectral decomposition of the estimated matrix of coefficients $\hat{B}$ to find the first eigenvalues and the associated eigenvectors. If $\hat{\phi}_1, \ldots, \hat{\phi}_K$ are the estimated eigenvectors, the corresponding eigenfunctions are approximated by $\hat{\Phi}_k(y_t) = \hat{\phi}_k' Z(t)$ (see Chen, Hansen, and Scheinkman 1999 for the choice of the partition and the asymptotic properties of the estimator).

Kernel-Based Estimation
This approach was introduced by Darolles, Florens, and Gourieroux (1998). These authors proposed the application of the nonlinear canonical analysis to a kernel-based estimator of the bivariate pdf. The estimated pdf is

$$\hat{f}(y_t,y_{t-1}) = \frac{1}{Th^2} \sum_{\tau=1}^{T} K\left(\frac{y_\tau - y_t}{h}\right) K\left(\frac{y_\tau - y_{t-1}}{h}\right), \qquad (12.27)$$

where K is a univariate kernel, and h is the bandwidth. We refer to Darolles et al. 1998 for the optimal choice of the bandwidth h and the asymptotic properties of the estimated canonical correlations and canonical directions.

12.2.7 Applications

A Monte Carlo Study
We first provide an illustration of the previous approach based on the simulated realizations of an Ornstein-Uhlenbeck process, that satisfies the stochastic differential equation [see (12.8)]

$$dy_t = \lambda(\mu - y_t)dt + \sigma dW_t.$$

This equation admits a solution that is a Gaussian process. It can be shown that the canonical analysis of the covariance operator associated with the discrete time process $(y_t, t \in Z)$ leads to the canonical correlations

$$\lambda_i = \exp(-i\lambda), \qquad i = 1, 2, \ldots \qquad (12.28)$$

The corresponding canonical variates are $\Phi_i(y) = \dfrac{1}{\sqrt{i!}} \, H_i\left(\dfrac{y}{\sigma_y}\right)$, $i = 1, 2, \ldots,$

where σ_y^2 is the variance of y_t, and H_i are the Hermite polynomials:

$$H_i(y) = \sum_{0 \le m \le [i/2]} \frac{i!}{(i-2m)! \, m! \, 2^m} (-1)^m y^{i-2m}. \qquad (12.29)$$

In particular, the first Hermite polynomials are

$$H_1(y) = y, \qquad H_2(y) = y^2 - 1. \qquad (12.30)$$

As an example, we simulate a path $(y_t, t = 1, 2, \ldots, T)$ of length $T = 250$ of the process with parameter values $\mu = 0$, $\lambda = 0.8$, and $\sigma = 0.5$. It is plotted in Figure 12.2.

We apply the kernel-based canonical analysis to the artificially gener-

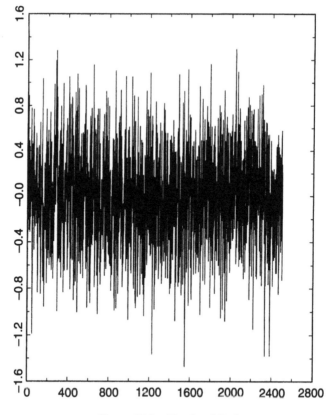

Figure 12.2   *Simulated Path*

Table 12.1   *Canonical Correlations*

			Order			
	1	2	3	4	5	6
λ_i	0.451	0.215	0.107	0.053	0.027	0.008
True value	0.449	0.202	0.091	0.041	0.018	0.008

ated data to estimate nonparametrically the first canonical correlations
and variates. The selected kernel is Gaussian: $K(x) = \dfrac{1}{\sqrt{2\pi}}\exp - (x^2/2)$. The
bandwidth is set at $h = 0.10$. The first six estimated canonical correlations
are given in Table 12.1, along with the corresponding true values.

The estimated first three canonical directions are displayed in Figure
12.3. We find the expected patterns, that is, an affine form of the first canonical direction and a quadratic one of the second canonical direction.

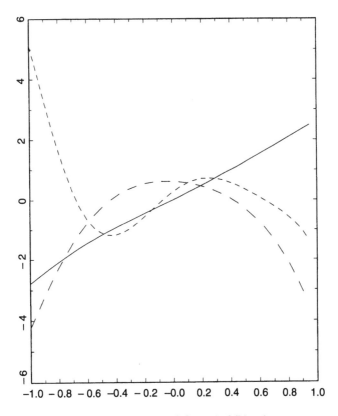

Figure 12.3   *Estimated Canonical Directions*

In the second step, by applying Demoura's approach (see system 12.18), we find nonparametric estimators of the drift and volatility functions. The estimators obtained from the simulated sample can be compared to their theoretical counterparts, which are an affine and a constant function for the drift and volatility, respectively. They are displayed in Figures 12.4 and 12.5 along with their confidence bands evaluated by bootstrap.

Application to the Alcatel Stock
The high-frequency data on the Alcatel stock were sampled at a constant interval of 20 minutes. They cover the period May 2, 1997, to August 30, 1998, and contain 1,705 observations. We perform a kernel-based estimation of the canonical decomposition using a Gaussian kernel and a bandwidth $h = 0.062$. We show in Figure 12.6 the first three current canonical directions Φ_1, Φ_2, and Φ_3, and in Figure 12.7, we show the first three lagged canonical directions ψ_1, ψ_2, and ψ_3.

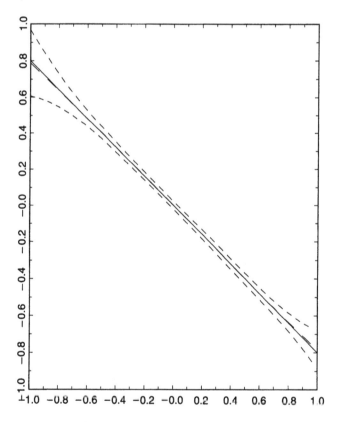

Figure 12.4   *Estimated Drift Function*

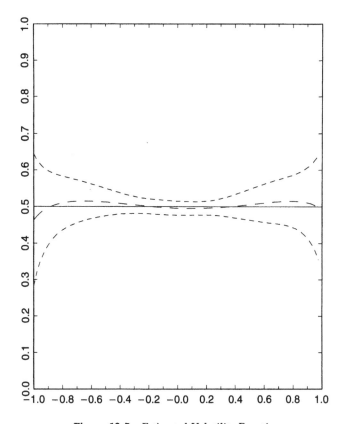

Figure 12.5 *Estimated Volatility Function*

We observe that the current and lagged canonical directions are not identical. Therefore, we reject the time reversibility hypothesis, as well as the possibility that the Alcatel returns follow a unidimensional diffusion model. Therefore, it is necessary to extend the model, for instance, by introducing a stochastic volatility or an additional jump component. Moreover, the first lagged canonical direction, which is the most informative function of the past, is not quadratic, contrary to an implicit assumption of the autoregressive conditionally heteroscedastic (ARCH) models, for instance. It displays an asymmetry due to its steeper slope for negative returns.

12.3 Methods Based on the Scale and Speed Functions

The approaches based on the scale and speed functions consist of replacing the initial parametrization of a diffusion equation by drift and volatil-

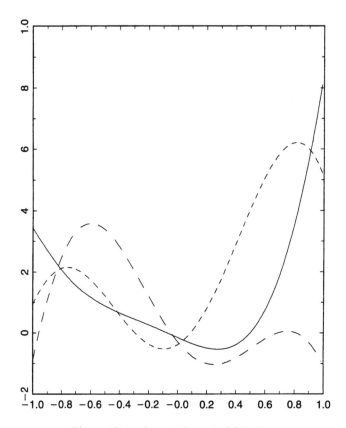

Figure 12.6   *Current Canonical Directions*

ity functions by another parametrization that is easier to estimate from discrete time data. We first recall the definitions of the scale and speed functions and explain their relevance for estimation of diffusion models. Next, we show how to estimate these functions from discretely valued observations.

12.3.1   *Instrinsic Scale and Intrinsic Time*

The objective is to simplify the dynamics of a diffusion process by applying appropriate scale and time deformations. The *scale deformation* changes the measurement unit in the space of all admissible values of the process, whereas the *time deformation* modifies the time unit (see Chapter 14) of its trajectory. These transformations, denoted by S and M, respectively, are applied in the following order:

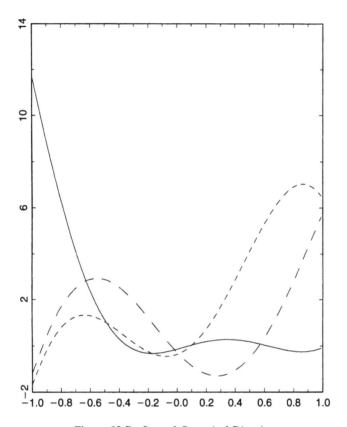

Figure 12.7 *Lagged Canonical Directions*

$$y_t \overset{S}{\Rightarrow} z_t = S(y_t) \overset{M}{\Rightarrow} x_t = z_{M(t)} = S[y_{M(t)}].$$

PROPOSITION 12.2: *There exists a pair of scale and time deformations such that* $x_t = z_{M(t)} = W_t^*$ *is a Brownian motion. The scale deformation can be set as*

$$S(y) = \int^y s(u)du, \qquad where \; s(y) = \exp - \int^y \frac{2\mu(u)}{\sigma^2(u)} du.$$

The time deformation can be selected to get

$$M(t) = \int^t m(y_u)du, \qquad where \; m(y) = \frac{1}{\sigma^2(y)s(y)}.$$

PROOF: First, let us study the effect of the scale deformation S. If $dy_t = \mu(y_t)dt + \sigma(y_t)dW_t$, we get, by Ito's formula,

$$dz_t = \left[\mu(y_t)S'(y_t) + \frac{1}{2}\sigma^2(y_t)S''(y_t)\right]dt + \sigma(y_t)S'(y_t)dW_t.$$

The transformation S is supposed to eliminate the drift:

$$\mu(y)S'(y) + \frac{1}{2}\sigma^2(y)S''(y) = 0.$$

We find $S(y) = \int^y s(u)du$, where $s(y) = \exp{-\int^y \frac{2\mu(u)}{\sigma^2(u)}du}$.

Therefore, the process (z_t) satisfies the diffusion equation

$$dz_t = \sigma(y_t)S'(y_t)dW_t$$

$$= \sigma[S^{-1}(z_t)]S'[S^{-1}(z_t)]dW_t.$$

Second, let us now introduce a time deformation of the type

$$M(t) = \int^t m(y_u)du = \int^t \frac{m[S^{-1}(z_u)]}{S'[S^{-1}(z_u)]}dz_u.$$

We find

$$dx_t = \left|\frac{dM_t}{dz}\right|^{1/2}\sigma[S^{-1}(z_t)]S'[S^{-1}(z_t)]dW_t$$

$$= \sigma(y_t)m(y_t)^{1/2}s(y_t)^{1/2}dW_t.$$

The time deformation is supposed to transform the initial volatility into a volatility equal to 1:

$$\sigma(y)m(y)^{1/2}s(y)^{1/2} = 1 \Leftrightarrow m(y) = \frac{1}{\sigma^2(y)s(y)}.$$

QED

Proposition 12.2 shows that it is equivalent to know the drift and volatility functions μ and σ^2 or the two functions S and M, called the *scale function* and *speed measure*, respectively. However, these functions may be difficult to estimate. Proposition 12.3 provides some useful interpretations in terms of conditional moments that may facilitate the approach.

We define $T(a)$, the first time when the process reaches the value a, starting from y at date $t = 0$. Let us now consider two constants $a < b$ and an initial value $y \in [a,b]$ (Figure 12.8).

PROPOSITION 12.3: *We have*

(i) $u(y) = P[T(b) < T(a)|Y_0 = y] = \dfrac{S(y) - S(a)}{S(b) - S(a)}$, $a < y < b$;

(ii) $v(y) = E[Min\ [T(a),T(b)]|Y_0 = y]$

$\quad = 2\left\{u(y)\int_y^b [S(b) - S(\xi))]m(\xi)d\xi + [1 - u(y)]\int_a^y [S(\xi) - S(a)]m(\xi)d\xi\right\}.$

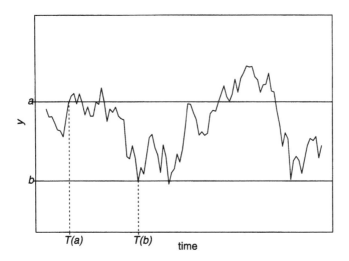

Figure 12.8 *Hitting Times*

PROOF: See Karlin and Taylor (1981).

Moreover the functions u and v can be deduced from the infinitesimal generator. More precisely they satisfy the differential equations given below.

PROPOSITION 12.4:

(i) *The function u is the solution of the differential equation*

$$\mu(y)\frac{du(y)}{dy} + \frac{1}{2}\sigma^2(y)\frac{d^2u(y)}{dy^2} = 0, \qquad \text{for } a \leq y \leq b,$$

with the boundary conditions $u(a) = u(b) = 1$.
(ii) *The function v is the solution of the differential equation*

$$\mu(y)\frac{dv(y)}{dy} + \frac{1}{2}\sigma^2(y)\frac{d^2v(y)}{dy^2} = -1, \qquad \text{for } a \leq y \leq b,$$

with the boundary conditions $v(a) = v(b) = 0$.

12.3.2   Estimation from Discrete-Valued Observations

Let us consider a continuous time process (y_t) that satisfies a diffusion equation and assume that we observe the dates at which this process takes integer values, as well as the associated values of the process (Figure 12.9).

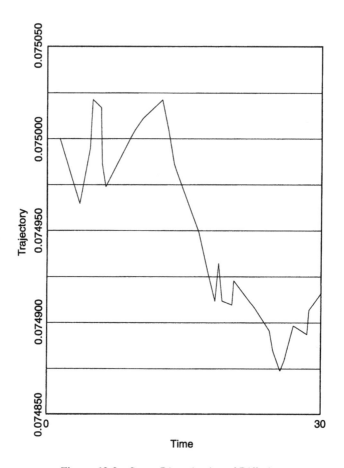

Figure 12.9 *Space Discretization of Diffusion*

Then, we can easily estimate the two expressions

$$u(x) = P[T(x+1) < T(x-1)|Y_0 = x],$$

$$v(x) = E(\text{Min }[T(x+1), T(x-1)]|Y_0 = x),$$

associated with $a = x-1$, $b = x+1$, for any integer x. Indeed, let us denote by $\tau_j(x), j = 1, \ldots, J_x$, the dates for which the process takes the value x, by $T_j(x+1)$ and $T_j(x-1)$, the first dates after $\tau_j(x)$ for which the process takes the values $x+1$ and $x-1$, respectively. The consistent estimators are

$$\hat{u}(x) = \frac{1}{J_x} \sum_{j=1}^{J_x} \mathbf{1}_{T_j(x+1)<T_j(x-1)},$$

$$\hat{v}(x) = \frac{1}{J_x} \sum_{j=1}^{J_x} [\text{Min }(T_j(x+1), T_j(x-1)) - \tau_j(x)].$$

The set $\hat{u}(x)$, x varying, provides an approximation of the function u for integer-valued arguments. It can be smoothed to approximate u for real arguments. The same approach can be applied to the function v. Finally, Proposition 12.4 can be used to derive nonparametric estimators of the drift and volatility functions by solving the bivariate system

$$
\begin{cases}
\hat{\mu}(y) \dfrac{d\hat{u}(y)}{dy} + \dfrac{1}{2}\hat{\sigma}^2(y) \dfrac{d^2\hat{u}(y)}{dy^2} = 0, \\[3mm]
\hat{\mu}(y) \dfrac{d\hat{v}(y)}{dy} + \dfrac{1}{2}\hat{\sigma}^2(y) \dfrac{d^2\hat{v}(y)}{dy^2} = -1,
\end{cases}
$$

for any value y.

This procedure was applied by Darolles, Gourieroux, and Le Fol (2000) to high-frequency data on the Elf-Aquitaine stock traded on the Paris Bourse. The authors considered signed trades, initiated by buy orders, and found that more than 92% of price movements were smaller than one tick (the one-tick price moves are equal to −1, 0, +1). They assumed that the discretely valued trading data were obtained from an underlying diffusion process by space value discretization. We show in Figure 12.10 the estimator of the scale function computed from the May 1998 sample.

Therefore, it is necessary to apply first an increasing convex function to the process y_t to get a Brownian motion under a well-chosen time deformation.

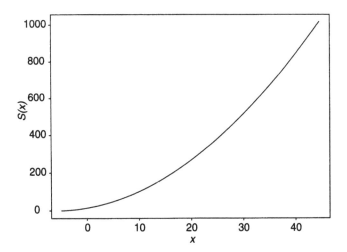

Figure 12.10 *Scale Function S for Elf-Aquitaine*

12.4   Method of Simulated Moments

Contrary to the approach based on the infinitesimal generator, the
method of simulated moments (MSM) does not require moment conditions in explicit form (see Duffie and Singleton 1993 for a particular appli-
cation). We select a priori some functions $g_i(y_t, y_{t-1}, \ldots, y_{t-p})$, $i = 1, \ldots, n$, that
depend on the present and p lagged values of the process. If this process
satisfies the stochastic differential equation

$$dy_t = \mu(y_t; \theta)dt + \sigma(y_t; \theta)dW_t, \tag{12.31}$$

and is stationary, then the expectation

$$Eg_i(y_t, y_{t-1}, \ldots, y_{t-p}) = m_i(\theta), \qquad i = 1, \ldots, n, \tag{12.32}$$

is a function of the parameters. In general, m_i has a complicated form;
therefore, the standard moment estimator (Hansen 1982)

$$\hat{\theta}_T = \operatorname*{Arg\,min}_{\theta} \sum_{t=1}^{T} [g(y_t, y_{t-1}, \ldots, y_{t-p}) - m(\theta)]' \Omega \sum_{t=1}^{T} [g(y_t, y_{t-1}, \ldots, y_{t-p}) - m(\theta)],$$

where Ω is a given definite symmetric matrix, cannot be computed even
numerically.

The principle of the method of simulated moments consists of replacing in the last criterion the unknown function m by an approximation
obtained from simulations. For this purpose, we require simulated values
$y_t^s(\theta)$, $t = 1, \ldots, ST$, compatible with the diffusion model (12.31) and the
value θ of the parameter (see Chapter 11, Section 11.3.3, for the description of the simulation approach). A good approximation of $m(\theta)$ is

$$\hat{m}_T^s(\theta) = \frac{1}{ST} \sum_{t=1}^{ST} g[y_t^s(\theta), \ldots, y_{t-p}^s(\theta)], \tag{12.33}$$

where ST is sufficiently large. Then, the MSM estimator is defined by

$$\hat{\theta}_T^s = \operatorname*{Arg\,min}_{\theta} \sum_{t=1}^{T} [g(y_t, y_{t-1}, \ldots, y_{t-p}) - \hat{m}_T^s(\theta)]' \Omega \sum_{t=1}^{T} [g(y_t, y_{t-1}, \ldots, y_{t-p}) - \hat{m}_T^s(\theta)],$$

or, equivalently, by

$$\hat{\theta}_T^s = \operatorname*{Arg\,min}_{\theta} [\hat{m}_T - \hat{m}_T^s(\theta)]' \Omega [\hat{m}_T - \hat{m}_T^s(\theta)], \tag{12.34}$$

where $\hat{m} = \frac{1}{T} \Sigma_{t=1}^{T} g(y_t, y_{t-1}, \ldots, y_{t-p})$.

This method is essentially a calibration approach that provides the
best possible match between the empirical moments based on the observations and those based on the simulated values.

This approach requires only the possibility of generating artificial observations on the model. Therefore, it can also be used in more general

cases, such as multivariate diffusion models, continuous time models with stochastic volatility, or models that include jump components.

12.5 Indirect Inference

Indirect inference also is a simulation-based method, although with a different criterion function. By the same argument as the one given above, this method can also be applied to stochastic volatility models and to diffusions with jumps. We first present the general principle, followed by an application to univariate continuous time models.

12.5.1 Principle

Suppose that we are interested in estimating the parameter θ, but the log-likelihood function $\Sigma_{t=1}^{T} \log f(y_t|\underline{y_{t-1}};\theta) = \Sigma_{t=1}^{T} \log f_t(\theta)$ (say) cannot be written in an explicit form. Empirically, a common approach consists of replacing the likelihood function by a simpler expression $\Sigma_{t=1}^{T} \log g(y_t|\underline{y_{t-1}};\theta) = \Sigma_{t=1}^{T} \log g_t(\theta)$, say, and in maximizing this modified log-likelihood function. Obviously, the replacement of f by g induces a specification error and likely results in inconsistent approximations of θ. Indirect inference is a simulation-based technique designed to correct for the asymptotic bias (see Gourieroux, Monfort, and Renault 1993; Gallant and Tauchen 1996). It requires two inputs: (1) simulated data compatible with the true model and the value θ of the parameter and (2) an auxiliary model (called an *instrumental model*) (Dhaene, Gourieroux, and Scaillet 1998) with a log-likelihood function $\Sigma_{t=1}^{T} \log g_t(\beta)$ that is easy to optimize numerically.

Indirect inference includes the following steps:

1. The estimation of the auxiliary parameter β from the instrumental model and the observations:

$$\hat{\beta}_T = \operatorname*{Arg\,max}_{\beta} \sum_{t=1}^{T} \log g_t(\beta).$$

2. The simulation of the true model for the value θ of the parameter, yielding an artificial series of length ST: $y_t^s(\theta)$, $s = 1, \ldots, ST$, and then the estimation of the auxiliary parameter from the instrumental model and the artificial data:

$$\hat{\beta}_{TS}^s(\theta) = \operatorname*{Arg\,max}_{\beta} \sum_{t=1}^{ST} \log g[y_t^s(\theta)|\underline{y_{t-1}^s}(\theta);\beta].$$

3. The last step is a calibration step, yielding the indirect inference estimator of θ defined by

$$\hat{\theta}_T^s = \operatorname*{Arg\,min}_{\theta} \; [\hat{\beta}_T - \hat{\beta}_{TS}^s(\theta)]' \Omega [\hat{\beta}_T - \hat{\beta}_{TS}^s(\theta)]. \qquad (12.35)$$

where Ω is a weighting matrix.

12.5.2 Efficient Method of Moments

An alternative approach has been introduced by Gallant and Tauchen (1996). It is based on an auxiliary model $g(y_t|y_{t-1};\beta)$ and makes use of the quasi-maximum likelihood (QML) estimator $\hat{\beta}_T$. This estimator satisfies the first-order condition

$$\frac{1}{T}\sum_{t=1}^{T} \frac{\partial \log g_t(\hat{\beta}_T)}{\partial \beta} = 0.$$

It converges asymptotically to the solution β_0^* of the limiting moment condition

$$E\left[\frac{\partial \log g(y_t|y_{t-1};\beta_0^*)}{\partial \beta}\right] = 0, \qquad (12.36)$$

called the *pseudo-true value*. The moment condition of (12.36) resembles a simulated method of moments condition. More precisely, Gallant and Tauchen consider the series $y_t^s(\theta)$, $s = 1, \dots , ST$, generated under the true model and find the solution of the following optimization:

$$\hat{\theta}^s = \operatorname*{Arg\,min}_{\theta} \; \left[\frac{1}{ST}\sum_{t=1}^{T}\sum_{s=1}^{S} \frac{\partial \log g(y_t^s(\theta)|y_{t-1}^s;\hat{\beta}_T)}{\partial \beta}\right]$$

$$\Omega\left[\frac{1}{ST}\sum_{t=1}^{T}\sum_{s=1}^{S} \frac{\partial \log g(y_t^s(\theta)|y_{t-1}^s;\hat{\beta}_T)}{\partial \beta}\right], \qquad (12.37)$$

where Ω is a weighting matrix. It has been proved that the estimators $\hat{\theta}^s$ and $\hat{\theta}^s$ given in (12.37) and (12.35) are asymptotically equivalent. This is a consequence of the interpretation of the objective function as a Wald test statistic [see (12.35)] and a Lagrange multiplier test statistic [see (12.37)], respectively. The efficiency of the estimator increases with the number of moments considered. In the limiting case of an auxiliary model with an infinite number of parameters, full efficiency is achieved. This explains the term *efficient method of moments* (EMM) used as a reference in the literature (Gallant and Tauchen 1996).

12.5.3 Application to Continuous Time Models

Let us consider a continuous time process satisfying a stochastic differential equation

$$dy_t = \mu(y_t;\theta)dt + \sigma(y_t;\theta)dW_t, \tag{12.38}$$

where (W_t) is a standard Brownian motion. When the available observations are sampled at integer dates $1, 2, \ldots, T$, it is generally impossible to determine the analytical form of the likelihood function. A common approach consists of replacing the initial continuous time model in (12.25) by its Euler discretization (see Section 11.3.1):

$$y_t = y_{t-1} + \mu(y_{t-1};\beta) + \sigma(y_{t-1},\beta)\varepsilon_t, \tag{12.39}$$

where (ε_t) is a Gaussian white noise. Next, we estimate β by the maximum likelihood method applied to the approximated model in (12.26) and likely conclude that the estimated parameter $\hat{\beta}$ provides a good approximation of the unknown θ. However, since the Euler discretization is an approximation, model (12.39) is misspecified, causing an asymptotic bias of its estimators, which may be arbitrarily large (see Section 12.5.4).

However, the Euler discretization can be used as an instrumental model in the indirect inference method. The idea is to introduce a second Euler discretization involving a very short time unit, $\delta = 1/10$ (say). More precisely, we define the process $(y_t^{\delta}, t = k\delta, k$ varying) such that

$$y_{(k+1)\delta}^{(\delta)} = y_{k\delta}^{(\delta)} + \delta\mu\left(y_{k\delta}^{(\delta)},\theta\right) + \sigma\left(y_{k\delta}^{(\delta)},\theta\right)\sqrt{\delta}\varepsilon_k^{(\delta)}, \tag{12.40}$$

where $\varepsilon_k^{(\delta)}$, k varying, is a Gaussian white noise. This finer Euler discretization can be used to simulate the continuous time process. Let us denote by $y_{k\delta}^{(\delta),s}(\theta)$, $k = 1, \ldots, T/\delta$, the simulated path corresponding to the parameter value θ, and $y_t^{(s)}(\theta) = y_t^{(\delta),s}(\theta)$, $t = 1, \ldots, T$, the values corresponding to the observation dates.

The indirect inference approach includes the three estimation steps outlined below:

1. Estimation of β from observations

$$\hat{\beta}_T = \text{Arg} \min_{\beta} \sum_{t=1}^{T} \left\{ -\frac{1}{2}\log \sigma^2(y_{t-1},\beta) - \frac{1}{2}\frac{[y_t - \mu(y_{t-1},\beta)]^2}{\sigma^2(y_{t-1};\beta)} \right\};$$

2. Estimation of β from simulations

$$\hat{\beta}_T^s(\theta) = \text{Arg} \min_{\beta} \sum_{t=1}^{T} \left\{ -\frac{1}{2}\log \sigma^2(y_{t-1}^{(s)}(\theta),\beta) - \frac{1}{2}\frac{[y_t^{(s)}(\theta) - \mu(y_{t-1}^{(s)}(\theta),\beta)]^2}{\sigma^2(y_{t-1}^{(s)}(\theta);\beta)} \right\};$$

3. Calibration

$$\hat{\theta}_T^s = \text{Arg} \min_{\beta} [\hat{\beta}_T - \hat{\beta}_T^s(\theta)]'\Omega[\hat{\beta}_T - \hat{\beta}_T^s(\theta)],$$

where Ω is a given matrix of weights.

12.5.4   A Monte Carlo Study

To give some insights into the magnitude of the bias of the maximum likelihood estimators of a Euler discretized diffusion and its correction by indirect inference, we consider an Ornstein-Uhlenbeck process

$$dy_t = k(\mu - y_t)dt + \sigma dW_t. \tag{12.41}$$

The exact discretization of this process corresponds to the Gaussian AR(1) model

$$y_t = \mu[1 - \exp - k] + (\exp - k)y_{t-1} + \sigma\left(\frac{1 - \exp(-2k)}{2k}\right)^{1/2}\varepsilon_t, \tag{12.42}$$

where (ε_t) is independent identically $N(0,1)$ distributed $[\text{IIN}(0,1)]$.

We can also consider the crude Euler discretization of the continuous time model, which is

$$y_t = y_{t-1} + k^*(\mu^* - y_{t-1}) + \sigma^*\varepsilon_t^*, \tag{12.43}$$

where ε_t^* is $\text{IIN}(0,1)$, and we distinguish the parameters k^*, μ^*, and σ^*, which have a different interpretation than the parameters k, μ, and σ.

In Figures 12.11 and 12.12, we compare three estimation methods for the volatility and mean reverting parameters, that is,

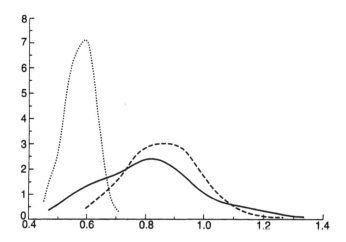

Figure 12.11   *Estimation of* k

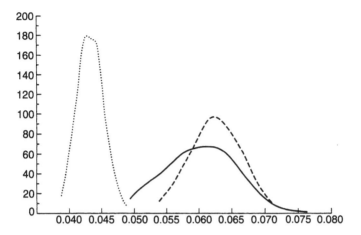

Figure 12.12 *Estimation of σ*

1. The true maximum likelihood estimator based on the exact discretization in (12.42) (the dashed line);
2. The quasi-maximum likelihood estimator based on the crude Euler discretization in (12.43) (the dotted line);
3. Its correction by indirect inference (the solid line).

The methods are applied to a sample of $T = 250$ observations, for which the parameters are $k = 0.8$, $\mu = 0.1$, and $\sigma = 0.06$. The indirect inference is applied with $S = 1$ replication and a time unit $\delta = 1/10$ for the simulations. We observe a large bias of the QML method based on the crude Euler discretization. Moreover, the indirect inference clearly corrects for the observed bias.

12.5.5 A Model for the Short-Term Interest Rate

Chan et al. (1992) have proposed the following family of models for the short-term interest rate:

$$dr_t = (\alpha + \beta r_t)dt + \sigma_0 r_t^\gamma dW_t. \tag{12.44}$$

The Brennan-Schwartz model (Brennan and Schwartz 1979) corresponds to (12.44) under the constraint $\gamma = 1$. Broze, Scaillet, and Zakoian (1995) have estimated this model for the rates of return on US Treasury bills with 1 month to maturity. Under their approach, the short-term interest rate is equivalent to a 1-month rate. The data cover the period January 1972 to November 1991 and contain 239 observations.

An extended version of the model is obtained by replacing the volatility term by

$$\sigma_t = \sigma_0(r_t^\gamma + \sigma_1).$$

Table 12.2 *Estimation from the Discretized Version*

	Parameter				
	α	$\beta+1$	σ_0	σ_1	γ
Estimation	0.23	0.97	0.094	−1.73	1

Its estimation by the exact likelihood method is not feasible due to the complicated pattern of volatility. Therefore, the ML has first been applied to the (misspecified) discretized version of the model under the constraint $\gamma \le 1$ (Table 12.2). Note that, contrary to what was said in the initial paper by Broze et al. (1995), this condition is not equivalent to a stationarity condition (Conley et al. 1997).

If these estimators were consistent for the parameters of the underlying continuous time model (which is not the case since they have been derived from the discretized version), we would have concluded that the model of Chan et al. is misspecified. Indeed, the constant term σ_1 in the volatility equation is different from 0. However, such a conclusion needs to be reconsidered after a bias correction of the estimators. The correction has been performed by indirect inference based on a finer discretization of the model with a time unit of 1/10 (Table 12.3).

The γ estimator still reaches the limiting point. The parameters α_1 and σ_1 are much more sensitive to the discretization effect. In particular, $\hat{\sigma}_1$ is now close to 0.

12.6 Summary

Generally, there are two types of estimation methods for the return data in continuous time. To the first category belong the exact methods, such as the maximum likelihood or the generalized method of moments. They are directly applicable whenever the dynamics of a series obeys a simple univariate diffusion equation. The second type of estimation method is simulation based. The simulation-based methods, such as the simulated

Table 12.3 *Estimation by Indirect Inference*

	Parameter				
	α	$\beta+1$	σ_0	σ_1	γ
Estimation	0.03	0.98	0.102	−0.08	1

method of moments and indirect inference, are applicable to more complicated processes, those featuring stochastic volatility or jumps, for example.

Since basic univariate diffusion models are misspecified when applied to data that span a long time, two approaches can be followed. The first one consists of using a simple diffusion model and the exact estimation method applied by rolling. At time t, the maximum likelihood estimator, for example, is computed from observations in the interval between $t - H$ and t. Then, at the next date, the set of observations is shifted by one point in time, and the estimate is updated. The Black-Scholes model is commonly used in this way, for example.

The second approach relies on a model that is valid for the whole period and takes into account complicated features, such as stochastic volatility or jumps. Then, it is necessary to employ the simulation-based estimation methods.

Similar remarks are made in the next chapter, in which data on prices of assets and their derivatives are examined. Exact estimation methods are performed on simple models fitted to rolling windows of observations across the sample.

13

Econometrics of Derivatives

IN CHAPTER 12, we explained how to estimate the parameters that characterize the price dynamics of various assets, such as stocks, bonds, and exchange rates given a series of observed prices. The aim of this chapter is inference, which accounts for additional information contained in option prices. There exist two approaches that differ with respect to the assumption on the type of market. Under the complete market hypothesis, the derivative price and the price of an asset are supposed to satisfy a deterministic relationship. We show that such a deterministic link is not compatible with statistical inference.

In the incomplete market framework, two types of parameters can be distinguished: parameters characterizing the dynamics of the basic asset price and parameters involved in the derivative pricing formula. We discuss the estimation of both types of parameters and the use of time series and cross-sectional techniques.

The first section deals with the Black-Scholes approach to option pricing. We first recall the Black-Scholes model and the option pricing formula and discuss the incompatibility between the model and statistical inference. Despite its misspecification, the Black-Scholes model offers a convenient framework for preliminary correction of option prices for the strike and maturity effects and for comparing option prices in practice. The corrected prices are called the *implied Black-Scholes volatilities*. The Black-Scholes volatilities at various maturities form an implied volatility surface.

The methods of derivative pricing on incomplete markets introduced in Chapters 8 and 12 were based either on some equilibria conditions or on the condition of the absence of arbitrage opportunities. We recall these results and review them in a general framework of stochastic discount factors, allowing the parameters that describe the underlying asset price dynamics to be distinguished from the parameters appearing in the risk-neutral density. Section 13.3 deals with estimation methods applicable to incomplete markets that make use of information contained in the prices of assets and their derivatives. The last two sections focus on some advanced problems of pricing complicated derivatives. Especially, the last section presents numerical methods of derivative pricing.

13.1   Analysis Based on the Black-Scholes Model

We consider the Black-Scholes model, which assumes a constant risk-free rate r and a geometric Brownian motion process of the price of the underlying asset

$$dS_t = \mu S_t dt + \sigma S_t dW_t. \tag{13.1}$$

We saw in Chapter 11 that, under the complete market hypothesis, the price of a European call with strike K and time to maturity H is uniquely determined by

$$C(t;H;K) = S_t \Phi(x_t) - K \exp(-rH)\Phi\left(x_t - \sigma\sqrt{H}\right), \tag{13.2}$$

where

$$x_t = \frac{\log[S_t/(K \exp -rH)]}{\sigma\sqrt{H}} + \frac{1}{2}\sigma\sqrt{H}, \tag{13.3}$$

and Φ is the cumulative distribution function (cdf) of the standard normal.

The option price can also be written as a function of the *moneyness-strike*, which is the ratio of the strike and spot price $k = K/S_t$.

We get

$$C(t;H;k) = S_t \Psi(\sigma;k;H;r), \tag{13.4}$$

where:

$$\Psi(\sigma;k;H;r) = \Phi(x) - k \exp(-rH)\Phi\left(x - \sigma\sqrt{H}\right), \tag{13.5}$$

and

$$x = -\frac{\log(k \exp -rH)}{\sigma\sqrt{H}} + \frac{1}{2}\sigma\sqrt{H}. \tag{13.6}$$

Thus, the volatility parameter σ appears in both the dynamic specification of the underlying price and in relations between the derivative prices, whereas the drift parameter appears in the dynamic equation only.

13.1.1   Inference from the Price of the Underlying Asset

Let us suppose that the assumptions of the Black-Scholes model are all satisfied. Given a sample of observations $S_1, \ldots, S_T$ on the price of the underlying asset, we can estimate the drift and volatility parameters; next, by applying the Black-Scholes formula in (13.2) and (13.3), we can approximate the derivative prices.

Estimation of the Drift and Volatility Parameters
By Ito's formula, we know that

$$d \log S_t = \left(\mu - \frac{\sigma^2}{2}\right)dt + \sigma dW_t,$$

which implies

$$\Delta \log S_t = \log S_t - \log S_{t-1} = \left(\mu - \frac{\sigma^2}{2}\right) + \sigma \varepsilon_t, \qquad (13.7)$$

where (ε_t) is a standard Gaussian white noise. We find the expression of the maximum likelihood (ML) estimators of the mean $v = \mu - \dfrac{\sigma^2}{2}$ and variance σ^2 of the log-differenced prices (see Section 12.1.1). They are equal to

$$\hat{v}_T = \frac{1}{T} \sum_{t=1}^{T} (\Delta \log S_t) = \overline{\Delta \log S_T}, \qquad (13.8)$$

$$\hat{\sigma}_T^2 = \frac{1}{T} \sum_{t=1}^{T} \left[\Delta \log S_t - \overline{\Delta \log S_T}\right]^2. \qquad (13.9)$$

These two estimators are independent and asymptotically normal with asymptotic variances $V\hat{v}_T = \dfrac{\sigma^2}{T}$, $V\hat{\sigma}_T^2 = \dfrac{2\sigma^4}{T}$.

Determination of a Current Option Price
Our objective is to evaluate the option price at the present time T. The current option price is defined by the formula:

$$C(T;H;k) = S_T \Psi(\sigma;k;H;r_T), \qquad (13.10)$$

where the risk-free rate is usually replaced by a 1-month interest rate evaluated at T or the interest rate at horizon H, if available. Since S_T and r_T are both observable, the derivative price can be approximated by

$$\hat{C}(T;H;k) = S_T \Psi(\hat{\sigma}_T;k;H;r_T). \qquad (13.11)$$

It is a counterpart of the Black-Scholes option price (13.10) with the unknown volatility replaced by its maximum likelihood estimator. By applying the δ-method and using the formula of the asymptotic variance of
$\hat{\sigma}_T^2$, we get a 95% prediction interval for the option price

$$\left[\hat{C}(T;H;k) \pm 2S_T \frac{\partial \psi}{\partial \sigma}(\hat{\sigma}_T;k;H;r_T) \sqrt{\frac{2}{T}} \hat{\sigma}_T^2\right]. \tag{13.12}$$

The length of the prediction interval depends on the sensitivity $\frac{\partial \psi}{\partial \sigma}$ of the
option price with respect to the volatility.

Prediction of a Future Call Price
Our objective is now to predict at T the option price corresponding to a
future time t. Let us consider a European call with maturity $T_0 > T$ and
strike K. At date $t > T$, prior to maturity, its Black-Scholes price is

$$C(t;T_0 - t;K) = S_t\Psi[\sigma;K/S_t;T_0 - t;r]. \tag{13.13}$$

At the prediction origin T, the risk-free rate, assumed to be constant in
the Black-Scholes model, can be replaced by the current value r_T. However, the future price of the underlying asset also has to be predicted
given all available information. We know that

$$\log S_t = \log S_T + \mu(t - T) + \sigma \sqrt{t - T}\varepsilon, \tag{13.14}$$

where ε is a standard normal variable independent of $\log S_T$, and $t \geq T$.
Therefore, conditional on the current price S_T, the future price S_t has a
log-normal distribution with mean $\log S_T + \mu(t - T)$ and variance $\sigma^2(t - T)$.
Conditional on S_T, the option price admits a distribution that is derived
from the distribution of S_t by the Black-Scholes transformation (13.13).

The explicit form of the conditional distribution of the option price
is easily obtained when t is equal to the option maturity T_0. Indeed, we
have $C(T_0;0;K) = (S_{T_0} - K)^+$, and the conditional distribution of the option
price is a truncated log-normal distribution.
It admits a point mass at 0 with probability

$$P[S_{T_0} - K < 0 | S_T] = P[\log S_{T_0} - \log K < 0 | S_T]$$

$$= P\left[\log S_T - \log K + \mu(T_0 - T) + \sigma \sqrt{T_0 - T}\varepsilon < 0\right]$$

$$= \Phi\left[\frac{-\log S_T + \log K - \mu(T_0 - T)}{\sigma\sqrt{T_0 - T}}\right],$$

and a continuous part for strictly positive values. Depending on the location of the mode of the log-normal distribution with respect to the strike,
we get one of the two patterns displayed in Figure 13.1.

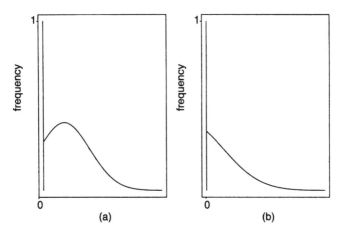

Figure 13.1 *Conditional Distributions of $(S_{T_0} - K)^+$*

When t is strictly less than the maturity T_0, the analytical expression of the conditional distribution is difficult to derive. In contrast, this distribution is easily obtained by simulations. Let us consider S independent drawings ε^s, $s = 1, \ldots, S$, from the standard normal distribution. Using formula (13.14), we generate simulated values of the future price of the underlying asset:

$$\log S_t^s = \log S_T + \hat{\mu}_T(t - T) + \hat{\sigma}_T\sqrt{t - T}\,\varepsilon^s, \qquad s = 1, \ldots, S, \qquad (13.15)$$

after replacing the unknown parameters by their estimators. Next, using formula (13.13), the simulated future option prices are

$$C_s(t, T_0 - t; K) = S_t^s\,\Psi(\hat{\sigma}_T; K/S_t^s; T_0 - t, r_T), \qquad s = 1, \ldots, S. \qquad (13.16)$$

The conditional distribution of the future option price is well approximated by the empirical distribution of the simulated values $C^s(t, T_0 - t; K)$. It is important to note that, to determine this conditional distribution, we need to estimate the drift parameter. Indeed, the parameter μ is necessary for predicting the future option price even though it does not appear explicitly in the Black-Scholes formula.

Some conditional distributions of future option prices are displayed in Figure 13.2.

13.1.2 The Incompatibility between the Black-Scholes Model and Statistical Inference

The previous section leaves us with an impression that, from a statistical point of view, the Black-Scholes model is a simple and convenient tool

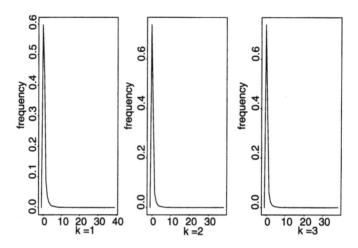

Figure 13.2 *Conditional Distributions of Future Option Prices*

for analysis. Recall that, from a sample of asset prices, we estimated the parameters μ and σ of the geometric Brownian motion and substituted σ into the option pricing formula. Statistical inference breaks down, however, when option prices are observed as well.

Let us further assume that at date t we have a complete sample of observations on the price S_t of the asset, the risk-free rate r_t, and two option prices with characteristics H_1,k_1 and H_2,k_2, respectively. From the Black-Scholes formula,

$$\begin{cases} C(t;H_1,k_1) = S_t\Psi(\sigma;k_1,H_1,r_t), \\ C(t;H_2,k_2) = S_t\Psi(\sigma;k_2,H_2,r_t). \end{cases}$$

The true value of the volatility should arise as the solution of this bivariate nonlinear system. Yet, in practice, the observed prices S_t, r_t, $C(t;H_1,k_1)$, and $C(t,H_2,k_2)$ are such that the system has no solution; as a consequence, the Black-Scholes model is immediately rejected by the data with probability 1.

The incompatibility stems from the unrealistic assumption of the Black-Scholes model on unique derivative prices, which implies a deterministic relationship between the asset price and option price. In reality, such deterministic relationships do not exist. Statistical inference makes sense only in the presence of a source of random variation or, more precisely of an error term, transforming the deterministic relationship into a stochastic one. Therefore, the Black-Scholes formula can be viewed instead as an approximate pricing formula:

$$C(t;H_1,k_1) = S_t\Psi(\sigma;k_1,H_1,r_t) + \eta_{1t},$$

$$C(t;H_2,k_2) = S_t\Psi(\sigma;k_2,H_2,r_t) + \eta_{2t},$$

where η_{1t} and η_{2t} are error terms. One has to realize, however, that the presence of the additional noises (η_{1t}) and (η_{2t}), for instance, results in an incomplete market framework (see Chapter 11) for which derivative prices are no longer unique.

13.1.3 Implied Volatilities

Definition
Nevertheless, the Black-Scholes formula remains a valuable tool for comparing option prices. Especially, it may be used for preliminary correction of the derivative price for the effects of residual maturity, moneyness-strike, and current asset price. This first-step correction leads to the so-called implied volatility. Thus, in spite of its name, an *implied volatility* is essentially a normalized option price.

Let us assume an observed option price of a call with residual maturity H and moneyness-strike k: $C(t;H;k)$, (say). Since the function Ψ in the Black-Scholes formula is a one-to-one function of volatility, there exists a unique volatility value such that

$$C(t;H,k) = S_t\Psi[\sigma_{BS}(t;H;k);k;H,r_t], \qquad (13.17)$$

where $\sigma_{BS}(t,H,k)$ is the implied volatility associated with the derivative with an observed price. It can essentially be viewed as a corrected option price for which the correction pertains to the aforementioned effects. This explains why, on derivative markets, options are often quoted in terms of their implied volatilities to facilitate price comparison.

If the assumptions of the Black-Scholes model were all satisfied, all implied volatilities would be equal and would coincide with the constant historical volatility σ. In fact, in the Black-Scholes world, all contingent claims are generated either by the risky and risk-free assets or by an option and risk-free asset. All options are equivalent; hence, their corrected prices are equal as well.

Comparison of Volatilities
In the real world, implied volatilities vary depending on the data, maturity, and strike. To illustrate this feature, Figure 13.3 shows various volatilities that correspond to the index Hang Seng of the Hong Kong stock exchange covering the period January 15, 1997, to January 12, 1999. The data contain (1) the historical volatility and (2) the implied volatility. Historical volatility consists of daily observations, each computed from a sam-

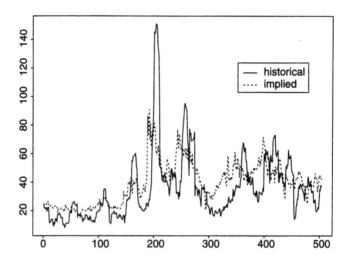

Figure 13.3 *Evolution of Historical and Implied Volatilities*

ple of daily data on 10 consecutive trading days. For implied volatility, the daily implied volatilities are derived by averaging the Black-Scholes implied volatilities of the six most frequently traded call and put options written on the index. Of course, the selection of these six derivatives is endogenous and varies in time.

The implied volatility series is less volatile than the historical series. This is a stylized fact, which can partly justify the interpretation of implied volatility as an expectation of future volatilities (see the variance bounds discussed in Chapter 8). Such an interpretation results from a reasoning based on an equilibrium model with rational expectations rather than the Black-Scholes model. Since the derivatives are introduced to hedge against the volatility risk, their demand and supply have to be functions of the expected future volatilities. Therefore, the equilibrium prices and the normalized equilibrium prices (i.e., the implied volatilities) also depend on these expectations.

Additional information on the joint dynamics of the historical and implied volatilities is provided by their autocorrelation functions (ACF), shown in Figure 13.4. The significant autocorrelations of historical volatilities are partly due to the overlapping of the periods from which averages are computed. The possible explanations of the larger values of autocorrelations of the implied volatilities are of two different types. First, if we interpret the implied volatilities as normalized prices, we expect a unit root price dynamics under the efficient (derivative) market hypothesis. Second, if we retain an expectation interpretation of implied volatility as

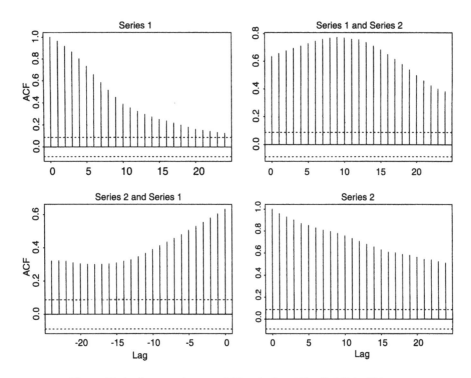

Figure 13.4 *Autocorrelogram of Historical and Implied Volatilities*

the average of expected future volatilities until the maturity, we again end up with the overlapping argument. However, the overlapping alone does not explain the entire values of implied autocorrelations, as seen by comparing them with the autocorrelations of historical volatilities. The temporal dependence revealed by the joint autocorrelogram of historical and implied volatilities suggests a bivariate autoregressive structure of the volatilities and implied volatilities, and likely the possibility to outperform the predictions based on generalized autoregressive conditional heteroscedastic models by introducing implied volatilities among the regressors. This stylized fact was noted first by Lamoureux and Lastrapes (1993). Table 13.1 shows the estimated coefficients from various ARCH regressions that include implied volatilities among the regressors.

The ARCH-type models are

$$y_t = \sigma_t \varepsilon_t,$$

where

$$\sigma_t^2 = a_0 + a_1 y_{t-1}^2 + a_2 \sigma_{BS,t-1}^2 + a_3 \sigma_{BS,t-1}.$$

Table 13.1 *Implied Volatility in ARCH Regression*

Constant	y^2_{t-1}	$\sigma^2_{BS,t-1}$	$\sigma_{BS,t-1}$
0.0004	0.3903	–	–
(4.58)	(9.47)	–	–
−0.0011	–	0.4E-4	–
(−4.52)	–	(7.72)	–
−0.0027	–	–	0.0005
(−5.70)	–	–	(7.26)
−0.0007	0.3143	0.3E-4	–
(−3.01)	(7.32)	(5.03)	–
−0.0018	0.3237	–	0.0003
(−3.77)	(7.58)	–	(4.75)

Moreover it has been observed that, when lagged volatilities are also included in the ARCH equation, their coefficients are not significant. In some sense, the lagged implied volatilities are more informative than the lagged historical volatilities for predicting future risks on the underlying asset.

Volatility Smile and Volatility Surface
It is also interesting to consider a given date t, maturity H, and implied volatilities corresponding to various moneyness-strikes. In general, for stock options, the implied volatilities plotted against the moneyness-strike form a parabola, with a minimum at $k = 1$ and slight asymmetry, due to greater slope for $k < 1$ than for $k > 1$. This particular pattern is called the *volatility smile*, and it is discussed further below.

However, this typical pattern is not observed in all derivatives, as shown in Figure 13.5, in which the volatility smiles for the dollar/yen options are displayed. As expected, the asymmetry is more difficult to detect in exchange rates. Indeed, the definition of the exchange rate depends on the selected currency of reference. A call option with dollars as the basic currency is similar to a put option with yen as the basic currency. Thus, there is no reason to justify an asymmetry to the right rather than to the left or vice-versa.

More generally, for any given date t, we can plot the implied volatilities as functions of both the maturity and moneyness-strike to obtain the so-called implied volatility surface (Figure 13.6). This surface illustrates the dependence of the smile effect on the maturity.

Alternatively, this dependence can be observed by plotting the smiles associated with various residual maturities. We provide in Figure 13.7 a

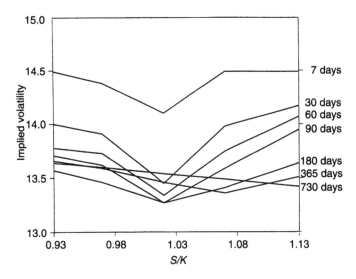

Figure 13.5 *Volatility Smiles, U.S. Dollar/Japanese Yen, September 1, 1997*

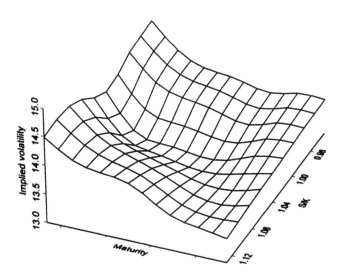

Figure 13.6 *Implied Volatility Surface, U.S. Dollar/Japanese Yen, September 1, 1997*

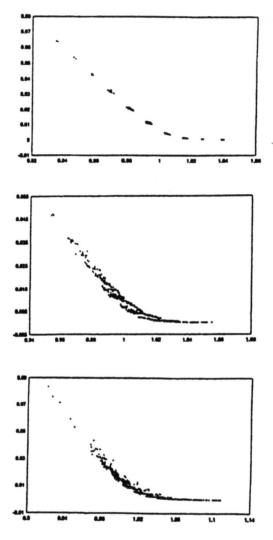

Figure 13.7 *Set of Volatility Smiles, S&P*

set of such figures for different dates and options on the Standard and
Poor's (S&P) Index.

13.1.4 *Reconstitution of the Implied Volatility Surface*

In practice, at each date t, there exists a very limited number of liquid
European calls (or puts) with prices that can be considered competitive.

Their characteristics are denoted by (H_j,k_j), $j = 1, \ldots, J_t$. Their observed prices are $C(t;H_j,k_j)$, and the implied volatilities are $\sigma_{BS}(t;H_j,k_j)$, $j = 1, \ldots, J_t$. These data can be used to infer an acceptable competitive price of a newly created derivative such as a call with characteristics (H,k) or to price a derivative that is not actively traded on the market. Equivalently, this information may serve to recover the price surface

$$(H,k) \rightarrow C(t;H,k),$$

or the implied volatility surface

$$(H,k) \rightarrow \sigma_{BS}(t;H,k).$$

There exist various heuristic approaches to fitting a smooth surface to a set of observed points (see the references at the end of this book). In finance, the variable represented by the surface is, in general, the implied volatility, for the following reasons. First, under the Black-Scholes framework, we should observe a flat surface, which is easy to recover. Moreover, fewer restrictions are imposed on the volatility surface than on the price surface [for instance, $C(t;H,k)$ is a decreasing function of k]. Below, we outline the methods that can be applied for obtaining the implied volatility surface (H and k varying) or simply the smile (k varying, fixed maturity).

Finally, note that there exists a large number of databases that include "complete" volatility surfaces. These surfaces have generally been estimated by one of the approaches described below. Thus, it is important to know the initial observed prices and the method of smoothing before using these volatility surfaces for further analysis.

Regression Approach
A natural idea is to introduce a parametric specification for the implied volatility surface:

$$\sigma_{BS}(t;H,k) \simeq a(H,k;\theta), \qquad \text{say}, \tag{13.18}$$

where θ is a vector parameter. Usually the selected parametric specification includes a constant function. Then, we approximate the implied volatility surface by $a(H_j,k_j;\hat{\theta}_t)$, where:

$$\hat{\theta}_t = \operatorname*{Arg\,min}_{\theta} \sum_{j=1}^{J_t} [\sigma_{BS}(t;H_j,k_j) - a(H_j,k_j;\theta)]^2. \tag{13.19}$$

The price surface is approximated by

$$\hat{C}(t;H,k) = S_t \psi[a(H,k;\hat{\theta}_t);k,H,r_t]. \tag{13.20}$$

This approach is designed to reproduce an implied volatility surface at a fixed time, that is, under a cross-sectional approach. As a consequence, the volatility surfaces are computed daily by practitioners. Since the parameter $\hat{\theta}_t$ is reestimated each day as well, a time series of varying parameters is generated as an additonal output.

EXAMPLE 13.1: Let us introduce a polynomial approximation of the implied volatility surface. For a polynomial of degree 2, we get

$$a(H,k;\theta) = a_0 + a_1 H + a_2 k + a_3 H^2 + a_4 Hk + a_5 k^2,$$

where $\theta = (a_0, a_1, a_2, a_3, a_4, a_5)'$. Furthermore, for a fixed maturity H, we obtain a parabolic smile. The level and curvature of the smile may depend on the maturity. Empirically, polynomials of higher degrees are required to capture asymmetric smiles.

The fact that the estimated volatility surface is not flat is an indication of misspecification in the Black-Scholes model. The parametric specification in (13.18) extends the standard Black-Scholes set of pricing formulas

$$C(t;H,k) = S_t \psi[a(H,k;\theta);k,H,r_t].$$

The sensitivities of the option price with respect to the arguments H and k are also modified. More precisely, we have

$$\frac{\partial C}{\partial H}(t;H,k) = S_t \frac{\partial \psi}{\partial \sigma}\frac{\partial a}{\partial H} + S_t \frac{\partial \psi}{\partial H}$$

$$= v_t \frac{\partial a}{\partial H} - \Theta_t,$$

where v_t and Θ_t denote the first derivatives of the Black-Scholes formula with respect to the volatility and maturity, respectively. They are called *vega* and *theta*, respectively.

Regressogram
The implied volatility surface can also be recovered by nonparametric methods. For instance, we can approximate the implied volatility associated with (H,k) by computing a weighted average of observed volatilities using as weights some functions of the derivative characteristics. For illustration, let us introduce a Gaussian kernel and two bandwidths η_H and η_k for the maturity and moneyness-strike, respectively. The approximated implied volatility can be defined as

$$\hat{\sigma}_{BS}(t;H,k) = \frac{\sum_{j=1}^{J_t} K\left[\dfrac{H-H_j}{\eta_H}\right] K\left[\dfrac{k-k_j}{\eta_k}\right] \sigma_{BS}(t;H_j,k_j)}{\sum_{j=1}^{J_t} K\left[\dfrac{H-H_j}{\eta_H}\right] K\left[\dfrac{k-k_j}{\eta_k}\right]}. \tag{13.21}$$

This is the so-called regressogram, or Nadarayah-Watson estimator, of the implied volatility function.

Hermite Polynomial Expansions

Other nonparametric approximations of the price surface are based on polynomial expansions. These methods allow for a choice of one among various possible basis of polynomials. For instance, Jarrow and Rudd (1982) considered Edgeworth expansions, whereas Madan and Milne (1994) proposed the introduction of Hermite polynomials. Let us describe the last approach after introducing first the definition and properties of Hermite polynomials.

The formula of a Hermite polynomial involves a derivative of the standard normal density. As we know, the probability density function (pdf) φ of the standard normal distribution admits derivatives of any order. These derivatives are written as products of φ and polynomials of increasing degrees. The Hermite polynomial of order k is defined by

$$H_k(x) = \frac{(-1)^k}{\sqrt{k!}} \frac{d^k \varphi(x)}{dx^k} \frac{1}{\varphi(x)}. \tag{13.22}$$

For example, the Hermite polynomials of low orders are

$$H_0(x) = 1, \qquad H_1(x) = x, \qquad H_2(x) = \frac{x^2 - 1}{2}, \qquad H_3(x) = \frac{x^3 - 3x}{6}.$$

The sequence of Hermite polynomials forms a basis of orthonormal functions with respect to the standard normal distribution φ:

$$\int H_k^2(x)\varphi(x)dx = 1, \qquad \forall k,$$

$$\int H_k(x)H_l(x)\varphi(x)dx = 0, \qquad \forall k \neq l. \tag{13.23}$$

Therefore, any function g can be decomposed on the orthonormal basis as

$$g(x) = \sum_{l=0}^{\infty} g_l H_l(x), \quad \text{where } g_l = \int g(x)H_l(x)\varphi(x)dx. \tag{13.24}$$

Let us now describe an application of the Hermite expansion to the Black-Scholes formula. Under the Black-Scholes model, the price of a derivative with residual maturity H and cash flow $g(S_{t+H})$ is

$$C(t,H,g) = \exp(-rH) \overset{\pi^{BS}}{E} [g(S_{t+H})|S_t]$$

$$= \exp(-rH)E\left[g\left(S_t \exp\left[\left(r - \frac{\sigma^2}{2}\right)H + \sigma\sqrt{H}u\right]\right)\right], \tag{13.25}$$

where u is a standard normal variable.

Instead of using a Gaussian distribution, Madan and Milne (1994) assumed a nonparametric specification of the risk-neutral density of the shock u. Let us pursue their approach. We get

$$C(t,H,g) = \exp(-rH)\ \overset{\pi}{E}\left[g\left(S_t\ \exp\left[\left(r-\frac{1}{2}\right)H + \sigma\ \sqrt{H}u\right]\right)\right]$$

$$= \exp(-rH)\ \overset{\pi}{E}\ g(S_t,H,\sigma^2,r;u) \qquad \text{(say)} \tag{13.26}$$

$$= \exp(-rH)\ \int g(S_t,H,\sigma^2,r;u)\pi(u)du.$$

Madan and Milne (1994) considered the Hermite expansion of the ratio of the latent risk-neutral density and the Black-Scholes Gaussian density:

$$\pi(u) = \left[\sum_{k=0}^{\infty} c_k H_k(u)\right]\varphi(u),$$

and truncated this expansion at a finite number of terms, say $k = K$:

$$\pi(u) \simeq \left[\sum_{k=0}^{K} c_k H_k(u)\right]\varphi\ (u). \tag{13.27}$$

The pricing formula now becomes

$$C(t,H,g) = \exp(-rH)\sum_{k=0}^{K} c_k \int g(S_t,H,\sigma^2,r,u)H_k(u)\varphi(u)du \tag{13.28}$$

$$= \exp(-rH)\sum_{k=0}^{K} c_k\gamma_k(g,S_t,H,\sigma^2,r), \qquad \text{say.}$$

The parameters r, σ^2, and c_k, $k = 0, \ldots, K$, are approximated by calibration, that is, by substituting the observed derivative prices into the following formula:

$$(\hat{r},\hat{\sigma}^2,\hat{c}_k) = \underset{r,\sigma^2,c_k}{\text{Arg min}} \sum_{j=1}^{J_t}\left\{C(t,H_j,g_j) - \exp(-rH_j)\sum_{k=0}^{K} c_k\gamma_k(g_j,S_t,H_j,\sigma^2,r)\right\}^2.$$

The calibration is performed directly on price volatilities, instead of implied Black-Scholes volatilities, to maintain the linearity of the approximation formula with respect to the parameters c_k, $k = 0, \ldots, K$, in the expansion.

Once an implied volatility or a call price surface has been recovered, it is common to display several surfaces jointly. The most interesting ones are (1) the price surface for the European calls, (2) the implied volatility surface, and (3) the implied state price densities. Let us explain how the implied state price densities can be inferred from the price surface of the European calls. The price of a European call is

$$C(t,H,K) = \exp(-rH)\ \overset{\pi}{E}((S_{t+H} - K)^+|S_t)$$

$$= \exp(-rH)\int(s - K)^+\pi_H(s|S_t)ds,$$

where $\pi_H(s\,|\,S_t)$ denotes the conditional risk-neutral density of S_{t+H} given S_t. By differentiating both sides of the pricing formula, we obtain (Breeden and Litzenberger 1978)

$$C(t,H,K) = \exp(-rH) \int_K^\infty (s-K)\pi_H(s\,|\,S_t)ds,$$

$$\frac{\partial C(t,H,K)}{\partial K} = -\exp(-rH) \int_K^\infty \pi_H(s\,|\,S_t)ds$$

$$\frac{\partial^2 C(t,H,K)}{\partial K^2} = \exp(-rH)\pi_H(K\,|\,S_t).$$

Thus, the computation of the second-order derivatives of the European call price with respect to the strike yields the family of state price densities as functions of the residual maturity.

13.1.5 Asymmetric Smile and Stochastic Volatility

The presence of the smile effect reveals various misspecifications of the Black-Scholes model. Let us take a closer look at the assumption of constant volatility. To explore its effect, we modify the formula by introducing a heterogeneous volatility.

The pricing formula becomes

$$C(t;H,k) = S_t \int \psi(\sigma,k,H;r)f(\sigma)d\sigma, \tag{13.29}$$

where f is the volatility distribution under the risk-neutral probability. The implied volatility $\sigma_{BS}(t;H,k)$ is the solution of

$$\psi\,[\sigma_{BS}(t;H,k),k,H;r)] = \int \psi(\sigma,k,H,r)f(\sigma)d\sigma.$$

PROPOSITION 13.1: *Under the condition* $r = 0$, *we have*

$$\sigma_{BS}(t,H,1/k) = \sigma_{BS}(t,H,k).$$

PROOF: We have

$$\psi(\sigma,k,H,0) = \Phi\left[\frac{-\log k}{\sigma\sqrt{H}} + \frac{1}{2}\sigma\sqrt{H}\right] - k\Phi\left[\frac{-\log k}{\sigma\sqrt{H}} - \frac{1}{2}\sigma\sqrt{H}\right],$$

and:

$$\psi(\sigma,1/k,H,0) = \Phi\left[\frac{\log k}{\sigma\sqrt{H}} + \frac{1}{2}\sigma\sqrt{H}\right] - 1/k\Phi\left[\frac{\log k}{\sigma\sqrt{H}} - \frac{1}{2}\sigma\sqrt{H}\right]$$

$$= 1 - (1/k) - \Phi\left[\frac{-\log k}{\sigma\sqrt{H}} - \frac{1}{2}\sigma\sqrt{H}\right]$$

$$+ (1/k)\Phi\left[\frac{-\log k}{\sigma\sqrt{H}} + \frac{1}{2}\sigma\sqrt{H}\right]$$

$$= 1 - (1/k) + (1/k)\psi(\sigma,k,H,0).$$

Let us denote by $\sigma_{BS}(k)$ the implied volatility. We deduce

$$\psi\left[\sigma_{BS}(1/k),1/k,H,0\right] = \int \psi(\sigma,1/k,H,0)f(\sigma)d\sigma$$

$$= 1 - (1/k) + (1/k)\int \psi(\sigma,k,H,0)f(\sigma)d\sigma$$

$$= 1 - (1/k) + (1/k)\psi[\sigma_{BS}(k),k,H,0]$$

$$= \psi[\sigma_{BS}(k),1/k,H,0].$$

Therefore, $\sigma_{BS}(1/k) = \sigma_{BS}(k)$ by the uniqueness of implied volatility. QED

In particular, the implied volatility is an even function of the log moneyness-strike log k. This implies a zero derivative at moneyness $\frac{\partial\sigma_{SB}(1)}{\partial k} = 0$ and an asymmetric smile when the implied volatility is plotted against k (and not log k).

13.2   Parameterized Pricing Formulas

In Chapters 8 and 11, we derived the pricing formulas for derivative assets based on either the equilibrium or absence of arbitrage conditions. In both cases, the price of the derivative was expressed as the conditional expectation of the discounted future cash flows with respect to a modified probability measure. Equivalently, it can be written as the conditional expectation of the future cash flow with respect to the historical probability measure after introducing a stochastic discount factor. In the first section, we give a general review of this class of models for which the stochastic discount factor admits a parametric specification. In the second section, we discuss the compatibility between the discount factor models and statistical inference.

13.2.1   Stochastic Discount Factor Models

We consider European derivatives backed on an underlying asset with price (S_t). The European derivative with residual maturity H and cash flow $g(S_{t+H})$ at date $t+H$ has a price $C(t;H,g)$. We assume that the price satisfies a stochastic discount factor model

$$C(t;H,g) = E[M_{t,t+H}g(S_{t+H})|I_t], \qquad (13.30)$$

where I_t denotes the information set of the representative investor, and $M_{t,t+H}$ is the discount factor for the period $[t,t+H]$. The information set includes various variables y^*, such as prices, macroeconomic variables, and volatility factors. They are called *state variables*. The discount factor depends on the history of these variables until the maturity date $t+H$. We assume a parametric specification of the discount factor

$$M_{t,t+H} = M(H; y^*_{t+H}; \alpha). \tag{13.31}$$

Under this parametric specification, we get

$$C(t;H,g) = E[M(H; y^*_{t+H}, \alpha) g(S_{t+H}) | y^*_t], \tag{13.32}$$

where the conditional expectation is taken with respect to the historical probability.

To obtain the expression of the derivative price, we have to compute the conditional expectation after specifying the conditional distribution of y^*_{t+H}, S_{t+H} given y^*_t. For ease of exposition, we assume that the price of the underlying asset belongs to the information set and that the process followed by state variables is Markov. The model contains a parametric specification of the state variable transitions. Let β denote the associated parameter. It is a vector that may possibly share some common components with the α parameter. By computing the conditional expectation in (13.25), we get a parametric specification of the derivative price as a function of the state variables y^*_t:

$$C(t;H,g) = \gamma(H,g; y^*_t; \alpha, \beta), \quad \text{say.} \tag{13.33}$$

EXAMPLE 13.2, CONSUMPTION-BASED CAPM: During the period $(t,t+1)$, between two consecutive portfolio updatings, the discount factor is [see (8.13)]

$$M_{t,t+1} = \frac{q_t}{q_{t+1}} \delta \frac{\dfrac{dU}{dc}(C_{t+1})}{\dfrac{dU}{dc}(C_t)},$$

where q_t is a consumer price index, and C_t is the aggregate consumption of physical goods. The pricing formula

$$p_t = E_t[p_{t+1} M_{t,t+1}],$$

is easily extended to larger horizons. For instance, we have

$$p_t = E_t[p_{t+1} M_{t,t+1}]$$
$$= E_t[E_{t+1}(p_{t+2} M_{t+1,t+2}) M_{t,t+1}]$$
$$= E_t (p_{t+2} M_{t,t+1} M_{t+1,t+2}), \quad \text{by iterated expectation.}$$

We deduce that $M_{t,t+2} = M_{t,t+1}M_{t+1,t+2}$, and more generally, $M_{t,t+H} = \Pi_{h=0}^{H-1} M_{t+h,t+h+1}$.

Next we select a power utility function, and write

$$M_{t,t+H} = \Pi_{h=0}^{H-1}\left[\frac{q_{t+h}}{q_{t+h+1}}\ \delta\left(\frac{C_{t+h+1}}{C_{t+h}}\right)^{\gamma}\right]$$

$$= \delta^H\frac{q_t}{q_{t+H}}\left(\frac{C_{t+H}}{C_t}\right)^{\gamma}.$$

Under the Consumption-Based Capital Asset Pricing Model (CCAPM), the information set of the investor includes the consumer price index, the consumption variable, and the prices of tradable assets. As shown in Section 8.1, the CCAPM is a semiparametric model that cannot provide derivative prices unless it is completed by a transition equation for the state variable (under the historical probability).

EXAMPLE 13.3, RECURSIVE UTILITY: Let us consider the Epstein-Zin model introduced in Section 8.2. The discount factor is

$$M_{t,t+H} = \Pi_{h=0}^{H-1}\left[\left[\delta\left(\frac{C_{t+h+1}}{C_{t+h}}\right)^{-(1-\rho)}\right]^{\alpha/\rho}\left(\frac{W_{t+h}}{W_{t+h+1}}\right)^{1-\alpha/\rho}\left(\frac{q_{t+h+1}}{q_{t+h}}\right)^{-\alpha/\rho}\right]$$

$$= \delta^{\alpha H/\rho}\left(\frac{C_{t+H}}{C_t}\right)^{-(1-\rho)\alpha/\rho}\left(\frac{W_t}{W_{t+H}}\right)^{1-\alpha/\rho}\left(\frac{q_{t+H}}{q_t}\right)^{-\alpha/\rho}.$$

The discount factor now depends on the evolution of the market portfolio value. Consequently, a market index has to be introduced among the state variables. By analogy to Example 13.2, the model also has to be completed by the transition equation of the state variable to provide derivative prices.

EXAMPLE 13.4, DERIVATIVE PRICING IN CONTINUOUS TIME: Let us consider an underlying asset with a price that satisfies the diffusion equation $dS_t = \mu(S_t)dt + \sigma(S_t)dW_t$. We saw in Section 11.4.3 that the discount factor is given by

$$M_{t,t+H} = \exp(-rH)\ \exp\left[-\int_t^{t+H}\frac{\mu_\tau - rS_\tau}{\sigma_\tau}dW_\tau - \frac{1}{2}\int_t^{t+H}\left(\frac{\mu_\tau - rS_\tau}{\sigma_\tau}\right)^2 d\tau\right],$$

when the derivative prices are assumed to depend on S_t only, and the state variable is $y_t^* = S_t$.

In contrast to the examples corresponding to equilibrium conditions, the dynamics of the state variable S_t and of the discount factor are now jointly specified. The parameterization involves the drift and volatility functions.

EXAMPLE 13.5, STOCHASTIC VOLATILITY MODEL: For a stochastic volatility model of the type

$$\begin{cases} dS_t = \mu S_t dt + \sigma_t S_t dW_t^S, \\ df(\sigma_t) = a(\sigma_t)dt + b(\sigma_t)dW_t^\sigma, \end{cases}$$

we derived in Section 11.5.3 the discount factor

$$M_{t,t+H} = \exp(-rH) \, \exp\left\{-(\mu - r)\int_t^{t+H} \frac{dW_\tau^S}{\sigma_\tau}\right.$$

$$\left. -\frac{1}{2}(\mu - r)^2 \int_t^{t+H} \frac{d\tau}{\sigma_\tau^2}\right\} \exp\left\{-\int_t^{t+H} v_\tau \, dW_\tau^\sigma - \frac{1}{2}\int_t^{t+H} v_\tau^2 d\tau\right\}.$$

To obtain a fully parametric model, we still have to introduce parametric specifications of the drift and volatility functions that appear in the volatility equation, as well as a parametric specification of the volatility premium (v_τ). The parameters of the volatility premium are not necessarily related to the parameters that characterize the dynamics of the state variable $y_t^* = (S_t, \sigma_t)$ under the historical probability. This allows selection of the most appropriate pricing formula in an incomplete market framework, in which an infinite number of pricing formulas are a priori admissible.

In the above examples, the conditional expectation that appears in the definition of the derivative price cannot be computed analytically in general and needs to be approximated by simulations (see Section 13.5 on Monte Carlo methods).

Also note that the discount factor models can be simplified if the sampling dates of the asset price process and the discount factor horizons are multiples of a fixed time unit, conventionally set equal to 1. Indeed, we can always write

$$M_{t,t+H} = \prod_{h=0}^{H-1} M_{t+h,t+h+1},$$

so that the discount factors over a unitary period need only to be specified. Simple models arise when

$$M_{t,t+1} = \exp m(y_t^*; \alpha), \qquad \text{say.} \qquad (13.34)$$

Then, we get

$$C(t;H,g) = E\left[\prod_{h=0}^{H-1}\exp\ m(y_{t+h}^*;\alpha)g(S_{t+H})\,\big|y_t^*\right]$$

(13.35)

$$= \gamma(H,g;y_t^*;\alpha,\beta), t, H \in \mathbb{N},$$

whereas the transition function also represents the dynamics at discrete dates. It is denoted by

$$f(y_{t+1}^*|y_t^*;\beta).$$

(13.36)

The complete model is a nonlinear state-space model with transition equation (13.36) and measurement equation (13.35) (see Chapter 9).

REMARK 13.1: The discrete time formula of the discount factor can also be used to approximate a continuous time pricing formula. For instance, the discount factor of the stochastic volatility model can be approximated by

$$M_{t,t+H} = \exp(-rH)\ \exp\left\{-(\mu - r)\sum_{\tau=t}^{t+H-1}\frac{\varepsilon_\tau^s}{\sigma_\tau} - \frac{1}{2}(\mu - r)^2\sum_{\tau=t}^{t+H-1}\frac{1}{\sigma_\tau^2}\right\}$$

$$\exp\left\{-\sum_{\tau=t}^{t+H-1}v_\tau\varepsilon_\tau^\sigma - \frac{1}{2}\sum_{\tau=t}^{t+H-1}v_\tau^2\right\},$$

where (ε_τ^s) and $(\varepsilon_\tau^\sigma)$ are independent sequences of independent identically distributed (i.i.d.) Standard Gaussian variables.

13.2.2 Compatibility with Statistical Inference

Let us now reconsider the question of compatibility between the stochastic discount factor model and statistical inference (see Section 13.1.2). For expositional convenience, we assume that, at any discrete date $t = 1, \ldots, T$, the econometrician observes

- the price S_t of the underlying asset;
- the price C_t of one derivative, for instance, of an at-the-money European call with residual maturity H and cash flow $g_t(S_{t+H}) = (S_{t+H} - S_t)^+$;
- other variables X_t, which are not asset prices.

The whole vector of observations is denoted by $y_t = (S_t, C_t, X_t')'$. We can now distinguish different cases depending on the respective dimensions of the vector of observations y_t and the vector of state variables y_t^*.

1. If the number of state variables is strictly less than the number of observed variables, a deterministic relationship between the observed variables is spuriously created, which is at odds with available data. Therefore, the stochastic discount factor model is rejected with proba-

bility 1. This is the situation discussed in Section 13.1.2 for the Black-Scholes model.

2. If the number of state variables is equal to the number of observed variables, in general we can recover the state variables from the observed ones. Moreover, the likelihood function is directly derived from the likelihood function associated with the state variables.

3. If the number of state variables is strictly larger than the number of observed ones, we have to integrate out some unobservable state variables to derive the observable likelihood function. Then, we can apply a filter to recover the unknown states.

13.3   Statistical Inference

Let us now discuss the estimation of parameters from observations on both the underlying asset, a derivative, and possibly some other variables *X*. We already presented consistent estimation methods for selected subsets of parameters. For instance, in the CCAPM model, the preference parameters can be estimated from the Euler conditions by the Generalized Method of Moments (GMM) (see Section 8.3). In the continuous time asset price models, the parameters of the diffusion equation can be estimated from the observations on (S_t) only (see Chapter 12). In this section, we apply a maximum likelihood approach jointly using the information on the underlying asset and derivative. We expect this method to be more efficient.

13.3.1   The Hull-White Model

Let us consider the stochastic volatility model in Example 13.4 with an Ornstein-Uhlenbeck log-volatility process:

$$d \log \sigma_t = a_0(a_1 - \log \sigma_t)dt + bdW_t^\sigma,$$

and a constant volatility premium v. The observed prices are S_t and the price of an at-the-money call $C_t = \gamma(S_t, \sigma_t; \theta)$, where

$$\gamma(S_t, \sigma_t; \theta) = E[M_{t,t+H}(S_{t+H} - S_t)^+ | S_t, \sigma_t],$$

$$M_{t,t+H} = \exp(-rH)\exp\left\{-(\mu - r)\int_t^{t+H} \frac{dW_\tau^S}{\sigma_\tau} - \frac{1}{2}(\mu - r)^2 \int_t^{t+H} \frac{d\tau}{\sigma_\tau^2}\right\}$$

$$\exp\left\{-v(W_{t+H}^\sigma - W_t^\sigma) - \frac{Hv^2}{2}\right\},$$

and the parameter vector is $\theta = (\beta, \alpha)$, with $\beta = (\mu, a_0, a_1, b)$, and $\alpha = (r, v)$. The parameter vector β characterizes the state variables dynamics, whereas the parameter α is associated specifically with the pricing formula. We denote by $f(S_{t+1}, \sigma_{t+1} | S_t, \sigma_t; \beta)$ the transition function of the state variables and by $\tilde{f}(S_{t+1} | \underline{S_t}; \beta)$ the transition function of the price (S_t) only.

Marginal Maximum Likelihood
A consistent estimator of β is the ML estimator based on the observed price of the underlying asset only:

$$\tilde{\beta}_T = \underset{\beta}{\text{Arg max}} \sum_{t=1}^{T} \log \tilde{f}(S_{t+1} | \underline{S_t}; \beta),$$

whenever β is identifiable from this partial information. In this optimization, $\tilde{f}$ generally has to be computed numerically.

Global Maximum Likelihood
The pair (S_t, C_t) satisfies a one-to-one relationship with the pair (S_t, σ_t):

$$\begin{cases} S_t = S_t, \\ C_t = \gamma(S_t, \sigma_t; \theta) \end{cases} \Leftrightarrow \begin{cases} S_t = S_t, \\ \sigma_t = \gamma^*(S_t, C_t; \theta). \end{cases}$$

where γ^* is the inverse of γ with respect to the volatility. The transition equation for prices is derived from the Jacobian formula

$$f^* (S_{t+1}, C_{t+1} | S_t, C_t; \theta) = \left| \frac{\partial}{\partial c} \gamma^*(S_t, C_t; \theta) \right| f[S_{t+1}, \gamma^*(S_{t+1}, C_{t+1}; \theta) | S_t, \gamma^*(S_t, C_t; \theta); \beta].$$

The maximum likelihood estimator of $\theta = (\beta, \alpha)$ is:

$$\hat{\theta}_T = \underset{\theta}{\text{Arg max}} \sum_{t=1}^{T} \log f^*(S_{t+1}, C_{t+1} | S_t, C_t; \theta).$$

In this optimization, both γ^* and $f(S_{t+1}, \sigma_{t+1} | S_t, \sigma_t)$ involve multiple integrals and have to be computed numerically (see Section 13.5).

Two-Step Method
A consistent estimation method, which is less efficient although easier to implement, relies on the marginal ML estimator of β and estimates α as

$$\hat{\alpha}_T = \underset{\alpha}{\text{Arg max}} \sum_{t=1}^{T} \log f^*(S_{t+1}, C_{t+1} | S_t, C_t; \alpha, \tilde{\beta}_T).$$

The various estimation methods presented in this section are maximum likelihood methods. Thus, the corresponding estimators feature standard asymptotic properties of the ML estimator. However, they cannot be applied directly since the pricing function γ, its inverse, and its derivative have no explicit form. For this reason, the pricing formulas have to be approximated by simulations before the optimizations are performed. We define the *maximum simulated likelihood estimator*

$$\hat{\theta}_T^s = \text{Arg} \max_{\theta} \sum_{t=1}^{T} \log f^{*s}(S_{t+1}, C_{t+1} \mid S_t, C_t; \theta),$$

where:

$$f^{*s}(S_{t+1}, C_{t+1} \mid S_t, C_t; \theta) = \left| \frac{\partial}{\partial c} \gamma^{*s}(S_t, C_t; \theta) \right| f(S_{t+1}, \gamma^{*s}(S_{t+1}, C_{t+1}; \theta) \mid S_t, \gamma^{*s}(S_t, C_t; \theta); \beta),$$

and γ^{*s} is the inverse of a Monte Carlo approximation of γ.

13.3.2 General Case

In the general case, the number of factors is strictly greater than the number of observed prices. Let us consider a sample of regularly spaced observations on the prices of K derivatives. The K-dimensional vector of derivative prices can be written as

$$C_t = \gamma(y_t^*; \theta), \qquad (13.37)$$

where the factor process satisfies the transition equation

$$f(y_{t+1}^* \mid y_t^*; \theta). \qquad (13.38)$$

The likelihood function of this nonlinear factor model has no analytical expression for two reasons: First we have to integrate out the unobservable factors, which requires computing integrals of dimension $(K - L)T$, where L is the number of factors. Second, the γ function is a conditional expectation without an analytical expression.

The estimation methods for the parameter θ all involve simulations (see Sections 9.3, 12.4, and 12.5). Let us, for instance, consider the method of simulated moments, with a number of moments set equal to the parameter dimension p. We denote by $b(C_t, C_{t-1})$ the p-dimensional price transformation, which is used for moment calibration.

Let us introduce the simulated paths of the factor process corresponding to the transition function $f(y_{t+1}^* \mid y_t^*; \theta)$ and the value θ of the parameter. They are denoted by $y_t^{*s}(\theta)$, $t = 1, \ldots, T$, $s = 1, \ldots, S$. Let us also denote by $\hat{\gamma}^{S^*}$ an approximation of γ obtained by a Monte Carlo method based on S^* replications (see Section 13.5).

Then, the MSM estimator of θ is the solution of the set of calibrating equations:

$$\frac{1}{T} \sum_{t=1}^{T} b(C_t, C_{t-1}) = \frac{1}{ST} \sum_{s=1}^{S} \sum_{t=1}^{T} b[\hat{\gamma}^{S^*}(y_t^{*s}(\theta), \theta), \hat{\gamma}^{S^*}(y_{t-1}^{*s}(\theta), \theta)]. \qquad (13.39)$$

The method involves two sets of simulations: the first one to approximate γ, and the second one to generate the factors. The method of simulated moments (MSM) estimator is consistent when both T and S^* tend to infinity (not necessarily S).

13.4 Stochastic Risk-Neutral Probability

We have discussed various procedures that allow approximation of the latent risk-neutral probability. Some heuristic approaches described in Section 13.1.4 are designed to provide an outcome at a fixed date. Therefore, the computations have to be performed daily. The reason is that heuristic methods do not account for latent factors that describe the dynamics of the state price densities. Thus, they are appropriate for a cross-sectional analysis, but not for prediction making. The dynamic parametric specifications of the risk-neutral density were introduced in Section 3.2. They contain a limited number of latent factors that allow for statistical inference on a limited number of derivative prices. However, the parametric models cannot be used when the number of derivatives increases in time since the order condition (see Section 13.2.2) is no longer satisfied.

One can argue that an appropriate specification needs to include the state prices (i.e., Arrow-Debreu prices) as the unobserved latent variables. Thus, the number of latent error terms has to be equal to the number of admissible states, that is, infinite. Equivalently, the risk-neutral probability could be assumed stochastic to accommodate the effect of the large amount of information unavailable to an econometrician. Such an approach was first introduced by Clement, Gourieroux, and Monfort (2000). We describe below the method of cross-sectional analysis of the state price density at a given residual maturity H; the original paper has an extension to a dynamic framework.

13.4.1 Stochastic Model for the State Price Density

We assume a state price density (for the residual maturity H). The price of a European derivative with cash flow $g(S_{t+H})$ is

$$C(t,H,g) = \int g(s)dQ_t(s), \qquad (13.40)$$

where $dQ_t(s) = Q_t(s+ds) - Q_t(s)$ is the price of the digital option providing \$1 at $t+H$ if S_{t+H} belongs to $[s, s+ds]$. This price includes the discounting and risk correction (i.e., the risk-neutral densities).

Due to insufficient information, the econometrician does not know the state price density exactly. The missing information can be accommodated by assuming a random state price measure. For a generic element of the probability space w, we get

$$C(t,H,g,w) = \int g(s)dQ_t(s,w). \tag{13.41}$$

Then, the derivative prices also depend on the generic element w and therefore are stochastic. This leads us to a specification with latent variables, in which we define (1) the distribution of the latent prices, that is, the distribution of the stochastic state price density $[dQ_t(s), s$ varying] and (2) the links between the observed derivative prices and the latent prices defined by (13.41).

Due to the linearity of measurement equation (13.41), the first- and second-order moments of the derivative prices are easy to derive from the first- and second-order moments of the state price density.

Let us define

$$E_w dQ_t(s,w) = dm_t(s), \tag{13.42}$$

$$Cov_w[dQ_t(s,w), dQ_t(s',w)] = \tilde{C}_t(ds,ds'), \tag{13.43}$$

$$V_w[dQ_t(s,w)] = C_t(ds), \tag{13.44}$$

where the expectation and variance are evaluated with respect to the distribution of the generic element of the probability space. We deduce

$$E_w C(t,H,g;w) = E_w \left[\int g(s)dQ_t(s,w) \right]$$

$$= \int E_w \left[g(s)dQ_t(s,w) \right] \tag{13.45}$$

$$= \int g(s)dm_t(s).$$

Similarly, we get

$$Cov_w[C(t,H,g,w), C(t,H,\tilde{g},w)]$$

$$= \int\int g(s)\tilde{g}(s')\tilde{C}_t(ds,ds') + \int g(s)\tilde{g}(s)C_t(ds). \tag{13.46}$$

13.4.2 Gamma Model

At this point, we can introduce a tractable specification of the stochastic valuation measure. Clement et al. (2000) proposed a gamma specification for at least the three following reasons:

1. It leads to a clear-cut factorization of the distribution into components corresponding to the zero-coupon price and risk-neutral probability.
2. It is close to a deterministic valuation formula, such as that of Black and Scholes.
3. The estimation and computation steps are easily performed by simulation-based inference methods.

DEFINITION 13.1: *The random measure Q_t is a gamma measure if and only if:*

(i) *it has independent increments, that is, the variables $Q_t([s_1,s_2]), \ldots,$ $(Q_t[s_{n-1},s_n])$ are independent for any n, $s_1 < s_2 \ldots < s_n$;*

(ii) *the variable Q_t $([s_1,s_2])$ follows a gamma distribution with parameters $v_t[s_1, s_2]$, and λ_t, where v_t is a positive deterministic measure on R^+, and λ_t is a positive real number.*

Therefore, the distribution of the random measure is characterized by a real λ_t and a deterministic measure v_t. Let us recall that the gamma distribution with parameters v, and λ has the density $f(y) = \frac{1}{\Gamma(v)} \exp(-\lambda y)\lambda^v y^{v-1} 1_{y>0}$, mean v/λ, and variance v/λ^2. We deduce the first- and second-order moments of the random measure under the gamma specification:

$$dm_t(s) = \frac{1}{\lambda_t} dv_t(s), \qquad C_t(ds) = \frac{1}{\lambda_t^2} dv_t(s), \qquad \tilde{C}_t(ds,ds') = 0, \qquad (13.47)$$

where the last equality results from the property of independent increments. Therefore, the second-order properties of derivative prices are

$$E_w C(t,H,g;w) = \frac{1}{\lambda_t} \int g(s)dv_t(s), \qquad (13.48)$$

$$V_w C(t,H,g;w) = \frac{1}{\lambda_t^2} \int g^2(s)dv_t(s), \qquad (13.49)$$

$$Cov_w[C(t,H,g;w),C(t,H,\tilde{g};w)] = \frac{1}{\lambda_t^2} \int g(s)\tilde{g}(s)dv_t(s). \qquad (13.50)$$

Equations (13.48)–(13.50) suggest the interpretations of the parameters v_t (.) and λ_t. For instance, $dv_t(s)/\lambda_t$ is the average digital option price, whereas λ_t measures the ex-ante uncertainty about this price. In the limiting case $\lambda_t \to +\infty$, we get a deterministic formula for derivative pricing that corresponds to the standard complete market framework.

EXAMPLE 13.6: As an illustration, we can extend the standard Black-Scholes model by allowing for stochastic state prices. We assume

$$v_t(ds) = \lambda_t \exp(-rH)\pi_t^{BS}(ds),$$

where π_t^{BS} is the Black-Scholes risk-neutral probability of S_{t+H} given S_t. Thus, we get

$$E_w C(t;H,g,w) = \exp(-rH) \int g(s)\pi_t^{BS}(ds),$$

that is, the Black-Scholes formula written as an expectation. The accuracy of the derivative prices is measured by

$$Cov_w[C(t,H,g,w),C(t,H,\tilde{g},w)] = \frac{1}{\lambda_t} \exp(-rH) \int g(s)\tilde{g}(s)\pi_t^{BS}(ds).$$

It depends on the Black-Scholes price of the derivative, whose cash flow is equal to the product $g(S_{t+H})\ \tilde{g}(S_{t+H})$. Thus introducing of a stochastic state price allows to evaluate the accuracy of the Black-Scholes formula by estimating the parameter λ_t.

13.5 Monte Carlo Methods

In general, derivative prices do not admit analytical expressions and have to be computed numerically. In this section, we consider approximations obtained by simulations. They are used not only to predict the derivative prices, but also to build the likelihood function when option prices are observed (see Section 13.3). We first recall various classical techniques to compute an integral by Monte Carlo experiments. Then, we discuss its implementation to option pricing. In particular, we explain how to use jointly the historical and risk-neutral densities in numerical computations.

13.5.1 The Approach

Let us consider an integral

$$I = \int a(z)dz, \tag{13.51}$$

which can be multidimensional. Although the function a is known, we cannot compute analytically the integral and find the value of I.

A Monte Carlo method consists in introducing f, a known pdf, and rewriting I as follows:

$$I = \int \frac{a(z)}{f(z)} f(z)dz = E_f\left[\frac{a(Z)}{f(Z)}\right]. \tag{13.52}$$

Thus, the integral I is an expectation, which can be approximated by an empirical average.

DEFINITION 13.2: *A Monte-Carlo estimator of I is:*

$$\hat{I}_S = \frac{1}{S} \sum_{s=1}^{S} \frac{a(z_s)}{f(z_s)},$$

where z_s, $s = 1, \ldots, S$, are independent drawings in the distribution f.

This estimator is unbiased of I, with a variance equal to

$$V(\hat{I}_S) = \frac{1}{S} V_f\left[\frac{a(Z)}{f(Z)}\right]. \tag{13.53}$$

Its variance depends on the selected distribution f, called the *importance function*. Intuitively, optimal accuracy is achieved when a/f is constant, that is, when f is proportional to a. However, the coefficient of proportionality $1/\int a(z)dz = 1/I$ is unknown. Nevertheless, accurate approximations can still be obtained when a and f have similar patterns.

There exist various possibilities to improve the general Monte Carlo approach:

First, let us select a symmetric distribution f. We can double the number of simulated realizations by considering z_s, as well as the same vector with the opposite sign $-z_s$. The estimator becomes

$$\hat{I}_S^a = \frac{1}{2S} \sum_{s=1}^{S} \left[\frac{a(z_s)}{f(z_s)} + \frac{a(-z_s)}{f(-z_s)} \right]. \tag{13.54}$$

This is a method involving antithetic variables. The estimator is unbiased, with a variance given by

$$V(\hat{I}_S^a) = \frac{1}{4S} V_f \left[\frac{a(Z)}{f(Z)} + \frac{a(-Z)}{f(-Z)} \right]. \tag{13.55}$$

The use of antithetic variables is intended to reduce the variance of the estimator and to enhance its efficiency. Such an improvement is achieved when the function a/f is almost symmetric.

Second, sometimes we know an approximation a_0 of a that is easy to integrate. Then, we can write

$$I = \int a(z)dz$$
$$= \int a_0(z)dz + \int [a(z) - a_0(z)]dz$$
$$= I_0 + \int [a(z) - a_0(z)]dz,$$

and estimate the value of I by

$$\hat{I}_S^0 = I_0 + \frac{1}{S} \sum_{s=1}^{S} \frac{a(z_s) - a_0(z_s)}{f(z_s)}. \tag{13.56}$$

The estimator is unbiased with variance

$$V(\hat{I}_S^0) = \frac{1}{S} V_f \left[\frac{a(Z) - a_0(Z)}{f(Z)} \right]. \tag{13.57}$$

13.5.2 Application to Option Pricing

Let us consider a risky asset with the price (y_t) that satisfies the diffusion equation

$$dy_t = \mu(y_t)dt + \sigma(y_t)dW_t. \qquad (13.58)$$

We changed the notation for the asset price from S_t to y_t to avoid confusion with the number S of replications. The corresponding risk-neutral model is

$$dy_t = ry_t dt + \sigma(y_t)dW_t. \qquad (13.59)$$

For computational ease the continuous time processes in (13.58) and (13.59) are replaced by their Euler discretized versions at a short time interval δ. For $\delta = 1$, these discretized models are

$$y_t = y_{t-1} + \mu(y_{t-1}) + \sigma(y_{t-1})\varepsilon_t, \qquad (13.60)$$

$$y_t = y_{t-1} + ry_{t-1} + \sigma(y_{t-1})\varepsilon_t. \qquad (13.61)$$

They correspond to the transitions

$$p_{t|t-1} = \frac{1}{\sigma(y_{t-1})} \varphi\left[\frac{y_t - y_{t-1} - \mu(y_{t-1})}{\sigma(y_{t-1})}\right], \qquad (13.62)$$

$$\pi_{t-1} = \frac{1}{\sigma(y_{t-1})} \varphi\left[\frac{y_t - y_{t-1} - ry_{t-1}}{\sigma(y_{t-1})}\right], \qquad (13.63)$$

under the historical and risk-neutral probabilities, respectively.

Let us now consider the pricing at t of a European option with residual maturity H and cash flow $g(y_{t+H})$. Its price is given by

$$C(t;H,g) = \exp(-rH)E_\pi[g(y_{t+H})|y_t]. \qquad (13.64)$$

The conditional expectation is an integral:

$$I = E_\pi[g(y_{t+H})|y_t]$$

$$\approx \int g(y_{t+H}) \prod_{h=1}^{H-1} \pi_{t+h|t+h-1}(y_{t+h}|y_{t+h-1}) \prod_{h=1}^{H-1} dy_{t+h}.$$

This integral admits different equivalent expressions:

$$I \approx \int g(y_{t+h}) \prod_{h=1}^{H-1} \frac{\pi_{t+h+h|t+h-1}(y_{t+h}|y_{t+h-1})}{p_{t+h|t+h-1}(y_{t+h}|y_{t+h-1})} \prod_{h=1}^{H-1} p_{t+h|t+h-1}(y_{t+h}|y_{t+h-1}) \prod_{h=1}^{H-1} dy_{t+h}$$

$$\qquad (13.65)$$

$$= \int g(y_{t+h}) \prod_{h=1}^{H-1} m_{t+h|t+h-1}(y_{t+h}|y_{t+h-1}) \prod_{h=1}^{H-1} p_{t+h|t+h-1}(y_{t+h}|y_{t+h-1}) \prod_{h=1}^{H-1} dy_{t+1}$$

which involve the stochastic discount factor.

I can also be defined in terms of future shocks under either the risk-neutral probability or the historical one. Let us denote $z = (\varepsilon_{t+1}, \ldots, \varepsilon_{t+H})'$ standard Gaussian shocks. We get

$$I = \int g^R(y_t, z) \prod_{h=1}^{H-1} \varphi(\varepsilon_{t+h}) \prod_{h=1}^{H-1} d\varepsilon_{t+h}, \tag{13.66}$$

where $g^R(y_t, z) = g(y_{t+H})$, and shocks are introduced recursively by using the risk-neutral recursive formula (13.61). We also have

$$I = \int g^{Hist}(y_t, z) \prod_{h=1}^{H-1} m^{Hist}_{t+h|t+h-1}(y_t, z) \prod_{h=1}^{H-1} \varphi(\varepsilon_{t+h}) \prod_{h=1}^{H-1} d\varepsilon_{t+h}, \tag{13.67}$$

where g^{Hist} and m^{Hist} are deduced from g and m by recursive substitution of shocks under the historical formula (13.60).

Let us now define:

$z^s = (\varepsilon^s_{t+h})$, independent drawings of a Gaussian white noise,

(y^s_{t+h}), independent drawings compatible with the risk-neutral dynamics in (13.61), conditional on y_t,

$(y^{Hist,s}_{t+h})$, independent drawings compatible with the historical dynamics in (13.60), conditional on y_t.

Monte Carlo estimators of the option price are:

$$\hat{I}_1 = \frac{1}{S} \sum_{s=1}^{S} g\!\left(y^{R,s}_{t+H}\right),$$

$$\hat{I}_2 = \frac{1}{S} \sum_{s=1}^{S} \left\{ g\!\left(y^{Hist,s}_{t+H}\right) \prod_{h=1}^{h-1} m_{t+h|t+h-1}\!\left(y^{Hist,s}_{t+h} \,\middle|\, y^{Hist,s}_{t+h-1}\right) \right\},$$

$$\hat{I}_3 = \frac{1}{S} \sum_{s=1}^{S} g^R(y_t, z^s),$$

$$\hat{I}_4 = \frac{1}{S} \sum_{s=1}^{S} \left[g^{Hist}\!\left(y_t, z^s\right) \prod_{h=1}^{H-1} m^{Hist}_{t+h|t+H-1}(y_t, z^s) \right].$$

It is easy to check that the estimators $\hat{I}_1$ and $\hat{I}_3$, $\hat{I}_2$ and $\hat{I}_4$ are similar.

These estimators can be improved in two regards. First, we can introduce antithetic variables and consider, for instance,

$$\hat{I}_3^a = \frac{1}{2S} \sum_{s=1}^{S} \left[g^R(y_t, z^s) + g^R(y_t, -z^s) \right],$$

$$\hat{I}_4^a = \frac{1}{2S} \sum_{s=1}^{S} \left[g^{Hist}(y_t, z^s) \prod_{h=1}^{H-1} m^{Hist}_{t+h|t+h-1}(y_t, z^s) \right.$$

$$\left. + g^{Hist}(y_t, -z^s) \prod_{h=1}^{H-1} m^{Hist}_{t+h|t+h-1}(y_t, -z^s) \right].$$

Second, we can also compute a part of the integral. For instance, let us approximate the initial price dynamics by the Black-Scholes one:

$$dS_t = \mu_0 S_t dt + \sigma_0 S_t dW_t.$$

If $g(y_{t+H}) = (y_{t+H} - K)^+$ corresponds to a European call, we get

$$I = E_\pi \left[(y_{t+H} - K)^+ | y_t \right]$$

$$= E_{\pi_0} \left[(y_{t+H} - K)^+ | y_t \right] + E_\pi [(y_{t+H} - K)^+ | y_t] - E_{\pi_0} [(y_{t+H} - K)^+ | y_t],$$

where E_{π_0} denotes the expectation under the risk-neutral Black-Scholes probability. As a consequence,

$$I = I_0 + \int (y_{t+H} - K)^+ \left[\prod_{h=1}^{H-1} \pi_{t+h|t+h-1}(y_{t+h} | y_{t+h-1}) \right.$$

$$\left. - \prod_{h=1}^{H-1} \pi^0_{t+h|t+h-1}(y_{t+h} | y_{t+h-1}) \right] \prod_{h=1}^{H-1} dy_{t+h}$$

$$= I_0 + E_\pi \left[(y_{t+H} - K)^+ \left(1 - \prod_{h=1}^{H-1} \frac{\pi^0_{t+h|t+h-1}(y_{t+h} | y_{t+h-1})}{\pi_{t+h|t+h-1}(y_{t+h} | y_{t+h-1})} \right) | y_t \right],$$

where I_0 is the Black-Scholes price. Therefore, the estimated option price is

$$\hat{I} = I_0 + \frac{1}{S} \sum_{s=1}^{S} \left[(y_{t+H}^{R,s} - K)^+ \left\{ 1 - \prod_{h=1}^{H-1} \frac{\pi^0_{t+h|t+h-1}(y_{t+h}^{R,s} | y_{t+h-1}^{R,s})}{\pi_{t+h|t+h-1}(y_{t+h}^{R,s} | y_{t+h-1}^{R,s})} \right\} \right].$$

The estimated derivative price is the Black-Scholes price, with a correction for the change of probability.

13.6 Summary

The Black-Scholes model of option pricing contradicts empirical evidence on time-varying volatilities. A way of detecting model misspecification is to solve the option pricing formula with respect to volatility by substituting for option price data collected on the market. The resulting implied volatilities differ numerically depending on the strike and maturity of the option value used in the calculation. Nevertheless, the time series of such implied volatilities and the implied volatility surfaces provide insightful information on the possible misspecifications of the Black-Scholes model. Typically, the presence of a smile effect can be due to the omitted stochastic volatility. A difficulty in the analysis of option prices stems from the definition of risk-neutral probability, under which asset prices are martingales. On an incomplete market, the risk-neutral probability is not uniquely defined. Parametric specifications of the underlying probability can be introduced through the stochastic discount factors. The corresponding additional parameters can be estimated by appropriate use of prices of both the underlying assets and the derivatives. These estimation techniques generally involve multiple integrals, which require Monte Carlo integration methods.

14

Dynamic Models for
High-Frequency Data

THE EXPANDING FINANCIAL MARKETS generate extremely large amounts of high-frequency data, which has become accessible for academic and commercial purposes. The availability of detailed information on trades and quotes is essentially due to the implementation of electronic trading systems, such as CAC (Cotation Assistée en Continu) (Paris Bourse, Toronto Stock Exchange [TSE], Chicago), SETS (London Stock Exchange), Xetra (Deutsche Börse), and TSA (Amsterdam Stock Exchange). The electronic trading systems fulfill vital tasks on stock markets. Especially,

1. They maintain an electronic order book (i.e., a record of submitted orders) ranked according to the goodness of price and time of entry. The systems also enter new incoming buy and sell orders into the order book, update the ranking, and automatically match the buy and sell orders.
2. They register the trades and therefore document the order execution. This implies that the recorded trade characteristics, such as the volume, price, and time, become legally binding terms of trade and are assumed to be free of measurement errors.
3. They serve to release information either in real time or in historical data files.

In the first section, we present a typology of financial markets and describe the trading mechanisms, types of orders, and order-matching procedures. Next, we discuss the tick-by-tick data arising from market transactions. In Section 14.2, we give some insights from the microstructure theory on heterogeneous behaviors of market participants and their effects on the trading process. In Section 14.3, we examine the dynamics

351

of trading prices and bid-ask quotes. We first present some stylized facts revealed by applications of standard ARMA-GARCH (autoregressive moving average–generalized autoregressive conditionally heteroscedastic) models. Next, we introduce the deformed time models that accommodate the dynamics of processes evolving in transaction time. The analysis is further extended to the modeling of bid and ask prices. Dynamic models for intertrade durations, which by construction resemble the ARCH and stochastic volatility models, are introduced in Section 14.4. Our interest in duration analysis is motivated by a close relationship between the intertrade durations and asset liquidity. Finally, Section 14.5 presents joint models of prices, volumes, and trading times.

14.1 The Markets

14.1.1 Typology of Markets

Quote-Driven versus Order-Driven Market
A market that is quote (or price) driven is characterized by the presence of *market makers*, who act as intermediaries between the buyers and the sellers. The responsibility of market makers (also called *dealers*) is to quote at any date t the buy and sell prices of stocks, called the *bid* and *ask* prices, denoted by b_t and a_t, respectively. An investor who wishes to buy (resp. to sell) a volume v of shares can immediately get stock from the dealer at the ask price a_t (resp. the bid price b_t). In practice, there exist several dealers j designated to trade the same asset on a given market, quoting possibly different ask and bid prices a_t^j, and b_t^j, $j = 1, \ldots, J$. Due to the variety of prices, an investor may compare the prices and bargain, especially in transactions involving large volumes.

The difference between ask and bid is called the *spread*. It represents a financial reward to the market maker for intermediation. The essential role of the market maker is to provide liquidity, that is, stand by to buy or sell an asset at any time, regardless of the quantity of shares. The task of the market maker therefore requires maintaining an inventory of stocks, which entails significant risk.

To ensure liquidity and fair prices, the dealers have to manage the asset inventories at their best. In the case of inventory misadjustments, they are obliged to sell or buy an asset from other dealers on the market. Such interdealer trades account for a large proportion of market transactions (approximately two-thirds on the Stock Exchange Automated Quotation [SEAQ] [London]).

The order-driven markets, in contrast, are managed without the intermediation of dealers. The orders submitted by investors are entered directly into an order book monitored by a computer system and often publicly displayed. Trades occur whenever orders are matched through an electronic medium according to the price and timing priority criteria. Thus, trades result directly from transactions concluded automatically between investors.

We can graphically represent the individuals involved in the trading procedures:

Quote-driven market

Buyer→Buying →Buying → Dealers ←Selling←Selling←Seller
       Broker   Firm's   Firm's   Broker
                trader   trader

Order-driven market

Buyer→Buying →Buying   ⇔   Selling←Selling←Seller
       Broker   Firm's   Electronic   Firm's   Broker
                trader   medium   trader

Call Auction versus Continuous Matching
The trading mechanisms allow for two different procedures of order matching; these are called *continuous trading* and *call auction*. Continuous matching refers to ongoing trading throughout the day, while a call auction takes place at predetermined times of day. These predetermined times can be fixed at 16:00, for example, or may depend on past market activity. An average intertrade duration is typically much larger on a call auction market than on a continuous trading market. Moreover, the trading price is often identical for all trades occurring at the same time under the call auction procedure, whereas it may differ across several orders filled simultaneously under continuous matching.

Typology
A stock exchange can use both matching procedures, depending on the time of day or asset liquidity. Most stock markets organize daily a call auction for all assets at the market opening. During this time (approximately one-half hour prior to the official opening time), incoming orders are collected while no trading occurs. At the opening time, 09:00, say, a market-clearing supply-demand equilibrium price is computed so that all queued orders with prices compatible with the equilibrium price are completely filled at this price. All remaining orders are entered into the order book. Call auctions for all stocks may also be held at market closures and

Table 14.1 *Typology*

Stock Exchange	Quote vs. Order Driven	Matching
Paris Bourse Toronto Stock Exchange	Order driven	Call auction at the opening and closing, continuous matching during the day
NYSE	Order driven with dealers	Call auction for opening, continuous auction during the day
TAIEX (Taiwan)	Order driven	Call auction with about 90 seconds between calls (continuous call)
SEAQ (London)	Quote driven	
NASDAQ	Quote driven	

at some predetermined times of day to exchange illiquid assets, called the *infrequently traded stocks*. In this chapter, we restrict our attention to trading mechanisms of frequently traded stocks.

Table 14.1 shows the procedures implemented on selected stock exchange markets.

14.1.2   Matching Procedure on Order-Driven Market

In this section, we consider an order-driven market with continuous matching. During the continuous trading session, all incoming orders are entered into the order book, illustrated in Table 14.2. The first three columns show the buy side of the market, while the next three columns represent the sell side. The orders are ranked with respect to the price per share. On the buy side, the first column gives the number of submitted orders, the middle one contains the price per share, and the third one shows all volume available at the announced price. The volume is aggregated across all investors on the Paris Bourse, while on the TSE,

Table 14.2 *Initial Situation, Alcatel, May 14, 1996, 10:04:37*

Buy Orders			Sell Orders			Last Trades		
1	490.60	964	491.00	950	2	10	490.60	10:04:37
3	490.00	200	491.20	1,000	1	247	491.00	10:03:59
2	489.00	650	491.40	975	1	147	491.00	10:03:59
1	488.50	500	491.50	600	1	453	491.00	10:03:53
5	488.00	638	491.80	230	1	1,000	491.00	10:03:42

each order is displayed in a separate row along with a trader identification code. Various types of orders and trade characteristics are examined below.

Initial Situation

The initial situation of the order book and recent trades of the Alcatel stock are displayed on the screen (see Table 14.2). Looking at the book, we can see that 490.60 is the best bid, which is the highest price anyone is willing to pay to own this stock. 491.00 is the best ask, which is the lowest price anyone would accept to sell the stock. There are 964 shares (resp. 950 shares), which are available at the best bid (resp. best ask). They correspond to a single order (resp. two orders).

The last three columns provide the records of recent trades, starting from the last one. The last transaction occurred at 10:04:37, when 10 shares were exchanged at a price of 490.60 per share. Two simultanous trades took place shortly before.

Incoming Buy Limit Order

A *limit order* specifies the maximum admissible price per share (for a buy order) or the minimum admissible price per share (for a sell order), along with the desired volume of stock. Consider a buy limit order entered at 10:05:01 for 2,000 shares at 491.20 per share. It can possibly match all sell orders in the first two lines of the order book (Table 14.2). Accordingly, the two orders in the first line on the sell side of the market are completely filled at 491.00 due to two simultanous trades of 500 and 450 shares, respectively.

We see that the buy order has begun trading at the best bid. It will now work down the sell side of the market, order by order, until it is filled or its limit price is reached.

In order to buy the remaining 1,050 shares, the buyer has to trade with the next-best offer after trading 950 shares at 491.00. Looking at the book in Table 14.2, the next-best sell order is displayed in the second line as an order to sell 1,000 shares. Thus, the incoming order will buy the next 1,000 shares at 491.20, and the third transaction occurs.

The incoming order has not been filled yet; there are still 50 shares outstanding. However, its limit price of 491.20 has been reached. The unfilled balance (i.e., $2,000 - 450 - 500 - 1,000 = 50$) cannot be matched and will book as the new best bid on the buy side. The aftermarket at 10:05:01 is shown in Table 14.3.

Three trades of the Alcatel shares at different prices per share have occurred. Due to the record accuracy of 1 second, market participants will perceive them as simultaneously executed (despite that the matching

Table 14.3 *Final Situation at 10:05:01, Buy Limit Order*

Buy Orders			Sell Orders			Last Trades		
1	491.20	50	491.40	975	1	1,000	491.20	10:05:01
1	490.60	964	491.50	600	1	450	491.00	10:05:01
1	490.00	200	491.80	230	1	500	491.00	10:05:01
3	489.00	650	492.00	3,200	3	10	490.60	10:04:37
2	488.50	500	492.10	700	1	247	491.00	10:03:59

time is less than 1/10 second). The prices received by the investors on the sell side of the market are 491.20 and 491.00. The price per share paid by the investor, who placed the incoming buy limit order, is:

$$\frac{950}{1,950}\, 491.00 + \frac{1,000}{1,950}\, 491.20 \approx 491.104$$

REMARK 14.1: The treatment of limit orders on a quote-driven market is different. The order will be kept by the broker until the market quote established by the dealer matches the investor's order price.

REMARK 14.2: In the first matching, the price of 491.00 gives privilege to the latest arrival (i.e., the buy order in our example, and not the sell order queued in the book). In this way, the order-matching system enhances asset liquidity.

Incoming Buy Market Order
A market order is assigned the best price from the opposite side of the market the moment it enters the computer system. If the incoming order is a market order to buy 2,000 shares, it is assigned the best offering price (i.e., 491.00 in our example). The order will buy as much stock as is available at that price and, if partially filled, will be booked on the buy side as the new best bid of 491.00.

We observe two simultanous trades at the same price per share. The aftermarket is shown in Table 14.4.

Table 14.4 *Final Situation at 10:05:01, Buy Market Order*

Buy Orders			Sell Orders			Last Trades		
1	491.00	1,050	491.20	1,000	1	450	491.00	10:05:01
1	490.60	964	491.40	975	1	500	491.00	10:05:01
3	490.00	200	491.50	600	1	10	490.60	10:04:37
2	489.00	650	491.80	230	1	247	491.00	10:03:59
1	488.50	500	491.90	300	1	147	491.00	10:03:59

Table 14.5 *Final Situation at 10:05:01, Better Price Limit Buy Order*

Buy Orders			Sell Orders			Last Trades		
1	490.60	964	491.40	925	1	50	491.40	10:05:01
1	490.00	200	491.50	600	1	1,000	491.20	10:05:01
3	489.00	650	491.80	230	1	450	491.00	10:05:01
2	488.50	500	492.00	3,200	3	500	491.00	10:05:01
5	488.00	638	492.10	700	1	10	490.60	10:04:37

Incoming Better Price Limit Order

There are times when an investor may wish to purchase or sell shares immediately, regardless of the price of the stock. For example, to prevent further loss on a stock that is falling sharply (with no end in sight), an investor may wish to sell his shares at whatever price is currently available. This type of order, when price is not specified, is called a *better price limit order*.

Let us now assume that the trader insists on buying 2,000 shares immediately. If entered as a market order, 950 shares will trade at 491.00, and the remaining 1,050 will book on the buy side. Suppose that the trader insists on a complete fill of 2,000 shares. To buy the remaining 1,050 shares, the buyer has to trade with the two next-best orders. Consequently, the buyer will buy 1,000 shares at 491.20 and an additional 50 shares at 491.40. To do so, the trader needs to enter a better price limit order. In Table 14.5, we get the aftermarket for four transactions concluded at three different trading prices.

Bids and Asks

The examples above give insights on the relationship between trading prices and bid-ask prices, as well as on the dynamics of bids and asks. Our reasoning focused on an incoming buy order since a sell order has analogous outcomes on the opposite side of the market.

The trading price coincides with the best ask when an incoming order is a market order. It is generally greater than the best ask for the other types of orders. Thus, the average trading price often falls outside the best bid–best ask interval that existed before the matching.

The transactions initiated by a buy order imply nondecreasing bid and ask prices. However, the spread can vary in any direction, and the bid-ask intervals before and after the trade can be disjointed.

14.1.3 Available Data

A standard database includes an extremely large amount of information concerning the transactions and the submitted orders.

Transaction Data

In Table 14.6, we provide an example of a trade record (without any intermediate quotes) for the Bank of Montreal stock traded on the TSE. The letter T in the first position pertains to "trade." It is followed by the date in format YYMMDD (Y = year, M = month, D = day) and the symbol of the stock "BMO." The next entry is the time stamp in the format HHMMSS (H = hour, M = minute, S = second), price in format $$$$CCC, and volume (nine digits). The following digits represent the input time HHMMSS, and the next two fields of three digits give the number of buyers and sellers. These entries are followed by a qualitative variable that describes the type of trader (whether registered) and a sequence of 0–1 indicators (not reported in Table 14.6) that specifies the terms of trade, such as delay, cancellation, special terms, correction, and so forth. The last entry in each line is a buyer or seller identification.

There are essentially three time series arising from these records: the trading prices, volumes, and trading times that yield intertrade durations.

Since the price per share may not be uniquely defined at a given transaction time in case of simultaneous trades, it is common to transform the price records prior to statistical analysis. Two solutions have been proposed in the literature.

First, we can aggregate the outcomes of multiple transactions concluded at the same date by computing the total traded volume and average price per share. Accordingly, the three transactions in Table 14.3 are replaced by a single aggregate trade of 1,950 shares at a price of 491.104 per share and assigned to the time mark 10:05:01. This standard practice generates artificial prices, which are not equal to integer multiples of the tick.

Table 14.6 High-frequency Data

T981001BMO	0943180053350000001000094330013063	1
T981001BMO	0943300053400000001000094350002028	1
T981001BMO	0944180053400000000400094430002081	1
T981001BMO	0944240053400000000700094440007081	1
T981001BMO	0944240053400000000300094440007084	1
T981001BMO	0944300053400000000600094450063081	1
T981001BMO	0944300053400000000300094450063084	1
T981001BMO	0945060053400000000300094510002081	1
T981001BMO	0945060053250000000400094510002063	1
T981001BMO	0945060053250000000200094510002026	1
T981001BMO	0945060053200000000500094510002084	1
T981001BMO	0945180053450000000500094530009076	1
T981001BMO	0945300053450000000500094550009079	1
T981001BMO	0946060053400000000100094610085009	1

A second approach preserves the discreteness of price values and assumes that the transactions are not exactly simultaneously executed, but are instead separated by 1-second intervals, say. Thus, we replace the three transactions in Table 14.3 concluded at 10:05:01 by the following three trades:

$$
\begin{array}{rcl}
1000 & 491.20 & 10:05:03 \\
450 & 491.00 & 10:05:02 \\
500 & 491.00 & 10:05:01
\end{array}
$$

It has to be emphasized that the data on transaction prices do not satisfy standard assumptions used in the theory of asset prices.

1. The trading prices do not exist in continuous time, but are instead irregularly spaced (separated by unequal time intervals).
2. At each trading date, the transaction price is not unique, and the average price per share depends on traded volumes.
3. The prices take discrete values equal to integer multiples of the tick.
4. The trading prices feature instantaneous fluctuations between bid and ask depending on the type of entering orders, which may either be buy or sell orders. Therefore, the trading price bounces between a slightly higher and a slightly lower value. This phenomenon is called the *bid-ask bounce*.

To illustrate the trade price dynamics, we show in Figure 14.1 a path of the trading price obtained from data transformed using the second approach.

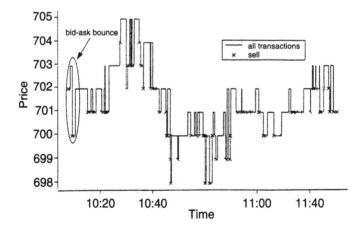

Figure 14.1 *Trading Price*

Bid-Ask Curves
Depending on the research interest, it is possible to extract from the order book data on various events other than trade or quote arrivals. Such events are, for example, the arrivals of orders that do not generate trades and remain queued in the order book or else order cancellations. This type of information is especially interesting in the analysis of investor behaviors, provided that their identity is known. Unfortunately, this information is often unavailable from the records for confidentiality reasons.

Another interesting research topic is the analysis of supply and demand functions documented in the order book. These functions can be directly inferred from the book. For example, by cumulating volumes on the buy side of the market, we obtain the total demand at a given price. We see in Table 14.7 that 964 shares are available at the proposed price of 490.60, and that $964 + 200 = 1,164$ shares available at the proposed price of 490.00, and so on. The supply function is obtained in a similar way by cumulating volumes on the sell side of the market.

Analytically, a buy limit order at a limit price b and volume v corresponds to an individual demand of the type

$$d(p) = v\mathbf{1}_{p\le b}.$$

Indeed, the investor accepts the volume v at any proposed price less or equal to b and rejects any transaction at a price higher than the limiting price. The aggregate demand derived by cumulating the individual demands is a stepwise function displayed in Figure 14.2.

It is also possible to derive the inverse demand and supply functions. More precisely, the inverse demand (supply) yields an ask curve (bid curve) that represents the price per share required to be paid (received) as a function of the requested (offered) volume. The ask curve is increasing, whereas the bid curve is decreasing. The best bid and ask prices correspond to the values of these curves for a small volume $v = 1$ (Figure 14.3).

Intraday Patterns
The time series formed by high-frequency data exhibit some typical periodic patterns. Let us consider the following series: trade intensity (num-

Table 14.7 *Computation of Bid and Ask Curves*

Buy Orders			Sell Orders				Last Trades		
1	490.60 964	964	950	950	491.00	2	10	491.60	10:04:37
3	490.00 200	1,164	1,950	1,000	491.20	1	247	491.00	10:03:59
2	489.00 650	1,814	2,925	975	491.40	1	147	491.00	10:03:59
1	488.50 500	2,314	3,525	600	491.50	1	453	491.00	10:03:53
5	488.00 638	2,952	3,755	230	491.80	1	1,000	491.00	10:03:42

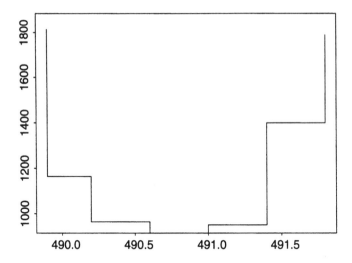

Figure 14.2   *Demand and Supply Curves*

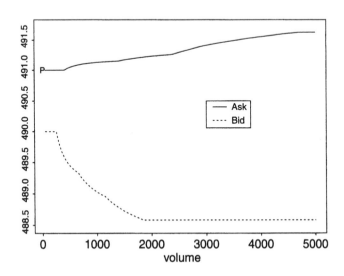

Figure 14.3   *Bid and Ask Curves*

ber of trades per hour, say), trade volatility, intertrade durations, and traded volumes. A trading day usually begins with heavy trading, coupled with high volatility and large volumes. During the lunch period, the market activity declines. At that time, fewer transactions are concluded, and fewer shares are exchanged. As well, trading prices become more homogeneous, resulting in lower volatility. A second spike in market activity occurs before the closure, when traders attempt to achieve target positions in various assets. In Figure 14.4, we observe the intraday evolution of the aforementioned series computed for the Bank of Montreal stock traded on the TSE. The volume, volatility, and trade intensity display similar behavior, resembling a U shape, throughout the day, in contrast to intertrade durations.

Empirical evidence also indicates the existence of periodic phenomena at lower frequencies, such as the so-called Monday effect and the January effect due to high market activity. The periodic patterns in high-frequency data are partly predictable. There exists yet another predictible component that characterizes the market behavior prior to major announce-

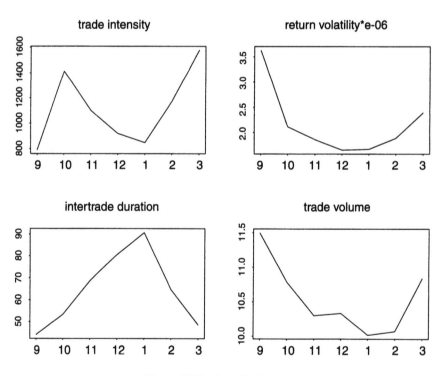

Figure 14.4 *Intraday Patterns*

ments. These announcements may, for example, be made by the National Bank concerning the prime rate, by the government in regular releases of macroeconomic data describing the state of economy, or by individual companies reporting their profits prior to shareholder meetings (see Andersen and Bollerslev 1998). These events are fully forecastable and trigger intense speculative trading, which increases price volatility.

14.2 Microstructure Theory

Microstructure theory has been developed to describe the behavior of various economic agents, transmission of information, and their effects on prices and volumes. The structural interpretations were derived mainly before the recent implementation of electronic trading systems. Therefore, they are not always adequate to explain contemporaneous financial markets. In this section, we sketch some of the main results and notions of microstructure theory and point out its limitations.

14.2.1 Components of the Bid-Ask Spread

The theory presented in this section concerns quote-driven markets. As pointed out, the spread on these markets acquires a particular importance since it represents the reward of the market maker. Recall that the bid-ask spread is the difference between ask and bid prices announced by a dealer at any fixed point in time. Current literature claims that the quoted spread must cover three cost components incurred by a dealer: order processing cost, inventory holding cost, and adverse information cost. We discuss these three cost components before turning our attention to the related microstructure theory.

Order Processing Cost
A market marker has to be compensated for the cost of effectuating transactions. Roll (1984) proposed a simple model to examine the effect of this compensation on the transaction price dynamics. He assumed that transactions take place at exogenous dates, which are regularly spaced. There exists a latent asset value, denoted by p_t^*, that is supposed to satisfy the random walk hypothesis, that is, the standard market efficiency hypothesis:

$$p_t^* = \sum_{\tau=1}^{t} \varepsilon_\tau^*,$$

where (ε_t^*) is a strong white noise. However, the observed transaction price p_t is not equal to the latent value since it includes the transaction cost. The associated cost component depends on the sign of the transaction, indicating whether it is a buy or a sell. We denote by Z_t the indicator variable, which takes the value $+1$ if it is a buy and the value -1 if it is a sell, and by η_t the unit cost at date 1. We assume that the processes (ε_t^*), (Z_t), and (η_t) are independent, and that (Z_t) and (η_t) are strong white noises. The distribution of Z_t is the uniform distribution on $\{-1, +1\}$. Thus, the transaction price is equal to the sum of the latent price and the cost correction term

$$p_t = p_t^* + Z_t\eta_t. \tag{14.1}$$

The introduction of a transaction cost component has the following consequences on the trade price dynamics.

PROPOSITION 14.1:

   (i) *The transaction price no longer satisfies the market efficiency hypothesis.*
   (ii) *The conditional and marginal distributions of the price change are mixtures of distributions.*
   (iii) *The first-order autocorrelation of the price change is negative and directly related to the spread size.*

   PROOF:

   (i) The prediction of the future transaction price is

$$E_t p_{t+1} = E_t p_{t+1}^* + E_t(Z_{t+1}\eta_{t+1})$$
$$= E_t p_{t+1}^* = p_t^*,$$

where I_t denotes the information, including the current and lagged quoted ask and bid prices; since these prices are $p_t^* \pm z_t$, the information includes the current and lagged values of p_t^*, η_t. Therefore, the martingale condition $E_t p_{t+1} = p_t$ is not satisfied by the transaction prices.
   (ii) The price change is

$$\Delta p_t = p_t - p_{t+1}$$
$$= p_t^* - p_{t-1}^* + Z_t\eta_t - Z_{t-1}\eta_{t-1}.$$

It admits the following forms, depending on the prevailing regime:

$$\Delta p_t = \varepsilon_t^* + \eta_t - \eta_{t-1}, \quad \text{if } Z_t = Z_{t-1} = 1,$$
$$= \varepsilon_t^* - \eta_t + \eta_{t-1}, \quad \text{if } Z_t = Z_{t-1} = -1,$$
$$= \varepsilon_t^* + \eta_t + \eta_{t-1}, \quad \text{if } Z_t = 1, Z_{t-1} = -1,$$
$$= \varepsilon_t^* - \eta_t - \eta_{t-1}, \quad \text{if } Z_t = -1, Z_{t-1} = 1.$$

The mixture of distributions arises as a consequence of switching regimes, determined by alternating buy and sell transactions.

(iii) Let us now compute the first-order autocovariance of price changes. We get

$$\text{Cov}(\Delta p_t, \Delta p_{t-1}) = \text{Cov}(\varepsilon_t^* + Z_t\eta_t - Z_{t-1}\eta_{t-1}, \varepsilon_{t-1}^* + Z_{t-1}\eta_{t-1} - Z_{t-2}\eta_{t-2})$$

$$= - V(Z_{t-1}\eta_{t-1}) \qquad \text{(by taking into account the independence between the variables)}$$

$$= - E(Z_{t-1}^2\eta_{t-1}^2) \qquad \text{(since } Z_{t-1} \text{ and } \eta_{t-1} \text{ are independent and } EZ_{t-1} = 0)$$

$$= - E(\eta_{t-1}^2) \qquad \text{(since } Z_{t-1}^2 = 1).$$

Therefore, the first-order autocovariance is negative and is linked to the average spread, defined as $2\sqrt{E(\eta_{t-1}^2)}$. The first-order autocorrelation of price changes is

$$\text{Corr } (\Delta p_t, \Delta p_{t-1}) = \frac{\text{Cov } (\Delta p_t, \Delta p_{t-1})}{V (\Delta p_t)}$$

$$= - \frac{E(\eta_{t-1}^2)}{V\varepsilon_t^* + 2V(Z_t\eta_t)}$$

$$= - \frac{E(\eta_t^2)}{V\varepsilon_t^* + 2E\eta_t^2}$$

$$= - \frac{1}{2 + V\varepsilon_t^*/V\eta_t}$$

Its absolute value is less than 0.5. It decreases when the transaction cost diminishes.

QED

Inventory Holding Cost
Another role of the market maker, who acts as a middleman on the stock market, is to maintain asset inventories to ensure a smooth flow of the trading process. The inventories partly result from past transactions and partly reflect the market maker's expectation about future orders. The literature examines the management of inventories in a setup of a monopolistic market maker and emphasizes the impact of inventory costs on the bid and ask prices (see, e.g., Garman 1976b; Amihud and Mendelson 1980; Ho and Stoll 1981; O'Hara and Olfield 1986). In this section, we discuss this effect in the restrictive framework of a simple static model and a deterministic environment.

We consider a call auction market. At time t, the market maker holds the stock x_t and quotes ask and bid prices a_t and b_t, respectively. These quoted prices are assumed independent of the order size. The market maker knows the demand and supply functions at date t; they are d_t and s_t, respectively. The objective function of the market maker includes two components: the first corresponds to the gain or loss incurred from trading and the second measures the cost due to misadjustment of the inventory level x_t. When x_t is too large, the maintenance of inventory becomes costly; when x_t is too small, the middleman has to acquire asset shares at a high price to satisfy client demand.

The optimization consists of maximizing

$$\max_{a_t, b_t} a_t d_t(a_t) - b_t s_t(b_t) - g[x_t - d_t(a_t) + s_t(b_t)],$$

where g is a penalty function that is decreasing for negative values of the term in the brackets, increasing for positive ones, and equal to 0 otherwise. The first-order conditions yield

$$\begin{cases} a_t \dot{d}_t(a_t) + d_t(a_t) + \dot{d}_t(a_t) \dot{g}[x_t - d_t(a_t) + s_t(b_t)] = 0, \\ b_t \dot{s}_t(b_t) + s_t(b_t) + \dot{s}_t(b_t) \dot{g}[x_t - d_t(a_t) + s_t(b_t)] = 0. \end{cases}$$

Where the dot denotes the first derivative with respect to time.

They are equivalent to

$$\begin{cases} a_t = -\dfrac{d_t(a_t)}{\dot{d}_t(a_t)} - \dot{g}[x_t - d_t(a_t) + s_t(b_t)], \\ b_t = -\dfrac{s_t(b_t)}{\dot{s}_t(b_t)} - \dot{g}[x_t - d_t(a_t) + s_t(b_t)]. \end{cases}$$

We deduce that

$$a_t - b_t = -\frac{d_t(a_t)}{\dot{d}_t(a_t)} + \frac{s_t(b_t)}{\dot{s}_t(b_t)}. \tag{14.2}$$

The bid and ask prices are such that $a_t \geq b_t$ since the demand function is decreasing and the supply function is increasing. The bid-ask spread depends on the pattern of demand and supply functions only and does not depend on the penalties for inventory misadjustment. Its magnitude is due to the monopolistic position of the market maker. Therefore, in the above framework, inventory costs mainly have an impact on the levels of bid and ask prices, rather than on their difference.

Adverse Information Cost

A common argument to justify the existence of the bid-ask spread relates to the asymmetry of information. An asymmetry of information arises when the specialist believes that he or she is trading with investors who have an informational advantage. The relation between the spread and the heterogeneity of traders with respect to their information has been studied by a number of authors (see, e.g., Copeland and Galai 1983; Glosten and Milgrom 1985; Glosten 1987; Easley and O' Hara 1987). We present below a typical equilibrium model for the quoted ask and bid prices.

The potential transaction dates, that is, the quoting dates, are exogenous and regularly spaced. A structural approach relies, in general, on a latent future value of the asset p^*_{t+1}, often called the *fundamental value* or *liquidation value*; its precise nature is not discussed (and is generally not discussed in the literature). There are two types of market participants, a market maker and informed traders. They share a common knowledge information at date t, denoted I_t, which can be used to predict the fundamental value, that is, to compute $\hat{p}_t = E(p^*_{t+1}|I_t)$.

Let us now assume that traders are more informed than the market maker and observe an additional signal (ψ_{t+1}). They can use this privileged information to improve their assessment of the fundamental value and adjust their portfolio allocations. Then, by entering a buy or sell order, they reveal a part of their information to the market maker, who can also update beliefs about p^*. More precisely, if the admissible orders are constrained to unitary volumes (a unit of volume may be equal to 100 shares, say), and if one order only can be entered at t, a risk-neutral market maker will quote the following ask and bid prices:

$$a_t = E(p^*_{t+1}|I_t, Z_t = 1), \quad b_t = E(p^*_{t+1}|I_t, Z_t = -1), \qquad (14.3)$$

that is, will take into account the sign of the potential order.

In summary we get various predictions of the future fundamental value:

$\hat{p}_t = E(p^*_{t+1}|I_t)$, based on the common knowledge information,
$\tilde{p}_t = E(p^*_{t+1}|I_t, \psi_{t+1})$, based on the information of the traders,
a_t and b_t, depending on the potential trader behaviors.

We need now to complete the model by describing the traders' behavior and writing the equilibrium condition for ask and bid prices. Let us first introduce the following assumptions.

ASSUMPTION A.14.1: *The (conditional) joint distribution of $(p^*_{t+1}, \psi_{t+1})'$ given I_t is a Gaussian distribution with mean $(m_{1,t}, m_{2,t})'$ and variance-covariance matrix*

$$\Sigma_t = \begin{pmatrix} \sigma_{11,t} & \sigma_{12,t} \\ \sigma_{12,t} & \sigma_{22,t} \end{pmatrix}.$$

ASSUMPTION A.14.2: *At the beginning of period t, one investor is randomly drawn from the set of all investors. This investor has an endowment w_t of the risk-free asset that is invested in a portfolio including the risk-free asset and the* *risky asset of interest. The investor also has an exponential utility function with absolute risk aversion coefficient A and evaluates the future portfolio wealth at the fundamental value.*

We implicitly assume the presence of different investors at different dates, with similar preferences and different endowments and access to information. We disregard how they will rebalance their portfolios in the future.

ASSUMPTION A.14.3: *The risk-free rate is $r_f = 0$.*

Let w_t denote the trader's endowment at the beginning of period t. There are three alternative actions the investor can take. The investor can submit a buy order for the risky asset, $Z_t = 1$; a sell order for the risky asset, $Z_t = -1$; or refrain from ordering the risky asset, $Z_t = 0$.

The associated expected utility levels are as follows: For the buy order,

$$E[\exp - A(w_t - a_t + p^*_{t+1}) | I_t, \psi_{t+1}] = -\exp - A(w_t - a_t)\exp[-AE(p^*_{t+1} | I_t, \psi_{t+1})$$
$$+ \frac{A^2}{2} V(p^*_{t+1} | I_t, \psi_{t+1})];$$

for the sell order,

$$E[-\exp - A(w_t + b_t - p^*_{t+1}) | I_t, \psi_{t+1}] = -\exp - A(w_t + b_t)\exp[-AE(p^*_{t+1} | I_t, \psi_{t+1})$$
$$+ \frac{A^2}{2} V(p^*_{t+1} | I_t, \psi_{t+1})];$$

and for no order, $E(-\exp - Aw_t | I_t, \psi_{t+1}) = -\exp(-Aw_t)$.

Let us denote the two first conditional moments of the future fundamental value by

$$E(p^*_{t+1} | I_t, \psi_{t+1}) = \alpha_t + \beta_t \psi_{t+1}, \tag{14.4}$$

where $\beta_t = \sigma_{12t}/\sigma_{22t}$, and $\alpha_t = m_{1t} - \beta_t m_{2t}$,

$$V(p^*_{t+1} | I_t, \psi_{t+1}) = \gamma_t^2, \tag{14.5}$$

where $\gamma_t^2 = \sigma_{11,t} - \sigma_{12,t}^2/\sigma_{22,t}$.

The endogenous decision of the trader is

$$Z_t = +1, \quad \text{if } \alpha_t + \beta_t \psi_{t+1} > a_t + \frac{A}{2} \gamma_t^2,$$

$$Z_t = 0, \quad \text{if } b_t - \frac{A}{2} \gamma_t^2 < \alpha_t + \beta_t \psi_{t+1} < a_t + \frac{A}{2} \gamma_t^2, \tag{14.6}$$

$$Z_t = -1, \quad \text{if } \alpha_t + \beta_t \psi_{t+1} < b_t - \frac{A}{2} \gamma_t^2.$$

The trader submits a buy order if the expected fundamental value is sufficiently high; the trader submits a sell order if the expected fundamental value is sufficiently low; no order is placed otherwise.

These alternatives are well defined whenever

$$a_t + \frac{A}{2}\gamma_t^2 > b_t - \frac{A}{2}\gamma_t^2$$

$$\Leftrightarrow a_t - b_t + A\gamma_t^2 > 0.$$

This condition is satisfied if $a_t - b_t \geq 0$.

Let us now examine the expressions of the bid and ask prices under a rational expectation hypothesis.

ASSUMPTION A.14.4: *The market maker knows the distribution of $p^*_{t+b}\psi_{t+1}$ conditional on the information I_t and the behavior of traders.*

Then, the ask and bid prices satisfy

$$\begin{cases} a_t = E[p^*_{t+1}|I_t, Z_t = +1], \\ b_t = E[p^*_{t+1}|I_t, Z_t = -1], \end{cases}$$

or, equivalently, if $\beta_t > 0$,

$$\begin{cases} a_t = E\left[p^*_{t+1}\Big|I_t, \psi_{t+1} > \left(a_t - \alpha_t + \frac{A}{2}\gamma_t^2\right)/\beta_t\right], \\ \\ b_t = E\left[p^*_{t+1}\Big|I_t, \psi_{t+1} < \left(b_t - \alpha_t - \frac{A}{2}\gamma_t^2\right)/\beta_t\right]. \end{cases} \tag{14.7}$$

We get a system of implicit equations of the type

$$\begin{cases} a_t = g_a(a_t; \alpha_t, \beta_t, \gamma_t, m_{2,t}, \sigma_{22,t}, A), \\ b_t = g_b(b_t; \alpha_t, \beta_t, \gamma_t, m_{2,t}, \sigma_{22,t}, A), \end{cases}$$

where g_a and g_b are known functions (see Appendix 14.1). By solving these equations, we derive the equilibrium ask and bid prices as functions of the parameters of the conditional distribution of $(p^*_{t+1}, \psi^*_{t+1})$ and of the absolute risk aversion coefficient. The equilibrium bid-ask prices satisfy the following relationship:

PROPOSITION 14.2:

(i) *The system of equilibrium equations is, for $\beta_t > 0$,*

$$a_t = m_{1,t} + \beta_t\sigma_{22,t}^{1/2}\mu\left[\frac{a_t - \alpha_t + \frac{A}{2}\gamma_t^2}{\beta_t\sigma_{22,t}^{1/2}} - \frac{m_{2,t}}{\sigma_{22,t}^{1/2}}\right],$$

$$b_t = m_{1,t} + \beta_t\sigma_{22,t}^{1/2}\mu\left[\frac{m_{2,t}}{\sigma_{22,t}^{1/2}} - \frac{b_t - \alpha_t - \frac{A}{2}\gamma_t^2}{\beta_t\sigma_{22,t}^{1/2}}\right],$$

where $\mu(x) = \varphi(x)/(1 - \Phi(x))$ is the hazard function of the standard normal distribution.

(ii) At equilibrium, we have

$$a_t \geq m_{1,t} = E(p_{t+1}^* | I_t) \geq b_t,$$

where the equality holds if $\beta_t = 0$, that is, if the signal is noninformative.

Although the quoted ask and bid prices are defined at any date t, these dates are not necessarily equivalent to the transaction dates. A transaction is concluded at date t if and only if $Z_t \neq 0$. Then, the transaction price is equal to $p_t = a_t \mathbf{1}_{Z_t=+1} + b_t \mathbf{1}_{Z_t=-1}$.

At this point, we need to remember that the analysis has been performed under quite restrictive assumptions, such as

1. The dates of order arrivals are exogenous.
2. The orders concern a unit of volume.
3. There is at most one order entered at a given date
4. The investors execute at most one trade on the market. All future rebalancing of their portfolios is performed out of the market.
5. If the market maker needs additional quantities of asset shares for inventory, the market maker does not buy them on the market, but instead from external sources.
6. The bid and ask prices are defined for a unit of volume.
7. The dynamics of the fundamental values, signals, and common information are not specified, except for Assumption A.14.1.

The attempts to relax some of these assumptions have not produced satisfactory results. The resulting models either feature higher complexity or yield unrealistic outcomes. To illustrate this issue, let us discuss the consequences of relaxing some selected assumptions.

First, for example, let us assume that the volume is not constrained to be equal to one unit. As a consequence, the market maker quotes entire bid-ask curves, and the equilibrum condition concerns these curves. Moreover, the information contained in each order now comprises Z_t, v_t. Therefore, it is no longer qualitative, but also quantitative. Under the mean-variance optimization framework, the demanded volume is

$$v_t = \frac{1}{A} V(p_{t+1}^* | I_t, \psi_{t+1})^{-1} (E(p_{t+1}^* | I_t, \psi_{t+1}) - a_t),$$

that is, an affine function of the signal ψ_{t+1}. Therefore, by observing the volume v_t, the market maker acquires the same information as the informed investor.

This difficulty can be circumvented by imposing heterogeneity of investors. Accordingly, we can assume that some traders are informed and receive the signal, while others are uninformed and possess the basic information I_t only. Then, at each date, one investor is drawn at random from the set of investors. Since the market maker does not know for sure whether this trader is informed, the market maker has more difficulty to recover the exact value of the signal ψ_{t+1}. At this point, researchers often assume that the probability of an investor being informed is exogenous and time independent, which seems unrealistic.

Second, to design a coherent structure of price dynamics, the fundamental value and the signal are often assumed time independent: $p^*_{t+1} = p^*$, $\psi_{t+1} = \psi$. Moreover, the common knowledge at time t is supposed to include the initial market information I_0 and the market data, that is, the lagged values of Z:

$$I_{t+1} = \{I_t, Z_t\}.$$

The information set implicitly includes the quoted ask and bid prices, which are functions of I_t, Z_t. In this framework, the market maker can learn the signal perfectly. More precisely, the sequences of ask and bid prices converge to the expected fundamental value $E(p^*|I_t,\psi) = E(p^*|I_0,\psi)$ of the informed trader. Consequently, the spread asymptotically tends to 0. In fact, the basic Glosten-Milgrom model assumes a single news component, which can always be learned by all market participants. In practice, there will be many informative shocks over time.

14.2.2 Timing of Orders

This section concerns the microstructure theory of order-driven markets. In particular, we investigate how the behaviors of individual traders determine the traded volume under an automatic order-matching procedure.

Exogenous Effect of Order-Matching Frequency in Automatic Systems
Let us consider a partition of the time T into two subperiods $[0,T_1]$ and $[T_1,T]$. We assume the exogeneity of order flows during these subperiods. They are determined by the demand and supply functions, denoted by D_1 and S_1, respectively, for the first subperiod and by D_2 and S_2, respectively, for the second one.

For comparison, let us first consider global matching at a predetermined time T. We aggregate the demands and supplies of the two subperiods, getting

$$D = D_1 + D_2, \qquad S = S_1 + S_2.$$

The market-clearing equilibrium price is p^a and the associated quantity traded at equilibrium is

$$v^a = D(p^a) = S(p^a).$$

Under the second scenario, the trading procedure is sequential, although limited to two call auctions. The first call auction takes place at an intermediate time T_1. At this time, the market clearing price is p_1, and the associated traded volume v_1 is such that

$$v_1 = D(p_1) = S(p_1).$$

The outstanding buy and sell orders arrived in the meantime and have not been matched yet; they are now entered into the book and aggregated with the order flows of the second subperiod. The second call auction is held at date T and deals with the demand $D^F = D_2 + (D_1 - v_1)^+$ and the supply $S^F = S_2 + (S_1 - v_1)^+$. These curves intersect at the price p_2, and the associated volume is

$$v_2 = D^F(p_2) = S^F(p_2).$$

The following proposition is proved in Appendix 14.2.

PROPOSITION 14.3:

    (i) The price p^a lies between prices p_1 and p_2.
    (ii) $v^a \leq v_1 + v_2$.
    (iii) If $p_1 < p_2$, the sellers, who are served at T by the global matching procedure, are also served by the sequential one. Similarly, if $p_1 > p_2$, the buyers, served at T by the global matching procedure, are also served by the sequential one.

Proposition 14.3 shows that the frequency of call auctions has direct consequences on the trading prices and volumes. An increase of the trading frequency from one to two call auctions causes an increase of the traded volume and creates more price volatility (since the unique price p^a is now replaced by the pair p_1, p_2 of distinct values). Therefore, it is natural to observe a positive dependence among the trading frequency, traded volume, and price volatility. Of course, this result assumes that investors do not adjust their demands and supplies to the new matching procedure.

Stripping of Individual Orders under Volume Constraint
Let us assume a sequence of call auctions held regularly at dates t, $t+1$, $\ldots$. We also assume linear ask curves (i.e., inverse supply): $a_t(v) = a_{0,t} + a_{1,t}v$. We consider at time t an investor, facing a short sell constraint, who is required to accumulate an exact volume v of shares at date $t+1$. The investor can acquire this quantity by buying at t the volume αv and buying the residual part $(1-\alpha)v$ at time $t+1$. The final cost is

$$C_{t+1}(\alpha) = \alpha v a_t(\alpha v) + (1-\alpha)v a_{t+1}[(1-\alpha)v]$$

$$= a_{0,t}\alpha v + a_{1,t}\alpha^2 v^2 + a_{0,t+1}(1-\alpha)v + a_{1,t+1}(1-\alpha)^2 v^2.$$

Let us restrict our analysis to the framework of perfect foresight. The investor selects the portion α of the order that minimizes $C_{t+1}(\alpha)$ under $0 \le \alpha \le 1$. The first-order derivative of the cost function is

$$\frac{dC_{t+1}(\alpha)}{d\alpha} = a_{0,t}v + 2a_{1,t}\alpha v^2 - a_{0,t+1}v - 2a_{1,t+1}(1-\alpha)v^2.$$

It is equal to zero for

$$\alpha = \frac{2a_{1,t+1}v - a_{0,t} + a_{0,t+1}}{2v(a_{1,t} + a_{1,t+1})}.$$

Therefore, the investor submits orders at both dates if $0 \le \alpha^* \le 1$ and at a single date otherwise. In particular, when the target volume is high, we have $\alpha^* \simeq \dfrac{a_{1,t+1}}{a_{1,t} + a_{1,t+1}}$. The stripping coefficient depends on the slopes of the ask curves only. Its expression reveals the relationship between the patterns of the ask curves and the distribution of volume per trade.

Similar results could be derived in a stochastic environment under the mean-variance portfolio optimizing behavior of the investor. The optimization criterion becomes

$$E_t C_{t+1}(\alpha) - \frac{A}{2} V_t C_{t+1}(\alpha)$$

$$= a_{0,t}\alpha v + a_{1,t}\alpha^2 v^2 + E_t(a_{0,t+1})(1-\alpha)v + E_t a_{1,t+1}(1-\alpha)^2 v^2$$

$$- \frac{A}{2} \{ V_t(a_{0,t+1})(1-\alpha)^2 v^2 + V_t(a_{1,t+1})(1-\alpha)^4 v^4 + 2\, Cov_t(a_{0,t+1}, a_{1,t+1})(1-\alpha)^3 v^3 \}.$$

This is a polynomial of degree four in α. The optimal order-stripping coefficient α depends on the uncertainty about the intercepts and slopes of the ask curves.

14.3 Price Dynamics

The analysis of price dynamics based on high-frequency data involves either trading prices or quoted bid and ask prices. In the first two sections, we consider the trading prices, signed and unsigned. We first present stylized facts documented by standard ARMA or GARCH applications. Next, we introduce deformed time models that take into account the difference between calendar and transaction times. In Section 14.3.3, we study the dynamics of the supply and demand functions, called the bid-ask curves, on an order-driven market.

14.3.1   Application of Autoregressive Moving Average and Generalized Autoregressive Conditionally Heteroscedastic Models

In early empirical studies of high-frequency data, standard ARMA or GARCH models were fitted to trading prices.

Calendar Time and Trading Time
Empirical evidence suggests that the estimated price dynamics heavily depends on the sampling of observations. Under a commonly implemented sampling scheme, the tick-by-tick data are sampled regularly in calendar time, for instance, with prices recorded every 5 minutes retained (or the closest trading price). Let us now introduce the concept of trading time measured on a time scale set by trade arrivals. Consequently, data are said to be sampled regularly in the trading time when, for instance, prices of every fifth trade are extracted regardless of their timing. Even in the case when the average time between consecutive trades is about 1 minute, the time series resulting from both sampling schemes feature different dynamics due to the variation of intertrade durations.

We can illustrate the time scale effect by comparing the trajectories of returns in calendar and trading times. The reader should be cautioned about different definitions of displayed returns. A return over five trades is a return existing in a random interval of calendar time. Therefore, it differs from a return calculated at a fixed horizon of 5 minutes.

We show in Figure 14.5 the paths of returns on the US$/DM (deutsche mark) exchange rate.

Distinct patterns are also exhibited by the autocorrelation functions (ACF) of returns sampled in calendar and trading times (Figure 14.6). Of course, one lag is associated here with 5 minutes and five trades, respectively. In calendar time, the returns feature strong persistence, whereas in trading time, they display a shorter memory.

In the reminder of this section, we consider trading prices sampled in calendar time.

Bid-Ask Bounce
We have mentioned that daily returns are expected to satisfy the weak white noise hypothesis, that is, to have statistically insignificant empirical autocorrelations. This stylized fact is evidenced by data sampled at very low frequencies, such as 1 week or 1 month. In contrast, the absence of serial correlation is no longer observed when the sampling frequency increases and, for example, autocorrelations of daily or intradaily returns are computed. Figure 14.7 shows the ACF of returns on the US$/DM exchange rate sampled at 1-minute intervals. We find a significant negative first-order autocorrelation, whereas the higher order correlations are

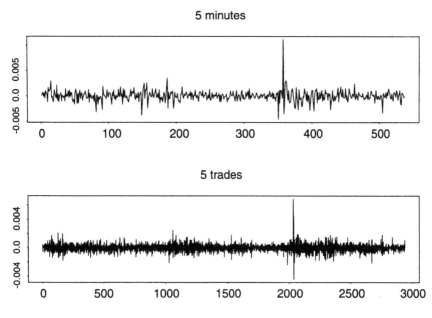

Figure 14.5 *Returns in Calendar and Trading Times*

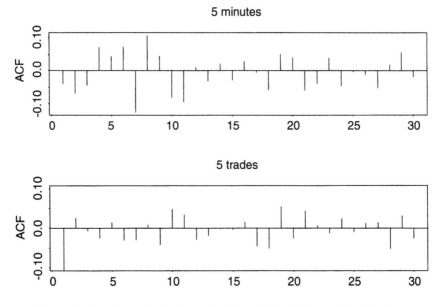

Figure 14.6 *Autocorrelation Function (ACF) in Calendar and Trading Times*

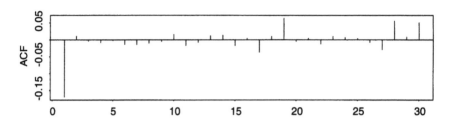

Figure 14.7 *Autocorrelation Function (ACF) in Calendar Time, Sampled at 1 Minute*

much smaller in absolute sense. This effect is due to the alternating trades initiated by buy and sell orders, that is due to the bid-ask bounce (see Section 14.2.1). It often disappears when autocorrelograms are computed from *signed trades*, for which buyer- and seller-initiated trades are distinguished.

Discrete-Valued Prices

Early applications of dynamic heteroscedastic models to daily returns on various assets employed simple models, such as the MA(1)–GARCH(1,1) process. Let us focus on an example for which returns on various assets were estimated under this setup, with fixed MA and GARCH orders set independent of individual assets. Such an approach allows for a comparison of various asset return dynamics with respect to the estimated autoregressive and moving average parameters of the drift and volatility equations. In particular, we can verify a stylized fact about the presence of a unit root in the volatility equation (see Chapter 6) documented from daily data. This stylized fact is not always confirmed by high-frequency data. Andersen and Bollerslev (1997b) estimated the MA(1)–GARCH(1,1) models for the US\$/DM exchange rates and Standard and Poor's (S&P) returns at different frequencies δ/k, where δ is given, and k varies from 1 to 10. We report in Table 14.8 the estimated values of the persistence coefficient of volatility in the GARCH equation.

Table 14.8 *Estimated Persistence Coefficient and Sampling Frequency*

Sampling Frequency	1	2	3	4	5	6	7	8	9	10
Persistence coefficient exchange rate	0.98	0.93	0.92	0.88	0.80	0.84	0.80	0.73	0.77	0.60
Persistence coefficient, S&P	0.995	0.99	0.98	0.98	1.00	0.97	0.96	0.96	0.93	0.93

We observe that, while the estimated coefficients are close to 1 at almost all frequencies in the S&P data, they are close to 1 only at low frequencies in the exchange rate data. Moreover, in the latter case, we do not observe the convergence of the persistence coefficient when k increases, as we would if the returns satisfied an underlying diffusion model. Some researchers refer to the discreteness of prices as a possible cause of this phenomenon. When the sampling frequency increases, the jump effects become stronger and induce high persistence. The empirical evidence on volatility persistence suggests a misspecification of GARCH models. This effect is easy to detect in data on a simple asset (such as an exchange rate), but is still very much present in market indexes despite that jumps are attenuated due to averaging.

14.3.2 Deformed Time

The aim of this section is to compare the dynamic properties of a price process measured on two alternative time scales. We introduced in Section 14.3.1 a simple example of time deformation by illustrating differences between the trajectories of returns in calendar time and in transaction time determined by trade arrivals. Potentially, a variety of alternative time scales can be created, depending on the definition of the time unit. This approach, called *time deformation*, is used to reveal or suppress some specific dynamic properties of data in calendar time. For example, a return trajectory can be smoothed by stretching the intervals between observations in a volatile period and by shrinking them in a period of market tranquility. The concept of time deformation is explained in detail below.

The Time Scales
We consider two time scales, the calendar time t, which takes continuous nonnegative values, and an alternative time z, which takes discrete nonnegative values. This latter time is called in the literature *intrinsic time, deformed time, market time,* or *business time*. The time-changing process, or *directing process (driving process)*, is an increasing process that determines the mapping from the calendar to the intrinsic time. It is denoted by

$$Z : t \in \mathbf{R}^+ \to Z_t \in \mathbf{N}.$$

EXAMPLE 14.1: The following increasing driving processes can be used in financial applications:

$N(t)$, which counts the number of transactions before t,
$V(t)$, which measures the total number of shares traded before t,
$C(t)$, which measures the total market value traded before t.

Let us now consider a price process of interest and its definitions with respect to both times. It is denoted by $(Y_z^*, z \in \mathbf{N})$ in intrinsic time and by $(Y_t, t \in \mathbf{R}^+)$ in calendar time. The two representations of the process are linked by the time deformation

$$Y_t = Y_{Z_t}^*, t \in \mathbf{R}^+. \tag{14.8}$$

Comparison of the Dynamics

To compare the dynamics of the processes Y and Y^*, it is necessary to impose assumptions concerning the joint distributions of the processes Y^* and Z. The distributional properties of the process Y follow from (14.8). We consider below stationary processes, although similar results are valid for processes with unit roots as well. The standard assumptions in the literature (see, e.g., Clark 1973; Stock 1988; Ghysels, Gourieroux, and Jasiak 1997) are as follows:

ASSUMPTION A.14.5: *The processes Y^* and Z are independent.*

ASSUMPTION A.14.6: *The process Y^* is strongly stationary.*

ASSUMPTION A.14.7: *The time deformation has strongly stationary increments, that is, the processes $(Z_t - Z_{t-t_1}, \ldots, Z_t - Z_{t-t_n})$ are strongly stationary for any $n, t_1, \ldots, t_n$.*

It is easy to show that the following proposition holds (see Ghysels et al. 1997).

PROPOSITION 14.4: *Under assumptions A.14.5–A.14.7, the process Y in calendar time is strongly stationary.*

We can now examine the first- and second-order properties of the two processes Y and Y^*. Let us introduce the expectations

$$m = E(Y_t), \qquad m^* = E(Y_z^*), \tag{14.9}$$

and the autocovariance functions

$$\gamma(\tau) = Cov(Y_t, Y_{t-\tau}), \qquad \gamma^*(h) = Cov(Y_z^*, Y_{z-h}^*). \tag{14.10}$$

The γ function is defined on $\mathbf{R}^+$, whereas the γ^* function is defined on $\mathbf{N}$.

PROPOSITION 14.5: *We have*

(i) $m = m^*$.
(ii) $\gamma(\tau) = E[\gamma^*(Z_t - Z_{t-\tau})]$.

In particular, $\gamma(0) = \gamma^*(0)$.

PROOF:

(i) By the law of iterated expectation, we get

$$m = E(Y_t) = E(Y_{Z_t}^*)$$
$$= EE(Y_{Z_t}^* | Z_t)$$

$$= Em^*$$
$$= m^*.$$

(ii) From the covariance decomposition equation, it follows that

$$\gamma(\tau) = Cov(Y_t, Y_{t-\tau})$$
$$= Cov(Y^*_{Z_t}, Y^*_{Z_{t-\tau}})$$
$$= Cov[E(Y^*_{Z_t}|Z), E(Y^*_{Z_{t-\tau}}|Z)] + E\ Cov(Y^*_{Z_t}, Y^*_{Z_{t-\tau}}|Z)$$
$$= Cov(m^*, m^*) + E[\gamma^*(Z_t - Z_{t-\tau})]$$
$$= E[\gamma^*(Z_t - Z_{t-\tau})].$$

QED

Random Walks
The first example of time deformation studied in the literature concerns the random walks (Clark 1973; Stock 1988; Mandelbrot and Taylor 1987). We assume that

ASSUMPTION A.14.8: *(Y^*_z) is a Gaussian random walk, that is, the differences $\Delta Y^*_z = Y^*_z - Y^*_{z-1}, z \in \mathbf{N^*}$ are independent identically distributed (i.i.d.) standard Gaussian variables.*

ASSUMPTION A.14.9: *For any calendar time unit δ, the differences $\Delta_\delta Z_n = Z_{n\delta} - Z_{(n-1)\delta}, n \in \mathbf{N^*}$, are i.i.d. variables.*

It is easily checked that the random walk property also holds for the process of interest expressed in calendar time.

PROPOSITION 14.6: *Under assumptions A.14.5 and A.14.7–A.14.9, the process Y is such that $\Delta_\delta Y_n = Y_{n\delta} - Y_{(n-1)\delta}, n \in \mathbf{N^*}$ are i.i.d. variables.*

PROOF:

(i) Let us first check the independence property. We get for $m \neq n$

$$P[\Delta_\delta Y_n \in A, \Delta_\delta Y_m \in B] = P[Y^*_{Z_{n\delta}} - Y^*_{Z_{(n-1)\delta}} \in A, Y^*_{Z_{m\delta}} - Y^*_{Z_{(m-1)\delta}} \in B]$$

$$= EP[Y^*_{Z_{n\delta}} - Y^*_{Z_{(n-1)\delta}} \in A, Y^*_{Z_{m\delta}} - Y^*_{Z_{(m-1)\delta}} \in B|Z],$$
(by iterated expectations),

$$= E\{P[Y^*_{Z_{n\delta}} - Y^*_{Z_{(n-1)\delta}} \in A|Z]P[Y^*_{Z_{m\delta}} - Y^*_{Z_{(m-1)\delta}} \in B|Z]\},$$
(by assumption A.14.8),

$$= E\{P[(Z_{n\delta} - Z_{(n-1)\delta})^{1/2}U \in A|Z]P[(Z_{m\delta} - Z_{m-1)\delta})^{1/2}V \in B|Z]\},$$
(where U and V are independent standard Gaussian variables)

$$= EP[(Z_{n\delta} - + Z_{(n-1)\delta})^{1/2}U \in A|Z]\ EP[(Z_{m\delta} - Z_{(m-1)\delta})^{1/2}V \in B|Z]$$
(by assumption A.14.9)

$$= P(\Delta_\delta Y_n \in A)P(\Delta_\delta Y_m \in B).$$

(ii) Let us now check if the variables $\Delta_\delta Y_n$, n varying, have the same distribution. We have

$$P[\Delta_\delta Y_n \in (y, y + dy)] = EP[(\Delta_\delta Z_n)^{1/2} U \in (y, y + dy) | Z]$$

$$\simeq dy E\left(\frac{1}{(\Delta_\delta Z_n)^{1/2}} \frac{1}{\sqrt{2\pi}} \exp - \frac{y^2}{2\Delta_\delta Z_n} \right).$$

Therefore, the probability density function (pdf) of $\Delta_\delta Y_n$ is independent of n since the variables $\Delta_\delta Z_n$, $n \in \mathbf{N}^*$, have identical distributions. QED

Proposition 14.6 has important implications with regard to the market efficiency hypothesis. Indeed, the property of market efficiency depends on the selected time scale. Therefore, it may hold in calendar time, but be violated in intrinsic time, or vice-versa. Proposition 14.6 provides a set of assumptions that ensure its validity in both times.

In Proposition 14.6, we have derived the pdf of the increment of Y in calendar time. By introducing a stochastic time deformation, this density becomes a mixture of Gaussian distributions due to the volatility effect of $\Delta_\delta Z_n$. Thus, time deformation induces the properties given below, which are similar to the properties featured by conditionally heteroscedastic processes (see Chapter 6 and Clark 1973).

PROPOSITION 14.7: *Time deformation may induce heavy tails of price increments.*

PROOF: We have

$$E(\Delta_\delta Y_n) = E[(\Delta_\delta Z_n)^{1/2} U] = 0,$$

$$E[(\Delta_\delta Y_n)^2] = E[(\Delta_\delta Z_n U^2) = E(\Delta_\delta Z_n),$$

$$E[(\Delta_\delta Y_n)]^4 = E((\Delta_\delta Z_n)^2 U^4) = 3E[(\Delta_\delta Z_n)]^2.$$

We derive the marginal kurtosis in calendar time:

$$k = \frac{E(\Delta_\delta Y_n)^4}{[E(\Delta_\delta Y_n)^2]^2}$$

$$= 3 \frac{[E(\Delta_\delta Z_n)^2}{[E(\Delta_\delta Z_n)]^2}$$

$$= 3 + \frac{V(\Delta_\delta Z_n)}{[E(\Delta_\delta Z_n)]^2},$$

which is larger than the benchmark value of 3 determined by the kurtosis of a Gaussian distribution. QED

Therefore, under the assumptions A.14.5 and A.14.7–A.14.9, we find Gaussian tails in the intrinsic time and heavier tails in the calendar time. The tail increase is a function of $\dfrac{V(\Delta_\delta Z_n)}{[E(\Delta_\delta Z_n)]^2}$, that is, it depends on the dispersion of the deformed time speed. In special cases, this effect may become so strong that the moments of the price increment distribution in calendar time will not exist.

PROPOSITION 14.8: *When the distribution of $\Delta_\delta Z_n$ is the inverse Gaussian pdf*
$$h(z) = \frac{1}{\sqrt{2\pi}} \frac{1}{z^{3/2}} \exp - \frac{1}{2z}, \text{ then } \Delta_\delta Y_n \text{ admits a Cauchy distribution.}$$

PROOF: The pdf of $\Delta_\delta Y_n$ is

$$g(y) = E\left[\frac{1}{\sqrt{2\pi}(\Delta_\delta Z_n)^{1/2}} \exp\left(- \frac{y^2}{2\Delta_\delta Z_n} \right) \right]$$

$$= \int_0^\infty \frac{1}{z^{1/2}\sqrt{2\pi}} \exp\left(-\frac{y^2}{2z} \right) \frac{1}{\sqrt{2\pi}} \frac{1}{z^{3/2}} \exp - \frac{1}{2z} \, dz$$

$$= \int_0^\infty \frac{1}{2\pi} z^{-2} \exp - \frac{1}{2z} (1 + y^2) dz$$

$$= \frac{1}{\pi} \frac{1}{1 + y^2}.$$

QED

Autoregressive Models
Another example of interesting dynamic properties concerns the autoregressive processes. Let us assume a Gaussian autoregressive process of price increments in intrinsic time:

$$Y_z^* = m + \rho(Y_{z-1}^* - m) + \sigma \varepsilon_z^*, \qquad 0 \le \rho < 1. \tag{14.11}$$

Then, at lag h, we get

$$Y_z^* = m + \rho^h (Y_{z-h}^*) + \sigma \left(\frac{1 - \rho^{2h}}{1 - \rho^2} \right)^{1/2} \varepsilon_z^*, \tag{14.12}$$

where $\varepsilon_z^* \sim N(0, 1)$.

We find that, conditional on the process Z,

$$Y_{Z_t}^* = m + \rho^{(Z_t - Z_{t-1})}(Y_{Z_{t-1}}^* - m) + \sigma \left(\frac{1 - \rho^{2(Z_t - Z_{t-1})}}{1 - \rho^2} \right)^{1/2} \varepsilon_t^*, \tag{14.13}$$

$$\Leftrightarrow Y_t = m + \rho^{(Z_t - Z_{t-1})}(Y_{t-1} - m) + \sigma \left(\frac{1 - \rho^{2(Z_t - Z_{t-1})}}{1 - \rho^2} \right)^{1/2} \varepsilon_t^*, \tag{14.14}$$

where (ε_t^*) is a Gaussian white noise.

Thus, we get an autoregressive model that features both stochastic volatility and stochastic correlation. These stochastic factors are nonlinear functions of the deformed time increments $Z_t - Z_{t-1} = \Delta Z_t$. In particular, this model can be considered an extension of the Hull-White type of model introduced in Chapters 11–13 since the additional stochastic features affect not only the volatility, but also the mean reverting parameter.

When assumptions A.14.5 and A.14.7–A.14.9 are satisfied, we can make explicit the marginal dynamics of the process Y after integrating the moments with respect to the time deformation. We know that

$$EY_t = EY^*_{Z_t} = m,$$

$$VY_t = VY^*_{Z_t} = \frac{\sigma^2}{1-\rho^2}.$$

Moreover,

$$
\begin{aligned}
\gamma(\tau) &= Cov(Y_t, Y_{t-\tau}) \\
&= E \; Cov \; (Y^*_{Z_t}, Y^*_{Z_{t-\tau}} | Z) \\
&= \frac{\sigma^2}{1-\rho^2} \; E\!\left(\rho^{Z_t - Z_{t-\tau}}\right) \\
&= \frac{\sigma^2}{1-\rho^2} \; E\!\left[\rho^{Z_t - Z_{t-1} + \ldots + Z_{t-\tau+1} - Z_{t-\tau}}\right] \\
&= \frac{\sigma^2}{1-\rho^2} \; \left[E\!\left(\rho^{Z_t - Z_{t-1}}\right)\right]^\tau.
\end{aligned}
$$

We deduce that the process Y in calendar time also admits a weak AR(1) representation, with an autoregressive coefficient $r = E(\rho^{\Delta Z_t}) \leq \rho^{E\Delta Z_t}$ by Jensen's inequality. If $E\Delta Z_t < 1$, we get $r < \rho$. If $E\Delta Z_t > 1$, we get either $r < \rho$ or $r > \rho$, depending on the distribution of ΔZ_t.

We can also compute the two first conditional moments of the process in calendar time. We obtain:

$$
\begin{aligned}
E[Y_t | \underline{Y_{t-1}}] &= E[E(Y_t | \underline{Y_{t-1}}, Z) | \underline{Y_{t-1}}] \\
&= E[m + \rho^{\Delta Z_t} (Y_{t-1} - m) | \underline{Y_{t-1}}] \\
&= m + E(\rho^{\Delta Z_t}) (Y_{t-1} - m).
\end{aligned}
$$

Thus, the conditional mean is an affine function of Y_{t-1}. The conditional variance is given by

$$
\begin{aligned}
V[Y_t | \underline{Y_{t-1}}] &= V[E(Y_t | \underline{Y_{t-1}}, Z) | \underline{Y_{t-1}}] + E[V(Y_t | \underline{Y_{t-1}}, Z) | \underline{Y_{t-1}}] \\
&= V[m + \rho^{\Delta Z_t}(Y_{t-1} - m) | \underline{Y_{t-1}}] + E\!\left[\sigma^2 \frac{1 - \rho^{2\Delta Z_t}}{1-\rho^2} | \underline{Y_{t-1}}\right] \\
&= V(\rho^{\Delta Z_t}) (Y_{t-1} - m)^2 + \sigma^2 E\!\left(\frac{1 - \rho^{2\Delta Z_t}}{1-\rho^2}\right).
\end{aligned}
$$

Time deformation induces conditional heteroscedasticity, which is a function of the squared term $(Y_{t-1} - m)^2$, but does not depend on squared innovations, contrary to ARCH models.

Statistical Inference

Statistical inference on time-deformed processes depends on (1) the available data, which may be tick by tick or regularly spaced; (2) observability of the time-deformation process; and (3) specification, which may be partly nonparametric. In any case, it is important to estimate all parameters, including the latent parameters of time deformation, along with the parameters that determine the dynamics in calendar time. The estimates of latent parameters are useful for option pricing and risk hedging. Moreover, it is insightful to recover the entire trajectory of time deformation whenever it is unobservable. In this section, we consider examples for which time deformation is either observable or defined as a parametric function of observable covariates. The case of unobservable factors would be treated as a special case of dynamic factor models considered in Chapter 9.

Intrinsic Time Autocorrelogram. Let us assume a sample of data in calendar time comprising both the series of interest and the time deformation process: Y_t, Z_t, $t = 1, \ldots, T$. A common approach consists of calculating the calendar time autocovariance γ using standard software. In our study, however, we are also interested in the intrinsic time autocovariance function γ^*. Although the function γ^* is defined for all admissible lags z, due to discreteness we may not be able to approximate it by its empirical counterpart since the number of pairs t, τ such that $Z_t - Z_\tau = z$, where z is given, is often be equal to 0. Therefore, some preliminary smoothing is required.

Before deriving the expression of the smoothed estimator, let us first consider the basic estimator of the autocovariance function in calendar time (for a demeaned process). It can be written as

$$\hat{\gamma}_T(h) = \frac{1}{T} \sum_{t=1}^{T} Y_t Y_{t+h}$$

$$\simeq \frac{1}{T} \sum_{t=1}^{T} \sum_{\tau=1}^{T} Y_t Y_\tau \mathbb{1}_{t-\tau=h}$$

$$\simeq \sum_{t=1}^{T} \sum_{\tau=1}^{T} Y_t Y_\tau \mathbb{1}_{t-\tau=h} \Big/ \sum_{t=1}^{T} \sum_{\tau=1}^{T} \mathbb{1}_{t-\tau=h}.$$

We replace the indicator function by a kernel function of the intrinsic time increments. The estimator is defined by

$$\hat{\gamma}_T^*(z) = \frac{\sum_{t=1}^{T} \sum_{\tau=1}^{T} Y_t Y_\tau \frac{1}{h_T} K\left[\dfrac{Z_t - Z_\tau - z}{h_T}\right]}{\sum_{t=1}^{T} \sum_{\tau=1}^{T} \frac{1}{h_T} K\left[\dfrac{Z_t - Z_\tau - z}{h_T}\right]}, \qquad (14.15)$$

where K is a kernel, and h_T is the bandwidth.

The asymptotic properties of this estimator were derived by Ghysels, Gourieroux, and Jasiak (1998).

PROPOSITION 14.9:

(i) $\hat{\gamma}_T^*(z)$ *is a consistent estimator of* $\gamma^*(z)$.
(ii) *It is asymptotically normal:*

$$\sqrt{Th_T}[\hat{\gamma}_T^*(z) - \gamma^*(z)] \xrightarrow{d} N\left[0, \frac{\int K^2(v)dv}{2\sum_{n=1}^{\infty} f_n(z)} V[Y_{z_0}^* Y_{z_0+z}^*]\right],$$

where f_n *is the pdf of* $Z_{t+n} - Z_t$.

The asymptotic variance of the smoothed autocorrelogram depends on the degree of conditional heteroscedasticity of Y^* since

$$V(Y_{z_0}^* Y_{z+z_0}^*) = V(Y_{z_0}^* E[Y_{z+z_0}^* | Y_{z_0}^*]) + E[Y_{z_0}^{*2} V(Y_{z+z_0}^* | Y_{z_0}^*)].$$

Parametric Specification of Time Deformation. Let us consider a Gaussian autoregressive model in intrinsic time:

$$Y_z^* = m + \rho(Y_{z-1}^* - m) + \sigma\varepsilon_z^*, \ \varepsilon_z^* \sim N(0, 1),$$

and the time deformation

$$Z_t = g(t, X_t; b), \qquad (14.16)$$

satisfying a deterministic relationship with observed variables X_t. From the definition of the process in calendar time, we get

$$Y_t = m + \rho^{\Delta g(t,X_t;b)} (Y_{t-1} - m) + \sigma\left[\frac{1 - \rho^{2\Delta g(t,X_t;b)}}{1 - \rho^2}\right]^{1/2} \varepsilon_t,$$

where $\Delta g(t,X_t;b) = g(t,X_t;b) - g(t-1,X_{t-1}; b)$.

The parameters b, m, ρ, and σ can be estimated by maximizing the (partial) likelihood function:

$$\log L_T = \sum_{t=1}^{T} \left\{ -\frac{1}{2} \log 2\pi - \frac{1}{2} \log \left[\sigma^2 \frac{1 - \rho^{2\Delta g(t,X_t;b)}}{1 - \rho^2} \right] \right.$$

$$\left. -\frac{1}{2} \frac{[y_t - m - \rho^{\Delta g(t,X_t;b)} (y_{t-1} - m)]^2}{\sigma^2} \frac{1 - \rho^2}{1 - \rho^{2\Delta g(t,X_t;b)}} \right\}.$$

Then, for the associated estimator of b, denoted $\hat{b}$, the time deformation at time t can be approximated by

$$\hat{Z}_t = g(t,X_t;\hat{b}). \tag{14.17}$$

Finally, it may be interesting to specify the time deformation so that

$$g(t,X_t;0) = t. \tag{14.18}$$

This would allow us to test the null hypothesis $H_0 = \{b = 0\}$ to check whether the autoregressive model of price increments is also valid in calendar time.

Binomial Tree and Time Deformation
Time deformation is a core issue in option pricing. Let us consider the binomial tree, which underlies the standard Black-Scholes formula (see Chapter 11). It has been implicitly assumed that the trading dates, which correspond to the nodes of the tree, are regularly spaced. Whenever they are irregularly spaced, it is still possible to apply the pricing formula associated with the binomial tree under the following conditions: (1) There exists an asset that is risk-free between the consecutive trading dates (i.e., nodes), and (2) the horizon of the investment is equal to an integer mutiple of these trading dates. However, standard risk-free assets and derivatives are written in calendar time. For example, a European call with a maturity of 6 months is equivalent to a call option with a stochastic maturity obtained by replacing the 6-month time by a random number of transactions corresponding to the residual period.

14.3.3 Bid-Ask Curves

The dynamics of trade characteristics, such as trading dates, prices, and volumes, are determined by the dynamics of the order book. We noted in Section 14.1.3 that the content of the order book can be summarized partly by the demand and supply functions, that is, the bid and ask curves. In this section, we present dynamic factor models for the bid and ask curves in transaction time.

Let us consider the nth transaction on a selected trading day. For the transaction n, the observed bid and ask curves, denoted by $a_n(v)$, and $b_n(v)$, depend on the varying volume. For illustration, we plot in Figures 14.8

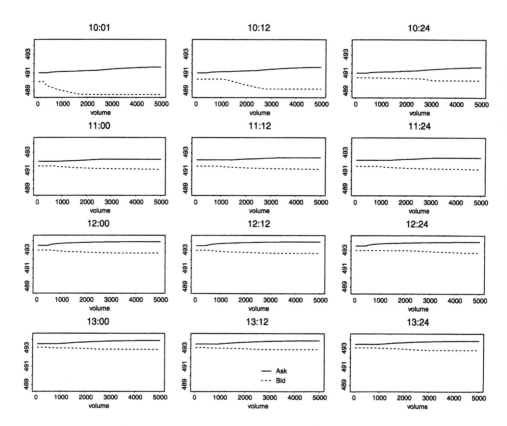

Figure 14.8   Bid and Ask Curves in the Morning, Alcatel

and 14.9 the bid and ask curves evaluated at different times of day for the Alcatel stock traded on the Paris Bourse.

Even though these curves are shifting throughout the day, some invariant patterns can still be revealed. We find that the vertical distance between the curves at small volumes is not related to the distance between them at larger volumes. There exist volume thresholds that distinguish the segments of curves that lie close to each other from the segments separated by a widening gap. These thresholds vary throughout the day. Moreover, the bid and ask curves are not symmetric beyond these thresholds. In terms of financial interpretation, the slopes of bid and ask curves represent the marginal effect of an additional unit of demand or supply on the price. The wider the discrepancy between the bid and ask curves, the higher the price volatility is. The slope asymmetry implies that the volatility can be different in the regimes of rising and falling prices. In

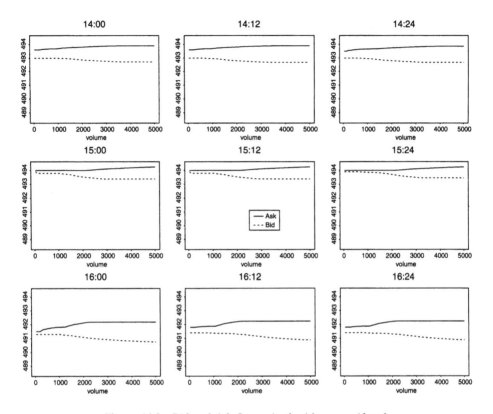

Figure 14.9 *Bid and Ask Curves in the Afternoon, Alcatel*

other words, it is linked to the so-called leverage effect captured by asymmetric ARCH models.

Gourieroux, Le Fol, and Meyer (1998) estimated a linear dynamic factor model (see Chapter 9) for the logarithms of bid and ask curves. Let us consider the two-factor model for log-transformed ask and bid quotes:

$$\begin{cases} \log a_t(v) = \alpha_0(v) + \alpha_1(v)F_{1,t} + \alpha_2(v)F_{2,t} + u_t(v), \\ \log b_t(v) = \beta_0(v) + \beta_1(v)F_{1,t} + \beta_2(v)F_{2,t} + v_t(v). \end{cases} \qquad (14.19)$$

The model includes the dynamic factors $F_{1,t}$ and $F_{2,t}$, the volume-dependent coefficients, and two error terms assumed independent of the factors. The errors, however, can be contemporaneously correlated across the bid and ask equations, as well as across pairs of ask prices associated with different volumes.

The ask data are doubly indexed by time and volume, and the factor decomposition is symmetric with respect to both indexes. For instance $F_{1,t}$ and $F_{2,t}$ are linear factors in a time factor representation of the log ask prices, whereas $\alpha_0(.)$, $\alpha_1(.)$, and $\alpha_2(.)$ are linear factors in a volume factor representation.

The estimation of this factor model of log bid-ask curves from data on the Alcatel stock produced the results below.

1. The time factors can be approximated by the mimicking factors:

$$\hat{F}_{1,t} = \log mid_t, \qquad \hat{F}_{2,t} = \log spread_t,$$

where $mid_t = \dfrac{1}{2}[a_t(50) + b_t(50)]$ is an average price of 50 shares, and $spread_t = a_t(2,000) - b_t(2,000)$ is the spread evaluated for 2,000 shares.
2. The dynamics of the mimicking factors is nonlinear autoregressive:

$$\Delta \log mid_t = -0.0002 + 0.0408|\Delta \log mid_{t-1}|,$$

$$\log spread_t = 0.333 + 0.203 \log spread_{t-1} - 37.33|\Delta\log mid_t|$$
$$+ 66.00|\Delta \log mid_{t-2}|.$$

3. The volume factors α and β are roughly piecewise linear functions with kinks at 1,000, 2,000, and 2,500 shares. Therefore, they are well approximated by splines of order 1 (Figure 14.10).

This example shows that

1. The middle price and the spread can be very informative when they are computed for appropriate volumes and not, as is traditional, for volumes equal to 1.
2. The factor models are useful for understanding the dynamics of curves, not just finite-dimensional variables.
3. Spline approximations of order 1 are especially appropriate for curves with path-dependent thresholds.

14.4   Intertrade Durations

In this section, we present dynamic models of intertrade durations. We denote by τ_n^m, $n = 1, \ldots, N^m$, $m = 1, \ldots, M$, the duration between the $(n-1)$th and the nth trades on day m. In the first section, we recall standard characteristics of a duration distribution, including the survivor function and the hazard function. In Section 14.4.2, we study the variation of empirical distributions of durations throughout the day. This provides a rationale for defining the activity and coactivity measures, which approximate intraday liquidity levels. The next two sections cover the

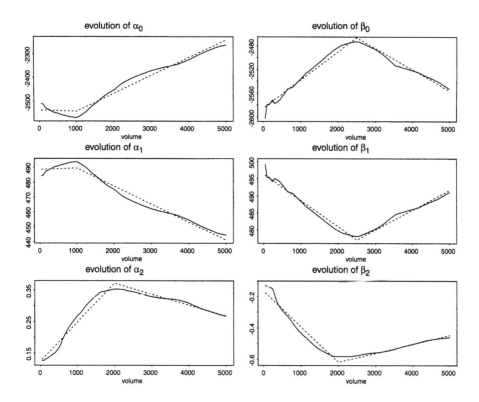

Figure 14.10 *Volume Factors and Spline Approximations*

modeling of intertrade durations. In particular, we introduce the extensions of the ARCH and stochastic volatility models that accommodate the duration dynamics. Finally, we introduce in the last section the weighted durations, which measure the time necessary to trade a given number of shares or a given market value.

14.4.1 Duration Distribution

The probabilities of various outcomes of a random experiment can be defined either by the probability density function f or the cumulative distribution function F. They are given by

$$f(y) = \lim_{dy \to 0} \frac{P[y < \tau \le y + dy]}{dy}, \tag{14.20}$$

$$F(y) = P[\tau \le y], \tag{14.21}$$

where τ denotes the variable of interest. For a nonnegative duration variable, the density and the cumulative distribution functions satisfy the relationship

$$f(y) = \frac{dF(y)}{dy}, \tag{14.22}$$

$$F(y) = \int_0^y f(\tau)d\tau. \tag{14.23}$$

The distribution of duration variables can be characterized by other functions, admitting interesting interpretations.

The *survivor function* S measures the probability of a large duration, that is, the risk of low liquidity. It is defined by

$$S(y) = P[\tau > y], y \in \mathbf{R}^+. \tag{14.24}$$

This is a decreasing function with limiting values $S(0) = +1, S(+\infty) = 0$. It satisfies

$$S(y) = 1 - F(y) = \int_y^{+\infty} f(\tau)d\tau. \tag{14.25}$$

The *hazard function* or *intensity* λ provides the instantaneous probability of occurrence of a trade after a time y when no trades have arrived; it is defined by

$$
\begin{aligned}
\lambda(y) &= \lim_{dy \to 0} \frac{1}{dy} P[y < \tau \le y + dy \,|\, \tau \ge y] \\
&= \lim_{dy \to 0} \frac{1}{dy} \frac{P[y < \tau \le y + dy]}{P[\tau \ge y]} \\
&= \frac{f(y)}{S(y)}.
\end{aligned}
\tag{14.26}
$$

From the hazard function, we derive the expression of the survivor function

$$
\begin{aligned}
\lambda(y) &= -\frac{1}{S(y)} \frac{dS(y)}{dy} \\
&= -\frac{d \log S(y)}{dy}.
\end{aligned}
$$

Therefore, we have

$$S(y) = \exp\left\{-\int_0^y \lambda(\tau)d\tau\right\}. \tag{14.27}$$

The elementary duration distribution is characterized by a constant hazard function $\lambda(y) = \lambda$. It means that the occurrence of a trade is independent of the time elapsed without trades. We immediately deduce from (14.27) that the associated duration distribution is such that

$$S(y) = \exp(-\lambda y)$$

$$\Leftrightarrow f(y) = \lambda \exp(-\lambda y).$$

This is the *exponential distribution*, with parameter λ, $\lambda > 0$. Its mean is equal to $E\tau = \lambda^{-1}$, whereas its variance is $V\tau = \lambda^{-2}$.

Other duration distributions introduced in the literature allow for different patterns of the hazard function.

EXAMPLE 14.2, GAMMA DISTRIBUTION: The family of gamma distributions is indexed by two positive parameters, v and λ. The $\gamma(v,\lambda)$ distribution admits the pdf

$$f(y) = \frac{1}{\Gamma(v)} \lambda^v y^{v-1} \exp - \lambda y, \qquad \text{for } y > 0,$$

where $\Gamma(v) = \int_0^\infty y^{v-1} \exp - y \, dy$. Its mean is equal to $E\tau = v/\lambda$, whereas its variance is $V\tau = v/\lambda^2$. It features an important property of invariance with respect to additivity of duration variables. For instance, if the intertrade durations are independent, with the same exponential distribution $\gamma(1, \lambda)$, then the duration between the trades n and $n+h$ follows the $\gamma(h, \lambda)$ distribution.

EXAMPLE 14.3, WEIBULL DISTRIBUTION: The Weibull distribution family is derived from the exponential family by a deterministic time deformation. The duration variable τ follows the Weibull distribution with parameters γ and λ, denoted by $W(\gamma, \lambda)$, if and only if $(\lambda\tau)^\gamma$ follows the exponential distribution $\gamma(1, 1)$. We deduce the hazard function, the survivor function, and the pdf:

$$\lambda(y) = \gamma\lambda(\lambda y)^{\gamma-1},$$

$$f(y) = \gamma\lambda(\lambda y)^{\gamma-1}\exp - (\lambda y)^\gamma,$$

$$S(y) = \exp - (\lambda y)^\gamma.$$

The hazard function is decreasing for $0 < \gamma < 1$ and increases otherwise. The first moments are

$$E\tau = \frac{1}{\lambda}\Gamma(1 + 1/\gamma), \quad V\tau = \lambda^{-2}[\Gamma(1 + 2/\gamma) - \Gamma(1 + 1/\gamma)^2].$$

EXAMPLE 14.4, THE BURR DISTRIBUTION: The hazard functions and pdf of the Burr distributions are given by

$$\lambda(y) = \frac{\xi y^{\xi-1}}{(1 + ay^\xi)},$$

$$f(y) = \frac{\xi y^{\xi-1}}{[1 + ay^\xi]^{\frac{a+1}{a}}},$$

where the parameters are constrained by $-\xi < 1 < \xi/a$, $a > 0$.
The family of Burr distributions includes

- the Weibull distributions in the limiting case $a \to 0$,
- the exponential distribution, when $a \to 0$ and $\xi = 1$,
- the log-logistic distribution.

14.4.2   Activity and Coactivity Measures

In this section, we examine the *trading intensity (rate)*, defined as the number of transactions concluded in a fixed time interval. The rationale for this approach is a duality between the modeling of duration dynamics and of the transaction rate dynamics. However, from the perspectives of a financial analyst interested in asset liquidity, the outcomes of both methods are equivalent.

The One-Asset Case
Before analyzing the temporal dependence of the transaction rate, it is important to eliminate potential sources of nonstationarities. For this reason, we need to investigate intraday periodicities, called the *intraday seasonalities*. Gourieroux, Jasiak, and Le Fol (1999) introduced a periodic model in which the transaction rate depends on the time of day:

$$P(\text{one trade between } t \text{ and } t + dt, \text{ day } m) = \lambda(t)dt + o(dt), \quad (14.28)$$

$$\begin{array}{l} P(\text{strictly more than one trade} \\ \text{between } t \text{ and } t + dt, \text{ day } m) = o(dt), \end{array} \quad (14.29)$$

where the time t is measured since the market opening on a given day m. Thus, λ depends on the time of day, but not on the day itself, which is the pertaining periodicity condition. Moreover, it does not depend on the entire trade history.

Let us denote by $N_m(t)$ the number of transactions on day m up to time t. It is known that

$$EN_m(t) = \int_o^t \lambda(u)du = \Lambda(t) \quad (\text{say}), \quad (14.30)$$

where Λ is the so-called cumulated hazard function.

A consistent estimator of the function Λ is obtained from trade observations on M consecutive days for a large M:

$$\hat{\Lambda}(t) = \frac{1}{M} \sum_{m=1}^{M} N_m(t). \quad (14.31)$$

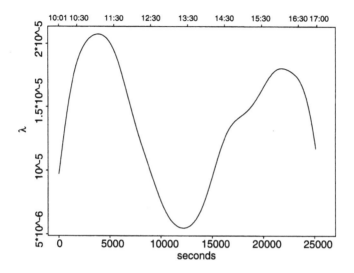

Figure 14.11 *Trading Rate, Alcatel*

Since the counting process $t \rightarrow N_m(t)$ is not differentiable, an estimator of the hazard function can only be derived after preliminary smoothing. A kernel estimator of the trading intensity λ is

$$\hat{\lambda}(t) = \frac{1}{M} \sum_{m=1}^{M} \sum_{n=1}^{N_m} \frac{1}{h_M} K \left[\frac{d_n(m) - t}{h_M} \right], \qquad (14.32)$$

where $d_n(m)$ is the time of the nth trade on day m, N_m is the total number of transactions, K is a kernel, and h_M is the bandwidth. The estimated trading rate for the Alcatel data is presented in Figure 14.11.

The trading rate is time dependent and features characteristic seasonal patterns: a low trade intensity shortly after the market opening and shortly before the closure; a minimal trade intensity at the lunch time; a high intensity at the opening of foreign markets, that is, the London Stock Exchange around 10:30 and the New York Stock Exchange (NYSE) around 15:30. The activity pattern is generally market dependent and varies across stock exchange markets. Especially, an M-shaped intensity is obtained for liquid assets traded on the Paris Bourse, while a U-shaped intensity is reported on the NYSE.

The Multiasset Framework
The previous analysis can be extended to a multiasset framework. For convenience, we consider two assets, 1 and 2. We define various periodic trading rates:

P (one trade between *t* and *t* + *dt*, day *m*, and this is a trade of asset 1
only) = $\lambda_{11}(t)dt + o(dt)$,

P (one trade between *t* and *t* + *dt*, day *m*, and this is a trade of asset 2
only) = $\lambda_{22}(t)dt + o(dt)$,

P (two trades between *t* and *t* + *dt*, day *m*, and these are trades of both
assets 1 and 2) = $\lambda_{12}(t)dt + o(dt)$,

P (no trades between *t* and *t* + *dt*, day *m*), = $1 - \lambda_{11}(t) - \lambda_{22}(t) - \lambda_{12}(t) + o(dt)$.

These various rates are related to counting processes that measure the
numbers of trades before *t* on day *m* for assets 1 and 2. They are denoted
by $N_m^1(t)$ and $N_m^2(t)$, respectively. Between *t* and *t* + *dt*, the increments of
the counting processes, that is, $N_m^1(t + dt) - N_m^1(t) = dN_m^1(t)$ and $N_m^2(t + dt) -
N_m^2(t) = dN_m^2(t)$, are either 0 or 1 if *dt* is sufficiently small.

We deduce that

$$E[dN_m^1(t)] \simeq \lambda_1(t)dt = [\lambda_{11}(t) + \lambda_{12}(t)]dt,$$

$$E[dN_m^2(t)] \simeq \lambda_2(t)dt = [\lambda_{22}(t) + \lambda_{12}(t)]dt,$$

$$V[dN_m^1(t)] \simeq \lambda_1(t)dt, \ V[dN_m^2(t)] \simeq \lambda_2(t)dt,$$

$$Cov[dN_m^1(t), \ dN_m^2(t)] \simeq \lambda_{12}(t)dt.$$

Thus, we can approximate the instantaneous trade occurrence at *t* by
the variance-covariance matrix

$$A(t) = \frac{1}{dt}V\begin{bmatrix} dN_m^1(t) \\ dN_m^2(t) \end{bmatrix} = \begin{bmatrix} \lambda_1(t) & \lambda_{12}(t) \\ \lambda_{12}(t) & \lambda_2(t) \end{bmatrix}. \tag{14.33}$$

This matrix measures the instantaneous liquidity risk and is similar
to the volatility-covolatility matrix that represents the risk on returns. Its
diagonal elements give the marginal trading rates of each asset (called
activity measures). The off-diagonal element λ_{12} is called the *coactivity measure*. It measures the intensity of simultaneous trades of both assets. Figure 14.12 shows the activity-coactivity measures for the stocks Alcatel and
St. Gobain traded on the Paris Bourse. The coactivity has been multiplied
by 2.10^6 to allow for a comparison.

14.4.3 *Autoregressive Conditional Duration*

The Models

In the spirit of ARCH models introduced for time series of returns, Engle
and Russell (1997, 1998a, 1998b) developed a similar specification for series
of durations. The basic idea consists of introducing a path-dependent time

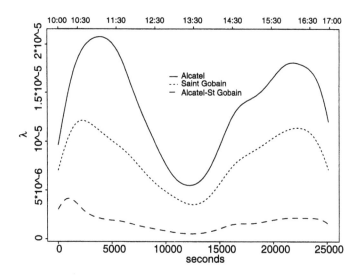

Figure 14.12 *Activity and Coactivity Measures, Alcatel–St. Gobain*

deformation such that the durations expressed on the new time scale are i.i.d.

More precisely, let us consider the sequence of observed durations τ_n, $n = 1, \ldots$. We denote by

$$\psi_n = a(\underline{\tau_{n-1}}), \tag{14.34}$$

a time scale function of the lagged durations. Then, we assume that

$$\tau_n / \psi_n = \varepsilon_n, \tag{14.35}$$

is a sequence of i.i.d. variables with the same distribution f. Expressions (14.34) and (14.35) define the family of autoregressive conditional duration (ACD) models. The ACD models differ by the assumptions on the functional form of time deformation and on the distribution of errors.

EXAMPLE 14.5: Engle and Russell proposed a type of ARMA dynamics for ψ_n: $\psi_n = w + \sum_{i=1}^{p} \alpha_i \tau_{n-i} + \sum_{j=1}^{q} \beta_j \psi_{n-j}$, where the parameters are nonnegative, $w > 0$, $\alpha_i \geq 0$, $\beta_j \geq 0$. This specification is analogous to the ARCH dynamics of volatilities (see Chapter 6) and is denoted ACD (p,q).

EXAMPLE 14.6: Bauwens and Giot (1998b) advocated a recursive equation of the log time deformation, which ensures the positivity of ψ_n without constraining a priori the autoregressive and moving average parameters. The idea is similar to that underlying exponential

GARCH models developed by Nelson (see Chapter 6). The logarithmic ACD (LACD) model is based on the recursive equation

$$\log \psi_n = w + \sum_{i=1}^{p} \alpha_i \tau_{n-i} + \sum_{j=1}^{p} \beta_j \log \psi_{n-j}.$$

EXAMPLE 14.7: Various assumptions can be imposed on the distribution of errors. Usually, they are assumed to belong to standard duration families presented in Section 14.4.1. By introducing a constant term into the ψ_n equation, we can always assume that the error term has a mean equal to 1. In particular, when ε_n admits an exponential distribution $\gamma(1,1)$, we get an exponential ACD (EACD) model. The Weibull ACD (WACD) model is obtained when ε_n follows a Weibull distribution with parameter γ, that is, when $\varepsilon_n^\gamma \sim \gamma(1, 1)$.

Stochastic Properties

The ACD models imply complicated nonlinear dynamics of durations. In particular, it is generally difficult to exhibit the (strong) stationarity conditions and to derive the marginal duration distribution. However, it is rather easy to study the conditional and marginal first- and second-order moments.

Let us note that relation (14.35) can be written as

$$\tau_n = \psi_n \varepsilon_n, \tag{14.36}$$

or as

$$\log \tau_n = \log \psi_n + \log \varepsilon_n. \tag{14.37}$$

From (14.37), we infer that

$$E(\tau_n | \underline{\tau_{n-1}}) = \psi_n E(\varepsilon_n | \underline{\tau_{n-1}}) = \psi_n, V(\tau_n | \underline{\tau_{n-1}}) = \psi_n^2 V(\varepsilon_n | \underline{\tau_{n-1}}) = \psi_n^2 \eta^2, \tag{14.38}$$

where η^2 is the variance of the distribution f. Thus, the first- and second-order conditional moments satisfy a deterministic relationship $V(\tau_n | \underline{\tau_{n-1}}) = \eta^2 [E(\tau_n | \underline{\tau_{n-1}})]^2$, which is path independent.

The expressions of the marginal mean and variance can be derived in special cases. Let us consider a WACD(1,1) model where

$$\psi_n = w + \alpha \tau_{n-1} + \beta \psi_{n-1}.$$

By taking the expectations on both sides, we get

$$E\psi_n = w + \alpha E\tau_{n-1} + \beta E\psi_{n-1} \Leftrightarrow E\tau_n = w + (\alpha + \beta)E\tau_{n-1}$$

$$\Leftrightarrow E\tau_n = \frac{w}{1 - \alpha - \beta}, \tag{14.39}$$

if the duration process is stationary.

A similar computation provides the marginal variance (see Engle and Russell [1998a]); we get

$$V\tau_n = (E\tau_n)^2 (V\varepsilon_n) \frac{1 - 2\alpha\beta - \beta^2}{1 - (\alpha + \beta)^2 - \alpha^2 V\varepsilon_n},\qquad(14.40)$$

where

$$V\varepsilon_n = \frac{\Gamma(1 + 2/\gamma)}{\Gamma(1 + 1/\gamma)^2} - 1.\qquad(14.41)$$

Semiparametric Estimation

A semiparametric ACD model for which the time deformation admits a parametric specification can be estimated by the quasi-maximum likelihood (QML). For example, in the following model,

$$\psi_n = a(\tau_{n-1}; \theta),\qquad(14.42)$$

the error distribution f is left unspecified. Under a QML method, the log-likelihood function can be computed as if the error terms were exponentially distributed. The associated quasi log-likelihood is

$$\log L(\theta) = \sum_{n=1}^{N} \log \left[\frac{1}{\psi_n} \exp\left(-\frac{\tau_n}{\psi_n} \right) \right]$$

$$= - \sum_{n=1}^{N} (\log \psi_n + \tau_n/\psi_n)\qquad(14.43)$$

$$= - \sum_{n=1}^{N} [\log a(\tau_{n-1}; \theta) + \tau_n/a(\tau_{n-1}; \theta)].$$

It has been proved by Gourieroux, Monfort, and Trognon (1984) that the QML estimator

$$\hat{\theta}_N = \underset{\theta}{\text{Arg min}} \ \log L(\theta),$$

is consistent of θ whatever is the unknown distribution f.

Given the estimated parameter $\hat{\theta}_N$, we find first the sequence of time deformations

$$\hat{\psi}_n = a(\tau_{n-1}; \hat{\theta}_N), \qquad n = 1, \ldots, N;$$

and second the residuals

$$\hat{\varepsilon}_n = \tau_n/\hat{\psi}_n, \qquad n = 1, \ldots, N.$$

In the next step, we can smooth the empirical distribution of the residuals to get a kernel estimator of the unknown error distribution f:

$$\hat{f}_N(\varepsilon) = \frac{1}{Nh_N} \sum_{n=1}^{K} K\left(\frac{\varepsilon - \hat{\varepsilon}_n}{h_N}\right), \tag{14.44}$$

where h_N denotes the bandwidth.

Parametric Estimation

When the distribution of the error term ε_n belongs to a given parametric family, we can perform the estimation by maximizing the associated likelihood function. For illustration, let us consider a WACD(1,1) model. The pdf of ε_n is $f(\varepsilon_n) = \gamma \varepsilon_n^{\gamma-1} \exp(-\varepsilon_n^\gamma)$, and the associated log-likelihood is

$$L = \sum_{n=1}^{N} [\log \gamma + (\gamma - 1) \log \tau_n - \gamma \log \psi_n - (\tau_n/\psi_{n+})^\gamma], \tag{14.45}$$

where $\psi_n = w + \alpha\tau_{n-1} + \beta\psi_{n-1}$. It can be optimized with respect to the parameters w, α, β, and γ.

14.4.4   Stochastic Volatility Duration Models

An important concept in the duration analysis is *conditional overdispersion*, defined as the ratio of the conditional variance and square conditional mean. It is easy to see that, for example, exponentially distributed i.i.d. durations feature constant conditional overdispersion. As well, the ACD processes presented in the previous section feature constant conditional overdispersion due to the assumption of a linear deterministic relationship between the conditional variance and squared conditional expectation. This is a drawback of ACD models since such a relationship is at odds with empirical evidence (see Figure 14.13).

A similar drawback has already been pointed out in the context of stock return analysis based on ARCH models. A remedy consists of allowing for independent variation of the two first-order conditional moments by introducing an additional error term to make the volatility stochastic. In this way, we obtained the so-called stochastic volatility model. By analogy Ghysels, Gourieroux, and Jasiak (1998a) introduced the stochastic volatility duration (SVD) model. Their approach is based on an alternative representation of exponential distributions with stochastic intensity rate.

1. Consider a static case for when the duration τ follows an exponential distribution with a stochastic, gamma-distributed intensity parameter. The duration can be written as:

$$\tau = X_1/\lambda = X_1/(aX_2), \quad a > 0, \tag{14.46}$$

where X_1 and X_2 are independent variables with distributions $\gamma(1, 1)$ and $\gamma(b,b)$, respectively. It is easily checked that the duration variable

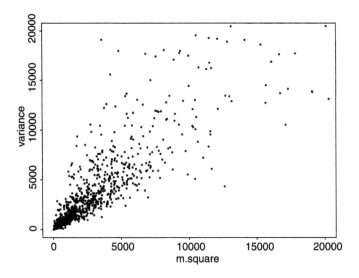

Figure 14.13 *Mean-Variance Representation of Durations*

τ admits a Pareto distribution with mean $E\tau = b[a(b-1)]^{-1}$ and variance $V\tau = b^3[a(b-1)]^{-2}(b-2)^{-1}$ for $b > 2$.

2. The gamma variables X_1 and X_2 can now be replaced by Gaussian simulators. Indeed, we can write

$$X_1 = H(1, F_1), \qquad X_2 = H(b, F_2), \tag{14.47}$$

where F_1 and F_2 are independent standard normal variables, $H(b, F) = G[b, \Phi(F)]$, $G(b,.)$ is the quantile function of the $\gamma(b, b)$ distribution, and Φ is the cumulative distribution function of the standard normal. Thus, we can express the duration variable τ as a deterministic nonlinear transformation of the bivariate Gaussian vector (F_1, F_2):

$$\tau = \frac{H(1, F_1)}{aH(b, F_2)}. \tag{14.48}$$

3. The SVD models are derived by imposing linear vector autoregressive moving average (VARMA) dynamics on the Gaussian factors (F_1, F_2).

As an illustration, let us consider the VAR(1) (vector autoregressive processs order 1) process. This SVD model is a nonlinear factor model defined by the measurement equation

$$\tau_n = \frac{H(1, F_{1n})}{aH(b, F_{2n})},$$

and the transition equation

$$F_n = \begin{pmatrix} F_{1n} \\ F_{2n} \end{pmatrix} = \psi F_{n-1} + (Id - \psi\psi')^{1/2} \, \varepsilon_n,$$

where (ε_n) is a bivariate Gaussian white noise $\varepsilon_n \sim N(0, Id)$.

By constraining the variance of the noise in the transition equation to an identity matrix and by setting the constant term equal to 0, we ensure that the marginal distribution of the factor F_n is $N(0, Id)$. As a consequence, the marginal distribution of the duration is of the Pareto type.

14.4.5 Weighted Durations

Until now, all durations in the sample were given equal weights regardless of the price and volume characteristics of the associated trade. Accordingly, in Section 14.4.2, while counting the number of transactions $N_m(t)$ before time t on day m, we attributed the same weight to all transactions. Under this approach, we cannot distinguish a trade of 100 shares from a trade of 10,000 shares. In this section, we explain how to assign adequate weights to trade counts and to define the resulting weighted durations. As an illustration, we consider the volume-weighted durations.

Let us introduce the cumulated volume traded before t on day m:

$$V_m(t) = \sum_{n=1}^{N_m(t)} v_n^m, \tag{14.49}$$

where v_n^m is the traded volume for transaction n on day m. When the time t varies, we get an increasing process of a (stochastic) time deformation. This process can be used to define weighted durations in the following way. Let us introduce a given volume threshold v_0, say. We can define the time $d_n^m(v_0)$, n varying, elapsed since the market opening on day m that is necessary to trade a volume nv_0:

$$d_n^m(v_0) = \inf \{ t : V_m(t) \geq nv_0 \}. \tag{14.50}$$

We get a series of volume-weighted durations between successive crossing times of the volume level v_0:

$$\tau_n^m(v_0) = d_n^m(v_0) - d_{n-1}^m(v_0). \tag{14.51}$$

The volume-weighted durations arise from mixing the volume per trade and the trading frequency effects.

Other weighted durations have also been proposed in the literature.

First, let us define the cumulated market value traded before t on day m:

$$C_m(t) = \sum_{n=1}^{N_m(t)} p_n^m v_n^m,$$

where p_n^m is the trading price per share for the trade n.

Then, we consider a market value threshold c_0 and define:

$$d_n^m(c_0) = inf\ \{t\ :\ C_m(t) \ge nc_0\},$$

$$\tau_n^m(c_0) = d_n^m(c_0) - d_{n-1}^m(c_0).$$

Second, we can also study duration between large price movements. Let us fix a number of ticks Δ, say. The price at t is defined by

$$p_m(t) = p_{N(t)}^m.$$

Then, we define:

$$\tau_1^m(\Delta) = inf\ \{t\ :\ |p_{N(t)}^m - p_0^m| > \Delta\},$$

$$\tau_2^m(\Delta) = inf\ \{t \ge \tau_1^m\ (\Delta)\ :\ |p_{N(t)}^m - p_{\tau_1^m(\Delta)}^m| > \Delta,$$

and so on.

14.5 Joint Analysis of Prices, Volumes, and Trading Dates

The challenging task of joint modeling of prices, volumes, and trading dates has been undertaken by a limited number of researchers (Engle and Russell 1998b; Darolles, Gourieroux, and Le Fol 2000; Hamilton and Jorda 1999). In the first section, we discuss the principles of joint modeling and explore the relationship between joint and individual series models, such as the ACD model of intertrade durations.

14.5.1 Basic Models

Let us first introduce the observed variables of interest, along with the notation used in the remainder of the section:

1. $m = 1, \ldots, M$ is the day index.
2. $n = 0,\ 1, \ldots,\ N_m$ is the transaction index on day m with $n = 0$ for opening.
3. d_n^m, is the nth transaction time on day m elapsed since the opening ($d_0^m = 0$).
4. τ_n^m is the duration between consecutive $(n-1)$th and nth transactions $\tau_n^m = d_n^m - d_{n-1}^m$.
5. p_n^m is the price of transaction n on day m; $x_n^m = p_n^m - p_0^m$ denotes the price modification since the opening.

6. v_n^m is the associated volume.

7. z_n^m is the variable taking 0–1 values to indicate if the trade is buyer or seller initiated: $z_n^m = 1$ if the price is an ask price and $z_n^m = 0$ if it is a bid price. This indicator variable is defined for all trades of the continuous session, excluding the opening.

Let us examine the joint distribution of d_n^m, p_n^m, v_n^m, z_n^m, $m = 1, \ldots, M$, $n = 1, \ldots, N_m$. When the number of observations is large, it can be written as a product of conditional distributions indexed by the day and transaction count:

$$L = \prod_{m=1}^{M} \prod_{n=0}^{N_m} l\left(d_n^m, p_n^m, v_n^m, z_n^m \mid \underline{d_{n-1}^m}, \underline{p_{n-1}^m}, \underline{v_{n-1}^m}, \underline{z_{n-1}^m}\right), \tag{14.52}$$

where $\underline{d_{n-1}^m}$ is the information that includes the past trading dates recorded on either the same day or the days before.

Dynamics of Market Openings and Intraday Movements
The matching procedure at market opening is generally different from the continuous order matching during the day. For this reason, it is important to distinguish the variables that characterize the opening period from those that characterize the intraday market activity. While all variables 1–7 listed above can potentially be used to characterize trades, we focus only on the joint dynamics of durations, prices, volumes, and trade initiating market side indicators. Their joint distribution can be decomposed as

$$L = \prod_{m=1}^{M} l\left(d_0^m, p_0^m, v_0^m \mid \underline{d_0^m}, \underline{p_0^m}, \underline{v_0^m}, \underline{z_0^m}\right)$$

$$\prod_{n=1}^{N} l\left(\tau_n^m, x_n^m, v_n^m, z_n^m \mid \underline{d_{n-1}^m}, \underline{p_{n-1}^m}, \underline{v_{n-1}^m}, \underline{z_{n-1}^m}\right). \tag{14.53}$$

The following assumptions allow us to establish a link between (14.53) and standard daily data models, as well as to compare the opening and continuous trading periods. They essentially concern the components of the likelihood decomposition.

ASSUMPTION A.14.10: *The conditional distribution of the opening trade characteristics depends on the past through the lagged opening trade characteristics on preceeding days. Let us denote*

$$\underline{d_0^{m-1}} = \left(d_0^{m-1}, d_0^{m-2}, \ldots\right), \qquad \underline{p_0^{m-1}} = \left(p_0^{m-1}, p_0^{m-2}, \ldots\right), \qquad \underline{v_0^{m-1}} = \left(v_0^{m-1}, v_0^{m-2}, \ldots\right),$$

we get

$$l\left(d_0^m,p_0^m,v_0^m \mid \underline{d_0^m},\underline{p_0^m},\underline{v_0^m},\underline{z_0^m}\right) = l\left(d_0^m,p_0^m,v_0^m \mid \underline{d_0^{m-1}},\underline{p_0^{m-1}},\underline{v_0^{m-1}}\right).$$

When both the opening and closure matching procedures are call auctions, we may impose similar assumptions on the opening and closure trade characteristics.

ASSUMPTION A.14.11: *The conditional distribution of intraday trade characteristics depends on their past values pertaining to the same day.*

Let us denote $\underline{d_{n-1}^m} = (d_{n-1}^m, d_{n-2}^m, \ldots, d_1^m)$ and use similar notation for other possible trade characteristics x_n given above; we get

$$l\left(\tau_n^m,x_n^m,v_n^m,z_n^m \mid \underline{d_{n-1}^m},\underline{p_{n-1}^m},\underline{v_{n-1}^m},\underline{z_{n-1}^m}\right)$$

$$= l\left(\tau_n^m,\ x_n^m,v_n^m,z_n^m \mid \underline{d_{n-1}^m},\underline{x_{n-1}^m},\underline{v_{n-1}^m},\underline{z_{n-1}^m},d_0^m,p_0^m,v_0^m\right),$$

in which the opening trade characteristics in the conditioning set are distinguished from those of the continuous matching.

ASSUMPTION A.14.12: *The intraday dynamics does not depend on the opening characteristics. This assumption is*

$$l\left(\tau_n^m,x_n^m,v_n^m,z_n^m \mid \underline{d_{n-1}^m},\underline{x_{n-1}^m},\underline{v_{n-1}^m},\ \underline{z_{n-1}^m},d_0^m,p_0^m,v_0^m\right)$$

$$= l\left(\tau_n^m,x_n^m,v_n^m,z_n^m \mid \underline{d_{n-1}^m},\underline{x_{n-1}^m},\underline{v_{n-1}^m},\underline{z_{n-1}^m}\right).$$

In the section below, we focus on this last density decomposition, while examining the dynamics of τ_n^m, x_n^m, v_n^m, and z_n^m.

Decompositions of Intraday Dynamics
The existing applications are focused on subsets of trade characteristics, like price changes and dates (Bauwens and Giot 1998a; Hamilton and Jorda 1999); prices, volumes, and dates (Engle and Russell 1998b); signed ask prices and trading dates (Darolles, Gourieroux, and Le Fol 2000). They all emphasize the discreteness of price changes with a limited number of admissible values. These specifications differ essentially with respect to the assumptions imposed on the structure of causal relationships between the variables. For expositional convenience, let us consider a bivariate series of price changes and trading dates, disregarding the influence of other variables. The conditional joint distribution of τ_n^m,x_n^m can be decomposed as

$$l\left(\tau_n^m,x_n^m \mid \underline{\tau_{n-1}^m},\underline{x_{n-1}^m}\right)$$

$$= l\left(\tau_n^m \mid x_n^m,\underline{\tau_{n-1}^m},\underline{x_{n-1}^m}\right)l\left(x_n^m \mid \underline{\tau_{n-1}^m},\underline{x_{n-1}^m}\right)$$

$$= l\left(\tau_n^m \mid \underline{\tau_{n-1}^m},\underline{x_{n-1}^m}\right)l\left(x_n^m \mid \tau_n^m,\underline{\tau_{n-1}^m},\underline{x_{n-1}^m}\right).$$

To use the ACD representation of duration dynamics, Engle and Russel (1998b) considered the second line of the decomposition given above and assumed that

$$l\left(\tau_n^m \mid \underline{\tau_{n-1}^m, x_n^m}\right) = l\left(\tau_n^m \mid \underline{\tau_{n-1}^m}\right),$$

that is, imposed a unidirectional noncausality from prices to trading dates. Darolles, Gourieroux, and Le Fol (2000) considered instead the first line of the decomposition and assumed

$$l\left(x_n^m \mid \underline{\tau_{n-1}^m, x_n^m}\right) = l\left(x_n^m \mid \underline{\tau_{n-1}^m}\right),$$

that is, imposed a unidirectional noncausality from trading dates to prices. The latter noncausality hypothesis has a direct financial interpretation. It means that lagged prices are fully informative to predict current prices, which is a weak form of the market efficiency hypothesis.

To illustrate the differences between these specifications, let us consider the conditional distribution

$$l\left(\tau_n^m \mid x_n^m, \underline{\tau_{n-1}^m, x_{n-1}^m}\right).$$

If the admissible price movements are restricted to $+1$, -1 only, and the ACD model is used to represent the duration dynamics, we obtain various forms of time deformation depending on the conditioning variables

$$\tau_n^m = \psi_n^m\left(x_n^m, \underline{\tau_{n-1}^m, x_{n-1}^m}\right)\varepsilon_n^m,$$

where the variables (ε_n^m) are i.i.d. The following terms

$$\psi_n^{m,+} = \psi_n^m\left(1, \ \underline{\tau_{n-1}^m, x_{n-1}^m}\right),$$

$$\psi_n^{m,-} = \psi_n^m\left(-1, \ \underline{\tau_{n-1}^m, x_{n-1}^m}\right).$$

define two forms of time deformation pertaining to the two admissible future price regimes. Their dynamics may be defined by a bivariate system like the following one:

$$\psi_n^{m,+} = a_{1,1}\mathbf{1}_{x_{n-1}^m=1} + a_{1,0}\mathbf{1}_{x_{n-1}^m=-1} + b_{1,1}\mathbf{1}_{x_{n-1}^m=1}x_{n-1}^m + b_{1,0}\mathbf{1}_{x_{n-1}^m=-1}x_{n-1}^m$$
$$+ c_{1,1}\mathbf{1}_{x_{n-1}^m=1}\psi_{n-1}^{m,+} + c_{1,0}\mathbf{1}_{x_{n-1}^m=-1}\psi_{n-1}^{m,+} + d_{1,1}\mathbf{1}_{x_{n-1}^m=1}\psi_{n-1}^{m,-} + d_{1,0}\mathbf{1}_{x_{n-1}^m=-1}\psi_{n-1}^{m,-}$$

$$\psi_n^{m,-} = \alpha_{1,1}\mathbf{1}_{x_{n-1}^m=1} + \alpha_{1,0}\mathbf{1}_{x_{n-1}^m=-1} + \beta_{1,1}\mathbf{1}_{x_{n-1}^m=1}x_{n-1}^m + \beta_{1,0}\mathbf{1}_{x_{n-1}^m=-1}x_{n-1}^m$$
$$+ \gamma_{1,1}\mathbf{1}_{x_{n-1}^m=1}\psi_{n-1}^{m,+} + \gamma_{1,0}\mathbf{1}_{x_{n-1}^m=-1}\psi_{n-1}^{m,+} + \delta_{1,1}\mathbf{1}_{x_{n-1}^m=1}\psi_{n-1}^{m,-} + \delta_{1,0}\mathbf{1}_{x_{n-1}^m=-1}\psi_{n-1}^{m,-}.$$

Eventually, various noncausality hypotheses can be tested by comparing the estimated coefficients. For instance, the lagged price change has no effect if $a_{1,1} = a_{1,0}$, $b_{1,1} = b_{1,0}$, $c_{1,1} = c_{1,0}$, $d_{1,1} = d_{1,0}$, $\alpha_{1,1} = \alpha_{1,0}$, $\beta_{1,1} = \beta_{1,0}$, $\gamma_{1,1} = \gamma_{1,0}$, $\delta_{1,1} = \delta_{1,0}$.

14.6 Summary

Electronic trading systems have increased the amount and variety of information about market mechanisms. This knowledge can be exploited to improve existing models by taking into account traded volumes, timing of trades, evolution of the order book, and noncompetitive behavior of some investors. The aim of this chapter was to define precisely the automatic trading system, describe the available data, and present some stylized facts. As well, we introduced dynamic models that can explain the patterns of prices, volumes, and trading dates. The analysis of high-frequency data is certainly one of the most promising fields for future research in financial econometrics. It also has the potential of providing important insights into financial theory. For example, in the future, it will allow rethinking of the notion of liquidity and incorporating the liquidity risk in efficient portfolio management.

Appendix 14.1: Equations Defining the Bid-Ask Prices

LEMMA 14.1: *If* $X \sim N(m, \sigma^2)$, *then*

(i) $E[X|X > a] = m + \sigma \mu \left(\dfrac{a - m}{\sigma} \right)$,

(ii) $E[X|X < a] = m + \sigma \mu \left(\dfrac{m - a}{\sigma} \right)$,

where $\mu(x) = \varphi(x)/[1 - \Phi(x)]$ *is the hazard function of the standard normal distribution.*

PROOF:

(i) Let us write $X = m + \sigma u$, where u is standard normal. We get

$$E(X|X > a) = E(m + \sigma u | m + \sigma u > a)$$

$$= m + \sigma E \left(u \middle| u > \frac{a - m}{\sigma} \right)$$

$$= m + \sigma \int_{(a-m)/\sigma}^{+\infty} u\varphi(u)du \left[1 - \Phi \left(\frac{a - m}{\sigma} \right) \right]^{-1}$$

$$= m + \sigma \mu \left(\frac{a - m}{\sigma} \right).$$

(ii) We get

$$E[X|X<a] = -E[-X| - X > -a]$$

$$= (-m) + \sigma\mu\left(\frac{-a - (-m)}{\sigma}\right)$$

$$= m + \sigma\mu\left(\frac{m - a}{\sigma}\right), \qquad \text{from (i).}$$

QED

Equations
Let us consider the equation that defines the ask quote. We can write

$$p^*_{t+1} = \alpha_t + \beta_t\psi_{t+1} + \gamma_t u,$$

where u and ψ_{t+1} are independent, $u \sim N(0, 1)$ and $\psi_{t+1} \sim N[m_{2,t}, \sigma_{2,2t}]$ conditional on I_t. Therefore,

$$a_t = E\left[p^*_{t+1}|I_t, \psi_{t+1} > \left(a_t - \alpha_t + \frac{A}{2}\gamma_t^2\right)/\beta_t\right]$$

$$= \alpha_t + \beta_t E\left[\psi_{t+1}|I_t, \psi_{t+1} > \left(a_t - \alpha_t + \frac{A}{2}\gamma_t^2\right)/\beta_t\right]$$

$$= \alpha_t + \beta_t\left\{m_{2,t} + \sigma_{22,t}^{1/2}\mu\left[\frac{a_t - \alpha_t + \frac{A}{2}\gamma_t^2}{\beta_t\sigma_{22,t}^{1/2}} - \frac{m_{2,t}}{\sigma_{22,t}^{1/2}}\right]\right\}$$

$$= m_{1,t} + \beta_t\sigma_{22,t}^{1/2}\mu\left[\frac{a_t - \alpha_t + \frac{A}{2}\gamma_t^2}{\beta_t\sigma_{22,t}^{1/2}} - \frac{m_{2,t}}{\sigma_{22,t}^{1/2}}\right].$$

Similarly, we get

$$b_t = E\left[p^*_{t+1}|I_t, \psi_{t+1} < \left(b_t - \alpha_t - \frac{A}{2}\gamma_t^2\right)/\beta_t\right]$$

$$= m_{1,t} + \beta_t\sigma_{22,t}^{1/2}\mu\left[\frac{m_{2,t}}{\sigma_{22,t}^{1/2}} - \frac{b_t - \alpha_t - \frac{A}{2}\gamma_t^2}{\beta_t\sigma_{22,t}^{1/2}}\right].$$

Appendix 14.2   Global or Sequential Matching

LEMMA 14.2: *The price p^a lies between p_1 and p_2.*

PROOF: The price p^a corresponds to a zero global excess demand:

$$\alpha(p^a) = 0,$$

where $\alpha(p) = D_1(p) + D_2(p) - S_1(p) - S_2(p)$ is a decreasing function. The price p_2 is such that

$$\alpha^*(p_2) = 0,$$

where $\alpha^*(p) = D_2(p) + (D_1(p) - v_1)^+ - S_2(p) - (S_1(p) - v_1)^+$ is a decreasing function.

Moreover, the price p_1 gives a null excess demand $D_1 - S_1$ or, equivalently, it solves

$$\beta(p_1) = 0,$$

where $\beta(p) = \alpha(p) - \alpha(p^*) = \min(0, D_1 - v_1) - \min(0, S_1 - v_1)$. This last function is decreasing, with positive values for $p < p_1$ and negative values otherwise. We can also note that

$$\alpha(p) = \alpha^*(p) + \beta(p).$$

Let us now consider the case $p_1 < p_2$ (the reasoning is similar in the opposite case). We get

$$\alpha(p_1) = \alpha^*(p_1) + \beta(p_1) = \alpha^*(p_1) > 0,$$
$$\alpha(p_2) = \alpha^*(p_2) + \beta(p_2) = \beta(p_2) < 0.$$

By the mean value theorem, we deduce that $p^a \in [p_1, p_2]$.
QED

LEMMA 14.3: *$v^a \leq v_1 + v_2$, and if $p_1 < p_2$, any seller served at T by the global matching is also served by the sequential procedure.*

PROOF: It is sufficient to prove the second part of the lemma, which has a first part that is a direct consequence. Let us now consider the sell orders in the sequential procedure.

If the limiting price is $p < p_1$ and the order enters in the first subperiod, it is filled at T_1.

If the limiting price is $p < p_1$ and the order enters in the second subperiod, it is filled at T.

If the limiting price is between p_1 and p_2, it is filled at T.

The result follows.
QED

15

Market Indexes

THE STOCK MARKET INDEXES play an important role in finance. They summarize joint evolution of multiple assets, provide proxies for market portfolios, and consequently allow testing of structural models such as the Capital Asset Pricing Model (CAPM). There exist derivatives written on stock indexes that belong to the most actively traded assets on stock markets. In the first section, we recall standard definitions of price indexes. The concept of stock market indexes is borrowed from consumption theory. Indeed, the first indexes ever built were the consumer price indexes. They were introduced into the literature at the end of the nineteenth century to examine the effect of gold mine discoveries on inflation (see, e.g., Laspeyres 1864; Jevons 1863, 1865; Kramar 1886; Nicholson 1887). Two widely used index formulas are the so-called Laspeyres and Paasche indexes; we compare their properties. The second section is devoted to the use and description of stock market indexes. In Section 15.3, we explain why a linear dynamic factor model fails to accommodate asset prices and market indexes simultaneously. Finally, in Section 15.4, we discuss the endogenous selection of weights and assets included in market indexes.

15.1 Price Indexes

15.1.1 Basic Notions

The use of stock market indexes follows from the tradition of computing standard consumer price indexes (see, e.g., Laspeyres 1864; Jevons 1865; Paasche 1870; Schumpeter 1905; Fisher 1922; Konus 1939). Therefore, it is insightful to recall the definitions of consumer price indexes before introducing the stock market indexes.

Let us consider two states, corresponding to two distinct dates, denoted 0 and 1. The consumption bundle includes n goods, with quantities
$q_0 = (q_{10}, \ldots, q_{n0})'$ in state 0 and $q_1 = (q_{11}, \ldots, q_{n1})'$ in state 1. The associated
price vectors are $p_0 = (p_{10}, \ldots, p_{n0})'$ and $p_1 = (p_{11}, \ldots, p_{n1})'$. The modification of consumer expenditure between the two states is

$$\frac{W_1}{W_0} = \frac{p_1' q_1}{p_0' q_0}$$

$$= \frac{p_1' q_1}{p_1' q_0} \frac{p_1' q_0}{p_0' q_0} \tag{15.1}$$

$$= \frac{p_0' q_1}{p_0' q_0} \frac{p_1' q_1}{p_0' q_1}.$$

The second factor of this multiplicative decomposition captures the
price effect for an unchanged bundle of goods, whereas the first factor
measures the quantity effect evaluated at the same price levels. The price
and quantity effects differ essentially in terms of weights, which may correspond to either state 0 or state 1. By convention, an index with weights
that correspond to state 0 is called the *Laspeyres index*. When the weights
correspond to state 1, it is called the *Paasche index*. We distinguish four
different indexes underlying decomposition (15.1), namely,

a Laspeyres index for prices

$$\mathcal{L}_{1/0}(p) = \frac{p_1' q_0}{p_0' q_0}, \tag{15.2}$$

a Paasche index for prices

$$\mathcal{P}_{1/0}(p) = \frac{p_1' q_1}{p_0' q_1}, \tag{15.3}$$

a Laspeyres index for quantities

$$\mathcal{L}_{1/0}(q) = \frac{p_0' q_1}{p_0' q_0}, \tag{15.4}$$

and a Paasche index for quantities

$$\mathcal{P}_{1/0}(q) = \frac{p_1' q_1}{p_1' q_0}. \tag{15.5}$$

Thus, the decomposition of the relative expenditure modification can be
written as

$$W_1/W_0 = \mathcal{L}_{1/0}(p)\mathcal{P}_{1/0}(q) = \mathcal{P}_{1/0}(p)\mathcal{L}_{1/0}(q). \tag{15.6}$$

15.1.2 Fixed-Base versus Chain Index

A multiplicative decomposition involving more than two states (i.e., dates) is rather complex. However, it has to be determined whenever a consumption pattern over a sequence of dates $t = 0, 1, 2, \ldots$ is examined. In such a case, several alternative approaches can be adopted.

Fixed Base
We can select a benchmark state (date), set by convention at $t = 0$, that is used to define the weights of the Laspeyres indexes at all future dates. Then, we have

$$W_t/W_0 = \mathcal{L}_{t/0}(p)\mathcal{P}_{t/0}(q)$$

$$= \frac{p_t'q_0}{p_0'q_0}\frac{p_t'q_t}{p_t'q_0}.$$

A set of coherent measures of price evolutions is defined by the ratio

$$I_t = \frac{p_t'q_0}{p_0'q_0}, \qquad t = 0, 1, \ldots, \tag{15.7}$$

which is called the index value with base 0. The corresponding evolution of the index between t and $t + h$ is

$$I_{t+h/t} = \frac{I_{t+h}}{I_t}.$$

This expression measures the change of the value of a fixed consumption bundle q_0 between t and $t + h$.

Chain Index
The benchmark state can be successively changed at each date (Marshall 1887). The idea is to consider the subsequent decompositions

$$\frac{W_t}{W_{t-1}} = \mathcal{L}_{t/t-1}(p)\mathcal{P}_{t/t-1}(q)$$

$$= \frac{p_t'q_{t-1}}{p_{t-1}'q_{t-1}}\frac{p_t'q_t}{p_t'q_{t-1}},$$

and to measure the price evolution between $t - 1$ and t by

$$I_{t/t-1} = \frac{p_t'q_{t-1}}{p_{t-1}'q_{t-1}}. \tag{15.8}$$

The price index is finally defined by

$$I_t = \prod_{\tau=1}^{t} I_{\tau/\tau-1}, \tag{15.9}$$

with $I_0 = 1$, by convention.

Alternatively, the composite indexes can be based on the Paasche formula, for which temporal consistency is ensured by the chain index

$$I_t^* = \prod_{\tau=1}^{t} I_{t/t-1}^*, \qquad \text{where } I_{t/t-1}^* = \frac{p_t' q_t}{p_{t-1}' q_t}.$$

Even though it seems more natural to select weights corresponding to date $t-1$ rather than weights corresponding to a future date t, we have to remember that decomposition formula (15.6) represents a mixture of the Laspeyres and Paasche indexes. Generally, when alternative states correspond to different dates, Laspeyres price indexes are selected. For international comparisons for which the states correspond to different countries, both indexes can be considered.

15.1.3 Comparison of Laspeyres and Paasche Indexes

The selection of weights may have a significant impact on the measure of price evolution. A comparison between the Laspeyres and Paasche indexes provides insights on the direction and magnitude of these effects. We consider again the two-state setup.

PROPOSITION 15.1:

(i) $\mathcal{L}_{1/0}(p) = \sum_{i=1}^{n} \alpha_{i0} \dfrac{p_{i1}}{p_{i0}}$, *where* $\alpha_{i0} = p_{i0} q_{i0} / p' _0 q_0$.

(ii) $\mathcal{P}_{1/0}(p) = \left(\sum_{i=1}^{n} \alpha_{i1} \dfrac{p_{i0}}{p_{i1}} \right)^{-1}$, *where* $\alpha_{i1} = p_{i1} q_{i1} / p'_1 q_1$.

This proposition is easily proved. It provides an interpretation of the composite Laspeyres index as an arithmetic average of elementary price changes with weights corresponding to the budget shares α_{i0} in situation 0. Similarly, the composite Paasche index is a harmonic average of elementary price changes with weights corresponding to the budget shares α_{i1} in state 1.

Proposition 15.2 is directly implied by the Jensen inequality.

PROPOSITION 15.2: *If the budget shares are invariant* $\alpha_{i0} = \alpha_{i1}, \ \forall i$, *then* $\mathcal{L}_{1/0}(p) \geq \mathcal{P}_{1/0}(p)$.

Even if the budget shares are not invariant, this inequality is often satisfied in practice. This is due to Proposition 15.3.

PROPOSITION 15.3:

$$\mathcal{L}_{1/0}(p) - \mathcal{P}_{1/0}(p) = -\mathcal{L}_{1/0}(q)^{-1} cov_{\alpha_0} \left(\frac{p_{1i}}{p_{i0}}, \frac{q_{i1}}{q_{i0}} \right),$$

where cov_{α_0} denotes the covariance computed using the weights α_{i0}, $i = 1, \ldots, n$.

PROOF: We get

$$\mathcal{L}_{1/0}(p) - \mathcal{P}_{1/0}(p)$$

$$= \frac{\sum_{i=1}^{n} p_{i1} q_{i0}}{\sum_{i=1}^{n} p_{i0} q_{i0}} - \frac{\sum_{i=1}^{n} p_{i1} q_{i1}}{\sum_{i=1}^{n} p_{i0} q_{i1}}$$

$$= \sum_{i=1}^{n} \alpha_{i0} \frac{p_{i1}}{p_{i0}} - \left(\sum_{i=1}^{n} \alpha_{i0} \frac{p_{i1}}{p_{i0}} \frac{q_{i1}}{q_{i0}} \right) \left(\sum_{i=1}^{n} \alpha_{i0} \frac{q_{i1}}{q_{i0}} \right)^{-1}$$

$$= - \left(\sum_{i=1}^{n} \alpha_{i0} \frac{q_{i1}}{q_{i0}} \right)^{-1} cov_{\alpha_0} \left(\frac{p_{i1}}{p_{i0}}, \frac{q_{i1}}{q_{i0}} \right).$$

QED

Standard consumption theory implies that this quantity is nonnegative. Indeed, if the elementary price ratio p_{i1}/p_{i0} is higher for good i, the good is perceived as expensive, and its consumption decreases. Therefore, we expect that q_{i1}/q_{i0} is a decreasing function of p_{i1}/p_{i0}. Hence, the covariance is negative, and the difference $\mathcal{L}_{1/0}(p) - \mathcal{P}_{1/0}(p)$ is positive.

15.2 Market Indexes

15.2.1 The Use of Market Indexes

Market indexes are designed for different purposes. They can be used as measures of asset price evolutions, benchmarks for evaluating the performance of portfolio management, support of derivatives, and economic indicators. Since these various functions are not entirely compatible, indexes with various characteristics need to be designed.

Measure of Asset Price Evolution
The indicator needs to allow for a clear and quick interpretation of the sign and size of price modifications. It has to be computationally simple and evaluated in practice from a limited sample of assets that quickly respond to shocks (i.e., are highly liquid). The weights may be set equal for all assets in the sample or else may depend on the current importance of assets in terms of their capitalization, that is, of the total capital corresponding to the issued shares.

Benchmark for Portfolio Management
Since a market index is often interpreted as the value of an efficient portfolio, it seems natural to assess the performance of a portfolio manager with respect to the performance of the market portfolio. We comment

below on the consequences of this practice on the composition of the market index.

First, in general, a portfolio manager adopts a dynamic strategy that involves frequent updating of the portfolio allocation. It is natural to compare the performance of this manager to the performance of the efficient dynamic portfolio that admits a priori time-varying allocations. Thus, it is preferable to select a benchmark with time-varying allocations (i.e., a chain index) instead of a Laspeyres index, which has a fixed allocation that corresponds to a static management scheme. This is the case when the market index is weighted by current capitalization.

Second, to assess personal performance, the manager takes into account the total return on his or her portfolio, including the modification of the portfolio value and cash flows received during the management period. Let us consider a stock index that can eventually account for the dividends:

$$\mathcal{L}_{t/t-1}(p) = \frac{\sum_{i=1}^{n} a_{i,t-1} p_{i,t}}{\sum_{i=1}^{n} a_{i,t-1} p_{i,t-1}}, \tag{15.10}$$

$$\mathcal{L}_{t/t-1}(p,d) = \frac{\sum_{i=1}^{n} a_{i,t-1}(p_{i,t} + d_{i,t})}{\sum_{i=1}^{n} a_{i,t-1} p_{i,t-1}}, \tag{15.11}$$

$$\mathcal{L}_{t/t-1}(p,d^*) = \frac{\sum_{i=1}^{n} a_{i,t-1}(p_{i,t} + d_{i,t}^*)}{\sum_{i=1}^{n} a_{i,t-1} p_{i,t-1}}, \tag{15.12}$$

where $a_{i,t-1}$ is the quantity in asset i for date $t-1$, $d_{i,t}$ is the dividend received between $t-1$ and t, and $d_{i,t}^*$ the dividend immediately reinvested in asset i. Therefore, it is useful to distinguish the *price index* (i.e., without dividends) from the *return index* (including dividends) since the modifications of the latter are always larger. The return index is an adequate benchmark for evaluation of portfolio performance, despite that in practice portfolio managers use price indexes, that are easier to outperform.

Third, finally note that market indexes are computed ex-post, that is, after observing the price. Such ex-post performance measures have to be distinguished from ex-ante measures, which take into account potential risk. Examples of such measures are the Sharpe performance coefficient (see Chapter 3) and the (conditional) Value at Risk (see Chapter 16).

Support of Derivatives
Options or futures on market indexes belong to the most frequently traded derivatives. They initially were introduced as hedging instruments against the market risk and are now used also by speculators, who try to benefit from transitory mispricing of these derivatives. The market indexes have to be updated very frequently (for instance, every 30 seconds)

to allow for frequent trading of the derivatives. They also have to be sufficiently volatile because otherwise risk on the market index would not be large enough, and the derivatives would be useless. As well, the way in which the selection and updating of weights is implemented has to prevent perfect arbitrage opportunities.

Economic Indicator

The stock indexes summarize the values of companies and reflect the underlying economic fundamentals. In this regard, they provide useful inputs into macroeconomic studies and national accounting. They can be compared to other price indexes, like consumer price indexes, which generally are Laspeyres indexes. For this type of application, the weights of Laspeyres market indexes need to ensure sectorial representativeness.

15.2.2 Main Stock Market Indexes

US Indexes

To the most commonly traded market indexes belong the indexes computed by Standard and Poor's (S&P), Dow Jones Company, or by major stock exchanges. The main indexes are weighted by current capitalization. The composite New York Stock Exchange (NYSE) and the NASDAQ (National Association of Securities Dealer Automated Quotation) are comprehensive indexes, including all assets that are quoted by these institutions. The composite NYSE includes about 1,600 stocks. The S&P 500 includes 500 stocks of the NYSE, representing about 80% of the capitalization. The S&P 100 includes the 100 most important ones. The S&P 400 Midcap includes 400 assets that do not belong to the S&P 500: 246 from the NYSE, 141 from the NASDAQ, and 13 from the AMEX (American Stock Exchange). The last three indexes support their own derivatives.

The Dow Jones is an index with equal weights. It includes 30 stocks that represent about 25% of the NYSE.

UK Indexes

The main indexes in the United Kingdom are jointly computed by the Financial Times and the London Stock Exchange (LSE). The FT-SE 100 (called *Footsie*) includes 100 assets that represent about 70% of the capitalization of the LSE. It is weighted by current capitalization and supports options and forward contracts.

The FT-30 includes 30 most important stocks, whereas the FT–Actuarial–All Shares is a general index. The latter index includes not only 650 stocks, but also bonds. It represents about 80% of the total capitalization.

Japanese Indexes

For a long time, the Nikkei was a market index with equal weights. The weights are now related to the capitalization. It includes about 225 stocks, for 70% of the total capitalization of the Tokyo Stock Exchange.

The TOPIX index is a comprehensive index for the first section of the Tokyo Stock Exchange (about 1,100 stocks). It is weighted by capitalization. Both indexes support their own derivatives.

French Indexes

French indexes are computed and diffused by the Paris Bourse (Euronext).

The CAC 40 (CAC is for Cotation Assistée en Continu, i.e., continuous quotation) is continuously computed and diffused every 30 seconds. It supports derivatives and includes 40 important stocks.

The general indexes SBF 120 and 250 (Société des Bourses Françaises) are computed daily. They include 120 and 250 assets, respectively, and take into account the sectorial representativeness.

The "indice second marché" is an index for emerging markets. It is computed daily and is a comprehensive index of the secondary market, with a highly volatile composition due to variation of companies who join or quit the index. Table 15.1 provides some insights on the dynamics of an emerging market.

Canadian Indexes

The Canadian indexes are managed by the Toronto Stock Exchange (TSE). The TSE 35 and TSE 100 include 35 and 100 of Canada's largest corporations, respectively. They support derivatives such as the TIPS 35 and TIPS

Table 15.1 *The Size of the Paris Secondary Market (1983–1991)*

Year	Number of Stocks (End of December)	Arriving		Quitting	
		Number	% of Total Capitalization	Number	% of Total Capitalization
1983	43	4			
1984	72	32	48%	3	30%
1985	127	56	51%	1	0.3%
1986	180	57	32%	4	8.6%
1987	258	87	36%	9	19%
1988	286	37	10%	9	17%
1989	298	39	13%	27	20%
1990	295	17	7%	20	14%
1991	288	13	2%	20	10%

100, which are portfolios that mimic the indexes. The TSE 300 composite index is the general index and includes 14 groups of companies.

15.2.3 Market Index and Market Portfolio

The test of the CAPM hypothesis is usually performed by regressing the asset returns (or gains) on the market portfolio return (or value modification). This regression may include an intercept that either is constant (Proposition 4.3) or depends on lagged variables (Proposition 6.4). Under the CAPM hypothesis, the intercept is equal to 0.

Market indexes are often used as proxies for the value of the market portfolio. This approximation may result in misleading conclusions on the CAPM hypothesis tests. This argument is known in the literature as the *Roll's critique* (Roll 1977). It is mainly due to the structure of market indexes with asset components that are time varying, whereas the market portfolio is theoretically based on a fixed set of assets. Contrary to the market portfolio, the weights in market indexes may be cap constrained. As well, the market indexes may or may not include dividends. A formal discussion of this problem is given below in the framework of an error-in-variable model.

Under the CAPM hypothesis, the regression model

$$Y_t = c + \beta Y_{m,t} + u_t,$$

where $Eu_t = 0$, $Cov(u_t, Y_{m,t}) = 0$, admits a zero intercept: $c = 0$. Let us assume that we approximate the market portfolio return $Y_{m,t}$ by the rate of increase of a market index $I_{m,t}$, say, and consider the regression

$$Y_t = c^* + \beta^* I_{m,t} + u_t^*,$$

where $Eu_t^* = 0$, $Cov(u_t^*, I_{m,t}) = 0$. We get

$$c^* = EY_t - \frac{Cov(Y_t, I_{m,t})}{V(I_{m,t})} E(I_{m,t}) \tag{15.13}$$

$$= \frac{Cov(Y_t, Y_{m,t})}{V(Y_{m,t})} E(Y_{m,t}) - \frac{Cov(Y_t, I_{m,t})}{V(I_{m,t})} E(I_{m,t}). \tag{15.14}$$

In general, this coefficient is different from 0. For instance, in the error-in-variable model,

$$I_{m,t} = Y_{m,t} + \eta_t,$$

where $E\eta_t = 0$, $Cov(\eta_t, Y_{m,t}) = 0$, $Cov(\eta_t, Y_t) = 0$, the intercept is equal to

$$c^* = \frac{Cov(Y_t,Y_{m,t})}{V(Y_{m,t})}E(Y_{m,t}) - \frac{Cov(Y_t,Y_{m,t})}{V(Y_{m,t}) + V\eta_t}E(Y_{m,t}) \qquad (15.15)$$

$$= Cov(Y_t,Y_{m,t})E(Y_{m,t})\left[\frac{1}{V(Y_{m,t})} - \frac{1}{V(Y_{m,t}) + V\eta_t}\right] \neq 0. \qquad (15.16)$$

The approximation of the market portfolio by a market index leads to a spurious rejection of the true CAPM hypothesis.

15.3 Price Index and Factor Model

By selecting a fixed portfolio to construct the Laspeyres index, we induce a lack of representativeness of the asset price dynamics in the long run. We first consider this problem when the relative asset price changes are i.i.d. Then, the analysis is extended to a dynamic model including factors.

15.3.1 Limiting Behavior of a Price Index

Let us consider the price changes $y_{i,t} = p_{i,t}/p_{i,t-1}$, $i = 1,\ldots,n$, and assume that the vectors $(y_{1,t},\ldots,y_{n,t})'$, t varying, are independent with identical distribution. We denote by μ and Ω the mean and variance-covariance matrix of $(\log y_{1,t},\ldots,\log y_{n,t})'$, respectively.

The price at date t can be written as

$$p_{i,t} = p_{i,0}y_{i,1}\cdots y_{i,t}$$
$$= p_{i,0}\exp\left\{\textstyle\sum_{\tau=1}^{t}\log y_{i,\tau}\right\}$$
$$= p_{i,0}\exp t\mu_i \exp\left\{\sqrt{t}\frac{1}{\sqrt{t}}\textstyle\sum_{\tau=1}^{t}(\log y_{i,\tau} - \mu_i)\right\}.$$

Therefore, for large t, we can apply the central limit theorem, yielding the approximation

$$p_{i,t} \simeq p_{i,0}\exp(t\mu_i)\exp\sqrt{t}u_i, \qquad (15.17)$$

where the vector $U = (u_1,\ldots,u_n)'$ is Gaussian with mean 0 and variance-covariance matrix Ω.

The above approximation can be used to derive an asymptotic absence of arbitrage opportunity (AAO) condition. Let us consider an investor with a fixed arbitrage portfolio allocation in assets i and j, where $\mu_i > \mu_j$. The allocation satisfies

$$a_i p_{i,0} + a_j p_{j,0} = 0,$$

and the portfolio value at t is

$$W_t = a_i p_{i,t} + a_j p_{j,t}$$

$$\sim a_i p_{i,0} \exp\left(t\mu_i + \sqrt{t}u_i\right) + a_j p_{j,0} \exp\left(t\mu_j + \sqrt{t}u_j\right),$$

for large t. We deduce that

$$P[W_t > 0] = P\left[u_i - u_j > \frac{1}{\sqrt{t}} \log\left(-\frac{a_i p_{i,0}}{a_j p_{j,0}}\right) - \sqrt{t}(\mu_i - \mu_j)\right],$$

tends to 1, when t tends to infinity. With a zero initial endowment, this static portfolio ensures asymptotically a positive gain with probability 1. We obtain the following condition of no asymptotic arbitrage opportunity:

PROPOSITION 15.4: *A necessary condition for asymptotic AOA is* $\mu_i = E \log y_{i,t} = \mu$, *independent of the asset.*
    Under this condition, we have $\lim_{t\to\infty}P[W_t > 0] = 1/2$.

REMARK 15.1: If there exists a risk-free asset with a constant rate r, the condition implies $E \log y_{i,t} = \log(1 + r)$, and by the Jensen inequality,

$$Ey_{i,t} = E(\exp \log y_{i,t}) > \exp(E \log y_{i,t}) = 1 + r.$$

Therefore, the condition is compatible with the existence of a risk premium.

From the above analysis of basic price evolutions, we can easily infer the asymptotic behavior of a Laspeyres price index. Let us consider the evolution of the price index between $t - 1$ and t. We get

$$\frac{\mathcal{L}_{t/0}(p)}{\mathcal{L}_{t-1/0}(p)} = \sum_{i=1}^{n} \left\{ \frac{q_{i,0}p_{i,0}\dfrac{p_{i,t-1}}{p_{i,0}}}{\sum_{i=1}^{n} q_{i,0}p_{i,0}\dfrac{p_{i,t-1}}{p_{i,0}}} y_{i,t} \right\} \qquad (15.18)$$

$$\simeq \sum_{i=1}^{n} \left\{ \frac{q_{i,0}p_{i,0} \exp\left(t\mu_i + \sqrt{t}u_i\right)}{\sum_{i=1}^{n} q_{i,0}p_{i,0} \exp\left(t\mu_i + \sqrt{t}u_i\right)} y_{i,t} \right\},$$

where the variables $y_{i,t}$, $i = 1, \ldots, n$, are independent of the asymptotic variables u_i, $i = 1, \ldots, n$. The relative change in the price index is a weighted average of the asset price changes $y_{i,t}$, $i = 1, \ldots, n$, with stochastic weights. Let us now discuss the choice of weights by distinguishing two cases.

For the first case, if the condition of asymptotic AOA is not satisfied, there is an asset, asset 1, say, with the highest mean μ_1. Then, the change of the index price tends to be driven by the change in the price of asset 1. Asymptotically, the Laspeyres index does not take into account the price movements of the whole set of assets.

In the second case, if the means μ_i, $i = 1, \ldots, n$, are equal, we get, asymptotically,

$$\frac{\mathcal{L}_{t/0}(p)}{\mathcal{L}_{t-1/0}(p)} \simeq \sum_{i=1}^{n} \mathbf{1}_{(u_i > u_j, \forall j \neq i)} y_{i,t}. \tag{15.19}$$

The index is no longer comprehensive for large t. However, the prevailing asset is now randomly selected, with the probability of any asset being drawn depending on the volatility-covolatility matrix Ω.

15.3.2 The Effect of Factors

The discussion can be extended to a dynamic factor representation of the relative changes of asset prices. Let us consider a linear factor model (see Chapter 9):

$$y_{i,t} = p_{i,t}/p_{i,t-1} = a_i' F_t + \varepsilon_{i,t}, \tag{15.20}$$

where (F_t) is strongly stationary and independent of the strong white noise $(\varepsilon_t) = (\varepsilon_{1,t}, \ldots, \varepsilon_{n,t})'$. Under the necessary condition of asymptotic AOA,

$$E \log(a_i' F_t + \varepsilon_{i,t}) = \mu, \qquad \text{independent of } i, \tag{15.21}$$

the change of the index is

$$\frac{\mathcal{L}_{t/0}(p)}{\mathcal{L}_{t-1/0}(p)} \simeq \left[\sum_{i=1}^{n} \mathbf{1}_{(u_i > u_j, \forall j \neq i)} a_i'\right] F_t + \sum_{i=1}^{n} \mathbf{1}_{(u_i > u_j, \forall j \neq i)} \varepsilon_t.$$

The Laspeyres index also satisfies a linear factor model with the same factors (F_t), but with stochastic coefficients instead. Therefore, only linear factor representations with stochastic coefficients provide a coherent specification of both asset price and composite index dynamics.

REMARK 15.2: The above result may not be valid for other types of indexes. To understand this point, let us consider a Paasche chain index. We get

$$\frac{\mathcal{P}_{t/0}(p)}{\mathcal{P}_{t-1/0}(p)} = \frac{\sum_{i=1}^{n} q_{i,t} p_{i,t}}{\sum_{i=1}^{n} q_{i,t} p_{i,0}} \frac{\sum_{i=1}^{n} q_{i,t-1} p_{i,0}}{\sum_{i=1}^{n} q_{i,t-1} p_{i,t-1}}$$

$$= \sum_{i=1}^{n} \left\{\frac{q_{i,t-1} p_{i,t-1}}{\sum_{i=1}^{n} q_{i,t-1} p_{i,t-1}}\right\} \frac{q_{i,t}}{q_{i,t-1}} \frac{p_{i,t}}{p_{i,t-1}} \left[\sum_{i=1}^{n} \left\{\frac{q_{i,t-1} p_{i,0}}{\sum_{i=1}^{n} q_{i,t-1} p_{i,0}}\right\} \frac{q_{i,t}}{q_{i,t-1}}\right]^{-1}.$$

The asymptotic expansion of the relative change involves both the price and quantity dynamics. Hence, factors driving the modification of the Paasche index are not only the price factors, but also quantity factors.

15.4 Endogenous Selectivity

In a standard consumer price index, the set of goods included in the index is invariant. This explains why we denoted the goods by $i = 1, \ldots,$ n without allowing for their dependence on either the date or the environment. Indexes of financial assets often become endogenously modified in time, leading to a change of their interpretation. Typically, as seen in Section 15.3, the choice of a fixed portfolio implies a lack of representativeness in the long run. Various schemes of endogenous selections of weights can be considered for the sake of representativeness or liquidity. Indeed, the index components have to be liquid for at least two reasons. The observed asset prices have to be competitive. Moreover, since several indexes support derivatives, any asset in the index has to be liquid enough to allow for arbitrage strategies.

15.4.1 Selection of the Weights

The decisions on substantial and sudden modifications of the index composition are usually taken by scientific committees, which have meeting dates that are never announced in advance to avoid speculative interventions on the markets. These committees may follow various policy rules, which are often based on a (static or dynamic) analysis of the underlying weights.

$$\pi_{i,t} = p_{i,t} q_{i,t} / \sum_{j=1}^{N_t} p_{j,t} q_{j,t}, \tag{15.22}$$

where $i = 1, \ldots, N_t$, and N_t is the total number of assets traded at period t. We describe below two approaches that allow transformation of the weights; these are often followed in practice.

Index with a Fixed Number of Assets
The main market indexes usually include a fixed number of assets, such as the S&P 100 on the NYSE, which includes 100 assets; the CAC 40 on the Paris Bourse, which includes 40 assets; and so on. The assets can be selected by considering the most important capitalizations. Let us consider a Laspeyres index with underlying weights $\pi_{i,t-1}$, $i = 1, \ldots, N_t$. We classify the assets by decreasing capitalization:

$$\pi_{(1),t-1} \geq \pi_{(2),t-1} \geq \ldots \pi_{(N_{t-1}),t-1},$$

and denote by i_j the index of the asset with rank j. Then, the price index with a given number N^0 of assets is such that

$$\mathcal{L}_{t/t-1}^0(p) = \frac{\sum_{j=1}^{N^0} \pi_{i_j,t-1} p_{i_j,t} / p_{i_j,t-1}}{\sum_{j=1}^{N^0} \pi_{i_j,t-1}}. \tag{15.23}$$

The evolution of this restricted index can differ from the evolution of an unrestricted index based on the set of all assets. Indeed, between $t-2$ and $t-1$, an asset may be removed from the selected basket if its weight diminishes significantly. It is sufficient that its price diminishes with respect to other asset prices. In contrast, a new asset may be included when its price increases significantly. Therefore, we get an endogenous selection scheme in which the price change of the newly included asset is generally above the average. Thus, we can expect the value of the restricted index $\mathcal{L}_{t/t-1}^0(p)$ to be greater than that of the unrestricted one.

Index with Cap
Let us consider an index that includes a given sample of assets:

$$\mathcal{L}_{t/t-1}(p) = \sum_{i=1}^{N} \pi_{i,t-1} p_{i,t}/p_{i,t-1},$$

where $\sum_{i=1}^{N} \pi_{i,t-1} = 1$. We now illustrate a nonlinear transformation of the weights, which is often performed in practice when some weights become too large. The reason is that such an underlying portfolio may not be sufficiently diversified. This is a typical situation on the Helsinki Stock Exchange, on which the largest stock represents about 50% of the market. To prevent this effect, an upper bound (a *cap*) on the weight values, 10%, say, can be imposed. The new weight bundle is derived by the following recursive algorithm.

1. The weights are ranked by decreasing value, and the weights larger than 10% are set equal to 10%; then, the other weights are transformed by a scale factor to make them sum to 1. We get a new set of weights $\pi_{i,t-1}^{(1)}$, $i = 1, \ldots, N$.
2. The previous approach is reapplied to the set $\pi_{i,t-1}^{(1)}$, $i = 1, \ldots, N$, and so on until all weights are set less than or equal to 10%. This final set of weights is used to construct the index.

To illustrate this technique, let us consider $N = 20$ and the initial weights (in %)

$$20, 9, 8, 6, 6, 6, 6, 3, \ldots, 3.$$

In the first step, we truncate the weight 20 to get

$$10, 9, 8, 6, 6, 6, 6, 3, \ldots, 3,$$

then, we rescale by 9/8 to get

$$10, 81/8, 9, 54/8, \ldots, 54/8, 27/8, \ldots, 27/8.$$

The second weight is larger than 10. Therefore, we apply the method again to get

$$10, 10, \frac{100-20}{100-10-81/8} 9, \ldots ,$$

which is the final set of weights since $\frac{100-20}{100-10-81/8} 9 < 10.$

15.4.2 Hedonic Index for Bonds

The construction of price indexes requires regularly observed asset prices from a time invariant sample of assets. This condition is not always satisfied, especially when we consider bonds or derivative assets. Indeed, liquid bonds (or derivatives) at date $t-1$ and date t generally do not have the same structure of cash flows. To describe this problem, we first consider an index for bonds in a complete market framework and then present the extensions to the incomplete market framework.

Complete Market
Let us consider a fixed portfolio of bonds, indexed by $i = 1, \ldots, n$, with quantities $q_{i,0}$, $i = 1, \ldots, n$. At date $t-1$, they pay cash flows $(f_{i,0}, f_{i,1}, \ldots, f_{i,H})$, $i = 1, \ldots, n$, at future dates $t, t+1, \ldots, t+H$ and have prices $p_{i,t-1}$, $i = 1, \ldots, n$. At date t, the bond prices are $p_{i,t}$, and the residual future cash flows are $(f_{i,1}, \ldots, f_{i,H})$, $i = 1, \ldots, n$. The modification of the Laspeyres index between $t-1$ and t is

$$\frac{\mathcal{L}_{t/0}(p)}{\mathcal{L}_{t-1/0}(p)} = \frac{\sum_{i=1}^n q_{i,0} p_{i,t}}{\sum_{i=1}^n q_{i,0} p_{i,t-1}}. \tag{15.24}$$

Under the complete market hypothesis, the bond prices can be written in terms of zero-coupon prices:

$$p_{i,t-1} = \sum_{h=0}^H f_{i,h} B(t-1,h),$$
$$p_{i,t} = \sum_{h=1}^H f_{i,h} B(t,h-1) = \sum_{h=0}^H f_{i,h+1} B(t,h),$$

setting by convention $f_{i,H+1} = 0$, $\forall i$.

By substituting into equation (15.24), we get

$$\frac{\mathcal{L}_{t/0}(p)}{\mathcal{L}_{t-1/0}(p)} = \frac{\sum_{i=1}^n q_{i,0}\left[\sum_{h=0}^H f_{i,h+1} B(t,h)\right]}{\sum_{i=1}^n q_{i,0}\left[\sum_{h=0}^H f_{i,h} B(t-1,h)\right]}$$

$$= \frac{\sum_{h=0}^H (\sum_{i=1}^n q_{i,0} f_{i,h+1}) B(t,h)}{\sum_{h=0}^H (\sum_{i=1}^n q_{i,0} f_{i,h}) B(t-1,h)}$$

$$= \frac{\sum_{h=0}^H (\sum_{i=1}^n q_{i,0} f_{i,h}) B(t,h)}{\sum_{h=0}^H (\sum_{i=1}^n q_{i,0} f_{i,h}) B(t-1,h)}$$

$$\frac{\sum_{h=0}^H (\sum_{i=1}^n q_{i,0} f_{i,h+1}) B(t,h)}{\sum_{h=0}^H (\sum_{i=1}^n q_{i,0} f_{i,h}) B(t,h)}$$

We get the decomposition

$$\frac{\mathcal{L}_{v0}(p)}{\mathcal{L}_{t-1/0}(p)} = \frac{\mathcal{L}_{v0}(B)}{\mathcal{L}_{t-1/0}(B)} e_t(s), \tag{15.25}$$

where $\mathcal{L}_{v0}(B)/\mathcal{L}_{t-1/0}(B)$ is the modification of a Laspeyres index on zero-coupon bonds, and $e_t(s)$ is a residual term that measures a structural effect. Indeed, the bond i, with the same name at dates $t-1$ and t, is not the same financial asset since its maturity has decreased, and the cash flow pattern became modified. Therefore, the index computed from bonds is a value index, which does not take into account the intermediate coupon payments. It still responds to the structural effect. Note that only the Laspeyres index computed from zero-coupon bonds has an interpretation as a price index.

Incomplete Market

Generally, the zero-coupon bonds are not actively traded on the market, and thus the associated prices are not observed. Therefore, the exact price index cannot be computed, but may be approximated instead by a dynamic model of the term structure. More precisely, by using such a model, we derive date-by-date predictions of the underlying zero-coupon prices $\hat{B}(t,h)$, say. Then, the modification of the index is approximated by

$$\frac{\hat{\mathcal{L}}_{v0}(B)}{\hat{\mathcal{L}}_{t-1/0}(B)} = \frac{\sum_{h=0}^{H} (\sum_{i=1}^{n} q_{i,0} f_{i,h}) \hat{B}(t,h)}{\sum_{h=0}^{H} (\sum_{i=1}^{n} q_{i,0} f_{i,h}) \hat{B}(t-1,h)}. \tag{15.26}$$

This approach is related to the theory of *hedonic price indexes* (see, e.g., Griliches 1961; Rosen 1974), introduced for consumption goods of varying quality. The idea underlying the hedonic index is to price the various qualities, or *characteristics*, and to consider next a consumption good as a portfolio of characteristics with a price that is inferred from the individual characteristic prices. The bond characteristics are various admissible maturities, and the cash flows represent the quantities of these characteristics.

15.5 Summary

A market index is commonly perceived as an empirical equivalent of the theoretical concept of market portfolio, a key ingredient of the CAPM model. It is important to realize, however, that market indexes have various structures and compositions. As a consequence, not all market indexes provide good approximations of the market portfolio. Section 15.1 introduced basic definitions of consumer price indexes, including the well-known Paasche and Laspeyres indexes, extended in Section 15.2 to market indexes. We discussed the practical use of market indexes with reference to their design and gave a brief overview of major stock market indexes. The following section illustrated the use of factor models to study market indexes. We showed that factor variables can efficiently account for the price and quantity effects, whenever random coefficients are introduced. More information on factor models can be found in Chapter 9. The last section concerned the choice of weights in constructing market indexes. This topic was investigated under the complete and incomplete market hypotheses.

16

Management of Extreme Risks

IN PREVIOUS CHAPTERS, risk on financial assets was measured by the conditional second-order moment representing the volatility. Recall that volatility-based risk underlies the mean-variance portfolio management rules and justifies the use of generalized autoregressive conditionally heteroscedastic (GARCH) and stochastic volatility models for predicting future risks.

The variance, however, provides a correct assessment of risk only under some specific conditions, such as the normality of the conditional distribution of returns and a constant absolute risk aversion of investors. It also adequately represents small risks. In particular, a measure of a small market risk on an asset of value X is based on the expected utility $E(U(X))$, which can be expanded into $U(E(X)) + 0.5\ U''[E(X)]V(X)$, revealing the importance of the two first moments. Such risks can be evaluated at short horizons from price processes with continuous trajectories. In contrast, the conditional variance shows poor performance as a measure of occasionally occurring extreme risks. This chapter introduces the models, risk measures, and optimal risk management rules under the presence of extreme risks.

The market risk is inherently related to the probability of occurrence of extreme events, that is, very large negative or positive returns. For any random return variable, the probability of extremely valued observations is reflected by the size of the tails of the distribution. The benchmark for heavy tails is determined by the normal distribution. Normally distributed data are characterized by a relatively low probability of extreme realizations, and the tails of their distribution taper off quickly. Indeed, a standard normal variable admits values greater than 1.96 in absolute sense only with 5% probability. In statistics, a standard measure of tails is the *kurtosis*, defined as the ratio $E[X^4]/[E[X^2]]^2$ for a zero-mean variable X.

It can be estimated by computing $\frac{1}{T}\Sigma x_t^4 / \left[\frac{1}{T}\Sigma x_t^2\right]^2$. Whenever this quantity exceeds 3 (i.e., the theoretical kurtosis of a standard normal), we say that the data feature excess kurtosis, or that their distribution is leptokurtic, that is, has heavy tails. There also exist other more sophisticated scalar measures of the thickness of tails. Among them we distinguish a classical measure called the *tail index*. It is introduced in the first section, along with the estimator of the tail index originally proposed by Hill (1975).

In Section 16.1, we review thick-tailed distributions commonly used in statistical analysis and introduce dynamic models that allow for path-dependent tails. The Value at Risk (VaR) is defined in Section 16.2. The VaR measures the maximum loss on a portfolio incurred within a fixed period with a given probability. It is used by bank regulators to define the minimum capital banks are required to hold to hedge against market risk on asset portfolios. We also show that the VaR can be interpreted as a conditional quantile and present selected quantile estimators. In Section 16.3, we analyze the sensitivity of the VaR to changes in portfolio allocations and study portfolio management when VaR is used as a measure of risk instead of volatility. Finally, in Section 16.4, we explain why standard constant absolute risk aversion (CARA) utility functions are not adapted to infrequent extreme risks and introduce a class of utility functions for extreme risk analysis.

16.1 Distributions with Heavy Tails

Empirical evidence suggests that the marginal and conditional distributions of returns feature heavy tails and therefore often admit extreme values. We show in Figure 16.1 the empirical distribution of returns on the Alcatel stock traded on the Paris Bourse in August 1996, sampled at 1-minute intervals. The density function is centered at 4.259E-6, and its variance and standard deviation are 9.771E-7 and 0.000989, respectively. The distribution is slightly asymmetric, with skewness coefficient −0.00246. The high kurtosis of 5.329689 is due to the presence of heavy tails stretched between the extreme values of −0.00813 and 0.007255. Of the probability mass, 90% is concentrated between −0.0017 and 0.001738. The interquartile range 0.000454 is 100 times smaller than the overall range 0.01538. The kurtosis of real-time data in general is lower than the kurtosis of data sampled regularly in calendar time, which is approximately 10 for the return series. This is a standard effect of random time deformation on the empirical distribution (see Chapter 14).

The shape of tails, although kernel smoothed in Figure 16.1, suggests the presence of local irregularities in the rate of tail decay. Indeed, slight

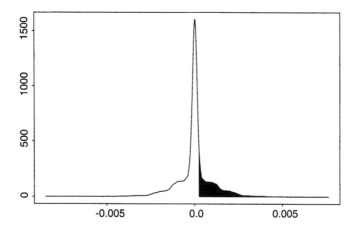

Figure 16.1 *Density of Returns, Alcatel*

lobes can easily be distinguished in both tails. They may be due to the discreteness of prices and preference of investors for round numbers (see Chapter 14). In the right tail, we observe a higher probability of returns taking values between 0.0012 and 0.0013 compared to the probability of those of a slightly smaller size (i.e., between 0.0010 and 0.0012). In the left tail, we recorded relatively more returns between −0.0014 and −0.0012 than those with marginally higher values.

16.1.1 Tail Index

Let us consider a continuous distribution on the real line with the probability density function (pdf) and cumulative distribution function (cdf) denoted by f and F, respectively. For example, let f be a conditional distribution of portfolio returns. The right (resp. left) tail encompasses extreme high (resp. low) values of y, which in the limit tend to $+\infty$ (or $-\infty$). The magnitude of the right tail can be inferred from the survivor function $1 - F(y)$, which determines the probability that the variable takes values greater than y. In particular, the survivor function can be used for comparing the size of tails of various distributions. We say that a distribution F^* more often admits large positive values than a distribution F, if

$$1 - F^*(y) > 1 - F(y), \qquad \text{for large } y.$$

In general, distributions can be compared in terms of asymptotic properties of the survivor function when y tends to $+\infty$. Below, we give some examples of analytical expression of survivor functions for selected distributions.

Gaussian Distribution

Let us denote by φ and Φ the pdf and cdf of the standard normal distribution, respectively. For large y, we get

$$\frac{1-\Phi(y)}{\varphi(y)} \sim \frac{1}{y} \Leftrightarrow 1-\Phi(y) \sim \frac{1}{\sqrt{2\pi}}\frac{1}{y}\exp\left(-\frac{y^2}{2}\right).$$

The survivor function tends very fast to 0. Therefore, the probability of extreme values of y is not very high.

Exponential Tail Distribution

Let us consider a symmetric distribution such that

$$F(y) = \begin{cases} \dfrac{1}{2}\exp(\lambda y), & \text{if } y < 0, \\[2mm] 1 - \dfrac{1}{2}\exp(-\lambda y), & \text{if } y > 0, \end{cases}$$

where λ is a positive parameter. The survivor function tends to 0 at an exponential rate, which is infinitely slower than for a Gaussian distribution.

Pareto Tail Distribution

Another thick-tailed symmetric distribution is characterized by the cumulative distribution function

$$F(y) = \begin{cases} \dfrac{1}{2}\dfrac{1}{(1-y)^\alpha}, & \text{if } y < 0, \\[2mm] 1 - \dfrac{1}{2}\dfrac{1}{(1+y)^\alpha}, & \text{if } y > 0. \end{cases}$$

for positive α. The survivor function tends to 0 at a slow hyperbolic rate, depending on the parameter α.

The extreme risk analysis classifies the distributions with respect to the type of tails. In practice, a heavy tail is generally of an exponential, or Pareto, type, that is, it assigns to the extremes a higher probability than the normal distribution and resembles the shape of exponential or Pareto tails. More precisely, a distribution is of *Pareto type* if we have

$$1 - F(y) \sim y^{-\alpha}L(y), \tag{16.1}$$

where L is a so-called slowly varying function at infinity:

$$\lim_{y\to\infty}\frac{L(\lambda y)}{L(y)} = 1, \qquad \forall \lambda > 0. \tag{16.2}$$

Examples of slowly varying functions are the constant and the logarithmic functions. Here, α is called the *tail index* of the distribution F. Note that the definition is given for the right tail, that is, $y \to +\infty$. An analogous definition for the left tail follows directly.

16.1.2 Hill Estimator

The tail index of a Pareto type of distribution can be estimated easily from a set of independent identically distributed (i.i.d.) observations y_1, ..., y_T. The idea is simply to fit a Pareto distribution to the largest values in the sample and to retain the corresponding maximum likelihood (ML) estimator of α (Hill 1975). More precisely, let us consider a Pareto distribution (with origin at $+1$) and a truncation point c. The truncated Pareto distribution has the pdf $f(y) = 1_{y>c} \dfrac{\alpha c^\alpha}{y^{\alpha+1}}$. The associated log-likelihood function is

$$\sum_{t=1}^{T} \log f(y_t) = \sum_{t=1}^{T} 1_{y>c} \{\log \alpha + \alpha \log c - (\alpha + 1) \log y_t\}.$$

The maximization with respect to α provides the ML estimator

$$\hat{\alpha}(c) = \sum_{t=1}^{T} 1_{y>c}(\log y_t - \log c) / \sum_{t=1}^{T} 1_{y>c},$$

where $\hat{\alpha}$ is a stepwise function with jumps at each observed value of y greater than the censoring threshold c. Let us rank the observations to obtain the order statistics, that is, the numbered observations arranged in ascending order:

$$y_{(1)} \leq y_{(2)} \ldots \leq y_{(T)}.$$

Then, the admissible values of $\hat{\alpha}(c)$ are

$$\hat{\alpha}_k = \hat{\alpha}(y_{(T-k)}) = \frac{1}{k} \sum_{j=0}^{k-1} \log y_{T-j} - \log y_{(T-k)}. \qquad (16.3)$$

It has been proved that $\hat{\alpha}_k$ tends to α when k tends to infinity with the number T of observations increasing at an appropriate rate.

Similar methods can be applied to an exponential type of distribution and the estimation of the λ parameter. We can estimate the exponential intensity rate λ by maximizing the likelihood function based on an exponential distribution with a domain restricted to extreme positive values.

16.1.3 Dynamic Specification of Extreme Risks

The standard conditionally heteroscedastic models are often based on a conditional Gaussian distribution of returns with a dynamic specification of the mean (ARMA) and variance (GARCH). As a consequence, the tails of these conditional distributions are equivalent to the thin Gaussian tails and are path independent, that is, invariant in time. A natural extension of this approach that allows for path-dependent tails consists of considering families of distributions that include more parameters, especially a tail parameter. Then, a wide range of dynamic patterns can be modeled by inducing time variation of the enlarged set of parameters. To suitable families belong the student distributions and Levy distributions, also called α–*stable*.

Let us focus on the Levy distributions, that is, one-dimensional distributions with four parameters:

a location parameter μ, $\mu \in R$,
a scale parameter γ, $\gamma \in R^+$,
a skewness parameter β, $\beta \in [-1,1]$,
a tail or stability parameter α, $\alpha \in (0, 2)$.

The density functions of stable distributions do not admit explicit expressions except for the following special cases:

$\alpha = 2$, $\beta = 0$, the normal distributions,
$\alpha = 1$, $\beta = 0$, the Cauchy distributions,
$\alpha = 0.5$, $\beta = 1$, the Levy distributions.

Nevertheless, their pdf $f(y;\mu,\gamma,\beta,\alpha)$ (say) can always be found numerically by inverting the characteristic function

$$\psi(t) = \exp\left\{ i\mu t - \gamma^\alpha |t|^\alpha \left[1 - i\beta \,\text{sign}\,(t) \tan\left(\frac{\alpha\pi}{2}\right) \right] \right\}. \tag{16.4}$$

Let us assume that the data have been conditionally standardized ($\mu = 0$, $\gamma = 1$), and focus on the parameters β and α.

Stochastic Parameter
Our purpose is to introduce dynamic, autoregressive skewness and tail parameters. Accordingly, we consider a stochastic parameter model for which the conditional distribution of y_t is

$$f(y_t;0,1,\beta_t,\alpha_t),$$

and the parameters satisfy a Gaussian VAR(1) model after appropriate nonlinear transformations:

$$\begin{pmatrix} \beta_t^* \\ \alpha_t^* \end{pmatrix} = m + A \begin{pmatrix} \beta_{t-1}^* \\ \alpha_{t-1}^* \end{pmatrix} + \varepsilon_t,$$

where (ε_t) is a Gaussian white noise with mean zero, and $\beta_t^* = \text{logit}\left(\dfrac{1+\beta_t}{2}\right)$, $\alpha_t^* = \text{logit}\left(\dfrac{\alpha_t}{2}\right)$ to ensure any admissible real values for α_t^* and β_t^*.

Autoregressive Simulators

An alternative dynamic specification was introduced by Gourieroux and Jasiak (1999a) and was estimated from high-frequency data. A stable variable y_t can be written as

$$y_t = \beta\left(1 - tan\frac{\alpha\pi}{2}\right) + \left(cos\left[arctan\left(\beta\ tan\frac{\alpha\pi}{2}\right)\right]\right)^{-1/\alpha}$$

$$\frac{sin\left[\alpha u_t + arctan\left(\beta\ tan\left(\frac{\alpha\pi}{2}\right)\right)\right]}{(cos\ u_t)^{1/\alpha}} \left\{\frac{cos\left[u_t(1-\alpha) - arctan\left(\beta tan\frac{\alpha\pi}{2}\right)\right]}{v_t}\right\}^{\frac{1-\alpha}{\alpha}} \quad (16.5)$$

$$= g(u_t, v_t; \alpha, \beta) \quad \text{(say)},$$

where u_t and v_t are independent variables with a uniform distribution on $\left(-\dfrac{\pi}{2}, \dfrac{\pi}{2}\right)$ and an exponential distribution, respectively. These underlying variables can be transformed into Gaussian variables $F_{1,t}$ and $F_{2,t}$ by considering

$$u_t = \pi\Phi(F_{1,t}) - \pi/2, \quad v_t = -\log[1 - \Phi(F_{2t})], \quad (16.6)$$

where Φ denotes the cdf of the standard normal distribution.

Next, an autoregressive specification with path-dependent skewness and tails is derived by considering the system of (16.5), (16.6), and the recursive equation

$$\begin{pmatrix} F_{1,t} \\ F_{2,t} \end{pmatrix} = \begin{pmatrix} \Phi_1 & 0 \\ 0 & \Phi_2 \end{pmatrix}\begin{pmatrix} F_{1,t-1} \\ F_{2,t-1} \end{pmatrix} + \begin{pmatrix} \sqrt{1-\Phi_1^2} & 0 \\ 0 & \sqrt{1-\Phi_2^2} \end{pmatrix}\begin{pmatrix} \varepsilon_{1t} \\ \varepsilon_{2t} \end{pmatrix},$$

where $(\varepsilon_{1t}, \varepsilon_{2t})'$ is a standard Gaussian white noise.

To illustrate the associated dynamic patterns, we fixed the parameters at $\alpha = 1.7$ and $\beta = 0.0$ (symmetric distribution) and generated a path of 3,000 observations (Figure 16.2). The values of the autoregressive parameters are $\Phi_1 = 0.1, 0.5, 0.8, 0.95$ and $\Phi_2 = 0.5$. When the coefficient Φ_1 increases, the magnitude of extreme values decreases, and more frequently, extreme values of both signs tend to follow themselves (i.e., to cluster).

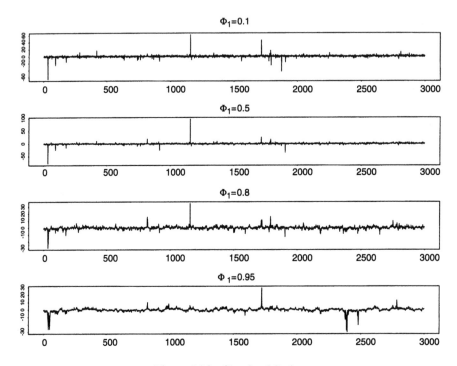

Figure 16.2   *Simulated Paths*

16.2   Value at Risk

The Value at Risk (VaR) is a measure of market risk, as well as a major determinant of the minimum capital banks are required to keep to cover potential losses arising from market risks. More precisely, the VaR equals the dollar loss on a portfolio that will not be exceeded by the end of a fixed period with a fixed probability. Let α be the probability in percentage. The bank regulators usually impose $\alpha = 1\%$ or, less often, 5%. Following a standard practice for portfolios of insurance contracts, the Basle Committee, which includes the governors of the main Central Banks, has introduced the requirement of a minimum capital amount to authorize the management of an asset portfolio over a given period. The capital charge, called the *market risk capital*, is computed from successive Values at Risk by a formula of the type

$$MRC_t = \max\left[VaR_{t-1}, \frac{k}{60} \sum_{i=1}^{60} VaR_{t-i} \right],$$

where the constant k is larger than 3 and typically is included between 3 and 4. In the first section, we explain the relationship between the VaR and the distribution of the incremental portfolio value. Next, we derive the expression of the VaR for Gaussian distributions and various heavy-tailed distributions. We also discuss the parametric and nonparametric methods of VaR estimation. Finally, alternative measures of the minimum required capital are described.

16.2.1 Definition

Let us consider a portfolio including n assets with fixed allocation $a = (a_1, \ldots, a_n)'$ between t and $t+h$ (say). At date t, the investor has the endowment $W_t(a) = a'p_t$ designated for the purchase of this portfolio and an additional *reserve amount* R_t (say), which is supposed to compensate potential adverse changes in prices. Essentially, the investor selects a reserve amount such that the global position (i.e., the portfolio value plus the reserve) may incur a loss with a predetermined small probability α at date $t+h$. This condition is $P_t[W_{t+h}(a) + R_t < 0] = \alpha$, where P_t is the conditional distribution of future prices. Thus, $-R_t$ is an α-quantile of the conditional distribution of the future portfolio value, called the *profit and loss* (P&L) distribution.

The *required capital* at time t is the sum of the initial endowment plus the reserve. It is denoted by

$$VaR_t = W_t(a) + R_t,$$

and characterized by the condition

$$P_t[W_{t+h}(a) - W_t(a) + VaR_t < 0] = \alpha. \tag{16.7}$$

It depends on the information that is available at date t, on the horizon h, on the portfolio allocation a, and on the loss probability α. We introduce explicitly these arguments into the VaR formula:

$$VaR_t = VaR_t(a,h,\alpha). \tag{16.8}$$

Condition (16.7) is equivalent to

$$P_t[a'(p_{t+h} - p_t) < -VaR_t] = \alpha. \tag{16.9}$$

Thus, the opposite of the VaR defined in (16.9) is an upper quantile at level α of the distribution of the change in portfolio value.

REMARK 16.1: The required capital and the reserve amount are identical for an *arbitrage portfolio*, which has a value at date t that is equal to 0.

16.2.2   The Gaussian Value at Risk

For convenience, we assume a unitary time horizon $h = 1$. When the prices are conditionally Gaussian, we get

$$P_t[a'(p_{t+1} - p_t) < -VaR_t] = \alpha$$

$$\Leftrightarrow P_t\left[\frac{a'(p_{t+1} - p_t) - a'(E_t p_{t+1} - p_t)}{[a'V_t p_{t+1} a]^{1/2}} < \frac{-VaR_t - a'(E_t p_{t+1} - p_t)}{(a'V_t p_{t+1} a)^{1/2}}\right] = \alpha \qquad (16.10)$$

$$\Leftrightarrow -VaR_t - a'(E_t p_{t+1} - p_t) = \Phi^{-1}(\alpha)\,(a'V_t p_{t+1} a)^{1/2}$$

$$\Leftrightarrow VaR_t = -a'(E_t p_{t+1} - p_t) + \Phi^{-1}(1 - \alpha)\,(a'V_t p_{t+1} a)^{1/2},$$

where $\Phi^{-1}(1 - \alpha)$ is the $1 - \alpha$ quantile of the standard normal distribution. The associated amount of reserve is

$$R_t = -a'E_t p_{t+1} + \Phi^{-1}(1 - \alpha)\,(a'V_t p_{t+1} a)^{1/2}.$$

In practice, the predetermined probability of loss is small, often equal to 1% or 5%. Thus, the Value at Risk is an increasing function of the portfolio value volatility and a decreasing function of the expected increment of the gain and of the loss probability. The required amount of reserve is nonnegative if and only if

$$\frac{a'E_t p_{t+1}}{(a'V_t p_{t+1} a)^{1/2}} < \Phi^{-1}(1 - \alpha),$$

that is, if the portfolio performance measure is too small. Otherwise, the reserve is negative, and there is a possibility of borrowing.

16.2.3   Estimation of the Value at Risk

We have seen that the opposite of the VaR is equivalent to an upper quantile associated with a conditional increment of the portfolio value

$$P_t[a'(p_{t+1} - p_t) < -VaR_t(a,\alpha)] = \alpha,$$

for a unitary horizon (say). Let us denote $y_t = \Delta p_t = p_t - p_{t-1}$ as the price increments and assume that they define a stationary process. Our task is to estimate the quantiles of the conditional distribution of $a'y_t = a'\Delta p_{t+1}$ from observations $y_1, \ldots, y_t$ (say). We can distinguish various approaches depending on the specification of the (y_t) dynamics. There exist parametric and nonparametric methods that allow for a more or less complex temporal dependence of returns.

Gaussian i.i.d Price Increments
The Gaussian i.i.d. price increments approach assumes that price increments are normally distributed. It consists of inverting the cumulative

normal distribution function that approximates the marginal distribution of returns evaluated at the mean and variance estimated from a sample of past returns. This procedure was suggested by J.P. Morgan (1996) and is often used for regulatory purposes. Let us denote by $\hat{\mu}$ and $\hat{\Omega}$ the empirical mean and variance-covariance matrix, respectively, of the price increments. These values can be plugged into formula (16.10), which defines the VaR under normality. The estimated VaR is

$$\widehat{VaR}_t(a,\alpha) = -a'\hat{\mu} + \Phi^{-1}(1-\alpha)\,(a'\hat{\Omega}a)^{1/2}. \qquad (16.11)$$

REMARK 16.2: When data feature nonstationarity, or if we want to adapt the approach to varying conditional distributions of returns, the method can be improved by computing the parameters by rolling, that is, by updating a sample of a fixed length, by adding the most recently observed return, and deleting the oldest observation from the sample. More precisely, we select a bandwidth of length p (say) and estimate the mean and variance sequentially from the window $y_{t-1}, \ldots, y_{t-p}$. Thus, $\hat{\mu}$ and $\hat{\Omega}$ depend on t and are updated for any new observation. Such summary statistics at different horizons are computed daily by Riskmetrics.

REMARK 16.3: The estimators $\hat{\mu}$ and $\hat{\Omega}$ may provide more or less accurate estimators of μ and Ω, respectively. Since the finite sample distribution of $(a'\hat{\mu}, a'\hat{\Omega}a)$ is known in the Gaussian case, we can find the distribution of the VaR estimate, as well as the corresponding confidence interval. Even if this feature is often disregarded by practitioners, it is important to keep in mind that the measure of risk is random and therefore risky itself.

Nonparametric Analysis of i.i.d. Price Increments
Obviously, the use of a normal approximation of the marginal return distribution results in underestimated tails and disregards excess kurtosis and skewness displayed by the empirical marginal distributions of returns. A natural idea is to replace the theoretical probability by an empirical frequency in the general VaR formula: $P[-a'y_{t+1} - VaR(a,\alpha) > 0] = \alpha$.
The empirical counterpart of this equation is

$$\frac{1}{T}\sum_{t=1}^{T} \mathbf{1}_{[-a'y_t - VaR(a,\alpha)>0]} = \alpha,$$

where $\mathbf{1}_{[.]}$ is an indicator function. The nonparametric approach is commonly implemented by banks. It is called *historical simulation* because it is based on the historical distribution. In reality, it involves no simulation at all. A serious limitation of this method is due to the discreteness of the T observed portfolio values, which implies that the above equation, in general, has no closed-form solution. It is thus preferable to smooth the estimator of the historical cdf. The smoothing yields the VaR as a continuous function of the portfolio allocation. For instance, we can replace the indicator function $1_{y>0}$ by $\Phi(y/h)$, where Φ is the cdf of the standard normal distribution, and h is a bandwidth. The smoothed estimated VaR is defined as the solution to

$$\frac{1}{T}\sum_{t=1}^{T}\Phi[(-a'y_t - \widehat{VaR}(a,\alpha))/h] = \alpha. \qquad (16.12)$$

In practice, this equation is solved numerically. The starting value of the algorithm can be set equal to the VaR derived under the normality assumption.

When T is large and h close to 0, the estimated VaR is asymptotically equivalent to

$$\sqrt{T}[\widehat{VaR}(a,\alpha) - VaR(a,\alpha)] \sim -\frac{1}{g_a[-VaR(a,\alpha)]}\frac{1}{\sqrt{T}}\sum_{t=1}^{T}[1_{a'y_t<-VaR(a,\alpha)} - \alpha],$$

where g_a denotes the pdf of $a'y_t$. In particular, when the price increments are i.i.d., the estimated VaR is asymptotically normal with mean $VaR(a,\alpha)$ and variance $\dfrac{1}{T}\dfrac{1}{g_a^2[-VaR(a,\alpha)]} G_a[-VaR(a,\alpha)] (1 - G_a[-VaR(a,\alpha)])$, where G_a is the cdf of $a'y_t$.

The accuracy depends on the size of the tails. As an illustration, let us consider an increment of the portfolio value with a left Pareto tail:

$$G_a(y) \sim \frac{1}{|y|^\gamma}, \qquad \text{for small } y.$$

We get

$$g_a(y) \sim \frac{\gamma}{|y|^{\gamma+1}},$$
$$-VaR(a,\alpha) \sim \alpha^{-1/\gamma},$$
$$\frac{G_a[-VaR(a,\alpha)]}{g_a^2[-VaR(a,\alpha)]} \sim \frac{1}{\gamma^2}[-VaR(a,\alpha)]^{\gamma+2} \sim \frac{1}{\gamma^2}\frac{1}{\alpha^{1+2/\gamma}}.$$

Thus, the variance of the estimated VaR increases when either γ or α decreases. Moreover, the term $\gamma^2\alpha^{1+2/\gamma}$ can be small when α or γ is small. In such a framework, the estimator is not very accurate, except for a very large number of observations T.

Semiparametric Analysis for i.i.d. Price Increments
When the loss probability α is small, the empirical quantile is estimated from a limited number of extreme observations. Therefore, the estimated

VaR may not be accurate. To circumvent this difficulty, we can estimate the quantile for a larger value α_0 (say) and deduce the VaR of interest from a parametric model of the tail. This is called the *model building* method. Let us assume, for instance, a Pareto type distribution, where we have approximately

$$1 - G_a(y) \sim cy^{-\beta}.$$

If we consider the right tail quantiles associated with the loss probabilities α_0 and α, with $\alpha_0 > \alpha$, we get

$$1 - G_a(VaR_\alpha) = \alpha \sim c(VaR_\alpha)^{-\beta},$$
$$1 - G_a(VaR_{\alpha_0}) = \alpha_0 \sim c(VaR_{\alpha_0})^{-\beta}.$$

We deduce that

$$\alpha_0/\alpha = [VaR_\alpha/VaR_{\alpha_0}]^\beta$$

$$\Leftrightarrow VaR_\alpha = VaR_{\alpha_0} \left(\frac{\alpha_0}{\alpha}\right)^{1/\beta}. \tag{16.13}$$

If, for instance, $\alpha = 1\%$, we can apply the quantile estimation described in the section on nonparametric analysis for the loss probability $\alpha_0 = 5\%$, estimate the tail index by Hill's method, and find the estimator

$$\widehat{VaR}_\alpha = \widehat{VaR}_{\alpha_0} \left(\frac{\alpha_0}{\alpha}\right)^{1/\beta}.$$

This means that we apply a correction depending on the tail index to the quantile estimator at $\alpha_0 = 5\%$ (see Danielsson and de Vries 1998 for different methods of this type).

Parametric Analysis Based on Conditional Gaussian Autoregressive Conditionally Heteroscedastic Models
We can extend the Gaussian approach to conditional distributions. Let us assume that the price increments satisfy a conditionally Gaussian model

$$l(y_t|y_{t-1}) = N[\mu(y_{t-1};\theta),\Omega(y_{t-1};\theta)],$$

where the conditional mean and variance admit parametric specifications. If $\hat{\theta}$ is a consistent estimator of the parameter θ, we can apply formula (16.10) to derive the estimated VaR:

$$\widehat{VaR}_t(a,\alpha) = -a'\mu(y_{t-1};\hat{\theta}) + \Phi^{-1}(1 - \alpha)[a'\Omega(y_{t-1};\hat{\theta})a)]^{1/2}. \tag{16.14}$$

Thus, the estimated VaR depends on the observed history.

Note that a number of ad hoc methods should be avoided. A typical example is the so-called exponentially weighted moving average (EWMA) model, which assumes $a'\mu(\underline{y}_{t-1};\theta) = 0$ and an IGARCH specification

$$\sigma_t^2(a) = \theta\sigma_{t-1}^2(a) + (1 - \theta)\,(a'\underline{y}_{t-1})^2,$$

for $\sigma_t^2(a) = a'\Omega(\underline{y}_{t-1};\theta)a$. First, the efficiency hypothesis is likely violated due to the presence of the risk premium. Second, the IGARCH specifications are not compatible for portfolios with different allocations. Recall that this was the main reason for introducing the factor ARCH model in Chapter 6. Despite these drawbacks, the EWMA is still used by Riskmetrics and seems to be quite hard to beat in practice.

Parametric Analysis Based on a Parametric Conditional Model
In a more general approach, we can introduce other conditional models that allow for path-dependent tails (see Section 16.1.3). If $F(y_t|\underline{y}_{t-1};\theta)$ denotes the conditional cdf of y_t given $\underline{y}_{t-1}$ and $\hat{\theta}_T$ is a consistent estimator of the parameter θ, the conditional VaR is estimated by solving the equation

$$1 - F_a[VaR(\underline{y}_{t-1})|\underline{y}_{t-1};\hat{\theta}_T] = \alpha, \qquad (16.15)$$

where F_a is the conditional cdf of $a'y_t$ given $\underline{y}_{t-1}$. For instance, we can select a family of multivariate distributions larger than the Gaussian family, like the multivariate Student t distribution, and introduce GARCH models with Student t distributed errors. However the quantile of the distribution of a linear combination of a vector of Student t variables has no explicit analytical form and requires a numerical approximation.

REMARK 16.4: It has also been suggested to extend the nonparametric approach to conditional distributions. A simple idea is to apply the historical simulation approach to the conditionally standardized portfolio values:

$$[a'y_t - a'\mu(\underline{y}_{t-1};\hat{\theta})]/[a'\Omega(\underline{y}_{t-1};\hat{\theta})a]^{1/2}.$$

Conditional Quantile Estimation
The conditional quantile estimation approach was suggested by Engle and Manganelli (1999). These authors introduced a recursive specification for the VaR corresponding to a given level α. For instance,

$$VaR_t = \beta_0 + \beta_1 VaR_{t-1} + \beta_2|y_{t-1}|.$$

By recursive substitutions, VaR_t is expressed as a function of the return history and the parameters

$$VaR_t = g(\underline{y}_{t-1}, \beta), \quad \text{(say)} \tag{16.16}$$

The parameter β is consistently estimated by applying the quantile regression of Koenker and Basset (1978), that is, by minimizing

$$\min_\beta \quad \Sigma_t\{\alpha[a'y_t - g(\underline{y}_{t-1};\beta)]\mathbf{1}_{a'y_t \geq g(\underline{y}_{t-1};\beta)} \tag{16.17}$$
$$\{+(1-\alpha)[g(\underline{y}_{t-1};\beta) - a'y_t]\mathbf{1}_{a'y_t \leq g(\underline{y}_{t-1};\beta)}\}.$$

This approach is applied to each risk level α and portfolio allocation a separately. Like the EWMA model, the VaR specifications are not compatible when α or a vary. Moreover, it may be useful to smooth the indicator function to ensure that the estimator of β is a continuous function of portfolio allocations.

Local Gaussian Approximation
Gourieroux and Jasiak (2000b) proposed estimation of local extreme risk from a Gaussian model and to replace the conditional mean and variance in the Gaussian formula (16.10) of the VaR by local approximations.

Let us assume a Markov process of returns. The entire information on the dynamics is contained in the joint distribution of (y_t, y_{t-1}), $f(y_t, y_{t-1})$ (say). We estimate a Gaussian approximation of this density in a neighborhood of the conditioning value of interest y_{T-1} (say) and of an extreme value $\tilde{y}$ for y_T, associated, for instance, with the marginal α upper quantile. The parameters of this approximation are the bivariate mean

$$\begin{bmatrix} \mu_1(\tilde{y}, y_{T-1}) \\ \mu_2(\tilde{y}, y_{T-1}) \end{bmatrix} = \mu \quad \text{and variance-covariance matrix}$$

$$\begin{bmatrix} \sigma_1^2(\tilde{y}, y_{T-1}) & \sigma_{12}(\tilde{y}, y_{T-1}) \\ \sigma_{12}(\tilde{y}, y_{T-1}) & \sigma_2^2(\tilde{y}, y_{T-1}) \end{bmatrix} = \Sigma.$$

These parameters are estimated by a local truncated log-likelihood method, that is, by maximizing

$$(\hat{\mu}, \hat{\Sigma}) = \text{Arg max}_{\mu\Sigma} \sum_{\tau=1}^{T} \left[\frac{1}{h^2} K\left(\frac{y_\tau - \tilde{y}}{h}\right) K\left(\frac{y_{\tau-1} - y_{T-1}}{h}\right) \log \varphi(y_\tau, y_{\tau-1}; \mu, \Sigma) \right]$$

$$-\sum_{\tau=1}^{T} \frac{1}{h^2} K\left(\frac{y_\tau - \tilde{y}}{h}\right) K\left(\frac{y_{\tau-1} - y_{T-1}}{h}\right)$$

$$\log \int\int \frac{1}{h^2} K\left(\frac{y_\tau - \tilde{y}}{h}\right) K\left(\frac{y_{\tau-1} - y_{T-1}}{h}\right) \varphi(y_\tau, y_{\tau-1}; \mu, \Sigma) dy_\tau dy_{\tau-1},$$

where $\varphi(y_t, y_{t-1}; \mu, \Sigma)$ denotes the pdf of the bivariate normal distribution with mean μ and variance Σ. From these estimators, we derive the approximated first- and second-order conditional moments

$$\hat{\mu}_{1|2}(\tilde{y}, y_{T-1}) = \hat{\mu}_1(\tilde{y}, y_{T-1}) - \frac{\hat{\sigma}_{1,2}(\tilde{y}, y_{T-1})}{\hat{\sigma}_2^2(\tilde{y}, y_{T-1})} \hat{\mu}_2(\tilde{y}, y_{T-1}),$$

$$\hat{\sigma}_{1|2}^2(\tilde{y}, y_{T-1}) = \hat{\sigma}_1^2(\tilde{y}, y_{T-1}) - \frac{\hat{\sigma}_{1,2}^2(\tilde{y}, y_{T-1})}{\hat{\sigma}_2^2(\tilde{y}, y_{T-1})},$$

which are used as inputs for the Gaussian VaR formula in (16.10).

We give in Figure 16.3 a comparison of the standard Gaussian VaR and the localized VaR for a portfolio that includes two stocks traded on the Toronto Stock Exchange: the Bank of Montreal and the Royal Bank. The data were sampled at 2-minute intervals and cover the month of October 1998. The proportion of the Bank of Montreal stock in the portfolio is given on the *x*-axis, whereas the VaR is measured on the *y*-axis. As expected, the localized VaR is much larger than the unlocalized VaR, revealing that the tails of returns are thicker than those of a Gaussian distribution. Moreover, the minimum extreme risk portfolio allocations (measured by the VaR) are significantly different under both approaches.

Note that the previous exercise concerns VaR at a very short horizon of 2 minutes. While such a risk measure is correct for intraday risk control, it cannot be used to derive the VaR at larger horizons of a day, week, or month. In such a case, returns sampled daily, monthly, or weekly seem more appropriate.

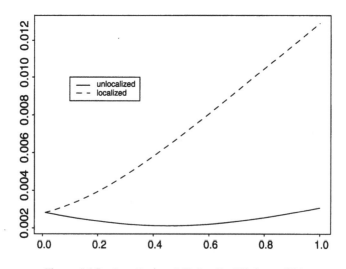

Figure 16.3 *Localized and Unlocalized Value at Risk*

16.2.4 Coherent Risk Measures

Despite its popularity among regulators, the VaR does not exactly correspond to standard risk measures implemented in the insurance industry. The reason is that it disregards the potential size of loss when it occurs. Artzner et al. (1997) proposed a constructive approach to evaluate the capital requirement; the approach is based on four desirable properties. Let $R_t[W]$ denote the required reserve amount for the future portfolio value W. The properties are monotonicity, invariance with respect to drift, homogeneity, and subadditivity.

Monotonicity
If W is more risky than W^* by the stochastic dominance of order 1, then $R_t(W) \geq R_t(W^*)$.

Invariance with Respect to Drift

$$R_t(W + c) = R_t(W) - c, \forall c, W.$$

The condition of invariance with respect to drift means that the required reserve should include the reserve already kept by the investor.

Homogeneity

$$R_t(\lambda W) = \lambda R_t(W), \qquad \forall \lambda \geq 0, \forall W.$$

Homogeneity is the condition of constant returns to scale. It is quite intuitive for λ close to 1, but not otherwise, especially for illiquid assets. Indeed, when an investor tries to sell quickly a stock of securities, the selling price per share in a lot of 200,000 shares is likely much lower than the selling price per share in a lot of 100,000 shares (see Chapter 14).

Subadditivity

$$R_t(W + W^*) \leq R_t(W) + R_t(W^*), \qquad \forall W, W^*.$$

Subadditivity, which is not "politically" neutral, points to an advantage of portfolio merging since it reduces the minimum required capital.

Homogeneity and subadditivity imply the convexity of the R function. It is easily checked that the standard reserve requirement associated with the VaR does not satisfy this condition. Artzner et al. (1997) have characterized the functions R that satisfy the conditions above. They are called *coherent risk measures*. In particular, the *expected shortfall* or *tail VaR*

$$TVaR(a, \alpha) = E_t[W_{t+1}(a) \,|\, W_{t+1}(a) - W_t(a) + VaR_t(a, \alpha) < 0], \qquad (16.18)$$

is a coherent risk measure. $TVaR(a,\alpha)$ is simply a (risk historical) pricing of a reinsurance contract, and the required reserve can be interpreted as a self-reinsurance.

16.3   Value at Risk Efficient Portfolios

Standard portfolio management rules are based on a mean-variance approach, for which risk is measured by the volatility of the future portfolio value. In this section, we reconsider the optimal portfolio allocation, with risk measured by the VaR. We first analyze the sensitivity of the VaR with respect to changes in the portfolio allocation. Next, we develop the corresponding theory of VaR efficient portfolios.

16.3.1   Sensitivity of the Value at Risk

Let us consider the VaR at horizon 1, defined by

$$P[a'\Delta p_{t+1} < -VaR_t(a,\alpha)] = \alpha.$$

The VaR depends on the portfolio allocation. Proposition 16.1 provides the analytical expressions of the first- and second-order derivatives of the VaR with respect to portfolio allocation (see Gourieroux, Laurent, and Scaillet 1999 for a proof).

PROPOSITION 16.1:

(i) $\dfrac{\partial VaR_t(a,\alpha)}{\partial a} = -E_t[\Delta p_{t+1} | a'\Delta\, p_{t+1} = -VaR_t(a,\alpha)].$

(ii) $\dfrac{\partial^2 VaR_t(a,\alpha)}{\partial a\partial a'} = \dfrac{\partial \log g_{a,t}}{\partial z}[-VaR_t(a,\alpha)]V_t[\Delta p_{t+1} | a'\Delta p_{t+1} = -VaR_t(a,\alpha)]$

$\qquad + \left\{\dfrac{\partial}{\partial z}V_t[\Delta p_{t+1} | a'\Delta p_{t+1} = z]\right\}_{z=-VaR_t(a,\alpha)},$

where $g_{a,t}$ denotes the conditional pdf of $a'\Delta p_{t+1}$.

Thus, the first- and second-order derivatives of the VaR can be written in terms of the first- and second-order conditional moments of price changes in a neighborhood of the VaR condition $a'\Delta p_{t+1} = -VaR_t(a,\alpha)$.

REMARK 16.5: The sensitivity of the VaR can be examined directly in the Gaussian case (see, e.g., Garman 1996, 1997). Let us denote by μ_t, and Ω_t the conditional mean and variance, respectively, of Δp_{t+1}. The VaR is given by

$$VaR_t(a,\alpha) = -a'\mu_t + \Phi^{-1}(1-\alpha)(a'\Omega_t a)^{1/2}.$$

We get

$$\frac{\partial VaR_t(a,\alpha)}{\partial a} = -\mu_t + \frac{\Omega_t a}{(a'\Omega_t a)^{1/2}}\Phi^{-1}(1-\alpha)$$

$$= -\mu_t + \frac{\Omega_t a}{a'\Omega_t a}[VaR_t(a,\alpha) + a'\mu_t]$$

$$= -E_t[\Delta p_{t+1}|a'\Delta p_{t+1} = -VaR_t(a,\alpha)].$$

16.3.2 The Optimization Problem

A portfolio selection rule based on probability of failure (also called the *safety first criterion*) was initially proposed by Roy (1952) (see Levy and Sarnat 1972; Arzac and Bawa 1977; Jansen, Koedijk, and de Vries 1998 for applications).

Let us consider a given budget w to be allocated at time t among n risky assets and a risk-free asset, with a risk-free interest rate r. The budget constraint at time t is

$$w = a_0 + a'p_t,$$

where a_0 is the amount invested in the risk-free asset and a the allocation in the risky assets. The portfolio value at the next date is

$$W_{t+1}(a) = a_0(1+r) + a'p_{t+1}$$
$$= w(1+r) + a'[p_{t+1} - (1+r)p_t]$$
$$= w(1+r) + a'Y_{t+1},$$

where Y_{t+1} is the excess gain. The required reserve amount for this portfolio is defined by

$$P_t[W_{t+1}(a) < -R_t(a_0,a;\alpha)] = \alpha. \tag{16.19}$$

It can be written in terms of the quantile of the risky part of the portfolio, denoted by $VaR_t(a,\alpha)$. This quantile is different from $VaR_t(a_0,a,\alpha) = w + R_t(a_0,a;\alpha)$. More precisely, we get

$$R_t(a_0,a,\alpha) + w(1+r) = VaR_t(a,\alpha),$$

where $VaR_t(a,\alpha)$ satisfies

$$P_t[a'Y_{t+1} < -VaR_t(a,\alpha)] = \alpha. \tag{16.20}$$

We define the VaR efficient portfolio as a portfolio with an allocation vector that solves the constrained optimization

$$\begin{cases} \max_a E_t W_{t+1}(a) \\ \text{subject to } R_t(a_0,a,\alpha) \le R^0, \end{cases}$$

where R^0 is a benchmark reserve level. This optimization is equivalent to

$$\begin{cases} \max_a a' E_t Y_{t+1} \\ \text{subject to } VaR_t(a,\alpha) \le VaR^0, \end{cases}$$

where $VaR^0 = R^0 + w(1+r)$.

PROPOSITION 16.2: *A VaR efficient portfolio satisfies the first-order condition*

$$E_t Y_{t+1} = \lambda^* E_t[Y_{t+1} | a^{*\prime} Y_{t+1} = -VaR^0],$$

where the Lagrange multiplier is determined by the constraint

$$VaR_t(a^*,\alpha) = VaR^0.$$

Thus, the first-order condition implies the proportionality between the expected excess gain and the expectation evaluated on the boundary of the risk contraint.

16.3.3   Estimation of Value at Risk Efficient Portfolios

Let us assume i.i.d. excess gains Y. For any allocation a, the VaR can be estimated as (see Section 16.2.3)

$$\frac{1}{T}\sum_{t=1}^{T} \Phi\left(\frac{-a'y_t - \widehat{VaR}(a,\alpha)}{h}\right) = \alpha,$$

where h is a bandwidth. Then, we can solve the problem of optimal allocation by applying a Gauss-Newton algorithm. The optimization in a neighborhood of an allocation $a^{(p)}$ becomes

$$\max_a a' EY_{t+1}$$

$$\text{subject to } VaR(a^{(p)},\alpha) + \frac{\partial VaR}{\partial a'}(a^{(p)}, \alpha)[a - a^{(p)}]$$

$$+ \frac{1}{2}[a - a^{(p)}]'\frac{\partial^2 VaR(a^{(p)},\alpha)}{\partial a \partial a'}[a - a^{(p)}] \le VaR^0.$$

This objective function admits the solution

$$a^{(p+1)} = a^{(p)} - \left[\frac{\partial^2 VaR}{\partial a \partial a'}(a^{(p)},\alpha)\right]^{-1}\frac{\partial VaR}{\partial a}(a^{(p)},\alpha)$$

$$+ \left[\frac{2[VaR^0 - VaR[a^{(p)},\alpha)] + Q(a^{(p)},\alpha)}{EY'_{t+1}\left[\frac{\partial^2 VaR}{\partial a \partial a'}(a^{(p)},\alpha)\right]^{-1} EY_{t+1}}\right]^{1/2} \left[\frac{\partial^2 VaR}{\partial a \partial a'}(a^{(p)}, \alpha)\right] EY_{t+1},$$

with $Q(a^{(p)},\alpha) = \frac{\partial VaR}{\partial a'}(a^{(p)},\alpha)\left[\frac{\partial^2 VaR}{\partial a \partial a'}(a^{(p)},\alpha)\right]^{-1}\frac{\partial VaR}{\partial a}(a^{(p)},\alpha).$

Next, the theoretical recursion is replaced by its empirical counterpart, in which the expectation EY_{t+1} is replaced by the empirical mean $\bar{y}_T$, whereas the VaR and its derivatives are replaced by their corresponding kernel estimates.

16.4 Utility Functions for Extreme Risks

In this section, we introduce a specification of infrequent extreme risks and show that an optimizing behavior based on expected CARA utility functions leads to zero demand for risky assets. Next, we introduce a class of utility functions that allows a strictly positively valued demand for risky assets.

16.4.1 A Drawback of Constant Absolute Risk Aversion Utility Functions

Let us assume that the distribution of excess asset returns is a mixture of two normal distributions

$$Y \sim \alpha N\left[m, \frac{1}{\alpha}\Omega_1\right] + (1-\alpha)N\left[m, \frac{1}{1-\alpha}\Omega_2\right], \tag{16.21}$$

with the same mean and weights α and $1 - \alpha$. The variance-covariance matrices are normalized according to the weights. Intuitively, if α is close to 0 (or to 1), there is an infrequently occurring regime of very large variance, that is, an extreme risk.

However, when the regime is unknown, the mean is equal to $\alpha m + (1-\alpha)m = m$, whereas the variance is $\alpha\frac{\Omega_1}{\alpha} + (1-\alpha)\frac{\Omega_2}{1-\alpha} = \Omega_1 + \Omega_2$. Therefore, the first- and second-order moments do not depend on the weights.

Let us now consider an investor with an absolute risk aversion coefficient $A = 1$. If the investor follows the standard mean-variance approach, the allocation of the efficient portfolio is

$$a^* = (\Omega_1 + \Omega_2)^{-1}m. \tag{16.22}$$

Alternatively, if an investor maximizes an expected CARA utility function, the optimal allocation solves the optimization objective

$$\tilde{a} = \text{Arg max}_a - E(\exp - a'Y)$$

$$= \text{Arg max}_a - \left\{\alpha \exp\left(-a'm + \frac{a'\Omega_1 a}{2\alpha}\right) + (1-\alpha) \exp\left(-a'm + \frac{a'\Omega_2 a}{2(1-\alpha)}\right)\right\}$$

Figure 16.4 displays the optimal allocations in a two-asset case, when

$$m = \begin{pmatrix} 1 \\ 1 \end{pmatrix}, \qquad \Omega_1 = \begin{pmatrix} 16 & 0 \\ 0 & 4 \end{pmatrix}, \qquad \Omega_2 = \begin{pmatrix} 4 & 0 \\ 0 & 16 \end{pmatrix}$$

for different weights.

In the non-Gaussian case, the mean-variance approach and the expected CARA utility approach yield very different portfolio allocations. The mean-variance approach provides a portfolio with equal allocations in the two assets for any value of α. The same allocations are obtained for the approach based on CARA utility function when $\alpha = 0.5$. However, when α is close to either 0 or 1, the demand $\tilde{a}$ for the risky assets tends to 0. Therefore, if investors believe in the CARA utility function, there is no market for infrequent extreme risks. This is a drawback of the class of CARA utility functions, which is therefore not adequate for the management of extreme risks.

16.4.2   The Left Integrable Risk Aversion Utility Functions

Gourieroux and Monfort (1998, 2000) characterized the utility functions to ensure a nondegenerate demand for assets with infrequent extreme risks.

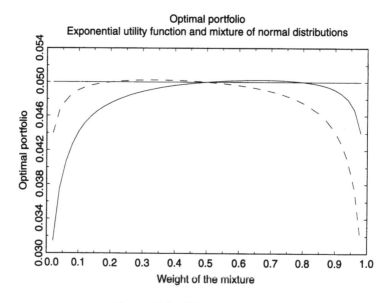

Figure 16.4   Efficient Allocations

PROPOSITION 16.3: *There exists a nonzero demand for infrequent extreme risks if and only if the utility function may be written as*

$$U(w) = -\int (w - x)^- dG(x) + cw,$$

where G is a cumulative distribution function, and c is a nonnegative scalar. These functions are called LIRA *(left integrable [absolute] risk aversion) utility functions.*

The associated expected utility has a simple interpretation. Indeed, we get, with $c = 0$,

$$E_W U(W) = -E_W E_X (W - X)^-,$$

where E_X and E_W are the expectations with respect to the distribution G and the return distribution, respectively. By commuting the expectations, we get

$$E_W U(W) = -E_X E_W (W - X)^- = -E_X P(X), \qquad (16.23)$$

where $P(X)$ is the expected cash flow of a European put written on the gain, with striking price X. The expected utility is the opposite of an average price for these puts, and the underlying distribution G defines the weights that correspond to various strikes.

16.4.3 Portfolio Management Based on Left Integrable Risk Aversion Utility

Let us assume i.i.d. excess returns and select a LIRA utility function with a distribution G and a scalar $c = 0$. The optimal allocation is the solution of

$$\bar{a} = \operatorname*{Arg\,max}_a E\left[-\int (a'Y + w - x)^- dG(x)\right],$$

where w denotes the initial endowment (under a zero risk-free rate). Consistent estimators of this optimal allocation are derived by replacing the theoretical expectations by empirical counterparts, either

$$\hat{a} = \operatorname*{Arg\,max}_a -\frac{1}{T}\Sigma_{t=1}^T \int (a'y_t + w - x)^- dG(x),$$

or

$$\hat{\hat{a}} = \operatorname*{Arg\,max}_a -\frac{1}{T}\Sigma_{t=1}^T (a'y_t + w - x_t^s)^-,$$

where x_t^s, $t = 1, \ldots, T$ are independent drawings in the distribution G.

16.5   Summary

A large part of the financial literature assumes that volatility is an appropriate measure of risk. However, this measure can be misleading in the presence of extreme risks due to the fat tails of the conditional distributions of returns. In this chapter, we described various types of distributions with fat tails and explained how to construct dynamic models with path-dependent tails. Next, we discussed an alternative risk measure proposed by financial regulators, called the VaR. The VaR defines the minimum capital required to be put aside for coverage of a financial loss with a fixed probability of occurrence. Any financial institution has to fulfill the minimum capital condition to acquire the authorization for managing portfolios. We showed that the VaR risk measure is related to a conditional quantile and explained how it can be computed in practice using either a parametric or a nonparametric approach. Finally, we discussed portfolio management in the presence of extreme risks. The management needs to be carried out with great care whenever a portfolio contains risky assets, such as derivatives or bonds with credit risk.

References

Abhyankar, A. (1995). Return and Volatility Dynamics in the FTSE 100 Stock Index and Stock Index Futures Markets, *Journal of Futures Markets*, 15, 457–488.

Abhyankar, A., D. Ghosh, E. Levin, and R. Limmack. (1997). Bid-Ask Spreads, Trading Volume and Volatility: Intra-day Evidence from the London Stock Exchange, *Journal of Business, Finance and Accounting*, 24, 343–362.

Abken, P., D. Madan, and S. Ramamurtie. (1996). *Estimation of Risk Neutral and Statistical Densities by Hermite Polynomial Approximations with an Application to Eurodollar Futures Options*, Discussion paper 96-5, Federal Reserve Bank of Atlanta, Atlanta, Ga.

Admati, A., and P. Pfleiderer. (1988). A Theory of Intraday Patterns: Volume and Price Variability, *Review of Financial Studies*, 1, 3–40.

Ait-Sahalia, Y. (1996). Nonparametric Pricing of Interest Rate Derivative Securities, *Econometrica*, 64, 527–560.

Ait-Sahalia, Y., and A. Lo. (1998). Nonparametric Estimation of State-Price Densities Implicit in Financial Asset Prices, *Journal of Finance*, 53, 499–547.

Akaike, H. (1974). Markovian Representation of Stochastic Processes and its Applications to the Analysis of Autoregressive Moving Average Processes, *Annals of the Institute of Statistical Mathematics*, 26, 363–387.

451

Akerlof, G. (1970). The Market for Lemons: Qualitative Uncertainty and the Market Mechanism, *Quarterly Journal of Economics*, 89, 488–500.

Altug, S., and P. Labadie. (1994). *Dynamic Choice and Asset Markets*, Academic Press, New York.

Amihud, Y., and H. Mendelson. (1980). Dealership Markets: Market Making with Uncertainty, *Journal of Financial Economics*, 8, 31–53.

———. (1982). Asset Price Behavior in a Dealership Market, *Financial Analysts Journal*, 38, May–June, 50–59.

———. (1987). Trading Mechanisms and Stock Returns: An Empirical Investigation, *Journal of Finance*, 42, 533–553.

———. (1991). Volatility, Efficiency and Trading: Evidence from the Japanese Market, *Journal of Finance*, 46, 369–395.

Ammer, J., and A. Brunner. (1997). Are Banks Market Timers or Market Makers? Explaining Foreign Exchange Profits, *Journal of International Financial Markets, Institutions and Money*, 7, 43–60.

Andersen, T., and T. Bollerslev. (1997a). Heterogenous Information Arrivals and Returns Volatility Dynamics, Uncovering the Long-Run in High Frequency Returns, *Journal of Finance*, 52, 975–1005.

———. (1997b). Intraday Periodicity and Volatility Persistence in Financial Markets, *Journal of Empirical Finance*, 4, 115–158.

———. (1998). DM-Dollar Volatility: Intraday Activity Patterns, Macroeconomic Announcements and Longer Run Dependencies, *Journal of Finance*, 53, 219–265.

Anderson, H., C. Granger, and A. Hall. (1990). *Treasury Bill Yield Curves and Cointegration*, Discussion paper 9024, University of California, San Diego.

Anderson, H., and F. Vahid. (1998). Testing Multiple Equation Systems for Common Nonlinear Components, *Journal of Econometrics*, 84, 1–36.

Anderson, T. W. (1971). *The Statistical Analysis of Time Series*, Wiley, New York.

Anderson, T. W., and L. Goodman. (1957). Statistical Inference about Markov Chains, *Annals of Mathematical Statistics*, 28, 89–109.

Arrow, K. (1959). Towards a Theory of Price Adjustment. In *The Allocation of Economic Resources*, M. Abramowitz et al., editors, 49–51. Stanford University Press.

———. (1964). The Role of Securities in the Optimal Allocation of Risk Bearing, *Review of Economic Studies*, 31, 91–96.

Arrow, K., and M. Nerlove. (1958). A Note on Expectations and Stability, *Econometrica*, 26, 297–305.

Artzner, P., F. Delbaen, J. Eber, and D. Heath. (1997). Thinking Coherently, *Risk*, 10, 68–71.

Arzac, E., and V. Bawa. (1977). Portfolio Choice and Equilibrium in Capital Markets with Safety First Investors, *Journal of Financial Economics*, 4, 277–288.

Baba, Y., R. Engle, D. Kraft, and K. Kroner. (1987). *Multivariate Simultaneous Generalized ARCH*, Discussion paper, University of California, San Diego.

Bachelier, L. (1900). Theory of Speculation. In *The Random Character of Stock Market Prices*, P. Costner, editor, MIT Press, Cambridge, 1964, reprint.

Bahra, B. (1996). Probability Distributions of Future Asset Prices Implied by Option Prices, *Bank of England Quarterly Bulletin*, 299–311.

Baillie, R., and T. Bollerslev. (1991). Intra-day and Intermarket Volatility in Foreign Exchange Rates, *Review of Economic Studies*, 58, 565–585.

Bakshi, G., C. Cao, and Z. Chen. (1997). Empirical Performance of Alternative Option Pricing Models, *Journal of Finance*, 52, 2003–2049.

Banz, R., and M. Miller. (1978). Prices for State Contingent Claims: Some Estimates and Applications, *Journal of Business*, 51, 653–672.

Barone-Adesi, G., and R. Whaley. (1987). Efficient Analytic Approximation of American Option Values, *Journal of Finance*, 42, 301–320.

Bassi, F., P. Embrechts, and M. Kafetzaki. (1997). Risk Management and Quantile Estimation. In *Practical Guide to Heavy Tails*, R. Adler, R. Feldman, and M. Taqqu, editors, Birkhauser, Boston.

Bates, D. (1991). The Crash of 87: Was it Expected ? The Evidence from Options Markets, *Journal of Finance*, 46, 1009–1044.

———. (1996a). Dollar Jump Fears, 1984–1992: Distributional Abnormalities Implicit in Currency Futures Options, *Journal of International Money and Finance*, 15, 65–93.

———. (1996b). Jumps and Stochastic Volatility: Exchange Rates Processes Implicit in Deutsche Mark Options, *Review of Financial Studies*, 9, 69–107.

Bauwens, L., and P. Giot. (1998a). *Introducing Price Information in the ACD Model with a Two State Transition ACD Model*, Discussion paper, CORE, Louvain, Belgium.

———. (2000). The Logarithmic ACD Model: An Application to the Bid/Ask Quote Process of Three NYSE Stocks, *Annales d'Economie et de Statistique*, 60, 117–149.

Beder, T. (1995). VaR: Seductive, but Dangerous, *Financial Analysts Journal*, 51, September–October, 12–21.

Berchtold, A. (1995). General Autoregressive Modelling of Markov Chains. In *Proceedings Volume of the 10th International Workshop on Statistical Modelling*, Geneva University, Discussion paper 9505, Springer-Verlag.

Biais, B. (1993). Price Formation and Equilibrium Liquidity in Fragmented and Centralized Markets, *Journal of Finance*, 48, 157–185.

Biais, B., T. Foucault, and P. Hillion. (1997). *Microstructure des Marchés Financiers*, Presses Universitaires de France, Collection Finance, Paris.

Biais, B., P. Hillion, and C. Spatt. (1995). An Empirical Analysis of the Limit Order Book and the Order Flow in the Paris Bourse, *Journal of Finance*, 5, 1655–1689.

Billingsley, P. (1961). *Statistical Inference for Markov Processes*, University Chicago Press, Chicago.

Billio, M., and A. Monfort. (1995). *Switching State Space Models*, Discussion paper, CREST, Paris.

Bissiere, C., and T. Kamionka. (1998). *Timing of Orders, Orders Aggressiveness and the Order Book of the Paris Bourse*, Toulouse University, Toulouse.

Black, F. (1972). Capital Market Equilibrium with Restricted Borrowing, *Journal of Business*, 45, 444–454.

———. (1976). Studies in Stock Price Volatility Changes. In *Proceedings of the 1976 Business and Economic Statistic Section*, 177–181. American Statistical Association, Alexandria, Va.

Black, F., and M. Scholes. (1973). The Pricing of Options and Corporate Liabilities, *Journal of Political Economy*, 81, 637–654.

Bloomfield, R., and M. O'Hara. (1999). Market Transparency: Who Wins and Who Loses? *Review of Financial Studies*, 12, 5–35.

Blume, M., and I. Friend. (1973). A New Look at the Capital Asset Pricing Model, *Journal of Finance*, 28, 19–33.

Bollerslev, T. (1986). Generalized Autoregressive Conditional Heteroskedasticity, *Journal of Econometrics*, 32, 307–327.

———. (1987). *A Multivariate GARCH Model with Constant Conditional Correlations for a Set of Exchange Rates*, Discussion paper, Northwestern University, Evanston, IL.

———. (1990). Modelling the Coherence in Short Run Nominal Exchange Rates: A Multivariate Generalized ARCH Model, *Review of Economics and Statistics*, 72, 498–505.

Bollerslev, T., R. Chou, and K. Kroner. (1992). ARCH Modelling in Finance: A Review of the Theory and Empirical Evidence, *Journal of Econometrics*, 52, 5–59.

Bollerslev, T., and I. Domowitz. (1993). Trading Patterns and Prices in the Interbank Foreign Exchange Market, *Journal of Finance*, 48, 1421–1443.

Bollerslev, T., R. Engle, and D. Nelson. (1994). ARCH Models. In *Handbook of Econometrics*, vol. 4, 2961–3040. R. Engle and D. McFadden, editors, Elsevier, Amsterdam.

Bollerslev, T., R. Engle, and J. Wooldridge. (1988). A Capital Asset Pricing Model with Time Varying Covariance, *Journal of Political Economy*, 96, 116–131.

Bollerslev, T., and M. Melvin. (1994). Bid-Ask Spreads and Volatility in the Foreign Exchange Market: An Empirical Analysis, *Journal of International Economics*, 36, 355–372.

Boos, D. (1984). Using Extreme Value Theory to Estimate Large Percentiles, *Technometrics*, 26, 33–39.

Box, G., and G. Jenkins. (1970). *Time Series Analysis: Forecasting and Control*, Holden-Day, San Francisco.

Box, G., and D. Pierce. (1970). Distribution of Residual Autocorrelation in Autoregressive Integrated Moving Average Time Series Models, *Journal of the American Statistical Association*, 65, 1509–1529.

Breeden, D. (1979). An Intertemporal Asset Pricing Model with Stochastic Consumption and Investment Opportunities, *Journal of Financial Economics*, 7, 265–296.

Breeden, D., and R. Litzenberger. (1978). Price of State Contingent Claims Implicit in Option Prices, *Journal of Business*, 51, 621–651.

Brennan, M., and E. Schwartz. (1979). A Continuous Time Approach to the Pricing of Bonds, *Journal of Banking and Finance*, 3, 135–153.

Brock, W., J. Lakonishok, and B. Le Baron. (1992). Simple Technical Trading Rules and the Stochastic Properties of Stock Returns, *Journal of Finance*, 47, 1731–1764.

Brown, B., and S. Maital. (1981). What Do Economists Know? An Empirical Study of Experts' Expectations, *Econometrica*, 49, 491–504.

Brown, S. (1989). The Number of Factors in Security Returns, *Journal of Finance*, 44, 1247–1262.

Broze, L., C. Gourieroux, and A. Szafarz. (1985). Solutions of Dynamic Linear Rational Expectations Models, *Econometric Theory*, 1, 341–368.

———. (1990). *Reduced Form of Rational Expectations Models*, Harwood Academic Publishers, London.

Broze, L., O. Scaillet, and J. M. Zakoian. (1995). Testing for Continuous Time Models of the Short Term Interest Rate, *Journal of Empirical Finance*, 2, 199–223.

Campa, J., and P. Chang. (1995). Testing the Expectations Hypothesis on the Term Structure of Implied Volatilities in Foreign Exchange Options, *Journal of Finance*, 50, 529–547.

Campbell, J. (1987). Stock Returns and the Term Structure, *Journal of Financial Economics*, 18, 373–399.

Campbell, J., A. Lo, and A. McKinlay. (1997). *The Econometrics of Financial Markets*, Princeton University Press, Princeton, N.J.

Campbell, J., and N. Mankiw. (1987). Are Output Fluctuations Transitory? *Quarterly Journal of Economics*, 102, 857–880.

Campbell, J., and R. Shiller. (1987). Cointegration and Test of Present Value Models, *Journal of Political Economy*, 95, 1062–1088.

———. (1988). Dividend Price Ratios and Expectations of Future Dividends and Discount Factors, *Review of Financial Studies*, 1, 195–228.

Canina, L., and S. Figlewski. (1993). The Informational Content of Implied Volatility, *Review of Financial Studies*, 6, 659–681.

Carpenter, J., P. Clifford, and P. Fearnhead. (1996). Sampling Strategies for Monte-Carlo Filters of Nonlinear Systems, *IEE Colloquium Digest*, 243, 611–613.

Chamberlain, G. (1983). Funds, Factors and Diversification in Arbitrage Pricing Models, *Econometrica*, 51, 1305–1323.

Chamberlain, G., and M. Rothschild. (1983). Arbitrage, Factor Structure and Mean Variance Analysis in Large Asset Markets, *Econometrica*, 51, 1281–1301.

Chan, K., Y. Chung, and H. Johnson. (1995). The Intraday Behavior of Bid-Ask Spreads for NYSE Stocks and CBOE Options, *Journal of Financial and Quantitative Analysis*, 30, 329–346.

Chan, K., G. Karolyi, F. Longstaff, and A. Sanders. (1992). An Empirical Comparison of Alternative Models of the Short Term Interest Rate, *Journal of Finance*, 47, 1209–1227.

Chatfield, C. (1975). *The Analysis of Time Series: Theory and Practice*, Chapman and Hall, London.

Chen, N., and J. Ingersoll. (1983). Exact Pricing in Linear Factor Models with Infinitely Many Assets: A Note, *Journal of Finance*, 38, 985–988.

Chen, X., L. Hansen, and J. Scheinkman. (1998). *Shape Preserving Estimation of Diffusion*, Discussion paper, University of Chicago, Chicago.

Chow, K., and K. Denning. (1993). A Simple Multiple Variance Ratio Test, *Journal of Econometrics*, 58, 385–401.

Christie, A. (1982). The Stochastic Behavior of Common Stock Variances: Value, Leverage and Interest Rate Effects, *Journal of Financial Economics*, 10, 407–432.

Christie, W., and P. Schultz. (1994). Why Do NASDAQ Market Markers Avoid Odd-Eight Quotes? *Journal of Finance*, 49, 1813–1840.

Clark, P. K. (1973). A Subordinated Stochastic Process Model with Finite Variance for Speculative Prices, *Econometrica*, 41, 135–155.

Clement, E., C. Gourieroux, and A. Monfort. (2000). Econometric Specification of the Risk Neutral Valuation Model, *Journal of Econometrics*, 94, 177–143.

Cochrane, J. (1991). Volatility Tests and Efficient Market: A Review Essay, *Journal of Monetary Economics*, 27, 463–485.

———. (1988). How Big is the Random Walk in GNP? *Journal of Political Economy*, 96, 893–920.

———. (2001). *Asset Pricing*, Princeton University Press, Princeton, N.J.

Conley, T., L. Hansen, E. Luttmer, and J. Scheinkman. (1997). Short-Term Interest Rates as Subordinated Diffusions, *Review of Financial Studies*, 10, 525–577.

Connor, G. (1984). A Unified Beta Pricing Theory, *Journal of Economic Theory*, 34, 13–31.

Cootner, P. (1969). *The Random Character of Stock Market Prices*, MIT Press, Cambridge.

Copeland, T., and D. Galai. (1983). Information Effects and the Bid-Ask Spread, *Journal of Finance*, 38, 1457–1469.

Cordella, T., and T. Foucault. (1999). Minimum Price Variations, Time Priority and Quote Dynamics, *Journal of Financial Intermediation*, 8, 141–173.

Corrado, C., and T. Su. (1996). S&P Index Option Tests of Jarrow and Rudd's Approximate Option Valuation Formula, *Journal of Futures Markets*, 16, 611–629.

Cox, J., and M. Rubinstein. (1985). *Options Markets*, Prentice-Hall, Englewood Cliffs, N.J.

Cox, J., J. Ingersoll, and S. Ross. (1985). A Theory of the Term Structure of Interest Rates, *Econometrica*, 53, 385–407.

Cox, J., S. Ross, and M. Rubinstein. (1979). Option Pricing: A Simplified Approach, *Journal of Financial Economics*, 7, 229–263.

Cox, S., and H. Miller. (1965). *The Theory of Stochastic Processes*, 2nd edition, Chapman and Hall, London.

Danielsson, J., and G. de Vries. (1998). *Beyond the Sample: Extreme Quantile and Probability Estimation*, Discussion paper 298, London School of Economics, London.

———. (2000). Value at Risk and Extreme Returns, *Annales d'Economie et de Statistique*, 60, 239–270.

Darolles, S., J. P. Florens, and C. Gourieroux. (1998). *Kernel Based Nonlinear Canonical Analysis*, Discussion paper 9855, CREST, Paris.

Darolles, S., C. Gourierioux, and G. Le Fol. (2000). Intraday Transaction Price Dynamics, *Annales d'Economie et de Statistique*, 60, 207–238.

Debreu, G. (1959). *Theory of Value*, Wiley, New York.

De Haan, L., and S. Resnick. (1980). A Simple Asymptotic Estimate for the Index of a Stable Distribution, *Journal of the Royal Statistical Society*, B, 42, 83–87.

De Jong, F., R. Mahieu, and P. Schotman. (1998). Price Discovery in the Foreign Exchange Market: An Empirical Analysis of the Yen/DMark Rate, *Journal of International Money and Finance*, 17, 5–27.

De Jong, F., and T. Nijman. (1997). High Frequency Analysis of Lead-Lag Relationships between Financial Markets, *Journal of Empirical Finance*, 4, 259–277.

Demoura, S. (1993). Theory and Application of Transition Operator to the Analysis of Economic Time Series. Necessary and Sufficient Conditions for Nonlinearities in Economic Dynamics; Aliasing Problem, manuscript.

Derman, E., and I. Kani. (1994). Riding on a Smile, *Risk*, 7, 32–39.

———. (1997). *Stochastic Implied Trees: Arbitrage Pricing with a Stochastic Term and Strike Structure of Volatility*, Quantitative Strategies Technical Notes, Goldman-Sachs. New York.

Dhaene, G., C. Gourieroux, and O. Scaillet. (1998). Instrumental Models, *Econometrica*, 66, 3, 673–688.

Dickey, D., and W. Fuller. (1979). Distribution of the Estimators for Autoregressive Time Series with a Unit Root, *Journal of the American Statistical Association*, 74, 427–431.

Dickey, D., and W. Fuller. (1981). Likelihood Ratio Statistics for Autoregressive Time Series with a Unit Root, *Econometrica*, 49, 1057–1072.

Diebold, F., and A. Inoue (1999). *Long Memory and Structural Change*, Discussion paper, Stern Business School, New York University, New York.

Diebold, F., and M. Nerlove. (1989). The Dynamic of Exchange Rate Volatility: A Multivariate Latent Factor ARCH Model, *Journal of Applied Econometrics*, 4, 1–22.

Ding, Z., R. Engle, and C. Granger. (1993). A Long Memory Property of Stock Market Returns and a New Model, *Journal of Empirical Finance*, 1, 83–106.

Domowitz, I. (1993). A Taxonomy of Automated Trade Execution Systems, *Journal of International Money and Finance*, 12, 607–631.

Domowitz, I., and J. Wang. (1994). Auctions as Algorithms: Computerized Trade Execution and Price Discovery, *Journal of Economic Dynamics and Control*, 18, 29–60.

Doob, J. (1953). *Stochastic Processes*, Wiley, New York.

Duan, J. C. (1994). Maximum Likelihood Estimation using Price Data of the Derivative Contracts, *Mathematical Finance*, 4, 155–167.

———. (1995). The GARCH Option Pricing Model, *Mathematical Finance*, 5, 13–32.

Duffie, D., and P. Glynn. (1997). Estimation of Continuous Time Markov Processes Sampled at Random Time Interval, Discussion paper, Graduate School of Business, Stanford University.

Duffie, D., and J. Pan. (1997). An Overview of Value at Risk, *Journal of Derivatives*, 4, 7–49.

Duffie, D., and K. Singleton. (1993). Simulated Moments Estimation of Markov Models of Asset Prices, *Econometrica*, 61, 929–952.

Dufour, A., and R. Engle. (1999). *The ACD Model: Predictability of the Time between Consecutive Trades*, Discussion paper, University of California, San Diego.

Dumas, B., J. Fleming, and R. Whaley. (1998). Implied Volatility Functions: Empirical Tests, *Journal of Finance*, 53, 2059–2106.

Dupire, B. (1994). Pricing with a Smile, *Risk*, 7, 18–20.

Easley, D., and M. O'Hara. (1987). Price, Trade Size, and Information in Securities Markets, *Journal of Financial Economics*, 19, 69–90.

———. (1992). Time and the Process of Security Price Adjustment, *Journal of Finance*, 47, 577–606.

Easley, D., N. Kiefer, M. O'Hara, and J. Paperman. (1996). Liquidity, Information and Infrequently Traded Stocks, *Journal of Finance*, 51, September 1405–1436.

El Jahel, L., W. Perraudin, and P. Sellin. (1998). *Value at Risk for Derivatives*, Discussion paper IFR 50, Birbeck College, University of London, London, UK.

Embrechts, P., A. McNeil, D. Straumann, and R. Kaufmann. (1999). Modelling Extremal Events for Insurance and Finance, 15th International Summer School of the Swiss Association of Actuaries.

Engle, R. (1982). Autoregressive Conditional Heteroskedasticity with Estimates of the Variance of UK Inflation, *Econometrica*, 50, 987–1008.

————. (2000). The Econometrics of Ultra High Frequency Data, *Econometrica*, 68, 1–22.

Engle, R., and C. Granger. (1987). Cointegration and Error Correction: Representation, Estimation and Testing, *Econometrica*, 55, 251–276.

Engle, R., C. Granger, and D. Kraft. (1984). Combining Competing Forecasts of Inflation Using a Bivariate ARCH Model, *Journal of Economics Dynamics and Control*, 6, 151–165.

Engle, R., and S. Kozicki. (1993). Testing for Common Features, *Journal of Business and Economic Statistics*, 11, 369–380.

Engle, R., D. Lilien, and R. Robbins. (1987). Estimating Time Varying Risk Premia in the Term Structure: The ARCH-M Model, *Econometrica*, 55, 391–407.

Engle, R., and S. Manganelli. (1999). *CaViar: Conditional Autoregressive Value at Risk by Regression Quantiles*, Discussion paper, University of California, San Diego.

Engle, R., and C. Mustafa. (1992). Implied ARCH Models from Option Prices, *Journal of Econometrics*, 52, 289–311.

Engle, R., V. Ng, and M. Rothschild. (1990). Asset Pricing with a Factor ARCH Covariance Structure: Empirical Estimates for Treasury Bills, *Journal of Econometrics*, 45, 213–237.

Engle, R., and J. Russell. (1997). Forecasting the Frequency of Changes in Quoted Foreign Exchange Prices with the Autoregressive Conditional Duration Model, *Journal of Empirical Finance*, 12, 187–212.

————. (1998a). Autoregressive Conditional Duration: A New Model for Irregularly Spaced Transaction Data, *Econometrica*, 66, 1127–1162.

————. (1998b). *Econometric Analysis of Discrete Valued, Irregularly Spaced Financial Transactions Data Using a New Autoregressive Conditional Multinomial Model*, Discussion paper, University of California, San Diego.

Epstein, L. (1992). Behavior Under Risk: Recent Developments in Theory and Application. In *Advances in Economic Theory*, vol. 2, 1–63. J. J. Laffont, editor, Cambridge University Press, Cambridge, UK.

Epstein, L., and S. Zin. (1989). Substitution, Risk Aversion and the Temporal Behaviour of Consumption and Asset Returns: A Theoretical Framework, *Econometrica*, 57, 937–968.

————. (1990). First Order Risk Aversion and the Equity Premium Puzzle, *Journal of Monetary Economics*, 26, 387–407.

————. (1991). Substitution, Risk Aversion and the Temporal Behaviour of Consumption and Asset Returns: An Empirical Investigation, *Journal of Political Economy*, 99, 263–286.

Falk, M. (1985). Asymptotic Normality of the Kernel Quantile Estimator, *Annals of Statistics*, 13, 428–433.

Fama, E. (1963). Mandelbrot and the Stable Paretian Hypothesis. In *The Random Character of Stock Market Prices*, P. Costner, editor, MIT Press, Cambridge, Mass., 1969, reprint.

———. (1965). The Behavior of Stock Market Prices, *Journal of Business*, 38, 34–105.

———. (1976). Forward Rates as Predictors of Future Spot Rates, *Journal of Financial Economics*, 3, 361–377.

———. (1984). The Information in the Term Structure, *Journal of Financial Economics*, 13, 509–528.

———. (1990). Term Structure Forecasts of Interest Rates, Inflation and Real Returns, *Journal of Monetary Economics*, 25, 59–76.

Fama, E., and J. McBeth. (1973). Risk, Return and Equilibrium: Empirical Tests, *Journal of Political Economy*, 81, 607–636.

Faust, J. (1992). When Are Variance Ratio Tests for Serial Dependence Optimal, *Econometrica*, 60, 1215–1226.

Feinstone, L. (1987). Minute by Minute: Efficiency, Normality and Randomness in the Intra-Daily Asset Prices, *Journal of Applied Econometrics*, 2, 193–214.

Fisher, I. (1896). "Appreciation and Interest," *Publications of the American Economic Association*, Nashville, Tenn., 23–29, 88–92.

———. (1922). *The Making of Index Numbers*, Houghton, Boston.

———. (1930a). *The Theory of Interest*, Macmillan, New York.

———. (1930b). *The Theory of Interest as Determined by Impatience to Spend Income and the Opportunity to Invest It*, Macmillan, New York.

Flavin, M. (1983). Excess Volatility in the Financial Markets: A Reassessment of the Empirical Evidence, *Journal of Political Economy*, 91, 929–956.

Flood, M., R. Huisman, K. Koedijk, and R. Mahieu. (1999). Quote Disclosure and Price Discovery in Multiple Dealer Financial Markets, *Review of Financial Studies*, 12, 37–59.

Foellmer, H., and P. Leukert. (1999). Quantile Hedging, *Finance and Stochastics*, 3, 251–273.

Follmer, H., and M. Schweizer. (1991). Hedging of Contingent Claims under Incomplete Information. In *Applied Stochastic Analysis*, Stochastic Monographs, vol. 5, 389–414. M. Davis and R. Elliott, editors, Gordon and Breach.

Forsyth, F., and R. Fowler. (1981). The Theory and Practice of Chain Price Index Numbers, *JRSS*, *A*, 144, 224–246.

Foster, F., and S. Viswanathan. (1993). Variations in Trading Volume, Return Volatility and Trading Costs: Evidence on Recent Price Formation Models, *Journal of Finance*, 48, 187–211.

Frankel, J., G. Galli, and A. Giovannini. (1996). *The Microstructure of Foreign Exchange Markets*, University of Chicago Press, Chicago.

Franses, P., and D. VanDijk. (2000). *Nonlinear Time Series Models in Empirical Finance*, Cambridge University Press, Cambridge.

Friedman, B. (1980). Survey Evidence and the Rationality of Interest Rate Expectations, *Journal of Monetary Economics*, 6, 453–465.

Friedman, M. (1957). *A Theory of Consumption Function*, National Bureau of Economic Research, New York.

Fuller, W. (1976). *Introduction to Statistical Time Series*, Wiley, New York.

Gallant, A., P. Rossi, and G. Tauchen. (1992). Stock Prices and Volume, *Review of Financial Studies*, 5, 199–242.

Gallant, A., and G. Tauchen. (1992). A Nonparametric Approach to Nonlinear Time Series Analysis, Estimation and Simulation. In *IMA Volumes on Mathematics and Its Applications*, Billinger, D., Caines, L., Geweke, J., Parzen, E., Rosenblatt, M., and Taggu, M. editors, Springer-Verlag, New York, 71–92.

———. (1996). Which Moments to Match, *Econometric Theory*, 12, 657–681.

Garbade, K., and W. Silber. (1979). Structural Organisation of Secondary Markets: Clearing Frequency, Dealer Activity and Liquidity Risk, *Journal of Finance*, 34, 577–593.

Garman, M. (1976a). *A General Theory of Asset Valuation under Diffusion State Processes*, Working Paper 50, University of California, Berkeley.

———. (1976b). Market Microstructure, *Journal of Financial Economics*, 3, 257–278.

———. (1996). Improving on VaR, *Risk*, 9, 61–63.

———. (1997). Taking VaR to Pieces, *Risk*, 10, 70–71.

George, T., G. Kaul, and M. Nilamendran. (1991). Estimation of Bid-Ask Spreads and Its Components: A New Approach, *Review of Financial Studies*, 4, 623–656.

Geweke, J. (1982). Measurement of Linear Dependence and Feedback between Multiple Time Series, *Journal of the American Statistical Association*, 77, 304–313.

Geweke, J., and S. Porter-Hudak. (1982). The Estimation and Application of Long Memory Time Series Models, *Journal of Time Series Analysis*, 4, 221–238.

Ghysels, E., C. Gourieroux, and J. Jasiak. (1997). Trading Patterns, Time Deformation and Stochastic Volatility in Foreign Exchange Markets. In *Nonlinear Modelling of High Frequency Financial Time Series*, 127–160. C. Dunis and B. Zhou, editors, Wiley, New York.

———. (1998a). Kernel Autocorrelogram for Time Deformed Processes, *Journal of Statistical Planning and Inference*, 68, 167–191.

———. (1998b). *Stochastic Volatility Duration Models*, Discussion paper, CREST, Paris.

Ghysels, E., A. Harvey, and E. Renault. (1996). Stochastic Volatility. In *Handbook of Statistics*, vol. 14, 119–192. G. Madala and C. Rao, editors. North Holland, Elsevier Science, Amsterdam.

Ghysels, E., and J. Jasiak. (1998). GARCH for Irregularly Spaced Financial Data: The ACD-GARCH Model, *Studies in Nonlinear Dynamics and Econometrics*, 2(4), 133–149.

Gibbons, M. (1982). Multivariate Tests of Financial Models: A New Approach, *Journal of Financial Economics*, 10, 3-27.

Glosten, L. (1987). Components of the Bid-Ask Spread and the Statistical Properties of Transaction Prices, *Journal of Finance*, 42, 1293-1308.

Glosten, L., and L. Harris. (1988). Estimating the Components of the Bid-Ask Spreads, *Journal of Financial Economics*, 21, 123-142.

Glosten, L., and P. Milgrom. (1985). Bid-Ask and Transaction Prices in a Specialist Market with Heterogeneously Informed Traders, *Journal of Financial Economics*, 14, 71-100.

Goodhart, C., and L. Figlivoli. (1991). Every Minute Counts in Financial Markets, *Journal of International Money and Finance*, 10, 23-52.

Goodhart, C., and M. O'Hara. (1997). High Frequency Data in Financial Markets: Issues and Applications, *Journal of Empirical Finance*, 4, 73-114.

Gourieroux, C. (1997). *ARCH Models and Financial Applications*, Springer-Verlag, New York.

Gourieroux, C., and J. Jasiak. (1998). Nonlinear Autocorrelograms: An Application to Intertrade Durations, *Journal of Time Series Analysis*, forthcoming.

———. (1999a). Dynamic Factor Models, *Econometric Reviews*, forthcoming.

———. (1999b). *Nonlinear Innovations and Impulse Response*, CEPREMAP DP 9906, Paris.

———. (1999c). *Nonlinear Persistence and Copersistence*, CREST, DP 9963, Paris.

———. (2000a). State Space Models with Finite Dimensional Dependence, *Journal of Time Series Analysis*, Vol. 22, 4.

———. (2000b). *Local Likelihood Density Estimation and Value at Risk*, Discussion paper, CREST, Paris.

———. (2001). Memory and Infrequent Breaks, *Economics Letters*, 70, 29-41.

Gourieroux, C., J. Jasiak, and G. Le Fol. (1999). Intra-Day Market Activity, *Journal of Financial Markets*, 2, 193-226.

Gourieroux, C., J. J. Laffont, and A. Monfort. (1982). Rational Expectations in Dynamic Linear Models: Analysis of the Solutions, *Econometrica*, 50, 409-425.

Gourieroux, C., J. P. Laurent, and O. Scaillet. (2000). Sensitivity Analysis of Values at Risk, *Journal of Empirical Finance*, 7, 225-246.

Gourieroux, C., and G. Le Fol. (1998). Modes de négociations et caractéristiques de marché, *Revue Economique*, 49, 795-808.

Gourieroux, C., G. Le Fol, and B. Meyer. (1998). Etude du Carnet d'Ordres, *Banques et Marches*, 36, 5-20.

Gourieroux, C., and A. Monfort. (1992). Qualitative Threshold ARCH Models, *Journal of Econometrics*, 52, 159-199.

———. (1995). *Statistics and Econometric Models*, Cambridge University Press, Cambridge, UK.

———. (1996). *Simulation Based Econometric Methods*, Oxford University Press, Oxford, UK.

————. (1997). *Time Series and Dynamic Models*, Cambridge University Press, Chapters 15, 16.

————. (1998). *The Econometrics of Efficient Frontiers*, Discussion paper 9834, CREST, Paris.

————. (2000). *Infrequent Extreme Risks*, Discussion paper, CREST, Paris.

Gourieroux, C., A. Monfort, and E. Renault. (1987). Kullback Causality Measures, *Annales d'Economie et de Statistique*, 617, 369–410.

————. (1993). Indirect Inference, *Journal of Applied Econometrics*, 8, 85–118.

————. (1995). Inference in Factor Models. In *Advances in Econometrics and Quantitative Economics*, 311–353. G. Maddala, P. C. B. Phillips, and T. Srinivasan, editors, Blackwell. Oxford, UK.

Gourieroux, C., A. Monfort, and C. Tenreiro. (2000). Kernel M-Estimators and Functional Residual Plots. In *Panel Data Econometrics: Future Directions*, 235–278. J. Krishnakumar and E. Ronchetti, editors, North Holland, Amsterdam.

Gourieroux, C., A. Monfort, and A. Trognon. (1984). Pseudo Maximum Likelihood Methods: Theory, *Econometrica*, 52, 681–700.

Gourieroux, C., and I. Peaucelle. (1992). Séries codépendantes: Application à l'hypothèse de Parité du Pouvoir d'Achat, *Revue d'Analyse Economique*, 68, 283–304.

Gourieroux, C., and J. Pradel. (1985). Direct Test of the Rational Expectation Hypothesis (with Special Attention to Qualitative Variables), *European Economic Review*, 30, 265–284.

Gourieroux, C., O. Scaillet, and A. Szafarz. (1997). *Econometrie de la Finance*, Economica, Paris.

Grammig, J., R. Hujer, S. Kokot, and K. Maurer. (1998). *Modeling the Deutsche Telekom IPO Using a New ACD Specification*, Discussion paper 55, Research Center on Quantification and Simulation of Economic Processes, Humboldt University, Berlin.

Granger, C. (1980). Long Memory Relationships and the Aggregation of Dynamic Models, *Journal of Econometrics*, 14, 227–238.

————. (1986). Developments in the Study of Cointegrated Economic Variables, *Oxford Bulletin of Economics and Statistics*, 48, 213–228.

Granger, C., and R. Joyeux. (1980). An Introduction to Long Memory Time Series Models and Fractional Differencing, *Journal of Time Series Analysis*, 1, 15–29.

Granger, C., and T. Terasvirta. (1999). Simple Nonlinear Time Series Model with Misleading Linear Properties, *Economic Letters*, 62, 161–165.

Granger, C. W. J. (1969). Investigating Causal Relations by Econometric Models and Cross Spectral Methods, *Econometrica*, 37, 424–439.

————. (1980). Testing for Causality: A Personal Viewpoint, *Journal of Economic Dynamics and Control*, 2, 329–352.

Griliches, Z. (1961). Hedonic Price Indexes for Automobiles: An Econometric Analysis of Quality Change. In *The Price Statistics of the Federal Government*, General Series No. 73, 137–196. Columbia University Press, New York.

Grinblatt, M., and S. Titman. (1983). Factor Pricing in a Finite Economy, *Journal of Financial Economics*, 12, 497–568.

Grossman, S., A. Melino, and R. Shiller. (1987). Estimating the Continuous-Time Consumption-Based Asset-Pricing Model, *Journal of Business and Economic Statistics*, 5, 315–327.

Grossman, S., and R. Shiller. (1981). The Determinants of the Variability of Stock Market Prices, *American Economic Review*, 71, 222–227.

Guillaume, D., M. Dacorogna, R. Dave, U. Muller, R. Olsen, and O. Pictet. (1997). From the Bird's Eye View to the Microscope: A Survey of New Stylized Facts of the Intra-daily Exchange Markets, *Finance and Stochastics*, 1, 95–126.

Guillaume, D., M. Dacarogna, and O. Pictet. (1995). *On the Intra-Daily Performance of GARCH Processes*, Working Paper, Olsen and Associates, Zurich.

Hafner, C. (1998). *Nonlinear Time Series Analysis with Appications to Foreign Exchange Rates Volatility*, Physica-Verlag, Contributions to Economics, Heidelberg, Germany.

Hall, R. (1988). Intertemporal Substitution in Consumption, *Journal of Political Economy*, 96, 221–273.

Hamao, Y., and J. Hasbrouck. (1995). Securities Trading in the Absence of Dealers: Trades and Quotes on the Tokyo Stock Exchange, *Review of Financial Studies*, 8, 849–878.

Hamilton, J. (1989). A New Approach to the Economic Analysis of Nonstationary Time Series and the Business Cycle, *Econometrica*, 57, 357–384.

———. (1990). Analysis of Time Series Subject to Changes in Regime, *Journal of Econometrics*, 45, 39–70.

———. (1994). *Time Series Analysis*, Princeton University Press, Princeton, N.J.

Hamilton, J., and O. Jorda. (1999). *A Model for the Federal Funds Rate Target*, Discussion paper, University of California, San Diego.

———. (1989). A New Approach to the Economic Analysis of Nonstationary Time Series and the Business Cycle, *Econometrica*, 57, 357–384.

———. (1990). Analysis of Time Series Subject to Changes in Regime, *Journal of Econometrics*, 45, 39–70.

Hannan, E. (1970). *Multiple Time Series*, Wiley, New York.

Hansen, L. (1982). Large Sample Properties of Generalized Method of Moment Estimators, *Econometrica*, 50, 1029–1054.

Hansen, L., and R. Hodrich. (1980). Forward Exchange Rates as Optimal Predictors of Future Spot Rates, *Journal of Political Economy*, 88, 829–853.

Hansen, L., and R. Jagannathan. (1991). Implications of Security Market Data for Models of Dynamic Economics, *Journal of Political Economy*, 99, 225–262.

Hansen, L., and S. Richard. (1987). The Role of Conditioning Information in Deducing Testable Restrictions Implied by Dynamic Asset Pricing Models, *Econometrica*, 54, 587–613.

Hansen, L., and J. Scheinkman. (1995). Back to the Future: Generating Moment Implications for Continuous Time Markov Processes, *Econometrica*, 63, 765–804.

Hansen, L., J. Scheinkman, and N. Touzi. (1998). Spectral Methods for Identifying Scalar Diffusions, *Journal of Econometrics*, 86, 1–32.

Hansen, L., and K. Singleton. (1982). Generalized Instrumental Variables Estimation of Nonlinear Rational Expectations Models, *Econometrica*, 63, 767–804.

———. (1983). Stochastic Consumption, Risk Aversion and the Temporal Behavior of Asset Returns, *Journal of Political Economy*, 91, 249–268.

Hansen, P., and S. Johansen. (1998). *Workbook on Cointegration*, Oxford University Press, Oxford, UK.

Hardle, W., and P. Vieu. (1992). Kernel Regression Smoothing of Time Series, *Journal of Time Series Analysis*, 13, 209–232.

Harrison, M., and S. Pliska. (1981). Martingales and Stochastic Integrals in the Theory of Continuous Trading, *Stochastic Processes and Their Applications*, 11, 215–260.

Harrison, J., and D. Kreps. (1979). Martingales and Arbitrage in Multiperiod Securities Markets, *Journal of Economic Theory*, 20, 381–408.

Hartmann, P. (1998). Do Reuters Spreads Reflect Currencies Differences in Global Trading Activity? *Journal of International Money and Finance*, 17, 757–784.

———. (1999). Trading Volumes and Transaction Costs in the Foreign Exchange Market: Evidence from the Daily Dollar-Yen Spot Data, *Journal of Banking and Finance*, 23, 801–824.

Harvey, A. (1989). *Forecasting, Structural Time Series and the Kalman Filter*, Cambridge University Press, Cambridge.

Harvey, A., E. Ruiz, and N. Shepard. (1994). Multivariate Stochastic Variance Models, *Review of Economic Studies*, 61, 247–264.

Hasbrouck, J. (1995). One Security, Many Markets: Determining the Contributions to Price Discovery, *Journal of Finance*, 45, 181–211.

Hasbrouck, J., and G. Sofianos. (1993). The Trades of Market Makers: An Empirical Analysis of NYSE Specialists, *Journal of Finance*, 48, 1565–1593.

Hausmann, J., A. Lo, and C. McKinlay. (1992). An Ordered Probit Analysis of Transaction Stock Prices, *Journal of Financial Economics*, 31, 319–379.

Hendry, D. (1986). Econometric Modelling with Cointegrated Variables: An Overview, *Oxford Bulletin of Economics and Statistics*, 48, 201–212.

Heston, S. (1993). A Closed Form Solution for Options with Stochastic Volatility with Applications to Bond and Foreign Currency Options, *Review of Financial Studies*, 6, 327–393.

Heynen, R. (1994). An Empirical Investigation of Observed Smile Patterns, *Review of Futures Markets*, 13, 317–354.

Heynen, R., A. Kenna, and T. Vorst. (1994). Analysis of the Term Structure of Implied Volatilities, *Journal of Financial and Quantitative Analysis*, 29, 31–56.

Hill, D. (1975). A Simple Approach to Inference About the Tail of a Distribution, *Annals of Statistics*, 13, 331–341.

Ho, T., and H. Stoll. (1981). Optimal Dealer Pricing under Transactions and Return Uncertainty, *Journal of Financial Economics*, 9, 47–73.

Hobson, D., and L. Rogers. (1998). Complete Models with Stochastic Volatility, *Mathematical Finance*, 8, 27–48.

Hosking, J. (1981). Fractional Differencing, *Biometrika*, 68, 165–176.

Houthakker, H. (1981). Systematic and Random Elements in Short Term Price Movements, *American Economic Review*, 51, 164–172.

Hsieh, D., and A. Kleidon. (1996). Bid-Ask Spread in Foreign Exchange Markets: Implication for Models of Asymmetric Information. In *The Microstructure of Foreign Exchange Markets*, 41–65. J. Frankel, G. Galli, and A. Giovannini, editors, University of Chicago Press, Chicago.

Huang, C., and R. Litzenberger. (1988). *Foundations for Financial Economics*, North Holland, New York.

Huang, R., and R. Masulis. (1999). Spreads and Dealer Competition Across the 24 Hours Trading Days, *Review of Financial Studies*, 12, 61–93.

Huang, R., and H. Stoll. (1996). Dealer Versus Auction Markets, *Journal of Financial Economics*, 41, 313–357.

———— (1997). The Components of the Bid-Ask Spread: A General Approach, *Review of Financial Studies*, 10, 995–1034.

Huberman, G. (1982). A Simple Approach to Arbitrage Pricing Theory, *Journal of Economic Theory*, 28, 183–191.

Huberman, G., S. Kandel, and R. Stambaugh. (1987). Mimicking Portfolio and Exact Arbitrage Pricing, *Journal of Finance*, 42, 1–9.

Hull, J., and A. White. (1987). The Pricing of Options on Assets with Stochastic Volatilities, *Journal of Finance*, 42, 281–300.

Hutchinson, J., A. Lo, and T. Poggio. (1996). A Nonparametric Approach to Pricing and Hedging Derivative Securities via Learning Networks, *Journal of Finance*, 49, 851–889.

Ingersoll, J. (1984). Some Results in the Theory of Arbitrage Pricing, *Journal of Finance*, 39, 1021–1039.

————. (1987). *Theory of Financial Decision Making*, Rowman and Littlefield, Totowa, N.J.

Ito, K. (1951). On Stochastic Differential Equations, *Memoirs of the American Mathematical Society*, 4, 1–51.

Jackwerth, J., and M. Rubinstein. (1996). Recovering Probability Distributions from Option Prices, *Journal of Finance*, 51, 349–369.

Jacobs, P. A., and P. A. W Lewis. (1978). Discrete Time Series Generated by Mixtures I: Correlation and Runs Properties, *Journal of the Royal Statistical Society*, 8, 40, 94–105.

———. (1993). Stationary Discrete Autoregressive-Moving Average Time Series Generated by Mixtures, *Journal of Time Series Analysis*, 4, 18–36.

Jain, P., and G. Joh. (1988). The Dependence between Hourly Prices and Trading Volume, *Journal of Financial and Quantitative Analysis*, 23, 269–284.

Jansen, D., and G. De Vries. (1991). On the Frequency of Large Stock Returns: Putting Booms and Busts into Perspective, *Review of Economics and Statistics*, 73, 18–24.

Jansen, D., K. Koedijk, and C. de Vries. (1998). *Portfolio Selection with Limited Downside Risk*, Maastricht University, Netherlands.

Jarrow, R., and A. Rudd. (1982). Approximate Valuation for Arbitrary Stochastic Processes, *Journal of Financial Economics*, 10, 349–369.

Jasiak, J. (1999). Persistence in Intertrade Durations, *Finance*, 19, 166–195.

Jevons, W. (1863). A Series Fall in the Value of Gold Ascertaine and Its Social Effects. In *Investigation in Currency and Finance*, vol. 3, Jevons, editor. Reprint, London, 1909.

———. (1865). The Variation of Prices and the Value of the Currency Since 1782. In *Investigation in Currency and Finance*, vol. 3, Jevons, editor. Reprint, London, 1909.

Jobson, J., and R. Korkie. (1982). Potential Performance and Tests of Portfolio Efficiency, *Journal of Financial Economics*, 10, 433–466.

Johansen, S. (1988). Statistical Analysis of Cointegration Vectors, *Journal of Economic Dynamics and Control*, 12, 231–254.

———. (1996). *Likelihood Based Inference in Cointegrated Vector Autoregressive Models*, Oxford University Press.

Jones, D., and V. Roley. (1983). Rational Expectation and the Expectations Model of the Term Structure: A Test Using Weekly Data, *Journal of Monetary Economics*, 12, 453–465.

Jorion, P. (1997). *Value at Risk: The New Benchmark for Controlling Market Risk*, Irwin, Chicago.

J.P. Morgan. (1996). *Risk Metrics Technical Document*, 4th edition, J.P. Morgan, New York.

Kallsen, J., and M. Taqqu. (1998). Option Pricing in ARCH Type Models, *Mathematical Finance*, 58, 13–26.

Kalman, R. (1960). A New Approach to Linear Filtering and Prediction Problem, *Journal of Basic Engineering*, 82, 34–45.

Kalman, R., and R. Bucy. (1961). New Results in Linear Filtering and Prediction Theory, *Journal of Basic Engineering*, 83, 95–108.

Kandel, E., and L. Marx. (1997). NASDAQ Market Structure and Spread Patterns, *Journal of Financial Economics*, 45, 61–89.

Kandel, S., and R. Staumbaugh. (1987). On Correlations and the Sensitivity of Inference about Mean-Variance Efficiency, *Journal of Financial Economics*, 18, 61–90.

Karatzas, I., and S. Shreve. (1988). *Brownian Motion and Stochastic Calculus*, Springer-Verlag, New York.

Karlin, S., and M. Taylor. (1981). *A Second Course in Stochastic Processes*, Academic Press, London.

Karpoff, J. (1987). The Relation Between Price Changes and Trading Volume: A Survey, *Journal of Financial and Quantitative Analysis*, 22, 109–126.

Kaufman, P. (1980). *Technical Analysis in Commodities*, Wiley, New York.

Kemeny, J., and J. L. Snell. (1976). *Finite Markov Chains*, Springer-Verlag, New York.

Kim, C. J. (1994). Dynamic Linear Models with Markov Switching, *Journal of Econometrics*, 60, 1–22.

Kim, O., and R. Verrechia. (1991a). Market Reactions to Anticipated Announcements, *Journal of Financial Economics*, 30, 273–310.

Kim, O., and R. Verrechia. (1991b). Trading Volume and Price Reaction to Public Announcements, *Journal of Accounting Research*, 29, 302–321.

King, M., E. Sentana, and S. Wadhwani. (1994). Volatility Links between National Stock Markets, *Econometrica*, 62, 901–933.

King, M., and S. Wadhwani. (1990). Transmission of Volatility between Stock Markets, *Review of Financial Studies*, 3, 5–33.

Kitagawa, G. (1987). Non Gaussian State Space Modeling of Nonstationary Time Series, *Journal of the American Statistical Association*, 82, 1032–1063.

Kleidon, A. (1986). Variance Bounds Tests and Stock Price Valuation Models, *Journal of Political Economy*, 94, 953–1001.

Kleidon, A., and I. Werner. (1993). *Round the Clock Trading: Evidence from UK Cross-Listed Securities*, Discussion paper, Stanford University, Stanford, Calif.

Koenker, R., and G. Basset. (1978). Regression Quantiles, *Econometrica*, 46, 33–50.

Kofman, J., and M. Martens. (1997). Interaction between Stock Markets: An Analysis of the Common Trading Hours at the London and New York Stock Exchange, *Journal of International Money and Finance*, 16, 387–414.

Kofman, J., and J. Moser. (1997). Spreads, Information Flows and Transparency Across Trading Systems, *Applied Financial Economics*, 7, 281–294.

Konus, A. (1939). The Problem of the Time Index of the Cost of Living, *Econometrica*, 7, 10–29.

Koopmans, L. (1964). On the Multivariate Analysis of Weakly Stationary Stochastic Processes, *Annals of Mathematical Statistics*, 35, 1765–1780.

Kramar, K. (1886). *Das Papiergeld in Oesterreich seit 1848*, Leipzig.

Kreps, D., and E. Porteus. (1978). Temporal Resolution of Uncertainty and Dynamic Choice Theory, *Econometrica*, 46, 185–200.

Kyle, A. (1985). Continuous Auctions and Insider Trading, *Econometrica*, 53, 1315–1336.

———. (1989). Informed Speculation with Imperfect Competition, *Review of Economic Studies*, 56, 317–356.

Lamoureux, C., and W. Lastrapes. (1993). Forecasting Stock Return Variance: Toward an Understanding of Stochastic Implied Volatilities, *Review of Financial Studies*, 6, 293–326.

Lancaster, H. (1968). The Structure of Bivariate Distributions, *Annals of Mathematical Statistics*, 29, 716–736.

Lancaster, T. (1990). *The Econometric Analysis of Transition Data*, Cambridge University Press.

Laspeyres, E. (1864). Hamburger Warenpreise 1851–1863, und die californishaustralischen Goldentdeckungen seit 1848. In *Jahrbucher fur Nationalokonomie und Statistik*, Von Bruno Hildebrand, editor, Bd III, Jena.

Lee, T., G. Judge, and A. Zellner. (1968). Maximum Likelihood and Bayesian Estimation of Transition Probabilities, *Journal of the American Statistical Association*, 63, 1162–1179.

Le Roy, S. (1973). Risk Aversion and the Martingale Model of Stock Prices, *International Economic Review*, 14, 436–446.

———. (1996). Stock Price Volatility. In *Handbook of Statistics*, vol. 14, G. Maddala and C. Rao, editors, North Holland, Amsterdam, 193–208.

Le Roy, S., and A. Porter. (1981). Stock Price Volatility: Tests Based on Implied Variance Bounds, *Econometrica*, 49, 555–574.

Levy, H., and M. Sarnat. (1972). Safety First. An Expected Utility Principle, *Journal of Financial and Quantitative Analysis*, 7, 1829–1834.

Lintner, J. (1965). Valuation of Risky Assets and the Selection of Risky Investments in Stock Portfolio and Capital Budgets, *Review of Economics and Statistics*, 47, 13–37.

Litzenberger, R., and K. Ramaswamy. (1979). The Effect of Personal Taxes and Dividends on Capital Asset Prices: Theory and Evidence, *Journal of Financial Economics*, 7, 163–169.

Liu, Y., V. Liu, and C. Wu. (1998). The Impact of Information Diffusion on Comparisons Among Various Trading Mechanisms, *Review of Quantitative Finance and Accounting*, 9, 301–326.

Ljung, G., and G. Box. (1978). On a Measure of Lack of Fit in Time Series Models, *Biometrika*, 66, 67–72.

Lo, A., and A. McKinlay. (1988a). Mean Reversion in Stock Returns, Evidence and Implications, *Journal of Financial Economics*, 22, 27–60.

———. (1988b). Stock Market Prices Do Not Follow Random Walks: Evidence from a Simple Specification Test, *Review of Financial Studies*, 1, 41–66.

———. (1989). The Size and Power of the Variance Ratio Test in Finite Samples: A Monte Carlo Investigation, *Journal of Econometrics*, 40, 203–238.

———. (1990). An Econometric Analysis of Infrequent Trading, *Journal of Econometrics*, 45, 181–211.

Lofton, T. (1986). *Trading Tactics: A Livestock Futures Anthology*, Chicago Mercantile Exchange.

Longin, F. (1997). *Beyond the VaR*, Discussion paper 97-011, ESSEC, Cergy.

Longstaff, F. (1992). *An Empirical Examination of the Risk Neutral Valuation Model*, Discussion paper, Ohio State University, Columbus, Ohio.

Lovell, M. (1986). Test of the Rational Expectation Hypothesis, *American Economic Review*, 76, 110–124.

Lucas, R. (1978). Asset Prices in an Exchange Economy, *Econometrica*, 46, 1429–1446.

Lutkepohl, H. (1993). *Introduction to Multiple Time Series Analysis*, Springer-Verlag, New York.

Lutz, F. (1940). The Structure of Interest Rates, *Quarterly Journal of Economics*, 55, 36–63.

Lyons, R. (1995). Tests of Microstructural Hypotheses in the Foreign Exchange Market, *Journal of Financial Economics*, 39, 321–351.

——. (1996). Optimal Transparency in a Dealer Market with an Application to Foreign Exchange, *Journal of Financial Intermediation*, 5, 225–254.

——. (1997). A Simultaneous Trade Model of the Foreign Exchange Hot Potato, *Journal of International Economics*, 42, 275–298.

——. (1999). "The Microstructure Approach to Exchange Rates." MIT Press, forthcoming.

MacDonald, I. L., and W. Zucchini. (1997). *Hidden Markov and Other Models for Discrete-Valued Time Series*, Chapman and Hall, London.

Madan, D., and F. Milne. (1994). Contingent Claims Valued and Hedged by Pricing and Investing in a Basis, *Mathematical Finance*, 4, 223–245.

Madanski, A. (1959). Least Squares Estimation in Finite Markov Processes, *Psychometrika*, 24, 137–144.

Madhavan, A. (1992). Trading Mechanisms in Securities Markets, *Journal of Finance*, 47, 607–641.

Madhavan, A., M. Richardson, and M. Roomans. (1997). Why Do Security Prices Change? A Transaction Level Analysis of NYSE Stocks, *Review of Financial Studies*, 10, 1035–1064.

Madhavan, A., and S. Smidt. (1991). A Bayesian Model of Intraday Specialist Pricing, *Journal of Financial Economics*, 30, 99–134.

——. (1993). An Analysis of Changes in Specialist Inventories and Quotations, *Journal of Finance*, 48, 1595–1628.

Malz, A. (1996). *Option-Based Estimates of the Probability Distribution of Exchange Rates and Currency Excess Returns*, Federal Reserve Bank of New York.

Mandelbrot, B. (1963). The Variations of Certain Speculative Prices, *Journal of Business*, 36, 394–419.

Mandelbrot, B., and H. Taylor. (1967). On the Distribution of Stock Price Differences, *Operations Research*, 15, 1057–1062.

Markowitz, H. (1952). Portfolio Selection, *Journal of Finance*, 7, 77–91.

——. (1976). *Portfolio Selection*, Yale University Press, New Haven, Conn.

Marshall, A. (1887). Remedies for Fluctuations of General Prices, *The Contemporary Revue*, March, 371–375.

Marten, M. (1998). Price Discovery in High and Low Volatility Periods: Open Outcry Versus Electronic Trading, *Journal of International Financial Markets, Institutions and Money*, 8, 243–260.

Massimb, M., and B. Phelps. (1994). Electronic Trading, Market Structure and Liquidity, *Financial Analysts Journal*, 50, 39–50.

McCullogh, R. E., and R. S. Tsay. (1994). Statistical Analysis of Economic Time Series via Markov Switching Models, *Journal of Time Series Analysis*, 155, 523–539.

McInish, T., and R. Wood. (1992). An Analysis of Intraday Patterns in Bid/Ask Spread for NYSE Stocks, *Journal of Finance*, 47, 753–764.

Mehra, R., and E. Prescott. (1985). The Equity Premium: A Puzzle, *Journal of Monetary Economics*, 15, 145–161.

Melino, A., and S. Turnbull. (1990). Pricing Foreign Currency Options with Stochastic Volatility, *Journal of Econometrics*, 45, 239–265.

Mendelson, H. (1982). Market Behaviour in the Clearing House, *Econometrica*, 50, 1505–1524.

———. (1987). Consolidation, Fragmentation and Market Performance, *Journal of Financial and Quantitative Analysis*, 22, 189–207.

Merton, R. (1972). An Analytical Derivation of the Efficient Portfolio Frontier, *Journal of Financial and Quantitative Analysis*, 7, 1851–1872.

———. (1973a). An Intertemporal Capital Asset Pricing Model, *Econometrica*, 41, 867–887.

———. (1973b). Rational Theory of Option Pricing, *Bell Journal of Economics and Management Science*, 4, 141–183.

———. (1976). Option Pricing when Underlying Stock Returns Are Discontinuous, *Journal of Financial Economics*, 3, 124–144.

Miller, M. (1988). *Financial Innovations and Market Volatility*, Basil Blackwell Publishers, Cambridge, UK.

Mills, T. (1993). *The Econometric Modelling of Financial Time Series*, Cambridge University Press, Cambridge.

Milne, F. (1988). Arbitrage and Diversification in a General Equilibrium Asset Economy, *Econometrica*, 56, 815–840.

Mossin, J. (1966). Equilibrium in Capital Asset Market, *Econometrica*, 35, 768–783.

Muller, U., M. Dacorogna, R. Olsen, O. Pictet, M. Schwarz, and C. Morgenegg. (1990). Statistical Study of Foreign Exchange Rates, Empirical Evidence of a Price Scale Law, and Intraday Analysis, *Journal of Banking and Finance*, 14, 1189–1208.

Mullineaux, D. (1978). On Testing for Rationality: Another Look at the Livingstone Price Expectations Data, *Journal of Political Economy*, 86, 329–336.

Murphy, J. (1986). *Technical Analysis of the Futures Markets*, New York Institute of Finance, New York.

Muth, J. (1961). Rational Expectations and the Theory of Price Movements, *Econometrica*, 29, 315–335.

Naidu, G., and M. Rozeff. (1994). Volume, Volatility, Liquidity and Efficiency on the Singapore Stock Exchange Before and After Automation, *Pacific Basin Financial Journal*, 2, 23–42.

Naik, N., A. Neuberger, and S. Viswanathan. (1999). Trade Disclosure Regulation in Markets with Negociated Trades, *Review of Financial Studies*, 12, 873–900.

Nandi, S. (1996). *Pricing and Hedging Index Options Under Stochastic Volatility*, Discussion paper, Federal Reserve Bank, Atlanta, Ga.

Nelson, D. (1990). ARCH Models as Diffusion Approximations, *Journal of Econometrics*, 45, 7–38.

———. (1990). Stationarity and Persistence in the GARCH(1,1) Models, *Econometric Theory*, 6, 318–334.

Nelson, D., and K. Ramaswamy. (1990). Simple Binomial Processes as Diffusion Approximations in Financial Models, *Review of Financial Studies*, 3, 393–430.

Nerlove, M. (1958). Adaptive Expectations and Cobweb Phenomena, *Quarterly Journal of Economics*, 73, 227–240.

Nicholson, J. (1887). The Measurement of Variations in the Value of the Monetary Standard, *Journal of the Royal Statistical Society*, 50.

Niederhoffer, V., and M. Osborne. (1966). Market Making and Reversal on the Stock Exchange, *Journal of the American Statistical Association*, 61, 897–916.

O'Hara, M. (1995). *Market Microstructure Theory*, Basil Blackwell Publishers, Oxford, UK.

O'Hara, M., and G. Olfield. (1986). The Microeconomics of Market Making, *Journal of Financial and Quantitative Analysis*, 21, 361–376.

Osborne, M. (1959). Brownian Motion in the Stock Market, *Operations Research*, 7, 145–173.

Paasche, H. (1870). Studien uber die Natur der Geldwertung und ihre pratische Bedeutung in den letzten Jahrzehnte auf Grund statistischen Detailmaterials entn. der Stadt Halle a./s., Jena. In *Sammlung nationalokonomischer und statisticher Abhandlungen des Staatswissenschaftlichen Seminars zu Hall*, J. Conrad, editor, B1.

Pagan, A. (1996). The Econometrics of Financial Markets, *Journal of Empirical Finance*, 3, 15–102.

Pagan, A., and W. Schwert. (1990). Alternative Models for Conditional Stock Volatility, *Journal of Econometrics*, 45, 267–290.

Pagano, M. (1989). Trading Volume and Asset Liquidity, *Quarterly Journal of Economics*, 104, 255–274.

Pagano, M., and A. Roell. (1996). Transparency and Liquidity: A Comparison of Auction and Dealer Markets, *Journal of Finance*, 51, 579–611.

Pagano, M., and A. Ruel. (1992). Auction and Dealerships Markets: What Is the Difference? *European Economic Review*, 36, 613–623.

Palm, F. (1996). GARCH Models of Volatility. In *Handbook of Statistics*, vol. 14, 209–240. G. Maddala and C. Rao, North Holland, Amsterdam.

Pegram, G. G. S. (1975). A Multinomial Model for Transitions Probability Matrices, *Journal of Applied Probability*, 12, 498–506.

———. (1980). An Autoregressive Model for Multilag Markov Chains, *Journal of Applied Probability*, 17, 350–362.

Peiers, B. (1997). A High Frequency Study on the Relationship between Central Bank Intervention and Price Leadership in the Foreign Exchange Market, *Journal of Finance*, 52, 1589–1614.

Petersen, M., and D. Fralkowski. (1994). Posted Versus Effective Spreads: Good Prices or Bad Quotes? *Journal of Financial Economics*, 35, 269–292.

Pham, H., and N. Touzi. (1996). Equilibrium State Price in a Stochastic Volatility Model, *Mathematical Finance*, 6, 215–236.

Phillips, P. (1991). Optimal Inference in Cointegrated Systems, *Econometrica*, 59, 283–306.

Poterba, J., and L. Summers. (1986). The Persistence of Volatility and Stock Market Fluctuation, *American Economic Review*, 76, 1142–1151.

———. (1988). Mean Reversion in Stock Returns: Evidence and Implications, *Journal of Financial Economics*, 22, 27–60.

Prechter, R., and A. Frost. (1985). *Elliott Wave Principle*, New Classics Library, Gainesville, Fla.

Quenouille, M. (1949). Approximate Tests of Correlation in Time Series, *Journal of the Royal Statistical Society*, B, 11, 68–84.

Raftery, A. (1985). A Model for High-Order Markov Chains, *Journal of the Royal Statistical Society*, 8, 47, 528–539.

Reiss, P., and I. Werner. (1998). Does Risk Sharing Motivate Interdealer Trading? *Journal of Finance*, 53, 1657–1703.

Revuz, A., and M. Yor. (1990). *Continuous Martingale Calculus*, Springer-Verlag, New York.

Richardson, M., and T. Smith. (1994). A Direct Test of the Mixture of Distributions Hypothesis: Measuring the Daily Flow of Information, *Journal of Financial and Quantitative Analysis*, 29, 101–119.

Richardson, M., and J. Stock. (1989). Drawing Inferences from Statistics Based on Multi-Year Asset Returns, *Journal of Financial Economics*, 25, 323–348.

Ridder, T. (1997). *Basics of Statistical VaR Estimation*, SGZ-Bank, Frankfurt, Germany.

Robinson, P. (1992). Semiparametric Analysis of Long Memory Time Series, *Annals of Statistics*, 22, 515–539.

Roll, R. (1977). A Critique of the Asset Pricing Theory's Test—Part One: Past and Potential Testability of the Theory, *Journal of Financial Economics*, 4, 129–176.

———. (1978). Ambiguity When Performance Is Measured by the Securities Market Line, *Journal of Finance*, 33, 1051–1069.

———. (1984). A Simple Implicit Measure of the Effective Bid-Ask Spread in an Efficient Market, *Journal of Finance*, 39, 1127–1139.

Romer, D. (1993). Rational Asset Price Movements without News, *American Economic Review*, 83, 1112–1130.

Rosen, S. (1974). Hedonic Prices and Implicit Markets: Product Differentiation in Pure Competition, *Journal of Political Economy*, 82, 34–55.

Ross, S. (1976). The Arbitrage Theory of Capital Asset Pricing, *Journal of Economic Theory*, 17, 254–286.

Roy, A. (1952). Safety First and the Holding of Assets, *Econometrica*, 431–439.

Rubinstein, M. (1976). The Valuation of Uncertain Income Streams and the Pricing of Options, *Bell Journal of Economics*, 7, 407–425.

———. (1994). Implied Binomial Trees, *Journal of Finance*, 69, 771–818.

Samuelson, P. (1965). Proof that Properly Anticipated Prices Fluctuate Randomly, *Industrial Management Review*, 6, 41–49.

SBF. (1995). *Les Indices de la Bourse de Paris*, Société de Bourses Françaises, Paris.

Schumpeter, I. (1905). *Die Methode der Index Zahlen*, Statistische Monatschrift, Jahrg X, Vienna.

Schwert, G. (1989a). Business Cycles, Financial Crises and Stock Volatility, *Carnegie-Rochester Conference Series on Public Policy*, 39, 83–126.

———. (1989b). Why Does Stock Market Volatility Change Over Time? *Journal of Finance*, 44, 1115–1153.

Scott, L. (1987). Option Pricing when the Variance Changes Randomly: Theory, Estimation and an Application, *Journal of Financial and Quantitative Analysis*, 22, 419–438.

Shanken, J. (1985). Multivariate Tests of the Zero-Beta CAPM, *Journal of Financial Economics*, 14, 342–348.

Sharpe, W. (1963). A Simplified Model for Portfolio Analysis, *Management Service*, 9, 277–293.

———. (1964). Capital Asset Prices: A Theory of Market Equilibrium Under Conditions of Risk, *Journal of Finance*, 19, 425–442.

Shephard, N., and M. Pitt. (1997). Likelihood Analysis of Non Gaussian Measurement Time Series, *Biometrika*, 84, 653–668.

Shiller, R. (1981). Do Stock Prices Move Too Much to Be Justified by Subsequent Changes in Dividends? *American Economic Review*, 71, 421–436.

———. (1982). Consumption, Asset Markets and Macroeconomic Fluctuations, *Carnegie-Rochester Conference Series Public Policy*, 17, 203–238.

———. (1989). *Market Volatility*, MIT Press, Cambridge.

———. (1990). The Term Structure of Interest Rates. In *Handbook of Monetary Economics*, vol. 1, B. Friedman and F. Hahn, editors, Chapter 12, North-Holland, Amsterdam.

Shiller, R., Y. Campbell, and K. Schoenholtz. (1983). Forward Rates and Future Policy: Interpreting the Term Structure of Interest Rates, *Brookings Papers on Economic Activity*, 1, 173–217.

Shimko, D. (1993). Bounds of Probability, *Risk*, 6, 33–37.

Shyy, G., and J. Lee. (1995). Price Transmission and Information Asymmetry in Bond Futures Markets: LIFFE versus DTB, *Journal of Futures Markets*, 16, 519–543.

Simon, D. (1989). Expectations and Risk in the Treasury Bill Markets: An Instrumental Variable Approach, *Journal of Financial and Quantitative Analysis*, 24, 357–365.

Smithson, C. (1996a). Value at Risk, *Risk*, 9, 25–27.

———. (1996b). Value at Risk (2), *Risk*, 9, 38–39.

Snell, A., and I. Tonks. (1995). Determinants of Price Quote Revisions on the London Stock Exchange, *Economic Journal*, 105, 77–94.

Stephan, H., and R. Whaley. (1990). Intraday Price Change and Trading Volume Relations in the Stock and Stock Option Markets, *Journal of Finance*, 45, 191–220.

Stock, J. (1987). Asymptotic Properties of Least Squares Estimates of Cointegrating Vectors, *Econometrica*, 55, 1035–1056.

———. (1988). Estimating Continuous Time Processes Subject of Time Deformation, *Journal of the American Statistical Association*, 83, 77–84.

Stock, J., and M. Watson. (1988). Testing for Common Trends, *Journal of the American Statistical Association*, 83, 1097–1107.

Stoll, H. (1978). The Supply of Dealer Services in Securities Markets, *Journal of Finance*, 33, 1133–1151.

———. (1989). Inferring the Component of the Bid-Ask Spread: Theory and Empirical Tests, *Journal of Finance*, 39, 1127–1139.

Stroock, D., and S. Varadhan. (1979). *Multidimensional Diffusion Processes*, Springer-Verlag, Berlin.

Stulz, R. (1998). *Derivatives, Risk Management and Financial Engineering*, Southwestern Publishing.

Stutzer, M. (1996). A Simple Nonparametric Approach to Derivative Security Valuation, *Journal of Finance*, 51, 1633–1652.

Subrahmanyam, A. (1991). Risk Aversion, Market Liquidity and Price Efficiency, *Review of Financial Studies*, 4, 417–442.

Szroeter, J. (1983). Generalized Wald Methods for Testing Nonlinear Implicit and Overidentifying Restrictions, *Econometrica*, 51, 335–348.

Tauchen, G., and M. Pitts (1983). The Price Variability-Volume Relationship on Speculative Markets, *Econometrica*, 51, 485–505.

Taylor, S. (1986). *Modelling Financial Time Series*, Wiley, London.

———. (1990). *Modelling Stochastic Volatility*, Discussion paper, University of Lancaster, UK.

———. (1994). The Magnitude of Implied Volatility Smiles: Theory of Empirical Evidence for Exchange Rates, *Review of Futures Markets*, 13, 355–380.

Taylor, S., and X. Xu. (1993). The Magnitude of Implied Volatility Smiles: Theory and Empirical Evidence for Exchange Rates, *Review of Futures Markets*, 13, 355–380.

Turnovski, S., and M. Wachter. (1972). A Test of the Expectation Hypothesis Using Directly Observed Wage and Prices Expectations, *Review of Economics and Statistics*, 54, 47–54.

Vahid, F., and R. Engle. (1993). Common Trends and Common Cycles, *Journal of Applied Econometrics*, 8, 341–360.

———. (1997). Codependent Cycles, *Journal of Econometrics*, 80, 199–221.

Vasicek, O. (1977). An Equilibrium Characterization of the Term Structure, *Journal of Financial Economics*, 5, 177–188.

Vogler, K. (1997). Risk Allocation and Inter-Dealer Trading, *European Economic Review*, 41, 1615–1634.

Wald, A. (1937). Zur Theorie der Preizindexziffern, *Zeitschrift fur National Okonomie*, 8, 179–219.

Wasserfallen, W., and H. Zimmermann. (1985). The Behavior of Intra-Daily Exchange Rates, *Journal of Banking and Finance*, 9, 55–72.

Wei, S., and J. Kim. (1997). The Big Players in the Foreign Exchange Market: Do They Trade on Information or Noise? National of Bureau of Economic Research, Working Paper 6256.

Weil, P. (1989). The Equity Premium Puzzle and the Risk-Free Rate Puzzle, *Journal of Monetary Economics*, 24, 401–421.

Weiss, A. (1984). ARMA Models with ARCH Errors, *Journal of Time Series Analysis*, 5, 129–143.

West, K. (1988). Bubbles, Fads and Stock Price Volatility: A Partial Evaluation, *Journal of Finance*, 43, 636–656.

Whittle, P. (1963). *Prediction and Regulation*, English Universities Press, London.

Wiener, N. (1923). Differential Space, *Journal of Mathematical Physics*, 2, 131–174.

———. (1924). Un problème de probabilités dénombrables, *Bulletin de la Société Mathématiqué de France*, 52, 569–578.

Wilson, T. (1996). Calculating Risk Capital. In *The Handbook of Risk Management and Analysis*, C. Alexander, editor, Wiley, Chichester, 193–232.

Wood, R., T. McInish, and J. Ord. (1985). An Investigation of Transaction Date for NYSE Stocks, *Review of Financial Studies*, 3, 37–71.

Working, H. (1934). A Random Difference Series for Use in Analysis of Time Series, *Journal of the American Statistical Association*, 29, 11–24.

Yadav, P., and P. Pope. (1992). Intraweek and Intraday Seasonalities in Stock Market Risk Premia: Cash and Futures, *Journal of Banking and Finance*, 16, 233–270.

Zellner, A. (1962). An Efficient Method of Estimating Seemingly Unrelated Regressions and Tests for Aggregation Bias, *Journal of the American Statistical Association*, 57, 348–368.

Zhou, B. (1996). High Frequency Data and Volatility in Foreign Exchange Rates, *Journal of Business and Economic Statistics*, 14, 45–52.

Index

Milton Keynes UK
Ingram Content Group UK Ltd.
UKHW010203091223
434043UK00004B/202

9 780691 242361